REVIEW OF
RESEARCH IN
EDUCATION

Review of Research in Education is published annually on behalf of the American Educational Research Association, 1430 K St., NW, Suite 1200, Washington, DC 20005, by SAGE Publishing, 2455 Teller Road, Thousand Oaks, CA 91320. Send address changes to AERA Membership Department, 1430 K St., NW, Suite 1200, Washington, DC 20005.

Member Information: American Educational Research Association (AERA) member inquiries, member renewal requests, changes of address, and membership subscription inquiries should be addressed to the AERA Membership Department, 1430 K St., NW, Suite 1200, Washington, DC 20005; fax 202-238-3250; e-mail: members@aera.net. AERA annual membership dues are $215 (Regular Members), $215 (Affiliate Members), $165 (International Affiliates), and $65 (Graduate Students), and $40 (Student Affiliates). **Claims:** Claims for undelivered copies must be made no later than six months following month of publication. Beyond six months and at the request of the American Educational Research Association, the publisher will supply missing copies when losses have been sustained in transit and when the reserve stock permits.

Subscription Information: All non-member subscription inquiries, orders, back-issue requests, claims, and renewals should be addressed to SAGE Publishing, 2455 Teller Road, Thousand Oaks, CA 91320; telephone (800) 818-SAGE (7243) and (805) 499-0721; fax: (805) 375-1700; e-mail: journals@sagepub.com; website: http://journals.sage pub.com. **Subscription Price:** Institutions: $397; Individuals: $72. For all customers outside the Americas, please visit http://www.sagepub.co.uk/customercare.nav for information. **Claims:** Claims for undelivered copies must be made no later than six months following month of publication. The publisher will supply missing copies when losses have been sustained in transit and when the reserve stock will permit.

Copyright Permission: To request permission for republishing, reproducing, or distributing material from this journal, please visit the desired article on the SAGE Journals website (journals.sagepub.com) and click "Permissions." For additional information, please see www .sagepub.com/journalspermissions.nav.

Advertising and Reprints: Current advertising rates and specifications may be obtained by contacting the advertising coordinator in the Thousand Oaks office at (805) 410-7763 or by sending an e-mail to advertising@sagepub.com. To order reprints, please e-mail reprint@ sagepub.com. Acceptance of advertising in this journal in no way implies endorsement of the advertised product or service by SAGE or the journal's affiliated society(ies). No endorsement is intended or implied. SAGE reserves the right to reject any advertising it deems as inappropriate for this journal.

Change of Address: Six weeks' advance notice must be given when notifying of change of address. Please send old address label along with the new address to ensure proper identification. Please specify name of journal.

International Standard Serial Number ISSN 0091-732X
International Standard Book Number ISBN 978-1-5443-8976-9 (Vol. 43, 2019, paper)
Manufactured in the United States of America. First printing, March 2019.

Printed on acid-free paper

REVIEW OF RESEARCH IN EDUCATION

Changing Teaching Practice in P–20 Educational Settings

Volume 43, 2019

Terri D. Pigott, Editor
Ann Marie Ryan, Editor
Charles Tocci, Associate Editor
Loyola University Chicago

AMERICAN EDUCATIONAL RESEARCH ASSOCIATION
FOUNDED 1916

⑤SAGE

Review of Research in Education

Changing Teaching Practice in P–20 Educational Settings

Volume 43

AMERICAN EDUCATIONAL RESEARCH ASSOCIATION

Tel: 202-238-3200 Fax: 202-238-3250
http://www.aera.net/pubs

FELICE J. LEVINE
Executive Director

MARTHA YAGER
Managing Editor

JOHN NEIKIRK
Director of Publications

JESSICA SIBOLD
Publications Associate

Contents

Cover image: istockphoto.com/andipantz

Introduction

Changing Teaching Practice in P–20 Educational Settings: Introduction to the Volume

CHARLES TOCCI
ANN MARIE RYAN
TERRI D. PIGOTT
Loyola University Chicago

Reflecting on a century of education reform efforts, Tyack and Cuban (1997) wrote, "To bring about improvement at the heart of education - classroom instruction . . . has proven to be the most difficult kind of reform" (p. 134). This historical insight about teaching practice, that it requires intensive and extensive effort to change, runs up against a popular and all-too-familiar canard that classroom teaching and learning remain unchanged over the past 100 years or more (Dorn, 2011; Watters 2015; Watters, Anderson, Neuschatz, & Kantrowitz, 2018). Like many public arguments about our education system, this argument is not about the demonstrable, factual truth. We know teaching practice has changed and continues to change because we have read about it (e.g., Cohen, 1988; Cuban, 1993), we have seen it, and we have made changes ourselves.

Nonetheless, there are clear historical consistencies that persist in pedagogy (Cuban, 1993; Tyack & Cuban, 1997). Dorn (2018) asserts that the "institutional and cultural dynamics of schooling" have produced both perennial teaching practices as well as spaces for educators to experiment, create, and implement new ideas. Drawing on Schon (1973), Cuban (2013) characterized the interplay between stable repertoires and reform initiatives within schools as representing "dynamic conservatism" (p. 3), that is, the typical product of change efforts is a minimal or incremental adaptation of current practice.

In turn, this means that year after year, millions of teachers work and tens of millions of students learn in classrooms that are complex composites of change and continuity. Our schools are an ensemble of historical developments and contemporary innovations that profoundly shape what happens in classrooms. For instance,

Review of Research in Education
March 2019, Vol. 43, pp. vii–xiii
DOI: 10.3102/0091732X19839068
Chapter reuse guidelines: sagepub.com/journals-permissions
© 2019 AERA. http://rre.aera.net

schools built to accommodate legal segregation, later integrated by court-approved plans, might now again be de facto segregated through complicated interactions between housing and school choice policies. In these schools, chalkboards gave way to whiteboards that are giving way to smartboards, on which teachers broadcast information to students sitting in tablet desks that supplanted wooden desks once bolted to the floor. And at the end of a series of such lessons, students will likely show that they have learned this information by answering multiple-choice questions, no longer on a quiz or scantron form but on a laptop accessing a Web-based proprietary learning management system. Every innovative practice is implemented within the constraints and opportunities of our educational histories.

As Tyack and Cuban (1997) explored, there are a number of forces that have served to maintain "the grammar" (p. 5) of schooling and resist sweeping changes: cultural beliefs, institutional habits, entrenched interests, and the decentralized yet highly interdependent structure of school systems. Efforts to make dramatic changes to classroom practice require a sustained investment of significant resources and often result in minor modifications to what it is that is already being done, an outcome that often burns out reformers before the work is complete. Reflecting on Tyack and Cuban's work as well as his own efforts to reimagine education through the use of computers, Papert (1997) dismissed the idea that any centralized grand plan could overhaul a system as complex as schooling. But Papert was hopeful that a "rich diversity" (p. 427) of new ideas and the change initiatives occurring throughout would evolve schools into more effective and meaningful educational institutions.

We take our cue for this volume from this historically grounded yet optimistic view of change to teaching practice. We know that teaching practice, while only one of the numerous factors that produce educational inequality, is central to the mission of improving schooling (RAND Corporation, 2012). We know that change is not the same as progress or improvement (Payne, 2008); we know that for all of the resources and time invested in reform initiatives, only some have broad, lasting impact (Schneider, 2014). Yet the aspirational purposes of our school system calls us to make changes in the pursuit of equity and excellence with our students, especially the most vulnerable and marginalized. Deeper, more sophisticated understandings of why, how, and under what conditions teaching changes in intentional, coordinated, sustained, and responsive ways are essential to the work.

What makes this such a complicated research endeavor is the many variables involved in teaching, including who is teaching, who is being taught, what is being taught, and in what contexts teaching occurs. Similar to the past, future decades will likely see significant changes in teacher (U.S. Department of Education, 2016) and student demographics, evolutions in academic content, the introduction of new instructional tools, and a proliferation of learning spaces—online and in person, formal and informal—where teaching takes place. Generic answers to the question "how do we change teaching practice" will not suffice. We need multidisciplinary approaches applied in a wide range of settings to generate findings that illuminate the common and the contingent elements involved in changing teaching practice. We require research that has meaningful transferability across learning spaces, teachers, and types of changes with careful consideration about how the particularities of place and time influence change processes. We believe this volume can spark these conversations by, for instance, bringing together a history of "race work" in the first half of the 20th century with an analysis of resistance to culturally relevant education in the early 21st century.

The chapters that follow span well-defined specializations as well as specific disciplinary and interdisciplinary approaches. They bring together varied strands of inquiry into applied problems of changing teaching practice that are typically siloed into different research specializations: education policy, organizational change, teacher learning, curriculum and teaching, data use, and teacher preparation. Across these specializations and disciplines used to investigate them, there are distinct literatures and different units of analysis. To bridge these differences, we ask readers to consider the following questions as they peruse the volume: How is change to practice conceptualized, evidenced, and analyzed? What are the key barriers, facilitators, and contextual factors affecting sustained change? How do institutional and social contexts shape efforts to change practice? How does teaching practice change relate to student learning? Finally, what have we learned from both successful attempts to change practice as well as failures? By posing such questions, the volume convenes a broader discussion among education researchers and research-interested practitioners seeking to understand a change to practice as a central problem. In turn, we hope this will promote more multidisciplinary work that can draw overlaps among specializations and consider multiple dimensions of practical change in teaching.

THE ORGANIZATION OF THIS VOLUME

Our goal in editing this volume has been to present high-quality reviews that examine change to teaching practice from a variety of perspectives and a range of disciplines with an eye toward the enormous scope of the field. This volume is not exhaustive nor is it comprehensive. It does not reflect exactly what we thought it would be when we published the call for proposals; the quality and creativity of the proposals broadened our view. Taken as a whole, we believe that this volume presents a compelling profile of the core challenges and opportunities facing those engaged in the work of changing teaching practice and those who research these efforts. We have organized the chapters into four sections in an effort to highlight major themes that emerge across the reviews.

The first section of this volume delves into the history and policy of changing teaching practice. Lauri D. Johnson and Yoon K. Pak begin in Chapter 1 with "Teaching for Diversity: Intercultural and Intergroup Education in the Public Schools, 1920s to 1970s." This 20th-century history of diversity work in classrooms highlights the intercultural education movement and pivots around *Brown v. Board of Education* (1954) examining the deeper connections running from the past through to our present day around the teaching and issues of race and structural racism. In Chapter 2, "From Mass Schooling to Education Systems: Changing Patterns in the

Organization and Management of Instruction," Donald J. Peurach, David K. Cohen, Maxwell M. Yurkofsky, and James P. Spillane revisit a previous *Review of Research in Education* chapter written by Cohen and Spillane (1992) to explore how policies focusing on promoting equity and excellence in educational outcomes have played out within the established structures of mass public schooling.

The second set of chapters consider the capacity of teachers to make changes. In Chapter 3, Katrina Liu and Arnetha F. Ball concentrate on "Critical Reflection and Generativity: Toward a Framework of Transformative Teacher Education for Diverse Learners." Through a review of the literature on teacher education, they ask, "How can we instill in preservice teachers a capacity and a motivation to change practice?" Rachel Garrett, Martyna Citkowicz, and Ryan Williams authored Chapter 4, "How Responsive Is a Teacher's Classroom Practice to Intervention? A Meta-Analysis of Randomized Field Studies." Their review concludes that teacher practice does change in response to professional development interventions but that there is also still a great deal to learn and research. Mary M. Kennedy discusses the assumptions underlying teacher professional development in Chapter 5, "How We Learn About Teacher Learning," and how researchers think about teacher learning. Chapter 6 by Megan McGlinn Manfra, "Action Research and Systematic, Intentional Change in Teaching Practice," focuses on teachers as self-directed learners engaged in the problems of changing practice at both practical and conceptual levels; there are success stories but also many barriers to overcome to strengthen and spread action research. The last review in this section by Rebecca Colina Neri, Maritza Lozano, and Louis M. Gomez, Chapter 7, "(Re)framing Resistance to Culturally Relevant Education as a Multilevel Learning Problem," engages in a rigorous examination of how we understand and find ways to overcome a key barrier to implementing culturally relevant educational practices, a change that is past due and powerfully argued in the research literature.

The third set of chapters review literature examining how to change practice in numerous settings in various ways. Miranda Suzanne Fitzgerald and Annemarie Sullivan Palincsar lead off this section with Chapter 8, "Teaching Practices That Support Student Sensemaking Across Grade and Disciplines: A Conceptual Review." The authors go below the techniques of teaching to examine how we know how children make sense of the world and then analyze how instruction can promote sensemaking; viewing change to practice from how students learn represents a necessary and productive complement to assessing practice by its outcomes. This is followed by Mariana Souto-Manning, Beverly Falk, Dina López, Lívia Barros Cruz, Nancy Bradt, Nancy Cardwell, Nicole McGowan, Aura Perez, Ayesha Rabadi-Raol, and Elizabeth Rollins's Chapter 9, "A Transdisciplinary Approach to Equitable Teaching in Early Childhood Education." Their review is a deep rethinking of the core ideas and assumptions of early childhood education, to move beyond increasing availability to powerful learning experiences that foster equity. Steve Graham takes on the critically important core skill of writing in Chapter 10, "Changing How Writing Is Taught." He reviews the past two decades of efforts to improve writing instruction, focusing on the specific barriers identified in the literature and making concrete recommendations to policymakers, administrators, teachers, and the public.

Complementing this review, Kara Mitchell Viesca, Kathryn Strom, Svenja Hammer, Jessica Masterson, Cindy Hammer Linzell, Jessica Mitchell-McCollough, and Naomi Flynn review literacy instruction through content areas in Chapter 11, "Developing a Complex Portrait of Content Teaching for Multilingual Learners via Nonlinear Theoretical Understandings." Using Deleuze and Guattari's rhizome concept to think anew about how teaching is deeply tied to context, the authors broaden the view of change to practice by identifying the myriad contextual factors involved. Rhonda S. Bondie, Christine Dahnke, and Akane Zusho tackle the complicated practice of differentiation in Chapter 12, "How Does Changing 'One-Size-Fits-All' to Differentiated Instruction Affect Teaching?" The chapter takes on the now well-established trope of differentiation to explore its developments and limitations, ultimately pushing for a new definition to move the field forward. Finally, Dolores Perin and Jodi Patrick Holschuh round this section out in Chapter 13, "Teaching Academically Underprepared Postsecondary Students." They discuss the research on teaching approaches for postsecondary students in developmental courses and suggest ways to improve their educational opportunities.

The final section of the volume centers on emerging issues for practice. In Chapter 14, Philip J. Piety begins with "Components, Infrastructures, and Capacity: The Quest for the Impact of Actionable Data Use on P–20 Educator Practice." He offers a broad survey of the subfields grouped under the heading of "data"—data-driven decision making, learning analytics, and educational data mining—and finds that there is little research evidence that data have informed or changed practice. In the end, the review looks to how the field might move to do so. Authors M. Shelley Thomas, Shantel Crosby, and Judi Vanderhaar review the newer interdisciplinary field of trauma-informed practice in Chapter 15, "Trauma-Informed Practices in Schools Across Two Decades: An Interdisciplinary Review of Research." The authors are a team from different fields—education, social work, professional—who analyze research related to trauma-informed practice now migrating into education and its implications for teachers and schools. Finally, Chapter 16 is authored by Julia Daniel, Karen Hunter Quartz, and Jeannie Oakes, who examine community schools and the impact they have on teaching practice, "Teaching in Community Schools: Creating Conditions for Deeper Learning." In a return to an older literature that viewed schools as inextricably part of their communities, the authors review recent work exploring those ties and analyze the extent to which deeper and expanded learning opportunities can be fostered through community schools.

Taken as a whole, these chapters consider some of the most critical problems facing educators and scholars today: how our history shapes our present-day possibilities, how we develop the capacity of educators to change and improve practice, the innumerable aspects that can be changed, which dimensions of teaching should we prioritize, and what emerging issues will shape this work in the coming years? Again, we do not imagine this volume of *Review of Research in Education* represents the full range of issues, approaches, and potential developments regarding change to teaching practice. Instead, we believe it provides an insightful profile of recent research on changing teaching practice that shines a light on the complexity, intricacy, and contingency involved on both the professional and scholarly sides of classroom instruction. Furthermore, across the volume we see ideas and the seeds of future projects that, in order to be undertaken with rigor and sensitivity, must be approached in ways that span disciplines, subfields, and the gaps between researchers and practitioners.

LOOKING FORWARD

Again, based on their historical study, Tyack and Cuban (1997) posited that change to teaching practice "will result in the future more from internal changes created by the knowledge and expertise of teachers than from the decisions of external policy makers" (p. 135). To this formulation, we would map education researchers in the space between and overlapping with practitioners, policymakers, and communities. This is a privileged position that allows us to investigate, collaborate, experiment, and deliberate with degrees of freedom and support unavailable to other stakeholders. And it is precisely because we are afforded these privileges that we researchers are obliged to work with determination and a morality attuned to the lives of our most vulnerable and marginalized youth. As a diverse community of scholars, we can fulfill these obligations through the concerted development and well-considered communication of knowledge about that most difficult kind of reform, changing classroom practice to be more equitable and just.

In pursuit of this aspiration, we see several core challenges that emerge as central for the next generation of research on change to teaching practice: fostering collaborative relationships across research fields and with practitioners to generate more robust scholarship, developing consistent and shared language to facilitate these partnerships, bringing educational history to bear to deepen and nuance our understandings, identifying the general elements of change in relation to the context- and practice-dependent elements, and articulating studies about teacher capacity and performance with research in institutional and sociocultural context.

It is our hope that this volume finds readers across the range of the American Educational Research Association (AERA)'s subfields and specializations, including research-interested practitioners within the organization, because it will be through collaboration across these distinctions that the next generation of literature will become more holistic, cross-disciplinary, methodologically sophisticated, and engaged with the complex realities of teaching and learning. Our students are depending on it.

ACKNOWLEDGMENTS

The editors thank the many people who made this volume possible. First and foremost, we thank the authors, who worked tirelessly to produce high-quality reviews on a short time line. We were fortunate to have such dedicated and talented scholars to work with. We also thank our reviewers who similarly worked with very tight turnarounds yet managed to provide feedback that was substantive, constructive, and thoughtful. And we extend our thanks to all the scholars that submitted proposals, whose excellent ideas made the selection process difficult and had a formative effect on this volume. Leann Zuhrmuhlen, our contact at SAGE, was instrumental in helping us manage the editorial process. Both Felice Levine and John Neikirk at AERA were indispensable guides and advisors from start to finish; we would not have been able to put out this volume without drawing on their knowledge and expertise. Thank you to the AERA Journal Publications Committee who selected our proposal and provided us the opportunity to address the vital issues shaping teaching practice. We thank our colleagues, friends, and family for their support, encouragement, and continual understanding. Finally, and most important, we thank teachers and students for their persistent and inspiring commitment to teaching and learning.

REFERENCES

Cohen, D. K. (1988). *Teaching practice: Plus ça change . . .* East Lansing, MI: National Center for Teacher Education.

Cohen, D. K., & Spillane, J. (1992). Policy and practice: Relations between governance and instruction. *Review of Research in Education, 18*(1), 3–49.

Cuban, L. (1993). *How teachers taught: Constancy and change in American classrooms, 1890-1990.* New York, NY: Teachers College Press.

Cuban, L. (2013). *Inside the black box of classroom teaching: Change without reform in American education.* Cambridge, MA: Harvard University Press.

Dorn, S. (2011, September 4). Being careless with education history [Blog post.] Retrieved from http://shermandorn.com/wordpress/?p=3780

Dorn, S. (2018, March 10). How the "industrial era schools" myth is a barrier to helping schools today [Blog post]. Retrieved from http://shermandorn.com/wordpress/?p=8558

Papert, S. (1997). Why school reform is impossible. *Journal of the Learning Sciences, 6,* 417–427.

Payne, C. (2008). *So much reform, so little change: The persistence of failure in urban schools.* Cambridge, MA: Harvard University Press.

RAND Corporation. (2012). *Teachers matter: Understanding teachers' impact on student achievement.* Santa Monica, CA: Author. Retrieved from https://www.rand.org/pubs/corporate_pubs/CP693z1-2012-09.html

Schneider, J. (2014). *From the ivory tower to the schoolhouse: How scholarship becomes common knowledge in education.* Cambridge, MA: Harvard University Press.

Schon, D. (1973). *Beyond the stable state.* New York, NY: W. W. Norton.

Tyack, D., & Cuban, L. (1997). *Tinkering towards utopia: A century of public school reform* (Rev. ed.). Cambridge, MA: Harvard University Press.

U.S. Department of Education. (2016). *The state of racial diversity in the educator workforce.* Washington, DC: Author. Retrieved from www2.ed.gov/rschstat/eval/highered/racial-diversity/state-racial-diversity-workforce.pdf

Watters, A. (2015, April 25). The invented history of the factory model of education [Blog post]. Retrieved from http://hackeducation.com/2015/04/25/factory-model

Watters, A., Anderson, B., Neuschatz, K., & Kantrowitz, L. (2018, October 16). *The history of the future of high school.* Retrieved from www.vice.com/en_us/article/j53vnk/the-history-of-the-future-of-high-school-v25n3

Chapter 1

Teaching for Diversity: Intercultural and Intergroup Education in the Public Schools, 1920s to 1970s

Lauri D. Johnson iD
Boston College

Yoon K. Pak
University of Illinois at Urbana-Champaign

This historiography chronicles educators' efforts to teach for diversity through heightening awareness of immigrant experiences as well as discrimination against minoritized religious and racial groups in public school classrooms from the 1920s through the 1970s. This curriculum and pedagogical work was couched under various terms, such as intercultural education, intergroup education, human relations, and cultural pluralism. Drawing from published secondary research literature as well as primary archival sources, we aim to disrupt commonly held views that intercultural education/intergroup education met its demise in the 1950s and show how curriculum and pedagogy shifted after the landmark 1954 ruling of Brown v. Board of Education toward improving intergroup relations within the context of school desegregation. In the end we identify common themes across the decades that include the failure to recruit and support a diverse teaching force, the importance of teacher-led curriculum and professional development, and the lack of a sustained focus on race and racism in classroom practices.

Democracy in group relations in human relations is gripping the American mind and consciousness. Next to the war it is the most discussed topic these days. If our democracy is to survive, we have to do something about it. Two-thirds of the world today is under the control of the colored races, and they are swiftly rising to power. This one fact has made us look at the undemocratic pictures at home, and in many cases, we do not like what we see.

—Lauretta Wieland, a teacher of home economics at Waukesha High School, Waukesha, Wisconsin (1945)[1]

Review of Research in Education
March 2019, Vol. 43, pp. 1–31
DOI: 10.3102/0091732X18821127
Chapter reuse guidelines: sagepub.com/journals-permissions
© 2019 AERA. http://rre.aera.net

How educators learn to teach for diversity is just as complicated today as it was in our recent educational history. From the 1920s, diversity work in classrooms was often couched under the umbrella terms of intercultural and intergroup education, which aimed to heighten awareness of immigrant experiences as well as discrimination against minoritized religious and racial groups. In this review of the literature, we aim to disrupt two aspects of the conventional wisdom about intercultural and intergroup education. First, we argue that intercultural and intergroup education did not witness a demise in the mid-1950s as some have suggested (Wechsler, 2012), including the authors of this chapter. Rather, the purposes shifted after the landmark 1954 ruling of *Brown v. Board of Education* toward efforts to improve intergroup relations within the context of school desegregation from the late 1950s well into the 1970s. Citing Hall's (2005) example, we argue for a "long intercultural/ intergroup education movement," which links democratic citizenship education with culture-based curriculum, prejudice reduction pedagogy, and school desegregation efforts.

Second, we challenge the typology of intercultural education beginning in the 1930s and evolving naturally into intergroup education/human relations in the 1950s and into multiethnic and multicultural education in the late 1960s and 1970s. History is much too complicated and nuanced to fit neatly into discrete categories, even as we admit our own shortcomings regarding this chronology. Indeed, delving back into the historical literature reveals that the practices of intercultural and intergroup education never faded away but inserted themselves in different ways, especially given the need to address the permanence of racism in U.S. society (Bell, 1992). While nonexhaustive in scope, we offer historical insights that apply to contemporary educational reform for diversity and inclusion. We acknowledge that diversity work in the schools, and all of its referents, is still difficult and fraught with myriad challenges but remains a necessary and worthy path for educators to pursue.

Early research syntheses on the topic in the *Review of Educational Research* noted a lack of common agreement on aims and practices from the outset. Giles, Pitkin, and Ingram (1946) asserted that intercultural education was designed "to improve understandings and practices of good human relations between individuals of many culture groups" (p. 39), while Cook (1947) argued that research on intergroup education was "for the most part, a goodwill literature, urging everyone to act *right*, to act *now*" (p. 266).

TERMINOLOGY

Historians have chronicled a variety of terms that refer to efforts by teachers and teacher educators to increase group understanding and combat racial and religious intolerance. Montalto (1982), who researched the history of progressive organizations such as the Service Bureau on Intercultural Education from 1924 to 1941, used the term intercultural education but also referred to diversity work during this period as intergroup, interhuman, human relations, and ethnic studies.

Selig (2008), who begins her focus with the 1920s, adopts the term "cultural gifts" to describe the contributions of immigrant and minority groups to American life during the interwar years (p. 2). Terms like intergroup education and human relations were particularly used in the 1950s to describe teacher workshops aimed at studying how diverse racial and ethnic groups could work together, but these terms sometimes appear in earlier decades in curriculum materials and descriptions of in-service workshops. While some scholars have argued that educators moved from a cultural gifts approach in the 1920s and 1930s, to intercultural education in the late 1930s and 1940s, and intergroup education in the 1950s, in practice educators who worked to reduce prejudice often conflated terms and notions of race and culture to describe their work well into the 1950s. On the one hand, this could be regarded as a deliberate way to avoid the thorny issue of U.S. race relations by subsuming race and the study of minoritized groups under the topic of culture. But given social science evidence beginning in the 1930s and 1940s, intercultural and intergroup educators might also have been intentional in not employing the term "race" and abiding by research developments on the fallacy of "race" at that time. The specific term intercultural education faded in the U.S. context but was taken up in Europe by the early 1980s to refer to pedagogical approaches aimed at improving the interaction between diverse cultural groups in response to increasing immigration from the former colonies of Africa and Asia to Western Europe.

Beginning from the 1930s intercultural and intergroup educators also referred to their own research and publications on diversity work with terms such as intercultural, intergroup, cultural pluralism, cultural contributions, human relations, and democratic human relations (see, e.g., Cole, 1953; Cook, 1947; DuBois, 1984; Taba & Wilson, 1946; Vickery & Cole, 1943). Perhaps seen as advancements in social science research, a special issue of the *Journal of Educational Sociology* (1945) was devoted to "Workshops on Intergroup Education." Some of the more notable articles include: "Human Development and Intergroup Education" (Davis & Havighurst, 1945); "Intergroup Education Workshops and School Problems" (Giles, 1945); "Group Living as a Part of Intergroup Education Workshops" (Mead, 1945), "Summer Workshops in Intergroup Education" (Seamans, 1945), and "Facing the Need for Intergroup Education" (Warren, 1945). The journal continued to publish on the topic with "A Frame of Reference for Intercultural Education" four years later (Kilpatrick, Stone, & Cole, 1949). *The Journal of Educational Sociology* was a consistent outlet for a range of publications up through the 1960s, including questioning the basis for intergroup education and gauging its impact on educators (see, e.g., Hager, 1950, 1956; Merideth & Burr, 1947; Snyder, 1962).

Harvard Educational Review published articles by notable social scientists such as Gordon Allport (1945) and education scholars where the usage of the terms intergroup and intercultural education were blurred (Chatto, 1945; Murra, 1945). A 1951 publication from a conference on the "Educational Problems of Special Cultural Groups" at Teachers College, Columbia University, essentially focused on race and intercultural education with lectures by Gordon Allport, Charles S. Johnson, Margaret Mead, and Eleanor Roosevelt (Bureau of Publications, 1951). For the purposes of this chapter, we employ the terms intercultural and intergroup to refer to the range of diversity work occurring in the nation's schools during this time period. As much as diversity continues to be a problematic term, we use it here in reference to those religious and racial groups who have been minoritized in U.S. society, including immigrants from Asia and Southern and Eastern Europe. However, we focus our attention on those curriculum topics and classroom strategies that pertained to race.

METHODOLOGY

This historiography surveyed secondary sources written about intercultural and intergroup education from the 1920s through the 1970s, which were identified through university online databases and website searches using keywords such as "intercultural education," "intergroup education," "multicultural education," "race relations," and "human relations." Major education research databases searched include Academic Search Premier, EBSCO, MegaFILE, Education Source, ERIC, JSTOR, and Google Scholar. To address the gaps in the historical record and contextualize these secondary sources, additional archival sources were located at the Wayne State University Archives of Labor History and Urban Affairs and University Archives, Detroit, Michigan; University of Pittsburgh Collections; Young Research Library, University of California, Los Angeles; Immigration History Research Center Archives, University of Minnesota; Social Welfare History Archives, University of Minnesota; and the Hoover Institution Archives, Stanford, California.

HISTORICAL DEVELOPMENT OF INTERCULTURAL AND INTERGROUP EDUCATION

Nicholas Montalto's (1982) historical account of the intercultural education movement arguably stands as the most detailed treatment on the topic, beginning his investigation in the 1920s with the passage of the 1924 Immigration Act (the Johnson-Reed Act).[2] This remains a departure from more recent studies that chronicle the start of intercultural education in the 1930s stemming from increased anti-Semitic incidents abroad and race riots at home. Couching the challenges of intergroup education as "specialized work for the second generation" (Montalto, 1982), some educators became increasingly concerned with how second-generation students were losing their ethnic identities and languages from Americanization programs that effectively succeeded all too well in erasing students' home cultures.

Historical work on Americanization and "English-only" programs in the schools indicate the degree to which a homogenous American identity necessitated a White, Western European, Protestant ideology for all minoritized students (see, e.g., Adams, 1995; Blanton, 2004; Fass, 1989; Lawrence, 2011; Olneck, 1989; Tamura, 1993). Noting the limitations of Americanization reform and to address the needs of the second generation of immigrants, concerted efforts to reimagine the meaning of *e pluribus unum* (out of many, one) for democratic citizenship ensued.[3] More than a decade later, the influential publication of Gunnar Myrdal's *An American Dilemma* (1944) brought attention to the gap between the ideals of democracy and the reality of race relations in U.S. schools.

Situated within the progressive era in education, the work of Rachel Davis DuBois, whose particular teaching units are explained later in this chapter, is credited by Montalto (1982) as the "one person more than any other responsible for setting a new agenda for American education" (p. 77) in intercultural and intergroup affairs. Her work in classrooms in the 1920s and 1930s in Woodbury, New Jersey, Philadelphia, and New York paved the way for important collaborations with scholars from Teachers College, Columbia University, and in developing networks to form the Service Bureau for Intercultural Education in 1933. The Progressive Education Association (PEA) was the first major sponsor of DuBois's intercultural education work and was one of many commissions and committees sponsored by the PEA. Although the Commission (and later Committee) for Intercultural Education received scant attention by Lawrence Cremin (1961) in *The Transformation of the School: Progressivism in American Education, 1876–1957* and Patricia Albjerg Graham (1967) in *Progressive Education: From Arcady to Academe: A History of the Progressive Education Association, 1919–1953*, the broadened scope of intercultural/intergroup education gained in popularity, occurring alongside PEA's sponsorship of the famed "Eight-Year Study" (Kridel & Bullough, 2007).

Like Montalto, Selig (2008) argues that the restriction of immigration in the 1920s redirected debate from political to cultural terms, which paradoxically allowed a pluralistic approach to culture to begin to take hold. In her view, the success of nativist efforts to restrict immigration meant progressive educators and activists could offer a more positive but romanticized vision of ethnic cultures. Scholars have noted that elements of a "cultural gifts" approach had also taken root earlier in New York City in the 1910s and 1920s through the activities of progressive school leaders such as Leonard Covello, who established the Italian language on equal footing with other foreign languages at Dewitt Clinton High School (Johanek & Puckett, 2007). In 1934, he would become the famed principal of Benjamin Franklin High School, where he encouraged his largely Italian and Puerto Rican students and their families to express and appreciate their unique cultural contributions and implored his teachers to incorporate community funds of knowledge as part of the high school curriculum (Covello, 1936). Covello enacted an antiassimilationist stance and community oriented approach to educational leadership at a time when the norms of White, Anglo-Saxon Protestantism were common in the majority of U.S. schools (see, e.g., Fass, 1989; Karier, 1986).

Some theorists at the time, such as Bruno Lasker (1929), took a structural approach and argued in his book *Race Attitudes in Children* that in order to reduce racial prejudice students from diverse backgrounds must learn together (providing early support for racially integrated schools). Lasker believed that institutional reform was more important than curriculum innovations.

How were teachers conceptualizing race and culture in their classrooms in the 1930s? Using teacher publications in educational journals, Burkholder (2011) describes the period from 1900 to 1938 as "race as nation." Teachers who wrote about their classroom lessons in these publications frequently used the race concept to refer to European immigrants, particularly during Americanization campaigns. During the interwar years, ethnic group contributions also included some elements of racial and religious diversity (Mirel, 2010; Selig, 2008). This "separate approach" to cultural pluralism equated "race" to what we might now describe as ethnic background and emphasized those positive cultural traits that were deemed socially valuable and most in line with America's democratic ideals. It portrayed America as a nation of immigrants who could succeed through individual effort (Selig, 2008). The years immediately following World War II brought about the teaching of race as a construct based on new scientific knowledge on the topic (Klineberg, 1945).

INTERCULTURAL AND INTERGROUP EDUCATIONAL DEVELOPMENTS

Much of the work within intercultural and intergroup education involved the production of curriculum materials at all grade levels, radio shows and films, teacher in-service workshops, and college courses and community relations projects to encourage democratic cultural pluralism and improve human relations. Perhaps most well-known in the 1930s were a series of CBS radio programs, school assembly programs, and curriculum units on the cultural contributions of individual racial and ethnic groups originally conceived by Davis DuBois a decade before the development of the Service Bureau and implemented in selected schools in New Jersey, metropolitan New York City, Philadelphia, Washington, D.C., and suburban Boston.

DuBois, a Quaker and history teacher from Woodbury, New Jersey, has been described as a "tireless champion of pluralism" (Selig, 2008, p. 10) whose Quaker upbringing and values were evidenced early on through interracial relationships in her youth and the discernment of a lifelong "concern" or calling to devote her "major energies to race relations" (Mufti, 2018, p. 27). Davis DuBois's approach to intercultural education, instituted first in 1924 as the Woodbury Plan, focused on three intertwined methods of teaching and learning: the emotional, the intellectual, and the situational (Lal, 2004).

Between 1933 and 1936, Davis DuBois formulated classroom materials related to the "Negro, Chinese, Japanese, and Jews" that focused on subjects such as American History, Literature, Music, Art, Economics, and Science (DuBois, 1936). The topics and group discussion questions in these units countered the prevailing norms of who constituted an American and challenged the very notions of democratic citizenship. A few references to Native Americans and introductory materials on Hispanics in the Southwest (with more attention to Spanish versus Mexican cultural influences) also surfaced.

For example, in investigating the Reconstruction Period in American History, Davis DuBois was deliberate in including works by Carter G. Woodson, Booker T.

Washington, and W. E. B. DuBois with the objective: "1) to show that some Negroes after the Civil War were fit and able to take part in local and national government; and 2) to show the part the Negro played in the period after the Civil War" (DuBois, 1936, para. 3). An excerpt by Woodson (1922) from *The Negro in Our History* further accentuates the message Davis DuBois wished to impart to students: "The charge that all Negro officers were illiterates, ignorant of the science of government, cannot be sustained. Some of them had undergone considerable training and had experienced sufficient mental development to be able to discharge their duties with honor" (pp. 249–251). In her "Suggested Class Situation," W. E. B. DuBois's *The Negro Citizen* served as the backdrop to critically analyze the meaning of "a system of color in the United States based on a legal and customary race distinction and discriminations having to do with separation in travel, in schools, in public accommodations, in residence and in family relations" (as quoted in DuBois, 1936, para. 5). Incorporating research by prominent African American scholars bolstered Davis DuBois's approach toward a curriculum that considered minority perspectives as well as a means to understanding the complex face of democracy and citizenship by raising issues rarely discussed in the public schools, even today.

The legal and constitutional questions of citizenship also extended to the classroom units on Chinese and Japanese immigrants in the United States. Davis DuBois developed a fact sheet on "Some Rules of Immigration and Citizenship" to provide background information on who was eligible for citizenship based on the 1790 limit to naturalization based on "free White persons" and the 15th Amendment passed during the Reconstruction Era to include "persons of African descent." The specific reference to the Chinese Exclusion Act of 1882 as well as the 1924 Immigration Act pointed to the limitations of naturalized citizenship and in some respects implicitly questioned the basis of such exclusionary policies, ultimately questioning why groups were denied equal rights under the law based on race, religion, and nationality. The classroom materials on Japan, particularly framed for English and History, aimed to have students consider further problems of democracy in relation to Asian immigrants. Davis DuBois outlined the general objectives: (1) to make students appreciate the desirability of Japanese as neighbors and citizens and (2) to influence them to take a fair attitude toward the feeling of Japanese on the Exclusion Act.

In particular, attitudes to be counteracted rested on the stereotypical view of the Japanese, and Asians for that matter, as unassimilable and unfit for citizenship. Such notions were quite advanced for the time as throughout the West Coast numerous anti-Asiatic leagues heightened the general public fears about the yellow peril and the threat to democracy if the Japanese, in particular, would be considered for citizenship.

To counter the idea of Asians as unfit for citizenship and thus undesirable, the story of Lue Gim Gong, a pioneer Chinese American, who invented a new breed of oranges in Florida, was featured in one of Davis DuBois's curriculum units and in an episode of her popular radio show *Americans All, Immigrants All.* Naturalized in the United States prior to the 1882 Exclusion law, Lue Gim Gong created a hardier brand of oranges that was able to resist the cold, known as the Lue Gim Gong Orange, which earned him the Wilder Medal awarded by the U.S. Department of Agriculture. By revealing his humble, honest, and Christian character, in DuBois's view, Gong represented what was best about Asian immigrants and signified that his allegiance to the United States was unquestioned, thus situating his legitimacy as an American.

While no individual stories of American success were highlighted in the section on the Japanese, Davis DuBois included references by authors who were sympathetic to the Japanese American communities in California, and their economic contribution to the agricultural industry. The message about the Japanese as hardworking, persevering, and potential model citizens (even though the second-generation were citizens by birth) served to underscore the viability of extending citizenship to Asians. The ultimate irony in framing Chinese and Japanese immigrants as those most deserving to be citizens, because of their unswerving Protestant work ethic, would become a double-edged sword in the 1960s when they became framed as model minorities in comparison with the plight of African Americans and Latinx during the Civil Rights Movement (Wu, 2014).

DuBois's "separate approach" to intercultural education came under fire by Stewart Cole, a religion professor and fellow intercultural educator who had become the Director of the Service Bureau and favored an emphasis on cultural unity in light of the impending war (Bohan, 2007). Anthropologists such as Ruth Benedict also argued against the separate approach to cultural pluralism, noting that U.S. children of immigrant background were third generation, and faced "universal problems." Benedict concluded that the melting pot and the retention of cultural traits presented two "false alternatives" (Selig, 2008).

A 1937 evaluation of the Service Bureau for Intercultural Education conducted by the General Education Board, the Rockefeller philanthropy that funded the organization and other "race"-based initiatives, came to the conclusion that the organization should ground its work in academic scholarship and deemphasize race, ethnicity, and nationality as categories of identity and separation (Lal, 2004). This view bypassed Davis DuBois's version of cultural democracy and questioned her administrative abilities, and in 1941, she was forced to resign her role in the organization by the board of directors (Bohan, 2007).

Despite the administrative wrangling among the leadership of the Service Bureau, especially between Davis DuBois and Stewart Cole, the publications by the Service Bureau provided a prominent voice in education for intercultural relations. The monthly newsletter *Intercultural Education News* published renowned progressive educators such as William Heard Kilpatrick, Frank Trager, and Stewart Cole, as well as other prominent scholars on race such as Gordon Allport, Alain Locke, and Ruth Benedict. A content analysis of the major articles available (1939–1948) reveals that from January 1942 through January 1945, more explicit attention was paid to race than to any other major issues of the time (see Table 1 for list of sample titles).

TABLE 1
Sample Article Titles Addressing Race and Anti-Semitism in *Intercultural Education News*, 1942 to 1945

Publication Date	Title of Article
January 1942	"Service Bureau Submits an Inquiry to Negro and White Educators"
	"Leaders Identify the Obstacles Impeding Democratic Race Practices"
April 1942	"American Youth Commission Studies Negro Youth Adjustment Problems"
	"Jews in a Gentile World: The Problem of Anti-Semitism and Its Implications for America"
June 1942	"The Evacuation of the West-Coast Japanese: A Test of Social Democracy"
	"The Myth of the Negro Past: A Review"
October 1942	"The Issue of Race in War and Peace"
	"The Exclusion and Relocation of Pacific Coast Japanese"
	"The Negro in the War of Four Freedoms"
January 1943	"Japanese American Student Relocation"
	"Negroes Also Have Feelings"
March 1943	"Good Neighbors on the Home Front: An Experiment in Mexican-American Relations"
	"Patterns of Negro Segregation"
	"Japanese Americans in the Victory Program"
June 1943	"The Role of Negro Americans in American History Textbooks"
	"Statement of Conference of White Southerners on Race Relations"
October 1943	"Hate Diseases: An Introduction to Anti-Semitism"
	"Our Race Problem—An Editorial"
January 1944	"Books about the Negro for Children"
	"Interracial Citizens' Committees"
March 1944	"New York City Education and Race Prejudice"
	"Our American Democracy of Minority Rights"
November 1944	"The Bigot in Our Midst"
January 1945	"Prejudice: Japanese-Americans: Symbol of Racial Intolerance"

Source. Intercultural Education News, 1942 to 1945.

INTERCULTURAL EDUCATION POLICIES

The development of school district policies that addressed racial discrimination in hiring and promoted intercultural curriculum was another strategy employed by intercultural educators in the 1940s. A national survey of selected schools conducted by the Bureau for Intercultural Education in 1947 reported that only 28 schools (from the 234 that returned the survey—out of a total of 493 surveys that were mailed out) had adopted intercultural education policies (Pitkin, 1947). While the survey yield was hardly representative, it did provide insights about the process of adopting school or district-wide policies. The Service Bureau's analysis of these 28 districts revealed that all the policies came about since 1942, with very little or no opposition. Most of these policies were intended to (1) clarify to the public and to the staff the official perspective of schools in providing education for improved intergroup relations; (2) offer a firm basis on which to consider applicants for positions and promotions; and (3) provide security to the school staff. National attention from the passage of the Fair Employment Act of 1941 invariably influenced school settings. Many of the schools expressed similar beliefs in their reasons for adopting such policies. A school official from Kalamazoo, Michigan, indicated that their policy statement was helpful to the employing official in the school system,

Having a single salary schedule is one thing, and having the Board go on record in favor of employing people because of competence and ability, rather than upon the basis of national background, color, religion, or some other factor, is something entirely different.

While there is little information about how these policies were implemented, the changing face of the schools' populations moved some school leaders to provide incremental improvements, at least in writing. Southern school districts were a different story altogether.[4]

According to Pitkin (1947), there appeared to be five major ways that the policies were developed and enacted. First, schools developed policies rooted out of community unrest and the growing attention to segregated neighborhoods in the North. The race riots in places such as Detroit, Michigan, and Gary, Indiana, necessitated school and community officials to pay attention and enact changes in their schools toward effective "human relations" (see description of the development of the Detroit policy below). Second, school districts, such as those in San Diego and Kalamazoo, may have already had an Intercultural Relations Committee that expressed support by the administration for their work. Third, local Boards of Education issued a simple statement that no discriminatory practices would take place in the hiring and assignment of school personnel. The New Jersey cities of Camden and Elizabeth followed this model. Fourth, an individual superintendent, in places such as Cambridge, Massachusetts, and Providence, Rhode Island, expressed a deep commitment and initiated action to enact changes in the schools. Finally, a Curriculum Committee, in the development of a school philosophy for democratic living incorporated the area of human relations to broadening and strengthening its goals for citizenship. Schools in Seattle and Berkeley, California, for example, developed curriculum materials reflecting these broad, democratic goals (see Table 2 for list of school districts that adopted intercultural education policies).

Some of the most prominent and effective intercultural education policies in the 1940s were the result of coordinated community activism. Detroit's Administrative Committee for Intercultural and Interracial Education, along with religious and community leaders, campaigned for months for the adoption of a far-ranging document

TABLE 2
School Districts That Adopted Intercultural Education Policies, 1942 to 1947

Year	City
1942	Bayonne, New Jersey
1943	Elizabeth, New Jersey; Newark, New Jersey
1944	Hartford, Connecticut; Pittsfield, Massachusetts; Omaha, Nebraska; McKeesport, Pennsylvania; Chattanooga, Tennessee
1945	San Diego, California; Stamford, Connecticut; New Orleans, Louisiana; Detroit, Michigan; Atlantic City, New Jersey
1946	Berkeley, California; San Bernardino, California; Gary, Indiana; Cambridge, Massachusetts; Battlecreek, Michigan; Camden, New Jersey; Zanesville, Ohio; Providence, Rhode Island
1947	Stockton, California; Kalamazoo, Michigan; Cleveland Heights, Ohio; Sharon, Pennsylvania; Milwaukee, Wisconsin
No dates	Duluth, Minnesota; Seattle, Washington

Source. Victor Pitkin, "Survey of Intercultural Policies of Selected School Systems," BIE Manuscript Collection, Box, 1 Folder: BIE, Department of Analysis and Research, Survey of Intercultural Policies of Selected School Systems, 1947. Immigration History Research Center Archives, University of Minnesota.

that would send a message to the rest of the country that Detroit was dealing aggressively with racial discrimination. On January 9, 1945, they were successful in their efforts, and the school board unanimously approved the Detroit Intercultural Code modeled on a similar policy that had been adopted by social service agencies in Detroit. The policy stated, "The school has responsibility for treating all people fairly regardless of race, creed, national origin, or economic status." Detroit's policy prohibited racial discrimination in the hiring and promotion of employees, prevented out-of-district transfers based on race in an effort to curb white flight, mandated staff development and teacher education in "sound intercultural concepts" and the "understanding of minority groups," and advocated that the curriculum "provide for each pupil the educational experiences best suited to meet his needs and abilities" (L. Johnson & Pak, 2005, p. 8). In his 10–year study of intercultural efforts in the Detroit schools, Detroit educator Harold J. Harrison points to the Intercultural Code as the most significant accomplishment of the district's intercultural education efforts. He notes that as a result of the policy personnel policies were realigned, the district refused to continue support for racially segregated summer camp programs and High Y activities, and school administrators even boycotted a local segregated golf club (Harrison, 1953). While there were some notable exceptions, the overwhelming majority of the 234 school district officials who were surveyed by the Bureau of Intercultural Education replied that "no intercultural problems exist[ed]" and that a focus on interracial issues in schools would "do more harm than good" (Pitkin, 1947).

WORLD WAR II: REDUCING PREJUDICE AND RACIAL CONFLICT

During the war years, the rise of fascism and Nazism in Europe, early Civil Rights demands in Northern Black communities, changing student demographics on the West Coast, and the outbreak of racial and ethnic conflict in cities would bring a heightened urgency to school-based efforts aimed at combating racial and religious intolerance (Fallace, 2018). Several historians note that during World War II, teachers focused on combating race prejudice in order to aid the war effort, promote democracy, and unify the nation (Burkholder, 2011; L. Johnson, 2006; Shaffer, 1996). Burkholder (2011) focuses on how the concept of race became reconstructed in American classrooms during the war years in opposition to Nazi propaganda through the efforts of prominent anthropologists such as Franz Boas and Ruth Benedict. The pamphlet *The Races of Mankind*, originally intended for American troops, asserted scientific racial equality, and contended that differences between racial groups were social and cultural rather than biological (Benedict & Weltfish, 1943). By 1945, three quarters of a million copies of the pamphlet were in circulation, and it was used in several New York City schools, for example, to "debunk" racist myths (Burkholder, 2007). In 1946, the United Auto Workers hired United Productions of America to create an animated short film based on the pamphlet titled "The Brotherhood of Man," which was distributed to union and community groups and featured in a yearly human relations film festival for New York City teachers sponsored by the Harlem Committee of the Teachers Union of New York City (L. Johnson, 2002). Although the visual characterizations in the film would be considered stereotyped caricatures by today's standards, the film underscored that human differences were based on environmental influences, not race.

Other uses of film in the classroom, such as the Human Relations Film Series at Benjamin Franklin High School, were designed to help students reflect critically on the root causes of social problems and link with the school's neighborhood action projects. Designed by Alice Keliher, the series utilized selected Hollywood films and asked teachers to focus on the larger question, "How can we help [adolescents] to relate [their] personal problems to broad social developments and the culture in which they live?" (as cited in Rabin, 2013, p. 61). Several of these films, such as *Fury*, foregrounded issues of race, although often in coded ways.[5]

Psychological Perspectives

A scientific approach to race meant that science could be used "as (a) shield" against racial prejudice (Locke, 1940), which teachers might incorporate into their pedagogy and curriculum. In Perillo's (2006) view, those New York City teachers who implemented intercultural education activities in their classroom aimed to heal the "damaged Black psyche" while improving the psychological health of White America—by creating not just democratic citizens but democratic personalities (see also Giles & Van Til, 1946). Zimmerman (2004) has characterized the campaign over integrating school textbooks as a psychological discourse, arguing that while "racism injured America's national image on the world stage . . . it injured African Americans' *self image* at home" (p. 48). In other locales such as Massachusetts, the Springfield Plan, which became the most widely publicized intercultural education program during the war years, viewed racial and religious prejudice as a mental and emotional disease, and aimed to "inoculate students against propaganda" through classroom activities that involved propaganda analysis and the development of "straight thinking" among students (L. Johnson, 2006). Olneck (1990) argues that intercultural education came to emphasize changing individual attitudes and behaviors toward others who differ, and to champion ideals of universal inclusion, participation, and nondiscrimination. Racial discrimination was seen as an individual psychological and attitudinal phenomenon, rather than a collective process embedded in historical and material conditions. In her book that relates the lessons of the intergroup education movement to multicultural education, Banks (2005) also notes that "intergroup educators focused their attention on prejudice and discrimination at the personal level and did not give much attention to the structures in American society that supported those perspectives" (p. 127).

Efforts to reduce prejudice through psychological explanations and remedies both competed with as well as complemented organizational efforts to alter race relations during the war years. In New York City, activists from the Teachers Union of New York City promoted Black history and intercultural curriculum materials, advocated hiring more African American teachers and administrators, and worked side-by-side with parents for school reform in predominantly Black neighborhoods such as Harlem and Bedford-Stuyvesant (L. Johnson, 2002). Community advocacy organizations such as the Citywide Citizens' Committee for Harlem (CWCCH) incorporated both psychological approaches to prejudice reduction as well as a focus on Black history, recruiting a more diverse teaching force, establishing playgrounds in city neighborhoods, and promulgating fair housing policies. As an interracial civic unity committee, their accomplishments included the passage of the first employment discrimination bill in New York State, a race discrimination amendment that denied city funding to segregated child care agencies, the establishment of an Advisory Committee on Human Relations at the Board of Education, an in-service course on intercultural education, and an extensive public education campaign to improve race relations in New York City. The CWCCH's aim to transform both the political and social landscape of New York City as well as the racial views of individual New Yorkers bridged the psychologically oriented prejudice reduction activities of intercultural education with early Civil Rights work (as cited in L. Johnson, 2017).

Responses to Racial Conflict

Intercultural education also served as a symbolic response to racial conflicts, at a time when "riots" and racial uprisings in cities across the country—Chicago, Detroit, Los Angeles, Harlem, Mobile Alabama, and Beaumont Texas—challenged the United States' international image and served as a stark reminder of the gap between the democratic promise of the American creed and the lived reality for many African Americans and other Students of Color (Myrdal, 1944). In the summer of 1943, America's racial and ethnic inequities donned a public face in the media and proved an embarrassment to America's foreign policy abroad (Dudziak, 2011; J. Hart, 2004) when graphic photographs in *Life Magazine* showed White mobs beating up Black residents in Detroit and setting their cars on fire while the police stood by (*Life Magazine*, 1943).

Vowing that it would "never happen in our community," civic unity committees sprang up in cities from Seattle to Boston. The Race Relations Institute at Fisk University reported that 145 new interracial committees for unity formed in 1943 alone following the Detroit riot (Race Relations Institute, 1943), and by 1948, according to the American Council on Race Relation, there were 1,134 educational "organizations, public and private concerned with the improvement of racial, religious, ethnic, or cultural relations in the United States" (American Council on Race Relations, 1948, p. i).

School officials in other Northern cities pointed to Detroit's experience as a cautionary tale, and Board member Mrs. F. B. Chalfant urged the Pittsburgh schools to adopt a district-wide curriculum focused on democratic citizenship in order to help the city avoid racial conflicts ("Democracy to Be Taught in Local Schools," 1943). Examples from two cities, Detroit and Los Angeles, indicate educators' classroom strategies and organizational responses to racial conflict.

Intercultural Education in Detroit

World War II had transformed Detroit into a "total industrial landscape," where jobs were plentiful and 50% of the workers were unionized. As Black and White workers from the South poured into the city to work in converted automobile factories, Detroit became the "arsenal of democracy" and the largest producer of military equipment in the country during the war years (Sugrue, 1996). The African American population of Detroit more than doubled during the 1940s, from 149,119, about 9% of the population, to 303,721, more than 16%. As the new migrants settled into predominantly White or Black neighborhoods, the city (and the city's schools) became increasingly racially segregated.

As Halvorson and Mirel (2013) note in their case study of intercultural education programs in Detroit, the city had a long history "as a racial and ethnic tinderbox" (p. 363). However, teaching about race was not unknown in the Detroit schools before 1943. African American administrator Charles A. Daly, principal of Garfield School (and later Miller High School) in Detroit, had infused Black history and Black literature in his school's curriculum in the late 1930s (Daly, 1938). Faced with a particular urgency after the summer racial conflicts, in the fall of 1943 Detroit School Superintendent Dr. Warren Bow appointed a group of teachers and administrators to form the Administrative Committee on Intercultural and Interracial Relations (later known as the Coordinating Committee for Democratic Human Relations). Local intercultural committees were established in 200 Detroit schools, an Instructional Committee took on the task of analyzing textbooks and creating bibliographies of multiethnic books, and the Committee on Interracial and Intercultural Understanding in the Schools worked with community groups (L. Johnson & Pak, 2005).

Detroit teachers and administrators visited other school districts, including Springfield, Massachusetts and New York City, to examine their intercultural programs and invited Chicago educator Madeline Morgan to address the committee about her widely publicized "Supplementary Units for the Course of Study in Social Studies," a K–8 Black history curriculum that was used in the Chicago schools (Hines, 2017). In conjunction with the State Committee on Intercultural Understanding, teachers and administrators also developed the intercultural curriculum guide *Building One Nation, Indivisible* (Detroit Public Schools, 1944) that was distributed to all Detroit schools. The introduction to this guide made direct reference to the recent racial conflicts and linked intercultural education with the fight against fascism and efforts to "make democracy real" for all Detroit residents.

Exemplary intercultural curriculum approaches and lessons from local Detroit schools were published in *Promising Practices in Intergroup Education* (Detroit Public Schools, 1946), which described 11 approaches, including the "cultural contributions" approach, the study of prejudice, providing vicarious experiences of discrimination, and community participation in democratic decision making (not dissimilar to classroom approaches to multicultural education in the 1980s and 1990s). A version of this publication was adopted by the National Bureau of Intercultural Education and distributed to school districts across the country during the 1940s.

The Detroit Federation of Teachers formed their own intercultural committee in 1944 and sponsored a series of lectures for teachers on "The Price and Profit of Race Prejudice," "The Teacher's Role in Intercultural Education," and "Clinical Approaches to Prejudice." Some of their more innovative intercultural activities included circulating a list of downtown restaurants who served all patrons without discrimination entitled *Will You Eat For Democracy?* and staging "Know How Teas" in the union hall where teachers would present effective classroom lessons which furthered democratic human relations under the slogan, "It's fun to be fooled, but it's more fun to know how" (Detroit Federation of Teachers, 1948). These combined school and community efforts would lead Charles S. Johnson of Fisk University to characterize the Detroit intercultural program as "the most practical and effective program of any of the major cities" (C. S. Johnson, 1945).

Intercultural Education in Los Angeles

Multicultural Los Angeles in the 1940s was a reflection of the expansive growth in the population of Southern California during the Depression in the 1930s (Garcia, 2018; Raftery, 1992). Between 1920 and 1930 Los Angeles' population doubled from 576,673 to 1,238,048, with migrants coming chiefly from the South and the Midwest. The resultant housing shortage and crowded living conditions stretched the limits of de facto segregated neighborhoods throughout the city. Between June 3 and June 10, 1943, the city of Los Angeles experienced the worst rioting it had seen in the 20th century. Incited by sensational newspaper stories and the proclamations of city officials, which fed a growing hysteria about juvenile delinquency among Mexican American youth, southern White servicemen who were on leave attacked young men who wore "drapes" or zoot suits.[6] The reverberations of the "Zoot Suit riots" were felt by Los Angeles school officials, who faced overcrowded classrooms and a massive teacher shortage. The Superintendent of the Los Angeles County schools requested assistance from the Bureau of Intercultural Education through progressive educator William Kilpatrick to appoint an individual from the Bureau to develop a program on human relations in the Los Angeles schools. Kilpatrick encouraged his colleague and friend, Stewart Cole, to visit Los Angeles for a 1–year period to see "what could be done to allay the fears and frustrations of the Spanish speaking youth during the war time and to help them intergrate [*sic*] more effectively in the public school" (Cole, n.d., p. 16). Following Kilpatrick's advice, Cole headed for Southern California intending to return after his year of consultation. Instead, he remained a Bureau representative on the West Coast and in 1945 helped establish the Pacific Coast Council on Intercultural Education and served as its executive director.

Cole had also worked to establish a notable intercultural education program in the San Diego schools in 1946 in conjunction with William Jack Stone and with the support of Superintendent Will Crawford (Pak, 2002). While the San Diego plan included local consultants and scholars to incorporate cultural contributions and bridge school and community efforts, in the Los Angeles schools, Cole placed an emphasis on building peace in a world community through reliance on a recent publication by UNESCO, the education branch of the United Nations. Cole's post–World War II vision of intercultural education argued that a concentration on global efforts for peace could increase democratic awareness in local schools and communities:

> If we are to achieve the human relationships essential for a peaceful world, we must find ways and means for getting many peoples, races, and nations to work together on behalf of common humanitarian purposes. In other words, we recognize that the world is constituted of a diversity of cultures and that the ways of peace lie in the direction of sound and democratic intercultural relations. So far as the public schools are concerned in this grand strategy, their program lies in the field of intercultural education on a world scale. (Cole, 1948–1949, p. 2)

The Preamble of UNESCO outlined the foundations for joining the principles of intercultural relations with world citizenship. Of particular importance were the statements on education for world peace: (1) to recognize our common humanity and innate equality; (2) to develop an understanding of living with different groups; (3) to develop attitudes of trust and recognition of socioeconomic interdependence; expand the democratic principles of justice, liberty, equality, and mutual respect across race, sex, language, and religion; (4) to encourage unrestricted pursuit of objective truth and the free exchange of ideas; and (5) to develop interest in and responsibility for meeting local, national, and international world problems.

Cole's director for the San Diego plan, William Stone, and other educators associated with the Pacific Coast Council on Intercultural Education, such as William Hartshorn and Edna Wiese, were involved in the development of the Los Angeles curriculum guide, *Developing Human Relations in the Elementary School*, which focused on the United Nations and UNESCO and learning to develop "world-mindedness" from the local to a global context. The introduction of the guide described each classroom as a "United Nations Organization in miniature with as many misunderstandings, prejudices, and conflicting ideas . . ." (Los Angeles City Schools, 1950, p. 4). The challenge afforded in such conditions required that teachers would help students "understand themselves and to live cooperatively and harmoniously with others" (Los Angeles City Schools, 1950, p. 1).

To meet those needs the guide outlined thirteen objectives including practicing democratic procedures, appreciating the interdependence of people, understanding children of other lands, developing sensitivity to needs of others, respecting the culture of all people, and developing a concept of a united world. More than half of the curriculum guide was devoted to an extensive discussion about the development of the United Nations in 1945 and the various commissions that were formed. Of particular salience in promoting human relations in the schools was "The Declaration of Human Rights" and the recognition that "the inherent dignity and the equal and inalienable rights of all members of the human family is the foundation of freedom, justice and peace in the world" (Los Angeles City Schools, 1950, p. 106). The primary target for UNESCO was the individual mind. The various "tools" for the mind came with implementing specific activities in all subject areas, including science and mathematics as well as arts and music, in order to broaden children's understanding of their place in the world. The Los Angeles intercultural program was briefly popular with progressive teachers in the early 1950s before it fell prey to the Cold War era's belief that the United Nations was a direct threat to American sovereignty and that the organization's covert aim was the implementation of a Communist world government (R. J. Hart, 2016).

UNIVERSITY-BASED PROJECTS

Post–World War II university-based projects to reduce prejudice and develop human relations were exemplified by the Intergroup Education in Cooperating Schools Project, which operated from 1945 to 1951. Led by social studies educator and curriculum theorist Hilda Taba, the project involved 260 teachers from 13 states and 18 school districts and was funded by the American Council on Education and the National Council of Christians and Jews (Sevier, 2009). Taba's approach brought together both the child-centered and social reconstructionist streams of progressive education with her focus on democratic human relations. She argued that "(progressive educators) have to furnish children with an opportunity to cultivate their ways of living together" (Taba, 1962, p. 215). Teachers involved in this project researched the intergroup interactions of their students through student diaries, sociograms, and observations of child-to-child interactions in the classroom and the playground (Sevier, 2008).

While some of these teacher education projects were labeled as intergroup education, other local school districts couched in-service courses in prejudice reduction and human relations as intercultural education into the late 1950s. In Pittsburgh, the American Service Institute of Allegheny County utilized social work graduate students from the University of Pittsburgh to teach prejudice reduction techniques to Pittsburgh teachers as well as provide classes and technical assistance to new immigrants who were applying for American citizenship. The Workshop in Intercultural Education, in collaboration with the University of Pittsburgh, staged a series of short courses to "deal with intergroup tensions in our modern community," which involved in-service teachers learning alongside of community leaders. Teaching strategies used in these courses included lectures, discussion groups, field trips, films, and sociodrama ("Intercultural Education Workshop," 1955).

In New York City, Puerto Rican migration to the city was influenced by the development of U.S. corporate interests, population growth, and increasing unemployment on the island. By 1946, there were 25,000 Puerto Rican students in the public schools, and a series of studies were commissioned by the NYC Board of Education to address language issues and their social and cultural needs (Thomas, 2010). Teacher education efforts included the development of the "Workshop-Field Study in Puerto Rican Education and Culture." Initiated in the summer of 1948 by Robert Speer, professor at New York University, 30 New York City teachers traveled to Puerto Rico for a 6–week course in conjunction with professors at the University of Puerto Rico and government officials (Dossick, 1952). As a culminating activity, participants were required to write an essay which included what they had learned about the historical, political, economic, and social development of Puerto Rico and listed "[their] preconceptions, attitudes, prejudices or generalizations about Puerto Rico and Puerto Ricans . . . and [indicate] whether they had been confirmed, moderated or eliminated" (Dossick, 1952, pp. 180–181). Asked to commit to making changes in their practice when they returned to their New York City classrooms, one of the participating teachers noted in the final essay,

The psychological effect of a trip to Puerto Rico by teachers cannot be overestimated. Puerto Rican parents and children will glow with pride and self respect on learning that New York teachers went to the Island to sit at the feet of their University scholars and government specialists to learn from them and to profit from their teaching. . . . We shall now be able to view the Puerto Rican children in relation to their cultural patterns (and) establish a closer relationship based upon a better understanding . . . (Dossick, 1952, p. 181)

Continuing for 20 years, this field study workshop was expanded to include other teachers from outside New York City who worked with Puerto Rican students.

RESISTANCE TO INTERCULTURAL EDUCATION

Intercultural education was not without its critics. Several historians have chronicled how conservative teacher associations in New York City (Burkholder, 2015), the Catholic press (L. Johnson, 2006), and anticommunist commissions during the Cold War era such as California's Tenney Commission (Pak, 2002), and New York's Rapp Coudert Committee associated progressive education and intercultural in-service courses with radical teachers and Communism (Taylor, 2013). Burkholder (2015) cites that as many as 25% of NYC teachers joined one of two conservative teacher associations during the war years (i.e., the American Education Association, known as the Signposters after their newsletter *The Educational Signpost* and the Teachers Alliance of New York City). Socially conservative teachers nationwide emphasized training in Christian morals, traditional academic curriculum, strict discipline, and unquestioning respect for authority (Laats, 2015). They supported the government crackdown on Communist teachers through the anticommunist Rapp Coudert Committee and opposed progressive education as a "Soviet plot designed to undermine adult authority and destroy American civilization" (Burkholder, 2015, p. 236). The Teachers Union of NYC was particularly hard hit when at least 400 New York City teachers resigned or were dismissed as a result of the cold war investigations (Hartman, 2008; L. Johnson, 2002).

In Los Angeles and throughout the state of California, radical teachers associated with intercultural education as well as progressive education writ-large were also in the grips of red-baiting tactics instituted by Senator Jack B. Tenney's State Un-American Activities Committee. Allegations of teacher involvement in Communist-front organizations were a regular feature of the Tenney committee, and members of teachers' unions, for example, were under greater scrutiny by increasingly conservative boards of education. The LA Federation of Teachers defended the tenure system and academic freedom, opposed crowded classes, critiqued the rash of loyalty oaths to intimidate teachers, and opposed the Board's action in eliminating the entire UNESCO program and the emphasis upon intercultural, interracial education from [the] schools and making UN instruction almost impossible as being 'Controversial' (Eisenberg, n. d.). The "controversial" topics that were essentially banned by the Board included the teaching of the Bill of Rights, implementing the UNESCO curriculum toward world citizenship, and intercultural education. Intercultural education was also critiqued by scholars on the Left who complained that it "promoted a dangerous form of cultural relativism that failed to hold individuals or nations responsible for ethically unjust deeds" (Burkholder, 2011, p. 91).

INTERCULTURAL AND INTERGROUP EDUCATION INTO THE 1970S

Some scholars have argued that intercultural/intergroup education ended in the mid-1950s, the victim of red baiting and a conservative nativist turn in national politics. While organizational funding for diversity work dried up in the 1950s, our historical research (and the research of others) would indicate that many individuals who engaged in diversity work remained active in promoting culturally responsive curriculum, race relations, and democratic citizenship throughout their educational careers. This lifetime commitment to "teach for diversity" was often expressed in new organizational venues or locales. For example, Halvorson and Mirel (2013) highlight the case of Norman Drachler, a high school social studies teacher who authored a section of Detroit's intercultural curriculum guide on immigrants in the 1940s, and his subsequent commitment to hiring African American teachers and administrators and promoting the revision of racist textbooks when he became Detroit's superintendent in the 1960s.

New York City activist Algernon Black, co-chair of the CWCCH during the war years, developed the Encampment for Citizenship in the late 1940s, an interracial experiment aimed at improving intergroup relations and citizenship education which continues until today. It involved youth (ages 17–24 years) from diverse religious, racial, social, and national backgrounds in a summer camp experience where they "learn[ed] the principles and techniques of citizenship in a liberal democracy by living it" (as quoted in L. Johnson, 2017, p. 283).

After Leonard Covello retired as principal of Benjamin Franklin High School in 1956 he took an active role in advocating for New York City's Puerto Rican community through his role as Education Consultant to the Migration Division of the Puerto Rican Department of Labor. He promoted citizenship programs, worked with Puerto Rican organizations, and organized conferences and workshops to raise awareness and pride in Puerto Rican history and culture (Thomas, 2010).

Rachel Davis Dubois promoted her version of cultural democracy, culture-based curriculum, and race relations until the end of her long life (she lived to be 101). After she left the Bureau of Intercultural Education, she founded the Workshop for Cultural Democracy, which pioneered the "group conversation" technique where teachers and neighborhood residents from different racial and cultural backgrounds came together, often in individual homes, to dialogue about their common experiences in an effort to reduce prejudice. After instituting a successful program at P.S. 165 on New York City's upper Westside after the war that brought together the school's Puerto Rican, Irish, and Jewish parents, Davis DuBois took her neighborhood-home festivals (known as "parrandas") to other cities (DuBois, 1955). In 1965, she was invited by Dr. Martin Luther King Jr. to join the Southern Christian Leadership Conference staff in order to facilitate interracial group conversations as part of their Operation Dialogue initiative (Martin Luther King Jr. to Rachel Davis DuBois, 1964; "Summary of Ninth Annual Convention," 1965). When Southern Christian Leadership Conference funding for this initiative ran out, Davis DuBois continued the interracial dialogues on her own by networking with Quaker and community organizations in 10 cities throughout the South and establishing the Atlanta Dialogue Center (DuBois, 1984). Later in the fall of 1969, she took her group conversation method (now labeled Quaker Dialogues) to several cities in Europe under the sponsorship of the Friends World Committee (Hadley, 1969; "Leinster Quarterly

Meeting," 1969). Unlike some intercultural educators, Davis DuBois maintained a hands-on focus on teaching practices which aimed to increase interracial understanding in schools, churches, and community organizations. In her autobiography, written toward the end of her life, she confessed that, "I have always thought of myself as a classroom teacher" (as cited in Bohan, 2007, p. 103).

Sevier (2008), in his oral history about the Intergroup Education in Cooperating Schools Project, found that several participants continued to develop and implement intergroup education curriculum until they retired. For instance, one of the teacher participants (Robert Stevens) went on to become the coordinator of multicultural curricula for the Los Angeles Public Schools while another (Elizabeth Brady) became a Professor at California State University Northridge.

Intercultural and intergroup educators also continued to research diversity and equity issues but shifted their focus. Hilda Taba (1947, 1953) called for increased evaluation of the effectiveness of intercultural education programs. William Vickery's (1953) assessment of intergroup education workshops focused on an overview of the general aims and objectives of the movement. In his literature review published in the late 1950s, Van Til (1959) notes that the passage of *Brown v. Board in Education* in 1954 meant that many intercultural educators switched to investigating racial integration in the schools. Some school districts broadened their curriculum to a human relations approach, which emphasized common human traits rather than cultural differences. It might also be interpreted that these were deliberate attempts to decenter race and racial unrest. Common in the literature in the late 1950s were phrases that emphasized positive, productive, and better intergroup and human relations within school communities toward democratic means (Hager, 1956; Kilpatrick, 1957).

In the 1960s through the 1970s, elements of intercultural and intergroup curricula were incorporated in desegregation efforts. For instance, activism by African American parents in the New York City schools in the late 1950s and early 1960s included demands for school integration (because predominately White schools had more resources), as well as the transformation of the school curriculum to make it more responsive to Black and Puerto Rican students, teacher training in human relations to help eradicate racist views, and more Black teachers and school leaders (Back, 2003; City-Wide Citizens Committee for Integrated Schools, 1964).

As school curricula and reports about intergroup professional development became publicly available, the focus on improving group relations in school desegregation and bussing resulted in programs reflecting many of the objectives of earlier intercultural education efforts. Schools in West Virginia (Gilbert & Sessions, 1969), Cleveland (Program for Action by Citizens in Education, 1970), Houston (Houston Council on Human Relations, 1972), Denver (Dennis, 1976), and the states of Ohio (Glick & Meinke, 1972) and Maryland (Maryland State Department of Education, 1973) reflected some of the trends at this time. Expansion of intergroup education occurred in suburban schools with multiracial student populations, such as in the

Norwalk-LaMirada Unified School District in California in the late 1960s and the early 1970s (California State Department of Education, 1968, 1971). However, some resource guides on interracial and intergroup education, such as those from predominantly White suburban school districts in the Kansas City area, tended to frame minoritized students from a deficit perspective. Phrases like "dealing with the problems of the multi-racial classroom" (Caliguri, 1970) were not uncommon, and reflected the tenor of the infamous Moynihan Report (Moynihan, 1965), which framed African Americans as "culturally deprived."

Teacher attitudes were also identified as an essential component in establishing positive intergroup relations in desegregated schools (Virag, 1973). Once again, terms such as intergroup, human relations, race relations, and intercultural education were referenced. Expanding on his previous work, in the late 1970s William Van Til coauthored a curriculum bulletin to "encourage better human relations among Americans of varied racial, religious, ethnic and socioeconomic backgrounds" and listed strategies for "true integration" (Dixon & Van Til, 1978).

With increasing immigration of non-English speakers from Asia and Latin America, intercultural and intergroup approaches were also reformulated for bilingual education programs. For example, the Southwest Intergroup Relations Council (1970) in Austin, Texas, spoke against the traditional "sink or swim" method of English instruction and advocated for students to acquire sufficiency in their home language while being taught English. An intercultural approach to bilingual education in Calexico, California, featured ways of developing understanding about biculturalism and the sociolinguistic processes of linguistically diverse schoolchildren (Nafus & Lavine, 1972).

IMPLICATIONS FOR THE FIELD OR LESSONS LEARNED

The historical evidence about teaching for diversity since the 1920s reveals a somewhat messier chronology for intercultural and intergroup education than previously proposed and similar challenges with regards to how teachers have dealt with race (or not) in classroom curriculum and pedagogy. Themes that resonate across the decades include the failure to recruit and support a diverse teaching force, the importance of teacher led curriculum and professional development, and the lack of a sustained focus on race and racism in classroom practices.

The Need to Diversify the Teaching Force

While many intercultural and intergroup programs in the 1940s and 1950s advocated for hiring a more diverse teaching force, they often ended up with token representation of Teachers of Color in their school districts.[7] To date, the national demographics of teachers in public schools remains largely White and female, with slightly higher numbers of Teachers of Color in charter schools (Loewus, 2017). Teachers of Color make up only 18% of our nation's teachers and many students from diverse backgrounds will never be taught by a Teacher of Color during their school career. Dilworth (2018) and others have advocated for a racially, ethnically, and linguistically diverse teaching force, noting that millennial Teachers of Color are more likely to hold higher expectations for Students of Color and integrate culturally responsive curriculum in their classrooms. While more Teachers of Color are being hired than in the past, they are also leaving the profession more quickly than White teachers. In addition to their instructional role, African American male teachers in particular are often expected to serve as disciplinarians with Students of Color, to prepare their students for racism outside of school, and be experts on questions of diversity. The "invisible tax" they pay for this work can lead to burnout (Bristol & Mentor, 2018; J. King, 2016).

The Importance of Teacher-Led Curriculum, Research, and Professional Development

Several homegrown intercultural education projects in school districts such as Detroit, Los Angeles, San Diego, Pittsburgh, and Springfield, Massachusetts, included committees of teachers who critically analyzed existing curriculum for bias, developed units which promoted cultural pluralism and prejudice reduction, and taught in-service courses for their peers. Sevier (2008) notes that the practice in the Intergroup Education in Cooperating Schools Project of enlisting teachers to write their own curriculum arose from the progressive philosophy that teachers should be more than implementers of curriculum. To make change in classroom practice one must "begin where the teachers were in terms of their own beliefs about diversity and tolerance and proceed from there" (Sevier, 2008, p. 129). Some project participants such as Ruth Hardiman, who taught Kindergarten at Gilpin Elementary in Denver Colorado, also conducted teacher research about community-based knowledge through parent interviews and home visits with all of her students' parents (Sevier, 2008).

In the face of prepackaged curriculum programs produced by a handful of international publishing companies, which are designed to align with state standards and testing regimes, we argue that current classroom teachers are *less* involved in grassroots efforts to teach for diversity than they were in the 1930s, 1940s, and 1950s. This failure to treat teachers as professionals means that they have fewer opportunities to develop classroom-based curriculum, conduct teacher research, and share best practices with other teachers.

The Ongoing Failure to Examine Race and Structural Racism

In turn, intercultural and intergroup education also underscored the limits of curriculum reform alone as a vehicle to change institutional practices regarding race and racism. Sokol (2014) notes that the Springfield Plan was "pioneering pluralism, but practicing segregation" as the curriculum units Springfield teachers created as well as their community-based tolerance efforts did not question residential racial segregation (p. 3).

Much like curricular reforms regarding multicultural education over the past four decades, the aims and purposes of intercultural and intergroup education were contested and ranged from the highly superficial to more structural attempts to combat prejudicial attitudes among educators and students. Efforts to examine race and racism were often sabotaged, however, by an approach that equated and conflated the experiences of different racial and ethnic groups in the racial hierarchy. For example, Taba, Brady, and Robinson (1952) noted that "all newcomers to America-no matter what their origin-had to win their way, to start at the bottom of the ladder" and had "low status because they were new or 'different,' not because they were German or Irish or Jewish or Mexican" (p. 90).

Talking about race and acknowledging power disparities in the racial hierarchy continues to struggle for prominence in classroom diversity work today. In part, this is because of the continuing "problematics of Whiteness" in teacher education programs where resources and efforts are focused on changing the views of the majority of candidates (who are White) rather than the recruitment and support of teacher candidates of Color. Few novice teachers learn to acknowledge culture and race, see themselves as members of students' communities, and link teaching with students' community-based knowledge (Sleeter, 2016, p. 1065). It is also influenced by the lack of classroom research on race, especially from multiracial and intersectional standpoints. Milner (2017), in his study of research on culturally relevant pedagogy, argues that the emphasis on race in scholarship on culturally relevant classroom practice has *decreased* in significance since the construct was first introduced over 20 years ago. He questions, "Where is the race in culturally relevant pedagogy?" Without a focus on race and the development of a critical consciousness by teachers and teacher candidates, culturally relevant or responsive pedagogy can become a "soft option" instead of a critical examination of how racial hierarchies are constructed and racial groups are disadvantaged. While some teacher education programs have adopted culturally sustaining pedagogies, which incorporate a more critical approach to the intersectionality between race, culture, and language (see Paris & Alim, 2017), we would argue that in practice, talking about race and learning about racism continue to be the most difficult practices to institutionalize in preparation programs for aspiring and in-service teachers.

As scholars (and former practitioners) of diversity work, we are painfully aware that we seem to be asking the same questions that intercultural and intergroup educators asked nearly a century ago. We are confounded by the continued structural challenges that persist to implement meaningful change for culture-based and antiracist pedagogy and practice. Yet all the while, we remain critically hopeful and steadfast for that moment when diversity work in the classroom can become the new standard.

NOTES

[1]From "Teaching Democracy and Intercultural Relations through Home Economics." Presented to an Educational Methods Class in Home Economics Education at the University of Wisconsin, August 1945. Butts, Box 2, Folder, "Wisconsin Workshop." R. Freeman Butts Papers, Accession No. 80114, 14.35/38, Boxes 1, 2, 3. Hoover Institution Archives, Stanford University, Stanford, California.

[2]Under this legislation Eugenic "science," also employed in Nazi Germany, was used to limit the number of immigrants from their respective countries to just 2% of immigrants from that group who were already living in the United States in 1890. This was established after

realizing that census numbers from 1900, 1910, and 1920 would "favor" the immigration of Southern and Eastern Europeans and Jews. Asian immigration was virtually curtailed by the passage of the 1882 Chinese Exclusion Act and the 1907 Gentlemen's Agreement affecting Japanese immigration.

[3]The work of Jane Addams' Hull House and Robert Park's Chicago School of Sociology did much to influence the scholarship at the time on immigrant families and youth as well as studies on race relations. While some of the particular findings and interpretations of Park and his colleagues as well as his predecessors remain questionable, the implications for immigration and minority communities and resultant social policy ramifications were profound. For more case studies on this, see, for example, Henry Yu's (2001) *Thinking Orientals: Migration, Contact, and Exoticism in Modern America* and Mario Rios Perez's (2012) *The Color of Youth: Mexicans and the Power of Schooling in Chicago, 1917–1939.*

[4]According to Pitkin's report, two Southern cities that reported having adopted policies were New Orleans, Louisiana, and Chattanooga, Tennessee. Given the realities of segregation in the South, these schools' policies of intercultural education obviously meant "separate but equal." In such circumstances, it would be easy for school officials to state: "We operate a school system which provides equal facilities and training and opportunities for all the elements of our population. We have a single salary schedule and there is no racial or grade level differential of any kind." Indeed, problems of race would be easy to ignore for the White majority in the South since they held the power differential in a social caste system. The perversion of intercultural education policies in these regions reflected how school officials could see their views as being entirely appropriate and "equal." Woyshner's (2018) recent scholarship about how Southern White students interpreted the inclusion of African American history and culture in their schools in the 1930s offers additional insights about how an initiative meant to foster tolerance may actually reinforce stereotypes about racial difference when implemented in racially segregated schools.

[5]The protagonist in *Fury*, played by Spencer Tracy, has been wrongly accused of kidnapping in a small Midwestern town and narrowly escapes lynching by a vigilante mob. After viewing the film, students in Louis Relin's English class at Benjamin Franklin High School discussed the causes of lynching and "one student vehemently protested the lack of a 'racial background' to the movie, only to be disputed by another student who insisted that 'everyone knew what the film was talking about'" (Rabin, 2013, p. 62).

[6]An emblem of ethnicity that challenged the conventions of fashion and adult authority, zoot suits were a mainstay of popular culture for Latinx youth in wartime Los Angeles (Pagan, 2003). Like Detroit, the relationship between the Los Angeles Police Department and the Mexican American community had deteriorated during the war years. While only a handful of servicemen were arrested during the riots, over 600 Mexican American youth were jailed. Progressive reformers and activists of the time, such as Carey McWilliams, called for expansive governmental services and attention to the mounting racial antagonisms and lack of economic opportunities. They believed that the "Zoot Suit Riots" stemmed from a complex host of factors rooted in California's history of legalized discrimination against People of Color (McWilliams, 1961).

[7]Following the AACTE Diversified Teaching Workforce Topical Action Group, we have capitalized the term *Teachers of Color* in this chapter to acknowledge their group standpoint and collective "sociopolitical histories of marginalization by education institutions, structures, policies, and practices, as well as transformative pedagogical and resistant community-based practices" (as cited in Carter Andrews et al., 2019, p. 10).

ORCID ID

Lauri D. Johnson iD https://orcid.org/0000-0002-4497-2376

REFERENCES

Adams, D. (1995). *Education for extinction: American Indians and the boarding school experience, 1875–1928.* Lawrence: University of Kansas.

Allport, G. W. (1945). Is intergroup education possible? *Harvard Educational Review, 15*(2), 83–76.

American Council on Race Relations. (1948). *Directory of agencies in intergroup education.* Washington, DC: Author.

Back, A. (2003). Exposing the "whole segregation myth": The Harlem Nine and New York City's school desegregation battles. In J. Theoharis, & K. Woodard (Eds.), *Freedom North: Black freedom struggles outside the South, 1940–1980* (pp. 65–91). New York, NY: Palgrave Macmillan.

Banks, C. A. M. (2005). *Improving multicultural education: Lessons from the Intergroup Education Movement, 1933–1959.* New York, NY: Teachers College Press.

Bell, D. (1992). *Faces at the bottom of the well: The permanence of racism.* New York, NY: Basic Books.

Benedict, R., & Weltfish, G. (1943). *The races of mankind.* New York, NY: Public Affairs Committee.

Blanton, C. K. (2004). *The strange career of bilingual education in Texas, 1836–1981.* College Station: Texas A&M University Press.

Bohan, C. H. (2007). A rebellious Jersey girl: Rachel Davis DuBois, intercultural education pioneer. In S. Totten, & J. Pederson (Eds.), *Addressing social issues in the classroom and beyond: The pedagogical efforts of pioneers in the field* (pp. 99–115). Charlotte, NC: Information Age.

Bristol, T., & Mentor, M. (2018). Policing and teaching: The positioning of Black male teachers as agents in the universal carceral apparatus. *The Urban Review, 50,* 218. https://doi.org/10.1007/s11256-018-0447-z

Bureau of Publications. (1951). *Cultural groups & human relations: Twelve lectures on educational problems of special cultural groups held at Teachers College, Columbia University, August 18 to September 7, 1949.* New York, NY: Teachers College, Columbia University.

Burkholder, Z. (2007). Out to debunk the bunk: Antiracist teaching in the 1940s and today. *Teachers College Record.* Retrieved from http://www.tcrecord.org

Burkholder, Z. (2011). *Color in the classroom: How American schools taught race, 1900–1954.* Oxford, England: Oxford University Press.

Burkholder, Z. (2015). "A war of ideas": The rise of conservative teachers in wartime New York City, 1938–1946. *History of Education Quarterly, 55,* 218–243.

California State Department of Education. (1968). *Improving ethnic distribution and intergroup relations: An advisory report to the Board of Education, Colton Joint Unified School District.* Sacramento, CA: Author.

California State Department of Education. (1971). *Intergroup relations and the education of Mexican American children: An advisory report to the Board of Education, Norwalk-La Mirada Unified School District.* Sacramento, CA: Author.

Caliguri, J. P. (1970). *Suburban interracial education projects: A resource booklet.* Kansas City: University of Missouri.

Carter Andrews, D. J., Castro, E., Cho, C. L., Petchauer, E., Richmond, G., & Floden, R. (2019). Changing the narrative on diversifying the teaching workforce: A look at historical and contemporary factors that inform recruitment and retention of Teachers of Color. *Journal of Teacher Education, 70*(1), 6–12.

Chatto, C. I. (1945). Springfield's experience with intergroup education. *Harvard Educational Review, 15,* 99–103.

City-Wide Citizens Committee for Integrated Schools. (1964, March 16). [Letter from Rev. Milton Galamison]. *Elliot Linzer collection* (Box1, Folder 6). New York, NY: Queens College Department of Special Collections and Archives.

Cole, S. (n.d.). *Transcriptions of Stewart Cole Tapes #1 of 2.* New York, NY: Bureau for Intercultural Education.

Cole, S. (1948–1949). *A guide-sheet for the committee on a teachers' manual on UNESCO for the schools of California.* Pacific Coast Council on Intercultural Education (Stewart Cole). The National Conference of Christians and Jews Collection, Social Welfare History Archives. Minneapolis: University of Minnesota.

Cole, S. G. (1953). Trends in intergroup education. *Religious Education, 48*(1), 29–37.

Cook, L. (1947). Chapter II: Intergroup education. *Review of Educational Research, 17,* 266–278.

Covello, L. (1936). A high school and its immigrant community: A challenge and an opportunity. *Journal of Educational Sociology, 9,* 331–346.

Cremin, L. (1961). *The transformation of the school: Progressivism in American education, 1876–1957.* New York, NY: Knopf.

Daly, C. A. (1938). Racial enrichment of the curriculum. *Journal of the National Education Association, 27,* 235–236.

Davis, A., & Havighurst, R. J. (1945). Human development and intergroup education. *Journal of Educational Sociology, 18,* 535–541.

Democracy to be taught in local schools. (1943, September 25). *Pittsburgh Courier,* p. 2.

Dennis, E. G. (1976). *Developing and implementing a viable intergroup education program in the Denver public schools.* Retrieved from https://files.eric.ed.gov/fulltext/ED124529.pdf

Detroit Federation of Teachers. (1948). Toward better racial relations in Detroit. *The American Teacher, 32,* 13–16.

Detroit Public Schools. (1944). *Building one nation indivisible.* Detroit, MI: Detroit Public Schools, Division of Instruction.

Detroit Public Schools. (1946). *Promising practices in intergroup education.* Detroit, MI: Board of Education.

Dilworth, M. (Ed.). (2018). *Millennial teachers of color.* Cambridge, MA: Harvard Education Press.

Dixon, R. J., & Van Til, W. (1978). Widening cultural horizons: Recommended approaches to intercultural education. *Curriculum Bulletin, XXXII,* 339.

Dossick, J. J. (1952). Fifth workshop: Field study in Puerto Rican education and culture. *Journal of Educational Sociology, 26,* 177–186.

DuBois, R. D. (1936). *Service Bureau for Intercultural Education, classroom materials, CA. 1933–1936.* Rachel Davis DuBois Papers, Immigration History Research Center Archives, University of Minnesota.

DuBois, R. D. (1955). *Know your neighbors: A handbook for group conversation leaders.* New York, NY: Workshop for Cultural Democracy.

DuBois, R. D. (1984). *All this and something more: Pioneering in intercultural education.* Bryn Mawr, PA: Dorrance.

Dudziak, M. (2011). *Cold war civil rights: Race and the image of American democracy.* Princeton, NJ: Princeton University Press.

Eisenberg, F. (n.d.). *Problem curriculum (subject matter and activity program) has been curtailed, censored, and limited by the present Board of Education.* Frances Eisenberg Papers: Communism and LA Schools, Department of Special Collections, Young Research Library, University of California, Los Angeles.

Fallace, T. (2018). American educators' confrontation with fascism. *Educational Researcher, 47*(1), 46–52.

Fass, P. (1989). *The outside-in book: Minorities and the transformation of American education.* Oxford, England: Oxford University Press.

Garcia, D. G. (2018). *Strategies of segregation: Race, residence, and the struggle for educational equality.* Oakland: University of California Press.

Gilbert, A. R., & Sessions, R. P. (1969). *Updating intergroup education in public schools: A study-action manual.* Buckhannon: West Virginia Wesleyan College.

Giles, H. H. (1945). Intergroup education workshops and school problems. *Journal of Educational Sociology, 18*, 522–525.

Giles, H. H., Pitkin, V. E., & Ingram, T. (1946). Problems of intercultural education. *Review of Educational Research, 16*(1), 39–45.

Giles, H. H., & Van Til, W. (1946). School and community projects. *Annals of the American Academy of Political and Social Science, 244*, 34–41.

Glick, I. D., & Meinke, D. L. (1972). *Assessment of an intervention curriculum unit in intergroup education.* Toledo, OH: Toledo University.

Graham, P. A. (1967). *Progressive education: From Arcady to academe: A history of the Progressive Education Association, 1919–1953.* New York, NY: Teachers College Press.

Hadley, H. M. (1969, January 24). Visiting among European friends by Rachel Davis DuBois—Introducing "Group Conversation" (Quaker Dialogue) [Letter to Margaret S. Gibbins]. Rachel Davis DuBois papers, Box 21, Folder 6, Rachel Davis DuBois Papers, Immigration History Research Center Archives, University of Minnesota.

Hager, D. J. (1950). Some observations on the relationship between social science and intergroup education. *Journal of Educational Sociology, 23*, 278–290.

Hager, D. J. (1956). New problems in intercultural education. *Journal of Educational Sociology, 30*, 162–167.

Hall, J. D. (2005). The long civil rights movement and the political uses of the past. *Journal of American History, 91*, 1233–1263.

Halvorson, A., & Mirel, J. (2013). Intercultural education in Detroit, 1943–1954. *Paedagogica Historica, 49*, 361–381.

Harrison, H. J. (1953). *A study of the work of the Coordinating Committee on Democratic Human Relations in the Detroit Public Schools from September, 1943 to June, 1952* (Unpublished doctoral dissertation). Wayne State University, Detroit, MI.

Hart, J. (2004). Making democracy safe for the world: Race, propaganda, and the transformation of U.S. foreign policy during World War II. *Pacific Historical Review, 73*, 49–84.

Hart, R. J. (2016). Battling minds: Conservatives, progressives, and UNESCO in post war United States. In I. Kulnazarova, & C. Ydesen (Eds.), *UNESCO without borders: Educational campaigns for international understanding* (pp. 35–51). London, England: Routledge.

Hartman, A. (2008). *Education and the cold war: The battle for the American school.* New York, NY: Palgrave MacMillan.

Hines, M. (2017). *The blackboard and the color line: Madeline Morgan and the alternative Black curriculum in Chicago's public schools, 1941–1945* (Unpublished doctoral dissertation). Loyola University Chicago, Chicago, IL.

Houston Council on Human Relations. (1972). *Black/Mexican-American project report.* Retrieved from https://eric.ed.gov/?id=ED068592

Intercultural Education Workshop set by Pitt and Council on Intercultural Education. (1955). Pittsburgh, PA: University of Pittsburgh Collections.

Johanek, M., & Puckett, J. L. (2007). *Leonard Covello and the making of Benjamin Franklin High School: Education as if citizenship mattered.* Philadelphia, PA: Temple University Press.

Johnson, C. S. (1945, November 24). [Letter to Miss Laurentine B. Collins]. Detroit Public Schools Community Relations Papers, Wayne State University Archives of Labor History and Urban Affairs and University Archives, Detroit, MI.

Johnson, L. (2002). "Making democracy real": Teacher union and community activism to promote diversity in the New York City public schools—1935–1950. *Urban Education, 37*, 566–588.

Johnson, L. (2006). "One community's total war against prejudice": The Springfield Plan revisited. *Theory & Research in Social Education, 34*, 301–323.

Johnson, L. (2017). "Educating for democratic living": The City-Wide Citizens' Committee on Harlem (CWCCH), 1941–1947. *Historia Social y de la Educacion/Social and Education History, 6*, 261–289.

Johnson, L., & Pak, Y. (2005, November). "There ain't no North any more": Racial conflict and the struggle for intercultural education in Detroit and Los Angeles Schools—1943–1950. Paper presented at the History of Education Society Annual Meeting, Baltimore, MD.

Karier, C. J. (1986). *The individual, society, and education: A history of American educational ideas* (2nd ed.). Urbana-Champaign: University of Illinois Press.

Kilpatrick, W. H. (1957). *Modern education and better human relations.* Retrieved from https://eric.ed.gov/?id=ED030706

Kilpatrick, W. H., Stone, W. J., & Cole, S. G. (1949). A frame of reference for intercultural education. *Journal of Educational Sociology, 22,* 555–572.

King, J. (2016, May 15). The invisible tax on teachers of color. *The Washington Post.* Retrieved from https://www.washingtonpost.com/opinions/the-invisible-tax-on-black-teachers/2016/05/15/6b7bea06-16f7-11e6-aa55-670cabef46e0_story.html?noredirect=on&utm_term=.86cffb309dec

King, M. L., Jr. (1964, December 29). [Letter to R. D. DuBois]. Rachel Davis DuBois Papers, Box 34, Folder 1. Immigration History Research Center Archives, University of Minnesota.

Klineberg, O. (1945). A scientific basis for intergroup education. *Harvard Educational Review, 15,* 117–121.

Kridel, C., & Bullough, R. V., Jr. (2007). *Stories of the eight-year study: Reexamining secondary education in America.* Albany: State University of New York Press.

Laats, A. (2015). *The other school reformers: Conservative activism in American education.* Cambridge, MA: Harvard University Press.

Lal, S. (2004). 1930s Multiculturalism: Rachel Davis DuBois and the Bureau for Intercultural Education. *Radical Teacher, 69,* 18–22.

Lasker, B. (1929). *Race attitudes in children.* New York, NY: Henry Holt.

Lawrence, A. (2011). *Lessons from an Indian day school: Negotiating colonization in northern New Mexico, 1902–1907.* Lawrence: University of Kansas.

Leinster quarterly meeting. (1969, November 21). *The Friend,* p. 1454.

Life Magazine. (July 5, 1943). Retrieved from https://www.oldlifemagazines.com/july-05-1943-life-magazine.html

Locke, A. (1940). With science as his shield: The educator must bridge our "great divides." *Frontiers of Democracy, 6*(53), 208–210.

Loewus, L. (2017, August 15). The nation's teaching force is still mostly white and female. *Education Week.* Retrieved from https://www.edweek.org/ew/articles/2017/08/15/the-nations-teaching-force-is-still-mostly.html

Los Angeles City Schools. (1950). *Developing human relations in the elementary school.* Los Angeles, CA: Author.

Maryland State Department of Education. (1973). *Toward understanding: Human relations in Maryland schools.* Retrieved from https://eric.ed.gov/?id=ED115640

McWilliams, C. (1961). *North from Mexico: The Spanish-speaking people of the United States.* New York, NY: Monthly Review Press.

Mead, M. (1945). Group living as a part of intergroup education workshops. *Journal of Educational Sociology, 18,* 526–534.

Merideth, D., & Burr, E. W. (1947). Some problems of evaluation in intergroup education. *Journal of Educational Sociology, 21*(1), 43–52.

Milner, R. (2017). Where's the race in culturally relevant pedagogy? *Teachers College Record, 119*(1), 1–32.

Mirel, J. (2010). *Patriotic pluralism: American education and European immigrants.* Cambridge, MA: Harvard University Press.

Montalto, N. (1982). *A history of the Intercultural Educational Movement, 1924–1941.* New York, NY: Garland.

Moynihan, D. (1965). *The Negro family: The case for national action.* Washington, DC: U.S. Department of Labor.

Mufti, K. (2018). Revisiting Rachel Davis DuBois' childhood and young adulthood: Reflections on the linked lives of an intercultural education pioneer. *Quaker Studies, 23,* 25–46.

Murra, W. F. (1945). Reading materials for intergroup education. *Harvard Educational Review, 15,* 147–155.

Myrdal, G. (1944). *An American dilemma: The Negro problem and modern democracy.* New York, NY: Harper.

Nafus, C., & Lavine, L. (1972). *Calexico intercultural design: Content analysis schedule for bilingual education programs.* Washington, DC: Division of Bilingual Education. Retrieved from https://eric.ed.gov/?q=ED080022&id=ED080022

Olneck, M. (1989). Americanization and the education of immigrants, 1900–1925: An analysis of symbolic action. *American Journal of Education, 97,* 398–423.

Olneck, M. (1990). The recurring dream: Symbolism and ideology in intercultural and multicultural education. *American Journal of Education, 2,* 147–174.

Pagan, E. (2003). *Murder at the Sleepy Lagoon: Zoot suits, race, & riot in wartime L. A.* Chapel Hill: University of North Carolina Press.

Pak, Y. (2002). "If there is a better intercultural plan in any school system in America, I do not know where it is": The San Diego City Schools intercultural education program, 1946–1949. *Urban Education, 37,* 588–609.

Paris, D., & Alim, S. (Eds.). (2017). *Culturally sustaining pedagogies: Teaching and learning for justice in a changing world.* New York, NY: Teachers College Press.

Perez, M. (2012). *The color of youth: Mexicans and the power of schooling in Chicago, 1917–1939* (Unpublished doctoral dissertation). University of Illinois, Champaign-Urbana, IL.

Perillo, J. (2006). White teachers and the Black psyche: Interculturalism and the psychology of race in the New York City high schools, 1940–1950. In B. Beatty, E. D. Cahan, & J. Grant (Eds.), *When science encounters the child: Education, parenting, and child welfare in 20th-Century America* (pp. 157–174). New York, NY: Teachers College Press.

Pitkin, V. E. (1947). *Survey of intercultural policies of selected school systems.* New York, NY: Bureau for Intercultural Education.

Program for Action by Citizens in Education. (1970). *A human relations curriculum development project created by the PACE Association.* Retrieved from https://eric.ed.gov/?id=ED045557

Rabin, L. (2013). The social uses of classroom cinema: A history of the human relations film series at Benjamin Franklin High School in East Harlem, New York City, 1936–1955. *Velvet Light Trap, 72,* 58–71.

Race Relations Institute. (1943). *A monthly summary of events and trends in race relations.* Nashville, TN: Fisk University.

Raftery, J. (1992). *Land of fair promise: Politics and reform in Los Angeles schools, 1885–1941.* Stanford, CA: Stanford University Press.

Seamans, H. L. (1945). 1945 Summer workshops in intergroup education. *Journal of Educational Sociology, 18,* 569–572.

Selig, D. (2008). *Americans all: The cultural gifts movement.* Cambridge, MA: Harvard University Press.

Sevier, B. R. (2008). The project in intergroup education and Sarason's modal process of change: A historical exemplar of educational reform. *Journal of Educational Change, 9,* 123–151.

Sevier, B. R. (2009). Between mutuality and diversity: The Project in Intergroup Education and the discourse of national unity in multicultural texts. *Educational Foundations, 23,* 21–47.

Shaffer, R. (1996). Multicultural education in New York City during World War II. *New York History, 77,* 301–332.

Sleeter, C. (2016). Wrestling with the problematics of whiteness in teacher education. *International Journal of Qualitative Studies in Education, 29,* 1065–1068.

Snyder, E. E. (1962). Social-cultural approach to intergroup education at the secondary school level. *Journal of Educational Sociology, 35,* 236–239.

Sokol, J. (2014). *All eyes on us: Race and politics from Boston to Brooklyn: The conflicted soul of the Northeast.* New York, NY: Basic Books.

Southwest Intergroup Relations Council. (1970). *A bilingual approach: Education for understanding.* Austin, TX: Author.

Sugrue, T. (1996). *The origins of the urban crisis: Race and inequality in postwar Detroit.* Princeton, NJ: Princeton University Press.

Summary of Ninth Annual Convention, Southern Christian Leadership Conference, August 9–13, 1965. Rachel Davis DuBois Papers, Box 34, Folder 5, Immigration History Research Center Archives, University of Minnesota.

Taba, H. (1947). What is evaluation up to and up against in intergroup education? *Journal of Educational Sociology, 21*(1), 19–24.

Taba, H. (1953). Research oriented programs in intergroup education in schools and colleges. *Review of Educational Research, 23,* 362–371.

Taba, H. (1962). *Curriculum development: Theory and practice.* New York, NY: Harcourt, Brace, & World.

Taba, H., Brady, E., & Robinson, J. T. (1952). *Intergroup education in public schools.* Washington, DC: American Council on Education.

Taba, H., & Wilson, H. E. (1946). Intergroup education through the school curriculum. *Annals of the American Academy of Political and Social Science, 244,* 19–25. doi:10.1177/000271624624400104

Tamura, E. (1993). *Americanization, acculturation, and ethnic identity: The Nisei generation in Hawaii.* Urbana: University of Illinois.

Taylor, C. (2013). *Reds at the blackboard: Communism, civil rights, and the New York City Teachers Union.* New York, NY: Columbia University Press.

Thomas, L. (2010). *Puerto Rican citizen: History and political identity in twentieth century New York City.* Chicago, IL: University of Chicago Press.

Van Til, W. (1959). Chapter V: Instructional methods in intercultural and intergroup education. *Review of Educational Research, 29,* 367–377.

Vickery, W. E. (1953). Ten years of intergroup education workshops. *Journal of Educational Sociology, 26,* 292–302.

Vickery, W. E., & Cole, S. G. (1943). *Intercultural education in American schools: Proposed objectives and methods.* New York, NY: Harper.

Virag, W. F. (1973, November). *Integrating the desegregated school: Some observations and suggestions.* Paper presented at the annual meeting of the National Council for Social Studies, San Francisco, CA.

Warren, J. E. (1945). Facing the need for intergroup education. *Journal of Educational Sociology, 18,* 513–521.

Wechsler, H. S. (2012). Making a religion of intergroup education: The National Conference of Christians and Jews, 1927–1957. *Journal of Ecumenical Studies, 47*(1), 3–40.

Woodson, C. G. (1922). *The Negro in our history.* Washington, DC: Associated Publishers.

Woyshner, C. (2018). "I feel I am really pleading the cause of my own people": US southern white students' study of African-American history and culture in the 1930s through art and the senses. *History of Education, 47,* 190–208. doi:10.1080/0046760X.2017.1420241

Wu, E. D. (2014). *The color of success: Asian Americans and the origins of the model minority.* Princeton, NJ: Princeton University Press.

Yu, H. (2001). *Thinking Orientals: Migration, contact, and exoticism in modern America.* New York, NY: Oxford University Press.

Zimmerman, J. (2004). Brown-ing the American textbook: History, psychology, and the origins of modern multiculturalism. *History of Education Quarterly, 44,* 46–69.

Chapter 2

From Mass Schooling to Education Systems: Changing Patterns in the Organization and Management of Instruction

Donald J. Peurach
David K. Cohen
University of Michigan

Maxwell M. Yurkofsky
Harvard University

James P. Spillane
Northwestern University

In the early 1990s, the logic and policies of systemic reform launched a press to coordinate the pursuit of excellence and equity in U.S. public education, with each other and with classroom instruction. There was little in that policy moment to predict that these reforms would sustain, and much to predict otherwise. Yet, nearly three decades hence, many public school districts are working earnestly to pursue the central aims of the reforms: all students engaging rich instructional experiences to master ambitious content and tasks at the same high standards. That begs a question: What happens when new educational ambitions collide with legacy educational institutions—not in a policy moment but across a historical moment? This chapter takes up that question by reviewing the rise of mass public schooling in pursuit of universal access, a historic pivot toward instructionally focused education systems in pursuit of excellence and equity, and changing patterns in instructional organization and management that follow. The lesson we draw is that, even amid incoherence and turbulence in education environments, sustained public, political, and policy support for new educational ambitions opens up new opportunities for those ambitions to manifest in the structures and the work of public school districts.

E very now and then, it's a good idea to take stock of where you've been, where you are, and where you might be headed. We think that now is a very good time to do exactly that.

Review of Research in Education
March 2019, Vol. 43, pp. 32–67
DOI: 10.3102/0091732X18821131
Chapter reuse guidelines: sagepub.com/journals-permissions
© 2019 AERA. http://rre.aera.net

Over a quarter century ago, two of us published a chapter in the 18th volume of the *Review of Research in Education* examining the relationships between policy-and-practice and governance-and-instruction (Cohen & Spillane, 1992). The chapter was published soon after the logic of systemic reform was taken up in federal education policy (Smith & O'Day, 1991).

That policy moment in the early 1990s launched a press to coordinate the pursuit of excellence and equity in public education, with each other and with classroom instruction. The logic and policies of systemic reform aimed to push public education beyond didactic pedagogies, basic facts, and rote skills toward ambitious instructional experiences and outcomes for *all* students. They also aimed for more coherent, powerful guidance for instruction from state and federal agencies in the form of curriculum frameworks, performance assessments, accountability standards, and professional preparation.

Yet these aims were complicated by two sets of problems. One set arose from the distribution of power and the inattention to instruction in U.S. public education. By the onset of systemic reform, public education had evolved as a mass schooling enterprise that provided universal access to schools but delegated primary responsibility for organizing and managing classroom work to teachers. Another set arose from the demands of ambitious instruction on those habituated to the pursuit of basic skills and rudimentary knowledge and, thus, on the supports needed to move beyond access to excellence and equity in classroom work.

The earlier chapter offered a prediction. Absent complementary efforts to reduce existing sources of influence, efforts at the federal, national, and state levels to guide instruction in more coherent, powerful ways would breed further incoherence in education environments and, with that, complicate (rather than support) the pursuit of ambitious instruction. Gerald Grant, editor of the 18th volume of the *Review of Research in Education*, described this predication as "profoundly pessimistic" (Grant, 1992, p. xi).

Our prediction of further incoherence has held. The logic of systemic reform has evolved into the logic of standards-and-accountability and been institutionalized in federal, national, and state policy. The logic of standards-and-accountability, in turn, has played out in interaction with the logics of markets-and-choice, research-and-evidence, and autonomy-and-professionalism to create new sources of influence in education environments, to redistribute influence among existing sources, and to exacerbate incoherence in instructional guidance.

Even so, an unanticipated development also appears to be emerging and, with it, cautious optimism. Many public school districts are working earnestly to move beyond mass public schooling to instructionally focused education systems pursuing the central aims of systemic reform: all students engaging rich instructional experiences to master ambitious content and demanding tasks at the same high standards.

And that's what has us thinking that now is a good time to take stock of where we've been, where we are, and where we might be headed.[1] We tackle the issues in four chunks. We begin by examining the rise of mass public schooling in pursuit of universal educational access. We continue by examining this historic pivot toward instructionally focused education systems in pursuit of excellence and equity in students' educational experiences and outcomes. We then examine changing patterns in the organization and management of instruction that follow. To conclude, we offer summary reflections, along with thoughts on further research that would both produce basic knowledge about the shift from mass schooling to education systems and support districts and schools in this work.

Covering so much ground in so few pages is like using a broad brush to paint a landscape on a postage stamp. Yet the resulting image is sufficiently vivid to get a clearer sense of what happens when new ambitions collide with legacy institutions—not in a policy moment spanning years but across a historical moment spanning decades.

FROM MASS PUBLIC SCHOOLING . . .

By "mass public schooling," we mean a government-sponsored enterprise that provides education for large numbers of students. Thus defined, the central function of mass public schooling is to afford instruction of some sort, to many students of some sort, in a school of some sort, to learn something of some sort, specifics of which are to be worked out in and through government agencies and others operating in the public sphere.

In the United States, from the nation's founding through its bicentennial, mass public schooling was a success, in that it expanded over time to provide access to K–12 schools for virtually all students. It was a curiosity, in that the government agencies and others responsible for working out the many specifics directed comparatively little attention to the central educational function of mass public schooling: the day-to-day work of classroom instruction. And it was a problem, in that this central educational function turned out not to work in ways that many people assumed.

Ambitions for Educational Access

The rise of mass public schooling in the United States was driven by expanding societal ambitions for access to public education. These ambitions had roots in the colonial New England, with requirements that local communities establish public schools to teach students (primarily White boys) to read and write to understand the Bible, contracts, and laws (Cremin, 1970). Ambitions grew with associations between public education and the moral foundation, social order, and economic advance of a functional democracy; the advent of compulsory attendance and child labor laws; and urbanization and mass immigration, and the need to socialize millions of new citizens (Graham, 1974; Mirel, 2010; Tyack & Hansot, 1982).

Yet a fundamental matter that drove the expansion of societal ambitions was the association of public education and social equality. In a new nation in which the roots of public education had quickly become entangled with differences in gender, class, ethnicity, and race, the common school movement of the mid-1800s sought to advance equity in public schooling for boys and girls, in urban and rural schools (Kaestle, 1983). As Horace Mann, father of the movement, famously argued:

"Education, then, beyond all other devices of human origin, is the great equalizer of the conditions of men—the balance-wheel of the social machinery" (Mann, 1848).

But with racism, xenophobia, and sexism both deeply institutionalized and long leveraged to limit access to public education, it was not until the 1970s that the United States realized ambitions for universal access to K–12 public schooling (Katznelson & Weir, 1985). This success was a positive outcome of social movements, court decisions, and federal policies of the 1940s to 1970s that sought equitable access to public education for students historically discriminated against on the basis of gender, religion, race, ethnicity, social class, and/or disability (Anyon, 2009). Chief among these were the civil rights and disability rights movements; *Méndez v. Westminster School District of Orange County* in 1947; *Brown v. Board of Education of Topeka* in 1954; *Lau v. Nichols* in 1974; the Elementary and Secondary Education Act of 1965; and the Education for All Handicapped Children Act of 1975.

Yet the assurance of universal access to public education did not bring with it the assurance of quality or equality in students' educational experiences and outcomes. Rather, court decisions and federal policies of the 1940s to 1970s focused chiefly on ensuring a "free appropriate public education" and a "basic floor of educational opportunity" for all students, absent accountability for results (*Board of Education v. Rowley*, 1982). The chief means of doing so was the equitable distribution of educational resources among schools, including funding, teachers, materials, and time.

From the origins of public schooling through the realization of universal access, reformers, educators, and society writ large assumed that if students were exposed to teachers and books in schools, they would learn. Public schooling was invented at a time when most Americans assumed that the mind was shaped by its circumstances. If so, it could be shaped by man-made institutions like schools. On these assumptions, if governments built schools, supplied them with teachers and books, and made sure students attended, students would learn. And if governments supplied schools with more and better teachers and books, students would learn more and better.

Few gave much consideration to what, in hindsight, presents as a fundamental matter: Differences that resources make in students' educational experiences and outcomes depend on uses to which those resources are put in day-to-day classroom instruction (Cohen, Raudenbush, & Ball, 2003). By this reasoning, if resources are used well, prospects for students' learning improve; if they are not used well, prospects diminish. But by the reasoning of the day, to provide resources was to provide education; resource allocation would cause teaching and learning. That was how the educational function of public schooling was widely assumed to work.

Establishing and Structuring the Enterprise

Ambitions for universal access to public schooling rose in interaction with efforts of the federal and state governments to structure the environments of public education to bring order to influences bearing on the establishment, resourcing, and activities of schools. Characteristic of nation-building, the efforts to structure education environments included formidable investment in macro-level infrastructures: foundational governance, financial, administrative, and legal arrangements at the federal and state levels as the backbone of a mass public schooling enterprise.

Yet public schooling emerged as a local undertaking in a new nation distrustful of central authority and designed to limit the power of central governments, with no constitutional authority over public education at the federal level and with rudimentary engagement in substantive educational matters at the state level. With that, among those established by central governments, two macro-level infrastructures were noticeably absent (Cohen, Peurach, Glazer, Gates, & Goldin, 2014; Cohen, Spillane, & Peurach, 2018). One was a centrally established educational infrastructure providing specific visions and designs for instruction, formal resources for instruction (e.g., content frameworks, curriculum materials, and assessments), and social resources for instruction (e.g., teachers). Another was a centrally established accountability infrastructure setting out standards for students' learning, means of measuring performance in relation to those standards, and incentives and sanctions tied to metrics and standards of performance.

Instead, a different type of macro-level educational infrastructure emerged, shaped only in part by agencies of federal and state governments. Societal visions for public schools came to focus less on their educational function and more on their organizational form: a socially shared image of a "real school" featuring age-graded classes, one teacher per classroom, content drawn from academic disciplines or vocations, and a school day that ran from 8:30 a.m. to 3:00 p.m. (Metz, 1989). The development of essential resources fell largely to a "school improvement industry," with commercial publishers, nonprofits, and other organizations developing formal resources for instruction and accredited colleges, universities, and other organizations developing teachers (Rowan, 2002; see also Peurach, Cohen, & Spillane, in press).

A different type of macro-level accountability infrastructure developed, as well, defined less by the specific actions of federal and state agencies and focused less on examining instructional effectiveness. Rather, this accountability infrastructure was defined more by societal understandings of schooling and focused more on according legitimacy and resources to schools through their compliance with structural forms and categories recognized and valued by society. John Meyer and Brian Rowan (1978) described this as the "schooling rule":

Education is a certified teacher teaching a standardized curricular topic to a registered student in an accredited school. The nature of schooling is thus socially defined by reference to a set of standardized categories, the legitimacy of which is publicly shared. (p. 219)

By this argument, the social value of schooling was more in its credentialing function (i.e., categorizing graduates) and less in its educational function (i.e., actually teaching them anything of substance and use).

As ambitions for educational access expanded deep into the 20th century, so, too, did education environments (Cohen & Spillane, 1992; Rowan, 2002). Federal and state agencies engaging public schooling grew. The school improvement industry grew, too, with more interests and organizations advancing more visions of a "real school," more formal resources for instruction, and more professional learning opportunities for teachers. As the press for equitable access grew, so, too, did the press for equitable distribution of resources among schools. And as more historically marginalized students were incorporated into public schools, the categories used to describe their educational needs grew: for example, behaviorally challenged, language impaired, physically impaired, and learning impaired.

Within the constraints and affordances of these plural, fragmented education environments, responsibility for working out the educational specifics fell on public school districts: local units of government operating under elected boards and responsible for funding, establishing, and operating public schools (Gamson & Hodge, 2016; Tyack, 2002). Public school districts evolved to take a conventional, hierarchical form: geographically defined enterprises featuring a central office and feeder patterns of elementary, middle, and high schools. The work of those leading these central offices and schools (i.e., superintendents, principals, and their associates and assistants) evolved, as well, to fall into three broad categories (Cuban, 1988):

- Political responsibilities focused on managing relationships with the school board, local constituents, and other units of government
- Administrative responsibilities focused on financial, operational, logistical, and bureaucratic functions
- Educational responsibilities focused on organizing and managing instruction

Political and administrative responsibilities drew much of the time and attention of local educational leaders; educational responsibilities drew far less. Many matters conspired to make this the case: for example, the time demands of political and administrative work, the limited instructional knowledge of local educational leaders, the desire of local educational leaders to legitimize themselves by identifying with the political and administrative work shared with other government and business leaders, tensions between management (i.e., leaders) and labor (i.e., teachers and teachers' unions), and distrust of central authority in district offices and schools that mirrored distrust in broader American society (Callahan, 1964; Cohen, 1985; Goodlad, 1978; Tyack & Hansot, 1982).

Chief among these matters was that public accountability for leaders' political and administrative responsibilities were much stronger than for their educational responsibilities. Local constituents expected their voices to be heard and their financial contributions to be used efficiently. Yet there was often little agreement among local constituents on the desired outcomes for schools, instructional methods, or means of measuring effectiveness. Within a given district, diversity in social class, race, ethnicity, and religion brought diversity in educational aspirations and values (Powell, Farrar, & Cohen, 1985). The matter of what to teach, how to teach, and toward what ends was contested at the societal level, as well, with basic facts and skills and didactic pedagogies as a détente, and with that détente mirroring anti-intellectualism in broader American society (Hofstadter, 1963).

While some leaders took on the responsibility of devising coherent, coordinated educational and accountability infrastructures at the local level, many public school districts evolved in ways that mirrored education environments, with weak, uncoordinated educational and accountability infrastructures to guide instruction and to assess effectiveness. As education environments became increasingly elaborated and communities more diverse, so, too, did the educational and accountability infrastructures of public school districts, with elementary schools likened to educational Christmas trees and high schools likened to shopping malls (Bryk, Sebring, Kerbow, Rollow, & Easton, 1998; Powell et al., 1985).

The Organization and Management of Instruction

Thus, in the United States, the rise of mass public schooling resulted in a curious state of affairs, with agencies of governments (federal, state, and local) and others in the public sphere doing little to work out the specifics of what was, ostensibly, the primary educational function of public schooling: the day-to-day work of classroom instruction. Put differently: U.S. public education had evolved as an enterprise characterized by access-oriented mass public schooling; it had not evolved as a collection of instructionally focused education systems among or within states.

But it wasn't that classroom instruction was *un*-organized or *un*-managed. Rather, it was that instruction was organized and managed, again, differently: only partially by government agencies and others in the public sphere and more by the street-level agents of governments—classroom teachers.

Working within the conventions of a "real school" absent accountability for student learning, public school districts organized and managed instruction primarily by constituting it: that is, by sorting students into schools, grades, tracks, classes, and supplemental/categorical programs; resourcing those instructional venues with certified teachers, curriculum materials, and other educational materials; and promoting students annually based on age and attendance (Cohen, 1985; Oakes, 1985). Beyond this type of administrative sorting and resourcing, the educational work of central offices and schools often stopped at classroom doors. Much of the educational work of public schooling was organized and managed in individual classrooms, with teachers delegated primary responsibility for collaborating with students and families to work out the educational specifics using the resources afforded them (Dreeban, 1973; Jackson, 1968; Lortie, 1975).

The result was a "loose coupling" between the political and administrative work of central office and school leaders, on one hand, and the educational work of teachers and students in classrooms, on the other (Meyer & Rowan, 1978). This pattern of instructional organization and management worked for many people. It allowed local educational leaders to respond to the societal press for mass public schooling and, with that, to associate with the professional managerial class. It allowed teachers to exercise discretion and judgment in organizing and managing their own work and, with that, to identify as human service professionals. It allowed students and families to fashion a public education aligned with their own educational aspirations and values. And it accommodated a broader society in which educational means and ends were contested.

This pattern of instructional organization and management also made sense, given common assumptions about the educational function of schooling: If schools were built, supplied with teachers and books, and students attended, then students would learn. This was the common sense of citizens voting on local operating levies, of state legislators voting on school aid appropriations, of campaigns for universal attendance and against school dropouts, and of researchers who generated evidence associating greater resource allocation with greater educational attainment. From this perspective, it is easy to see why so much education policy—local, state, and, later, federal—had focused on resource allocation and attendance. It is also easy to see why few educators, reformers, or policymakers saw difficulty with these policies, worried about outsourcing a great deal to nongovernmental organizations, or even recognized fragmentation and incoherence in educational and accountability infrastructures.

But even if it worked for (and made sense to) many people, this pattern of instructional organization and management was also deeply problematic. The problems began in central offices and schools. While many historically marginalized students experienced quality educational opportunities, many others found their basic floor of educational opportunity lowered by the sorting of students into neighborhood schools segregated by race, ethnicity, and class; by assignment to low-level academic and vocational tracks; and by placement into remedial supplemental/categorical programs (Gamoran & Mare, 1989; Oakes, 1985). Resourcing often exacerbated these problems, with more poorly trained and less qualified teachers often overrepresented in districts, schools, and academic tracks serving large numbers of historically marginalized students (Lankford, Loeb, & Wyckoff, 2002; Jacob, 2007). Those teachers worked absent coherent guidance for practice, support from leaders, or accountability for much more than maintaining order.

The problems continued with the delegation of responsibility for instructional organization and management to individual classrooms. One matter was that by the standards of other human service professions, the professional preparation of teachers was widely regarded as weak and lacking a shared professional knowledge base to support and coordinate the exercise of judgment and discretion (Dreeban, 1973; Jackson, 1968; Lortie, 1975). Moreover, working in the privacy of their own classrooms and structurally isolated from colleagues, teachers had little opportunity to learn to coordinate and use the often incoherent and uncoordinated educational resources afforded them for their day-to-day work with students (Little, 1990). Instead, teachers often refashioned new resources to support existing ways of working or simply rejected them, carrying on largely as they, themselves, were taught: by focusing on basic facts and rote skills using didactic pedagogies (Cohen, 1990; Cuban, 1993; Lortie, 1975).

Challenges overcoming weaknesses in professional knowledge were exacerbated by the organization and management of districts as a whole. These were enterprises that appeared expertly designed to undermine collegial learning: hierarchical, bureaucratic, geographically distributed enterprises lacking mechanisms for the lateral exchange of knowledge among schools, the reciprocal exchange of knowledge between schools and central offices, and the accumulation and redistribution of knowledge by central offices (Glazer & Peurach, 2015).

Ironically, problems in the organization and management of instruction were exacerbated by a press to improve educational quality, by moving beyond a focus on basic facts and rote skills to a focus on complex thinking, reasoning, and problem solving. The press ran from the 1950s into the 1970s, roughly in parallel to the press for universal access, motivated by the security and economic threats from abroad, the cognitive revolution (and its influence on education), and growing debates about instructional methods and quality.

But new ambitions to improve educational quality ran into and through the institution of mass public schooling. Concerns with educational quality drove the development of a federally supported "innovation infrastructure" featuring agencies, institutes, centers, laboratories, grant-funded projects, and clearinghouses, thus further balkanizing macro-level educational infrastructures that produced still more resources lacking in guidance, supports, and accountability (Peurach, Penuel, & Russell, 2018). These new resources were disseminated to districts and schools that were creating new sorting mechanisms that often further segregated students by race, ethnicity, and social class: for example, magnet schools, gifted and talented programs, and college preparatory academic tracks. And new curricula, materials, and other instructional resources were allocated to classrooms where teachers, again, either rejected them or refashioned them, whether to support established instructional approaches or to develop some combination of the old and the new (Cohen, 1989, 1990; Dow, 1991).

Despite these problems, this pattern of sorting-resourcing-and-delegating persisted. One reason is that exposure to resources can yield returns, as evidenced by research associating resources and educational attainment (Greenwald, Hedges, & Laine, 1996). Yet, while resource allocation is an essential condition for instruction, it neither controls nor determines instruction. Much depends on how schools, teachers, students, and others use resources. The partial truth, commonsense power, and political pervasiveness of the ideas underlying this pattern of sorting-resourcing-and-delegating—along with the centuries-long investment of government and educators in it—greatly complicated even recognizing problems with it, never mind disrupting them.

While hard for many to see, the problems were more transparent to others. From the late 1800s into the mid-1900s, champions of the progressive education movement challenged public schools as sorting mechanisms serving economic purposes and sought to reform them as egalitarian foundations for democratic participation (Cremin, 1964). Yet it was seminal social research of the 1960s and 1970s—the first of its kind to combine big data, new statistical methods, and massive computational power—that provided evidence of a formidable average achievement gap between Black and White students, questions about the relationship between educational resources and student achievement, and arguments that schools were doing little to reduce achievement disparities among students (Coleman et al., 1966; Jencks et al., 1972). Subsequent research on determinants of resource use (e.g., teachers' knowledge, opportunities for practice-based learning, and instructional leadership) would soon reveal how much had been missing in common assumptions about how the educational function of schooling worked.

Thus, by the 1970s, a press for mass public schooling that had gained currency with the common school movement had yielded "one best system": a dominant pattern of instructional organization and management stitched deeply into the institutions and culture of American society but one that was also bound up with questions about U.S. public education as the great equalizer (Tyack, 1974). The progressive education movement had stalled, owing to the absence of both the understandings and infrastructures needed to realize its ambitions in classrooms. The press for universal access and for educational quality were working in tension with each other, and in weak relation with instruction: Many historically marginalized students were experiencing instruction of questionable quality, while efforts to improve quality were reinforcing the pattern (and the problems) of sorting-resourcing-and-delegating. And evidence challenging common assumptions about the educational function of public schooling was increasingly plain to see.

... TO INSTRUCTIONALLY FOCUSED EDUCATION SYSTEMS

By an "instructionally focused education system," we mean a mass public schooling enterprise that takes on, as a central matter, guiding and supporting the educational work of schools: classroom instruction. What moves an instructionally focused education system beyond mass public schooling is how the enterprise works out the specifics of teaching and learning. An instructionally focused education system is not an enterprise in which government agencies and others constitute instruction and, then, delegate to individual teachers primary responsibility for organizing and managing their day-to-day work in ways (and toward ends) that they, themselves, determine. Rather, an instructionally focused education system is one in which government agencies and others operating in the public sphere interact in mutually reinforcing ways to organize and manage instruction in and among classrooms in pursuit of agreed-upon ends. By this definition, an instructionally focused education system *is* a mass public schooling enterprise, and much more.

From the 1980s to the present, the U.S. public education enterprise has shown signs of moving beyond mass public schooling toward instructionally focused education systems, in the direction of agreed-upon ends that, historically, had been elusive: improving the quality of educational experiences and outcomes for all students while, at the same time, reducing disparities among them. This movement has played out in and through the established architecture of mass public schooling: expanding (but still limited) federal and state engagement in the educational work of public schooling, a continued (if not increased) dependence on the school improvement industry for essential formal and social resources, and public school districts still bearing primary responsibility for working out the educational specifics. The result is new ambitions colliding with legacy institutions, with new questions about instructional organization and management emerging from the fray.

Ambitions for Excellence and Equity

In the United States, the shift toward instructionally focused education systems has been driven by expanding societal ambitions: beyond *universal access* to public schooling to *excellence and equity* in public education—not as parallel pursuits and in tension but as coordinated with each other and, together, with classroom instruction.

As discussed above, these ambitions have roots in reform movements, social movements, and policy movements running into the 1960s, and these ambitions have expanded in the time since. But to say that excellence and equity were (and are) emerging as broad societal ambitions is not to say that there is social consensus on the meaning of "excellence" and "equity" or on how best to realize those ambitions. Rather, such matters were (and are) widely contested. After all, these broad societal ambitions are emerging in and from a distributed, decentralized, plural national education enterprise accustomed to accommodating and institutionalizing educational differences and unaccustomed to establishing and pursuing shared educational understandings, purposes, goals, and approaches.

One marker of the expanding, coordinated press for excellence and equity is a set of movements, court decisions, and policies with roots in 1970s that overlapped the press for universal access. For example,

- The effective schools movement challenged institutionalized patterns of instructional organization and management, famously anchored in arguments and evidence that "we can, whenever and where ever we choose, successfully teach all children whose schooling is of interest to us" (Edmonds, 1979, p. 23).
- State court decisions introduced the legal concept of adequacy (vs. equity) in justifying differential distribution of resources among public school districts to ensure comparable educational quality for all students *(Robinson v. Cahill*, 1973).
- In 1979, federal policy establishing the U.S. Department of Education as a cabinet-level federal agency was premised, most fundamentally, on two congressional findings:

(1) education is fundamental to the development of individual citizens and the progress of the Nation; (2) there is continuing need to ensure equal access for all Americans to educational opportunities of a high quality, and such educational opportunities should not be denied because of race, creed, color, national origin, or sex. (Department of Education Organization Act of 1979; https://www.gpo.gov/fdsys/pkg/STATUTE-93/pdf/STATUTE-93-Pg668.pdf)

The press for excellence and equity carried into the 1980s, in no small part due to a rapidly expanding federal role. This included the U.S. Department of Education establishing the National Commission on Educational Excellence, which, in its famous, scathing 1983 report, linked fundamental risks to national security, the economy, democratic processes, and social equality to weaknesses in the educational function of mass public schooling, including academic content, expectations for students' learning, instructional time, and teacher quality, preparation, and work conditions (National Commission on Educational Excellence, 1983). It also included the U.S. Department of Education publishing, in 1984, the first ever national report presenting evidence of state-by-state disparities in educational performance as related to educational resources and population characteristics (Ginsburg, Noell, & Plisko, 1988).

Debates about excellence, equity, and their relation to classroom instruction carried well beyond the federal government into the plural environments of U.S. public education. Responding to concerns with federal overreach, the nation's governors reasserted the state role in public education and introduced the notion that long-established local autonomy over educational specifics should be linked to new accountability for results (National Governors Association, 1986). Responding to concerns about increased government bureaucracy, advocates argued for raising the professional status of teachers as the primary resource for high-quality instruction (Carnegie Forum on Education and the Economy Nation, 1986). Also responding to concerns about government bureaucracy, critics called for shifting from democratic to market control of public education to empower families and to drive innovation (Chubb & Moe, 1988).

Toward moving from public debate to public policy, the historic Charlottesville Education Summit of 1989 ended with leaders from the executive branches of the federal and state governments agreeing to six National Education Goals affirming a commitment to access (via goals for preK education, high school retention, and positive school climates) while also affirming new commitments to excellence and equity (via goals for realizing world-class public education by the year 2000 that positioned *all* U.S. students for academic success and civic participation). The National Education Goals were introduced in the State of the Union Address by President George H. W. Bush in January 1990 and approved by the National Governors Association in February 1990, with the National Education Goals Panel established in July 1990, to monitor progress (Vinovskis, 1999).

Transforming the Enterprise

By historical standards, the 1980s were remarkable. In a national education enterprise characterized both by its limited central governance and its diversity of educational aspirations, the newly created federal Department of Education was instrumental in catalyzing federal/state collaboration in establishing a parsimonious set of shared education goals that, while largely symbolic, aimed to structure the national education reform agenda around the coordinated pursuit of excellence and equity.

But, again, different conceptions of excellence, equity, and their pursuit were (and continue to be) widely contested, not only among national-level policy elites as discussed above but also among advocates and grassroots reformers who conceptualize excellence as anchored in preparation for democratic participation, equity as anchored in principles of social justice, and their pursuit as anchored in the empowerment of families and communities.

Even so, the debates and compromises of the 1980s and early 1990s began to build consensus around operational conceptions that would soon drive federal and state policy. Excellence would center more narrowly on improving outcome measures for all students (and not privileging the success of some while neglecting others). Equity would center on reducing disparities in outcome measures among students, such that, as quality increased, gaps between students would narrow (and not sustain or expand). Realizing these ambitions, finally, would require comprehensive, coordinated initiatives aimed at transforming U.S. public education from an access-oriented mass public schooling enterprise to a collection of instructionally focused education systems.

Efforts to transform U.S. public education began in the 1990s as a sort of "addition without subtraction," with new ambitions for (and conceptions of) excellence and equity advanced within the institutionalized architecture of mass public schooling (Cohen & Spillane, 1992). Rather than reducing the many interests, organizations, and enterprises operating in U.S. education environments, federal and state agencies took on even more active roles in structuring new resources, incentives, and sanctions aimed at bringing macro-level actors into tighter coordination with each other and into deeper engagement with instruction.

But to say that federal and state agencies took on more active roles is neither to suggest that norms and designs for limited central government had evaporated, nor to suggest that these agencies had evolved to resemble education ministries with authority and capabilities to provide comprehensive, substantive educational support to districts and schools. Quite the opposite. The educational specifics would continue to be worked out by public school districts, motivated and supported (in principle) by increasingly coordinated and instructionally focused education environments.

A framework for moving the U.S. public education enterprise beyond mass public school toward instructionally focused education systems was mapped out in a seminal paper on "systemic reform" by Smith and O'Day (1991). The logic of systemic reform was anchored in reviews of research on effective schools and districts (Purkey & Smith, 1983, 1985); bolstered by new evidence of conditions under which public schools could, in fact, have a powerful equalizing effect on students (Heyns, 1978; Heyns, 1987); and shaped by contemporaneous efforts in states (e.g., Vermont, Kentucky, New York, California, and South Carolina) and professional associations (e.g., the National Council of Teachers of Mathematics) to establish (and to support the use of) coordinated content standards, teaching standards, assessments, and evaluations as resources for instructional improvement.

With that, the logic of systemic reform sought to effect coherent local educational and accountability infrastructures long missing in U.S. public school districts, anchored in a shared vision for teaching and learning that would drive resource selection, professional development, and student assessment. Local work would be motivated and supported by coherent macro-level educational and accountability infrastructures featuring coordinated, state-level academic content standards, performance standards, and accountability assessments that moved beyond basic skills toward cognitively demanding content and tasks; curricula and other educational resources aligned with those standards and assessments; and preservice and in-service professional development aligned with those standards, assessments, and resources.

The logic of systemic reform was quickly taken up in federal policies that aimed to move states, districts, and schools toward these types of coherent, coordinated educational and accountability infrastructures, notably, the Goals 2000–Educate America Act of 1994 and the Improving America's Schools Act of 1994. Working in tandem, these two federal policies resourced and incentivized (a) the development of state standards and assessments and (b) school-wide improvement responsive to state standards and assessments.

Yet the logic and policies of systemic reform were introduced into a highly politicized reform context without tamping down the many voices and interests that, through the debates of the 1980s, had driven excellence and equity to the center of the national education reform agenda. Moreover, new voices and interests soon emerged that sought to champion, shape, and even challenge that agenda: for example, the Annenberg Institute for School Reform, the Education Trust, and the Civil Rights Project.

Given the plural environments of U.S. public education, the coherence so central to the logic of systemic reform soon gave way to multiple policy logics advanced simultaneously by the federal government, state governments, and philanthropists since the 1990s, each privileging different approaches to improving educational quality and reducing disparities:

- Standards-and-accountability aimed at (a) raising standards and building consensus around ambitions for students' learning and measures of student outcomes and (b) catalyzing improvement using incentives and sanctions
- Markets-and-choice aimed at empowering families to pursue their educational aspirations and values, creating competition among schools, and stimulating entrepreneurship and innovation
- Research-and-evidence aimed at privileging science over fads, improving quality and accountability in the school improvement industry, and driving the use of data in decision making and practice
- Autonomy-and-professionalism aimed at (a) maintaining local discretion among districts and schools and (b) leveraging the knowledge and capabilities of teachers and leaders as resources for addressing the specific needs of students, schools, and communities

The proliferation of policy logics has driven the expansion of macro-level infrastructures supporting mass public schooling. For example, since the 1990s, governance infrastructures have expanded to include new categories of public school districts (e.g., state takeover districts, turnaround zones, and charter school networks) and new forms of oversight (e.g., mayoral control, operating boards, and authorizing agencies). Financial infrastructures have expanded to include new federal funding to support school-wide improvement, new state-level funding schemes to reduce disparities among districts, policies supporting open enrollment across districts, and formidable philanthropic investment. Administrative infrastructures have expanded to include new public reporting of student achievement, behavior, attendance, attainment, and school and district quality.

While these policy logics are not necessarily in conflict, their proliferation has exacerbated one of the primary problems that the logic of systemic reform sought to address: incoherence and turbulence in macro-level educational and accountability infrastructures. For example, consider the following:

- The introduction of standards articulating visions for students' learning as advanced by states, professional associations, and national consortia across increasing numbers of academic content areas, all constantly evolving and changing
- The introduction of new categories of formal resources (e.g., benchmark assessments and data systems, designs for coordinating between general education and special education, whole school improvement programs and networks), along with the introduction of a national-level infrastructure to evaluate and publicize their impacts on student outcomes
- The launch of new efforts within and beyond colleges and universities to advance the professional preparation and continuing education of teachers as the essential social resource for instruction, crossed by efforts to support alternative paths into teaching and the creation of alternative graduate schools of education
- The introduction of ever-evolving accountability assessments as advanced by states and national consortia, evaluation strategies for teachers and local educational leaders tied to student performance, and ever-evolving criteria for evaluating aggregate and subgroup performance among students within schools and districts

The incoherence and turbulence go further, to include the rise of opposition motivated by concerns with growing federal and state engagement, the increasing role of philanthropy, and the loss of local democratic control in defining and pursuing excellence and equity in public education (Burch, 2009; Holme, Diem, & Welton, 2014; Peurach & Scott, 2012; Reckhow, 2013; Tompkins-Stange, 2016). Of particular concern is the pursuit of narrow, outcome-focused, policy-determined conceptions of excellence and equity at the expense of conceptions valued more highly among local families and communities. For some families and communities, this opposition is expressed by simply opting out of state assessments. For those seeking to influence their students' day-to-day educational experiences, the challenge has become one of organizing in new ways to exercise collective voice in complex reform contexts where influence is often traded at the level of organizations rather than individuals (Peurach & Yurkofsky, 2018).

Finally, none of this has done anything to subtract from legacy concerns with "real schools" and "schooling rules" that draw attention to the organizational façade of schools over their educational substance. Instead, the incoherence and turbulence have created counterincentives for districts and schools to engage in a sort of "ritualized rationality" in which they use technical ceremonies to signal a positive response to the press of standards, assessments, research, and evidence, though with little connection to day-to-day classroom instruction (Peurach et al., 2018; Yurkofsky, 2017). It has also created new organizational categories that can be used to signal a positive responsive to excellence and equity though, again, without making deep changes in classroom instruction: for example, pursuing "21st-century skills" and "deeper learning" using "culturally responsive pedagogies" and "restorative practices" supported by "research-based," "research-validated," and "standards-aligned" curriculum materials, all under the guidance of "highly qualified teachers" engaged in "data-driven decision making" and "PDSA cycles" in "professional learning communities."

Transforming the Organization and Management of Instruction

In policy environments pressing for excellence and equity in educational *outcomes*, the challenge for public school districts charged with working out the specifics is to ensure excellence and equity in students' educational *experiences*. As with education environments, the matter for public school districts is, again, one of addition without subtraction. For local school leaders, the political and administrative work of mass public schooling continues, though complicated by increasing incoherence in education environments, crossed by varying conceptions of excellence and equity among local stakeholders, and bound up with personal accountability for educational responsibilities that many had long marginalized. Indeed, education environments do not present uniformly across public school districts as some sort of objective reality, nor do teachers, families, and community constituents regard the priorities and agendas established in those environments in similar ways. Rather, the essential task for local educational leaders is to "craft coherence," by identifying, understanding, and working among these many influences and interests—possibly competing, possibly complementary, possibly extraneous—in charting promising paths forward (Honig & Hatch, 2004).

In the face of formidable challenges, many public school districts are, indeed, taking up the work of refashioning themselves as instructionally focused education systems in ways responsive to the societal and policy press for excellence and equity (e.g., Duke, 2005; F. M. Hess, 2006; Kirp, 2013; O'Day, Bitter, & Gomez, 2011; Reville & Coggins, 2007). To varying degrees of success, central offices and schools are collaborating with each other (and, in some cases, with external partners) to guide and support instruction with the aim of improving quality and reducing disparities. Some are advancing coordinated, strategic plans for comprehensive district redesign; others are muddling through in ways that are more incremental and evolutionary; and all are balancing the increased engagement of central offices and schools with endemic uncertainties in classroom life requiring that teachers retain some amount of discretion over their day-to-day work.

Concurrently, researchers are working to conceptualize, theorize, and guide the work of redesigning mass public schooling enterprises as instructionally focused education systems.[2] Common themes running through this research include an emphasis on five core domains of activity as integral to these systems:

- *Managing environmental relationships* to selectively bridge, buffer, and reconcile among competing influences and resources in local and broader environments that bear on how the district understands and pursues excellence and equity in classroom instruction: for example, family/community aspirations and values, federal and state policies, philanthropists' agendas, and education research and resources (Honig & Hatch, 2004; Spillane, 2009)
- *Building educational infrastructure* that coordinates (a) visions for instructional practice, (b) formal instructional resources, such as instructional models, curricula, and assessments, and (c) social instructional resources, such as understandings, norms, values, and relationships among teachers, leaders, and students (Hopkins, Spillane, Jakopovic, & Heaton, 2013; Leithwood, Louis, Anderson, & Wahlstrom, 2004; Peurach & Neumerski, 2015)
- *Supporting the use of educational infrastructure in practice* by developing teachers' professional knowledge and capabilities through means such as workshops, practice-based coaching and mentoring, and collegial learning (Cohen, 2011; Cohen et al., 2003)
- *Managing performance* both for (a) continuous improvement, as via iterative, evidence-driven design, implementation, and evaluation, and (b) accountability, as via the use of evidence and standards to assess instructional processes and outcomes (Boudett, City, & Murnane, 2005; Bryk, Gomez, Grunow, & LeMahieu, 2015; Datnow & Park, 2014; Mintrop, 2016)
- *Distributing instructional leadership* beyond established administrative roles to new leadership roles and teams responsible for performing, coordinating, and managing all of the preceding (Elmore, 2000; Spillane, 2006)

Efforts by researchers to bundle these domains of activity into coherent frameworks to guide practice and research rest on a common theory. The more attention to (and coordination among) these domains of activity, the farther districts move in the direction of coherent, instructionally focused education systems; the farther districts move in the direction of coherent, instructionally focused education systems, the more able they will be to respond to the press to raise the quality of students' educational experiences and outcomes on average and to reduce disparities among them (Bryk, Sebring, Allensworth, Luppescu, & Easton, 2010; Cobb, Jackson, Henrick, Smith, & the MIST Team, 2018; Forman, Stosich, & Bocala, 2017; S. M. Johnson, Marietta, Higgins, Mapp, & Grossman, 2014).

Thus, the image that emerges from this shift toward instructionally focused education systems is not one of "enterprises transformed" but one of "enterprises transforming." Federal, state, and local governments are working in interaction with nongovernmental enterprises to guide and support instruction in ways that they hadn't historically, in response to societal ambitions for public education that have expanded considerably.

But this shift toward instructionally focused education systems is emerging in and from a "one best system" in which an institutionalized pattern of instructional organization and management was interacting with increased federal engagement to raise questions about quality and inequality in public schooling. Moreover, in the decades immediately prior, when earlier ambitions aimed at improving educational quality ran into and through this same mass public schooling enterprise, it was mass public schooling that took the hand.

That, then, begs new questions: What happens when ambitions for instructionally focused education systems collide with institutionalized mass public schooling? What new patterns (if any) emerge in the organization and management of instruction in public school districts?

CHANGING PATTERNS IN THE ORGANIZATION AND MANAGEMENT OF INSTRUCTION

Thus, new societal ambitions for excellence and equity in public education are accumulating atop continuing ambitions for universal access to public schooling, with these ambitions pressing public school districts to develop as instructionally focused education systems while sustaining themselves as engines of mass public schooling. A question that follows is whether new patterns of organization and management are emerging from this collision between ambitions and institutions.

To probe for patterns of instructional organization and management, we conducted a comprehensive and systematic analysis of the research literature on the redesign of conventional public school districts (urban, suburban, and rural) and alternative public school districts (state takeover districts, turnaround zones, and charter school networks), from 1995 to the present (see the appendix). Rather than one best system (old or new), we identified four primary types of systems:

- Managerial education systems
- Market-driven education systems
- Federated education systems
- Networked education systems

Each of these four system types has a characteristic theory of action. Each associates closely with specific theories of (and approaches to) district redesign that have gained or maintained currency since the mid-1990s. And each has a characteristic distribution among central offices and schools of the five domains of work essential to instructionally focused education systems: that is, managing environmental relationships, building educational infrastructure, supporting use, managing performance, and distributing instructional leadership.

Our assertion is not that these four types are enacted by public school districts in some pure form. For example, each of these types can be pursued symbolically. Districts can build elaborate educational infrastructures that signal attention to excellence and equity to key constituents, while doing little to support the use of those infrastructures in practice. Each can also be pursued as a sort of hybrid, with whole districts or individual schools collaborating with external partners (e.g., Cohen et al., 2014; Peurach & Neumerski, 2015). And it is possible for a public school district to be a composite of different approaches to instructional organization and management in different contexts (e.g., in different content areas; in general education, special education, and supplemental/compensatory education; in elementary, middle, and high schools; in neighborhood schools and magnet schools; and in low- and high-performing schools).

Rather than asserting these as normative standards, we offer them as ideal types: heuristics for analyzing, empathetically and critically, instructional organization and management in specific public school districts. The value of this typology rests on its usefulness as an interpretive framework for reasoning about instructional organization and management as work distributed among central offices and schools, across multiple instructional contexts, over time.

Managerial Education System

A managerial education system is characterized by a standard educational approach developed by the central office and administered consistently, district-wide. The theory of action is that the consistent, district-wide use of a high-quality educational approach will improve educational opportunities and outcomes on average while also reducing disparities between schools and classrooms. A managerial education system operates in accord with strategies for organizing and managing instruction that feature hierarchical role relationships and procedural work controls (e.g., Rowan, 1990; Trujillo, 2014).

In a managerial education system, the primary responsibility for building educational infrastructure lies in the central office: devising an instructional vision, developing or acquiring formal resources that provide detailed guidance for practice (supported by evidence of effectiveness), and developing norms that encourage "working within the system." The work of managing environmental relationships focuses on discerning state accountability requirements and resources for meeting them, as well as engaging families and communities to build buy-in around centrally developed infrastructure. The central office supports schools in using this educational infrastructure through professional development and coaching, with performance management focused primarily on holding schools accountable to standards for classroom practice and for bottom-line results. These activities require central office instructional leadership over instructional design, professional development, and assessment and evaluation.

The breadth of instructional leadership in the central office narrows the scope of instructional leadership in schools, with principals (along with their associates and assistants) functioning as agents of the central office in administering centrally designed educational infrastructure. The primary focus of school administrators is to support the use of centrally developed educational infrastructure in practice, with performance management focused again on faithful use and bottom-line results. Infrastructure-building and environmental management focus on cultivating understanding and buy-in among teachers, families, and community members of central office decisions and designs.

The pattern of activity that characterizes a managerial education system first emerged from our review of accounts and critiques of redesign efforts in urban public school districts at the onset of standards and accountability (e.g., Elmore & Burney, 1999; F. M. Hess, 2006; Ravitch, 2010; Reville & Coggins, 2007). This pattern was also evident in accounts of urban districts transitioning to standardized curricula coupled with high-stakes assessments (e.g., Diamond, 2012; Hallett, 2010; P. E. Johnson & Chrispeels, 2010); in accounts of instructional improvement in large, fragmented, historically bureaucratic school districts (e.g., Daly, Finnigan, Jordan, Moolenaar, & Che, 2014; Farrell, 2015; Hubbard et al., 2006); and in accounts of charter school networks that feature standardized instructional visions absent affordances for school-level adaptation (e.g., Lake, Dusseault, Bowen, Demeritt, & Hill, 2010; Torres, 2014).

Market-Driven Education System

While a managerial education system is characterized by a standard educational approach, a market-driven education system is characterized by the differentiation of educational approaches among schools, with families and communities advocating for (and choosing among) schools that are aligned with their educational values and aspirations. The theory of action is that introducing market competition while reducing central office control will stimulate school-level entrepreneurship and innovation aimed at improving quality and reducing disparities in ways responsive to families, communities, and broader policy pressures. A market-driven education system operates in accord with many principles of portfolio management as a strategy for reforming public school districts (Bulkley, Henig, & Levin, 2010; Hill, 2006; Lake & Hill, 2009).

Where the central office of a managerial system is the primary locus of redesign activity, the central office of a market-driven system functions more as an arbiter of school-level design activity. Key functions of the central office are to manage relationships with communities (to ensure educational alternatives responsive to diverse aspirations and values) and policy environments (to establish achievement targets for schools). Performance management focuses on holding schools accountable for meeting enrollment and achievement targets, reconstituting or closing those that do not, and constituting new schools as alternatives. These activities focus central office instructional leadership primarily on monitoring community and policy environments, goal setting, and evaluation.

In contrast to administering centrally designed educational infrastructure (as in a managerial education system), schools in a market-driven education system have primary responsibility for building educational infrastructure. They devise a school-specific instructional vision, create or acquire formal resources that support that vision, and cultivate a social organization that balances innovation and creativity with family/community responsiveness. That, in turn, places a premium on managing environmental relationships (to discern the aspirations and values of families/communities) and supporting the use of infrastructure in practice (to ensure that aspirations and values are represented in instruction). It also places a premium on managing performance both for continuous improvement (to iteratively refine infrastructure and supports for use) and accountability for bottom-line results (as set by choice-making families and the central office). These responsibilities require that schools develop all of the instructional leadership capabilities of the central office of a managerial education system, in addition to the marketing and advertising capabilities required of competitive markets.

The pattern of activity that characterizes a market-driven education system first emerged from our review of accounts of mayoral and state-directed district redesign (Cucchiara, Gold, & Simon, 2011; Glazer & Egan, 2018; Jabbar, 2016; Wong, 2011). Though they blur lines with managerial and federated systems, this pattern was also evident in accounts of redesign in urban districts that coordinated academic accountability with intradistrict choice programs such as pilot schools, magnet schools, and charter schools (Dauter & Fuller, 2016; Knoester, 2011; O'Day et al., 2011).

Federated Education System

A federated education system is characterized by independence among schools in devising their educational approaches within parameters established by the central office, balanced by an ethos of community and cooperation (in contrast to the competition and accountability of market-driven systems). The theory of action is that knowledge, capabilities, and values in schools and communities are essential resources for organizing and managing instruction in ways that improve quality and reduce disparities, with the central office providing supports to enable success and structuring constraints to ensure a level of district-wide coherence. Thus, where managerial and market-driven systems locate primary responsibility for education design activity either in the central office or in schools, a federated system features a more balanced distribution of design activity between central offices and schools. A federated education system operates in accord with principles of site-based/school-based management, distributed/participatory leadership, and commitment-oriented management strategies (David, 1995; Rowan, 1990; Spillane, 2006).

Where a hallmark of a market-driven system is a lean central office, a federated education system shares the more extensive instructional leadership capabilities of a managerial system, though directed at constraining (but not standardizing) educational approaches among schools. Infrastructure building focuses on establishing principles, frameworks, and guidance for school-level decision making (e.g., a district-wide educational mission, a curriculum scope-and-sequence, and core instructional values), though it can also include selecting infrastructure components to be used district-wide (e.g., an instructional model, textbook series, or assessment). That, in turn, has central offices managing environmental relationships to reconcile infrastructure-building efforts with policy expectations, externally available resources, and family/community aspirations and values. Performance management focuses on supporting schools' use of centrally developed resources, holding schools accountable for working within centrally devised constraints, and sharing accountability for their success.

For schools in a federated education system, a common feature is a participatory leadership team that includes teachers, administrators, and, possibly, family and community representatives. With that, the work of managing environmental relationships goes beyond building buy-in and soliciting input (as with managerial and market-driven systems) to the possibility of incorporating family/community representation into school-level redesign activity, including devising school-specific educational infrastructure within bounds established by the central office. Efforts to support use and manage performance focus on (a) working collegially to realize school-specific educational aspirations and values in classroom instruction and (b) working iteratively and collaboratively to refine educational infrastructure and supports for use.

The pattern of activity that characterizes a federated education system first emerged in our review of accounts of the decentralization reforms in the Chicago Public Schools, where local communities were given high levels of autonomy over schools (Bryk et al., 1998; Engel, 2013; G. A. Hess, 1995). This pattern of activity was also evident in accounts of suburban district redesign that blend central office guidance with school-level decision making (Brown, Anfara, & Roney, 2004; Dooley & Assaf, 2009), in accounts of redesign featuring school-level instructional leadership and mentoring (Honig & Rainey, 2014; Lussier & Forgione, 2010; Terosky, 2014; Youngs, 2007), and in accounts of central offices buffering schools from environmental turbulence to support school-level instructional improvement (Honig, 2012).

Networked Education System

Like a managerial system, a networked education system features a common, district-wide educational approach. However, in contrast to the standardization-and-administration that characterizes managerial systems, a networked education system is characterized by the central office and schools collaborating to develop, use, and refine a conventional, district-wide educational approach. The theory of action is that establishing, maintaining, and continuously refining common ways of working, district-wide, create potential both to elevate the quality of routine educational work consistently across schools and to address particular educational needs and problems among schools, classrooms, and students (thereby reducing disparities). A networked education system operates in accord with principles of evolutionary learning systems, networked improvement communities, and design-based improvement (Bryk et al., 2015; Fishman, Penuel, Allen, Cheng, & Sabelli, 2013; Peurach, Glazer, & Lenhoff, 2016).

As in a managerial system, the central office in a networked system has primary responsibility for building and maintaining district-wide educational infrastructure. However, efforts to support the use of centrally developed infrastructure balance faithful implementation (to establish conventional, high-quality classroom instruction, district-wide) and school-level discretion (to address school-specific needs and problems). In contrast to the accountability focus of managerial systems, performance management focuses on continuous improvement, with the central office leveraging school-level adaptations as a resource for refining educational infrastructure and supports for use. Managing environmental relationships focuses chiefly on identifying research and research-based resources to inform redesign activity, with outreach to families and communities focused on building buy-in around the district-wide educational approach. These responsibilities require many of the instructional leadership capabilities of managerial and federated education systems, complemented by capabilities to manage distributed, collaborative learning and improvement.

With the central office responsible for building and maintaining educational infrastructure, schools focus most centrally on supporting the use of infrastructure and managing performance in ways that parallel the work of the central office. Efforts to support use balance conventions (to maintain district-wide coherence and quality) with discretion (to address school-specific needs and problems). Performance management focuses on the use of iterative, continuous improvement cycles to structure collegial problem solving and adaptation, with positive adaptations fed back to the central office for potential use, district-wide. In schools, the work of managing environmental relationships involves building buy-in around the district-wide educational approach and engaging families and communities in adapting that approach to the local context. With that, school-level instructional leadership focuses on practice-based professional learning and problem solving, family/community outreach, and evidence-based continuous improvement.

The pattern of activity that characterizes a networked education system first emerged from our review of district and school redesign featuring different forms of research-practice partnerships that draw on the principles of design and continuous improvement (Cobb et al., 2018; Penuel & Gallagher, 2017; Peurach, 2011). This pattern was also evident in accounts of charter school networks, urban districts, and suburban districts that coordinate detailed, district-wide instructional visions with opportunities and support for school-level adaptation and feedback (e.g., Hopkins et al., 2013; Lake et al., 2010; Stein & D'Amico, 2002; Woodworth, David, Guha, Wang, & Lopez-Torkos, 2008).

AMBITIONS AND INSTITUTIONS

With our review of the literature in hand, we return to the questions that motivated it: What happens when ambitions for instructionally focused education systems collide with institutionalized mass public schooling? What new patterns (if any) emerge in the organization and management of instruction in public school districts?

Our answer to the second question is as reported immediately above. The shift from access to excellence and equity in public education—and the consequent shift beyond mass public schooling to instructionally focused education systems—has given rise to at least four types of systems, each with a characteristic theory of action, a close association with a current theories of/approaches to district redesign, and a characteristic distribution of essential work among central offices and schools.

Our answer to the first question is as reported above, also, and elaborated below. When ambitions collide with institutions, we don't see enterprises transformed. Rather, we see enterprises transforming, with new solutions emerging and taking form, though fashioned from (and coexisting with) the very problems that they seek to solve.

Reprise

New ideas, organizations, and practices are always filtered through and/or patched onto inherited ideas, organizations, and practices. This is the case in our analysis of education environments, which appear to be transforming to advance the instructional focus of macro-level educational and accountability infrastructures, though without reducing incoherence and without reducing the appeal of educational form over educational function. This is the case in our analysis of the work of local educational leaders, whose roles appear to be transforming to take up new categories of educational work alongside more (and more complex) political and administrative work that risks drawing their attention away.

This is also the case in our analysis of the types of systems emerging from those efforts. For example, each type is a response to an institutionalized pattern of instructional organization and management characterized by hierarchical organizational arrangements, sorting-resourcing-and-delegating, and learning challenges that followed. Yet this very architecture is central to three of the four system types: managerial, market-driven, and federated systems. That, in turn, leaves these three system types vulnerable to some of the very problems that each seeks to solve. Consider the following:

- All three of these system types (i.e., managerial, market-driven, and federated systems) have the central office in a position of power and authority over schools in establishing the fundamental strategy or approach for system redesign—in a public education enterprise famously distrustful of centralized power and authority, even within public school districts.

- All three depend on essential resources that, in the past, have either not been used effectively or evoked new problems: for example, the detailed instructional guidance of managerial systems (long interpreted by teachers as an unwelcome bureaucratic intervention into their professional work), the license for creativity in market-driven systems (long used by teachers to refashion new resources in ways that support existing practice), and the professional community of federated systems (among teachers who have long valued privacy and autonomy).
- All three seek to manage performance either in central offices or schools for continuous learning and improvement, yet with inheritances of hierarchy complicating the exchange, accumulation, and use of practical knowledge: for example, the lack of reciprocal and lateral relationships between central offices and schools and, in market-driven and federated systems, the beliefs in school-by-school differentiation that complicate collaborative learning.

Networked systems, the fourth system type, seek to manage these very problems: for example, by structuring reciprocal and lateral relations among the central office and schools and by using detailed routines to establish a formal and social foundation for professional practice, problem solving, and learning. However, networked education systems often exist as novel organizational arrangements within districts that manage other work hierarchically and bureaucratically. That introduces risks that detailed routines—the fundamental resource used to establish conventional practice, build social infrastructure, and capture and move knowledge—will be interpreted and used as bureaucratic implements to strong-arm teachers.

And then there is the risk that any one of these four types can be enacted symbolically: for example, a public school district that manages environmental relationships, builds educational infrastructure, and distributes instructional leadership to signal responsiveness to the press for excellence and equity, while doing little to support use or to manage performance. This is the legacy of loose coupling alive in the moment. From that follows the risk that students will still be sorted into schools and classrooms that have different expectations for (and beliefs in) possibilities for their academic success, that those schools and classrooms will be provided incoherent and uncoordinated resources, and that teachers will be delegated primary responsibility for organizing and managing instruction for the students assigned to them using the resources afforded them.

Introspection

Thus, while many public school districts are working earnestly to move beyond mass public schooling to instructionally focused education systems, these efforts are playing out where ambitions and institutions collide. Progress of this sort is measured, with new solutions coexisting with legacy problems. Progress of this sort is slow: nearly 30 years and counting, in the case of the shift from mass schooling to education systems. Progress of this sort must be evaluated against the 300+ years required to establish universal access to public education.

But progress of this sort is possible only with sustained public, political, and policy support over long periods of time. Indeed, even if such support creates and exacerbates incoherence in education environments, the fact that it is *sustained* appears to open up possibilities for new societal ambitions to manifest in the work of public school districts. That is the most important lesson that we have learned in writing this chapter.

When two of us wrote our earlier chapter for the *Review of Research in Education* at the outset of systemic reform, we recognized that initial policy moment as one of truly remarkable change and challenge in its ambitions for classroom instruction. We also worried that neither government agencies nor others in the public sphere had much capability to deliver on those ambitions. And that, we noted, is why most education reforms to that point were short-lived. But we were writing *at* a policy moment, not *across* a historical moment. We did not take seriously the possibility that systemic reform would not only persist but would also sink deep roots over nearly three decades, twisted-and-tangled in the institutions of mass public schooling.

Anticipation

With this chapter, we attended much more to how public school districts have responded to reforms that have far outlived our earlier expectations. We see reasons for hope, not only in the type of system redesign activity on which we report here but also in (a) continued research suggesting possibilities of a powerful equalizing effect of schooling on students (e.g., Downey, von Hippel, & Broh, 2004) and (b) new research suggesting possibilities to improve achievement on average and to reduce disparities among diverse students at a very large scale (Cohen et al., 2014; Reardon & Hinze-Pifer, 2017; Rowan, Correnti, Miller, & Camburn, 2009).

As we anticipate the coming decades, a central matter becomes that of sustaining the ambitions of these reforms as they collide with the institutions of mass public schooling. Nobody knows how this matter will play out. Much is likely to depend on the continued state embrace of the Common Core State Standards, on the engagement of philanthropists and nongovernment agencies, and on the engagement of teachers and families. The same holds for the Next Generation Science Standards. But this state-level activity will be playing out in interaction with unprecedented political turbulence at the federal and national levels. To say that this turbulence is a wild card is to risk serious understatement.

Whatever the ebbs and flows of politics and policies, as long as societal ambitions to improve educational quality and reduce inequality persist, our conjecture is that public school districts will be pressed to move beyond functioning as engines of mass public schooling to functioning as instructionally focused education systems, with local education leaders, teachers, families, and communities collaborating to work out the specifics.

As they do, further research is needed that examines and explains variation among the full range of public school districts in the following:

- Their movement toward instructionally focused education systems
- The role of policy and philanthropy in motivating and supporting this movement
- Patterns of instructional organization and management that emerge within and among them (perhaps consistent with the system types described here; perhaps consistent with other system types not yet evident in the literature)
- Performance levels of particular types of education systems in particular school, district, and state contexts

Yet, as we reflect on the mountains of research that we reviewed in writing this chapter, three emerging, interdependent genres strike us as especially promising for actually supporting districts in this work. Each aims to help districts in working and learning in new ways. Each would gain power if conducted longitudinally (to experience and examine system redesign over time) and comparatively (to experience and examine differences among content areas, levels of schooling, states, and even nations). They are the following:

- Research that aims to produce practical theory and guidance for organizing and managing instructionally focused education systems (e.g., Bryk et al., 2010; Forman et al., 2017; S. M. Johnson et al., 2014)
- Research that engages educational professionals, community constituents, and university researchers in collaborative design, problem solving, and improvement (e.g., Bryk et al., 2015; Cobb et al., 2018; Penuel & Gallagher, 2017)
- Research that positions external evaluators in reciprocal, developmental learning relationships with local education leaders (e.g., Peurach et al., 2016)

But these emerging genres of research are ambitions all their own, in collision with deeply institutionalized traditions of research and innovation that understand and pursue knowledge, its development, and its use in very different ways (Peurach, 2016; Peurach et al., 2018). Their continued development and widespread use will also require sustained public, political, and policy support.

Coda

As we imagine the potential power of these new genres of research, we remind ourselves of the intergenerational movement that they seek to support and sustain: the long historical arc of U.S. public education in and from which ambitions for excellence and equity have emerged and with which they collide.

Absent sustained public, political, and policy support, the collision between ambitions and institutions is not much of a collision at all. Institutions take the hand every time. With sustained public, political, and policy support, the collision becomes a version of societal plate tectonics: a slow grinding between new and inherited traditions of thought and action, each a powerful force. Seismic events do occur: A champion finds voice, judges see light, and policymakers find common cause. But, most often, the earth changes slowly but profoundly, while the ground on which we stand looks surprisingly familiar—until it's not.

So has it been with the shift in societal ambitions beyond access to excellence and equity in public education. So is it likely to be with the shift beyond access-oriented mass public schooling to instructionally education systems.

APPENDIX

Searching and Analyzing the Literature

To probe for new patterns of instructional organization and management, we conducted a comprehensive and systematic analysis of the research literature. Below, we detail our methods for sampling categories of districts, searching the literature, and analyzing our sources. We also reflect on limitations in our approach.

Sampling Categories of Districts

For this analysis, we sampled conventional public school districts (urban, suburban, and rural) and alternative public school districts (state takeover districts, turnaround zones, and charter school networks), because they are the mass public schooling enterprises in the United States that are in most direct contact with the political and policy activity pressing for instructionally focused education systems. Our conjecture was that there would be sufficient variation among these categories of public school districts to probe for different patterns of instructional organization and management.

We did not sample large-scale religious education enterprises (e.g., Catholic, Jewish, or Lutheran) or large-scale, philosophically aligned enterprises (e.g., Montessori or Rudolf Steiner), because they are in less direct contact with the political and policy activity pressing for instructionally focused education systems. Furthermore, we did not sample "hybrid" enterprises in which nonprofit or for-profit organizations support central offices and/or schools in district redesign. While hybrid enterprises do engage the same political and policy presses as public school districts, our prior research suggests that political and administrative matters (e.g., lack of formal authority and the lack of institutionalized funding structures) have them doing so differently from public school districts (Cohen et al., 2014). We reserve comparisons with and among public, religious, philosophically aligned, and hybrid education enterprises for future analyses.

Searching the Literature

Our primary approach to identifying sources was to use ProQuest to search the ERIC database for peer reviewed articles since 1995 using a standard set of keywords (e.g., "system," "organization," "district," "network," "local education agency," "instruction," and "teaching"). We focused primarily on peer-reviewed research in academic journals as a quality criterion, given the proliferation of books, foundation reports, and think tank reports on district redesign (a good deal of which are of questionable quality and independence). We focused on articles published since 1995, because this is the year after which the logic of system reform was first operationalized in federal policy and at which time empirical research focusing on it was first published. To supplement our primary search, we also included selected reports and books: for example, federally funded reports on charter school networks and rural school districts and books from peer-reviewed university presses.

This approach yielded over 1,700 articles, reports, and books. We then reviewed titles and abstracts to identify research that took entire districts and schools (rather than targeted components of districts and schools) as the primary units of analysis. To establish reliability, we randomly sampled sources, independently coded them to determine if they met these criteria, and then discussed and resolved disagreements. The process yielded 205 sources that became the focus of our search for patterns of instructional organization and management.

Analyzing Our Sources

We coded the 205 resulting resources using the five core work domains detailed in our main analysis. Because nearly 40% of our sources focused on urban districts, we began there, by writing and comparing analytic memos identifying patterns of work activity and its distribution among central offices and schools. Our analysis of urban districts yielded six system types: early iterations of what we ultimately came to describe as managerial, market-driven, federated, and networked systems; "hybrid" systems as described in our sampling procedures; and "symbolic" systems featuring structural changes absent connections to classroom practice. We then refined our provisional typology by repeating these analytic procedures for the other five categories of public school districts, reconciling them with our provisional typology, and refining the typology as we moved forward.

As our analysis converged on these six system types, we then reconciled them with theoretical, conceptual, and practical research on district redesign (a) to develop an interpretation of the theory of action and assumptions underlying each and (b) to draw principles and language to use in representing them. For purpose of this analysis, we do not report our findings on hybrid systems, because we did not systematically search for research on hybrid systems and for the reasons discussed above, under sampling. Furthermore, we do not identify a symbolic system as a type of instructionally focused education system, because it does not meet our definition.

Limitations

One matter that tempers our analysis is the general paucity of peer-reviewed research on the redesign of public school districts as instructionally focused education systems. Most of the literature on district redesign examines either (a) political and administrative matters or (b) targeted educational interventions. Moreover, of the research that did examine comprehensive district redesign, much took the form of evaluations that "blackboxed" exactly the organizational dynamics of interest to us. Indeed, in searching the literature, we were struck by its isomorphism both with legacy conceptions of educational innovation and improvement (e.g., research focused on targeted interventions) and with current policy priorities (e.g., research focused on identifying "what works"). Genres of research focused on understanding *how* complex, systemic, large-scale instructional improvement work actually plays out (and opportunities to publish such research) appeared to be comparatively thin, despite the ubiquitousness of such work in public school districts. For those who see value in the type of future research that we suggest in this analysis, these matters are cause for concern.

Second, even though our methods were comprehensive and systematic, they were neither exhaustive nor scientific. Though surprised by the general paucity of peer-reviewed research, we were also struck by the abundance of nonacademic publications providing insights into redesign activity in public school districts. If approached with care, our strong hunch is that there is much to be learned from these sources. Furthermore, our analytic approach, even while grounded in our research-based "five core domains" framework, was inductive and interpretive. That is why we offer the resulting typology as a collection of ideal types, the value of which lies in their usefulness (and not as normative standards to be found in the world in pure form). In the near future, we will be advancing additional research that (among other things) uses these system types to construct vignettes of actual public school districts, such that the ideal types described here are complemented by illustrative cases.

Indeed, a primary criticism of our analysis would be that there is much more to be examined, and that other analytic approaches would reveal a more elaborate typology of education systems than represented here. We welcome this line of criticism, because it makes one of our fundamental points. This is not a moment in which some new, "one best system" appears to be emerging. Rather, it appears to be a moment of divergence, exploration, and variety, bounded by institutionalized patterns of organization and management, emerging logics and new understandings, and local affordances and inventiveness.

ACKNOWLEDGMENTS

Work on this chapter was supported by the Spencer Systems Study at Northwestern University and University of Michigan, funded by a research grant from the Spencer Foundation (SP0034639-201600066). The authors gratefully acknowledge reviewers and others who provided comments on earlier drafts and presentations, as well as the members of our research team: Naomi Blaushild, Kathryn Gabriele, Daniella Hall, Whitney Hegseth, Christine M. Neumerski, Melissa Ortiz, and Jennifer Seelig. All opinions and conclusions expressed in this chapter are those of the authors and do not necessarily reflect the views of any funding agency.

NOTES

[1] This analysis is one product of the Spencer Systems Study at Northwestern University and the University of Michigan. The analysis draws from (and extends) earlier analyses examining dilemmas endemic to the redesign of education systems (Cohen et al., 2018), possibilities for engaging families and communities in the redesign of public school districts (Peurach & Yurkofsky, 2018), system-environment interactions in developing and leveraging educational infrastructure for instructional improvement (Spillane, Seelig, Cohen, Peurach, & Blaushild, 2018), and the engagement of nongovernmental organizations in the redesign of public school districts, in the United States and cross-nationally (Peurach et al., in press). Components of the

analysis were first presented in the *Cooper Annual Leadership for Learning Lecture* at the University of Virginia (Peurach, 2018) and at the April 2018 meeting of the American Educational Research Association (Peurach, Yurkofsky, Spillane, & Cohen, 2018). Future publications from Spencer Systems Study will go further by (among other things) providing detailed vignettes and examples of the four types of education systems identified in this analysis.

 [2] The "five domains" framework presented here (along with "four systems" typology developed below) were previously presented in a digest of this chapter published as a policy brief by the National Education Policy Center (Peurach & Yurkofsky, 2018). The policy brief situates this same framework and typology in a specific "use context" (i.e., family and community engagement in district redesign), as a resource for states, advocates, and reformers in supporting deeper family and community engagement in efforts to improve students' day-to-day lives in classrooms.

REFERENCES

Anyon, J. (2009). Progressive social movements and educational equity. *Educational Policy, 23*, 194–215.

Board of Education v. Rowley, 458 U.S. 176 (1982).

Boudett, K. P., City, E. A., & Murnane, R. J. (Eds.). (2005). *Data Wise: A step by step guide to using assessment results to improve teaching and learning.* Cambridge, MA: Harvard Education Press.

Brown, K. M., Anfara, V. A. Jr., & Roney, K. (2004). Student achievement in high performing, suburban middle schools and low performing, urban middle schools: Plausible explanations for the differences. *Education and Urban Society, 36*, 428–456.

Bryk, A. S., Gomez, L. M., Grunow, A., & LeMahieu, P. G. (2015). *Learning to improve: How America's schools can get better at getting better.* Cambridge, MA: Harvard Education Press.

Bryk, A. S., Sebring, P. B., Allensworth, E., Luppescu, S., & Easton, J. Q. (2010). *Organizing school for improvement: Lessons from Chicago.* Chicago, IL: The University of Chicago Press.

Bryk, A. S., Sebring, P. B., Kerbow, D., Rollow, S., & Easton, J. Q. (1998). *Charting Chicago school reform: Democratic localism as a lever for change.* New York, NY: Routledge.

Bulkley, K. E., Henig, J. R., & Levin, H. M. (2010). *Between public and private: Politics, governance, and the new portfolio model for urban school reform.* Cambridge, MA: Harvard Education Press.

Burch, P. (2009). *Hidden markets: The new education privatization.* New York, NY: Routledge.

Callahan, R. E. (1964). *Education and the cult of efficiency: A study of the social forces that have shaped the administration of the public schools.* Chicago, IL: University of Chicago Press.

Carnegie Forum on Education and the Economy Nation. (1986). *A nation prepared: Teachers for the 21st century.* New York, NY: Carnegie Corporation.

Chubb, J. E., & Moe, T. M. (1988). Politics, markets, and the organization of schools. *American Political Science Review, 82*, 1065–1087.

Cobb, P., Jackson, K., Henrick, E., Smith, T. M., & the MIST Team. (2018). *Systems for instructional improvement; Creating coherence from the classroom to the district office.* Cambridge, MA: Harvard Education Press.

Cohen, D. K. (1985). Origins. In A. G. Powell, E. Farrar, & D. K. Cohen (Eds.), *The shopping mall high school: Winners and loser in the educational marketplace* (pp. 223–308). Boston, MA: Houghton Mifflin.

Cohen, D. K. (1989). Teaching practice: Plus que ca change. In P. W. Jackson (Ed.), *Contributing to educational change: Perspectives on research and practice* (pp. 27–84). Berkeley, CA: McCutchan.

Cohen, D. K. (1990). A revolution in one classroom: The case of Mrs. Oublier. *Educational Evaluation and Policy Analysis, 12*, 311–329.

Cohen, D. K. (2011). *Teaching and its predicaments*. Cambridge, MA: Harvard University Press.

Cohen, D. K., Peurach, D. J., Glazer, J. L., Gates, K. G., & Goldin, S. (2014). *Improvement by design: The promise of better schools*. Chicago, IL: University of Chicago Press.

Cohen, D. K., Raudenbush, S. W., & Ball, D. L. (2003). Resources, instruction, and research. *Educational Evaluation and Policy Analysis, 25*, 119–142.

Cohen, D. K., & Spillane, J. P. (1992). Policy and practice: The relations between governance and instruction. *Review of Research in Education, 18*(1), 3–49.

Cohen, D. K., Spillane, J. P., & Peurach, D. J. (2018). The dilemmas of educational reform. *Educational Researcher, 47*, 204–212.

Coleman, J. S., Campbell, E. Q., Hobson, C. J., McPartland, J., Mood, A. M., Weinfeld, F. D., & York, R. L. (1966). *Equality of educational opportunity*. Washington, DC: National Center for Educational Statistics.

Cremin, L. A. (1964). *The transformation of the school: Progressivism in American education, 1876–1957*. New York, NY: Vintage Books.

Cremin, L. A. (1970). *American education: The colonial experience, 1607–1783*. New York, NY: Harper & Row.

Cuban, L. (1988). *The managerial imperative and the practice of leadership in schools*. Albany: State University of New York Press.

Cuban, L. (1993). *How teacher taught: Constancy and change in American classroom, 1890-1990*. New York, NY: Teachers College Press.

Cucchiara, M. B., Gold, E. V. A., & Simon, E. (2011). Contracts, choice, and customer service: Marketization and public engagement in education. *Teachers College Record, 113*, 2460–2502.

Daly, A. J., Finnigan, K. S., Jordan, S., Moolenaar, N. M., & Che, J. (2014). Misalignment and perverse incentives: Examining the politics of district leaders as brokers in the use of research evidence. *Educational Policy, 28*, 145–174.

Datnow, A., & Park, V. (2014). *Data-driven leadership*. San Francisco, CA: Jossey-Bass.

Dauter, L., & Fuller, B. (2016). Student movement in social context: The influence of time, peers, and place. *American Educational Research Journal, 53*, 33–70.

David, J. L. (1995). The who, what, and why of site-based management. *Educational Leadership, 53*(4), 4–9.

Diamond, J. B. (2012). Accountability policy, school organization, and classroom practice: Partial recoupling and educational opportunity. *Education and Urban Society, 44*, 151–182.

Dooley, C. M., & Assaf, L. C. (2009). Contexts matter: Two teachers' language arts instruction in this high-stakes era. *Journal of Literacy Research, 41*, 354–391.

Dow, P. B. (1991). *Schoolhouse politics: Lessons from the Sputnik era*. Cambridge, MA: Harvard University Press.

Downey, D. B., von Hippel, P. T., & Broh, B. A. (2004). Are schools the great equalizer? Cognitive inequality during the summer months and the school year. *American Sociological Review, 69*, 613–635.

Dreeban, R. (1973). The school as a workplace. In W. Traver (Ed.), *Second handbook of research on teaching* (pp. 450–473). New York, NY: Rand McNally.

Duke, D. L. (2005). *Education empire: The evolution of an excellent suburban school system*. Albany: State University of New York Press.

Edmonds, R. (1979). Effective schools for the urban poor. *Educational Leadership, 37*(1), 15–24.

Elmore, R. F. (2000). *Building a new structure for school leadership*. Washington, DC: Albert Shanker Institute.

Elmore, R. F., & Burney, D. (1999). Investing in teacher learning: Staff development and instructional improvement. In L. Darling-Hammond & G. Sykes (Eds.), *Teaching as the learning profession: Handbook of policy and practice* (pp. 263–291). San Francisco, CA: Jossey-Bass

Engel, M. (2013). Problematic preferences? A mixed method examination of principals' preferences for teacher characteristics in Chicago. *Educational Administration Quarterly, 49*, 52–91.

Farrell, C. C. (2015). Designing school systems to encourage data use and instructional improvement: A comparison of school districts and charter management organizations. *Educational Administration Quarterly, 51*, 438–471.

Fishman, B. J., Penuel, W. R., Allen, A.-R., Cheng, B. H., & Sabelli, N. (2013). Design-based implementation research: An emerging model for transforming the relationship of research and practice. *National Society for the Study of Education Yearbook, 112*, 136–156.

Forman, M. L., Stosich, E. L., & Bocala, C. (2017). *The internal coherence framework: Creating conditions for continuous improvement in schools.* Cambridge, MA: Harvard Education Press.

Gamoran, A., & Mare, R. D. (1989). Secondary school tracking and educational inequality: Compensation, reinforcement, or neutrality? *American Journal of Sociology, 94*, 1146–1183.

Gamson, D. A., & Hodge, E. M. (2016). Education research and the shifting landscape of the American school district, 1816 to 2016. *Review of Research in Education, 40*(1), 216–249.

Ginsburg, A. L., Noell, J., & Plisko, V. W. (1988). Lessons from the wall chart. *Educational Evaluation and Policy Analysis, 10*(1), 1–12.

Glazer, J. L., & Egan, C. (2018). The ties that bind: Building civic capacity for the Tennessee Achievement School District. *American Educational Research Journal, 55*, 928–964. doi:10.3102/0002831218763088

Glazer, J. L., & Peurach, D. P. (2015). Occupational control in education: The logic and leverage of epistemic communities. *Harvard Educational Review, 85*, 172–202.

Goodlad, J. I. (1978). Educational leadership: Toward the third era. *Educational Leadership, 35*, 322–331.

Graham, P. A. (1974). *Community & class in American education, 1865-1918.* New York, NY: John Wiley.

Grant, G. (1992). Introduction. *Review of Research in Education, 18*(1), xi–xx.

Greenwald, R., Hedges, L. V., & Laine, R. D. (1996). The effect of school resources on student achievement. *Review of Educational Research, 66*, 361–396.

Hallett, T. (2010). The myth incarnate: Recoupling processes, turmoil, and inhabited institutions in an urban elementary school. *American Sociological Review, 75*, 52–74.

Hess, F. M. (Ed.). (2006). *Urban school reform: Lessons from San Diego.* Cambridge, MA: Harvard Education Press.

Hess, G. A. (1995). *Restructuring urban schools: A Chicago perspective.* New York, NY: Teachers College Press.

Heyns, B. (1978). *Summer learning and the effects of schooling.* New York, NY: Academic Press.

Heyns, B. (1987). Schooling and cognitive development: Is there a season for learning? *Child Development, 58*, 1151–1160.

Hill, P. T. (2006). *Put learning first: A portfolio approach to public schools.* Retrieved from https://www.crpe.org/sites/default/files/pub_portfolio_putlearningfirst_feb06.pdf

Hofstadter, R. (1963). *Anti-intellectualism in American life.* New York, NY: Random House.

Holme, J. J., Diem, S., & Welton, A. (2014). Suburban school districts and demographic change: The technical, normative, and political dimensions of response. *Educational Administration Quarterly, 50*, 34–66.

Honig, M. I. (2012). District central office leadership as teaching: How central office administrators support principals' development as instructional leaders. *Educational Administration Quarterly, 48*, 733–774.

Honig, M. I., & Hatch, T. (2004). Crafting coherence: How schools strategically manage multiple, external demands. *Educational Researcher, 33*(8), 16–30.

Honig, M. I., & Rainey, L. R. (2014). Central office leadership in principal professional learning communities: The practice beneath the policy. *Teachers College Record, 116*.

Hopkins, M., Spillane, J. P., Jakopovic, P., & Heaton, R. M. (2013). Infrastructure redesign and instructional reform in mathematics: Formal structure and teacher leadership. *Elementary School Journal, 114*, 200–224.

Hubbard, L. A., Stein, M. K., & Mehan, H. (2006). *Reform as learning: School reform, organizational culture, and community politics in San Diego.* New York, NY: Routledge.

Jabbar, H. (2016). The visible hand: Markets, politics, and regulation in post-Katrina New Orleans. *Harvard Educational Review, 86*, 1–26.

Jackson, P. W. (1968). *Life in classrooms.* New York, NY: Holt, Rinehart & Winston.

Jacob, B. A. (2007). The challenges of staffing urban schools with effective teachers. *Excellence in the Classroom, 17*, 129–153.

Jencks, C., Smith, M., Acland, H., Bane, M. J., Cohen, D., Gintis, H., . . . Michelson, S. (1972). *Inequality: A reassessment of the effect of family and schooling in America.* New York, NY: Basic Books.

Johnson, P. E., & Chrispeels, J. H. (2010). Linking the central office and its schools for reform. *Educational Administration Quarterly, 46*, 738–775.

Johnson, S. M., Marietta, G., Higgins, M. C., Mapp, K. L., & Grossman, A. S. (2014). *Achieving coherence in district improvement: Managing the relationship between the central office and schools.* Cambridge, MA: Harvard Education Press.

Kaestle, C. F. (1983). *Pillars of the republic: Common schools and American society, 1780-1860.* New York, NY: Hill & Wang.

Katznelson, I., & Weir, M. (1985). *Schooling for all: Class, race, and the decline of the democratic ideal.* New York, NY: Basic Books.

Kirp, D. L. (2013). *Improbable scholars: The rebirth of a great American school system and a strategy for America's schools.* New York, NY: Oxford University Press.

Knoester, M. (2011). Is the outcry for more pilot schools warranted? Democracy, collective bargaining, deregulation, and the politics of school reform in Boston. *Educational Policy, 25*, 387–423.

Lake, R., Dusseault, B., Bowen, M., Demeritt, A., & Hill, P. (2010). *The National Study of Charter Management Organization (CMO) Effectiveness. Report on interim findings.* Seattle, WA: Center on Reinventing Public Education.

Lake, R. J., & Hill, P. T. (2009). *Performance management in portfolio school districts.* Retrieved from https://www.crpe.org/sites/default/files/pub_dscr_portfperf_aug09_0.pdf

Lankford, H., Loeb, S., & Wyckoff, J. (2002). Teacher sorting and the plight of urban schools: A descriptive analysis. *Educational Evaluation and Policy Analysis, 24*, 37–62.

Leithwood, K., Louis, S. K., Anderson, S., & Wahlstrom, K. (2004). *Review of research: How leadership influences student learning.* Minneapolis: University of Minnesota, Center for Applied Research and Educational Improvement.

Little, J. W. (1990). The persistence of privacy: Autonomy and initiative in teachers' professional relations. *Teachers College Press, 91*, 509–536.

Lortie, D. C. (1975). *Schoolteacher: A sociological study.* Chicago, IL: The University of Chicago Press.

Lussier, D. F., & Forgione, P. D. Jr. (2010). Supporting and rewarding accomplished teaching: Insights from Austin, Texas. *Theory Into Practice, 49*, 233–242

Mann, H. (1848). *Twelfth annual report for 1848 of the Secretary of the Board of Education of Massachusetts.* Retrieved from https://archives.lib.state.ma.us/handle/2452/204731

Metz, M. H. (1989). Real school: A universal drama amid disparate experience. In D. Mitchell & M. Goertz (Eds.), *Education politics for the new century: The twentieth anniversary yearbook of the Politics of Education Association* (pp. 75–91). London, England: Falmer Press.

Meyer, J. W., & Rowan, B. (1978). The structure of educational organizations. In M. W. Meyer (Ed.), *Schools and society: A sociological approach to education* (pp. 217–225). San Francisco, CA: Jossey-Bass.

Mintrop, R. (2016). *Design-based school improvement: A practical guide for education leaders.* Cambridge, MA: Harvard Education Press.

Mirel, J. E. (2010). *Patriot pluralism: Americanization education and European immigrants.* Cambridge, MA: Harvard University Press.

National Commission on Educational Excellence. (1983). *A nation at risk: The imperative for educational reform.* Washington, DC: U.S. Government Printing Office.

National Governors Association. (1986). *Time for results: The governors' 1991 report on education.* Washington, DC: Author.

Oakes, J. (1985). *Keeping track: How schools structure inequality.* New Haven, CT: Yale University Press.

O'Day, J. A., Bitter, C. S., & Gomez, L. M. (2011). *Education reform in New York City: Ambitious change in the nation's most complex school system.* Cambridge, MA: Harvard Education Press.

Penuel, W. R., & Gallagher, D. J. (2017). *Creating research-practice partnerships in education.* Cambridge, MA: Harvard Education Press

Peurach, D. J. (2011). *See complexity in public education. Problems, possibilities, and success for all.* New York, NY: Oxford University Press.

Peurach, D. J. (2016). Innovating at the nexus of impact and improvement: Leading educational improvement networks. *Educational Researcher, 45,* 421–429.

Peurach, D. J. (2018, March). *From mass public schooling to educational systems: Changing patterns in the organization, management, and improvement of instruction.* University Council for Educational Administration Cooper Lecture, University of Virginia, Charlottesville, VA.

Peurach, D. J., Cohen, D. K., & Spillane, J. P. (in press). Governments, markets, and instruction: Considerations for cross-national research. *Journal of Educational Administration.*

Peurach, D. J., Glazer, J. L., & Lenhoff, S. W. (2016). The developmental evaluation of school improvement networks. *Educational Policy, 30,* 606–648.

Peurach, D. J., & Neumerski, C. M. (2015). Mixing metaphors: Building infrastructure for large scale school turnaround. *Journal of Educational Change, 16,* 379–420.

Peurach, D. J., Penuel, W. R., & Russell, J. L. (2018). Beyond ritualized rationality: Organizational dynamics of instructionally-focused continuous improvement. In C. James, D. E. Spicer, M. Connolly, & S. D. Kruse (Eds.), *The Sage handbook of school organization* (pp. 465–489). Thousand Oaks, CA: Sage.

Peurach, D. J., & Scott, J. (2012). Have allowing and encouraging private corporations to participate in public education positively affected school governance? In R. C. Hunter, F. Brown, & S. Donahoo (Eds.), *Debating issues in American education: Vol. 7. School governance* (pp. 165–186). Thousand Oaks, CA: Sage.

Peurach, D. J., & Yurkofsky, M. (2018). *Organizing and managing instruction in US public school districts: Considerations for families, communities, and states.* Boulder, CO: National Education Policy Center.

Peurach, D. J., Yurkofsky, M., Spillane, J. P., & Cohen, D. K. (2018, April). *Designing and creating educational systems: A review of research.* Paper presented at the Annual Meeting of the American Educational Research Association. New York, NY.

Powell, A. G., Farrar, E., & Cohen, D. K. (1985). *The shopping mall high school: Winners and losers in the educational marketplace.* Boston, MA: Houghton Mifflin.

Purkey, S., & Smith, M. S. (1983). Effective schools: A review. *Elementary School Journal, 83,* 427–452.

Purkey, S., & Smith, M. S. (1985). School reform: The district policy implications of the effective schools literature. *Elementary School Journal, 85,* 352–389.

Ravitch, D. (2010). *The death and life of the great American school system.* New York, NY: Basic Books.

Reardon, S. F., & Hinze-Pifer, R. (2017). *Test score growth among public school students in Chicago, 2009-2014.* Retrieved from https://cepa.stanford.edu/content/test-score-growth-among-chicago-public-school-students-2009-2014

Reckhow, S. (2013). *Follow the money: How foundation dollars change public school politics.* New York, NY: Oxford University Press.

Reville, S. P., & Coggins, C. (Eds.). (2007). *A decade of urban school reform: Persistence and progress in the Boston Public Schools.* Cambridge, MA: Harvard Education Press.

Robinson v. Cahill, 62 N.J. 473 (1973).

Rowan, B. (1990). Commitment and control: Alternative strategies for the organizational design of schools. *Review of Research in Education, 16,* 353–389

Rowan, B. (2002). The ecology of school improvement: Notes on the school improvement industry in the United States. *Journal of Educational Change, 3,* 283–314.

Rowan, B., Correnti, R. J., Miller, R. J., & Camburn, E. M. (2009). School improvement by design: Lessons from a study of comprehensive school reform programs. In G. Sykes, B. Schneider, & D. Plank (Eds.), *AERA handbook on education policy research* (pp. 637–651). New York, NY: Routledge.

Smith, M. S., & O'Day, J. A. (1991). Systemic school reform. In S. H. Fuhrman & B. Malen (Eds.), *The politics of curriculum and testing: The 1990 yearbook of the Politics of Education Association* (pp. 233–267). New York, NY: Falmer Press.

Spillane, J. P. (2006). *Distributed leadership.* San Francisco, CA: Jossey-Bass.

Spillane, J. P. (2009). *Standards deviation: How schools misunderstand education policy.* Cambridge, MA: Harvard University Press.

Spillane, J. P., Seelig, J. L., Cohen, D. K., Peurach, D. J., & Blaushild, N. (2018, April). Managing environments and instruction in designing educational systems: A comparative analysis of six schools systems organizing for instruction in the US. Paper presented at the 2018 meeting of the American Educational Research Association, New York, NY.

Stein, M. K., & D'Amico, L. (2002). Inquiry at the crossroads of policy and learning: A study of a district-wide literacy initiative. *Teachers College Record, 104,* 1313–1344.

Terosky, A. L. (2014). From a managerial imperative to a learning imperative: Experiences of urban, public school principals. *Educational Administration Quarterly, 50,* 3–33.

Tompkins-Stange, M. (2016). *Policy patrons: Philanthropy, education reform, and the politics of influence.* Cambridge, MA: Harvard Education Press.

Torres, A. C. (2014). "Are we architects or construction workers?" Re-examining teacher autonomy and turnover in charter schools. *Education Policy Analysis Archives, 22*(124), 1–24.

Trujillo, T. (2014). The modern cult of efficiency: Intermediary organizations and the new scientific management. *Educational Policy, 28,* 207–232.

Tyack, D. (1974). *The one best system: A history of American urban education.* Cambridge, MA: Harvard University Press.

Tyack, D. (2002). Forgotten players: How local school districts shaped American education. In A. M. Hightower, M. S. Knapp, J. A. Marsh, & M. W. McLaughlin (Eds.), *School districts and instructional renewal* (pp. 9–24). New York, NY: Teachers College Press.

Tyack, D., & Hansot, E. (1982). *Managers of virtue: Public school leadership in America, 1820-1980.* New York, NY: Basic Books.

Vinovskis, M. A. (1999). *The road to Charlottesville: The 1989 Education Summit.* Washington, DC: National Education Goals Panel.

Wong, K. K. (2011). Redesigning urban districts in the USA: Mayoral accountability and the diverse provider model. *Educational Management Administration & Leadership, 39,* 486–500.

Woodworth, K. R., David, J. L., Guha, R., Wang, H., & Lopez-Torkos, A. (2008). *San Francisco bay area KIPP schools: A study of early implementation and achievement, final report.* Menlo Park, CA: SRI International.

Youngs, P. (2007). District induction policy and new teachers' experiences: An examination of local policy implementation in Connecticut. *Teachers College Record, 109,* 797–837.

Yurkofsky, M. (2017). *The restructuring of educational organizations: From ceremonial rules to technical ceremonies* (Unpublished qualifying paper). Harvard Graduate School of Education, Cambridge, MA.

Chapter 3

Critical Reflection and Generativity: Toward a Framework of Transformative Teacher Education for Diverse Learners

KATRINA LIU
University of Nevada, Las Vegas

ARNETHA F. BALL
Stanford University

This chapter provides a critical and synthesizing review of the literature on issues related to preparing teachers for diverse learners from historical and theoretical standpoints, reviewing more than 50 years of calls for teacher education reform and efforts to prepare White teachers and teachers of color for racial, ethnic, and linguistic diversity in schools and communities. It finds that the limited success of such efforts is the result of policy changes that overemphasize recruitment and underemphasize retention, and calls for restructuring teacher education programs and research that focuses on critical reflection and generativity that can lead to transformative practices in the classroom. The authors argue for a (re)new(ed) emphasis on community-based teacher preparation grounded in critical reflection and generativity, which facilitates and promotes transformative teacher education that prepares teachers to teach diverse student populations.

The American public education system from its inception in the late 19th century to the present day has struggled with fundamental contradictions in its structures, practices, and functions in society. For example, there has long been a basic contradiction between the democratic impulses of many of the American founders (Dewey, in particular) and the use of the schools to support the racial, gender, and language hierarchies integral to U.S. society. More recently, use of field placement for the final stages of teacher education was intended to improve real-world training for preservice teachers, but this quickly raised awareness among teacher educators that student teachers could learn negative attitudes and behaviors from their mentor

Review of Research in Education
March 2019, Vol. 43, pp. 68–105
DOI: 10.3102/0091732X18822806
Chapter reuse guidelines: sagepub.com/journals-permissions
© 2019 AERA. http://rre.aera.net

teachers. Furthermore, throughout the 20th century the desire for an extended, apprenticeship-based training system for teachers has foundered on the need for more teachers than such a system could possibly produce, prompting shortcuts in teacher education that once again reinforced inequity. The American public education system has also struggled because, while more and more has been demanded from teachers, they continue to be paid far less than other fields requiring a college degree. As a result, there is a chronic shortage of qualified teachers, especially in science and math and in schools that require teachers with the skills, dispositions, and knowledge needed to teach diverse student populations.

In 1969, B. Othanial Smith published *Teachers for the Real World*, the outcome of 2 years of work by the Steering Committee and Task Force of the National Institute for Advanced Study in Teaching Disadvantaged Youth. The report suggested that teacher education programs failed to provide adequate preparation for teachers to effectively teach "disadvantaged youth":

Racial, class, and ethnic bias can be found in every aspect of current teacher preparation programs. The selection processes militate against the poor and minority. The program content reflects current prejudices; the methods of instruction coincide with learning styles of the dominant group. Subtle inequities are reinforced in institutions of higher learning. (p. 3)

Noting 50 years of efforts to improve teaching and teacher education, including a study of his own (Smith, 1980), Smith nevertheless called for radical reforms in teacher education programs regarding their approach to teaching about diversity and equity, warning, however, that

unless there is scrupulous self-appraisal, unless every aspect of teacher training is carefully reviewed, the changes initiated in teacher preparation as a result of the current crises will be, like so many changes which have gone before, "merely differences which make no difference." (Smith, 1969, p. 3)

Since the 1969 Smith report, many reforms have been proposed for teacher education programs. Yet it would appear that—as he warned—success in teaching for diversity and equity remains as elusive now as it was 50 years ago. For that reason, it seems appropriate that we revisit the topic of changing teacher preparation practices to teach diverse learners in K–12 schools.

REVIEW METHOD

This chapter investigates the question "How is change in teaching practices and teacher education programs designed to prepare teachers to teach diverse learners conceptualized, facilitated and transformed?" through a critical and synthesizing review of the research literature. We set the context by reviewing 27 national studies of (or calls for the reform of) teacher education from 1929 to 2016. A thematic analysis of this literature provided a sense of the large movements in teacher education reform, which then guided our survey of research on preparing teachers for diverse classrooms to focus on approaches from multicultural education, critical race theory, and community-based teacher preparation. The second phase of the survey used systematic keyword searches of the ERIC database, including teacher education and Whiteness, teacher education and critical race theory, teacher education and multicultural teacher education programs, and so on, producing 10,500 hits. Focusing on teacher preparation shrank this list to 2,000 items; we then examined the texts for empirical studies on preparing White students to handle diversity versus recruiting, preparing, and retaining teachers of color, yielding 50 core studies. Having conducted this review, we then turn to the threads connecting the limited success of these approaches: the need to base research on actual teaching and learning practices in classrooms, the need to encourage critical reflection for transformative learning to be systematically applied throughout teacher education practice, and the need to expose teachers and teacher education programs to generative theory, which has the power to stimulate and support real change in teachers' practices. We conclude by offering a framework for developing promising practices that combines critical reflection and generativity in a model that can bring about real transformation in individual teachers and teacher education programs.

DEFINING STUDENT DIVERSITY

A review of literature on teacher education reform shows that the 1969 Smith Report is one of the earliest acknowledgments of student diversity, although he does not use the word *diversity*. Smith spoke of *disadvantaged youth*, a term that moved from a sociological association with poverty to encompass other kinds of disadvantage in the 1960s. In Smith's formulation, disadvantaged youth (1) are denied choice in careers; (2) lack any semblance of political power and are even denied an opportunity to learn how democratic decision making takes place; (3) are stigmatized as culturally disadvantaged, excluded from the broader cultural activities, and have their own culture denigrated; and (4) are denied inter- and intrapersonal competence, segregated from the larger society, and labeled as socially or emotionally disturbed if they protest against the inequity of the situation (pp. 3–4). Smith's definition avoids specifying groups that could be labeled *disadvantaged*, choosing instead to focus on the social costs they face by being so labeled. More recent notions of diversity tend to focus on the ways in which groups diverge from a norm that, by and large, itself remains undefined—indeed, the norm has largely become defined by repeatedly adding ways in which students diverge from it. Nevertheless, the overlap of "disadvantaged" with more recent notions of diversity is clear.

Most attempts to define diversity in education are also lists. For example, Zeichner (1996) lists social class, ethnicity, race, and language and Banks and Banks (2010) list gender, social class, ethnic, racial, or cultural characteristics. The National Council for Accreditation of Teacher Education (NCATE; 2008) defines "diversity" as "differences among groups of people and individuals based on ethnicity, race, socioeconomic status, gender, exceptionalities, language, religion, sexual orientation, and geographical area," and the InTASC Teaching Standards that many teacher education programs have adopted states that "all learners bring to their learning varying experiences, abilities, talents, and prior learning, as well as language, culture, and family and community values" (Council of Chief State School Officers, 2013). Note that although members of all the groups listed by the various definitions are probably subject to the social costs Smith (1969) identified as "disadvantaged," by focusing on how students diverge from the undefined norm, the lists erase the fundamental social inequities that affect some groups more intensively than others. In other words, if all differences participate in "diversity," then they become "differences which make no difference" (p. 3).

With the conceptual weakness of "diversity," it is no surprise that teacher education programs are quick to use the term *diversity* but "share no unified definition of what an educator prepared for diversity actually looks like, how such an educator should get prepared, or how his or her preparation could best be assessed" (Pollock, Deckman, Mira, & Shalaby, 2010, p. 212). We agree with Zeichner (1996) that an adequate definition of diversity must be broad and inclusive, but at the same time it must be effective for the purpose at hand, be it teacher preparation or research. For that reason, we choose to look more to the social costs identified by Smith—marginalization, denigration, segregation, and denial of competence—in choosing the kind of diversity to examine. For purposes of this chapter, we focus on racial, ethnic, and linguistic diversity for the following reasons: First, the racial and ethnic diversity in K–12 schools has increased dramatically in the last decades. In 1972, only 22% of the school population were students of color; as of 2014–2015, White students are now a minority in K–12 public schools, with no single racial or ethnic group in the majority (Institute of Education Sciences, 2016, Table 7, p. 48). In 5 of the 10 largest school districts, students of color comprise more than 90% of the total school enrollment (see Table 1). Yet the teacher corps and the teacher education professoriate remain overwhelmingly White; the resulting "cultural divide" between teachers and teacher educators on one side, and students and communities on the other, "undermines efforts to prepare interculturally competent teachers" (Zeichner, 2003, p. 493).

Second, the number of students who are English language learners or speakers of nonstandard variants of English is significant and growing. For example, California's residents speak roughly 200 officially recognized languages; nearly 45% use languages other than English in their homes. Black African immigrants represent one of the fastest growing segments of the U.S. immigrant population, increasing by about 200% during the 1980s and 1990s and by 100% during the 2000s (Capps, McCabe, & Fix, 2012); moreover, California has the fifth largest Black population in the country and is home to about 900,000 African Americans under the age of 25. Some 22 years after the Oakland Unified School District sparked fierce debate by declaring Ebonics a distinct language, native-born Black students remain the most misunderstood, misidentified, and underserved population of English language learners.

Third, these three forms of diversity are more consistently studied in the literature. For example, apart from a handful of calls for the inclusion of religion in

TABLE 1

Student Demographic of 10 Largest School Districts

School District	Los Angeles Unified School District (2017–2018)	Chicago Public Schools (2017–2018)	Puerto Rico Department of Education (2017–2018)	Miami-Dade County Public Schools (2017–2018)	Clark County School District (2017–2018)	Broward County Public Schools	Houston Independent School District	Hillsborough County Public Schools	Orange County Public Schools	Palm Beach County School District
% of White Students	9.8	10.2	0.1	6.9	24.5	22.3	8.6	34.9	27.8	32.6
% of Students of color	90.2	89.8	99.9	93.1	75.5	77.7	91.4	65.1	72.2	67.2

cultural relevant education (Aronson, Amatullah, & Laughter, 2016; Kimani & Laster, 1999), research on religious diversity is overwhelmingly done outside the United States; empirical research is rare, and it tends to focus on teacher and student beliefs. Diversity in gender and sexual orientation (often handled in tandem) is more significant, yet, as debates over intersectionality have revealed, has complicated interactions with race and ethnicity that scholars rarely attempt to tackle.

Finally, we take seriously the concerns articulated by Gutiérrez and Rogoff (2003), González (2005), Ladson-Billings (2009), Milner (2009, 2014, 2017), Howard (2013), and others that the overuse of "cultural" diversity, and especially the way in which it has replaced race at the center of multicultural education, means that culture has "lost much of its utility as a way to describe the diversity within society" (González, 2005, p. 36). Research indicates that prospective teachers in particular tend to avoid recognizing that race and ethnicity are important aspects of diversity and instead use socially safer terms such as *culture* (Ladson-Billings, 2009; Howard, 2013). Howard (2013) specifically cautions against "reductive notions of culture" that essentialize minority groups with stereotypical assumptions (p. 2001), while Milner (2017) argues that race needs to be recentered and reemphasized in the fight to support students of color with what they rightfully and highly deserve.

With this focus of diversity on race, ethnicity, and language, we now explore how teacher education programs have tried to prepare teachers for diverse students. We begin with a survey of teacher education reform in general, and with respect to diversity, and then discuss existing approaches to preparing teachers to teach diverse students.

CALLS FOR REFORM IN TEACHER EDUCATION

A review of approximately 30 calls for action in reforming teacher education from the first third of the 20th century to the present day (Table 2) indicates that they can be periodized into five phases, each adding new concerns to those of the previous phase:

1. 1929–1945: Developing teachers' classroom skills and civic responsibility
2. 1946–1968: Professionalizing teaching through clinical training and licensure
3. 1969–1982: Intensifying professionalization, growing awareness of student diversity
4. 1983–1996: Sense of crisis in U.S. education, need for diverse teacher corps
5. 1997–present: Development of alternatives to "traditional" teacher education and concern about U.S. "competitiveness" in international assessments (Program for International Assessment [PISA])

The first phase, bookmarked by the Great Crash and the end of World War II (WWII), featured three major reports, the Commonwealth Teacher Training Study (Charters et al., 1929), the U.S. Office of Education National Survey (1939), and the American Council on Education's report, *Teachers for Our Times*

TABLE 2
Teacher Education Reform Reports

Year	Report
1929	Commonwealth Teacher Training Study
1933	U.S. Office of Education National Survey
1944	American Council on Education, *Teachers for Our Times*
1946	American Council on Education, *The Improvement of Teacher Education*
1956	AACTE, *Teacher Education for a Free People*
1961	National Commission in Teacher Education and Professional Standards of National Education Association, *New Horizons for the Teaching Profession*
1963	American Council Study, aka the *Conant Report* (published as *The Education of the American Teachers*, New York, NY: McGraw-Hill)
1969	U.S. Office of Education, Ball State University, and a subcontract through AACTE, the Smith Report, *Teachers for the Real World*
1976	AACTE *Report of the Bicentennial Commission on Education for the Profession of Teaching*
1982	NCATE, *Standards for the Accreditation of Teacher Education*
1983	National Commission on Excellence in Education: *A Nation at Risk*
1985	AACTE National Commission for Excellence in Teacher Education, *A Call for Change in Teacher Education*
1985	NCATE, Standards, procedures, and policies for the accreditation of professional teacher education units
1986	Task Force on Teaching as a Profession, *A Nation Prepared: Teachers for the 21st Century* (aka the *Carnegie Report*)
1986	ATE Blue Ribbon Task Force, *Visions of Reform: Implications for the Education Profession*
1986	Holmes Group, *Tomorrow's Teachers: A Report of the Holmes Group*
1989	Holmes Group, *The Holmes Group One Year On*
1990	Holmes Group, *Tomorrow's Schools: Principles for the Design of Professional Development Schools*
1991	Holmes Group, *Toward a Community of Learning: The Preparation and Continuing Education of Teachers. A Report of the Curriculum Committee of the Holmes Group to University and School Faculty Engaged in Educating Teachers* (Prepared by Griffin, G.)
1992	Holmes Group, *Embracing Cultural Diversity in Colleges of Education: Minority Recruitment and Retention*
1995	Holmes Group, *Tomorrow's Schools of Education: A Report of the Holmes Group*
1997	Darling-Hammond, for the National Commission on Teaching & America's Future, *Doing What Matters Most: Investing in Quality Teaching*
2006	Kirby, McCombs, Barney, and Naftel, for the RAND Corporation, *Reforming Teacher Education: Something Old, Something New*
2010	NCATE, *Transforming Teacher Education Through Clinical Practice: A National Strategy to Prepare Effective Teachers. Report of the Blue Ribbon Panel on Clinical Preparation and Partnerships for Improved Student Learning*
2011	U.S. Department of Education, *Our Future, Our Teachers: The Obama Administration's Plan for Teacher Education and Reform*
2012	Klein, Rice, and Levy, for the Council on Foreign Relations, *U.S. Education Reform and National Security*
2016	Mitchell and King, *A New Agenda: Research to Build a Better Teacher Preparation Program*

Note. AACTE = American Association of Colleges for Teacher Education; NCATE = National Council for Accreditation of Teacher Education; ATE = Association of Teacher Education.

(1947). This trio of reports form a logical sequence, with the first constituting a functional analysis of teachers' classroom practices across the country, the second calling for a national focus on improving teachers' competence in classroom skills, and the third arguing for the civic responsibility of teachers in a democratic society. Although this period evinces an awareness of the need for effective teachers at both the classroom and community levels, there is no clear push for changes to teacher training in order to satisfy this need.

The second phase, beginning just after the end of WWII in 1946 and ending at the height of the Vietnam War in 1968, represents a major push toward the professionalization of teacher training, licensing, and assessment. In a series of studies and reports, organizations such as the American Council on Education (American Council on Education Commission on Teacher Education, 1946; Conant, 1963/2001), the American Association of Colleges for Teacher Education (AACTE; Cottrell & Cooper, 1956), and the National Education Association (Lindsey, 1961) developed detailed suggestions for teacher education, laying the foundation for what is now sometimes described as "traditional" teacher education. All the reports agreed on the need for teachers to be trained as undergraduate students at universities with some combination of liberal arts and education coursework, and to get preservice clinical experience under the joint supervision of university-based teacher educators and mentor teachers in the schools. Although the groups did not agree on where responsibility for licensure should lie, all agreed that the requirements for licensure should be decided by universities and be based on research into teaching and learning. Little attention was paid in this period to the social, economic, and political ferment in the larger U.S. society—there is no reflection in policy recommendations, for example, of the fight to eliminate Jim Crow in the south or of the growing race-based inequalities in the north. Even the titles of the reports—*The Improvement of Teacher Education* (American Council on Education Commission on Teacher Education, 1946), *New Horizons for the Teaching Profession* (Lindsey, 1961), *The Education of American Teachers* (Conant, 1963/2001)—reflect the managerial attitude prevalent in this phase.

The next phase continues this managerial attitude through such events as the 1976 Bicentennial Commission on Education for the Profession of Teaching (an AACTE project) and the publication of the first standards for teacher education by the NCATE in 1982. However, as the title of the 1969 report by the AACTE, *Teachers for the Real World* (Smith, 1969), suggests, the tumultuous changes that had been taking place outside schools of education were beginning to percolate into policy. Indeed, that report appears to be the earliest attempt to address the diversity of the student body, expending considerable space to speaking of "disadvantaged youth" as similar only in their marginalization, but "as different from one another as the children of other elements of the population" (p. 13).

The fourth phase corresponds to a period of major crisis and upheaval in education, heralded by the publication of *A Nation at Risk* in 1983. This report, although not directly concerned with teacher education, laid out in stark terms an apparent crisis in K–12 student achievement as measured by performance on SAT exams, in comparison to historical scores as well as international ones. Although strongly criticized on methodological and ideological grounds, the sense of crisis engendered by the report as well as a subset of the nearly 40 policy recommendations (notably, the use of standardized testing of student learning) have become permanent features of the U.S. education landscape. Subsequent to *A Nation at Risk* (National Commission on Education, 1983), further reports on education in general and teacher education in particular became a nearly annual event. Major landmarks include the 1985 AACTE report *A Call for Change in Teacher Education* (National Commission for Excellence in Teacher Education, 1985) and two competing reports in 1986, one by a group of politicians and businesspeople assembled by the Carnegie Forum on Education and the Economy (*A Nation Prepared: Teachers for the 21st Century*) and the other by the Holmes Group of education school deans (*Tomorrow's Teachers*). All the groups continued the emphasis on professionalization in their report, but the Holmes Group is distinguished for continuing to issue reports into the early 1990s and for launching and intensifying efforts to diversify the teacher workforce as a means of addressing both the growing diversity of the student body and the issues with achievement identified by *A Nation at Risk*. In particular, the Holmes Group required its member institutions to work on "recruiting minority students and faculty" and reporting the results, beginning with their 1989 report *The Holmes Group: One Year On*, through their calls for professional development schools (1990) and teacher learning communities (1991), culminating with a report entirely focused on the issue in 1992, *Embracing Cultural Diversity in Colleges of Education: Minority Recruitment and Retention* (Blankenship, 1992). Interestingly, although there have been many critiques of both the Carnegie and Holmes approaches to professionalizing teacher education (Caldwell, 1986; Cockrell, Mitchell, Middleton, & Campbell, 1999; Darling-Hammond, 1986; Fullan, Galluzzo, & Morris, 1998; Gottlieb & Cornbleth, 1989; Hawley, 1986; Johnson, 1987, 1990; to name just a few), rarely has the focus on teachers and teacher educators of color found in the Holmes Group's efforts merited comment.

Finally, the current phase, which begins with Darling-Hammond's 1998 *Doing What Matters Most: Investing in Quality Teaching*, builds on the proposals for professionalizing teachers that developed in the previous phases but replaces much of the concern about diversity and equity evidenced in the Holmes Group reports with a focus on national competitiveness. Recall that *A Nation at Risk* raised the issue of national competitiveness with an international comparison of SAT scores and K–12 curricula; in the late 20th and early 21st centuries this was intensified with the creation and application of international standardized testing, particularly those of the PISA. This has ushered in a strong neoliberal emphasis to the policy suggestions, including a focus on the economic value of schooling as opposed to knowledge or community engagement, and a move toward privatizing both K–12 education and teacher preparation. Thus, although some of the same organizations that had been issuing reports for years continued to re-present older prescriptions for teacher education, such as NCATE's (2010) *Transforming Teacher Education Through Clinical Practice*, new players from the private sector and the national security disciplines weighed in as well: Kirby, McCombs, Barney, and Naftel (2006), for the RAND Corporation; Klein, Rice, and Levy (2012), for the Council on Foreign Relations; and Mitchell and King (2016), for Bellwether Education Partners, a 501(c)(3) organization founded by venture capitalists and charter school operators including representatives from EdVentures, Inc., and Teach for America.

In sum, reports and calls for action in reforming teacher education through most of the 20th century and into the 21st only begin to recognize student diversity with the 1969 Smith report, and teacher diversity only with the Holmes Group reports from 1986 to 1992. None of the calls for action have elevated the needs of students of color or teachers of color to the level of other issues deemed "crises," such as the drop in SAT scores decried in *A Nation at Risk* or the fears of economic competition driving later PISA comparisons. Moreover, because they employ a managerial mindset, even the reports of the Holmes Group fail to fully diagnose the barriers facing the recruitment, retention, and success of students and teachers of color, providing little advice beyond promoting adequate funding and mentoring of teachers of color. Finally, all the reports since the end of WWII have advocated clinical practice as an important element of teacher preparation. However, there appears to be no recognition of the possibility that clinical practice could reinforce negative aspects of school and society, in spite of research suggesting just that as early as the original Harvard-Lexington summer program (Goldhammer, 1966).

CHANGES IN TEACHER EDUCATION PRACTICE

It is clear from the literature and policy reports that teacher education programs need to change future teachers' teaching practice to better support diverse learners. Teacher education programs have indeed responded to this demand and have implemented different approaches to address the issues of teaching diverse students. In general, these approaches fall into two categories: (1) preparing White prospective teachers to teach diverse students and (2) recruiting and preparing prospective teachers of color to teach diverse students. Below we provide a review of the practices and outcomes of these two types of teacher education practice.

Preparing White Teachers for Diverse Students

In the years since *A Nation at Risk*, three major approaches to preparing White teachers for diverse students have been developed: multicultural education, critical race theory, and community-based learning.

Multicultural Education and Critical Race Theory

Two approaches to teacher education emphasizing social justice have taken shape over the past 50 years, both of which are employed by teacher educators and research-ers. The older of the two, multicultural education, grows out of a desire to have schools fully reflect the pluralism of post-WWII society, particularly in the aftermath of the civil rights movements of the 1950s and 1960s. Some years later, scholars and teacher educators such as Gloria Ladson-Billings applied the ideas of critical race theory to education in general, and teacher education in particular. In subsequent years critical race theory has greatly influenced multicultural education, so we treat the two together.

Although the roots of multicultural education go back farther, it is generally considered to have taken shape in the 1970s, simultaneously in the United States, the United Kingdom, and Australia (Banks, 1974; Bullivant, 1972; Gay, 1977; Grant, 1975). There are several major surveys of multicultural education in the literature beginning as early as 1976 (Gibson, 1976) but none that specifically address research from the standpoint of diversity and efficacy in both classroom and teacher education programs. Sleeter and Grant (1987) observed that these early surveys, organized by a combination of target population, long-term goals, and assumptions about cultural differences, "failed to distinguish between related but different approaches" (p. 422). Therefore, they typologized 127 articles and books on multicultural education in terms of approaches to pedagogy but did not address research or teacher education. Some 15 years later, Bennett (2001) assayed an even broader survey of works on multicultural education using the concept of literary genre to develop four clusters of "genres of research" covering curriculum revision and reform, equity pedagogy, multicultural competence, and societal equity (p. 174). However, Bennett's survey is not limited to research and includes materials such as K–12 textbooks, curriculum reform proposals, and works that are broadly descriptive but not based in systematic research.

The broad literature reviews by Sleeter and Grant (1987) and Bennett (2001) are certainly highly valuable to educators and researchers, but neither provides a pathway for transformation of either classroom teaching or teacher preparation. They do dem-onstrate the enormous scope of research and pedagogy associated with multicultural education, and that in itself points to definitional problems in the approach. In spite of the use of the word "culture," in the beginning multicultural education was more closely linked with notions of race, ethnicity, and linguistic diversity and had a some-what contentious relationship with the identity politics of gender, sexual orientation, and disability. As early as 1974, Banks warned against the expansion of multicultural education away beyond race and ethnicity, arguing that race and ethnicity are so fundamental to American inequity that they must be addressed first, and that bring-ing in other ways people identify in groups would harm the causes of both sides. A year later, Grant identified a tension between the goals of multicultural education and competency-based teacher education, warning that viewing multicultural education as a set of skills transmissible through professional development would not address the primary goal: eliminating race-based inequities built into the American school system (Grant, 1975).

Critical race theory, by contrast, prioritizes the experience of minority communities of color over that of White teachers, even in the branches of critical race theory that are specifically concerned with the concepts and mechanisms of Whiteness (e.g., critical Whiteness theory). From the standpoint of critical race theory, educational institutions and practices function to perpetuate White supremacy, so the goal of teacher education should be to enable teachers to recognize, acknowledge, and change those institutions and practices. Critical race theory is more visible in research on teacher education than in teacher education programs themselves, typically used as a framework for interpretation and analysis of programs and participants. Nevertheless, it has now deeply affected the stated goals of multicultural teacher education programs, even if it has not produced a unique set of methods for teacher educators.

Notwithstanding early warnings by Banks and Grant, and repetitions over the years, including, most recently, Milner (2017), the two issues they identified have largely defined multicultural education in both practice and research. Originally envisioned as a set of approaches to change school culture, especially the relationship between a school and its surrounding community, it has become a standard pedagogical subject in a large number of teacher education programs, focusing on educating the large White majority of preservice teachers rather than increasing the ranks of teachers of color. As a result, both the majority of teacher education programs and the majority of research on multicultural teacher education focus on the efficacy of teaching White teachers to teach "students of diversity"—to change the mind-set of White preservice and in-service teachers through some combination of self-reflection and exposure to students of color. How to accomplish this has remained unclear; Banks has long advocated teaching "multiple dimensions" of multicultural education in his influential textbook (Banks, 1995), whereas Sleeter recently argued for targeting specific resistant practices of White preservice teachers, focusing their learning about multicultural education on understanding interest convergence, color blindness, and experiential knowledge—concepts drawn from critical race theory (Sleeter, 2017).

Regardless of the specific conception of multicultural education, recent examples of coursework in the literature still emphasize self-reflection and/or exposure to students of color. For example, Davis (2009) used "critical consultation" between White preservice teachers and students of color in their placements to encourage the preservice teachers to discard their habitual deficit thinking, Souto-Manning (2011) built a course using theatrical role-playing methods to raise the awareness of racism among White preservice teachers, and Matias and Mackey (2016) constructed a course focused on self-reflection to try to accomplish the same ends. Several scholars advocate autobiography or other narrative inquiry methods to encourage self-reflection around multicultural issues (Fits Fulmer,

2012; Rieger, 2015). The consistent reportage of a single course focused on multicultural education underscores the observation by Grant and Koskela (1986), Zeichner (1993), and others that multicultural teacher education tends to be handled with a single course (or inservice workshop) rather than being integrated into the curriculum. Given the centrality of self-reflection and exposure to students of color to these multicultural teacher education programs, it is reasonable to predict that this "one-shot approach" (Zeichner, 1993) would have limited effectiveness—and, indeed, several scholars (Amos, 2010; Evans-Winters & Hoff, 2011; Philip & Benin, 2014) suggest that, far from infusing White teachers with a sense of social justice, isolating multicultural content from the rest of the curriculum reinforces their unexamined assumptions about race and ethnicity.

Parallel to the multicultural education courses in teacher education programs, research since the 1990s on the efficacy of such courses has focused on assessing changes in White teachers' attitudes toward students of color (e.g., Deering & Stanutz, 1995; Gomez, 1994; Goodwin, 1994). This research almost exclusively relies on the self-reports of White teachers, with researchers interpreting statements made by teachers in surveys, interviews, and professional portfolios. Researchers tend to employ a critical framework for analysis, usually critical race theory or critical Whiteness theory, typically in the context of self-study with small-scale, qualitative case study methods, to determine how well White preservice or in-service teachers have "learned" multicultural education. Horton and Scott (2004) employed Freire's generative themes to examine the responses of four White preservice teachers to a multicultural education program, locating each participant in one of the stages of racial identity development suggested by Helms (1990). They found that far from encouraging notions of pluralism, short-term multicultural education courses may stimulate more rigid notions of White identity. Amos (2010), working with a framework of critical Whiteness theory, observed similar behavior, and went so far as to title his article "They Don't Want to Get it!" using a quote from one of the preservice teachers of color about their White classmates to summarize the problem: White preservice teachers dominate discussion in multicultural education classes, in part because the structures of teacher education encourage such dominance (Rieger, 2015).

In sum, it appears that consciousness raising through dedicated coursework and exposure to students of color has not produced the transformation of White teachers that early multicultural education theorists once envisioned. Moreover, even when White teachers claim transformation, their actual classroom behavior has not been examined.

Community-Based Learning in Teacher Preparation

Another, more recent approach to preparing teachers for diverse students draws from ideas of community-based learning in an effort to address the tension and distrust between teachers and parents (Graue, 2005; Graue & Brown, 2003). As Graue

(2005) observes, "There are significant discrepancies in perceptions between school people and parents about school efforts and family involvement in education" (p. 158), which are further exacerbated by racial and cultural differences between poor parents of color and the largely White middle-class teacher corps (Bryk & Schneider, 2002; Meier, 2002; Noguera, 2001; Tschannen-Moran, 2004).

Zeichner, Bowman, Guillen, and Napolitan (2016) suggest that addressing these problems requires that teachers know about the communities in which their students grow, develop respectful and trusting relations with students' families and other adults in their communities, and make use of this knowledge and these relationships to support their students' learning. Murrell (2000) calls this type of teacher a "community teacher" who

develops the contextualized knowledge of culture, community, and identity of children and their families as the core of their teaching practice. Community teachers possess the "multicultural competence" they need for accomplished practice in the communities they teach. Community teachers are individuals who typically live and work in the same under resourced urban neighborhoods and communities where students from diverse backgrounds live and go to school. (p. 340)

Because of the relatively recent nature of this approach, there is only limited research on preparing future teachers to work with families and communities (Cochran-Smith & Villegas, 2017; Graue, 2005; Zeichner et al., 2016). Nevertheless, the research that exists suggests that it is a promising approach.

Zeichner et al. (2016) conducted a review of the history of interaction between schools, families, and communities, finding that the idea that teachers should interact with families and communities goes back to the progressive era but that the rationales for developing the relationships vary dramatically, from racist attempts to sanction and correct parental child-rearing strategies to collaborative attempts to build humane educational spaces. Over the past two decades, education researchers and policymakers have attempted to require working with family and community in teacher education programs through performance standards—for example, InTASC Model Standard 10 states that teachers should "take responsibility . . . to collaborate with learners, families, colleagues, other school professionals, and community members to ensure learner growth, and to advance the profession" (Council of Chief State School Officers, 2013). However, researchers have found that the epistemologies and purposes behind these approaches vary dramatically (Evans, 2013; Zeichner et al., 2016). Zeichner et al. (2016) provide a three-tiered typology of teacher-family-community relations within teacher education (involvement, engagement, and solidarity) to distinguish the epistemological groundings, the educational purposes, and the implementation requirements of these approaches. Teacher-family-community involvement is school-centric with an ultimate goal of increasing academic performance, focusing on "school staff to share their knowledge and expertise with families and community providers" (Zeichner et al., 2016, p. 278). Involvement is the most common approach when teacher education programs address the topic at all (Evans, 2013).

The second type, teacher-family-community engagement, acknowledges the knowledge and experience or "community funds of knowledge" (Moll, Amanti, Neff, & González, 1992) to help teachers better understand and serve their students. Techniques of engagement include home visits (Schlessman, 2012; Vesely, Brown, & Mehta, 2017), community walks organized by families and community leaders (Henderson & Whipple, 2013), and listening sessions (Zeichner et al., 2016). Research shows positive learning outcomes from prospective teachers, such as increasing awareness of personal biases and prejudices, increasing understanding of cultural diversity, recognizing strengths and assets of diverse families and communities, and developing confidence and skills to approach and communicate with families and community members (Vesely et al., 2017).

The third type, teacher-family-community solidarity, indicates sustained engagement among teachers, families, community activists, and teacher unions in the joint struggle over pedagogical content and assessment for educational equity for all children. Approaches include setting up community panels with parents and community leaders as panelists (Zeichner et al., 2016), engaging community members as mentors for prospective teachers (Guillen & Zeichner, 2018; Zeichner, et al., 2016), and community and teacher educators co-constructing teacher education programs (Fickel, Abbiss, Brown, & Astall, 2018; Zeichner et al., 2016). These approaches represent a more democratic and transformative framework of teacher education, decentering the power of teacher educators and the traditional curriculum in preparing teachers.

As Sleeter and Soriano (2012) warn, there are perils in transcending the barriers between schools and communities, but at the same time there is great promise in building a relationship of solidarity between schools and marginalized communities, including dispelling "negative myths about diverse populations in particular contexts" and building relationships based on communication, respect, and mutuality (p. 3). Building solidarity between schools and communities is by no means easy work, but it is, as Dobbie and Richards-Schuster (2008) observe, "perhaps the most crucial yet under-theorized process in organizing people for social change" (p. 318). Nevertheless, restructuring teacher education from the standpoint of community-based learning is predicated on the belief "in the educability of all students, thus providing students from different social backgrounds, with diverse levels of ability and behavioral dispositions, opportunities to learn together to live together" (Lopez, Montecinos, Rodriguiz, Calderon, & Contreras, 2012, p. 23). As such, it holds out the hope of fulfilling the promise of multicultural education and critical race theory in education of educating all children equitably.

Recruiting, Preparing, and Retaining Teachers of Color to Teach Diverse Learners

Considering the recruitment, preparation, and retention of teachers of color is a different approach that seeks to change the makeup of the teacher corps, and not accept the overwhelming Whiteness of education as natural. Villegas and Irvine

(2010) identified three research-based rationales for increasing the supply of teachers of color: (1) Teachers of color serve as role models for all students, (2) teachers of color can improve the academic outcomes and school experiences of students of color, and (3) more teachers of color are needed to reduce the acute shortage of educators for high-needs urban schools. In addition, our society benefits when all students, regardless of their background, grow up seeing diverse adults in positions of authority (King, 2016). King's (2016) point is an important one: All students need the opportunity to experience a multiethnic teaching force in order to unlearn racist stereotypes they might have internalized in other settings (Villegas & Irvine, 2010). Research proves that teachers of color in the K–12 workforce benefit all students, inspiring students of color to work toward success and helping White students eliminate bias against people of color (Sleeter, 2001). Furthermore, Villegas and Irvine (2010) found that teachers of color have more favorable views of students of color, including more positive perceptions regarding their academic potential, and there is evidence that students of color view schools as more welcoming and perform better on a variety of academic outcomes if they are taught by teachers of color who are likely to have "inside knowledge" (Ingersoll & May, 2011) due to similar life experiences and cultural backgrounds (Villegas & Irvine, 2010). Thus, it is important to have a diverse population of teachers to meet the needs of all students.

Recruitment

As discussed above, the current teaching force, although becoming slightly more diverse, still remains about 82% White (U.S. Department of Education, Policy and Program Services Department, Office of Planning, Evaluation and Policy Development, 2016). Due to the documented benefits of diversifying the teacher force, teacher education programs and policymakers have called for recruiting and retaining more teachers of color since the mid-1980s (see the review of calls for teacher education reform above; also see Ingersoll & May, 2011, 2016; Irvine, 1988; Villegas, Strom, & Lucas, 2012). Villegas et al. (2012) summarized four specific recruitment strategies pushed by the Education Commission of the States (1990) to recruit more teachers of color: (1) early recruitment and college entrance support programs targeting promising pre-college students, (2) partnerships between 2- and 4-year colleges to facilitate the transition of community college students into 4-year colleges, (3) career ladder programs for paraprofessionals, and (4) final incentives such as scholarships, forgivable loans, and signing bonuses. Literature indicates that teacher education programs have adopted all of these strategies in the past two decades to recruit prospective teachers of color (see Gist, 2014; Schultz, Gillette, & Hill, 2011; Toshalis, 2012; Valenzuela, 2017; Villegas & Davis, 2007). In addition, teacher education programs also have made efforts to recruit undergraduates of color at their institutions with undeclared majors, but this approach is not considered very effective because the number of students of color who matriculate directly at 4-year colleges is limited (Villegas & Davis, 2007).

Retention

The 1992 Holmes Group report *Embracing Cultural Diversity in Colleges of Education: Minority Recruitment and Retention Project* called for a complete strategy from recruitment through training to mentorship of in-service teachers of color to support diversification of the administrative population as well as the teacher corps. However, while much attention has been given to recruitment of prospective teachers of color, less research demonstrates what teacher education programs have done to retain them. Practices for retaining students of color in teacher education programs have primarily focused on providing academic support in the form of additional instructional assistance through tutoring, learning communities, and exam preparation workshops as well as social support through developing cohorts of students of color, sponsoring cultural events, and providing forms of counseling and advisement (Gist, 2014). In addition to these approaches, some urban teacher residency programs adopt a mentorship approach to provide both academic and social and emotional support to prospective teachers of color (Berry et al., 2008). Currently, there are approximately 50 residency programs nationwide that use mentorship approaches (Carver-Thomas, 2018).

Preparation

Compared to the efforts to recruit and retain prospective teachers of color, less empirical research has been reported on the preparation of prospective teachers of color to teach diverse students (Gist, 2017; Gist, Flores, & Claeys, 2014; Rogers-Ard, Knaus, Epstein, & Mayfield, 2013; Sleeter, Neal, & Kumashiro, 2014; Villegas & Davis, 2008). The curriculum, instructional strategies, and fieldwork in most teacher education programs that emphasize the preparation of middle-class, White teachers (Cochran-Smith et al., 2015) take little consideration of the diversity of prospective teachers (Gist, 2014; 2017; Kohli, 2019), nor have they focused much attention on the specific needs of prospective teachers of color in learning to teach diverse students in K–12 classrooms (Brown, 2014). Two examples come from Brown's (2014) review of literature on preparing preservice teachers of color: Quiocho & Rios, 2000 found that preservice teachers of color often feel that their education programs are not preparing them to teach "effectively, both students from diverse backgrounds and across multiple school contexts," while Téllez (1999) finds that teacher education programs fail to engage the knowledge prospective teachers of color possess as well as fail to prepare them to teach all students. Our own review of the literature shows that research on prospective teachers of color primarily focuses on two areas: (1) experiences of prospective teachers of color in teacher education programs and (2) how teacher educators support prospective teachers to develop awareness of their identity, their cultural and linguistic assets, and/or their bias and limitations.

The first area focuses on the cultural and social isolation (Ladson-Billings, 2001; Schultz, Gillette, & Hill, 2008), institutional racism (Gay, 2005; Irizarry, 2007;

Villegas & Davis, 2008; Woodson & Pabon, 2016), and ideological and curricular challenges (Milner, 2008; Philip, 2010) that prospective teachers of color experience in teacher education programs. Ladson-Billings (2001) documented the experience of a prospective teacher of color who considered dropping out of her program due to a lack of diversity in the program, remaining only after two other prospective teachers of color joined the program and they were able to work together to support each other. Irizarry (2007) and Kohli (2014) both documented how prospective teachers of color endured institutional racism such as overtly racist comments or actions and racial hierarchies. Similarly, Kohli (2019) studied 11 women teachers of color about their teacher preparation experiences, finding that they believed their teacher preparation programs not only marginalized them in their preparation but also continued to negatively affect their careers as they entered the field with limited tools to resist racialized structures. Gist (2017) explored the program and pedagogical experiences of teacher candidates of color, finding that prospective teachers experience a lack of culturally and linguistically responsive learning in their teacher education programs. Similarly, Philip (2013) documented the experience of a prospective teacher of color who entered the teacher education program with a strong commitment to equity and social justice but found that the strengths gained through college student activism were overlooked and that the teacher education program failed to help her understand the nuances, strengths, and limitations of her activist stances within the context of classroom teaching and institutional change within schools.

The second area of research on prospective teachers of color focuses primarily on how teacher educators facilitate and support prospective teachers of color in developing a deeper understanding of who they are, where they are situated in the society, what assets they have, or what biases they bring through approaches such as critical reflection and collaborative dialog (Clark & Flores, 2001; DePalma, 2008; Kohli, 2012, 2014; Téllez, 1999). Villegas and Davis (2008) argued that teacher educators need to create a safe space conducive to critical dialogue in the preparation of prospective teachers of color. Similarly, Clark and Flores (2001) focused on how providing pedagogical approaches can support the ethnic identity development of Latinx teacher candidates to increase efficacious beliefs in their ability to enact culturally responsive pedagogy. Multiple studies (DePalma, 2008; Evans-Winters & Hoff, 2011; Horton & Scott, 2004; Matias & Mackey, 2016) indicate that the habits of privilege on the part of White preservice teachers and the general structures and assumptions of Whiteness in teacher education programs combine to amplify the voices of White students and silence those of students of color, even in multicultural education courses intended to accomplish the opposite. Kohli (2014), as well, found that prospective teachers of color felt that critical dialogue on internalized racism within teacher preparation was essential to developing pedagogy that challenged racial inequality. These approaches provide valuable pedagogical guidance for teacher educators regarding how to recognize and cultivate the cultural and linguistic strengths of prospective teachers of color.

In summary, research on the implications of prospective teachers' race and/or ethnicity has focused primarily on recruiting and retaining prospective teachers of color in teacher education programs. Little attention is given to the preparation of prospective teachers of color, and even less is given to how prospective teachers of color carry out the teaching tasks of teaching diverse learners. The practice of recruiting more students of color to teacher education programs, to a certain extent, helps diversify the K–12 teaching force. However, the practice of diversifying the prospective teachers pool through recruitment without further changes to teacher education curriculum, pedagogy, and instruction is problematic for three reasons.

First is the problem of interest convergence. Although Milner's (2006) research shows that exposure to peers of color dramatically improves the ability of White prospective teachers to empathize with students of color and implement culturally responsive teaching, he has also repeatedly observed that race has rarely had a central place in American teacher education (Milner, 2003, 2017; Milner & Laughter, 2015). Brown (2014) concurs, saying,

> While the call for recruiting more teachers of color is well founded, they exist in and help to maintain a system of interest convergence wherein teacher education programs can boast about efforts to bring in more teacher candidates of color while simultaneously not transforming the kinds of normative culture, knowledge, and experiences that are valued, maintained, and offered to these individuals. (pp. 339–340)

Second is the problem of the misconceived effect of cultural-match. Although literature on prospective teachers of color suggests that their cultural awareness and personal experiences are assets for teaching all students, especially students of color (Jackson & Knight-Manuel, 2019; Villegas & Davis, 2008), prospective teachers of color need preparation in order to teach diverse students effectively (Achinstein & Aguirre, 2008; Achinstein & Ogawa, 2011; Mabokela & Madsen, 2007). Zeichner (1996) argues that even when teachers and students share a significant part of their cultural background, teacher educators cannot assume that teachers can easily translate cultural knowledge into culturally relevant pedagogy (Montecinos, 1995). Similarly, Gay (2000) asserted, "Similar ethnicity between students and teachers may be potentially beneficial, but it is not a guarantee of pedagogical effectiveness" (p. 205). Moreover, research shows that teachers of color, if not critically assessing their assumptions and practices, have the potential to pathologize students of color, reinforcing deficit thinking (Achinstein & Aguirre, 2008; Jackson & Knight-Manuel, 2019) and internalizing racism due to socialization in a White culture and oppressive schooling system (Kohli, 2014). Teacher educators should not assume that prospective teachers of color are immediately ready to tap their knowledge and experiences in teaching diverse students; rather, as Jackson and Knight-Manuel (2019) suggest, teacher education programs need to create spaces purposefully for prospective teachers of color to critically examine their own sociopolitical consciousness. While Sleeter and Milner (2011) are careful not to assert that diversifying the teaching force is a panacea for increasing student achievement and student learning opportunities, they do propose that the research on the value of diversifying the teaching force is too compelling to ignore the potential benefits for students of color and for all students.

Third is the problem of Whiteness in teacher education. Prospective teachers of color need support to navigate the racialized teacher education programs; teacher education programs should also build curriculum and field experience on prospective teachers of color's cultural capital (Yosso, 2005) or funds of knowledge (Moll et al., 1992). Furthermore, educational funding inequities at all levels disproportionately affect students of color, including teacher education students, exposing them to sub-standard educational experiences at every point in their K–16 schooling (Lau, Dandy, & Hoffman, 2007). This, in turn, makes success more difficult and attrition more likely (Ahmad & Boser, 2014). In addition, once students of color become teacher education candidates, their programs are often predominantly White (Ladson-Billings, 2005) with curriculum, pedagogy, methods, and field experiences con-structed to prepare White teachers, and thus fail to provide the types of social, cultural, emotional, and academic support that students of color need to successfully complete the program (Gist, 2014; Sleeter & Thao, 2007). Prospective teachers of color then encounter marginalization and discrimination in teacher education pro-grams similar to their experiences in the K–12 system (Burant, 1999; Parker & Hood, 1995; Sleeter, 2001).

Summary of Changes in Teacher Education Practices

In sum, our review above on changing teacher education practices to produce teachers able to teach diverse students effectively shows that primary changes brought about generally focus on the areas of prospective teachers' beliefs, attitudes, and understandings; however, there are fewer studies that investigate how those changes bring about changes in classroom practice (Anderson & Stillman, 2013; Cochran-Smith et al., 2015). By *practice*, we mean "teacher candidates learning how to do the actual tasks of teaching" (Cochran-Smith et al., 2015, p. 117). However, much research that claims to study how teacher preparation influences prospective teachers' professional practice does not investigate their actions in classroom contexts because practice is considered "teacher candidates being engaged as reflective and inquiring professionals" (Cochran-Smith et al., 2015, p. 117). This type of research has primar-ily engaged prospective teachers in talking about, analyzing, or reflecting on their teaching, and thus research data on practice are primarily based on prospective teach-ers' reflections, self-reports, surveys, and interviews. Based on a thorough review of research on the preparation of teachers for urban and high-needs contexts, Anderson and Stillman (2013) find a disproportionate emphasis on belief and attitude change among prospective teachers with relatively little evidence for the development or change in actual teaching practice. They also find a tendency toward reductive views of culture and context. Cochran-Smith et al. (2015) provide similar findings in their extensive review of teacher education research, arguing, "We need more research that goes beyond assuming that changing teacher candidates' beliefs necessarily leads to different behaviors and actions in their classrooms" (p. 117).

Thus we need to know more about what changes preservice teachers actually implement in their day-to-day teaching practices in order to be able to assess the impact of teacher education programs on their teaching practices. As Hong (2012) argues, a radical shift is needed from reported values and beliefs to "transformative practice" (p. 30). Research grounded in observations of classroom teaching indicates that in spite of required training on multicultural education, differentiated instruction, and teaching for social justice, most White preservice and in-service teachers do not actually internalize these approaches or the philosophy underlying them. Rather, they are adept at performing a shallow approximation when given incentives and the opportunity to construct a carefully bounded example—but otherwise most teachers operate comfortably within the unconsidered privilege structure of the White majority (Thomas & Liu, 2012; Liu, 2015, 2017). According to Mezirow (1990, 2000), attitudes and assumptions are important and subject to critical reflection; however, no matter how critical the reflection sounds or how great the apparent change in attitude, real change happens only with the transformation in actions—which we are referring to as "critical reflection for transformative learning." This belief is based on our review of the literature, which confirms that most teacher education research does not provide guidance on shifting our focus from apparent attitude changes to actual change in teachers' practices. The next section reviews the research on critical reflection to facilitate transformative learning and the model of generative change as a framework that actually accounts for a process that facilitates change in teachers' classroom practices. We further propose that critical reflection and generativity be integrated throughout community-based teacher education programs to fill the existing gap as promising practices that transform teaching and teacher education for the benefit of diverse students.

CHANGING TEACHING PRACTICES THROUGH TRANSFORMATIVE TEACHER EDUCATION FOR DIVERSE STUDENTS

Recognition of the fundamental problems in the educational system, and by extension in the teacher education system, has grown in the past 50 years, heralded by the 1969 Smith report and truly launched by the 1983 *Nation at Risk* report. Part of that recognition has involved critiques of U.S. educational institutions for failing to set and meet standards of "rigor." As a result, standards-based approaches have continued to have a loud voice in the debates, leading to teacher education reform proposals that emphasize training teachers to follow the standards. For example, Hollins (2011) proposes reforming teacher education by focusing a conventional teacher education program (combining academic coursework with short- and medium-term field experiences) explicitly on InTASC and NCATE standards in order to enable teachers to develop constructivist curricula within the framework of the standards.

Two recent articles lay out more radical arguments for the construction and potential correction of the problems with teacher education in the United States: Zeichner's (2003) "The Adequacies and Inadequacies of Three Current Strategies to Recruit, Prepare, and Retain the Best Teachers for All Students" (hereafter referred to as "Adequacies") and Kretchmar and Zeichner's (2016) "Teacher Prep 3.0: A Vision for Teacher Education to Impact Social Transformation" (hereafter referred to as "Teacher Prep 3.0"). These two review-essays take slightly different approaches in examining trends in U.S. teacher education reform, but both build toward Kretchmar and Zeichner's vision of the next generation in teacher education programs, Teacher Prep 3.0. Beginning from "an understanding that education reform alone is insufficient to address the significant challenges of poverty" (Kretchmar & Zeichner, 2016, p. 427), the authors argue that the key to successfully addressing these issues is neither defending the current system through technical modification ("Teacher Prep 1.0") nor replacing it with privatized credentialing ("Teacher Prep 2.0") but in linking education reform to broader movements for social justice in the context of the specific communities of which the schools are a part. In other words, Teacher Prep 3.0 should be controlled neither by university teacher education faculty nor by wealthy entrepreneurs and their enabling politicians but rather by the communities that the schools are intended to serve—creating "community teachers." This might be done through developing grow-your-own-teacher programs, by bringing community members into the student teaching and evaluation process, or by moving teacher education classes completely out into the community. Thus, regardless of the specific approach, the result is clearly community-based teaching.

When read against 50 years of education reform and efforts to prepare teachers for racially, ethnically, and linguistically diverse learners, Kretchmar and Zeichner's (2016) Teacher Prep 3.0 presents both promise and challenge. The promise—developing educational and social equity in tandem—is clear; the challenge is how to fulfill that promise. In the previous pages we laid out the case that the limited success of previous attempts is a direct result of two problems: (1) a failure to base both teacher preparation and research on teacher preparation in classroom actions, not just in coursework and reflective, self-reported statements, and (2) a failure to focus efforts for transformation both on the level of the individual teacher and at a broader institutional and community level. The first problem results in preservice teachers talking the talk but not walking the walk; the second problem leaves even successful individuals isolated in an unresponsive institution as well as insulated from the communities that nurture their students. In the final pages of this chapter we present a framework that serves as an example of a model that addresses the problems highlighted above and that successfully accomplishes the vision of Teacher Prep 3.0— through the synthesis of critical reflection for transformative learning at work on every level of the model of generative change that is imbedded within a framework of community-based teaching.

CRITICAL REFLECTION FOR TRANSFORMATIVE LEARNING

Critical reflection is a hermeneutic approach to individual learning going back at least to Donald Schön (1983) and Zeichner and Liston (1996), if not John Dewey (1933), and is typically considered to involve repeated reexamination of one's assumptions about knowledge and understanding, particularly those that are socially, politically, or culturally based. For example, drawing from the philosophical work on reflection by van Manen (1977), as well as Liston and Zeichner's (1991) social reconstructionist approach, Dinkelman (1999) defines critical reflection as follows:

Deliberation about wider social, historical, political, and cultural contexts of education, and deliberation about relationships between educational practice and the construction of a more equitable, [just], and democratic society. (p. 332)

Or, as he puts in more succinctly later, "deliberation on the moral and ethical dimensions of education practice" (Dinkelman, 2000, p. 195). Similarly, Larrivee (2000) combines critical inquiry and self-reflection to define critical reflection as involving "examination of personal and professional belief systems, as well as the deliberate consideration of the ethical implications and impact of practices" (p. 294). What is clearly missing, as Cochran-Smith et al. (2015) critiqued, is a focus on how teachers carry out instructional practice based on reflection: They all seem to suggest a cognitive process as the solution to improved teaching, rather than using that reflection as the basis for change in the classroom.

Other scholars, however, do take the step from thinking to action. For example, Brookfield (1995) argues that "reflection in and of itself is not enough; it must always be linked to how the world can be changed" (p. 217), a position that resonates with Mezirow's (1990) idea that critical reflection is necessary for changing both how teachers teach and learners learn—what he terms *transformative learning*: "Reflective discourse and its resulting insights alone do not make for transformative learning. Acting upon these emancipatory insights, a praxis is also necessary" (p. 354). Drawing on thinkers from Dewey to Mezirow, Liu (2015) links the practice of critical reflection with the goal of transformative action for social justice, defining critical reflection as

a process of constantly analyzing, questioning, and critiquing established assumptions of oneself, schools, and the society about teaching and learning, and the social and political implications of schooling, and implementing changes to previous actions that have been supported by those established assumptions for the purpose of supporting student learning and a better schooling and more [just] society for all children. (pp. 144–145)

Liu (2015) then takes this definition and develops a full hermeneutic approach to critical reflection for transformative learning based on Brookfield's (1995) work, including a cycle of six steps of assumption analysis, contextual awareness, imaginative speculation, reflective skepticism, reflection-based action, and reflection on

FIGURE 1
The Hermeneutic Cycle of Critical Reflection for Transformative Learning

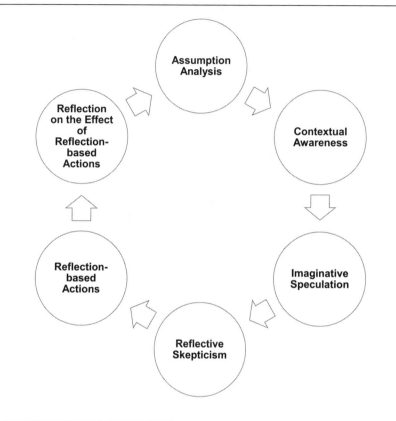

Note. Adapted from Liu (2015, p. 148).

reflection-based action. Figure 1 provides a visual representation of the hermeneutic cycle of critical reflection for transformative learning.

Key to this model is the systematic movement from rethinking basic assumptions to taking action to transform learning by both teacher and students. We argue that critical reflection for transformative learning in individual teachers' classrooms has the potential to further transform practice in the larger teacher education community for social and educational equity as envisioned by Kretchmar and Zeichner's (2016) Teacher Prep 3.0 for three reasons.

First, it provides clear guidance for teacher educators to guide prospective teachers in a process of intellectual work starting with analyzing and critiquing prior assumptions about diverse learners, especially those grounded on longstanding, taken-for-granted deficit models, recognizing that those assumptions are socially constructed in specific historical and cultural contexts, then actively searching for alternatives to the ways in which diverse learners are failed by our current educational systems. These steps form the basis for prospective teachers to call into question the current assumptions and institutional structures that have guided current practices of teaching diverse students. At this point, teacher educators do not stop their work—they continue to guide prospective teachers to implement alternative actions in their teaching, and further analyze the effect of the reflection-based actions on student learning, upon which they may make further decisions on whether the reflection-based actions better support diverse students, triggering another cycle of critical reflection for transformative learning.

Second, Liu's (2015) stages of critical reflection for transformative learning, when adopted by classroom teachers, can help them develop into transformative intellectuals who "develop a discourse that unites the language of critique with the language of possibility, so that social educators recognize they can make changes" (Giroux, 1988, p. 128). As transformative intellectuals, teachers can take an active role in reshaping curriculum and pedagogy for diverse learners through their own research-based actions, and by working with the larger community on the basis of shared knowledge as well as a shared commitment to social and educational equity. One problem in the work of preparing reflective teachers is the focus of facilitating reflection by individual prospective teachers with little attention to collaborative reflection among the community of prospective teachers, teacher educators, mentor teachers, and community members (Zeichner & Liu, 2010). We argue that integrating critical reflection in Teacher Prep 3.0 will enable university-based teacher education programs, schools, and the local community to work together on a more democratic basis to prepare the next generation of teachers—as the former prospective teachers become in-service teachers, they work with the community to further implement Teacher Prep 3.0.

Third, Liu's model of critical reflection for transformative learning provides a valuable framework for research on the content of and procedures for prospective teachers' reflection on teaching diverse students (see, e.g., Liu, 2017). It further provides a critical lens to guide teacher educators to conduct research on the real actions of prospective teachers in their teaching—whether or not their reflection brings about transformative actions in teaching diverse students. A focus on how prospective teachers actually teach diverse students has been long missing in teacher education research on preparing teachers to teach diverse students, much of which stops at collecting and analyzing prospective teacher's self-reported data such as written reflections (Anderson & Stillman, 2013; Cochran-Smith et al., 2015). Research based on classroom actions as well as written reflections can help teacher education researchers gain a better understanding of how to improve their own support for prospective teachers to achieve transformative learning. For example, teacher educators can foster prospective teachers' critical reflection by prompting them to engage in dialog within the teacher education community in Teacher Prep 3.0, to explore their assumptions more deeply, to situate an educational problem in the larger social-political context, and to ground their discussion in specific examples of their teaching practices in the classroom through approaches such as classroom observations and video-recorded lessons. Therefore, the framework, on one hand, points out the importance of focusing on prospective teachers' teaching practices and, on the other, guides teacher educators to analyze prospective teachers' actions to determine whether or not they are transformative in terms of teaching diverse learners.

Generative Theory as a Framework for Transformative Practice and the Preparation of Teachers for Diversity

Critical reflection can effect changes at the classroom level, but what about the larger institutional changes that are also necessary? Here we turn to *generativity* for an answer. Generativity is the generation of new or novel behavior in problem solving (Epstein, 1996), a complex psychosocial construct that describes how an individual responds to societal demands, inner desires, conscious concerns, beliefs, and commitments. The concept was meant to include productivity and creativity in accomplishing things that make the world a better place; it has also been described as a concern for one's legacy that leads to concrete goals and, most important for our considerations, to transformative actions. The notion of *generativity* dates back to noted psychoanalyst Erik Erikson (1963), who first used the term in his theory of the stages of psychosocial development. From its very beginning, the term has denoted a concern for guiding the next generation. Building on the work of Erikson, de St. Aubin and McAdams (1995) provided a conceptual and methodological framework for the scientific study of generativity in the context of a life span theory of personality development. Generative actions—including the behaviors of creating, maintaining, and offering to others—reciprocally influence subsequent generative commitments.

It has been noted that today's teachers are required to enter classrooms that neither they nor their teacher educators have ever seen or taught in before. These culturally and linguistically complex classrooms are diverse, posing challenges that teachers have not been fully prepared to meet. Teacher education programs can address these unmet needs by producing teachers able to generate new behaviors in the form of pedagogical problem solving. According to Erikson (1963), generativity theory provides a formal, empirically based theory of ongoing behavior in novel environments that can be used to engineer creative action. Research by Epstein (1996) on generative theory suggests that the generative mechanisms that underlie creativity are universal—but these mechanisms are not used by many classroom teachers because teacher education programs tend to promote uniformity and discourage the expression of novel or unusual ideas (Ball, 2006). Students who do not conform are seen as troublemakers. In kindergarten, virtually all children are creative; however, very few children express much creativity in school by the end of the first grade. This is not because of some sudden change in the brain's functioning. Rather, it is due entirely to the school's demand that children be taught to conform and that children's creativity be discouraged. The expression of creativity depends on a set of competencies that underlie successful performance, but these competencies are rarely taught in schools or teacher education programs. In general, our society views creativity as the nearly exclusive property of the privileged or the antisocial. However, generativity theory provides a powerful framework to understand the creative process, supporting the notion that, with appropriate training, almost anyone can display a high degree of creative action (Epstein, 1996).

In 2001, Franke, Carpenter, Levi, and Fennema reported a study on "teachers' generative change" as a consequence of their involvement in professional development, documenting how teachers who participated in a professional development program on understanding the development of students' mathematical thinking continued to implement the principles of the program four years after it ended. Twenty-two teachers participated in follow-up interviews and classroom observations; all of them maintained some use of children's thinking, and 10 continued learning about children's thinking.

The theme running throughout the literature on generativity over the past 70 years is conceiving of generativity as a formal, predictive theory of creative behavior or activity on the part of individuals. Building on this research, Ball (2009) proposed that theories of generativity provide an excellent framework to explain the process by which teachers engage in transformative change that can make a difference in the classroom lives of diverse student populations. Given the reality that almost 40% of teachers entering the classrooms report that they do not feel adequately prepared for the challenges that await them, we need to look to generative theories to guide teacher education in their transformation of program practices. Building on the work of Erickson (1963), Epstein (1996), and Franke et al. (2001), and influenced by Bandura's (1977, 1997) self-efficacy theories, Ball (2009) combined generative theory and teacher efficacy in a model designed to prepare teachers who believe in their potential ability to affect positive change in the lives of their students and who also think in generative ways to incorporate creative transformative action in their classroom practices in order to meet the needs of 21st-century students. A teacher's sense of efficacy is critical to his or her effectiveness in bringing transformative action into the classroom. By design, the teachers in Ball's courses engaged with new perspectives, new ideas, new theories, and new voices through assigned readings, discussions and critical reflective writing, and required interactions with diverse learners to facilitate metacognitive awareness, ideological becoming, and internalization. The outcome was teachers entering the classroom having increased their sense of metacognitive awakening, agency, advocacy, and efficacy in their culturally and linguistically diverse classrooms through these professional development experiences.

Based on longitudinal research spanning national boundaries, Ball (2009) proposed a model based on research grounded in theories of generativity and conducted in teacher professional development programs. Based on the analysis of teachers' written critical reflections, classroom observations, and discourse analysis of classroom interactions and interview data collected over a decade in the United States and

South Africa, the data support the development of a model of generative change explaining how professional development can be internalized by teachers, subsequently serving as a heuristic to help them change their individual programs of instruction. Drawing on that data, the four stages in the *model of generative change* were designed to stimulate, facilitate, and support real change in teachers' practices as teachers embraced generative thinking in their journeys toward becoming effective teachers of diverse student populations. Building on the work of Vygotsky (1962), Bakhtin (1991), and Bandura (1977, 1997), the four stages facilitating teachers' development of a change-oriented mindset include metacognitive awareness, a sense of agency, a sense of advocacy, and the development of a personal voice concerning the education of diverse students. Ball (2009) documents teachers' development of generative knowledge and illustrates how teachers drew on that knowledge in thinking about students and teaching to support transformative action and creative changes in classroom practices to meet the needs of historically marginalized students.

Ball (2009) argues that in order to effectively teach in culturally diverse classrooms, teachers must learn how to be reflective, introspective, critical, and generative in their thinking. For example, teachers can increase their metacognitive awareness, agency, and efficacy by engaging in Liu's (2015) stages of critical reflection throughout their development via the model of generative change. Ball defines generativity as the teachers' ability to continually add to their knowledge and understanding by reflecting on and connecting their personal and professional knowledge with the knowledge that they gain from their students and the students' community, which results in actions that include the production of knowledge and classroom practices that are creative and useful in meeting the needs of their students. See Figure 2.

This research emphasizes the importance of preparing teachers to learn from their students and community in order to teach diverse students effectively, and to become action-oriented generative thinkers in their classrooms through pedagogical problem-solving behaviors, creativity, and a sense of efficacy. This is accomplished as teachers progress through a carefully designed program that facilitates their development of metacognitive awareness, agency, advocacy, and personal voice concerning the education of diverse students (see Ball, 2006, 2009). Ball found that, as teacher educators model critical reflection and generativity for prospective teachers throughout the teacher education program, changes in teachers' practices occur. In addition, she found that as prospective teachers are exposed to the work of scholars like Henry Giroux (1988), they begin to consider how they can develop into transformative intellectuals as they critically reflect on the "need to develop a discourse that unites the language of critique with the language of possibility, so that social educators recognize they can make changes" (p. 196). As generative thinking transformative intellectuals, teachers can take an active role in reshaping curriculum and pedagogy for diverse learners through their own research-based actions, and work with the larger community on the basis of shared knowledge as well as a shared commitment to social and educational equity. This development enables the school and community to work together with teachers and teacher educators on a more collaborative basis to

FIGURE 2

Model of Generative Change: The Processes Through Which Teachers Develop Voice, Generativity, and Efficacy in Their Development Toward Transformative Change

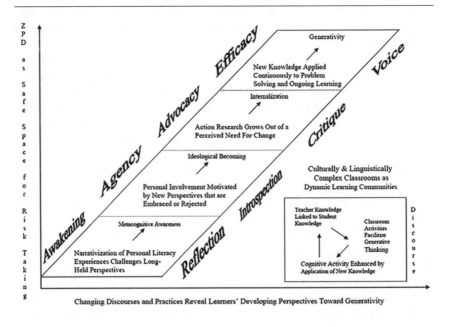

Note. Reprinted from Ball (2009).

prepare the next generation of teachers. Thus, the model of generative change serves as a framework that facilitates and accounts for the process of transformation and changing teachers' practices. In her 2012 American Educational Research Association Presidential Address, Ball discussed how teachers, teacher educators, and education researchers can take what we know from research and put it to effective use in designing policy and classroom practice. The essay challenged researchers to individually and collectively move away from "research designed as mere demonstrations of knowledge toward generative research that has the power to close the knowing–doing gap in education—research that is designed to inform others, influence others' thinking, and inspire others to action" (Ball, 2012, p. 283).

CONCLUSION

This chapter investigates the question "How is change in teaching practices and teacher education programs designed to prepare teachers to teach diverse learners conceptualized, facilitated, and transformed?" Through a critical and synthesizing review of the research literature, we have taken an interdisciplinary approach to a review of the literature related to issues of diversity and diversifying the teaching force. We have documented the calls for reform of teacher education from 1929 to the present, especially with respect to teaching diverse learners, and existing research on teacher education practices in preparing teachers for diverse classrooms, focusing on approaches from multicultural education, critical race theory, and community-based teacher preparation. We then considered research on the need to base research on teaching and learning in real classroom practice, the need to encourage critical reflection for transformative learning to be systematically applied throughout teacher education practice, and the need for critical reflection and generativity, which—when combined in systematic ways within the context of a community-based teacher education program—can support and facilitate real change in teachers' practices and promote transformative teacher education that prepares teachers to teach diverse student populations. Finally, based on this review, we have proposed an example of a model that combines critical reflection and generativity that can be used as a framework to bring about real transformation in teaching and teacher education for both individual teachers and the teacher education community.

REFERENCES

Achinstein, B., & Aguirre, J. (2008). Cultural match or culturally suspect: How new teachers of color negotiate sociocultural challenges in the classroom. *Teachers College Record, 110*(8), 1505–1540.

Achinstein, B., & Ogawa, R. (2011). *Change(d) agents: New teachers of color in urban schools.* New York, NY: Teachers College Press.

Ahmad, F. Z., & Boser, U. (2014). *America's leaky pipeline for teachers of color: Getting more teachers of color into the classroom.* Washington, DC: Center for American Progress.

American Council on Education Commission on Teacher Education. (1946). *The improvement of teacher education: A final report by the Commission on Teacher Education.* Washington, DC: American Council on Education.

American Council on Education Commission on Teacher Education. (1947). *Teachers for our times: A statement of purposes by the Commission on Teacher Education.* Washington, DC: American Council on Education.

Amos, Y. T. (2010). "They don't want to get it!" Interaction between minority and White preservice teachers in a multicultural education class. *Multicultural Education, 17*(4), 31–37.

Anderson, L., & Stillman, J. (2013). Student teaching's contribution to preservice teacher development: A review of research focused on the preparation of teachers for urban and high-needs contexts. *Review of Educational Research, 83*(1), 3–69.

Aronson, B., Amatullah, T., & Laughter, J. (2016). Culturally relevant education: Extending the conversation to religious diversity. *Multicultural Perspectives, 18*(3), 140–149.

Bakhtin, M. M. (1991). *Dialogic imagination: Four essays by M. M. Bakhtin* (C. Emerson & M. Holquist, Trans.). Austin: University of Texas Press.

Ball, A. F. (2006). *Multicultural strategies for education and social change: Carriers of the torch in the United States and South Africa.* New York, NY: Teachers College Press.

Ball, A. F. (2009). Toward a theory of generative change in culturally and linguistically complex classrooms. *American Educational Research Journal, 46*(1), 45–72.

Ball, A. F. (2012). Presidential address: To know is not enough: Knowledge, power, and the zone of generativity. *Educational Researcher Journal, 41*(8), 283–293.

Bandura, A. (1977). Self-efficacy: Toward a unifying theory of behavioral change. *Psychological Review, 84*(2), 191–215.

Bandura, A. (1997). *Self-efficacy: The exercise of control.* New York, NY: Freeman.

Banks, J. A. (1974). *Multicultural education: In search of definitions and goals.* Syracuse, NY: National Academy of Education.

Banks, J. A. (1995). Multicultural education and curriculum transformation. *Journal of Negro Education, 64*(4), 390–400.

Banks, J. A., & Banks, C. A. M. (2010). *Multicultural education: Issues and perspectives* (8th ed.). New York, NY: Wiley.

Bennett, C. (2001). Genres of research in multicultural education. *Review of Educational Research, 71*(2), 171–217.

Berry, B., Montgomery, D., Curtis, R., Hernandez, M., Wurtzel, J., & Snyder, J. (2008). *Creating and sustaining urban teacher residencies: A new way to recruit, prepare, and retain effective teachers in high-needs districts.* Washington, DC: Aspen Institute and the Center for Teaching Quality. Retrieved from https://files.eric.ed.gov/fulltext/ED512419.pdf

Blankenship, C. S. (1992). *Embracing cultural diversity in colleges of education: Minority recruitment and retention project.* Salt Lake City: Graduate School of Education, University of Utah.

Brookfield, S. D. (1995). *Becoming a critically reflective teacher.* San Francisco, CA: Jossey-Bass.

Brown, K. D. (2014). Teaching in color: A critical race theory in education analysis of the literature on preservice teachers of color and teacher education in the US. *Race Ethnicity and Education, 17*(3), 326–345.

Bryk, A., & Schneider, B. (2002). A grounded theory of relational trust. In A. Bryk & B. Schneider (Eds.), *Trust in schools: A core resource for improvement* (pp. 124–144). New York, NY: Russell Sage Foundation.

Bullivant, B. M. (1972). The cultural reality of curriculum development. *Education News, 13*(9), 14–17.

Burant, T. J. (1999). Finding, using, and loving voice: A pre-service teacher's experiences in an urban educative practicum. *Journal of Teacher Education, 50*(3), 209–219.

Caldwell, M. (1986). *Initial teacher certification/licensing: An analysis of the Carnegie Task Force recommendations for a national board for professional teaching standards.* Charlottesville: Virginia University Bureau of Educational Research.

Capps, R., McCabe, K., & Fix, M. (2012). *Diverse streams: African migration to the United States.* Washington, DC: National Center on Immigrant Integration Policy. Retrieved from https://www.migrationpolicy.org/pubs/CBI-AfricanMigration.pdf

Carnegie Forum on Education and the Economy. (1987). *A nation prepared: Teachers for the 21st century: The report of the Task Force on Teaching as a Profession, Carnegie Forum on Education and the Economy, May 1986.* Washington, DC: The Forum.

Carver-Thomas, D. (2018). *Diversifying the teaching profession: How to recruit and retain teachers of color.* Palo Alto, CA: Learning Policy Institute. Retrieved from https://learningpolicyinstitute.org/product/diversifying-teaching-profession-report

Charters, W. W., & Waples, D., Educational Research Committee., & Commonwealth Fund. (1929). *The Commonwealth teacher-training study.* Chicago, IL: University of Chicago Press.

Clark, E. J., & Flores, B. B. (2001). Who am I? The social construction of ethnic identity and self-perceptions in Latino preservice teachers. *Urban Review, 33*(2), 69–86.

Cochran-Smith, M., & Villegas, A. M. (2017). Research on teacher preparation: Charting the landscape of a sprawling field. In D. Gitomer & C. Bell (Eds.), *Handbook of research on teaching* (5th ed., pp. 439–538). Washington, DC: American Educational Research Association.

Cochran-Smith, M., Villegas, A. M., Abrams, L., Chavez-Moreno, L., Mills, T., & Stern, R. (2015). Critiquing teacher preparation research: An overview of the field, Part II. *Journal of Teacher Education, 66*(2), 109–121.

Cockrell, K. S., Mitchell, R. D., Middleton, J. N., & Campbell, J. O. (1999). The Holmes Scholars Network: A study of the Holmes Group initiative for the recruitment and retention of minority faculty. *Journal of Teacher Education, 50*(2), 85–93.

Conant, J. B. (2001). *The education of American teachers.* New York, NY: McGraw-Hill. (Original work published 1963)

Cottrell, D. P., & Cooper, R. M. (1956). *Teacher education for a free people [by] Russell M. Cooper [and others].* Oneonta, NY: American Association of Colleges for Teacher Education.

Council of Chief State School Officers. (2013). *InTASC model core teaching standards and learning progressions for teachers 1.0.* Washington, DC: Author. Retrieved fromhttps://ccsso.org/sites/default/files/2017-12/2013_INTASC_Learning_Progressions_for_Teachers.pdf

Darling-Hammond, L. (1986). We need schools willing and able to use Carnegie's "Teachers for the 21st Century." *Teacher Educator, 22*(2), 29–32.

Darling-Hammond, L. (1998). *Doing what matters most: Investing in quality teaching: A discussion.* Sacramento, CA: CSU Institute for Education Reform.

Davis, D. E. (2009). Preparing white student teachers through a critical consultative model. *International Journal of Progressive Education, 5*(2), 1–23.

Deering, T. E., & Stanutz, A. (1995). Preservice field experience as a multicultural component of a teacher education program. *Journal of Teacher Education, 46*(5), 390–394.

DePalma, L. (2008). The voice of every black person: Brining authentic minority voices into multicultural dialog. *Teaching and Teacher Education, 24*(3), 767–778.

De St. Aubin, E., & McAdams, D. P. (1995). The relations of generative concern and generative action to personality traits, satisfaction with life, and ego development. *Journal of Adult Development, 2*(2), 99–112.

Dewey, J. (1933). *How we think: A restatement of the relation of reflective thinking to the educative process.* Chicago, IL: Henry Regnery.

Dinkelman, T. (1999). Critical reflection in a social studies semester. *Theory & Research in Social Education, 27*(3), 329–357.

Dinkelman, T. (2000). An inquiry into the development of critical reflection in secondary student teachers. *Teaching and Teacher Education, 16*(2), 195–222.

Dobbie, D., & Richards-Schuster, K. (2008). Building solidarity through difference: A practice model for critical multicultural organizing. *Journal of Community Practice, 16*(3), 317–337.

Epstein, R. (1996). *Cognition, creativity, and behavior.* Westport, CT: Praeger.

Erikson, E. H. (1963). *Childhood and society* (2nd ed.). New York: Norton.

Evans, M. (2013). Educating preservice teachers for family, school, and community engagement. *Teaching Education, 24*(2), 123–133.

Evans-Winters, V. E., & Hoff, P. T. (2011). Aesthetics of white racism in pre-service teacher education: A critical race theory perspective. *Race Ethnicity and Education, 14*(4), 461–479.

Fickel, L., Abbiss, J., Brown, L., & Astall, C. (2018). The importance of community knowledge in learning to teach: Foregrounding Maori cultural knowledge to support preservice teachers' development of culturally responsive practice. *Peabody Journal of Education, 93*(3), 285–294.

Fits Fulmer, D. E. (2012). *Autobiographical meaning making, practitioner inquiry, and White teachers in multicultural education* (Unpublished EdD dissertation). University of Pennsylvania, Philadelphia.

Franke, M., Carpenter, T., Levi, L., & Fennema, E. (2001). Capturing teachers' generative change: A follow-up study of professional development in mathematics. *American Educational Research Journal, 38*(3), 653–689.

Fullan, M., Galluzzo, G., & Morris, P. (1998). *The rise and stall of teacher education reform.* Washington, DC: American Association of Colleges for Teacher Education.

Gay, G. (1977). Changing conceptions of multicultural education. *Educational Perspectives, 16*(4), 4–9.

Gay, G. (2000). *Culturally responsive teaching.* New York, NY: Teachers College Press.

Gay, G. (2005). Politics of multicultural teacher education. *Journal of Teacher Education, 56*(3), 221–228.

Gibson, M. A. (1976). Approaches to multicultural education in the United States: Some concepts and assumptions. *Anthropology and Education Quarterly, 7*(4), 7–18.

Giroux, H. (1988). *Teachers as intellectuals: Toward a critical pedagogy of learning.* Granby, MA: Bergin & Garvey.

Gist, C. (2014). *Preparing teachers of color to teach: Culturally responsive teacher education in theory and practice.* New York, NY: Palgrave Macmillan.

Gist, C. (2017). Voices of aspiring teachers of color: Unraveling the double bind in teacher education. *Urban Education, 52*(8), 927–956.

Gist, C. D., Flores, B. B., & Claeys, L. (2014). Competing theories of change: Critical teacher development. In C. Sleeter, L. Neal, & K. Kumashiro (Eds.), *Addressing the demographic imperative: Recruiting, preparing, and retaining a diverse and highly effective teaching force* (pp. 19–31). New York, NY: Routledge.

Goldhammer, R. (1966). *A critical analysis of supervision in instruction in the Harvard-Lexington summer program.* Cambridge, MA: Harvard University.

Gomez, M. L. (1994). Teacher education reform and prospective teachers' perspectives on teaching "Other people's" children. *Teaching and Teacher Education, 10*(3), 319–344.

González, N. (2005). Beyond culture: The hybridity of funds of knowledge. In N. González, L. Moll, & C. Amanti (Eds.), *Funds of knowledge: Theorizing practices in households, communities, and classrooms* (pp. 29–46). Mahwah, NJ: Lawrence Erlbaum.

Goodwin, A. L. (1994). Making the transition from self to other: What do preservice teachers really think about multicultural education? *Journal of Teacher Education, 45*(2), 119–131.

Gottlieb, E. E., & Cornbleth, C. (1989). The professionalization of tomorrow's teachers: An analysis of US teacher education reform rhetoric. *Journal of Education for Teaching, 15*(1), 3–12.

Grant, C. A. (1975). *Sifting and winnowing: An exploration of the relationship between multicultural education and CBTE.* Madison: University of Wisconsin Teacher Corps Associates Program.

Grant, C. A., & Koskela, R. A. (1986). Education that is multicultural and the relationship between preservice campus learning and field experiences. *Journal of Educational Research, 79*(4), 197–204.

Graue, E. (2005). Theorizing and describing preservice teachers' images of families and schooling. *Teachers College Record, 107*(1), 157–185.

Graue, E., & Brown, C. P. (2003). Preservice teachers' notions of families and schooling. *Teaching and Teacher Education, 19*(7), 719–735.

Guillen, L., & Zeichner, K. (2018). A university-community partnership in teacher education from the perspective of community-based teacher educators. *Journal of Teacher Education, 69*(2), 140–153.

Gutiérrez, K. D., & Rogoff, B. (2003). Cultural ways of learning: Individual traits or repertoires of practice. *Educational Researcher, 32*(5), 19–25.

Hawley, W. D. (1986). Holmes report: A critical analysis of the Holmes Group's proposals for reforming teacher education. *Journal of Teacher Education, July-August,* 47–51.

Helms, J. (1990). *Black and white racial identity: Theory, research and practice.* Westport, CT: Greenwood Press.

Henderson, A., & Whipple, M. (2013). How to connect with families. *Educational Leadership, 70*(9), 44–48.

Hollins, E. R. (2011). Teacher preparation for quality teaching. *Journal of Teacher Education, 62*(4), 395–407.

Holmes Group. (1986). *Tomorrow's teachers.* East Lansing, MI: Author.

Holmes Group. (1989). *Holmes Group: One year on.* East Lansing, MI: Author.

Hong, S. (2012). *A cord of three strands: A new approach to parent engagement in schools.* Cambridge, MA: Harvard Education Press.

Horton, J., & Scott, D. (2004). White students' voices in multicultural teacher education preparation. *Multicultural Education, 11*(4), 12–16.

Howard, T. C. (2013). *Black male(d): Peril and promise in the education of African American males.* New York, NY: Teachers College Press.

Ingersoll, R., & May, H. (2011). *Recruitment, retention and the minority teacher shortage.* Philadelphia, PA: Consortium for Policy Research in Education. Retrieved from http ://www.cpre.org/sites/default/files/researchreport/1221_minorityteachershortagerepor trr69septfinal.pdf

Ingersoll, R., & May, H. (2016). *Minority teacher recruitment, employment, and retention: 1987-2013* (Research brief). Retrieved from https://learningpolicyinstitute.org/sites/default /files/product-files/Minority_Teacher_Recruitment_Employment_Retention%20 _BRIEF.pdf

Institute of Education Sciences. (2016). *Projections of education statistics to 2023* (NCES 2015-o73). Washington, DC: U.S. Department of Education National Center for Education Statistics.

Irizarry, J. (2007). Home-growing teachers of color: Lessons learned from a town-gown partnership. *Teacher Education Quarterly, 34*(4), 87–102.

Irvine, J. J. (1988). An analysis of the problem of the disappearing Black educator. *Elementary School Journal, 88*(5), 503–514.

Jackson, I., & Knight-Manuel, M. (2019). "Color does not equal consciousness:" Educators of color learning to enact a sociopolitical consciousness. *Journal of Teacher Education, 70*(1), 65–78. doi:10.1177/0022487118783189

Johnson, W. R. (1987). Empowering practitioners: Holmes, Carnegie, and the lessons of history. *History of Education Quarterly, 27*(2), 221–240.

Johnson, W. R. (1990). Inviting conversations: The Holmes Group and tomorrow's schools. *American Education Research Journal, 27*(4), 581–588.

Kimani, M. H., & Laster, B. P. (1999). Responding to religious diversity in the classroom. *Educational Leadership, 56*(7), 61–63.

King, J. (2016, May 15). The invisible tax on teachers of color. *The Washington Post.* Retrieved from https://www.washingtonpost.com/opinions/the-invisible-tax-on-black-teachers/2016/05/15/6b7bea06-16f7-11e6-aa55-670cabef46e0_story.html

Kirby, S. N., McCombs, J. S., Barney, H., & Naftel, S. (2006). *Reforming teacher education: Something old, something new.* Santa Monica, CA: RAND Corporation.

Klein, J. I., Rice, C., & Levy, J. (2012). *U.S. education reform and national security* (Independent Task Force Report No. 68). New York, NY: Council on Foreign Relations.

Kohli, R. (2012). Racial pedagogy of the oppressed: Critical interracial dialogue for teachers of color. *Equity & Excellence in Education, 45*(1), 1–16.

Kohli, R. (2014). Unpacking internalized racism: Teachers of color striving for racially just classrooms. *Race Ethnicity and Education, 17*(3), 367–387.

Kohli, R. (2019). Lessons for teacher education: The role of critical professional development in teacher of color retention. *Journal of Teacher Education, 70*(1), 39–50. doi:10.1177/0022487118767645

Kretchmar, K., & Zeichner, K. (2016). Teacher Prep 3.0: A vision for teacher education to impact social transformation. *Journal of Education for Teaching, 42*(4), 417–433.

Ladson-Billings, G. (2001). *Crossing over to Canaan.* San Francisco, CA: Jossey-Bass.

Ladson-Billings, G. (2005). Is the team all right? Diversity and teacher education. *Journal of Teacher Education, 56*(3), 229–234.

Ladson-Billings, G. (2009). Race still matters: Critical race theory in education. In M. W. Apple, W. Au, & L. A. Gandin (Eds.), *The Routledge international handbook of critical education* (pp. 110–122). New York, MY: Routledge.

Larrivee, B. (2000). Transforming teaching practice: Becoming the critically reflective teacher. *Reflective Practice, 1*(3), 293–307.

Lau, K., Dandy, E., & Hoffman, L. (2007). The pathways program: A model for increasing the number of teachers of color. *Teacher Education Quarterly, 34*(4), 27–40.

Lindsey, M. (1961). *New horizons for the teaching profession: A report of the task force on new horizons in teacher education and professional standards.* Washington, D.C: National Commission on Teacher Education and Professional Standards, National Education Association of the United States.

Liston, D., & Zeichner, K. (1991). *Teacher education and the social conditions of schooling.* New York, NY: Routledge.

Liu, K. (2015). Critical reflection as a framework for transformative learning in teacher education. *Educational Review, 67*(2), 135–157.

Liu, K. (2017). Creating a dialogic space for prospective teacher critical reflection and transformative learning. *Reflective Practice, 18*(6), 805–820.

Lopez, V., Montecinos, C., Rodriguiz, J. I., Calderon, A., & Contreras, J. F. (2012). Enacting solidarity to address peer-to-peer aggression in schools: Case studies from Chile. In C. Sleeter & E. Soriano (Eds.), *Creating solidarity across diverse communities* (pp. 23–43). New York, NY: Teachers College Press.

Mabokela, R. O., & Madsen, J. M. (2007). "Color-blind" and "color-conscious" leadership: A case study of desegregated suburban schools in the USA. *International Journal of Leadership in Education, 8*(3), 186–206.

Matias, C. E., & Mackey, J. (2016). Breakin' down Whiteness in antiracist teaching: Introducing Critical Whiteness pedagogy. *Urban Review, 48*(1), 32–50.

Meier, D. (2002). *In schools we trust: Creating communities of learning in an era of testing and standardization.* Boston, MA: Beacon.

Mezirow, J. (Ed.). (1990). *Fostering critical reflection in adulthood: A guide to transformative and emancipatory learning.* San Francisco, CA: Jossey-Bass.

Mezirow, J. (2000). *Learning as transformation: Critical perspectives on a theory in progress.* San Francisco, CA: Jossey Bass.

Milner, H. R., IV. (2003). Reflection, racial competence, and critical pedagogy: How do we prepare pre-service teachers to pose tough questions? *Race Ethnicity and Education, 6*(2), 193–208.

Milner, H. R., IV. (2006). Preservice teachers' learning about cultural and racial diversity: Implications for urban education. *Urban Education, 41*(4), 343–375.

Milner, H. R., IV. (2008). Critical race theory and interest convergence as analytical tools in teacher education policies and practices. *Journal of Teacher Education, 59*(4), 332–246.

Milner, H. R., IV. (2009). African-American males in urban schools: No excuses—teach and empower. In H. R. Milner (Ed.), *Diversity and education: Teachers, teaching, and teacher education* (pp. 5–16). Springfield, IL: Charles C. Thomas.

Milner, H. R., IV. (2014). Culturally relevant, purpose-driven learning & teaching in a middle school social studies classroom. *Multicultural Education, 21*(2), 9–17.

Milner, H. R., IV. (2017). Where's the race in culturally relevant pedagogy? *Teachers College Record, 119*(1), 1–32.

Milner, H. R., IV, & Laughter, J. (2015). But good intentions are not enough: Preparing teachers to center race and poverty. *Urban Review, 47*(2), 341–363.

Mitchell, A. L., & King, M. S. (2016). *A new agenda: Research to build a better teacher preparation program.* Chicago, IL: Bellwether Education Partners.

Moll, L. C., Amanti, C., Neff, D., & González, N. (1992). Funds of knowledge for teaching: Using a qualitative approach to connect homes and classrooms. *Theory Into Practice, 31*(2), 132–141.

Montecinos, C. (1995). Culture as an ongoing dialogue: Implications for multicultural teacher education. In C. Sleeter & P. McLaren (Eds.), *Multicultural education, critical pedagogy, and the politics of difference* (pp. 269–308). Albany: State University of New York Press.

Murrell, P. C., Jr. (2000). Community teachers: A conceptual framework for preparing exemplary urban teachers. *Journal of Negro Education, 69*(4), 338–348.

National Commission for Excellence in Teacher Education. (1985). *A call for change in teacher education.* Washington, DC: American Association of Colleges for Teacher Education.

National Commission on Education. (1983). *A nation at risk: The imperative for educational reform.* Washington, DC: U.S. Department of Education.

National Council for Accreditation of Teacher Education. (2008). *NCATE standards revision: Glossary additions and edits.* Washington, DC: Author. Retrieved from http://www.ncate.org/~/media/Files/caep/accreditation-resources/ncate-standards-2008.pdf?la=en

National Council for Accreditation of Teacher Education. (2010). *Transforming teacher education through clinical practice: A national strategy to prepare effective teachers: Report of the Blue Ribbon Panel on Clinical Preparation and Partnership for Improved Student Learning.* Washington, DC: Author.

Noguera, P. (2001). Transforming urban schools through investments in the social capital of parents. In S. Saegart, J. P. Thompson, & M. Warren (Eds.), *Social capital and poor communities* (pp. 189–212). New York, NY: Russell Sage Foundation.

Parker, L., & Hood, S. (1995). Minority students vs. majority faculty and administrators in teacher education: Perspectives on the clash of cultures. *Urban Review, 27*(2), 159–174.

Philip, T. M. (2010). Moving beyond our progressive lenses: Recognizing and building on the strengths of teachers of color. *Journal of Teacher Education, 62*(4), 356–366.

Philip, T. M. (2013). Experience as college student activists: A strength and a liability for prospective teachers of color in urban schools. *Urban Education, 48*(1), 44–68.

Philip, T. M., & Benin, S. Y. (2014). Programs of teacher education as mediators of White teacher identity. *Teaching Education, 25*(1), 1–23.

Pollock, M., Deckman, S., Mira, M., & Shalaby, C. (2010). "But what can I do?" Three necessary tensions in teaching teachers about race. *Journal of Teacher Education, 61*(3), 211–224.

Quiocho, A., & Rios, F. (2000). The power of their presence: Minority group teachers and schooling. *Review of Educational Research, 70*(4), 485–528.

Rieger, A. (2015). Making sense of White identity development: The implications for teacher education. *Multicultural Learning and Teaching, 10*(2), 211–230.

Rogers-Ard, R., Knaus, C. B., Epstein, K. K., & Mayfield, K. (2013). Racial diversity sounds nice; systems transformation? Not so much: Developing urban teachers of color. *Urban Education, 48*(3), 451–479.

Schlessman, E. (2012). When are you coming to visit? Home visits and seeing our students. *Rethinking Schools, 27*(2). Retrieved from https://www.rethinkingschools.org/articles/when-are-you-going-to-come-visit-home-visits-and-seeing-our-students

Schön, D. A. (1983). *The reflective practitioner.* New York, NY: Basic Books.

Schultz, B., Gillette, M., & Hill, D. (2008). A theoretical framework for understanding Grow Your Own Teachers. *The Sophist's Bane, 4*(1), 69–80.

Schultz, B., Gillette, M., & Hill, D. (2011). Teaching as political: Theoretical perspectives for understanding the grow your own movement. In E. Skinner, M. Garreton, & B. Schultz

(Eds.), *Grow your own teachers: Grassroots change for teacher education* (pp. 5–21). New York: Teachers College Press.

Sleeter, C. E. (2001). Preparing teachers for culturally diverse schools: Research and the overwhelming presence of whiteness. *Journal of Teacher Education, 52*(2), 94–106.

Sleeter, C. E. (2017). Critical race theory and the Whiteness of teacher education. *Urban Education, 52*(2), 155–169.

Sleeter, C. E., & Grant, C. (1987). An analysis of multicultural education in the United States. *Harvard Educational Review, 57*(4), 421–444.

Sleeter, C. E., & Milner, H. R., IV. (2011). Researching successful efforts in teacher education to diversify teachers. In A. F. Ball & C. Tyson (Eds.), *Studying diversity in teacher education* (pp. 81–103). Lanham, MD: Rowman & Littlefield.

Sleeter, C. E. Neal, L. I., & Kumashiro, K. K. (2014). *Diversifying the teacher workforce: Preparing and retaining highly effective teachers.* New York, NY: Routledge.

Sleeter, C. E.., & Soriano, E. (Eds.). (2012). *Creating solidarity across diverse communities: International perspectives in education.* New York, NY: Teachers College Press.

Sleeter, C. E., & Thao, Y. (2007). Guest editors' introduction: Diversifying the teaching force. *Teacher Education Quarterly, 34*(4), 3–8.

Smith, B. O. (1969). *Teachers for the real world.* Washington, DC: American Association of Colleges for Teacher Education.

Smith, B. O. (1980). *A design for a school of pedagogy.* Washington, DC: U.S. Department of Education.

Souto-Manning, M. (2011). Playing with power and privilege: Theatre games in teacher education. *Teaching and Teacher Education, 27*(6), 997–1007.

Téllez, K. (1999). Mexican-American preservice teachers and the intransigency of the elementary school curriculum. *Teaching and Teacher Education, 15*, 555–570.

Thomas, M., & Liu, K. (2012). The performance of reflection: A grounded analysis of prospective teachers' eportfolios. *Journal of Technology and Teacher Education, 20*(3), 305–330.

Toshalis, E. (2012). The rhetoric of care: Preservice teacher discourses that depoliticize, deflect, and deceive. *Urban Review, 44*(1), 1–35.

Tschannen-Moran, M. (2004). *Trust matters: Leadership for successful schools.* San Francisco, CA: Jossey-Bass.

U.S. Department of Education, Policy and Program Services Department, Office of Planning, Evaluation and Policy Development. (2016). *The state of racial diversity in the educator workforce.* Retrieved from http://www2.ed.gov/rschstat/eval/highered/racial-diversity/state-racial-diversity-workforce.pdf

U.S. Office of Education. (1939). *Statistics of higher education: 1937-38.* Washington, DC: Author.

Valenzuela, A. (2017). *Grow Your Own Educators programs: A review of the literature with an emphasis on equity-based approach* (Intercultural Development Research Association report). Retrieved from http://www.idraeacsouth.org/wp-content/uploads/2017/12/Grow-Your-Own-Educator-Programs-Lit-Review-IDRA-EAC-South-2017.pdf

van Manen, M. (1977). Linking ways of knowing with ways of being practical. *Curriculum Inquiry, 6*(3), 205–228.

Vesely, C. K., Brown, B. E., & Mehta, S. (2017). Developing cultural humility through experiential learning: How home visits transform early childhood preservice educators' attitudes for engaging families. *Journal of Early Childhood Teacher Education, 38*(3), 242–258.

Villegas, A. M., & Davis, D. (2007). Approaches to diversifying the teaching force: Attending to issues of recruitment, preparation, and retention. *Teacher Education Quarterly, 34*(4), 137–147.

Villegas, A. M., & Davis, D. (2008). Preparing teachers of color to confront racial/ethnic disparities in educational outcomes. In M. Cochran-Smith, S. Feiman-Nemser, &

J. McIntyre (Eds.), *Handbook of research in teacher education: Enduring issues in changing contexts* (pp. 583–605). Mahwah, NJ: Lawrence Erlbaum.

Villegas, A. M., & Irvine, J. J. (2010). Diversifying the teaching force: An examination of major arguments. *Urban Review, 42*(3), 175–192.

Villegas, A. M., Strom, K., & Lucas, T. (2012). Closing the racial/ethnic gap between students of color and their teachers: An elusive goal. *Equity & Excellence in Education, 45*(2), 283–301.

Vygotsky, L. S. (1962). *Thought and language.* Cambridge: MIT Press.

Woodson, A., & Pabon, A. (2016). "I'm none of the above": Exploring themes of heteropatriarchy in the life histories of Black male educators. *Equity & Excellence in Education, 47*(1), 57–71.

Yosso, T. (2005). Whose culture has capital? A critical race theory discussion of community cultural wealth. *Race Ethnicity and Education, 8*(1), 69–91.

Zeichner, K. M. (1993). *Educating teachers for cultural diversity: NCRTL special report.* East Lansing, MI: National Center for Research on Teacher Learning.

Zeichner, K. (1996). Educating teachers for cultural diversity. In K. Zeichner, S. Melnick, & M. L. Gomez. (Eds.), *Currents of reform in preservice teacher education* (pp. 133–175). New York, NY: Teachers College Press.

Zeichner, K. (2003). The adequacies and inadequacies of three current strategies to recruit, prepare, and retain the best teachers for all students. *Teachers College Record, 105*(3), 490–515.

Zeichner, K., Bowman, M., Guillen, L., & Napolitan, K. (2016). Engaging and working in solidarity with local communities in preparing the teachers of their Children. *Journal of Teacher Education, 67*(4), 277–290.

Zeichner, K., & Liston, D. (1996). *Reflective teaching: An introduction.* Englewood Cliffs, NJ: Lawrence Erlbaum.

Zeichner, K., & Liu, K. (2010). A critical analysis of reflection as the goal of teacher education. In N. Lyons (Ed.), *Handbook of reflection and reflective inquiry: Mapping a way of knowing for professional reflective inquiry* (pp. 67–84). New York, NY: Springer.

Chapter 4

How Responsive Is a Teacher's Classroom Practice to Intervention? A Meta-Analysis of Randomized Field Studies

RACHEL GARRETT
MARTYNA CITKOWICZ
RYAN WILLIAMS
American Institutes for Research

While teacher effectiveness has been a particular focus of federal education policy, and districts allocate significant resources toward professional development for teachers, these efforts are guided by an unexplored assumption that classroom practice can be improved through intervention. Yet even assuming classroom practice is responsive, little information is available to inform stakeholder expectations about how much classroom practice may change through intervention, or whether particular aspects of classroom practice are more amenable to improvement. Moreover, a growing body of rigorous research evaluating programs with a focus on improving classroom practice provides a new opportunity to explore factors associated with changes in classroom practice, such as intervention, study sample, or contextual features. This study examines the question of responsiveness by conducting a meta-analysis of randomized experiments of interventions directed at classroom practice. Our empirical findings indicate that multiple dimensions of classroom practice improve meaningfully through classroom practice-directed intervention, on average, but also find substantial heterogeneity in the effects. Implications for practice and research are discussed.

Policymakers, practitioners, and researchers have all recognized the salience of having highly effective teachers in all of our nation's classrooms. Research repeatedly has demonstrated the importance of teacher quality for student achievement, beyond other school-level characteristics (Aaronson, Barrow, & Sander, 2007; Goldhaber, 2002; Rivkin, Hanushek, & Kain, 2005; Rockoff, 2004). The influence of teachers

Review of Research in Education
March 2019, Vol. 43, pp. 106–137
DOI: 10.3102/0091732X19830634
Chapter reuse guidelines: sagepub.com/journals-permissions
© 2019 AERA. http://rre.aera.net

can persist over time, with research linking teaching quality in elementary and middle schools to college attendance (Chamberlin, 2013).

Federal education policy has had a long-standing interest in teacher effectiveness, but it has put a particular focus on effective teachers over the past 15 years. This began with the requirements for highly qualified teachers in every school, as mandated by the No Child Left Behind Act in 2002. This was followed by the federal Race to the Top competition and the No Child Left Behind waivers, which both continued to place significant emphasis on ensuring effective instruction, primarily through a focus on more robust teacher evaluation systems. More recently, federal accountability requirements for teacher evaluation have been loosened in the Every Student Succeeds Act reauthorization, but states and districts continue to place a strong emphasis on teaching quality and to allocate significant resources toward professional development for teachers (Jacob & McGovern, 2015).

Alongside the increased focus on teacher effectiveness in education policy, the field of education research has witnessed a substantial increase in rigorous education research in instruction. As shown in Figure 1, a search of the literature for randomized controlled field studies that include a focus on developing classroom practice demonstrates this uptick. The research likely has responded to both the policy impetus and the related need from the field to understand how to support and promote effective instruction through professional learning programs for teachers.

Yet despite the empirical evidence that teachers play an important role in student learning, and the volume of research on interventions that aim to improve classroom practice, an underlying, fundamental question has not yet been addressed: To what extent is a teacher's classroom practice responsive to intervention?

The purpose of this study is to examine the question of responsiveness by conducting a meta-analysis of randomized experiments of interventions directed at classroom practice. We consider how changes in classroom practice may vary by specific aspects of practice, how heterogeneity of effects may relate to features of the interventions, and we seek to identify if there are particularly effective approaches to teacher professional learning. Through this work, we address the following set of questions, which have implications for future design of teacher professional learning programs, and for study design:

1. How does a teacher's classroom practice respond to intervention?
2. Are specific aspects of classroom practice more or less responsive?
3. Are particular intervention features (e.g., coaching, video and technology components, intervention length) associated with improvements in classroom practice?

We find that classroom practice is responsive, and interventions directed toward classroom practice are, on average, able to have meaningful and positive impacts. However, we also find substantial heterogeneity in effects, indicating that programs vary in their ability to improve classroom practice. Our results further indicate that

FIGURE 1
Number of References per Year of Randomized Field Studies That Target Classroom Practice

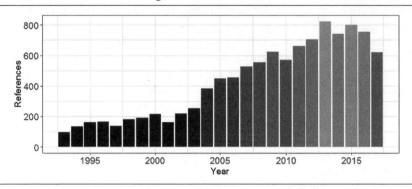

Note. The figure shows the citation returns from an EBSCO Host search of the previous 25 years, by year, for the following search string: ("classroom practice" OR instruction OR "instructional practice" OR "classroom practice" OR "teacher effectiveness") AND (intervention OR strateg* OR program OR treatment) AND (experiment OR "randomized experiment" OR "randomized trial" OR "randomized control").

interventions with a more limited dosage of treatment tend to produce similar effects to those with more intensive approaches. To present our study, the rest of the chapter is organized as follows. First, we summarize earlier studies that reviewed the research on teacher professional learning and present our theoretical framing. Next, we describe our approach. We then present our findings, and conclude with a discussion of the implications of our findings for practice and future research.

Previous Reviews of Research on Teacher Professional Learning

Several researchers have conducted reviews of research on the effects of interventions that target practice for teachers in K–12 settings. For example, Ingersoll and Strong (2011) focused on the effects of induction programs on beginning teachers and found positive effects for classroom practices in the majority of the 15 studies they reviewed. Slavin, Lake, Hanley, and Thurston (2012, 2014) focused on interventions of science instruction and found positive effects on student achievement for science teaching methods that focused on enhancing teachers' classroom instruction, but no effects for curriculum-focused teaching methods (i.e., programs that provide science kits to teachers), suggesting the importance of addressing classroom practice as a mediator to improving student outcomes. Gersten et al. (2009) found 42 studies to include in their syntheses of mathematics instructional interventions for students with disabilities and estimated positive and statistically significant mean effects for nearly all the aspects of classroom practice they studied. McKenna, Shin, and Ciullo (2015) also focused on instruction for students with disabilities and found some evidence of improved teacher use of targeted classroom practices across their 11 studies.

Other reviews have focused on sorting approaches used in teacher training and development, which may or may not contain an empirical synthesis. For example, Kennedy (2016) conducted a systematic review of the teacher professional development literature that focused on rigorous research studies that included student achievement outcomes. She identified 28 studies that met her inclusion criteria and was able to compute effect size estimates, which she sorted across the focal ideas teachers were expected to learn and the strategies for helping teachers execute those ideas in their practice. The review did not, however, contain a quantitative synthesis. Certainly many others have categorized the literature (e.g., Blank & de las Alas, 2009; Scher & O'Reilly, 2009; Timperley, Wilson, Barrar, & Fung, 2007). However, as Kennedy (2016) notes, most do not empirically examine the average effectiveness of these strategies for student or teacher outcomes, nor do they advance our understanding of differential effects among strategies. Most of these reviews also focus on understanding the relationship between professional learning strategies and student outcomes, without investigating the degree to which they affect intermediate outcomes like classroom practice.

A more recent study by Kraft, Blazar, and Hogan (2018) conducted a meta-analysis of coaching intervention effects. The authors identified 60 studies for which the intervention included coaching for pre-K–12 teachers and included a measure of classroom practice or student achievement as an outcome. The authors found positive effects of coaching on both classroom practice (0.49 standard deviations) and student achievement (0.18 standard deviations). However, the study did not consider effects separately for teachers working in pre-K and K–12 settings, which is likely an area worth further understanding given the substantial differences between the pre-K and grade school teaching forces and their working conditions (Herzfeldt-Kamprath & Ullrich, 2016). Furthermore, while the study provides insights about the benefits of teacher coaching, more can be learned from the broader literature on teacher professional learning.

Thus, while these published reviews show positive effects for improving teachers' classroom practices and student achievement, they are limited in scope as each is focused on particular types of interventions (e.g., coaching, induction programs, or science instruction) and specific types of samples (e.g., beginning teachers or students with disabilities). More inclusive meta-analyses across a range of intervention types—for both pre-K and K–12 settings—can help the field better understand how professional learning programs can change teachers' classroom practices, and ultimately student achievement outcomes. In addition, further disaggregating the effects by the features of the intervention, sample, setting, and classroom observation measure is important to produce a clearer picture of what interventions work, for whom, and when.

Theoretical Framework

This work is guided by a simple theoretical framework that captures the underlying impetus behind the range of policies and resources dedicated to improving teacher

FIGURE 2
Theoretical Framework for Classroom Practice

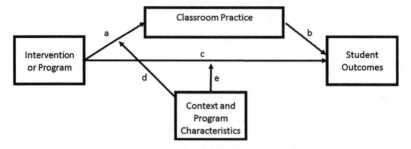

effectiveness. As shown in Figure 2, an intervention or program directed toward classroom practice is hypothesized to bring changes in classroom practice (Path *a*) as well as changes in student outcomes (Path *c*). In this framing, changes in student outcomes have a direct relationship with the classroom practices they experience (Path *b*), and the impact of the intervention or program on student outcomes is mediated by the changes in classroom practice (Paths *a* × *b*). Studies may examine only the direct effect of intervention on student outcomes (Path *c*) for a variety of design and logistical reasons and, therefore, may assume that observed effects on students happen indirectly, through Paths *a* and *b*, rather than through other programmatic mechanisms such as materials, curricula, or student supports. Also, there may be factors that moderate the programs' effects on classroom practice and student outcomes (Paths *d* and *e*), such as the context in which the program took place (e.g., characteristics of the students, teachers, or schools participating) or the features of the program (e.g., use of a coaching component, including a focus on data use).

This meta-analysis looks across the literature on classroom practice interventions to build knowledge about the extent to which this theoretical structure holds for Paths *a* and *d*. Existing quantitative syntheses that build knowledge across primary studies largely have focused on providing information for Paths *a* or *c*, but for specialized programs or populations. The research also offers little information to understand moderation effects that can account for the heterogeneity of program effectiveness across settings, populations, and interventions, illustrated by Paths *d* and *e*. This gap in the research represents a critical, untapped opportunity, given the more recent surge of rigorous research in classroom practice-directed interventions (see Figure 1).

APPROACH

Our study was designed to examine the responsiveness of classroom practice as measured through classroom observations. We define the study eligibility criteria, search strategy, study coding, effect size computation, and model estimation approach below.

Eligibility Criteria

To be eligible for inclusion in this meta-analysis, primary studies needed to meet the following criteria:

1. The study sample includes in-service teachers working in kindergarten to Grade 12.
2. The study evaluates an intervention that aims to improve classroom practices for supporting student academic learning (e.g., reading, math, science, social studies). Interventions may include professional development, training, and coaching for teachers. Curriculum interventions without a teacher training component that included a classroom practice focus were excluded.
3. The study design is a randomized control trial with randomization taking place at the teacher level or higher. The study must also include a control group.
4. The study uses a measure of classroom practice as measured through classroom observations.
5. The study is written in English.
6. The study provided sufficient information to calculate an effect size estimate and variance.

No restrictions were placed on actual study location or study year.

Literature Search and Retrieval

Our process of identifying relevant studies related to classroom practice effects as measured through classroom observations is graphically presented in Figure 3. We describe the process in detail below.

Database Search

We conducted electronic database searches of Web of Knowledge,[1] ERIC, Academic Search Premier, and PsycINFO on May 4, 2016. The search was limited to English language–only studies and studies including Grades pre-K–12.[2] No time frame restriction was imposed on the search.

We used the following search terms in our database search:

In title/subject/abstract: [Teacher OR educator OR "education* professional" OR instructor] AND ["Teach* practice" OR "instruction* approach" OR pedagogy OR practice OR enactment OR "classroom practice" OR "classroom performance" OR "teach* effectiveness" OR "teach* performance" OR "teach* efficacy" OR "instruction* efficacy" OR "teach* quality" OR "instruction* quality" OR "instruction* practice" OR "educat* practice" OR "educat* approach" OR "educat* quality" OR "educat* efficacy" OR "educat* effectiveness" OR "educat* performance"] AND [Intervention OR treatment OR program OR policy OR "professional development" OR training]
AND

FIGURE 3
Classroom Practice Meta-Analysis Literature Search and Retrieval Process

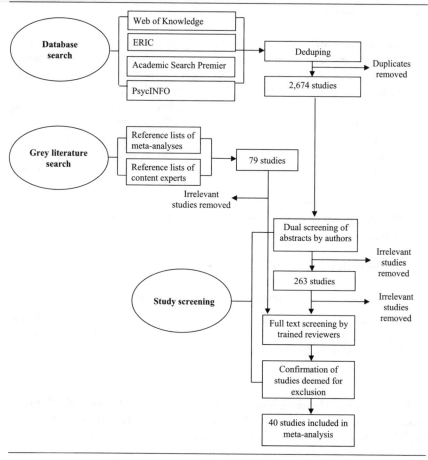

In full text: randomiz* OR "random* assign*"
NOT
In Subject: postsecondary or post-secondary or "higher ed*" or adult or nontradi-
tional or college or universit*

After removal of duplicate studies, the database search yielded 2,674 studies.

Abstract and Title Screening

As represented in Figure 3, the three authors screened the titles and abstracts of
studies using the eligibility criteria defined in the previous section. Because abstracts
do not always specify whether the classroom practice measure is observation-based, we

only required that the abstract indicate that classroom practice was measured at all, rather than specifically measured using observations. All 2,674 studies were assigned to dual title and abstract screening, such that each study could be screened by two authors. Any discrepancies were resolved by consensuses between the two authors.

We conducted our title and abstract screening using abstrackr, a free, open-source tool that uses machine learning technology to semiautomate the screening process (Wallace, Small, Brodley, Lau, & Trikalinos, 2012). Using our criteria, we indicated whether a study was eligible for inclusion in our meta-analysis using the "Yes", "Maybe," and "No" options. Learning which studies are most pertinent, abstrackr prioritized the screening of studies most likely to be relevant to our meta-analysis. Of the 2,674 studies, we dual-screened 2,018 studies. At this point, abstrackr indicated that the remaining 656 studies had a less than 0.5 probability of inclusion (Wallace et al., 2012). The first author screened the titles (and, when relevant, abstracts) of the 656 low-probability studies to verify their exclusion and agreed that all 656 should be excluded. Of the 2,018 screened studies, 263 studies were labeled as "Yes" or "Maybe" for inclusion and the full text was pulled for further screening.

Gray Literature Search

We searched for gray, or unpublished, literature using two methods. First, we scanned the reference lists of 16 meta-analyses focused on examining classroom practice (identified using the search above). Second, we reached out to experts in the field who provided us with lists of studies that include interventions for teachers and observations of classroom practice. We screened the titles and abstracts of these studies using our eligibility criteria defined above. Excluding studies our previous search identified, this search yielded an additional 79 studies for potential inclusion and for which the full text was pulled for further screening.

Full Text Screening

Four screeners screened the full text of the 342 studies that were deemed for potential inclusion based on their titles and abstracts. Ten percent of the studies that were screened out by the screeners were also screened by one of the authors. All dual-screened studies marked for exclusion were confirmed for exclusion by one of the authors. We screened the full text using the following criteria: (1) the study is a randomized control trial; (2) the study includes an observation-based measure of classroom practice; (3) the study includes an analysis that compares treatment and control group teachers on the observation-based classroom practice measure; and (4) the study provides sufficient information to calculate an effect size estimate and variance. We also selected studies that included Grades K–12 samples and set aside studies solely focused on pre-K.[3] The interventions and outcomes found in the pre-K studies differ drastically from the types of interventions and outcomes in the K–12 studies; thus, we plan to conduct a separate meta-analysis focused on interventions for pre-K teachers. Forty studies met our final inclusion criteria.

Study Coding

Four coders coded the 40 studies included from our review. Twenty percent of the studies were also coded by one of the authors. Any coding discrepancies were examined and resolved by one of the authors.

We coded available information from the studies using Cronbach's (1982) UTOS (units, treatments, outcomes, and settings) framework for generalizability. Coding focused on extracting core descriptive information from the identified studies as well as characteristics that could explain, at least in part, observed heterogeneity in classroom practice effects (i.e., potential moderators). Before coding began, the research team identified items related to the content of this meta-analysis, such as intervention features, classroom practice domains, and measurement features, by drawing on the expertise of the research team and in consultation with other content experts who have conducted large-scale professional learning experiments. Our goal was to strike a balance between comprehensiveness and feasibility. As such, we recognize there may be a number of other study features that warrant further inquiry.

To code intervention features, the study team reviewed the qualitative descriptions provided in the texts. An intervention feature was coded as "present" if there was a clear description of the feature, and otherwise was considered not present if there was either (1) a clear description that the feature was not used or (2) there was no information to make a determination either way.

To code the classroom practice measures, the study reviewed the descriptions provided in each study. The study conceptualized broad domains and constructs within those domains using the observable portions of *The Framework for Teaching Evaluation Instrument* (Danielson, 2013) as a guideline. Classroom practices were categorized into either classroom environment or instructional domains where possible, and where the measures descriptions were too general to assign to either of those two domains, they were categorized into an overall effectiveness domain. Where feasible, we further categorized measures into constructs within the classroom environment and instructional domains. Within environment, we were able to identify measures that fell into categories including classroom culture, classroom management, or that aggregated over multiple aspects of environment. Within instruction, we were able to categorize measures that related to instructional format, discourse (which included questioning), student engagement and measures that again aggregated over multiple aspects of instruction. We also categorized practices that were specific to mathematics or English language arts content (e.g., use of decoding strategies).

A copy of the codebook is included in Appendix A (available in the online version of the journal). The codes included the following:

- *Study-level information*: authors, publication type, citation, and the year of publication (if published)
- *Sample characteristics (U)*: sample sizes (districts, schools, teachers, and students), student demographic composition (i.e., percent eligible for free or reduced price

lunch, percent sample minority, percent sample special education, and percent sample English learners), and years of teaching experience
- *Intervention characteristics (T)*: intervention features (e.g., coaching, video and technology components), delivery mechanisms (e.g., in person vs. online coaching), and intervention dosage (i.e., intervention length in weeks and hours spent on intervention)
- *Outcome information (O)*: the broad domains of the classroom practice outcomes measured in the study (e.g., classroom environment, instruction, overall effectiveness) and constructs within those domains (e.g., classroom management, instructional format), and observation timing (i.e., during intervention, directly after, after time passed, or a combination)
- *Setting information (S)*: grade level and level of randomization
- *Effect size information*: summary statistics of impact estimate (e.g., means and standard deviations, *t* tests, *F* tests, χ^2 tests, models, effect sizes and their types), and variance estimates of the outcome

Lack of information precluded the study team from coding for all of the information identified in the codebook. For example, the included studies often provided limited information on sample characteristics, and frequently did not include any information on the reliability of the classroom observation instruments used. The analyses therefore focused on the codes that produced sufficient information for empirical investigation.

Computing Effect Sizes

Meta-analysis relies on effect sizes, which provide a common metric for synthesis across studies that measure outcomes on different scales. Effect sizes encode both the direction and the magnitude of the relationship between intervention and outcomes (Hedges & Olkin, 1985; Lipsey & Wilson, 2001). For this meta-analysis, we computed the standardized mean difference (SMD) effect size for all classroom practice outcomes reported in each study. We computed SMDs using reported summary statistics, including means and standard deviations, *t* tests, *F* tests, χ^2 tests, regression model estimates, and effect sizes in other metrics. The equations for calculating the SMD, or converting other effect size metrics to the SMD, can be found in Borenstein, Hedges, Higgins, and Rothstein (2009).

Appropriate summary statistics were not available to calculate SMDs for all effects. We queried authors for the missing information, which yielded little extra information for coding purposes.

Hedges's Small Sample Correction

An SMD is generally estimated using Cohen's *d*-index:

$$d = \frac{\bar{y}^T - \bar{y}^C}{s},$$

where $\bar{y}^T$ and $\bar{y}^C$ are the sample means of the treatment and control groups, respectively, and s is the total pooled within-group standard deviation.[4] To account for small studies, we applied Hedges's (1981) small sample bias correction to the computed d effects:

$$g = d\left[1-\left(\frac{3}{4df-1}\right)\right],$$

where df denotes the degrees of freedom, equal to $N^T + N^C - 2$. The variance of g is

$$v_g = \frac{N^T + N^C}{N^T N^C} + \frac{g^2}{2\left(N^T + N^C - 2\right)},$$

where N^T and N^C are the total sample sizes of the treatment and control groups, respectively.

Adjusting for Nesting

In education, students are often nested within teachers who are then nested within schools and districts. In our set of studies, teachers were generally nested, or clustered, within schools. To account for this two-level nesting, when possible, we adjusted the computed effect sizes and their variances using Hedges's (2007) corrections[5]:

$$g_2 = g\sqrt{1-\frac{2*(n-1)*\rho}{N-2}}$$

and

$$V_{g2} = \left(\frac{N}{N^T N^C}\right)\left(1+(n-1)\rho\right)+\frac{g_2^2}{2h_{g2}},$$

where N is the total sample size in the study, n is the average number of teachers per school, ρ is the intraclass correlation coefficient,[6] and h is the effective degrees of freedom, given by

$$h_{g2} = \frac{(N-2)\left[(N-2)-2(n-1)\rho\right]}{(N-2)(1-\rho)^2 + n(N-2n)\rho^2 + 2(N-2n)\rho(1-\rho)}.$$

META-ANALYSIS

To estimate our meta-analytic mean effects, we employed random- and mixed-effects models for which studies are considered a random sample of possible studies, allowing us to generalize to a hypothetical population of studies by incorporating the between-study heterogeneity statistic τ^2 (Hedges & Vevea, 1998). The following is the mean-only random-effects model used to estimate the overall weighted mean of all observed classroom practice effects:

$$g_{jk} = \beta_0 + u_k + e_{jk},$$

where g_{jk} is the jth effect size estimate from study k[7]; β_0 is the mean effect; u_k is a study-level random error term, assumed to be normally distributed with a mean of zero, and between-study variance τ_u^2; e_{jk} is the sampling error for effect size j in study k, assumed to be normally distributed with a mean of zero and sampling variance σ_e^2; and the weights are computed as the inverse of the variance plus the estimated between-study variance, or $w_{jk} = 1/(v_{jk} + \hat{\tau}_u^2)$ (Borenstein et al., 2009). We employed the mean-only model to estimate weighted mean effects on *all* observed outcomes as well as separate effects for each classroom practice outcome domain and construct.

Examining Sources of Heterogeneity

To examine the heterogeneity of the observed classroom practice effects, we employed mixed-effects models that include intervention intensity (length and hours), timing of the observational measurement, intervention features, grade band, teacher experience, and study characteristics (publication year and sample size), separately, as moderators in the model. We tested moderators one at a time due to power constraints and also to avoid issues of correlation among the moderators (e.g., intervention length correlating with types of outcomes). For each of these moderators, the mixed-effects model is defined as follows:

$$g_{jk} = \beta_0 + \beta_1 X_{jk} + \text{Domain}_{jk} + u_k + e_{jk},$$

where β_1 is the estimated fixed effect of moderator X_{jk} and Domain_{jk} is a vector of fixed effects controlling for the classroom practice outcome domain.

Due to an excess of missing information, we were not able to estimate mixed-effects models for all of the variables coded (e.g., student characteristics). And, for the variables (or moderators) we did include in our analyses, only subsets of studies were included in each analysis due to some missingness across studies. As a result, we often lack power to detect statistically significant effects and discuss the results in terms of the magnitudes (or size) of the effects.

Estimating Heterogeneity

We estimated heterogeneity using I^2. I^2 represents the percentage of variation across studies that is due to heterogeneity rather than chance and may be thought of as the proportion of total variation in the treatment effects that is due to variation between studies (Higgins & Thompson, 2002; Higgins, Thompson, Deeks, & Altman, 2003). The I^2 statistic may be estimated as follows:

$$I^2 = 100(Q - df)/Q,$$

where Q is Cochran's (1950) measure of heterogeneity:

$$Q = \sum w_{jk} \left(g_{jk} - \hat{\mu}_F \right)^2$$

and w_{jk} and $\hat{\mu}_F$ denote the weights and weighted average, respectively, from the fixed effects model.[8] Q follows a χ^2 distribution with $df = j - 1$.

To further characterize variation in how classroom practice responds to intervention, we also provide a 95% prediction interval for the estimated average effect (i.e., Borenstein, Higgins, Hedges, & Rothstein, 2017). The prediction interval provides the range of effect sizes that one would expect to see in future studies 95% of the time, based on the current analysis. Operationally, a 95% prediction interval is defined as follows:

$$PI_{95\%} = \hat{\beta}_0 \pm 1.96 \left(\hat{\tau} \right),$$

where $\hat{\beta}$ is the average effect size estimate and $\hat{\tau}$ is the square root of the estimated between-study heterogeneity parameter (i.e., the estimated standard deviation of true population effects), estimated with restricted maximum likelihood.

Adjusting for Effect Size Dependencies

Most studies included multiple effects per study due to the measurement of multiple outcomes or samples. Effects from the same study are dependent on one another and may be correlated, and these dependencies are not fully corrected through specifying study-specific random effects in the analytic model. To account for these effect size dependencies and adjust the variance of the model estimates, we used robust variance estimation when estimating our random- and mixed-effects models. The equations for robust variance estimation can be found in Hedges, Tipton, and Johnson (2010) and Tipton (2014), and the R package, *robumeta*, is available in Fisher and Tipton (2015). We set ρ, the within-study effect-size correlation used to fit the correlated effects meta-regression models to 0.53, based on the overall mean effect across all studies.

Adjusting for Publication Bias

Although we tried to combat publication bias by searching for gray literature, we realize it is not possible to track down every unpublished classroom practice study ever conducted. Thus, we explored the impact of publication bias on each meta-analysis using Citkowicz and Vevea's (2017) beta-density weight-function model.[9] The selection model provides adjusted meta-analytic mean estimates and tests for publication bias, allowing us to examine the degree to which publication bias is an issue in the given meta-analysis. Moreover, the model allows for the inclusion of moderators into the model, allowing us to examine publication bias in the mixed-effects models.

FINDINGS

Results of the Search Process

Using this approach for the systematic literature search, we identified 40 studies for inclusion (see Figure 3 for a depiction of the literature search and retrieval process and Table 1 for the list of included studies). Because studies typically included multiple outcomes, we extracted 321 effects from the 40 included studies.

The studies were coded for all relevant effect sizes for impacts on instructional practice, in addition to coding for a range of intervention, observation measure and contextual factors. See Table 2 for summary information on the studies and the study features that were coded. Full references for the coded studies can be found in Appendix B (available in the online version of the journal).

Meta-Analytic Findings

In our discussion of the meta-analytic findings, we focus primarily on the magnitudes of the effects. Drawing on guidelines from the What Works Clearinghouse (Institute of Education Sciences, 2017), we consider effect sizes (or differences in effect sizes when making group comparisons) of 0.10 to 0.25 medium sized and suggestive, and effect sizes greater than 0.25 sufficiently large to be of substantive interest.

As explained earlier, the nature of moderator or subgroup meta-analyses typically offers limited power, and so relying solely on standard significance tests may be insufficient for interpreting results. Therefore, we examine significance and also discuss the effect sizes and the prediction intervals associated with the average effects.

We find that, on average, the randomized field trials targeting classroom practice yielded a positive, statistically significant effect of 0.42 (0.07) standard deviations based on classroom observations, as presented in Table 3. While this is promising, our results also give caution: We observed a substantial amount of heterogeneity across effect sizes. Our estimated I^2 indicates that 73% of the total variation in our estimates of the treatment effect is due to heterogeneity between effects rather than within effects (e.g., sampling error). Moreover, our absolute effect sizes range from –0.94 to

TABLE 1

Studies Included in Meta-Analysis

Study	Number of Effects	Number of Teachers	School Level	Outcome Domains	Intervention Features
Grigg, Kelly, Gamoran, and Borman (2013)	18	285	Elementary	Instruction	Group training
Cordray, Pion, Brandt, Molefe, and Toby (2012)	8	172	Elementary	Instruction	Individual training, group training, instructional materials
C. C. Johnson and Fargo (2010)	1	14	Middle	Overall effectiveness	Individual training, group training, instructional materials
Nelson-Walker et al. (2013)	13	42	Elementary	Instruction	Individual training, group training, instructional materials
Lowry (2007)	4	53	Elementary, middle, high	Instruction	Individual training, group training
Cappella et al. (2015)	4	120	Elementary	Classroom environment	Group training, instructional materials
Nugent et al. (2016)	6	92	Middle, high	Instruction, overall effectiveness	Individual training, group training
Gregory, Allen, Mikami, Hafen, and Pianta (2014)	5	87	Middle, high	Classroom environment, instruction	Individual training, group training
DeCesare, McClelland, and Randel (2017)	6	74	Elementary	Classroom environment, instruction, overall effectiveness	Individual training, group training
Parkinson, Salinger, Meakin, and Smith (2015)	2	130	Elementary	Classroom environment, instruction	Individual training, group training, instructional materials
Doabler (2010)	3	65	Elementary	Instruction	Individual training, group training
Reinke, Herman, and Dong (2014)	1	105	Elementary	Classroom environment	Individual training, group training

(continued)

TABLE 1 (CONTINUED)

Study	Number of Effects	Number of Teachers	School Level	Outcome Domains	Intervention Features
Wanzek et al. (2015)	2	24	Middle	Classroom environment, overall effectiveness	Individual training, group training, instructional materials
Abry, Rimm-Kaufman, Larsen, and Brewer (2013)	1	239	Elementary	Overall effectiveness	Individual training, group training, instructional materials
Meyers et al. (2016)	4	158	Middle	Classroom environment, instruction	Individual training, group training
Ottmar, Rimm-Kaufman, Larsen, and Berry (2015)	2	88	Elementary	Instruction, overall effectiveness	Individual training, group training
Evertson (1989)	69	29	Elementary, middle	Classroom environment, instruction	Group training
Goodson, Wolf, Bell, Turner, and Finney (2010)	3	128	Elementary	Classroom environment, instruction	Individual training, group training
Ottmar, Rimm-Kaufman, Berry, and Larsen (2013)	1	88	Elementary	Instruction	Individual training, group training
Simmons (2010)	5	60	Middle	Classroom environment	Individual training, group training
Motoca et al. (2014)	22	138	Middle	Classroom environment	Individual training, group training
Santagata, Kersting, Givvin, and Stigler (2011)	3	44	Middle	Instruction	Individual training, group training
Faraclas (2015)	6	24	Middle, high	Classroom environment, instruction, overall effectiveness	Individual training, group training
Supovitz (2013)	4	64	Elementary	Instruction	Individual training, group training
Doabler et al. (2014)	7	129	Elementary	Instruction	Group training, instructional materials
Jacob, Hill, and Corey (2017)	4	57	Elementary	Instruction	Group training
L. D. Johnson et al. (2014)	10	43	Elementary, middle	Classroom environment	Individual training, instructional materials

(continued)

TABLE 1 (CONTINUED)

Study	Number of Effects	Number of Teachers	School Level	Outcome Domains	Intervention Features
Garet et al. (2016)	6	165	Elementary	Instruction	Individual training, group training
Garet et al. (2008)	12	330	Elementary	Instruction	Individual training, group training
Brown, Jones, LaRusso, and Aber (2010)	3	82	Elementary	Classroom environment, instruction	Individual training, group training, instructional materials
Matsumura, Garnier, and Spybrook (2012)	3	93	Elementary	Instruction	Individual training, group training
Garet et al. (2017)	12	997	Elementary, middle	Classroom environment, instruction	Individual training, group training
Connor et al. (2011)	1	25	Elementary	Instruction	Individual training, group training, instructional materials
Vadasy, Sanders, and Logan Herrera (2015)	30	61	Elementary	Instruction	Group training, instructional materials
Gersten, Dimino, Jayanthi, Kim, and Santoro (2010)	6	81	Elementary	Instruction	Group training, instructional materials
Glazerman et al. (2008)	6	631	Elementary, middle	Classroom environment, instruction	Individual training, group training
Baker, Santoro, L., Biancarrosa, and Baker (2015)	1	39	Elementary	Instruction	Individual training, group training, instructional materials
Bos et al. (2012)	9	527	Middle	Instruction, overall effectiveness	Individual training, group training, instructional materials
Garet et al. (2010)	12	358	Middle	Instruction	Individual training, group training, instructional materials
Blazar and Kraft (2015); Kraft and Blazar (2013, 2017)	6	184	Elementary, middle, high	Classroom environment, instruction	Individual training, group training

TABLE 2
Study Characteristics

	N	k
Year of publication		
Prior to 2013	16	148
2013 or later	24	173
Teacher sample size		
Less than 100 teachers	28	222
100 or more teachers	12	99
Years of teaching experience		
Up to 10 years	14	91
More than 10 years	19	196
School levels included		
Grades K–5	29	246
Grades 6–8	17	182
Grades 9–12	5	27
Intervention features		
Individual training	33	177
Regular coach	10	59
Structured protocol for coaching	15	118
Instructional materials	16	110
Teacher-driven learning	6	26
Technology enhanced	9	57
Focus on using data to inform instruction	10	61
Active learning/practice in training	17	92
Intervention length		
≤26 weeks	8	99
>26 to ≤52 weeks	17	124
>52 weeks	9	67
Intervention hours		
≤20 hours	9	144
>20 hours to ≤100 hours	14	112
>100 hours	6	23
Timing of observational measurement		
Mid-stream/during	10	91
Directly after	30	151
After time passed	2	14
Combination	12	75
Total	40	321

Note. N = number of studies; k = number of effect sizes.

TABLE 3
Overall Mean Effects and Mean Effects by Instructional Practice Constructs

Construct	M	SE	Confidence Interval		N	k	I^2	τ^2	Prediction Interval	
			Lower	Upper					Lower	Upper
All effects	0.42	0.07	0.28	0.56	40	321	72.60	0.16	-0.38	1.22
Broad domain										
Classroom environment	0.27	0.08	0.10	0.44	17	112	51.76	0.07	-0.24	0.78
Instruction	0.46	0.08	0.29	0.63	32	198	76.69	0.18	-0.38	1.30
Overall effectiveness	0.49	0.29	-0.20	1.18	8	11	84.90	0.44	-0.82	1.79
Constructs within broad domains										
Classroom environment										
Aggregate environment[a]	0.32	0.13	-0.03	0.67	6	22	52.37	0.07	-0.21	0.85
Classroom culture	0.16	0.06	0.01	0.31	9	32	41.02	0.03	-0.21	0.53
Classroom management	0.43	0.24	-0.17	1.02	7	58	57.02	0.24	-0.52	1.38
Instruction										
ELA content	0.55	0.16	0.13	0.96	6	49	84.70	0.30	-0.53	1.62
Math content	0.31	0.04	0.20	0.41	7	21	0.00	0.00	0.31	0.31
Instructional format	0.21	0.08	0.03	0.40	10	22	16.07	0.01	0.00	0.43
Discourse[b]	0.28	0.10	0.05	0.50	11	43	53.07	0.08	-0.26	0.82
Student engagement	0.46	0.12	0.14	0.79	6	11	69.12	0.11	-0.18	1.10
General/aggregate instruction[c]	0.64	0.20	0.20	1.07	15	35	85.78	0.34	-0.50	1.78

Note. Rho (ρ) was set to 0.53, based on the overall mean effect across all studies. ELA = English language arts; N = number of studies; k = number of effect sizes; I^2 = proportion of the total variance due to between effect size heterogeneity; τ^2 = total effect size heterogeneity.

[a]"Aggregate environment" includes measures that aggregated across two or more items capturing classroom environment.

[b]"Discourse" construct includes questioning, discussion, and formative assessment.

[c]"General/aggregate instruction" includes measures that aggregated across two or more items capturing instruction, or overall instructional measures.

2.76 standard deviations, with a 95% prediction interval of –0.38 to 1.22. This indicates that while classroom practice is responsive to intervention, there is substantial variation in the average population effects. Additionally, in our subgroup analyses that focus on specific aspects of instruction, the findings consistently demonstrate positive and mostly significant results across the different constructs, ranging from 0.16 (0.06) for classroom culture to 0.64 (0.20) for general instruction (see Table 3). Again, the findings further indicate substantial variability in effects across studies (with the exception of mathematics content) as observed by the wide confidence and prediction intervals and the high I^2s, ranging from 16% to 86%.

Additionally, we considered how the timing of a classroom observation measurement could be associated with the effect sizes, presented in Table 4. We did this through a moderator analysis that considered differences among effects that were measured during an intervention (i.e., while the intervention was ongoing and active), immediately after it ended (i.e., the first postintervention outcome assessment), or after some period of time had passed after the intervention (i.e., after the first postintervention outcome assessment). We found the largest effects among classroom observations measured right after an intervention completed (0.31), and only slightly smaller effects after time had passed (0.29) and during the intervention (0.26). While the differences were not statistically significant, this suggests that teachers may experience contemporaneous improvements in practice during interventions, which may taper off some shortly after an intervention ends but then plateau and potentially maintain for some time.

Intervention Intensity

We conducted additional moderator analyses to explore differences in effect sizes by the length of time over which an intervention occurred, the number of hours of the intervention, and when the observation of instruction occurred (Table 4). Appendix D (available in the online version of the journal) presents supplemental moderator analysis tables that include confidence and prediction intervals for the conditional means.

We first explored how intervention intensity could relate to effects by considering the total weeks the intervention lasted from start to end. Based on the patterns we observed in our data, we created three mutually exclusive categories, indicating whether an intervention lasted 26 weeks or fewer, over 26 and up to 52 weeks, or over 52 weeks long. We used the category indicating the shortest duration (26 weeks or fewer) as our reference group and conducted moderator analyses comparing the two longer duration categories to this group. We found the largest mean effects among interventions that lasted 26 or fewer weeks (0.43) compared with those that lasted 26 to 52 weeks (a mean of 0.28, or –0.15 *SD* lower than the reference group), and compared with interventions that lasted over 52 weeks (a mean of 0.24, or –0.19 *SD* lower than the reference group). Again, while the differences were not significant, we consider the magnitude of the differences suggestive. While not shown, when plotting effects by length of intervention, we noticed that studies of interventions with a

TABLE 4

Mean Effects by Timing of Observations and Intervention Intensity

Intervention Feature	M	SE	N	Δ From Reference Group	SE	p Value
Timing of observational measurement						
Mid-stream/during (reference group)	0.26	0.13	10			
Directly after	0.31	0.10	30	0.05	0.12	0.67
After time passed	0.29	0.50	2	0.03	0.51	0.96
Combination	0.36	0.15	12	0.10	0.17	0.56
Intervention length						
≤26 weeks (reference group)	0.43	0.23	8			
>26 to ≤52 weeks	0.28	0.17	17	−0.15	0.31	0.63
>52 weeks	0.24	0.16	9	−0.19	0.30	0.54
Intervention hours						
≤20 hours (reference group)	0.37	0.14	9			
>20 hours to ≤100 hours	0.39	0.14	14	0.02	0.16	0.90
>100 hours	0.33	0.16	6	−0.04	0.19	0.83

Note. Rho (ρ) was set to 0.53, based on the overall mean effect across all studies. N = number of studies; Δ = difference between the reference group and group of interest (i.e., the slope estimate $\hat{\beta}_g$).

longer duration had more variation in effects (i.e., the effects were not as consistent) compared with shorter duration studies, which tended to cluster around a particular mean effect.

To approach the question of intervention intensity slightly differently, we also examined differences in means by the number of program hours reported. Again, we empirically derived three categories based on our data, this time categorizing interventions according to whether they lasted 20 hours or fewer, over 20 up to 100 hours, or over 100 hours. We used the smallest category (20 hours or fewer) as our reference group to compare against the two longer duration categories. We found no significant or substantive differences comparing those with 20 or fewer hours to interventions with 20 to 100 hours or greater than 100 hours. This suggests that teachers are just as likely to benefit in less intensive interventions than more intensive ones.

Intervention Features

Of the intervention features that we analyzed in the moderator meta-analyses (Table 5), we did not find any statistically significant outcomes indicating particularly salient approaches to professional learning, but the magnitude of the results suggests a number of potential insights.

We examined effect sizes associated with interventions that had an individualized training component. Of the 33 interventions that included an individualized

TABLE 5
Mean Effects by Intervention Features

Intervention Feature	M	SE	N	Comparison Feature	M	SE	N	Δ	SE	p Value
Individual training	0.33	0.09	33	No individual training	0.17	0.11	8	0.16	0.11	0.17
Established coach	0.14	0.13	10	Other coach	0.42	0.12	18	0.28	0.16	0.09
In-person + remote training	0.43	0.22	6	In-person only	0.31	0.13	23	0.12	0.25	0.64
Structured observation protocol for coaching	0.21	0.10	15	No structured observation protocol used/described	0.49	0.15	18	-0.28	0.17	0.11
Active learning/practice	0.43	0.15	17	No active learning/practice described	0.25	0.09	24	0.18	0.15	0.23
Focus on using data to inform instruction	0.45	0.22	10	No focus on using data	0.26	0.10	30	0.19	0.24	0.44
Instructional materials	0.38	0.14	16	No instructional materials	0.27	0.10	24	0.11	0.17	0.53
Teacher-driven learning	0.34	0.25	6	Not teacher driven	0.31	0.09	34	0.03	0.26	0.92
Technology enhanced	0.37	0.19	9	No technology	0.29	0.11	31	0.07	0.23	0.75
Summer + school year	0.29	0.09	21	No summer	0.39	0.12	19	-0.10	0.08	0.23

Note. Rho (ρ) was set to 0.53, based on the overall mean effect across all studies. N = number of studies; Δ = difference between the group means (i.e., the slope estimate $\hat{\beta}_1$).

component (most often coaching), the average effect was 0.33, which was 0.16 standard deviations higher than the mean effects from the 8 interventions that did not include an individualized component (with a mean of 0.17). In a closer look among the subset of 33 interventions with individualized training, we compared effect sizes for interventions that used an established coach or trainer, such as using an established building or district-based coach or a full-time professional development provider, compared with effect sizes where someone took on the coach or trainer role specifically for the purposes of the study. We found that mean effects for the 10 studies that had an established coach (0.14) were smaller than the mean effects for the 18 studies that had a coach who either took on the coach role specifically for study or for whom there was no description (0.42). The difference in effects was 0.28 standard deviations, although this was again not statistically significant. We also found that interventions using a combination of remote and in-person coaching had higher mean effects by 0.12 standard deviations compared with interventions with only in-person training. Surprisingly, we found lower mean effects (0.28 standard deviation lower average) among studies that identified using a structured protocol for observation and feedback (0.21), compared with studies that allowed ad hoc feedback processes or that simply didn't specify the process in the intervention description (0.49).

We found several other potential indications of useful intervention features, all with insignificant but medium-sized differences in mean effects comparing among groups. Specifically, we found positive differences in group means in favor of interventions that provide teacher active learning opportunities to apply and practice the instructional skills during the training (0.18), training teachers to use data to guide their instruction (0.19), and including instructional materials (0.11). On the other hand, interventions that lasted over the school year and summer (0.29) produced smaller effects than interventions that did not include time over the summer (0.39). The other intervention features we considered—descriptions of teacher-driven learning and technology-enhanced learning experiences—yielded small changes, falling below our threshold of 0.1 to indicate something of potential substantive interest.

Grade Band and Teacher Experience

When considering the grade span of teachers included in a study (Table 6), our findings suggest that, compared with studies that included elementary school teachers (0.30), studies with middle school teachers had smaller average effects (0.27) and studies with high school teachers had larger mean effects (0.49). Neither of these were significantly different. We view the differences by grade band as suggestive of differences worth noting. However, given the small number of studies and effect sizes that include high school teachers, we interpret these results with extra caution.

TABLE 6
Mean Effects by Grade Band and Teacher Experience

Teaching Grade Span	No			Yes			Δ	SE	p Value
	M	SE	N	M	SE	N			
Grades K–5	0.33	0.17	11	0.30	0.10	29	–0.03	0.19	0.86
Grades 6–8	0.38	0.11	23	0.27	0.11	17	–0.11	0.16	0.49
Grades 9–12	0.28	0.09	35	0.49	0.33	5	0.20	0.35	0.59
More than 10 years of teaching experience	0.12	0.11	14	0.36	0.13	19	0.24	0.16	0.14

Note. Rho (ρ) was set to 0.53, based on the overall mean effect across all studies. N = number of studies; Δ = difference between the group means (i.e., the slope estimate $\hat{\beta}_1$). Studies with teachers across multiple grade bands are included in each category; therefore, the groups are not mutually exclusive.

While information on years of experience for teacher samples was often unreported or reported inconsistently, we were able to classify samples as averaging more than 10 years of experience or less among the studies that presented teacher experience information. Analyses indicated that impacts based on samples of teachers with 10 or more years of experience were higher (0.24 standard deviations) than impacts from samples of teachers with fewer than 10 years of experience, although for both groups the means were still positive (0.36 for the more experienced samples and 0.12 for the less experienced samples). Unfortunately, due to limited and inconsistent reporting about teacher characteristics across studies, we were not able to examine other teacher characteristics.

Study Features

Table 7 presents results from several additional analyses that consider features of the research studies. First, we wanted to consider whether the field was potentially getting more effective in developing useful teacher learning experiences, and so we looked separately at studies published more recently, that is, 2013 or later, compared with those published before 2013. We did not find meaningful differences in this comparison. Given the recent interest in coaching in particular, we looked at studies using this publication year divide among the interventions that included an individualized training component. We found some suggestion that more recent studies have been more effective (0.17 *SD* higher means) among these studies.

Finally, we compared impacts from studies with fewer than 100 teachers with those with 100 or more teachers. Analyses indicate an average effect size that is 0.25 standard deviations larger among the studies with fewer teachers, which meets our criteria for being of substantive interest, and this is also the one contrast we found that was statistically significant. While not examined through this study, one potential explanation is that studies with more teachers represent scale-up studies and

TABLE 7
Mean Effects by Study Features

Study Feature	No			Yes					
	M	SE	N	M	SE	N	Δ	SE	p Value
Study published in 2013 or later	0.25	0.13	16	0.33	0.10	24	0.08	0.15	0.61
Study published in 2013 or later (individual component only)	0.19	0.14	14	0.36	0.11	19	0.17	0.17	0.32
Total teacher N was less than 100	0.16	0.11	12	0.41	0.10	28	0.25	0.12	0.05

Note. Rho (ρ) was set to 0.53, based on the overall mean effect across all studies. N = number of studies; Δ = difference between the group means (i.e., the slope estimate $\hat{\beta}_1$).

reflect the difficulties of scaling teacher professional development. Alternatively, this may be a sign of publication bias, since studies with fewer teachers would need larger effects to be statistically significant, and therefore of interest for publication. We discuss publication bias next.

Publication Bias

The results of the publication bias analyses indicate that substantial publication bias is present in our set of meta-analyses. Using Citkowicz and Vevea's (2017) beta-density weight-function model, the overall estimate of 0.34[10] was adjusted upward to 0.86 standard deviations.[11] This result implies that larger effect size estimates with smaller p values are underrepresented in the literature that we synthesized; the opposite direction of what is typically associated with publication bias. The adjustment might not be as substantial with the inclusion of quasi-experimental study effect size estimates, given that they tend to be larger than randomized controlled trial results (Cheung & Slavin, 2016). Tables C1 and C2 in Appendix C (available in the online version of the journal) also present the publication bias results for the individual construct analyses and moderator analyses. With a few exceptions, the results are similar across all analyses such that the adjusted estimate is larger when adjusted for publication bias. While the true population effects are likely somewhere between the unadjusted and adjusted estimates, our analyses do not provide strong evidence of selective reporting as a function of statistical significance. That is, the estimated average effect is likely an underestimate of the true population effect.

DISCUSSION
Is Classroom Practice Responsive When Targeted Through Professional Learning Programs?

Our results indicate that interventions directly targeting classroom practice through professional learning can bring about meaningful shifts in practice as measured through classroom observation. We find that the effects of these interventions are on average positive, and the magnitude of the changes in classroom practice are substantively notable. Moreover, these findings generalize across multiple domains and subconstructs of observed classroom practice. This indicates that the responsiveness of classroom practice is not tied to a specific aspect of observable practice, and likewise that interventions can support teachers in developing different types of classroom practice skills. From this, we conclude that teachers stand to benefit from professional learning opportunities designed to promote their classroom practice development across a range of areas.

Moreover, our results suggest that teachers can continue to develop their expertise over their career. Although we could only examine the relationship of teacher experience with responsiveness of practice in a coarsened way due to limitations in reporting of teacher experience in the studies, our results are suggestive of greater intervention effects for samples of teachers with an average teaching tenure of more than 10 years. This may be surprising given prior research noting that novice teachers have lower instructional effectiveness and make particularly large improvements during their first years on the job (Desimone, Hochberg, & McMaken, 2016; Kini & Podolsky, 2016). Given the poor quality of information available for us to meta-analyze teacher experience, we do not wish to make too much of this finding, other than to point out the implication that classroom practice likely is a malleable factor for teachers across a range of tenure years, and even experienced teachers may be able to make observable and substantive shifts in their practice.

Can We Identify "Active Ingredients" in Professional Learning That Are Associated With Positive Changes in Classroom Practice?

While our findings provide strong evidence for the responsiveness of classroom practice when targeted through professional learning opportunities, the findings also highlight an important caution about the wide variability of how much classroom practice actually changes through a given intervention or implementation. The studies in this meta-analysis yielded effect sizes that varied from large and negative, to small and negligible, and to large and positive. This variation creates uncertainty about how much classroom practice will change in a given instance, and requires further exploration to understand identifiable sources of the heterogeneity in classroom practice outcomes.

One key question is then whether we can identify specific approaches to professional learning that appear particularly beneficial to promoting positive shifts in classroom practice; our findings did not uncover any "silver bullet" to promote effective classroom practices, but the results do suggest several things. First, our findings indicate the promise of including some kind of individual, personalized training component for teachers to develop their classroom practice. This likely aligns with conventional wisdom that individualized professional learning (e.g., coaching) is beneficial—reflected in the fact that only 8 of the 41 interventions[12] studied did not include some kind of individual component—but our meta-analysis provides empirical evidence to support the idea.

Beyond individualized training, our results suggest two other professional learning features worth noting. Our findings suggest the benefit of allowing teachers active learning opportunities where they may directly engage with or apply what they are learning during the context of the training. This coincides with earlier research that has identified the importance of allowing teachers active learning opportunities in professional development for yielding improvements in instruction (Desimone, Porter, Garet, Yoon, & Birman, 2002) and research that has found classroom practice improves when teachers are given opportunities for deliberate practice of instruction across multiple settings (Ericsson, 2006; Grossman, Hammerness, & McDonald, 2009; Lampert et al., 2013). We used a liberal approach to capturing active learning opportunities, considering it part of an intervention either through a specific description of the active learning opportunity or if the study simply stated that the approach included active learning, for example. We recognize that we were only able to capture this very broadly, which likely implies measurement error, but that measurement error would attenuate the findings and so the extent to which we see positive benefits in light of this is particularly interesting. Last, we also find suggestive evidence in support of helping teachers use student data to inform their instruction. Research has pointed to the increased emphasis of data-driven decision making to inform instruction over the last decade in response to accountability policy initiatives, but actual practices implemented vary and are inconsistent (Datnow & Hubbard, 2015). With the increased prevalence of available data and the suggested benefit through these findings, this may be an aspect of professional learning worth further study.

In contrast to these areas of promise, our findings also shed some light on what may be less useful or necessary for supporting development of teacher classroom practice. Specifically, we find no indication that interventions that have higher number of hours or last over a longer window of time provide enhanced benefits to classroom practice. In some ways this is counterintuitive, since *prima facie*, further support would presumably be linked to increased benefits. However, this result was also found in a meta-analysis of coaching studies (Kraft et al., 2018). One potential explanation is that longer, more intensive professional learning interventions may include a broader focus, while shorter interventions may include more narrowly targeted focal areas, producing larger effects in those targeted areas. For example, some researchers argue that teachers master complex forms of instruction when they first work on smaller routines and then build up to more complex activity (e.g., see Cai et al., 2017a, 2017b; Kraft & Blazar, 2017).

Is Classroom Practice Responsive Enough to Target in Short-Cycle Professional Learning Approaches?

Building on the finding that shorter, less intensive interventions yielded similar outcomes to those that were longer and more intensive, our results further suggest that classroom practice is malleable and responsive to intervention quickly enough to target in short-cycle professional learning approaches. We find that classroom practice effects measured midstream to the intervention were not meaningfully lower compared with when they were observed after the intervention, indicating that it is responsive and improvements can be found even before an intervention is fully implemented. Taken together with the findings that a larger dosage is not necessarily needed, this suggests that short-cycle, continuous improvement efforts to address classroom practice may be successful, and in fact may be an efficient way to support improvements in classroom practice.

What Are the Implications for Scaling Interventions to Improve Classroom Practice?

While these findings support the promise of improving classroom practice through intervention, they may also suggest the challenges in scaling programs. As discussed previously, our analysis contrasting studies with greater than 100 teachers to those with fewer indicated smaller benefits to classroom practice among studies including more teachers. This was the only moderator we analyzed that was both of substantive size and statistically significant. We also found that among studies with an individualized training component, there were larger effects in studies that either described using a coach that provided services specifically for the study or did not provide a description of the coach background compared with studies that described coaches as individuals who regularly provide coaching outside the study context. This may possibly reflect the difficulties of scale-up as well, since delivering professional learning across a larger group of teachers typically requires working with local coaches and trainers. In our data, the average number of teachers per study with an established coach was 154.5 teachers, compared with 111.6 teachers among studies that engaged people to coach specifically for study purposes or did not describe the coaches' backgrounds, lending some support to this connection. In smaller studies, such as efficacy trials, the program developers may be more likely to deliver the training and require fewer coaches. Larger studies may require more coaches and introduce greater variation in coaching effectiveness and implementation fidelity. Taken together, our findings provide further impetus to the field that continued research and work is needed to understand how to deliver effective professional learning opportunities focused on classroom practice at scale.

Directions for Future Research

Educator instructional effectiveness continues to be an important area of policy and a focal area for educators where substantial resources are spent. The findings from this meta-analysis provide strong empirical support for the potential to improve classroom practice through professional learning interventions, although research must continue to seek the most effective ways to provide useful learning opportunities. One critical next step will be to continue the meta-analysis of these studies to identify links between changes in classroom practice with changes in student outcomes. While large-scale, rigorous research on content-focused professional development has produced disappointing results in terms of improvements to student achievement, there is a need to identify the professional learning approaches or types of classroom practices that are most often associated with improved student outcomes and thus may provide a focus for new professional learning programs (Garet, Heppen, Walters, Smith, & Yang, 2016), and further meta-analyses tying changes in classroom practice to changes in student outcomes may help meet this need.

Our results also provide guidance for the design of research studies. For example, the average effect sizes identified through this work can inform power calculations when designing new research. These results support powering a study for larger effect sizes for classroom practice outcomes, compared with effects for student achievement outcomes (Hedges & Hedberg, 2007). The heterogeneity of the distribution of observed effects can also inform Bayesian analytic approaches that need estimates of not only the mean but also the level of uncertainty based on the expected distribution. Furthermore, our ability to understand effects of interventions would be enhanced by more in-depth information about implementation and implementation context (e.g., Hill, Corey, & Jacob, 2018). This could be achieved through mixed-methods approaches that provide deeper and qualitative explorations of how interventions were implemented and teacher experiences both during the professional learning and as they seek to apply their learning to the classroom. Future research thus can use the insights from these findings to inform evaluation design and analysis, as we work as a field to continue to build knowledge in the critical area of effective teaching.

ACKNOWLEDGMENTS

The authors thank Jane Coggshall, Mike Garet, Josh Polanin, Andrew Wayne, and members of the O2 Lab at American Institutes for Research for helpful comments and suggestions.

NOTES

Supplemental material is available for this article in the online version of the journal.

[1]The Web of Knowledge search was performed only in Social Science Citations and Social Science Conference Proceedings. Moreover, Web of Knowledge does not support full-text searching, thus the search was conducted in the default fields, as opposed to the fields specified in our search terms.

[2]The studies were grouped into those focused solely on Pre-K and Grades K–12 due to their differing focuses on interventions and outcomes only after the literature search was completed.

[3]The authors are currently in the process of conducting a separate study focusing on pre-K samples.

[4]The pooled standard deviation may be computed by $\sqrt{\dfrac{\left(N^T - 1\right)S_T^2 + \left(N^C - 1\right)S_C^2}{N^T + N^C - 2}}$.

[5]Adjustment is not necessary if teachers are randomly assigned within schools and school fixed effects are included in the analysis model.

[6]The intraclass correlation represents the amount of variance that is found between the

clusters (or teachers), relative to the total variation. It may be estimated by $\rho = \dfrac{\sigma_B^2}{\sigma_B^2 + \sigma_W^2}$,

where σ_B^2 and σ_W^2 are the between- and within-cluster variances. These were rarely reported by study authors. For studies where ρ, or information to calculate ρ, was not reported, we imputed the average of all calculated ρs, 0.18.

[7]When each sample in the analysis produces a single effect size, $j = k$.

[8]The fixed-effects model is estimated using the same approach as the random-effects model, with the exception that the fixed-effects model assumes that the effects are homogenous and omits the between-study heterogeneity statistic τ^2 from the model.

[9]Citkowicz and Vevea's (2017) beta-density weight-function model uses the beta density to explicitly model the selection process, or process by which studies are assumed to be chosen for publication. It then adjusts the meta-analytic results for publication bias by multiplying the usual probability density function for the effect-size model (i.e., a standard meta-analytic model) by the selection model.

[10]The overall estimate presented in Table 3 (0.42) is computed while adjusting for effect size dependencies. Currently, no publication bias method exists that allows for the simultaneous adjustment of effect size dependencies and publication bias. Thus, our publication bias adjustment is conducted on the meta-analytic mean that is unadjusted for effect size dependencies (0.34).

[11]We also used Vevea and Hedges's (1995) step-function model to adjust the meta-analytic estimates for publication bias and obtained similar results. The overall estimate was also adjusted upward, to 0.68 standard deviations.

[12]One study included two interventions, resulting in 41 interventions across 40 studies.

REFERENCES

Aaronson, D., Barrow, L., & Sander, W. (2007). Teachers and student achievement in the Chicago public high schools. *Journal of Labor Economics, 25*, 95–135.

Blank, R. K., & de las Alas, N. (2009). The effects of teacher professional development on gains in student achievement: How meta-analysis provides scientific evidence useful to education leaders. Retrieved from https://eric.ed.gov/?id=ED544700

Borenstein, M., Hedges, L. V., Higgins, J. P. T., & Rothstein, H. R. (2009). *Introduction to meta-analysis* (1st ed.). Chichester, England: Wiley.

Borenstein, M., Higgins, J. P. T., Hedges, L. V., & Rothstein, H. R. (2017). Basics of meta-analysis: I^2 is not an absolute measure of heterogeneity. *Research Synthesis Methods, 8*, 5–18. doi:10.1002/jrsm.1230

Cai, J., Morris, A., Hohensee, C., Hwang, S., Robison, V., & Hiebert, J. (2017a). Clarifying the impact of educational research on learning opportunities. *Journal for Research in Mathematics Education, 48*, 230–236.

Cai, J., Morris, A., Hohensee, C., Hwang, S., Robison, V., & Hiebert, J. (2017b). Making classroom implementation an integral part of research. *Journal for Research in Mathematics Education, 48*, 342–347.

Chamberlin, G. E. (2013). Predictive effects of teachers and schools on test scores, college attendance, and earnings. *Proceedings of the National Academy of Sciences of the United States of America, 110*(43), 17176–17182.

Cheung, A. C. K., & Slavin, R. E. (2016). How methodological features affect effect sizes in education. *Educational Researcher, 45*, 283–292. doi:10.3102/0013189X16656615

Citkowicz, M., & Vevea, J. L. (2017). A parsimonious weight function for modeling publication bias. *Psychological Methods, 22*, 28–41. doi:10.1037/met0000119

Cochran, W. G. (1950). The comparison of percentage in matched samples. *Biometrica, 37*, 256–266. doi:10.1093/biomet/37.3-4.256

Cronbach, L. J. (1982). *Designing evaluations of educational and social programs* (1st ed.). San Francisco, CA: Jossey-Bass.

Danielson, C. (2013). *The framework for teaching evaluation instrument.* Princeton, NJ: Danielson Group.

Datnow, A., & Hubbard, L. (2015). Teachers' use of assessment data to inform instruction: Lessons from the past and prospects for the future. *Teachers College Record, 117*(4), 1–26.

Desimone, L., Hochberg, D., & McMaken, J. (2016). Teacher knowledge and instructional quality of beginning teachers: Growth and linkages. *Teachers College Record, 118*(5), 1–54.

Desimone, L., Porter, A., Garet, M., Yoon, K., & Birman, B. (2002). Effects of professional development on teachers' instruction: Results from a three-year longitudinal study. *Educational Evaluation and Policy Analysis, 24*, 81–112.

Ericsson, K. A. (2006). The influence of experience and deliberate practice on the development of superior expert performance. In K. A. Ericsson, N. Charness, P. J. Feltovich, & R. R. Hoffman (Eds.), *The Cambridge handbook of expertise and expert performance* (pp. 683–703). Cambridge, England: Cambridge University Press.

Fisher, Z., & Tipton, E. (2015). *robumeta: Robust variance meta-regression* (R package version 1.6). Retrieved from http://CRAN.R-project.org/package=robumeta

Garet, M. S., Heppen, J. B., Walters, K., Smith, T. M., & Yang, R. (2016). *Does content-focused teacher professional development work? Findings from three Institute of Education Sciences studies* (NCEE 2017-4010). Washington, DC: National Center for Education Evaluation and Regional Assistance, Institute of Education Sciences, U.S. Department of Education. Retrieved from http://ies.ed.gov/ncee/pubs/20174010/pdf/20174010.pdf

Gersten, R., Chard, D., Jayanthi, M., Baker, S., Morphy, P., & Flojo, J. (2009). Mathematics instruction for students with learning disabilities: A meta-analysis of instructional components. *Review of Educational Research, 79*, 1202–1242.

Goldhaber, D. D. (2002). The mystery of good teaching. *Education Next, 2*, 50–55.

Grossman, P., Hammerness, K., & McDonald, M. (2009). Redefining teaching, re-imagining teacher education. *Teachers and Teaching: Theory and Practice, 15*, 273–289.

Hedges, L. V. (1981). Distribution theory for Glass's estimator of effect size and related estimators. *Journal of Educational Statistics, 6*, 107–128. doi:10.2307/1164588

Hedges, L. V. (2007). Effect sizes in cluster-randomized designs. *Journal of Educational and Behavioral Statistics, 32*, 341–370. doi:10.3102/1076998606298043

Hedges, L. V., & Hedberg, E. (2007). Interclass correlation values for planning group-randomized trials in education. *Educational Evaluation and Policy Analysis, 29*, 60–87.

Hedges, L. V., & Olkin, I. (1985). *Statistical methods for meta-analysis.* San Diego, CA: Academic Press.

Hedges, L. V., Tipton, E., & Johnson, M. C. (2010). Robust variance estimation in meta-regression with dependent effect size estimates. *Research Synthesis Methods, 1*, 39–65.

Hedges, L. V., & Vevea, J. L. (1998). Fixed- and random-effects models in meta-analysis. *Psychological Methods, 3*, 486–504.

Herzfeldt-Kamprath, R., & Ullrich, R. (2016). *Examining teacher effectiveness between preschool and third grade.* Washington, DC: Center for American Progress. Retrieved from https://cdn.americanprogress.org/wp-content/uploads/2016/01/19064517/P-3TeacherEffectiveness2.pdf

Higgins, J. P. T., & Thompson, S. G. (2002). Quantifying heterogeneity in a meta-analysis. *Statistics in Medicine, 21*, 1539–1558. doi:10.1002/sim.1186

Higgins, J. P. T., Thompson, S. G., Deeks, J. J., & Altman, D. G. (2003). Measuring inconsistencies in meta-analyses. *British Medical Journal, 327*, 557–560.

Hill, H., Corey, D., & Jacob, R. (2018). Dividing by zero: Exploring null results in a mathematics professional development program. *Teachers College Record, 120*(6), 1–42.

Ingersoll, R. M., & Strong, M. (2011). The impact of induction and mentoring programs for beginning teachers, the impact of induction and mentoring programs for beginning teachers: A critical review of the research, a critical review of the research. *Review of Educational Research, 81*, 201–233. doi:10.3102/0034654311403323

Institute of Education Sciences. (2017). *What Works Clearinghouse: Standards handbook* (Version 4.0). Washington, DC: U.S. Department of Education. Retrieved from https://ies.ed.gov/ncee/wwc/Docs/referenceresources/wwc_standards_handbook_v4.pdf

Jacob, A., & McGovern, K. (2015). *The mirage: Confronting the hard truth about our quest for teacher development.* Retrieved from https://tntp.org/assets/documents/TNTP-Mirage_2015.pdf

Kennedy, M. M. (2016). How does professional development improve teaching? *Review of Educational Research, 86*, 945–980. doi:10.3102/0034654315626800

Kini, T., & Podolsky, A. (2016). *Does teaching experience increase teacher effectiveness? A review of the research.* Palo Alto, CA: Learning Policy Institute, 2016. Retrieved from https://learningpolicyinstitute.org/sites/default/files/product-files/Teaching_Experience_Report_June_2016.pdf

Kraft, M. A., & Blazar, D. (2017). Individualized coaching to improve classroom practice across grades and subjects: New experimental evidence. *Educational Policy, 31*, 1033–1068.

Kraft, M. A., Blazar, D., & Hogan, D. (2018). The effect of teacher coaching on instruction and achievement: A meta-analysis of the causal evidence. *Review of Educational Research, 88*, 547–588. doi:10.3102/0034654318759268

Lampert, M., Franke, M., Kazemi, E., Ghousseini, H., Turrou, A. C., . . . Crowe, K. (2013). Keeping it complex: Using rehearsals to support novice teacher learning of ambitious teaching. *Journal of Teacher Education, 64*, 226–243.

Lipsey, M. W., & Wilson, D. B. (2001). *Practical meta-analysis.* Thousand Oaks, CA: Sage.

McKenna, J., Shin, M., & Ciullo, S. (2015). Evaluating reading and mathematics instruction for students with learning disabilities: A synthesis of observation research. *Learning Disability Quarterly, 38*, 195–207.

Rivkin, S. G., Hanushek, E. A., & Kain, J. F. (2005). Teachers, schools and academic achievement. *Econometrica, 73*, 417–458.

Rockoff, J. E. (2004). The impact of individual teachers on student achievement: Evidence from panel data. *American Economic Review, 94*, 247–252.

Scher, L., & O'Reilly, F. (2009). Professional development for K–12 math and science teachers: What do we really know? *Journal of Research on Educational Effectiveness, 2*, 209–249.

Slavin, R. E., Lake, C., Hanley, P., & Thurston, A. (2012). *Effective programs for elementary science: A best-evidence synthesis.* Baltimore, MD: Johns Hopkins University, Center for Research and Reform in Education.

Slavin, R. E., Lake, C., Hanley, P., & Thurston, A. (2014). Experimental evaluations of elementary science programs: A best-evidence synthesis. *Journal of Research in Science Teaching, 51*, 870–901.

Timperley, H., Wilson, A., Barrar, H., & Fung, I. (2007). *Teacher professional learning and development: Best evidence synthesis iteration.* Wellington, New Zealand: Ministry of Education.

Tipton, E. (2014). Small sample adjustments for robust variance estimation with meta-regression. *Psychological Methods, 20*, 375–393. doi:10.1037/met0000011

Vevea, J. L., & Hedges, L. V. (1995). A general linear model for estimating effect size in the presence of publication bias. *Psychometrika, 60*, 419–435.

Wallace, B. C., Small, K., Brodley, C. E., Lau, J., & Trikalinos, T. A. (2012). Deploying an interactive machine learning system in an evidence-based practice center: abstrackr. In *Proceedings of the 2nd ACM SIGHIT International Health Informatics Symposium* (pp. 819–824). New York, NY: Association for Computing Machinery.

Chapter 5

How We Learn About Teacher Learning

MARY M. KENNEDY
Michigan State University

This chapter examines research on professional development, or PD, focusing specifically on underlying assumptions about the nature of teaching and the nature of teacher learning. It examines PD programs according to their assumptions about what teachers need to learn, and it examines PD studies according to how and when they expect to see evidence of teacher learning. The chapter seeks to provide a broad view of how we think about teaching and teacher learning and to examine our underlying assumptions both about teaching and about how PD is expected to improve teaching. With respect to program effectiveness, the chapter raises questions about the extent to which effective PD programs can be replicated; with respect to our study designs, it raises questions about how teacher learning occurs and when and how we should expect to see program effects on teachers' practices. The chapter also offers some suggestions for future research design.

Human beings have taught one another for centuries, and for most of that time everyone invented their own approaches to teaching, without the guidance of mentors, administrators, teacher educators, or professional developers. Today, teachers receive guidance from almost every corner. They are formally certified to teach, and once certified, they continue to take additional courses, called *professional development*, or PD, throughout their teaching careers. In addition, states and school districts also regulate many aspects of their work through performance appraisals and student assessments.

This chapter addresses a specific portion of guidance called professional development, or PD. Literature on PD has grown substantially over time, and standards for research have also changed. Twenty years ago, I reviewed studies of PD effectiveness within math and science education (Kennedy, 1998), limiting my review to studies that provided evidence of student achievement and that included a comparison group. I found only 12 such studies, most of which are not acceptable by today's

Review of Research in Education
March 2019, Vol. 43, pp. 138–162
DOI: 10.3102/0091732X19838970
Chapter reuse guidelines: sagepub.com/journals-permissions
© 2019 AERA. http://rre.aera.net

standards. Some had very small samples, some did not randomly assign teachers to groups, and some provided instructional materials as well as PD, so that the effects of the PD were confounded with the effects of the materials. Since then, the literature has grown substantially, so that we are able to raise our standards for what counts as a "good study." Two years ago, I reviewed 28 studies of PD (Kennedy, 2016), all of which used random assignment. Since then, even more such studies have been published. For this chapter, I now raise my standards again and remove studies that were based on fewer than 20 teachers.[1]

PD studies represent our way, as researchers, of learning about teacher learning. We generate hypotheses about what good teaching consists of, about what teachers need to learn in order to do good teaching, or about what kind of activities or experiences provoke learning in teachers. Then we try different kinds of interventions to see how they work. It is not a perfect system, for every PD study simultaneously involves all three of these types of hypotheses: what teachers need to learn, how they learn, and how we will know whether they have learned enough. Thus, a given study of PD can fail if any one of these hypotheses is wrong, and we may not know where our error is. Furthermore, teachers themselves may learn about teaching independently, in ways we don't see. They take formal courses, they read things, they ruminate about their own experiences, and they seek advice from colleagues. They may even get a brainstorm about their teaching while watching a movie.

My aim in this chapter is to examine our existing oeuvre of experimental research on PD both from the standpoint of what we have learned about teacher learning and from the standpoint of what we have learned about *how to learn* about teacher learning—that is, how to design informative studies. I begin with a brief overview of how we think about teaching as a phenomenon.

FIRST IMPRESSIONS OF TEACHING

Teaching is, among other things, a cultural activity. We have all spent thousands of hours observing teachers and participating in classroom activities, and we have all formed a variety of different and sometimes contradictory thoughts about teaching. Here I offer five observations about our current understandings of teaching.

Our Learning Begins in Childhood

Learning about teaching is different from learning about any other occupation, in that our learning begins when we are children. As we watch our own teachers, we develop ideas about what they are doing, why they are doing it, what effect their work has on us, and so forth. The sociologist Dan Lortie (1975) referred to this extended period as an "apprenticeship of observation" and pointed out that this kind of occupational familiarity is unique to the profession of teaching. All of us—those who become teachers, those who become education researchers, and everyone else—have spent roughly 12,000 hours watching teachers through our child-eyes, developing our own conceptions about what the job entails and what makes some teachers better than others.

But the ideas we form about teaching are *naive* in the sense that they are formed without any awareness of what really causes events to turn out as they do. Just as a child might form the naive conception that the sun circles around the earth, she/he might form the conception that teaching practice comes naturally, or is effortless, because teachers always appear to know what to do. Moreover, we remain confident in our judgments that one teacher is "better" than another.

This is an important preface to any discussion about learning about teaching because our impressions could be wrong. We may be aware of the effect of a teacher's actions but not what its purpose was. We see their actions but not their thoughts, their goals, their motives, their frustrations. Moreover, we don't see *what they see*, from their vantage point at the front of the classroom and from their vantage point of trying to lead the class in a particular direction. This lack of awareness, in turn, can lead us to think that teaching practices come naturally or that the decisions about "what to do next" are always self-evident in the moment.

I became especially aware of the difference between an observer's view and a teacher's view in a study of teachers' in-the-moment decision making (Kennedy, 2005, 2010b). When I asked teachers about discrete actions they took during a lesson, they nearly always referred to something they saw at that moment. Teachers would say "I could see that Billy was about to jump out of his seat," or "I realized I didn't have enough handouts to go around," or "Juan rarely speaks and I wanted to encourage him." These conversations reveal a highly contingent aspect of teaching that is quite different from our naive conceptions of teachers as entirely self-directed and always knowing what to do next.

As Researchers, We Like Idealized Models of Teaching

In the 1970s, a federal program called *Follow Through* supported the development and field-testing of different models of teaching (McDaniels, 1975) that exemplified different teaching ideals. One model, for instance, was based on the research of the French psychologist, Jean Piaget, while another was based on behaviorist theories of learning, a third on the concept of open classrooms, and a fourth on the concept of a *Responsive Environment*. Each model developer was called a sponsor, and sponsors were funded to train teachers in specific schools to implement their models. Eventually over a dozen such models were developed and field-tested in schools throughout the country.

Models are useful to researchers because they provide us with a nomenclature that can be used in our research to distinguish among teachers. Researchers today continue to design, study, and evaluate different models of teaching. Some models derive from naive conceptions of teaching, some from theories of student learning, and some from empirical evidence of relationships between specific teaching practices and student learning. But many still embrace the naive view of the teacher as always in full control of the classroom, still failing to recognize the contingent nature of teaching. This view of teaching practice as entirely in the teachers' control leads to what social psychologists call *Attribution Error*, a tendency to assume that the behaviors we observe in others are caused entirely by their own character, not by the situations they are confronting.

We Are Guilty of Attribution Error

Since we tend to assume teaching comes naturally, and that teachers are entirely in control of events in their classrooms, we also assume that whatever behaviors we see are purposeful, rather than spurious responses to events. Here is an example of an attribution error I made several years ago when observing a fifth-grade mathematics teacher, Ms. Katlaski. It was the first period of the day, and she had been on hall duty that morning. When the bell rang, she entered the room and spent less than a minute looking at the text to remind herself what the lesson was about. It was about multiplying whole numbers with fractions. Students had previously learned how to multiply whole numbers with each other, and how to multiply fractions with each other. Today they would learn to solve a problem involving both a whole number and a fraction: $9 \times 2/3$. Her plan had been to show them that they could convert the 9 into 9/1, so that they could then use computation strategies they had already learned. To open the lesson, Katlaski asked the rhetorical question of how to convert 9 into a fraction. She was not really expecting an answer, but in this case, someone called out, Multiply 9 by 4/4. The student's proposal was technically correct, but it would be mathematically more difficult to solve if you are 9 years old. Katlaski's solution, converting the 9 to 9/1, would have yielded this computation:

$$9/1 \times 2/3 = 18/3 = 6.$$

The student's solution would have yielded this computation:

$$36/4 \times 2/3 = 72/12 = 6.$$

Katlaski knew that the student's proposal would be too complicated for her students to follow, so she immediately faced a dilemma: accept the student's solution and solve the problem on the board, even if most students couldn't follow it, or reject the student's solution. In a fluster, she said, "No, that won't work."

Katlaski's behavior would imply that she did not know her mathematics, but her real problem was a logistical one of how to respond to a proposal that would be difficult for her students to follow (Kennedy, 2010a). The term "attribution error" refers to this tendency to attribute the actions of others to stable personal traits rather than to the situations in which they find themselves. In Katlaski's case, the situation presented something she wasn't ready for, and an unknowing observer could easily attribute that error to a lack of sufficient content knowledge. Because we are all vulnerable to the assumption that teachers always know what to do, we are especially guilty, even as grown-ups and even as researchers, of attributing teachers' actions to their content knowledge or their character traits rather than to the situations they face.

We Expect PD to Solve All the Problems We See

In the past several decades, the number and variety of PD programs developed for teachers, and often required of them, have continuously increased. By 2001, teacher unions were adding PD requirements into their contracts, typically stipulating the number of hours of PD they should be taking each year (see, e.g., Bredeson, 2001). One recent study (TNTP, 2015) found some school districts that spent an average of $18,000 *per year per teacher* on PD. Yet education literature is replete with articles about the need for even more of it. A Web search for "professional development for teachers" yields dozens of sites advocating more or better PD for teachers. And as advocacy for PD has increased, so has research on PD.

My aim in this paper is to examine the research on PD from two perspectives: First, what have we learned about the benefits of these PD programs for teachers and students? Second, what have we learned about *how to study* the benefits of PD for teachers? For this analysis, I rely on a population of 29 PD studies that (a) include a minimum of 20 teachers, (b) include at least one measure of student achievement as an outcome, (c) include a comparison group, and (d) rely on some form of random assignment to allocate teachers to treatment and comparison conditions.[2] This population of studies is large enough to enable us to examine patterns in their findings and perhaps generate some useful hypotheses about when, why, or how PD can be helpful. All of these studies involve formal PD programs. That is, people from somewhere outside the school held scheduled meetings with teachers in order to alter teachers' practices in some specific way.

All the studies in this review have a comparison group, but I also rely here on a comparison *study*, in which the treatment of interest involves pairing relatively weaker teachers with other teachers in their own schools.

An Alternative to PD: Let Teachers Help Each Other

When researchers bring their idealized models of teaching into schools, there are at least two ways they can go wrong. They could be wrong about the effectiveness of their idealized model of teaching, or their PD could fail to address the myriad contingencies of teaching and thereby provide no benefit to teachers. A useful contrast to formal PD, therefore, is the system teachers often rely on informally, which is to seek guidance from one another and share tips about how to handle various contingencies. I found one study (Papay, Taylor, Tyler, & Laski, 2016) that pursues this idea. These researchers asked school principals to pair teachers whose practices fell below district standards with other teachers whose performances were higher. Although there was an official "curriculum" for this peer-to-peer support system, which was based on the district's performance assessment system, this program itself was very flexible: Principals were at liberty to decide which teachers from one group would be paired with which teacher from the other group. Then, mentors were free to do or say whatever they wanted to their protégés, and protégés were free to accept or reject their mentors' advice. The researchers hoped that the mentor teachers would discuss specific practices in which protégés were known to be less effective, but there were no rules regarding the content or format of these conversations. One teacher might present a specific behavior as a requirement, to be done at least twice every day, while another might cast it as useful in specific types of situations.

This program provides a useful alternative to conventional PD with conventional curricula: The program had no cost, no formal schedule, and no uniform curriculum. Formal PD programs have all these things—standards, goals, models of good practice, admonitions, and so forth—but they also have substantial cost and take up a lot of teachers' time. Since virtually all approaches to PD will be more expensive, we should expect them to demonstrate greater value than this simple "bootstrap" approach.

HOW DO WE MEASURE THE BENEFITS OF PD?

Throughout the history of education research, we have estimated the benefits of experimental programs with tests of statistical significance. These tests tell us the likelihood of achieving an outcome by chance, but they do not help us estimate the practical relevance of the effect itself. Effect sizes, on the other hand, allow us to place all differences between groups on the same standardized scale, typically ranging from –1 to +1, regardless of what outcome measure is used and what research design is used. An early advocate for the use of effect sizes, Jacob Cohen (1988) offered some rough guidelines for defining the meaningfulness of different effect sizes. He suggested that an effect size of 0.20 could be considered small, one of 0.50 could be considered medium, and one of 0.80 could be considered large. Now, as more and more researchers have presented their findings in the effect size metric, we know that Cohen's proposed standard were far too optimistic. Hill, Bloom, Black, and Lipskey (2008) recently reviewed the effects found by real researchers in real studies and found that effect sizes were shockingly small relative to the norms proposed by Cohen. In elementary schools, for instance, when effects were typically measured using standardized achievement tests, experimental treatment effects averaged only 0.07, far smaller than Cohen's proposed "small" effect of 0.20. When the content of the test was more narrowly defined, the average effect jumped to 0.23 and when it was even more specialized, it jumped to 0.44. As a result, education studies are more likely to find larger effects in middle schools and high schools, where tests are subject-specific and their content is more advanced.

These averages do not mean that larger effects are not possible, nor that we have not generated larger effects. They are *averages* across a wide range of educational interventions. Still, they give us a sense for the kind of outcomes we might expect, so the first thing we might ask about PD programs is how they compare with the effects of other kinds of education interventions. For this analysis, following Hill et al. (2008), I first sorted programs according to whether their outcome measures were broad or narrow. The majority of studies in my population were located in elementary schools and relied on broad standardized achievement tests. Only a handful used more narrowly focused outcome measures—one working with teachers of English language learners and a few others working on specific science topics.

Table 1 presents average effect sizes for studies using these two kinds of outcomes.[3] The top two rows of Table 1 provide two possible benchmark values against which to compare studies using broader outcome measures. First, we see the average effect size of all education studies examined by Hill et al. (2008), which was 0.07, and then we see the effect size of the "bootstrap" program described above, a program that simply pairs more effective teachers with less effective teachers.

After these rows in Table 1 are two rows showing the average effects of PD programs, first those that were evaluated with broad achievement tests in mathematics and language arts, and then those with specialized tests in the sciences or in English language learning. Finally, to help us understand the value of a second set of outcomes, the last line of Table 1 shows the average effect size Hill and others found when their studies used more narrow measures.

This comparison is not very encouraging. On average, our myriad expensive PD programs are almost indistinguishable from Papay et al.'s (2016) inexpensive bootstrap approach that encourages teachers to help one another. Yet most of these programs are far more expensive and time-consuming.

Still, the programs gathered here are quite various, and it behooves us to examine them further to see what else we might learn about the potential for PD to improve teaching practice. In the remainder of this chapter, I use patterns of program effects to address a variety of questions about how PD works and what we can expect from it.[4]

WHAT DO TEACHERS NEED TO LEARN?

The central premise underlying all PD is that there is something the researcher knows about teaching that teachers do not know. Over time, our hypotheses about what that is have shifted, and this shift largely reflects changes in how researchers themselves conceptualized the practice of teaching. So my first examination of PD literature sorts studies according to their hypotheses about what teachers need to learn. The most common hypotheses involve specific procedures, content knowledge, or strategies and insights.

Procedures

One stream of research focuses on what teachers are *doing*, often with little regard to *why* they did those things or to what their students were doing. This was the first approach we used to define the practices of teaching. A vocal advocate for this line of work, Nate Gage (1977) argued that the field needed a *scientific basis* for what had previously been thought of as "the art of teaching." To this end, researchers tried to partition teaching into a collection of discrete practices and then see which practices were correlated with student achievement gains. Once they became convinced that they had identified a set of such behaviors, they began devising PD programs to teach those behaviors to teachers.

TABLE 1
Overall Effects of Professional Development

Source of Study Effect Sizes	Average 1-Year Effect Sizes
Hill, Bloom, Black, and Lipskey's (2008) expected value for standardized tests	0.07
Papay, Taylor, Tyler, and Laski's (2016) bootstrap study	0.12 (1 study)
All elementary math or language professional development programs	0.10 (20 studies)
Topic-specific professional development programs	0.27 (4 studies)
Hill et al.'s expected value for narrower content tests	0.44

I found seven experimental studies that were designed to prescribe specific things teachers should do. Most focused on generic teaching practices such as questioning techniques or management techniques. One (Borman, Gamoran, & Bowdon, 2008) provided highly specified behavioral guidance on how to implement a new science curriculum. For instance, here is a passage from the teachers' manual describing a single fourth-grade unit (*Rot It Right: The Cycling of Matter and the Transfer of Energy. 4th Grade Science Immersion unit*, 2006):

- To set the tone for this investigation as an exploration, generate a class discussion and class list about what plants need for growth and development.
- Use the Think Aloud technique to model how to refine a wondering into a good scientific investigation. From the students' list about what plants need, form the question—What effect does sunlight have on radish plant growth and development?
- Continue the Think Aloud to model assembling the Terraqua Columns using proper experimental procedures, and designing an experiment that has only one factor that is varied.
- Have students record and explain their predictions for each set of columns for later reference. (p. 21)
- . . .

Content Knowledge

The second stream of work focuses on teachers' content knowledge. Interest in content knowledge arose relatively early in our history of PD research, and it derived from a study of teaching *behaviors* (Good & Grouws, 1979). These authors tested a PD model that stipulated a sequence of lesson segments for mathematics lessons. The guideline suggested that teachers spend about 8 minutes reviewing concepts that had been previously taught, then spend 20 minutes in "development," which involved introducing new concepts and questioning students to make sure they understood them, then move to a homework assignment, and so forth. But as the researchers watched teachers try to implement this relatively simple lesson framework, they came to see that teachers had great difficulty with the phase called "development." At first, the researchers tried to solve this problem by defining "development" more clearly, telling teachers that it was where they should attend to relationships between concepts and procedures, to students' confusions, and so forth. Ultimately, they concluded that teachers could not enact this step because they lacked sufficient *content knowledge.* A few years later, Lee Shulman (1986a, 1986b, 1987) actively sought to redirect the field away from behavioral depictions of teaching practice and toward a focus on teachers' knowledge.

This shift in attention from discrete teaching behaviors toward content knowledge is an example of researchers themselves learning about teaching. PD programs based on prescribed behaviors were part of an effort to be more scientific and objective, but they also represented a relatively naive conception of teaching, which is, after all, a "knowledge" profession.

Notice, though, that when I say that the field has shifted from behavioral admonitions to content knowledge, I do not mean that the former approach has entirely disappeared. In fact, the science program described just above is an example of a relatively recent addition to our PD oeuvre, but rather than teaching teachers science content, it teaches them the procedures they should use to teach that content.

I found five studies of PD that focused on teachers' content knowledge. Four addressed mathematical content (Garet et al., 2010; Garet et al., 2011; Garet et al., 2016; Jayanthi, Gersten, Taylor, Smolkowski, & Dimino, 2017; Niess, 2005); the fifth (Garet et al., 2008) focused on language arts. These programs tend to look a lot like conventional college classrooms, with teachers playing the role of students. There may be lectures, there may be question-and-answer sessions, there may be small-group discussions, and there may even be textbooks and homework.

Content knowledge continues to be a popular theme in discussions about what teachers need to know, but it is possible that our perception that teachers' content knowledge is seriously deficient could derive from attribution errors such as I experienced with Ms. Katlaski. This view is also relatively naive, in that it overlooks things like motivation, organization, representation, and so forth.

Strategies and Insights

The 1986 *Handbook of Research on Teaching* introduced yet another conception of teaching. It included a chapter about myriad decisions teachers make throughout their lessons (Clark & Peterson, 1986). This chapter depicted the practice of teaching as a process of continuous decision making as teachers interpreted and responded to events as they unfold in the classroom. It suggested that much of what we observed in classrooms was not planned behavior but rather spontaneous responses to unfolding events.

The realization that the behaviors we see might be contingent on circumstances led to yet a third approach to PD, one that focused on how to interpret events as they unfolded and how to respond to them strategically. Instead of prescribing specific teaching moves, these programs offered insights into how students make sense of their lessons and offered broad strategies for engaging and responding to their students. They often provide coaches or mentors who could visit teachers within their classrooms or to convene groups of teachers locally to share and compare their experiences.

I found 17 programs that focused on insights and strategies. They are quite various in their design, but a prominent theme has to do with gaining a deeper understanding of how students think and why they say or do what they do.

The earliest study in this group (Carpenter, Fennema, Peterson, Chiang, & Loef, 1989) focused on elementary school mathematics. The authors met with teachers in a small discussion group and showed teachers a series of videotaped interviews with students. The tapes were intended to show teachers how students made sense of mathematical relationships. As the group examined and discussed these videos, teachers gained better understanding of the content itself, but they also developed a better understanding about how their students thought about that content and how to interpret the things their students said. The program made no prescriptions about what teachers should actually *do*. That was largely up to them.

The proliferation of PD programs focusing on strategic teaching again reflects what we researchers ourselves have learned about teaching. As we have become more aware of the many contingencies involved in teaching, we have shifted our focus away from telling teachers what to do and toward deepening their understanding of their students so that they can make better in-the-moment judgments about how to respond to students.

PROGRAM EFFECTS

Do these different conceptions of teaching make a difference? The easiest way to compare these three approaches to PD is to focus on a subset of programs with common study designs. In this case, I compare 22 programs that all worked with teachers for a single academic year and used a general achievement test to measure student achievement. Figure 1 arrays the effects of these programs along a horizontal scale. Each program is characterized by a single circle. The figure does not include the science or English language learner studies, where test metrics can yield different effect sizes, or the studies that worked with teachers for only a portion of the year.

You can see that program effects are quite various across these studies, and that many of them appear to be less effective (though more expensive) than the bootstrap program, whose effect of 0.12 is shown in the top row. However, a larger fraction (2/3) of studies in the third group program yielded program effects larger than the 0.12 benchmark.[5]

FIGURE 1
Distribution of 1-Year Program Effects by Conceptions of Teaching

	-0.2	-0.1	zero	0.1	0.2	0.3	
Bootstrapping study				O			
Procedures		O O				O	O
Content Knowledge		O O O	O			O	
Insights and Strategies	O			O OO	OOO OO	OOO O	

The third conception also appears to be more widespread, with 13 research groups testing programs based on this vision of teaching. Thus we might benefit from a closer look at this approach to PD. Teachers are nearly always aware of multiple things continuously unfolding in their classrooms. They see that Ronald is confused, that Juanita is getting restless, that Mark is eager to show off what he has figured out, that someone has spilled something sticky on the floor near her desk, that the room is getting too hot because the janitor has not yet fixed the heater, and that the lunch bell will ring in 10 minutes. Regardless of what teachers plan to do during a given lesson, their in-the-moment actions are often responses to these in-the-moment observations. They want to suppress the show-off, calm down the fidgeter, help the confused student, open the window, and make sure the lesson reaches an appropriate closure before the bell rings. Then the mess can be cleaned up.

Strategic thinking is not merely about finding the best way to achieve the lesson goal; it is also about *seeing* things that might interfere with or facilitate the direction of the lesson, watching for signs of restlessness or confusion, inventing ways to avoid or capitalize on these moments, and generally being aware of what all the students are thinking and doing. Much of the strategically oriented PD had to do with interpreting students' comments and recognizing signs of confusion or disorientation that need to be addressed. I suspect that one reason why strategically oriented PD was more successful is that it helped teachers get better at *seeing signals* within their own classrooms.

These programs offer two thing that are often missing when programs focus on procedures or content knowledge. One is classroom artifacts. Many of these programs rely on videotapes of classroom events, examples of student work, interviews with children, or other artifacts that demonstrate to teachers the issues on which they want to focus. Thus, conversations about teaching are not about universal methods but about interpreting and responding to specific types of situations. Second, the people who provide this sort of PD tend to be people who have themselves spent a great deal of time in classrooms and are cognizant of all these nuances of classroom life. They themselves have an intimate familiarity with the complications of teaching. They are not merely telling teachers what to do or what to say; they are showing teachers what to *look for*. Which raises another question:

Can We "Package" Successful PD Programs?

An important reason for conducting research is to be able to identify effective practices so that others can adopt them. We want to be able to "package" effective programs and distribute them to a wider audience. But what if program effectiveness depends on the PD provider's own personal knowledge of classroom life, on his or her ability to spontaneously generate examples or to spontaneously notice things while visiting teachers' classrooms? If the quality of the message depends on the provider's intimate knowledge of classroom life, other providers, even when trained in the PD approach, might not be able to achieve the same outcomes.

Figure 2 presents a rough attempt to test this "intimate knowledge" hypothesis. It separates programs provided by their original developers from programs that were packaged by institutions. Figure 2 shows the same array of program effects as Figure 1, except in this case, packaged programs are marked with "X's" rather than with "O's."

Notice that almost all the "X's" reside on the negative end of the distribution, while the "O's" are all on the positive side. This pattern creates an interesting dilemma, for it suggests that our large-scale studies, the kind of studies researchers value most, are not effective at raising student achievement. There may be many reasons for this disparity, of course, having to do with the logistical difficulties of orchestrating large-scale studies or with the kinds of study samples used, but since my purpose is to examine our assumptions about teacher learning, I want to focus here on the hypothesis that these differences derive from packaged PD.

What exactly do I mean by "packaged" PD programs? In the following paragraphs, I contrast pairs of programs within each row, one program that I consider to be locally developed with a counterpart that appears to be packaged. To the extent possible, I strive to pair programs whose content and goals are comparable. However, I have not actually tested these pairs of studies to see whether their differences are statistically significant.

Procedural Knowledge

In one of the first studies of PD ever conducted, a group of researchers (Anderson, Evertson, & Brophy, 1979) generated a list of procedures that had been shown to be related to student learning, converted these into a list of recommended practices, and accompanied each recommendation with very brief rationale. For instance, one said, "The introduction to the lesson should give an overview of what is to come in order to mentally prepare the students for the presentation." Another said, "It is also at the beginning of the lesson that new words and sounds should be presented to the children so that they can use them later when they are reading or answering questions." The PD itself was remarkably brief, consisted of a single 3-hour orientation, during which the principal investigator presented the list as a whole, discussed its use, and allowed teachers to ask questions. They then asked teachers to try to use these admonitions for the entire school year. The program had a yearlong effect of 0.24 on student achievement, the second-most effective procedural program shown in Figure 2.

FIGURE 2
Distribution of Program Effects for Packaged Versus Original Programs

	-0.2	-0.1	zero	0.1	0.2	0.3
Bootstrapping study				O		
Procedures		XX			O	O
Content Knowledge		X X X	X		O	
Insights and Strategies	X		X O O	OOO OO	OOO O	

Now for the contrast: A few years after that study was done, another group (Coladarci & Gage, 1984) took the same list of admonitions and *mailed* it to a group of teachers to see if they could get the same effect. I consider this mailed list of admonitions to be a packaged message in part because it is more impersonal but also because there was no opportunity to discuss or clarify any of the admonitions, help teachers envision the kind of situations where they would be applicable, or respond to any questions. This mailed-in program had an effect of –0.04, compared to the 0.24 from the original study.

Subject Matter Knowledge

In general, all of the programs providing content knowledge looked roughly like college courses: Meetings were held in classroom-like settings, PD providers gave lectures and demonstrations, engaged in question-and-answer sessions, and formed teachers into small groups to solve practice problems. Sometimes programs also provided local coaches who visited teachers in their classrooms. This classroom format is not surprising; it is the customary way subject matter has always been taught, and it fits our perception of subject matter knowledge as universal, residing outside of specific situations. Yet only one of these programs was effective.

How did this program differ from the others? It is the only one that relied on local faculty who knew the local community, knew the schools and teachers, and could gear their presentations to these audiences. Furthermore, they were not given their curricula but instead taught courses they had designed themselves. They also tailored the program for teachers by frequently modeling the teaching of their content and by sponsoring an online forum where teachers could discuss issues with one another throughout the academic year. These activities helped teachers translate the content into their own situations.

In contrast, the less effective programs provided a uniform curriculum to all localities and hired presenters to teach this prespecified curriculum. Nothing in the programs was tailored to the unique needs or interests of participating teachers, nor is it clear whether the hired presenters were allowed to modify their program in response to the unique needs of their audiences. Nor is it clear whether the presenters had the kind of intimate knowledge of classroom life that would enable them to generate spontaneous teaching examples or story problems that would be meaningful to teachers.

Strategies

I use the term *strategic* to distinguish programs that are focused on interpreting events and adapting instruction to circumstances. In general, strategies are more flexible than procedures, more responsive to unique circumstances, and more responsive to differences among students.

One of the most effective of these programs (Gersten, Dimino, Jayanthi, Kim, & Santoro, 2010) introduced first-grade teachers to research findings regarding early reading instruction, and did this by helping teachers incorporate these findings into their local lesson plans. Teachers met in groups throughout the academic year to jointly plan their reading lessons, and throughout these meetings, they were regularly introduced to new research findings. Each planning meeting followed a four-step process: First, teachers would report what happened when they implemented their previously planned lessons. Then they would discuss their newest report on research findings. In this phase, the group facilitator focused their attention on the central concepts to make sure everyone understood them. In the third phase, they would review the publisher's recommended lesson and discuss its strengths and weaknesses. Finally, they would work together to design a lesson of their own that incorporated the research principle they had just read about. Thus, in this PD, even though the program gave teachers a standardized curriculum, it did so by embedding the content into the lesson planning process. Each planning group made sense of the findings in the context of its own classrooms and then directly applied the new knowledge into their next lessons.

There is another program that also taught teachers about findings from reading research, but instead of working with teachers and helping them incorporate the findings into their lesson plans, this program packaged the material and presented it to teachers through a series of daylong seminar sessions, each accompanied by a textbook. So both programs wanted teachers to get better at teaching language arts, and both aimed to do so by introducing teachers to research findings in that area. The first had an effect size of 0.23 and appears in the "strategy" row of Figure 2, while the second had an effect of 0.05 and appears in the "content knowledge" row of Figure 2.

By definition, strategic programs are less amenable to packaging. They aim to engage teachers in classroom-based problem-solving and to help them "see" their own classrooms differently, a goal that seems to require program faculty who have intimate familiarity with classroom life, so much so that they can help their teachers interpret their own experiences differently.

One program in this group has been working toward standardization for several years, and its progress might be instructive here. The Cognitively Guided Instruction program, or CGI, was initially designed and tested by a group of mathematics faculty and graduate students at the University of Wisconsin in 1989 (Carpenter et al., 1989). At that time it was a unique program, one of the first programs to move away from direct instruction and toward strategic thinking. It had a modest effect of 0.13. But the authors, along with their colleagues and graduate students, continued to use CGI in their college courses and in local PD programs for many years and to expand its influence. After about 10 years, they developed a guide for workshop leaders (Fennema, Carpenter, Levi, Franke, & Empson, 1999). Then, after another 10 years had passed, the younger generation of CGI mathematics educators (Jacobs, Franke, Carpenter, Levi, & Battey, 2007) carried out a second experimental test of CGI and achieved a much higher effect of 0.26. Presumably, this improvement reflected a series of refinements over time as all the members of this group became more familiar with teachers and their needs.

After that, some members of this group decided to create a formal organization to provide PD and related services. Called the Teachers Development Group, this organization sought to further disseminate the concept of CGI by providing written materials and making PD available on a broader scale. In other words, they sought to *package* the CGI program. But large-scale expansion runs the risk of relying on inexperienced PD providers who may have neither the personal, situated understanding of the program that the founders had nor the intimate knowledge of how teachers responded to CGI.

Now we have yet a third test (Schoen, LaVenia, Tazaz, & Faraina, 2018) of CGI, this one based on the new packaged version of the program. This new packaged version of CGI yielded an average effect of zero.

These three tests of CGI represent three different levels of PD provider experience. In the first test, yielding an effect of 0.13, the providers had knowledge of student learning and had experience teaching teachers in their classes but had no experience providing a PD program. In the second, yielding an effect of 0.23, program staff had knowledge of how children learn as well as more experience providing PD. But in the third study, yielding an average effect of 0.0, the program had been packaged for large-scale distribution, and I suspect local providers lack the kind of intimate familiarity with classroom life that is needed to help teachers alter their perceptions of their own experiences.

The pairs of outcomes I share here, of course, could reflect nothing more than ordinary statistical variations. However, the *pattern* of differential program effectiveness, across over 20 independent studies, raises important questions about the reliability of program effectiveness and, ultimately, about value of our PD research if our findings cannot be reliably expanded or replicated. Even if my hypothesis about packaging is wrong, we still need to think more about how we define salient program features that should be part of any replication effort and whether program staff experiences are a necessary "feature" of the program.

HOW DOES NEW KNOWLEDGE "TRAVEL" FROM PD TO STUDENT LEARNING?

The three groupings I outlined above suggest that different programs have different tacit theories about the kind of change that is needed. Some PD providers believe that if they teach a set of specific procedures to teachers, and teachers implement them, those specific behaviors will foster student learning. If we teach content knowledge, we are assuming that teachers will be more able, on their own, to teach that content. But we still know very little about how to actually foster these changes, or about how much time is needed to foster such change. In an effort to help teachers make these changes, many PD providers send mentors or coaches into the schools, people who visit teachers within their classrooms and help them "see" new things and try new things. Thus, we may think about PD as having a cascading sequence of influences that looks like this:

PD → Coaches → Teachers → Students

The modal PD program works with teachers throughout a single full academic year, implying that researchers expect teachers to be able to alter habits and routines relatively quickly, and adopt their new recommendations relatively quickly. But there is another timing problem inherent in this approach to PD: Researchers typically measure changes in student achievement *during that same academic year*. This schedule is popular in part because student achievement is typically measured by school districts at the end of each academic year. So a PD provider who comes in, say September, might consider last spring's school test as his pretest. Normally, we think of causes as preceding effects, so this schedule raises a variety of questions: How quickly do we expect teachers to alter their practice based on what they have just learned? Do we expect them to alter their methods the next day? Within a week or a month? On the other hand, if change is slow, and if teachers need time to alter their habits, can we expect to see the effect of that change on student achievement gains that are measured concurrent with the treatment itself?

These complications with PD research designs invite questions about the array of program effects, for virtually all of them could be underestimating program effects: Students' annual achievement gains are almost always the result of teaching events that occurred before the PD has had its full influence.

But there are also scenarios that would lead us to *overestimate* effectiveness: Suppose teachers privately dislike the approaches being taught but comply with them only to be polite or to get their coaches to leave them alone. If this occurred, we might see a gain during the program year, but the gain would reflect *compliance* rather than genuine learning and it would go away the following year.

These scheduling problems provide another example of an area in which we need to learn more about *how to learn* about teacher learning, how to design our studies, and how to map exposure to PD with changes in practice and, in turn, changes in student learning. Most important, we need to learn more about whether program effects are sustained over time, and whether they accumulate over time.

Do Program Effects Last Over Time?

The modal study design, which measures student learning concurrent with program implementation, is built on the tacit assumption that learning is immediate throughout the program year. But much of teaching practice is habitual, and teachers may need more time to generate new practices.

Furthermore, the role of time may vary across programs. Those offering procedures might be hoping to save teachers the problem of translation by providing precise behavioral guidance in the first place. Those offering content knowledge skirt the question of whether behaviors need to change. Those offering insights, on the other hand, depend heavily on teachers' own intentions to determine what gets changed. Teachers could reject a new idea altogether or, conversely, discover more situations where the new insight applies.

If we could follow changes in student learning across multiple years, we might see that different patterns of *teacher* learning yield different patterns of *student* learning as well.

Only five studies followed teachers into a second year and measured their students' achievement during that next year. These studies provide some clues about what happens to new ideas over the long term. That is, assuming that teachers benefit from a program in the first place, is the effect sustained into a new year? Figure 3 plots changes in student achievement from the end of Year 1 to the end of Year 2. That is, the beginning of the line represents program effects at the end of one year. From that starting point, a horizontal line means program effects were sustained through the second year, and while downward trending lines might mean that teachers either forgot or purposefully abandoned the program's ideas, an upward trend might suggest that teachers not only sustained their knowledge but also continued to find more ways to incorporate new ideas into their practices so that students benefitted even more during the follow-up year.

There are only slight differences among these lines, suggesting that in general, teachers in all programs roughly sustained what they had learned during Year 1. Those programs that had negligible effects during Year 1 had almost the same negligible effects at the end of Year 2. Their lines are virtually horizontal.

Programs that had a moderate effect in Year 1, however, invite some interesting hypotheses about teacher learning. They imply that teachers continued to improve their effectiveness during the second year, even though their programs were no longer helping them. One hypothesis might be that teachers may need time to digest new ideas and to fully incorporate them into their practices. If so, the traditional 1-year study may not be sufficient to fully understand program effects. One of these delayed effects came from the bootstrap program. Below, I examine the other two.

The topmost line represents results from a program in science (Heller, Dahler, Wong, Shinohara, & Miratrix, 2012). The study addressed only a single unit (electricity) in the science curriculum and provided teachers with knowledge about electricity as well as deeper insights into how students learn about electricity. For the

FIGURE 3
Delayed Effects From Different Approaches to Professional Development

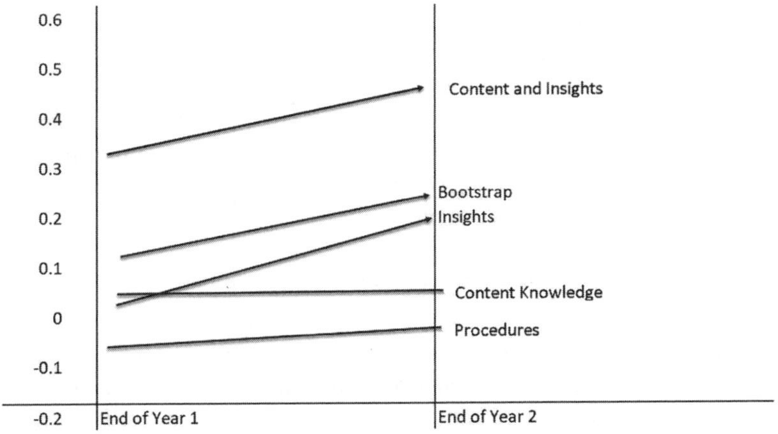

<table>
<tr><td>0.6</td></tr>
<tr><td>0.5</td><td>Content and Insights</td></tr>
<tr><td>0.4</td></tr>
<tr><td>0.3</td></tr>
<tr><td>0.2</td><td>Bootstrap</td></tr>
<tr><td></td><td>Insights</td></tr>
<tr><td>0.1</td></tr>
<tr><td>0</td><td>Content Knowledge</td></tr>
<tr><td></td><td>Procedures</td></tr>
<tr><td>-0.1</td></tr>
<tr><td>-0.2</td><td>End of Year 1</td><td>End of Year 2</td></tr>
</table>

'insights" part, they tested three approaches: Some teachers examined their own students' work, others examined written cases of real teaching episodes, and still others examined their own experiences as learners. All three approaches had strong effects, and Figure 4 shows their average effectiveness.

The other program (Allen, Pianta, Gregory, Mikami, & Lun, 2011) consisted of ongoing consultations between teachers and mentors. Teachers videotaped sample lessons approximately every 2 weeks and sent their tapes to an online "teaching partner." Then the two of them would talk about the lesson. The nature of these conversations helps us understand the difference between prescriptions and insights. Instead of correcting teachers' behaviors, prescribing recommended practices, or evaluating what they saw on the video, these mentors used "prompts" to help teachers examine and think about specific events that had occurred. For instance, a "nice work" prompt might say, "You do a nice job letting the students talk. It seems like they are really feeling involved. Why do you think this worked?" And a "consider this" prompt might look like this:

One aspect of "Teacher Sensitivity" is when you consistently monitor students for cues and when you notice they need extra support or assistance. In this clip, what does the boy in the front row do that shows you that he needs your support at this moment? What criteria did you use to gauge when to move on?

Notice that the teaching partner was not directly recommending any specific procedures or rules for teachers to follow, but there was a set of concepts the mentor wanted teachers to understand. Teaching partners posed questions that might help teachers think harder about their classroom experiences, about the relationship between their own behaviors and the behaviors of their students, and about the enacted meaning of these concepts.

This kind of conversation, of course, requires that mentors themselves must be able to select revealing moments for examination, and must be able to pose provocative questions rather than recommend specific behaviors. If such a program wanted to expand, it would not be easy for them to hire more mentors, or even to define their selection criteria. As PD providers shift their programs away from procedures and knowledge and toward strategic thinking, they depend more and more on PD providers who themselves have enough depth of experience that they can recognize "teachable moments" within the PD process.

Do Program Effects Accumulate Over Time?

Although the bulk of programs spent a single academic year with teachers, there were a handful that continued to interact with teachers for a second year, and one remained for a third year. These programs may have added more content to their curriculum during their second and third years, or perhaps they used that time to reinforce their original ideas, making sure teachers would not fall back into bad habits from the past. In either case, these programs provide an opportunity for us to look at potential cumulative effects. That is, do additional years of engagement yield additional improvements in student learning?

Six programs spent more than one academic year with their teachers. Five spent a second year and the sixth spent both a second and a third year. Their results are shown graphically in Figure 4.

As with Figure 3, the beginning of each line reflects the program effects at the end of the first year of the program. Overall, this chart looks remarkably similar to Figure 3 in its distribution of Year 1 effects. Both charts include a couple of programs whose first-year effects were relatively small, and whose effects didn't change much during Year 2. Together, these charts suggest that programs with weak first-year effects failed to produce either delayed effects or cumulative effects later on.

The remaining slopes, those that started with greater Year 1 effects, show only slight changes during Year 2 and may reflect nothing more than random variations in outcomes. They certainly do not suggest that extended programs are adding a noticeable benefit. But a comparison of Figures 3 and 4 invites some interesting hypotheses about teacher learning. Figure 3 suggests that teachers might be continuing to grow during Year 2 as they find more ways to incorporate new ideas into their practices. That is, when programs spend one year with them, teachers then spend the next year further refining their new understandings and further improving their practice. But Figure 4 suggests that when programs spend a second year with them, the program may actually interfere with teachers' need to consolidate their new knowledge, so that second-year program effects tend to drift downward. While the data we have so far are sketchy, they do suggest that we need to design longer term studies if we are to gauge the full effects of our programs.

FIGURE 4
Cumulative Program Effects

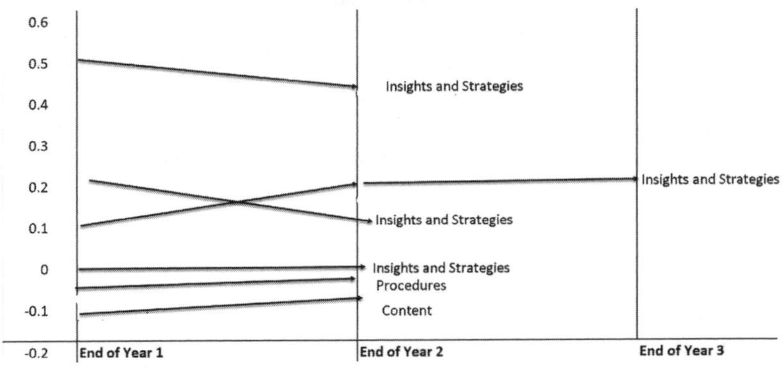

WHERE TO NEXT?

The first study I described here (Anderson et al., 1979) was conducted almost 40 years ago, and I suspect it was the first experimental study of PD ever published in an educational journal. In the intervening years, education researchers have continued to pursue questions about what makes one teacher better than another, and about how we can provide guidance that would help teachers improve their practice. Many of our efforts have been naive in the sense that we thought teaching was much simpler than it has turned out to be.

I sorted these PD programs into three ways of thinking about how to improve teaching: one focusing on teaching behaviors, one on increasing content knowledge, and one on strategic thinking. The evidence we have now suggests that the third approach has had the greatest positive impact on teachers' effectiveness. Furthermore, there is some evidence that this approach enables teachers to *continue* to improve their own practice independently after the formal PD is finished. I suspect that the reason for this delayed success has to do with its emphasis on purpose, which in turn helps teachers function autonomously after the PD providers are gone.

I hope over time it will become customary for PD researchers to follow teachers for at least one full school year beyond the program's duration. As Huberman (1993) pointed out a long time ago, teachers are essentially tinkerers. They are accustomed to working in isolation, they depend heavily on their own personal innovations, and they depend on automated habits and routines. It makes sense, then, that they would need time to incorporate new ideas into their habits and routines. Though a few studies have followed teachers for a year beyond their treatment, the data shown here are too skimpy to yield any firm conclusion.

An important remaining problem has to do with replication. The most effective PD programs appear to be designed and carried out by people who have gained deep personal knowledge of the intricacies of teaching. The patterns shown above suggest that their effectiveness is at least partially a function of this intimate knowledge. It is not clear whether or how PD providers can share this form of knowledge with other PD providers, thus raising questions about whether these programs can be expanded very much. We have reached a situation in which our knowledge about how to conduct productive PD is increasing but our ability to spread that knowledge is not. Meantime, teachers are being "treated" with ever-increasing volumes of packaged PD, at great expense to school districts and with almost no benefit for themselves or their students.

NOTES

[1]The present population of studies differs from the 2016 review as follows: (a) It excludes four studies whose samples included fewer than 20 teachers; (b) it removes one study that did not use random assignment and that I had mistakenly included earlier; (c) it includes four studies that followed teachers for less than a full academic year (my 2016 criteria required a minimum full academic year minimum); and (d) it adds six studies published since that review was completed.

[2]Randomization can be done in many ways. Researchers may assign individual teachers, whole school populations, or subgroups of teachers within schools. Sometimes they solicit volunteers first and then assign only volunteers to groups. The most common mistake in PD research is to solicit volunteers for their program, then seek out a group of *seemingly* comparable teachers for a comparison. This design overlooks the importance of motivation to learn as a factor in learning, and I rejected all of the studies based on matched groups.

[3]Readers are referred to my earlier article (Kennedy, 2016) in the *Review of Educational Research* for computational details.

[4]The following analysis is not intended to draw conclusions about relative program effectiveness but rather to use outcome patterns to generate hypotheses about teacher learning and about how PD fosters learning.

[5]I have not formally tested for differences among discrete program effects. Study sample sizes ranged from 20 to over 400 with more recent studies using larger samples.

STUDIES EXAMINED

Allen, J. P., Pianta, R. C., Gregory, A., Mikami, A. Y., & Lun, J. (2011). An interaction-based approach to enhancing secondary school instruction and student achievement. *Science, 333*, 19, 1034–1037.

Anderson, L. M., Evertson, C. M., & Brophy, J. E. (1979). An experimental study of effective teaching in first-grade reading groups. *Elementary School Journal, 4*, 193–223.

Babinski, L., Amendum, S. J., Knotek, S. E., Sanche, M., & Malone, P. (2018). Improving young English learners' language and literacy skills through teacher professional development: A randomized controlled trial. *American Educational Research Journal, 55*, 117–143.

Borman, G. D., Gamoran, A., & Bowdon, J. (2008). A randomized trial of teacher development in elementary science: First-year achievement effects. *Journal of Research on Educational Effectiveness, 1*, 237–264.

Campbell, P. F., & Malkus, N. N. (2011). The impact of elementary mathematics coaches on student achievement. *Elementary School Journal, 111*, 430–454.

Carpenter, T. P., Fennema, E., Peterson, P. L., Chiang, C.-P., & Loef, M. (1989). Using knowledge of children's mathematics thinking in classroom teaching: An experimental study. *American Educational Research Journal, 26*, 499–531.

Coladarci, T., & Gage, N. L. (1984). Effects of a minimal intervention on teacher behavior and student achievement. *American Educational Research Journal, 21*, 539–555.

Duffy, G. G., Roehler, L. R., Sivan, E., Rackliffe, G., Book, C., Meloth, M. S., . . . Bassiri, D. (1987). Effects of explaining the reasoning associated with using reading strategies. *Reading Research Quarterly, 22*, 347–368.

Garet, M. S., Cronen, S., Eaton, M., Kurki, A., Ludwig, M., Jones, W., . . . Sztejnberg, L. (2008). *The impact of two professional development interventions on early reading instruction and achievement.* Washington, DC: National Center for Educational Evaluation and Regional Assistance, Institute of Education Sciences. Retrieved from http://ies.ed.gov/ncee/pdf/20084031

Garet, M. S., Helpen, J. B., Walters, K., Parkinson, J., Smith, T. M., Song, M., . . . Yang, R. (2016). *Focusing on mathematical content knowledge: The impact of content-intensive teacher professional development.* Washington, DC: U.S. Department of Education.

Garet, M. S., Wayne, A. J., Stancavage, F., Taylor, J., Eaton, M., Walters, K., . . . Doolittle, F. (2011). *Middle school mathematics professional development impact study: Findings after the second year of implementation.* Washington, DC: U.S. Department of Education. Retrieved from http://ies.ed.gov/pubsearch/pubsinfo.asp?pubid=NCEE20114024

Gersten, R., Dimino, J., Jayanthi, M., Kim, J. S., & Santoro, L. E. (2010). Teacher study group: Impact of the professional development model on reading instruction and student outcomes in first grade classrooms. *American Educational Research Journal, 47*, 694–739.

Glazerman, S., Isenberg, E., Dolfin, S., Bleeker, M., Johnson, A., Grider, M., & Jacobus, M. (2010). *Impacts of comprehensive teacher induction: Final results from a randomized controlled study.* Washington, DC: National Center for Education Evaluation. Retrieved from https://files.eric.ed.gov/fulltext/ED565837.pdf

Good, T. L., & Grouws, D. A. (1979). The Missouri Mathematics Effectiveness Project: An experimental study in fourth grade classrooms. *Journal of Educational Psychology, 71*, 355–362.

Greenleaf, C. L., Litman, C., Hanson, T. L., Rosen, R., Boscardin, C. K., Herman, J., . . . Jones, B. (2011). Integrating literacy and science in biology: Teaching and learning impacts of reading apprenticeship professional development. *American Educational Research Journal, 48*, 647–717.

Heller, J. I., Dahler, K. R., Wong, N., Shinohara, M., & Miratrix, L. W. (2012). Differential effects of three professional development models on teacher knowledge and student achievement in elementary science. *Journal of Research in Science Teaching, 49*, 333–362.

Jacobs, V. R., Franke, M. L., Carpenter, T., Levi, L., & Battey, D. (2007). Professional development focused on children's algebraic reasoning in elementary school. *Journal for Research in Mathematics Education, 38*, 258–288.

Jayanthi, M., Gersten, R., Taylor, M. J., Smolkowski, K., & Dimino, J. (2017). *Impact of the developing mathematical ideas professional development program on grade 4 students' and teachers' understanding of fractions.* Washington, DC: National Center for Educational Evaluation and Regional Assistance.

Matsumura, L. C., Garnier, H. E., Correnti, R., Junker, B., & Bickel, D. D. (2010). Investigating the effectiveness of a comprehensive literacy coaching program in schools with high teacher mobility. *Elementary School Journal, 111*, 35–62.

McMeeking, L. B. S., Orsi, R., & Cobb, R. B. (2012). Effects of a teacher professional development program on the mathematics achievement of middle school students. *Journal for Research in Mathematics Education, 43*, 159–181.

Myers, C. V., Molefe, A., Brandt, W. C., Zhu, B., & Dhillon, S. (2016). Impact results of the eMints professional development validation study. *Educational Evaluation and Policy Analysis, 38* 455–476.

Niess, M. (2005). Oregon ESEA Title IIB MSP: Central Oregon Consortium. Corvallis: Department of Science and Mathematics Education, Oregon State University.

Papay, J. P., Taylor, E. S., Tyler, J. H., & Laski, M. (2016). *Learning job skills from colleagues at work: Evidence from a field experiment using teacher performance data.* Cambridge, MA: National Bureau of Economic Research.

Penuel, W. R., Gallagher, L. P., & Moorthy, S. (2011). Preparing teachers to design sequences of instruction in earth science: A comparison of three professional development programs. *American Educational Research Journal, 48,* 996–1025.

Roth, K. J., Garnier, H. E., Chen, C., Lemmens, M., Schwille, K., & Wickler, N. I. Z. (2011). Videobased lesson analysis: Effective science PD for teacher and student learning. *Journal for Research in Science Teaching, 48,* 117–148.

Sailors, M., & Price, L. R. (2010). Professional development that supports the teaching of cognitive reading strategy instruction. *Elementary School Journal, 110,* 301–322.

Santagata, R., Kersting, N., Givvin, K. B., & Stigler, J. W. (2011). Problem implementation as a lever for change: An experimental study of the effects of a professional development program on students' mathematics learning. *Journal of Research on Educational Effectiveness, 4,* 1–24.

Schoen, R. C., LaVenia, M., Tazaz, A. M., & Faraina, K. (2018). *Replicating the CGI experiment in diverse environments: Effects of Year 1 on student achievement.* Tallahassee: Florida State University Learning Systems Institute.

Supovitz, J. (2013, April). *The linking study: An experiment to strengthen teachers' engagement with data on teaching and learning.* Paper presented at the American Educational Research Association conference, San Francisco, CA. Retrieved from https://files.eric.ed.gov/fulltext/ED547667.pdf

REFERENCES

Allen, J. P., Pianta, R. C., Gregory, A., Mikami, A. Y., & Lun, J. (2011). An interaction-based approach to enhancing secondary school instruction and student achievement. *Science, 333,* 19, 1034–1037.

Anderson, L. M., Evertson, C. M., & Brophy, J. E. (1979). An experimental study of effective teaching in first-grade reading groups. *Elementary School Journal, 4,* 193–223.

Borman, G. D., Gamoran, A., & Bowdon, J. (2008). A randomized trial of teacher development in elementary science: First-year achievement effects. *Journal of Research on Educational Effectiveness, 1,* 237–264.

Bredeson, P. V. (2001). Negotiated learning: Union contracts and teacher professional development. *Education Policy Analysis Archives, 9.* Retrieved from https://epaa.asu.edu/ojs/article/viewFile/355/481

Carpenter, T. P., Fennema, E., Peterson, P. L., Chiang, C.-P., & Loef, M. (1989). Using knowledge of children's mathematics thinking in classroom teaching: An experimental study. *American Educational Research Journal, 26,* 499–531.

Clark, C. M., & Peterson, P. L. (1986). Teachers' thought processes. In M. C. Wittrock (Ed.), *Handbook of research on teaching* (3rd ed., pp. 255–296). New York, NY: Macmillan.

Cohen, J. (1988). *Statistical power analysis for the behavioral sciences.* Hillsdale, NJ: Lawrence Erlbaum.

Coladarci, T., & Gage, N. L. (1984). Effects of a minimal intervention on teacher behavior and student achievement. *American Educational Research Journal, 21,* 539–555.

Fennema, E., Carpenter, T., Levi, L., Franke, M. L., & Empson, S. B. (1999). *Children's mathematics: Cognitively guided instruction: A guide for workshop leaders.* Portsmouth, NH: Heinemann.

Gage, N. L. (1977). *The scientific basis of the art of teaching.* New York, NY: Teachers College Press.

Garet, M. S., Cronen, S., Eaton, M., Kurki, A., Ludwig, M., Jones, W., . . . Sztejnberg, L. (2008). *The impact of two professional development interventions on early reading instruction and achievement.* Washington, DC: National Center for Educational Evaluation and Regional Assistance, Institute of Education Sciences. Retrieved from http://ies.ed.gov/ncee/pdf/20084031

Garet, M. S., Helpen, J. B., Walters, K., Parkinson, J., Smith, T. M., Song, M., . . . Yang, R. (2016). *Focusing on mathematical content knowledge: The impact of content-intensive teacher professional development.* Washington, DC: U.S. Department of Education.

Garet, M. S., Wayne, A. J., Stancavage, F., Taylor, J., Eaton, M., Walters, K., . . . Doolittle, F. (2011). *Middle school mathematics professional development impact study: Findings after the second year of implementation.* Washington, DC: U.S. Department of Education. Retrieved from http://ies.ed.gov/pubsearch/pubsinfo.asp?pubid=NCEE20114024

Garet, M. S., Wayne, A. J., Stancavage, F., Taylor, J., Walters, K., Song, M., . . . Hurlburt, S. (2010). *Middle school mathematics professional development impact study: Findings after the first year of implementation.* Washington, DC: U.S. Department of Education. Retrieved from http://ies.ed.gov/ncee/pubs/20104009/

Gersten, R., Dimino, J., Jayanthi, M., Kim, J. S., & Santoro, L. E. (2010). Teacher study group: Impact of the professional development model on reading instruction and student outcomes in first grade classrooms. *American Educational Research Journal, 47,* 694–739.

Good, T. L., & Grouws, D. A. (1979). The Missouri Mathematics Effectiveness Project: An experimental study in fourth grade classrooms. *Journal of Educational Psychology, 71,* 355–362.

Heller, J. I., Dahler, K. R., Wong, N., Shinohara, M., & Miratrix, L. W. (2012). Differential effects of three professional development models on teacher knowledge and student achievement in elementary science. *Journal of Research in Science Teaching, 49,* 333–362.

Hill, C. J., Bloom, H. S., Black, A. R., & Lipskey, M. W. (2008). Empirical benchmarks for interpreting effect sizes in research. *Child Development Perspectives, 2,* 172–177.

Huberman, M. (1993). The model of the independent artisan in teachers' professional relations. In J. W. Little, & M. W. McLaughlin (Eds.), *Teachers' work: Individuals, colleagues, context* (pp. 11–50). New York, NY: Teachers College Press.

Jacobs, V. R., Franke, M. L., Carpenter, T., Levi, L., & Battey, D. (2007). Professional development focused on children's algebraic reasoning in elementary school. *Journal for Research in Mathematics Education, 38,* 258–288.

Jayanthi, M., Gersten, R., Taylor, M. J., Smolkowski, K., & Dimino, J. (2017). *Impact of the Developing Mathematical Ideas professional development program on grade 4 students' and teachers' understanding of fractions.* Washington, DC: National Center for Educational Evaluation and Regional Assistance.

Kennedy, M. M. (1998). *Form and substance in inservice teacher education.* Madison: University of Wisconsin National Institute for Science Education. Retrieved from www.msu.edu/~mkennedy/publications/valuePD.html

Kennedy, M. M. (2005). *Inside teaching: How classroom life undermines reform.* Cambridge, MA: Harvard University Press.

Kennedy, M. M. (2010a). Attribution error and the quest for teacher quality. *Educational Researcher, 39,* 591–598.

Kennedy, M. M. (2010b). *Teacher assessment and the quest for teacher quality: A handbook.* San Francisco, CA: Jossey Bass.

Kennedy, M. M. (2016). How does professional development improve teaching? *Review of Educational Research, 86,* 945–980.

Lortie, D. C. (1975). *Schoolteacher: A sociological study.* Chicago, IL: University of Chicago Press.

McDaniels, G. L. (1975). The evaluation of follow through. *Educational Researcher, 4*(11), 7–11.

Niess, M. (2005). *Oregon ESEA Title IIB MSP: Central Oregon Consortium.* Corvallis: Department of Science & Mathematics Education, Oregon State University.

Papay, J. P., Taylor, E. S., Tyler, J. H., & Laski, M. (2016). *Learning job skills from colleagues at work: Evidence from a field experiment using teacher performance data.* Cambridge, MA: National Bureau of Economic Research.

Rot it right: The cycling of matter and the transfer of energy. 4th grade science immersion unit. (2006). Los Angeles, CA: SCALE. Retrieved from http://fastplants.org/pdf/scale/rotitright2006.pdf

Schoen, R. C., LaVenia, M., Tazaz, A. M., & Faraina, K. (2018). *Replicating the CGI experiment in diverse environments: Effects of Year 1 on student achievement.* Tallahassee: Florida State University Learning Systems Institute.

Shulman, L. S. (1986a). Those who understand: Knowledge growth in teaching. *Educational Researcher, 15*(2), 4–14.

Shulman, L. S. (1986b). Paradigms and research programs in the study of teaching: A contemporary perspective. In M. C. Wittrock (Ed.), *Handbook of research on teaching* (3rd ed., pp. 3–36). New York, NY: Macmillan.

Shulman, L. S. (1987). Knowledge and teaching: Foundations of the new reform. *Harvard Educational Review, 57*, 1–22.

TNTP. (2015). *The Mirage: Confronting the hard truth about our quest for teacher development.* New York, NY: Author. Retrieved from https://tntp.org/publications/view/the-mirage-confronting-the-truth-about-our-quest-for-teacher-development

Chapter 6

Action Research and Systematic, Intentional Change in Teaching Practice

MEGHAN MCGLINN MANFRA
North Carolina State University

Action research shifts the paradigm of contemporary educational reform by emphasizing inquiry and placing teachers at the center of research-into-practice. By situating teachers as learners, action research offers a systematic and intentional approach to changing teaching. When working as part of a community of practice, action researchers engage in sustained professional learning activities. They explore issues of everyday practice and work to bring about change. This review highlights action research studies from across four subject areas— English language arts, mathematics, science, and social studies—and is premised on the notion that changing teaching practice is connected to understanding how teachers learn. Specifically, it focuses on understanding changes in teacher pedagogical content knowledge, disciplinary inquiry, and critical pedagogy through action research. Findings suggest that we must go beyond current conceptualizations of teacher learning as process-product, cognitive, and situative to view teaching as inquiry. Successful efforts to change practice through action research have demonstrated the value of engaging teachers as active participants in education research. At the same time, the field must overcome barriers including the marginalization of action research, logistical issues associated with conducting action research, and the dissemination of findings.

Contemporary educational reform has focused mainly on top-down, outside-in approaches to changing teaching practice (Gottlieb, 2014; McGuinn, 2012). Rather than rely on teacher judgment and teacher decision making in the classroom (Biesta & Stengel, 2016), databases of "evidence-based" practices describe "what works" in education (Farley-Ripple, May, Karpyn, Tilley, & McDonough, 2018; Institute of Educational Sciences, 2017). However, current research demonstrates that teaching practice is little affected by top-down, one-size-fits-all approaches to educational reform (Fullan, 2010; Hofman, de Boom,

Review of Research in Education
March 2019, Vol. 43, pp. 163–196
DOI: 10.3102/0091732X18821132
Chapter reuse guidelines: sagepub.com/journals-permissions
© 2019 AERA. http://rre.aera.net

Meeuwisse, & Hofman, 2012). Short-duration workshops in particular appear to have little impact on improving teacher practice (Hammerness, Darling-Hammond, & Bransford, 2005). Rather, professional learning opportunities must be connected to everyday practice, sustained and prolonged, and conducted as part of community of practice to bring about real change in teaching (Fullan, 2010; Hawley & Valli, 1999; Putnam & Borko, 2000).

Action researchers engage in "systematic and intentional inquiry" (Cochran-Smith & Lytle, 2009, p. 142) or "systematic, self-critical enquiry" (Stenhouse, 1985). The focus is on bringing about change in practice, improving student outcomes, and empowering teachers (Mills, 2017). Following a cycle of inquiry and reflection, action researchers collect and analyze data related to an issue(s) of practice. By situating teachers as scholars and knowledge producers, action research fundamentally shifts the culture of contemporary school reform and offers an antidote to educational reform efforts that de-professionalize teachers (Elliot, 1976; Kincheloe, 2003; McNiff, 2016).

This review explores action research literature focused on changing teaching practice to answer the following:

- How has change in teaching practice been conceptualized, evidenced, and analyzed in action research?
- What are the key barriers affecting intentional, coordinated, and sustained change through action research?

To conduct this review of the literature, I engaged in an iterative process to identify relevant studies beginning with major databases. The methodological aim was to conduct "a substantive, thorough, sophisticated literature review" in order "to advance our collective understanding" (Boote & Beile, 2005, p. 3). In keeping with Shulman's (1999) notion of "generativity," it provides a basis for future work in the area of action research and teacher learning.

By tracing action research literature across four subject areas—English language arts (ELA), mathematics, science, and the social studies—it reflects contemporary emphasis on these subjects in the public school "core" curriculum and professional development literature (Brady, 2010) and provides a basis for comparative analysis. The results contribute to the scholarship of teaching, especially with regard to improving pedagogical content knowledge (PCK), integrating disciplinary inquiry into instruction, and engaging teachers and students in critical pedagogy. Collectively these findings require us to reconsider the manner in which we position teachers as learners and make connections between research and practice.

CONCEPTUALIZING TEACHER LEARNING

This review is premised on the notion that changing teaching practice is connected to understanding how teachers learn. Russ, Sherin, and Sherin (2016) identify three perspectives of teacher learning and teaching as: "process-product"—"teaching as a set of actions;" "cognitive modeling"—"teaching as a way of thinking;" and "situative and sociocultural perspective"—"teaching as interacting." However, findings from the action research literature demonstrate the need to add a fourth category: teaching as inquiry.

Teacher learning conceptualized as "process-product" reduces teaching to a set of actions. From the process-product perspective, teacher learning involves changing teacher actions, independent of the context of the classroom. Relevant research focuses on teacher training, often around a series of indiscriminate teaching skills such as "wait time" (e.g., Tobin, 1987), "indirect teaching" (Flanders, 1970), and lesson planning (C. M. Clark et al., 1979). Here teacher learning is measured based on the extent to which teachers demonstrate fidelity to a particular model of pedagogy.

Teacher learning as cognitive modeling focuses on the mental life or "practical wisdom" of teachers (Biesta & Stengel, 2016, p. 37). Here teacher knowledge is context-dependent, and PCK represents "that special amalgam of content and pedagogy that is uniquely the province of teachers, their own special form of professional understanding" (Shulman, 1987, p. 8). PCK includes knowledge of subject matter and curriculum, knowledge of students, and pedagogical knowledge.

From this perspective, for teachers to learn, they must have authentic, prolonged, and sustained experiences that connect to their everyday work. As teachers translate content knowledge through the filter of their knowledge of learners and the educational context in which they practice, what emerges is their knowledge of teaching. To gauge teacher learning, researchers seek to understand the mental processes of teachers and how those processes change based on experience (Van Driel & Berry, 2012). They rely on indirect evidence of teacher knowledge "to make claims about the knowledge that teachers must possess in order to talk/behave in those ways" (Russ et al., 2016, p. 399).

Within the situative perspective, teacher learning and changes in practice are placed in "their larger social, physical, cultural, and historical contexts" (Russ et al., 2016, p. 402). According to Putnam and Borko (2000), this perspective "focuses researchers' attention on how various settings for teachers' learning give rise to different kinds of knowing" (p. 6). Research in this vein includes classroom discourse and developing "equitable communities that empower a range of students" (Russ et al., 2016, p. 404). Often this approach focuses on understanding how communities of teachers negotiate change, including changes to community norms, identities and roles, and teaching strategies.

ACTION RESEARCH AS A FOURTH PERSPECTIVE

Although the cognitive and situative perspectives align most closely with action research, they nonetheless situate teachers in traditional roles, outside of the research endeavor. According to Cochran-Smith and Lytle (1993), missing in these perspectives are "the voices of the teachers themselves, the questions that teachers ask, and the interpretive frames that teachers use to understand and to improve their own classroom practices" (p. 7). Action research represents a fourth perspective on teacher learning — teaching as inquiry.

Through action research, teachers' beliefs, their professional identities, and their levels of expertise change (Warren, Doorn, & Green, 2008). As they engage in systematic reflection, teacher action researchers improve their PCK as they reflect on practice, modifying and "fine-tuning" the knowledge base (Zeichner & Noffke, 2001). At the same time, engaging in action research empowers practitioners to bring about both practical and critical social change in their schools and communities (Vaughan & Burnaford, 2015; Zeichner, 2001). As a result, action research studies often focus on the needs of diverse learners and aim to create socially just and culturally relevant educational experiences (Price, 2001; Price & Valli, 2005; Storms, 2013).

The inquiry perspective addresses some of the challenges associated with teacher learning from both cognitive and situative perspectives, including, for example, the need for teachers to engage in active problem solving to develop subject-specific knowledge (Shulman, 1987), to "unlearn" practices that are no longer successful (e.g., Sherin, 2002), and to improve practice while also changing the context in which that practice occurs (Zeichner & Noffke, 2001). Through the process of engaging in action research, inquiry becomes a part of the identity of the teacher—teaching *is* inquiry (Cochran-Smith & Lytle, 2009; Jaworski, 2003; McNiff, 2016). As the teacher becomes situated as a learner, the processes of learning and teaching cannot be separated. The epistemology of action research is one of knowledge in action, and the emphasis is on change through action (Hendricks, 2009; McNiff, 2016).

Theory and practice are not separated in action research—theory emerges from systematic and intentional reflection on practice (Loughran, 2002). According to Hendricks (2009), "Knowledge is something that action researchers do—their living practice" (p. 3). Since the emphasis is on change, the inquiry is generative. The theories *of* action or theories *in* action that emerge from action research not only describe but also bring about change in pedagogy and teaching practice. For example, according to van Manen (1990), "Our ability [as action researchers] to bring to language (theorize) our insights becomes the measure of our thoughtfulness," and this "enables me to enrich and make more thoughtful my future pedagogical experience;" the result is more than just intellectual but a "matter of pedagogical fitness" and greater "mindfulness towards children" (p. 156). By engaging in systematic and intentional inquiry, teacher action researchers theorize and act to improve teaching with greater mindfulness or cognition about the impact those practices have on students.

APPROACHES TO ACTION RESEARCH

Within the action research literature there is frequent discussion about differences between action research and other related methodologies (see Borko, Whitcomb, & Byrnes, 2008; Noffke & Somekh, 2009; Reason & Bradbury, 2008). There are also concerns about various approaches to action research, including "first-, second-, and third-person" action research (Reason & Torbet, 2001); action research "as social inquiry," "as ways of knowing within communities," and "practical inquiry" (Cochran-Smith & Lytle, 1999, p. 17); or technical, practical, and emancipatory action research (see Grundy, 1982; Kemmis, McTaggart, & Nixon, 2014).

Theorizing about various approaches is perhaps part of a larger process of legitimatizing action research within the academy or "[a] form of tribalism and territorialism that specified what counts as 'legitimate' action research" (McNiff, 2016, p. 33). Proponents of critical action research critique "benign" forms of action research that fail to address systemic sociocultural and political issues that shape schooling (Kemmis et al., 2014; Kincheloe, 1995). Practical action research is viewed as "practical-deliberative" research (McKernan, 1996) with a focus on developing "practical reasoning" (Kemmis et al., 2014, p. 11) to "enhance practical knowledge" (Cochran-Smith & Lytle, 1999, p. 19).

Nonetheless there is common ground among the approaches when it comes to changing teaching practice. A common element across all forms of action research is the manner in which they diverge from more "traditional," techno-rationalist forms of research (Kemmis, 2006; Kemmis et al., 2014; Lincoln, 1998; McNiff, 2016). Due to the nature of the action research process, teachers who begin a project engaged in practical inquiry can move toward critical inquiry (see Kinsler 2010; Rust & Meyer, 2006; van Manen, 1990). Teachers understand that teaching is complex and that it cannot be divided into practical and critical concerns. "Missing within the gap between practical and critical action research is a sense of the nuance of teacher practice—the reality of classroom life that is mutually steeped in practical and critical concerns" (Manfra, 2009a, p. 41). These concerns are revealed through a systematic process of data collection and analysis focused on changing teaching. Given the marked differences between contemporary paradigms of education research and teacher learning, action research methodology provides a fourth, distinct approach to conceptualizing teacher learning through inquiry.

TEACHING AS INQUIRY

The analysis of action research literature within the fields of ELA, mathematics, science, and social studies reveals a common theme toward improving subject matter teaching practice through inquiry. To improve teacher learning and PCK, action research has been integrated into professional learning programs for experienced and preservice teachers across the subject areas. The result has been integrating theory into practice and developing theory through practice. These action research studies offer new insights about practical pedagogical experience through critical interpretation of practice (van Manen, 1990). They focus on integrating discipline-specific pedagogies and, in some cases, more culturally relevant or critical pedagogies to improve teaching. Most of the studies draw on social science or ethnographic methods to collect evidence to describe and analyze changes in teaching practice. Across the studies, the findings and the theories that emerged to describe those findings became an integral part of practice for the action researchers. Collaborative approaches appear to be most effective at supporting teachers in changing teaching practice. Of particular importance is the shift toward viewing teaching as a form of inquiry.

ACTION RESEARCH AND CHANGING TEACHING PRACTICE IN ELA EDUCATION

Within the ELA field, there is a marked emphasis on challenging traditional modes of education research by bridging theory and practice through action research (Wittrock, 2005). Here it is assumed that teachers have access to important insider knowledge (Athanases, 2011). Relevant studies cover a range of topics relevant to the discipline. By situating understanding within the context of practice, "the knowledge authority is placed inside the learning community" (Bloome, Chapman, & Freebody, 2011, p. 356). As a result, much of the action research effort within the field has focused on impacting teacher PCK, especially as part of university-school partnerships that facilitate the creation of communities of inquiry.

ELA Teachers as Learners

Action research conducted by preservice and experienced English teachers focuses on changing the teaching of reading and writing and emphasizes the importance of understanding the experiences of students as a basis for improving teaching (e.g., Ballenger, 1996, 1999; Burns, 2009; Douillard, 2003; Gallas, 2003; Lee, 1993; Sayer, 2005; Silvers, 2001). Based on her analysis of action research data, Gallas (2003) described changing her teaching to focus more on student imagination, storytelling, and comprehension. Similarly, Lee (1993) integrated new strategies based on her findings to teach literacy skills and writing to better match the experiences of her students. Douillard (2003) revised her writing assessments to provide her students with clear prompts and more detailed rubrics to capture more nuance in student writing. Here the reports described how teaching changed as a result of the action research and provided insight about pedagogical strategies that are effective with students. According to Fecho (2004), "My current understandings about how literacy is taught and learned shape decisions about my practice; my implementation of those decisions, aided by systematic reflection, further shapes my evolving theory" (p. 29).

In reporting on action research, the teachers developed greater mindfulness toward their students, which improved their "pedagogical fitness" (van Manen, 1990). This process included becoming "an astute observer of the students' thinking processes, by taking instructional cues from the tacit and expressed views of the students" (Silvers, 2001, p. 561). By becoming students of their students, these action researchers became better teachers. Burns (2009), based on her analysis of samples of elementary students' writing, drawings, and discussions over the course of a month-long unit, described being better able to gauge student readiness to confront complex issues.

In some cases, improved mindfulness meant addressing misperceptions about students. For example, Burton's ability to interrogate student writing behavior changed as he engaged in action research: "It was only through the processes of acting and reflecting over time that he later began to view Alan [his student] as a 'methodical' rather than a 'reluctant' writer" (Burton & Seidle, 2005, p. 200). Ballenger (1996, 1999) documented how her action research in a preschool classroom led her to change her preconceptions about early literacy practices and, in turn, shift her teaching. As the only American in a Haitian preschool, Ballenger (1996) was "forced to reconsider [her] beliefs, to try to understand what lay behind them" (p. 317). Hankins (1999) came to a similar conclusion in her reflection of her experiences as a second-grade teacher, writing that action research enabled her to not only listen but also hear her students.

Meta-analyses of action research conducted in ELA classrooms suggest that engaging in systematic and intentional reflection about practice improves teacher PCK and positively affects student learning outcomes. Pella (2015) followed five teachers over 3 years and nine cycles of lesson study. She found that the teacher action researchers developed more sophisticated pedagogical reasoning and improved their teaching of persuasive writing. Limbrick, Buchanan, Goodwin, and Schwarcz (2010) collected data over a 2-year period to understand the experiences of 20 elementary teachers engaged in action research. They concluded that the teachers experienced "enhanced pedagogical and content knowledge of writing" and they noted "marked gains for students on a standardized test of writing" (p. 897).

The positive impact of conducting action research on pedagogical decision making and PCK also appears in teacher education literature in English education (Vaughan & Burnaford, 2015). Here action research has been integrated into preservice education to help novice teachers "retheorize" their initial assumptions and beliefs (Scherff, 2012). For instance, Hillocks (2007) required preservice teachers to prepare, test, reflect on, and refine teaching strategies for narrative writing. As a result, they appeared to internalize the process of systematic reflection as an integral part of teaching writing. Bentley (2013) also found that, by studying their experiences as action researchers, preservice teachers developed, "'insider knowledge' as writers, thus affecting their beliefs and practices for teaching writing" (p. 218).

Critical Issues

Within ELA classrooms, action researchers have also investigated strategies for changing teaching practice to more effectively teach subject matter content in diverse contexts (Fecho & Allen, 2005). Again the theme of mindfulness appears in the work, although the intentionality is much more critically oriented. Fecho (2001) set out to open up "dialogue around issues of race and social justice" in his classroom (p. 10). Of particular importance for him was understanding "ways threat transacts in a critical inquiry classroom" (p. 10). Delp's action research study (see Freedman & Delp, 2007; Freedman, Delp, & Crawford, 2005) was situated within an untracked ELA classroom in an urban high school. The aim was to create "grand dialogic zones" in diverse whole-class settings. She adapted her curriculum and teaching to the needs of her students by providing explicit directions to support their engagement in classroom dialogue. This work parallels Christensen's (1989, 1990, 1993) action research focused on integrating critical inquiry about written texts in untracked English classes.

It appears that critical action research projects arose from practical concerns such as student engagement. For example, Lee (1993) implemented action research to integrate the African American social discourse of "signifying" to teach literary interpretation. Perminder, a fourth-grade teacher, participated in a Canada-wide action research project focused on developing multiliteracies pedagogy (Giampapa, 2010) to improve student achievement. As these action researchers changed their teaching practice they found evidence of a positive impact on student outcomes. When Lee (1993) compared her "experimental" approach to a control group, she found statistically significant gains from the pretest to the posttest. As a result of his action research, Fecho and his students developed "deeper and more complicated understandings of racial and ethnic issues in general" (Fecho, 2003, p. 285).

Within ELA classrooms, teachers also use participatory action research (PAR) to engage students actively in interrogating critical issues. Tendero (1998) describes the "Write for Your Life Project" in which she worked with 14 middle school girls to investigate the issue of teen pregnancy. As a result of their inquiry, the girls published a booklet on the subject. Sturk (1992) engaged her students in a PAR project that focused on caring for senior citizens in their community. Their work gained attention from community members and, as a result of their experiences, students became more politically active.

Collaborative and University-School Partnerships in ELA

Action research has been a major precept of the National Writing Project (NWP), enabling widespread participation of teachers from diverse contexts. It originated in 1974 with the Bay Area Writing Project as a university-school partnership. Today teachers in every state participate in NWP professional development projects (NWP, 2008; St. John & Stokes, 2008), and universities across the country continue to provide outreach and support. The NWP (2008) has significantly affected student achievement in writing as well as the adaption of action research as a form of professional learning (MacLean & Mohr, 1999). From its inception the NWP has taken an explicit equity stance that is reflected in the work of affiliated projects.

In projects that have evolved out of the NWP work, including the Pathway Project (Olson & Land, 2007) and M-CLASS (Freedman et al., 1999), teachers formed communities of practice and pursued lines of inquiry focused on marginalized youth. Over an 8-year period the Pathways Project included 55 teacher action researchers focused on ensuring English language learners developed the necessary academic language to be successful in school. The M-CLASS project created a national network of action researchers focused on literacy and multicultural education in urban schools.

It included a university-based partnership that provided support for school-based action researchers. The project also relied on site directors affiliated with the NWP in each city. In both cases the teacher participants were empowered to drive the direction of the projects and the inquiry: to "take ownership of the project and develop materials to contribute to the intervention" (Olson & Land, 2007, p. 277). According to Freedman, Simons, Kalnin, Casereno, and the M-Class Teams (1999), a major goal for the action researchers was to collect data based on practice and to use the data to provide narratives of successful strategies for teaching literacy.

The NWP and its affiliated projects, such as the School Research Consortium (Baumann, Schockley, & Allen, 1996) and the First-Ring Suburban Initiative (Cercone, 2009), influenced the work of many teachers and their students. From this work emerged new understandings about strategies for teaching literacy, particularly in urban schools. Delp (1999) began to engage in action research during her participation in the M-CLASS teacher research project and the Bay Area and NWP. Resnick (1996) and Chin (1996) participated in the Urban Sites Writing Network of the NWP, where community was a dominant theme. As teacher action researchers they developed new understandings and beliefs about the power of connecting school and home communities.

Across the projects the authors provided evidence of the positive impacts of participating in action research, including positive impacts on ELA teacher professional identities and improving teaching of ELA in diverse educational environments. Dipardo and Schnack (2004) and Smith and Connolly (2005) described partnerships between university-based researchers and teacher action researchers or "insider/outsider" research teams. For the teacher action researchers, collaboration provided an opportunity to study teaching practice more systematically. Stock (1993) credited her participation in an informal group of action researchers with colleagues from Saginaw schools and the University of Michigan as key to enabling her analysis of data. At the same time the teacher perspective proved invaluable to the university-based researchers as a means for understanding the outcomes of practice (Smith & Connolly, 2005).

ACTION RESEARCH AND CHANGING TEACHING PRACTICE IN MATHEMATICS EDUCATION

Within mathematics education, researchers continue to advocate for efforts to "acknowledge, critique, or challenge the research–practice link" (Langrall, 2014, p. 155) and seek improved collaboration between researchers and K–12 educators (The Linking Research and Practice Task Force, 2005; National Council of Teachers of Mathematics, 2005). As in other fields, advocates of action research in mathematics education focus on the value of teachers taking an inquiry stance (Doerr & Tinto, 2000; Kyei-Blankson, 2014; Lampert, 1990, 2001). Notable within the field are university-based collaborative action research projects that have engaged in a range of approaches to scaffolding inquiry as part of mathematics teacher professional learning.

Mathematics Teachers as Learners

Through the process of conducting an action research study in mathematics classrooms, teachers become learners. For example, an action researcher reported,

I have learned and will continue to learn in my classroom. There has been a paradigm shift in my thinking regarding what goes on with research and with students and how I can use research ideas to help my students. (Kyei-Blankson, 2014, p. 1059)

The experience of engaging in systematic inquiry about practice appears to change mathematics teachers' views about research and practice and impacts their PCK.

Reflective inquiry results in changing teaching practices specific to disciplinary understanding (Heaton & Mickelson, 2002; Jaworski, 2006; Katz & Stupel, 2016). For example, in Lampert's (1990) action research study she wanted her students to "know" mathematics as a discipline and "to challenge conventional assumptions about what it means to know mathematics (p. 35). To monitor the impact of her changes in teaching, she collected data over a course of a unit on teaching exponents and monitored student discourse as they developed arguments for their mathematical problem solving. She found that her students were able to develop both skills and content knowledge about exponents as well as develop fairly sophisticated disciplinary understanding about mathematical reasoning. In a similar study focused on improving student understanding of disciplinary knowledge, Hackenberg (2010) conducted an action research study focused on creating "mathematical caring relations (MCRs)" in her sixth-grade classroom. As a result of her study, she contended that integrating MCRs improved her "personal teaching efficacy" and influenced "students' construction of mathematical self-concepts" (p. 269). In these instances, the action researchers changed their teaching practices to improve student outcomes relevant to specific mathematics learning outcomes. Jaworski (2006) explains, "Improvement of mathematics learning in classrooms is fundamentally related to development in teaching, and that teaching develops through a learning process in which teachers and others grow" (p. 187).

This learning is evident in methods course work that engaged preservice mathematics teachers in reflective inquiry about their practice of using inquiry. For example, Betts, McLarty, and Dickson (2017) reported on their project to study the integration of inquiry into math education through the 4D cycle planning model. As a result of their inquiry, they concluded, for the preservice teachers, their understandings about inquiry "are enriched by applying the theory of inquiry to practice, by interpreting the theory and practice of inquiry, and developing their own personal, practical and professional theories of teaching using inquiry" (p. 10).

The embedded design of engaging preservice teachers in reflective inquiry about inquiry-based teaching also positively impacted preservice mathematics teachers in developing "mathematics subject matter knowledge (MSMK)" (Hourigan & O'Donoghue, 2015) and skills to assess students (Bragg, 2017; Zevenbergen, 2001) and also appears in action research focused on integrating inquiry into mathematics teaching and learning more generally (Betts et al., 2017; Bragg, 2017; Katz & Stupel, 2016; Mostofo, 2014; Zevenbergen, 2001). As a result of their inquiries, both the teacher educators and preservice teachers developed more nuanced understanding of the value of inquiry and the best approaches for integrating it into mathematics instruction. Across the cases, the action research cycle appeared to have positively affected the teacher educators' professional learning as well as that of the preservice math teachers in their courses.

Critical Issues

Through PAR studies, mathematics teachers changed their practice by engaging students in deliberative inquiry about sociopolitical issues that affect their daily lives (Gellert, Hernández, & Chapman, 2013). For example, Raygoza (2016) described a project in her course "Viewing and Changing the World Through Mathematics." After completing a series of scaffolded learning activities designed to connect math content to sociopolitical issues, her Algebra I students embarked on a project to investigate school food and health justice. As a result of her inquiry, her students demonstrated new understandings about research, mathematics concepts, and social justice issues. She concluded that the process of engaging students as researchers necessitated a shift toward more democratic ways of interacting within the classroom.

Collaborative and University-School Partnerships in Mathematics Education

Large-scale action research projects that included multiple mathematics teachers engaged in collaborative inquiry provided further evidence of the manner in which action research can shift PCK. In these studies, new strategies or tools for teaching were introduced, most of which were supported by federal funding. When comparing across these projects, there are examples of both tight and loose control over the direction of the action research.

In several of the projects the university-based partners facilitated the action research of participating teachers by introducing tightly scaffolded procedures for conducting the inquiry. For example, the Contemporary Teaching and Learning Mathematics program (Clarke et al., 2009) engaged early-career, elementary mathematics teachers in creating self-analysis portfolios to record and share the findings of their reflective inquiry. Similarly, Attorps and Kellner (2017) described a school-university partnership designed to improve student understanding of key math concepts. They introduced pedagogical and professional-experience repertoires linked to content representation. Muir and Beswick (2007) also introduced a protocol into the research of participating teachers— the Supporting Classroom Reflection Process. They reported that the protocol provided a necessary scaffold for maximizing the teachers' professional learning experiences.

Here the university-based facilitators found evidence that introducing the protocols within an action research framework positively influenced PCK. Scott, Clarkson, and McDonough (2012) noted shifts in math lesson planning that endured months after the project. Attorps and Kellner (2017) concluded, "Our results illustrate[d] how the pedagogical tools used in this project promoted teacher learning about teaching practices that made a difference for pupils" (p. 326), and Muir and Beswick (2007) found that through the process, the teachers developed effective strategies for teaching numeracy.

Gningue, Schroder, and Peach (2014) described a National Science Foundation–funded project in which they introduced more scaffolding of teacher inquiry over time. The main purpose of the project was to encourage middle and high school math teachers in integrating inquiry-based approaches to instruction. For many of the teachers, the new approaches to teaching required the teachers to depart "in significant ways from 'traditional' instruction" (p. 19). To support this pedagogical shift, the project team engaged two cohorts of over 40 teachers in conducting action research. In the second round, they guided the teachers through shorter duration inquiry projects described as a "cycle of teaching and inquiry model." They found the second approach to action research more effective in changing teachers' practices.

In other collaborative action research projects, the teacher action researchers were offered more choice over the topic of inquiry. The Mathematics Teacher Enquiry Project (Jaworski, 1998) engaged six teachers over an 18-month period in studies of self-chosen aspects of their own mathematics teaching. Herbel-Eisenmann (2009) described a 4-year project with eight math teachers engaged in individual research focused on the topic of communication in the mathematics classroom. Doerr and Tinto (2000) led the Mathematics Teacher/Researchers Collaborating for Collaboration in the Classroom project, funded in part by a Teacher Enhancement grant. In their project, "teachers were asked to rethink their practice but were not told what to change" (p. 248).

Across the more open-ended projects, the teacher participants reported improved efficacy regarding their ability to conduct action research and to make connections between their research and their teaching practice. For example, Jaworski (1998) noted that despite differences in the focus of their action research projects, all of the teachers pursued inquiry rooted in disciplinary teaching and learning. Herbel-Eisenmann (2009) noted that teacher reports described changes in classroom communication and discourse appropriate for the mathematics classroom. According to Doerr and Tinto (2000), as the mathematics teachers studied a range of issues related to practice, they "developed a new sense of creating a knowledge base" for mathematics teaching and learning (p. 250). Across these studies, the authors described positive impacts on the PCK of the mathematics teachers engaged in action research and documented changes in teaching. It seems that, regardless of the level of scaffolding, the teachers developed a new sense of efficacy as they adopted an inquiry stance.

ACTION RESEARCH AND CHANGING TEACHING PRACTICE IN SCIENCE EDUCATION

Action research has been integrated into professional learning opportunities for preservice and experienced teachers to increase content knowledge and science PCK

(Roth, 2007). Van Driel, Berry, and Meirink (2014) specifically draw distinctions between action research approaches in science education that "promote real-world applications" for changing teaching practice, from other education research methodologies that seek to measure and standardize "knowledge for teachers" (p. 866). The stance of action research, situating teachers as learners, connects action research to constructivist and inquiry-based approaches long advocated for within the field. According to Loughran (2014), "Teacher research stands out as a most productive approach to teacher learning and pedagogical change" (p. 821)

Science Teachers as Learners

Science teachers engaged in action research take on new roles in the classroom as learners and as theorizers. The "teacher-as-learner stance" plays a significant role in changing teaching practice as teachers integrate theories into practice (Loughran, 2014). Through their action research Geelan (1996) adopted "critical constructivism" and Fitzpatrick (1996) described "adopting a constructivist philosophy" (p. 59). Northfield's study of his practice as a "science teacher learner" also provided evidence of his reflections on practice and the impact on his professional understanding (see Loughran & Northfield, 1996).

Across these action research projects in science education, we find evidence of the embedded nature of inquiry as both the process and the outcome of action research—science teachers who engage in inquiry, adopting an inquiry stance, appear to change their teaching toward integrating more inquiry-based approaches into instruction. For example, based on their synthesis of preservice teachers' action research, Justi and van Driel (2006) determined that the action research cycle, particularly reflection on action, stimulated the development of PCK, especially with regard to integrating inquiry into science education. Similarly, Beyer and Davis (2012) engaged preservice teachers in inquiry related to adapting science curriculum materials in lesson planning. Over time, as the preservice teachers continued a cycle of inquiry and reflection about their planning, their PCK with regard to integrating inquiry-based teaching improved. Similarly, Maor (1999) focused on the experiences of Mark, who implemented action research with his biology students and described shifts in his PCK as he integrated inquiry-based teaching into the classroom. In these instances, Loughran (2014) notes teachers become "active learners of science, congruent with the ideas of constructivism" (p. 811).

Within science education, action research projects focus on improving science content knowledge to improve PCK and change practice. For example, Falk (2012) synthesized the experiences of elementary teachers who participated in a professional development program focused on electricity and electrical circuits. As part of their professional learning, the teachers taught a unit on the topic while collecting formative assessment data from their students. As a result of their research, the teachers developed new content knowledge that influenced their PCK related to teaching the topic and assessing student learning. Similarly, Geddis (1996) and Berry and Milroy (2002) described engaging science teachers in improving their subject matter knowledge through reflective inquiry. The teachers they worked with developed a better under-standing of effective teaching strategies and their professional identities as teachers shifted. For example, Berry and Milroy (2002) made connections between teacher action research and student learning about atomic theory. Through the process of sys-tematic inquiry about science teaching, the action researchers experienced cognitive disequilibrium. Halai's (2012) meta-synthesis of 20 qualitative action research studies conducted by experienced science teachers suggested that the teachers

developed an understanding of the theory and practice of the innovative strategy implemented and found that the transformation of their science content knowledge to 'fit' the new ways of teaching was the most challenging and rewarding part of their research. (p. 387)

Here action researchers revisioned their approaches to teaching science content as they learned through inquiry in action.

Collaborative and University-School Partnerships in Science Education

When action research was conducted as part of the work of communities of prac-tice (Wenger, 1998), science teachers experienced much-needed support in conduct-ing their inquiry. As in other subject areas, these projects engaged science teachers in making explicit their tacit knowledge of teaching while building trusting and sup-portive relationships with colleagues (Baird & Northfield, 1992). In the case of the Project for the Enhancement of Effective Learning, the emphasis was on "placing the teacher at the center of learning" so that "real change in school science can become a reality" (Baird & Mitchell, 1986, p. 820).

Evidence of change in teaching took many forms in these projects, including the development of new science curriculum (Loughran, Smith, & Berry, 2011). In Fleer and Grace's (2003) project, elementary science teachers adopted a "teacher-as-learner stance" within a community of practice; student experiences improved as a result of their teachers' participation. Similarly, Akerson, Cullen, and Hanson (2009) docu-mented an action research project that led to changes in teachers' views about the nature of science and, in turn, influenced student understanding.

Critical Issues

Within science education research PAR "actively addresses the inequalities in school and community" (Treagust, Won, & Dutt, 2014, p. 12) and is conducted in partnership with local communities, often in economically disadvantaged settings (Elmesky & Tobin, 2005). For example, Bouillion and Gomez (2001) worked with younger students through their Chicago River Project. Here they engaged elementary aged students from a low-income neighborhood in a science project to investigate the illegal dumping of waste. Changes in teaching included the integration of hands-on activities, which resulted in marked improvements in students' "ability to access information, form questions, share ideas, and analyze and compare data" (p. 888).

ACTION RESEARCH AND CHANGING TEACHING PRACTICE IN SOCIAL STUDIES EDUCATION

Action research within the social studies seems to have followed a similar arc as in other fields. Due in part to the prominence of qualitative and interpretive studies over the past decades, action research studies have appeared in major research journals in the field and have been integrated into social studies teacher education. It is notable, however, that action research is not more prominent in the field of social studies given the field's long-standing focus on democratic education and inquiry-based teaching (Johnston, 2006; Manfra, 2017). This may be due to relatively less federal funding to support large-scale social studies professional development programs and the marginalization of the field at the elementary level. Nonetheless, the extant literature on social studies action research, according to Boyle-Baise (2012), is based on "puzzlements" that lead to scholarly questions such as: "How can I mount an investigation of these personally significant questions?" (p. 27). Similar to other fields, social studies action research challenges traditional notions of education research and serves as an "effective means of professional growth" (p. 29).

Social Studies Teachers as Learners

The main body of action research literature in the field of social studies education focuses on improving student disciplinary understanding of history. This seems to reflect similar trends in social studies research in general that emphasizes history education. Action research studies focused on the topic of history education provide evidence of changing teaching practice and positive impacts on students.

VanSledright (2002, 2004) documented his long-term action research in a fifth-grade classroom to teach students to think like historians. He described how he "studied my own practice and collected data on what the students gained from the experience" (VanSledright, 2004, p. 232). As a result of his action research he turned "typical history teaching upside down" by integrating historical investigation into the classroom (p. 232) and documented how students developed a more nuanced understanding of the past as they adopted critical approaches to analyzing historical evidence.

The focus on historical investigation and integrating disciplinary inquiry to improve student understanding of history is echoed in other studies in the elementary grades. For instance, McCormick (2008) modified her teaching by integrating inquiry into a unit on the American Revolution with her fifth-grade students, Kelley (2006) introduced a modified approach to inquiry-based teaching with her kindergarten students during the "Our Town" unit she developed, and Jensen (2008) integrated historical research and structured debates into her fifth-grade classroom. Based on their research, the teachers found that changing their practices shifted instruction and learning in the classroom. In their mixed-methods action research study, Bosma, Rule, and Krueger (2013) collected quantitative data related to student learning outcomes as well as qualitative data to document changes in teaching and student experiences. Based on their findings, they determined that fifth-grade students retained historical content knowledge after reading graphic novels. Across the examples, the action researchers related changes in their teaching practice with improved student learning.

At the secondary level, action researchers in the field of social studies education also focused on more effectively teaching history content knowledge and skills associated with the discipline. Brooks (2008), Foster (1999), and Kohlmeier (2004, 2006) required students to analyze primary source sets in order to develop disciplinary habits related to historical investigation. The data they collected were used to refine their teaching practice. For instance, Kohlmeier (2006) collected a variety of data, including samples of student work and records of classroom discussions. As a result of her action research, she found that providing students with primary sources from "ordinary" people, along with scaffolds to guide their inquiry and writing, provided an effective approach to teaching historical content.

Brooks (2008) and Zagora (2011) studied the integration of writing as a tool to assess student historical understanding and argumentation. Brooks (2008) collected data including student work samples and interview data to compare the effectiveness of two different types of writing assignments in her eighth-grade social studies classroom. As a result of her analysis she found that both the first person and third person writing assignments yielded similar outcomes. To initiate her study, Zagora (2011) collected baseline data from students through survey questions. Over the course of her action research she developed a series of short writing assignments to support student content knowledge acquisition and improve their writing skills.

In addition to teaching content knowledge more effectively, historical empathy features prominently as an area of concern among action researchers in the social studies. In terms of changing her teaching practice, Brooks (2008) found, "The evidence produced by this investigation supports the assertion that a first-person writing assignment can both contribute to, and detract from, the development of historical empathy" (p. 144). Building off of Jensen's (2008) action research, D'Adamo and Fallace (2011) found that when given the choice between various genres of historical writing, first-person writing seemed most conducive to exploring issues related to historical empathy.

Collectively these studies emphasized disciplinary content knowledge and PCK. Assumed here is that changes in teaching practices coincided with improvements in teachers' PCK (Russ et al., 2016) or "professional understanding" (Shulman, 1987, p. 8). According to Martell (2015), "My teacher research became an outlet for a more systematic questioning of my curriculum decisions and teaching practices" (p. 54). Students were able to understand historical contexts and different points of view from the past as their teachers modified their teaching practices.

Within university-based teacher education programs, action research has also focused on PCK for history classrooms. For example, J. S. Clark (2014) focused on engaging preservice social studies teachers in historical thinking through the use of graphic novels and Christou and Bullock (2014) assigned students to conduct historical investigations. Across these examples, the teacher educators engaged in action research to refine their own professional learning in pursuit of improving the practices of future social studies teachers.

Critical Issues

In addition to changing teaching related to the skills of the disciplines, action researchers within the field of social studies have engaged in studies to bring about more critical and socially just social studies education (Stanley & Nelson, 1986). According to Johnston (2006), through action research, practitioners "unmask our prejudices and biases, study our own social justice agendas in practice, and learn from what students can tell us about their points of view and their learning" (p. 75). Across these examples, the teacher action researchers adopt an inquiry stance to reflect on the impact of changes in teaching practice on student experiences. These changes included teaching new curriculum, such as the *Teaching the Levees* curriculum (Thomas-Brown, 2010), integrating music and poetry to "provide a forum for discussion and critical analyses of larger societal issues (Sánchez, 2007, p. 651), "throwing" out the textbook (Martell & Hashimoto-Martell, 2012), and adopting antiracist pedagogy (Husband, 2010). Across these examples, the authors build on critical race theory. For instance, Sanchez (2007) based her action research on Bell and Griffin's (1997) strategies to help students "increase personal awareness" and "expand knowledge" (Bell & Griffin, 1997, p. 47). Martell (2015) referred to culturally relevant pedagogy to replace textbooks with reading packets. Here the teacher action researchers changed their teaching practices by integrating theory into practice to bring about more equitable and just social studies education.

As a practitioner engaged in teacher research, I found strong evidence that replacing the textbook was necessary to help my students better see that history is interpreted . . . and to empower my students to see themselves as part of history. (Martell & Hashimoto-Martell, 2012, p. 317)

Manfra (2009b) provided portraits of four experienced social studies teachers who began their projects seeking to make their teaching more culturally relevant for students. They sought to better understand their students' experiences and devised strategies for meeting their needs. They accomplished this by reading the work of critical race theorists, consulting with their colleagues, and becoming students of their students. To pursue their inquiry, they relied on critical theory to articulate not only what they observed but also what they aspired to achieve in their classrooms. Combined, these portraits demonstrate "the potential for teacher research to lead to critical inquiry, empowerment, and change in social studies classrooms" (p. 156).

Social studies teacher educators have also conducted action research as a method for engaging preservice social studies teachers in more critical reflection. This work has focused on integrating specific teaching strategies, such as the "Praxis Inquiry Protocol" (Lang, 2010) and community-based inquiries (Hyland & Noffke, 2005). Others have widened the scope of their work to focus on democratic education

(Wade, 1999) and integrating critical topics into social studies teacher education (Reidel & Salinas, 2011). For instance, in her "critical action research study," James (2008) collected data from her social studies methods classes over three semesters to better understand the reluctance of preservice teachers to engage students in historical interpretation about "difficult moral" topics. Dinkelman (1999, 2000) took a wide-angle lens in his action research study to determine the extent to which his teaching strategies supported critical reflection in his social studies methods classes. According to Crowe and Dinkelman (2010) self-study provides a particularly rich approach for social studies teacher educators to negotiate the multiple meanings and purposes of social studies education. Collectively this work "contribute(s) in a systematic, reflective way" to social studies teacher education (Adler, 2008, p. 345). Across the studies, the teacher educators employed metacognitive approaches to encourage preservice teachers to critically examine the beliefs that inform their practice and make connections between the inquiry assignments and their future work as teachers.

University-based PAR studies interrogated social justice issues in the social studies by engaging students more centrally in the action research process. For example, Mitchell and Elwood's (2012) project focused on "*counter-mapping* to resist hegemonic ways of representing space" (p. 158). Their aim was to engage students in exploring contemporary public and civic spaces. Data included the maps the students created and Mitchell and Ellwood's written observations and reflections. As result of their investigation, students appeared to develop insights about geo-spatial relationships to historical political events.

University-School Partnerships

Compared to the other subject areas reviewed here, there are noticeably fewer collaborative action research projects linking universities and schools. Crocco, Faithfull, and Schwartz (2003) and B. B. Levin and Rock (2003) integrated action research methods in their work with two different professional development schools. Preservice and experienced social studies teachers worked along-side university based researchers to study issues related to social studies teaching and learning. Similarly, Catapano and Song (2006) facilitated professional development about the Kids Voting curriculum with preservice social studies teachers and then analyzed data from their action research projects focused on integrating the curriculum in the classroom.

Two notable examples were part of larger funded projects focused on teaching about race and racism in schools: the Multicultural Education Instructional Support Team that emerged from The African and African-American Curriculum Project (Brennan & Noffke, 2000; Noffke, Clark, Palmeri-Santiago, Sadler, & Shujaa, 1996) and the 3-year Teaching About Race Relations program (Stenhouse, Verma, Wild, & Nixon, 1982). In both cases, university-based facilitators supported and studied the work of school-based teacher action researchers. Their work revealed the potential for action research to serve as a methodology for confronting critical issues in schools as well as outlined the complexity of this work. Brennan and Noffke (2000) suggested that important gains were made to create a community of teachers more attuned to issues of race. Yet they also noted that changing teaching for White teacher participants began with an examination of "their own personal identities as a precursory but also concomitant aspect to the engagement in collaborative struggle for social and educational change" (p. 72). Stenhouse et al.'s (1982) analysis of action research reports from across 40 participating schools also indicated various levels of teacher resistance and change. Both studies provide examples for the field of social studies to facilitate larger collaborative action research projects between university-school participants.

TEACHING AS INQUIRY

Action research across the subject areas provides further evidence of the limits of the process-product approach to teacher learning. It also suggests the need to go beyond cognitive and situative perspectives to consider a fourth perspective of teaching as inquiry. Across the studies, action research becomes a way of knowing (Lytle & Cochran-Smith, 1990) or "a way of being" (Jaworski, 2004) as teachers continuously reflect on and refine their teaching. Successful efforts to change practice through action research demonstrate the value of engaging teachers as active participants. According to Russ et al. (2016), "The long-term trajectory of teacher learning [is] complex" (p. 402). In order to leverage action research to bring about systematic, intentional change in teaching, we need to address barriers to coordinated and sustained action research across the disciplines.

LEGITIMIZING ACTION RESEARCH

A major barrier to systematic change in teaching practice through action research is the way education research has been traditionally defined (Apple, 1993; Appadurai, 2006). A common approach is to refer to a "two-community metaphor" in which the research community includes "those responsible for generating scholarship," including "producers" from "traditional academic institutions as well as think-tanks" (Farley-Ripple et al., 2018, p. 237). The "practice community" includes "all school and district practitioners: school district administrators, principals, interventionists, and teachers" (p. 237). At the same time, "rigorous" research designs have been limited to randomized, quasi-experimental, or correlational research (Elementary and Secondary Education Act of 2018; Institute of Educational Sciences, 2017; Sparks, 2016; Viadero, 2004). Members of the practice community are often excluded from fully participating since "rigorous" designs require "control" groups (teachers and educators are ethically obligated to meet the needs of *all* students), are often costly and time-intensive, and require large sample sizes. One effect has been for teachers to question their ability to conduct research (Martell, 2016). As long as education research is defined as the purview of academic researchers, action research will continue to be marginalized.

Trustworthiness

Similar questions about rigor and validity or "trustworthiness" have come from within the action research community (Huang, 2010). Zeichner (1993) warned against the "uncritical glorification of action research" (p. 200), and Kincheloe (2003) urged that "teachers must join the culture of researchers if a new level of educational rigor and quality is ever to be achieved' (p. 18). Responses have ranged from working to redefine "notions of validity and generalizability" within action research as "quite different from traditional criteria" (Cochran-Smith & Lytle, 2009, p. 43) to critiquing the "Western consciousness that devalues and distrusts collective and critical self-reflection as a source of legitimate understanding" (McTaggart, 1997, p. 41). Others have adopted language similar to social science research to strengthen the validity of their work. For example, Hyland and Noffke (2005) described steps to "distance ourselves from the data in some way and to check our own interpretations" (p. 373), including blinding the data, purposefully looking for contradictions, and seeking out areas of practice in need of improvement.

There are also concerns related to preservice teachers conducting action research, especially given the short duration of student teaching internships and "question(s) about ownership" (Burnaford, Fischer, & Hobson, 2001, p. 211). According to Phillips and Carr (2009), "The question of trustworthiness in preservice teacher action research arises from this context and brings to the forefront the unique and multiple positions of the preservice teacher as 'guest,' 'student,' 'teacher,' and 'researcher'" (p. 209). Preservice teachers control little about the environment in which they student-teach. At the same time their development as teachers is just emerging. All of this makes it difficult for their action research to have a long-term impact on their teaching (Volk, 2010).

These constraints, however, do not appear to be insurmountable compared to the benefits associated with conducting action research. According to Phillips and Carr (2009), "Such research allows preservice teachers to demonstrate critical competencies of a professional educator as they practice a cycle of assessment, planning, and implementation based upon data collected in the classroom" (p. 208). Findings from this review highlight the important role action research can play in providing preservice teachers with a voice and an opportunity to systematically reflect on their development as teachers. More specifically, through action research, preservice teachers across the subject areas improved their PCK as they engaged in reflective inquiry.

Issues Related to Dissemination

The impact of action research on the larger teacher education and education research community will continue to be limited if findings are not shared with audiences beyond the communities in which the action research studies take place (Altrichter, Feldman, Posch, & Somekh, 2008; Kemmis & McTaggart, 1992; Lampert, 2008, 2010; Mills, 2017). In this present review, most of the literature was published in academic texts, often with at least one coauthor from an institution of higher education. It did not capture action research studies that may have been shared at conferences or in smaller settings. Some have argued that academic journals need to begin accepting more action research articles (McFeetors, 2012). Yet there exist very different incentive structures that may hinder publishing efforts by practitioners. Without wider dissemination of action research, it will continue to be difficult to disrupt the traditional two-community metaphor of research and practice.

Structural Constraints

Additional constraints include structural factors that limit the work of action researchers. These include "ordinary school pressures" that "distract from and interrupt research" (Jaworski, 1998, p. 20), such as standardized achievement tests, curriculum maps, class schedules, and workloads (Christenbury & Scherff, 2018; Gningue et al., 2014; Kyei-Blankson, 2014; Mirra, Filipiak, & Garcia, 2015). In schools with a great deal of curriculum standardization and control, teachers may feel forced to "'teach' in hiding" (Christenbury & Scherff, 2018) when they try new teaching practices. These factors also limit the amount of time and resources practitioners have for participating in collaborative action research groups and disseminating their findings.

Although this review demonstrated the potential for collaborative action research to mitigate some of these structural factors, it is not always successful. Problems occur when members of the community feel underprepared or unsure about how to engage in action research (Judah & Richardson, 2006) or if there are conflicting conceptions of what constitutes research (Feldman & Minstrell, 2000). This work can be "risky business" for teachers (Lytle, 1993). For instance, Doerr and Tinto (2000) describe unexpected anger and resentment directed at teacher action researchers from their colleagues.

Time

Teachers frequently cite time as a major constraint preventing them from conducting action research (Best & Kahn, 2006; Boud & Walker, 1998; Feldman & Minstrell, 2000). For example, one teacher reported, "There just isn't enough time. I think research-based learning would have a huge impact in the classroom, but finding the time is a necessary part" (Kyei-Blankson, 2014, p. 1061). Since time is such a major obstacle, it is not surprising that much of the extant literature on action research is produced through funded university-school partnerships or in teacher education programs (M. Levin & Martin, 2007). According to Volk (2010), "Release time, resources, and awards may go a long way in helping to support teachers' research efforts" (p. 329).

Co-Option

Efforts to reduce constraints have included making action research more explicitly a part of the day-to-day work of teachers. In these instances, there is concern that action research may be co-opted by institutional and managerial forces (Adelman,

1999; Judah & Richardson, 2006). Ethical issues raised include whether or not teachers can still experience the emancipatory potential of action research when they are required to conduct action research by school administrators (Alberta Teachers' Association, 2000; Judah & Richardson, 2006). In the current review, the projects ranged from those that were tightly scaffolded by university-based partners and those that were more open-ended. The tension remains to seek out the best possible outcomes for teachers, their students, and other stakeholder groups and to clarify whose best interests are being served.

CHANGING TEACHING THROUGH INQUIRY

Despite the constraints raised in the research literature, there is ample evidence to suggest that action research provides teachers and teacher educators a systematic and intentional approach to changing teaching. Action research has been integrated into the four fields reviewed here in a variety of ways, including in investigations of individual teacher's classrooms, through communities of practice, and more democratic and critical pedagogy. Findings indicate that action research leads to improvement in PCK, which in turn leads to positive outcomes for students.

Action researchers from the four fields can learn from each other about the potential of inquiry to change teaching practice. The history of action research in English education demonstrates the power of coordinated and sustained efforts, such as the NWP, to engage teachers in communities of practice focused on changing teaching in diverse contexts. Action research in math and science education demonstrates how action research can be integrated into professional learning focused on subject matter knowledge and PCK. Findings from action research in the social studies parallel those in other subject areas to demonstrate the potential for inquiry to be integrated into teaching as well as a tool for improving professional practice and bringing about more socially just education. Collectively action research from the four subject areas contributes to the scholarship of teaching. According to Hutchings and Shulman (1999), a scholarship of teaching requires teachers to "frame and systematically investigate questions related to student learning . . . improving their own classroom but to advancing practice beyond it" (p. 13). Action research provides a method for this kind of systematic investigation.

Action research is predicated on changing practice through experience. This experience leads to disequilibrium, requiring teachers to question and affirm their professional knowledge. Within the action research reports cited here, the teachers developed mindfulness through engaging in metacognitive reflection that led to new knowledge and practice. According to Wade (1999), "The end results of action research may inform theory or be applicable to others' practice, but their most immediate and useful purpose is the contribution they make toward the transformation of one's own teaching" (p. 76).

In discrete, explicit ways the action researchers provided insights into the development of their PCK. Whereas other research within the cognitive and situative perspective relies on observational data to make judgments about the "mental life" and professional knowledge of teachers, here the teacher education community gains access to insider knowledge. Action research reveals the complex interplay of classroom teaching, the role of reflection, and ways to respond to the unique contexts of practice.

Need for University-Based Partnerships

It appears that action research is hard for teachers to sustain without support or encouragement (Martell, 2016; Volk, 2010). Working with university-based researchers can provide intellectual support and resources to develop communities of inquiry (Akerson et al., 2009; Baird & Northfield, 1992; Clarke et al., 2009; Jaworski, 2006). University faculty also provide leadership and external funding to support school-based initiatives to integrate action research for school improvement (Doerr & Tinto, 2000; Kyei-Blankson, 2014; Volk, 2010).

These collaborative relationships may also help to ensure the high quality of action research. Whereas some worry that action research may be used to "further solidify and justify practices that are harmful to students" (Zeichner, 1994, p. 66), evidence provided in this review suggests positive gains for both teachers and students when action research was the primary work of communities of practice. These communities provide a forum for critical feedback for action researchers and a means for disseminating findings. In many instances university educators introduce teachers to new ideas (theories) about teaching and strategies or protocols to put these ideas into action (M. Levin & Martin, 2007). They also provide mentoring for publishing written accounts of action research studies.

Action Research and Educational Reform

By situating teachers as learners, action research offers a systematic and intentional approach to improving PCK and changing teaching. Action research shifts the paradigm of contemporary educational reform by emphasizing inquiry and situating the teacher at the center of research-into-practice. Action research emerged from "growing understanding among groups of education researchers that school reform, educational improvement, and social welfare in general are going nowhere without the active participation of those who have in the past been the so-called 'targets' of improvement" (Lincoln, 1998, p. 21). Today we must sustain this work by building on the findings of previous studies. This includes creating the conditions for teachers to access their own power and change their practice through systematic inquiry. The active participation of teachers in education research to change teaching practice is warranted given our understanding of how teachers learn and the complex and situated nature of the daily work of teachers (Hawley & Valli, 1999). Through sustained, prolonged, and collaborative approaches to action research, systematic and intentional changes in teaching can occur.

REFERENCES

Adelman, K. (1999). Crosscurrents and riptides: Asking about the capacity of the higher education system. *Change, 1*(1), 20–27.

Adler, S. (2008). The education of social studies teachers. In L. Levstik & C. Tyson (Eds.), *Handbook of research in social studies education* (pp. 329–350). New York, NY: Routledge.

Akerson, V. L., Cullen, T. A., & Hanson, D. L. (2009). Fostering a community of practice through a professional development program to improve elementary teachers' views of nature of science and teaching practice. *Journal of Research in Science Teaching, 46,* 1090–1113.

Alberta Teachers' Association. (2000). *Action research guide for Alberta teachers.* Edmonton, Alberta, Canada: Author. Retrieved from https://www.teachers.ab.ca/sitecollection documents/ata/publications/professional-development/actionresearch.pdf

Altrichter, H., Feldman, A., Posch, P., & Somekh, B. (2008). *Teachers investigate their work: An introduction to action research across the professions* (2nd ed.). London, England: Routledge

Appadurai, A. (2006). The right to research. *Globalisation, Societies and Education, 4,* 167–177.

Apple, M. (1993). *Official knowledge: Democratic education in a conservative age.* New York, NY: Routledge.

Athanases, S. Z. (2011). Research as praxis documenting the dialectical relationship between theory and practice. In D. Lapp & D. Fisher (Eds.), *Handbook of research on teaching the language arts* (3rd ed., pp. 358–363). London, England: Routledge.

Attorps, I., & Kellner, E. (2017). School-university action research: Impacts on teaching practices and pupil learning. *International Journal of Science and Math Education, 15,* 313–330.

Baird, J. R., & Mitchell, I. J. (Eds.). (1986). *Improving the quality of teaching and learning: An Australian case study—the PEEL project.* Melbourne, Victoria, Australia: Monash University Printery.

Baird, J. R., & Northfield, J. R. (1992). *Learning from the PEEL experience.* Melbourne, Victoria, Australia: Monash University Printery.

Ballenger, C. (1996). Learning the ABCs in a Haitian preschool: A teacher's story. *Language Arts, 73,* 317–323.

Ballenger, C. (1999). *Teaching other people's children: Literacy and learning in a bilingual classroom.* New York, NY: Teachers College Press

Baumann, J. F., Schockley, B., & Allen, J. (1996). Methodology in teacher research: Three cases (Perspectives in Reading Research No. 10). Athens, GA: National Reading Research Center. Retrieved from https://files.eric.ed.gov/fulltext/ED392017.pdf

Bell, L., & Griffin, P. (1997). Designing social justice education courses, In M. Adams, L. Bell, & P. Griffin (Eds.), *Teaching for diversity and social justice: A sourcebook* (pp. 44–58). New York, NY: Routledge.

Bentley, E. (2013). Supernovas and superheroes: Examining unfamiliar genres and teachers' pedagogical content knowledge. *English Education, 45,* 218–246.

Berry, A., & Milroy, P. (2002). Changes that matter. In J. Loughran, I. Mitchell, & J. Mitchell (Eds.), *Learning from teacher research* (pp. 196–221). New York, NY: Teachers College Press.

Best, J., & Kahn, J. (2006). *Research in education.* Boston, MA: Pearson.

Betts, P., McLarty, M., & Dickson, K. (2017). An action research project by teacher candidates and their instructor into using math inquiry: Learning about relations between theory and practice. *Networks, 19*(1), 1–14.

Beyer, C. J., & Davis, E. A. (2012). Learning to critique and adapt science curriculum materials: Examining the development of preservice elementary teachers' pedagogical content knowledge. *Science Education, 96,* 130–157.

Biesta, G. J. J., & Stengel, B. S. (2016). Thinking philosophically about teaching. In D. H. Gitmoer & C. A. Bell (Eds.), *Handbook of research on teaching* (5th ed., pp. 7–66). Washington, DC: American Educational Research Association.

Bloome, D., Chapman, T., & Freebody, P. (2011). Complexity, multiplicity, timeliness, and substantive engagement. In D. Lapp & D. Fisher (Eds.), *Handbook of research on teaching the English language arts* (3rd ed., pp. 353–357). London, England: Routledge.

Boote, D. N., & Beile, P. (2005). Scholars before researchers: On the centrality of the dissertation literature review in research preparation. *Educational Research, 34*(6), 3–15.

Borko, H., Whitcomb, J. A., & Byrnes, K. (2008). Genres of research in teacher education. In M. Cochran-Smith, S. Feiman-Nemser, & K. E. Demers (Eds.), *Handbook of research on teacher education: Enduring questions in changing contexts* (3rd ed., pp. 1017–1049). New York, NY: Routledge.

Bosma, K., Rule, A. C., & Krueger, K. S. (2013). Social studies content reading about the American Revolution enhanced with graphic novels. *Social Studies Research and Practice, 8*(1), 59–76.

Boud, D., & Walker, D. (1998). Promoting reflection in professional courses: The challenge of context. *Studies in Higher Education, 23*, 191–206.

Bouillion, L. M., & Gomez, L. M. (2001). Connecting school and community with science learning: Real world problems and school–community partnerships as contextual scaffolds. *Journal of Research in Science Teaching, 38*, 878–898.

Boyle-Baise, M. (2012). Teachers-as-researchers: Following your puzzlement. *Social Studies and the Young Learner, 24*(4), 27–29.

Brady, M. (2010). *What is worth learning?* Charlotte, NC: Information Age.

Bragg, L. (2017). Action research on the application of variation theory in mathematics teacher education. *Mathematics Teacher Education and Development, 19*(1), 121–136.

Brennan, M., & Noffke, S. E. (2000). Social change and the individual: Changing patterns of community and the challenge for schooling. In H. Altrichter & J. Elliott (Eds.), *Images of educational change* (pp. 66–75). Philadelphia, PA: Open University Press.

Brooks, S. (2008). Displaying historical empathy: What impact can a writing assignment have? *Social Studies Research and Practice, 3*(2), 130–146.

Burnaford, G., Fischer, J., & Hobson, D. (2001). *Teachers doing research: The power of action through inquiry.* Mahwah, NJ: Lawrence Erlbaum.

Burns, T. J. (2009). Searching for peace: Exploring issues of war with young children. *Language Arts, 86*, 421–430.

Burton, F. R., & Seidle, B. L. (2005). Teacher researcher projects from the elementary school teacher's perspective. In J. Flood, D. Lapp, & J. R. Squire (Eds.), *Methods of research on teaching the English language arts: The Methodology chapters From the Handbook of Research on Teaching the English Language Arts* (2nd ed., pp. 195–210). New York, NY: Routledge.

Catapano, S., & Song, K. H. (2006). Let's collaborate and infuse citizenship education: Kids voting in primary classrooms. *Social Studies Research and Practice, 1*(1), 55–66.

Cercone, J. (2009). We're smarter together: Building professional social networks in English education. *English Education, 41*, 199–206.

Chin, C. (1996). "Are you the teacher who gives parents homework?" In H. Banford, M. Berkman, C. Chin, C. Cziko, B. Fecho, D. Jumpp, . . . M. Resnick, *Cityscapes: Eight views from the urban classroom* (pp. 145–163). Berkeley, CA: National Writing Project.

Christenbury, L., & Scherff, L. (2018). Embracing enduring tensions in English education. *English Journal, 107*(5), 14–19.

Christensen, L. (1989). Writing the word and the world. *English Journal, 79*, 14–18.

Christensen, L. (1990). Teaching standard English: Whose standard? *English Journal, 80*, 36–40.

Christensen, L. (1993). Tales from an untracked class. *Rethinking Schools, 7*(2), 19–23.

Christou, T., & Bullock, S. M. (2014). Learning and teaching about social studies and science: A collaborative self-study. *The Social Studies, 105*(2), 80–90.

Clark, C. M., Gage, N., Marx, R., Peterson, P., Stayrook, N., & Winne, P. (1979). A factorial experiment on teacher structuring, soliciting, and reacting. *Journal of Educational Psychology, 71*, 534–552.

Clark, J. S. (2014). Teaching historical agency: Explicitly connecting past and present with graphic novels. *Social Studies Research and Practice, 9*(3), 66–80.

Clarke, D., Downton, M., Roche, A., Clarkson, A., Scott, P., McDonough, A., . . . Hamilton, L. (2009). *Contemporary teaching and learning of mathematics 2008: Report to CEO Melbourne*. Melbourne: Mathematics Teaching and Learning Research Centre, Australian Catholic University.

Cochran-Smith, M., & Lytle, S. L. (1993). *Inside/outside: Teacher research and knowledge*. New York, NY: Teachers College Press.

Cochran-Smith, M., & Lytle, S. L. (1999). The teacher research movement: A decade later. *Educational Researcher, 28*(7), 15–25.

Cochran-Smith, M., & Lytle, S. L. (2009). *Inquiry as stance: Practitioner research for the next generation*. New York, NY: Teachers College Press.

Crocco, M. S., Faithfull, B., & Schwartz, S. (2003). Inquiring minds want to know: Action research at a New York City professional development school. *Journal of Teacher Education, 54*(1), 19–30.

Crowe, A. R., & Dinkelman, T. (2010). Self-study and social studies: Framing the conversation. In A. R. Crowe (Ed.), *Advancing Social Studies Education Through Self-Study Methodology* (pp. 1–19). New York, NY: Springer.

D'Adamo, L., & Fallace, T. (2011). The multigenre research project: An approach to developing historical empathy. *Social Studies Research and Practice, 6*(1), 75–88.

Delp, V. (1999). We soar together: Studying literature in a heterogeneous classroom. In S. W. Freedman, E. R. Simons, J. S. Kalnin, A. Casareno, & The M-CLASS Teams (Eds.), *Inside city schools: Investigating literacy in multicultural classrooms* (pp. 179–196). New York, NY: Teachers College Press.

Dinkelman, T. (1999). Critical reflection in a social studies methods semester. *Theory & Research in Social Education, 27*, 329–357.

Dinkelman, T. (2000). An inquiry into the development of critical reflection in secondary student teachers. *Teaching and Teacher Education, 16*, 195–122.

Dipardo, A., & Schnack, P. (2004). Expanding the web of meaning: Thought and emotion in an intergenerational reading and writing program. *Reading Research Quarterly, 39*, 14–37.

Doerr, H. M., & Tinto, P. P. (2000). Paradigms for teacher-centered, classroom-based research. In A. E. Kelly & R. A. Lesh (Eds.), *Handbook of research design in mathematics and science education* (pp. 240–253). Mahwah, NJ: Routledge.

Douillard, K. (2003). Writing matters: Exploring the relationship between writing instruction and assessment. In A. Clarke & G. Erickson (Eds.), *Teacher inquiry: Living the research in everyday practice* (pp. 9–19). New York, NY: Routledge Falmer.

Elementary and Secondary Education Act. (As amended through P. Law 115–224, Enacted July 31, 2018). Retrieved from https://legcounsel.house.gov/Comps/Elementary%20 And%20Secondary%20Education%20Act%20Of%201965.pdf

Elmesky, R., & Tobin, K. G. (2005). Expanding our understandings of urban science education by expanding the roles of students as researchers. *Journal of Research in Science Teaching, 42*, 807–828. doi:10.1002/tea.20079

Elliot, J. (1976). Preparing teachers for classroom accountability. *Education for Teaching, 100*, 49–71.

Falk, A. (2012). Teachers learning from professional development in elementary science: Reciprocal relations between formative assessment and pedagogical content knowledge. *Science Education, 96*, 265–290.

Farley-Ripple, E., May, H., Karpyn, A., Tilley, K., & McDonough, K. (2018). Rethinking connections between research and practice in education: A conceptual framework. *Educational Researcher, 47*, 235–245.

Fecho, B. (2001). "Why are you doing this?" Acknowledging and transcending threat in a critical inquiry classroom. *Research in the Teaching of English, 36*(1), 9–37.

Fecho, B. (2003). Yeki bood/Yeki na bood: Writing and publishing as a teacher researcher. *Research in the Teaching of English, 37*, 281–294.

Fecho, B. (2004). *Is this English? Race, language, and culture in the classroom.* New York, NY: Teachers College Press.

Fecho, B., & Allen, J. (2005). Teacher inquiry into literacy, social justice, and power. In J. Flood, D. Lapp, & J. R. Squire (Eds.), *Methods of research on teaching the English language arts: The methodology chapters from the Handbook of Research on Teaching the English Language Arts* (2nd ed., 211–244). NY: Routledge.

Feldman, A., & Minstrell, J. (2000). Action research as a research methodology for the study of the teaching and learning of science. In E. Kelly & R. Lesh (Eds.), *Handbook of research design in mathematics and science education* (pp. 429–455). Mahwah, NJ: Lawrence Erlbaum.

Fitzpatrick, B. (1996). The application of constructivist learning strategies to the redesign of the lower secondary science curriculum. In M. W. Hackling (Ed.), *Proceedings of the 21st annual conference of the Western Australian Science Education Association* (pp. 59–64). Retrieved from https://ro.ecu.edu.au/cgi/viewcontent.cgi?article=7743&context=ecuworks

Flanders, N. A. (1970). *Analyzing teaching behavior* (Vol. 16). Oxford, England: Addison-Wesley.

Fleer, M., & Grace, T. (2003). Building a community of science learners through legitimate collegial participation. In J. Wallace & J. Loughran (Eds.), *Leadership and professional development in science education: New possibilities for enhancing teacher learning* (pp. 116–133). London, England: Routledge Falmer.

Foster, S. J. (1999). Using historical empathy to excite students about the study of history: Can you empathize with Neville Chamberlin? *The Social Studies, 13*(1), 1–7.

Freedman, S. W., & Delp, V. (2007). Conceptualizing a whole-class learning space: A grand dialogic zone. *Research in the Teaching of English, 41*, 259–268.

Freedman, S. W., Delp, V., & Crawford, S. M. (2005). Teaching English in untracked classrooms. *Research in the Teaching of English, 40*, 62–126.

Freedman, S., Simons, E., Kalnin, J., Casereno, A., & the M-Class Teams. (1999). *Inside city schools: Investigating literacy in multicultural classrooms.* New York, NY: Teachers College Press.

Fullan, M. (2010). *All systems go: The change imperative for whole system reform.* Thousand Oaks, CA: Sage.

Gallas, K. (2003). *Imagination and literacy: A teacher's search for the heart of learning.* New York, NY: Teachers College Press.

Geddis, A. N. (1996). Science teaching and reflection: Incorporating new subject-matter into teachers' classroom frames. *International Journal of Science Education, 18*, 249–265.

Geelan, D. R. (1996). Learning to communicate: Developing as a science teacher. *Australian Science Teachers Journal, 42*, 30–43.

Gellert, U., Hernández, R. B., & Chapman, O. (2013). Research methods in mathematics teacher education. In M. A. Clements, A. J. Bishop, C. Keitel, J. Kilpatrick, & F. K. S. Leung (Eds.), *Third international handbook of mathematics education* (pp. 327–360). New York, NY: Springer.

Giampapa, F. (2010). Multiliteracies, pedagogy, and identities: Teacher and student voices from a Toronto elementary school. *Canadian Journal of Education, 33*, 407–431.

Gningue, S. M., Schroder, B., & Peach, R. (2014). Reshaping the "glass slipper": The development of reflective practice by mathematics teachers through action research. *American Secondary Education, 42*(3), 18–29.

Gottlieb, D. (2014). *Education reform and the concept of good teaching.* New York, NY: Routledge

Grundy, S. (1982). Three modes of action research. *Curriculum Perspectives, 2*(3), 23–34.

Hackenberg, A. J. (2010). Mathematical caring relations in action. *Journal for Research in Mathematics Education, 41*, 236–273.

Halai, N. (2012). Developing understanding of innovative strategies of teaching science through action research: A qualitative meta-synthesis from Pakistan. *International Journal of Science and Mathematics Education, 10*, 387–415.

Hammerness, K., Darling-Hammond, L., & Bransford, J., (with Berliner, D., Cochran-Smith, M., McDonald, M., & Zeichner, K.). (2005). How teachers learn and develop. In L. Darling-Hammond & J. Bransford (Eds.), *Preparing teachers for a changing world: What teachers should learn and be able to do* (pp. 358–389). San Francisco, CA: Jossey-Bass.

Hankins, K. (1999). Silencing the lambs. In J. Allen (Ed.), *Class actions: Teaching for social justice in elementary and middle school* (pp. 61–71). New York, NY: Teachers College Press.

Hawley, W. D., & Valli, L. (1999). The essentials of effective professional development: A new consensus. In L. Darling-Hammond & G. Sykes (Eds.), *Teaching as the learning profession: Handbook of policy and practice* (pp. 127–150). San Francisco, CA: Jossey-Bass.

Heaton, R. M., & Mickelson, W. T. (2002). The learning and teaching of statistical investigation in teaching and teacher education. *Journal of Mathematics Teacher Education, 5*, 35–59.

Hendricks, C. (2009). *Improving schools through action research: A comprehensive guide for educators* (2nd ed.). Upper Saddle River, NJ: Pearson.

Herbel-Eisenmann, B. (2009). Introduction to the project, the people, and the reflective activities. In B. Herbel-Eisenmann & M. Cirillo (Eds.), *Promoting purposeful discourse. Teacher research in mathematics classrooms* (pp. 3–28). Reston, VA: National Council of Teachers of Mathematics.

Hillocks, G. (2007). *Narrative writing: Learning a new model for teaching.* Portsmouth, NH: Heinemann.

Hofman, R. H., de Boom, J., Meeuwisse, M., & Hofman, W. H. A. (2012). Educational innovation, quality, and effects: An exploration of innovations and their effects in secondary education. *Educational Policy, 27*, 843–866.

Hourigan, M., & O'Donoghue, J. (2015) Addressing prospective elementary teachers' mathematics subject matter knowledge through action research. *International Journal of Mathematical Education in Science and Technology, 46*(1), 56–75.

Huang, H. B. (2010). What is good action research? Why the resurgent interest? *Action Research, 8*(1), 93–109.

Husband, T. (2010). He's too young to learn about that stuff: Anti-racist pedagogy and early childhood social studies. *Social Studies Research and Practice, 5*(2), 61–75.

Hutchings, P., & Shulman, L. S. (1999). The scholarship of teaching: New elaborations, new developments. *Change: The Magazine of Higher Education, 31*(5), 10–15.

Hyland, N. E., & Noffke, S. E. (2005). Understanding diversity through social and community inquiry: An action research study. *Journal of Teacher Education, 56*, 367–381.

Institute of Educational Sciences. (2017). *What Works Clearinghouse.* Retrieved from http://ies.ed.gov/ncee/wwc/

James, J. H. (2008). Teachers as protectors: Making sense of preservice teachers' resistance to interpretation in elementary history teaching. *Theory & Research in Social Education, 36*, 172–205.

Jaworski, B. (1998). Mathematics teacher research: Process practice and the development of teaching. *Journal of Mathematics Teacher Education, 1*, 3–31.

Jaworski, B. (2003). Research practice into/Influencing mathematics teaching and learning development: Towards a theoretical framework based on co-learning partnerships. *Educational Studies in Mathematics, 54,* 249–282.

Jaworski, B. (2004). Grappling with complexity: Co-learning in inquiry communities in mathematics teaching development. In *Proceedings of the 28th international conference of the International Group for the Psychology of Mathematics Education* (pp. 17–36). Retrieved from https://files.eric.ed.gov/fulltext/ED489178.pdf

Jaworski, B. (2006). Theory and practice in mathematics teaching development: Critical inquiry as a mode of learning in teaching. *Journal of Mathematics Teacher Education, 9,* 187–211.

Jensen, J. (2008). Developing historical empathy through debate: An action research study. *Social Studies Research and Practice, 3*(1), 55–56.

Johnston, M. (2006). The lamp and the mirror: Action research and self studies in the social studies. In K. C. Barton (Ed.), *Research methods in social studies education: Contemporary issues and perspectives* (pp. 57–83). Greenwich, CT: Information Age.

Judah, M., & Richardson, G. H. (2006). Between a rock and a (very) hard place: The ambiguous promise of action research in the context of state mandated teacher professional development. *Action Research, 4*(1), 65–80.

Justi, R., & van Driel, J. H. (2006). The use of the interconnected model of teacher professional growth for understanding the development of science teachers' knowledge on models and modelling. *Teaching and Teacher Education, 22,* 437–450.

Katz, S., & Stupel, M. (2016). Enhancing elementary-school mathematics teachers' efficacy beliefs: A qualitative action research. *International Journal of Mathematical Education in Science and Technology, 47,* 421–439. doi:10.1080/0020739X.2015.1080314

Kelley, L. (2006). Learning to question in kindergarten. *Social Studies Research and Practice, 1*(1), 45–54.

Kemmis, S. (2006). Participatory action research and the public sphere. *Educational Action Research, 14,* 459–476.

Kemmis, S., & McTaggart, R. (1992). *The action research planner* (3rd ed.). Geelong, Victoria, Australia: Deakin University Press.

Kemmis, S., McTaggart, R., & Nixon, R. (2014). *The action research planner: Doing critical participatory action research.* New York, NY: Springer.

Kincheloe, J. L. (1995). Meet me behind the curtain: The struggle for a critical post modern action research. In P. L. McLaren & J. M. Giarelli (Eds.), *Critical theory and educational research* (pp. 71–90). Albany: State University of New York Press.

Kincheloe, J. L. (2003). *Teachers as researchers: Qualitative inquiry as a path to empowerment* (2nd ed.). New York, NY: Rutledge.

Kinsler, K. (2010). The utility of educational research for emancipatory change. *Action Research, 8,* 171–189.

Kohlmeier, J. (2004). Experiencing world history through the eyes of ordinary women. *Social Education, 68,* 470–476.

Kohlmeier, J. (2006). "Couldn't she just leave?" The relationship between consistently using class discussions and the development of historical empathy in a 9th grade world history course. *Theory & Research in Social Education, 24,* 34–57.

Kyei-Blankson, L. (2014). Training math and science teacher-researchers in a collaborative research environment: Implications for math and science education. *International Journal of Science and Mathematics Education, 12,* 1047–1065.

Lampert, M. (1990). When the problem is not the question and the solution is not the answer: Mathematical knowing and teaching. *American Educational Research Journal, 27*(1), 29–63.

Lampert, M. (2001). Teaching problems and the problems of teaching. *Journal of Mathematics Teacher Education, 5*(2), 187–199.

Lampert, M. (2008). Knowing teaching: The intersection of research on teaching and qualitative research. *Harvard Educational Review, 70*(1), 86–99.

Lampert, M. (2010). Learning teaching in, from, and for practice: What do we mean? *Journal of Teacher Education, 61*(1–2), 21–34.

Lang, D. E. (2010). Diversity, democracy, and documentation: A self-study path to sharing social realities and challenges in a field-based social studies curriculum methods course. In A. R. Crow (Ed.), *Advancing social studies education through self-study methodology* (pp. 71–86). New York, NY: Springer.

Langrall, W. C. (2014). Linking research and practice: Another call to action? *Journal for Research in Mathematics Education, 45*, 154–156.

Lee, C. D. (1993). *Signifying as a scaffold for literary interpretations: The pedagogical implications of an African American discourse genre* (Research Report Series). Urbana, IL: National Council of Teachers of English.

Levin, B. B, & Rock, T. C. (2003). The effects of collaborative action research on preservice and experienced teacher partners in professional development schools. *Journal of Teacher Education, 54*, 135–149.

Levin, M., & Martin, A. (2007). The praxis of educating action researchers. *Action Research, 5*, 219–229.

Limbrick, L., Buchanan, P., Goodwin, M., & Schwarcz, H. (2010). Doing things differently: The outcomes of teachers researching their own practice in teaching writing. *Canadian Journal of Education/Revue canadienne de l'éducation, 33*, 897–924.

Lincoln, Y. S. (1998). From understanding to action: New imperatives, new criteria, new methods for interpretive researchers. *Theory & Research in Social Education, 26*, 12–29.

Loughran, J. (2002). Teacher as researcher: The PAVOT project. In J. Loughran, I. Mitchell, & J. Mitchell (Eds.), *Learning from teacher research* (pp. 3–18). New York, NY: Teachers College Press.

Loughran, J. J. (2014). Developing understandings of practice: Science teacher learning. In N. G. Lederman & S. K. Abell (Eds.), *Handbook of research on science education* (Vol 2, pp. 811–829). London, England: Routledge.

Loughran, J. J., & Northfield, J. R. (1996). *Opening the classroom door: Teacher, researcher, learner.* London, England: Falmer Press.

Loughran, J. J., Smith, K., & Berry, A. (2011). *Scientific literacy under the microscope: A whole school approach to science teaching and learning.* Rotterdam, Netherlands: Sense.

Lytle, S. (1993). Risky business. *The Quarterly of the National Writing Project and the Center for the Study of Writing and Literacy, 25*(1), 20–23.

Lytle, S., & Cochran-Smith, M. (1990). Learning from teacher research: A working typology. *Teachers College Record, 92*(1), 83–103.

MacLean, M. S., & Mohr, M. M. (1999). *Teacher-researchers at work.* Berkley, CA: National Writing Project.

Manfra, M. M. (2009a). Action research: Exploring the theoretical divide between practical and critical approaches. *Journal of Curriculum and Instruction, 3*(1), 32–46.

Manfra, M. M. (2009b). Critical inquiry in the social studies classroom: Portraits of critical teacher research. *Theory & Research in Social Education, 37*, 156-191.

Manfra, M. M. (2017). Practitioner research in the social studies: Findings from action research and self-study. In M. M. Manfra & C. M. Bolick (Eds.), *The Wiley handbook of social studies research* (pp. 132–167). Malden, MA: Wiley.

Maor, D. (1999). Teachers-as-learners: The role of multimedia professional development program in changing classroom practice. *Australian Science Teachers Journal, 45*(3), 45–50.

Martell, C. C. (2015). Learning to teach culturally relevant social studies: A White teacher's retrospective self-study. In P. Chandler (Ed.), *Doing race in social studies: Critical perspectives* (pp. 41–60). New York, NY: Information Age.

Martell, C. C. (2016). Teaching emerging teacher-researchers: Examining a district-based professional development course. *Teaching Education, 27*(1), 88–102.

Martell, C. C., & Hashimoto-Martell, E. A. (2012). Throwing out the textbook: A teacher research study of changing texts in the history classroom. In H. Hickman & B. J. Porfilio (Eds.), *The new politics of the textbook: Critical analysis in the core content areas* (pp. 305–320). Boston, MA: Sense.

McCormick, T. M. (2008). Historical inquiry with fifth graders: An action research study. *Social Studies Research and Practice, 3*(2), 119–129.

McFeetors, P. J. (2012). Enhancing students' mathematical learning through focused teacher growth. *Journal for Research in Mathematics Education, 43*, 651–657.

McGuinn, P. (2012). Stimulating reform: Race to the Top, competitive grants, and the Obama education agenda. *Educational Policy, 26*(1), 136–159.

McKernan, J. (1996). *Curriculum action research: A handbook of methods and resources for the reflective practitioner.* London, England: Kogan Page.

McNiff, J. (2016). *You and your action research project* (4th ed.). New York, NY: Routledge.

McTaggart, R. (1997). *Participatory action research: International contexts and consequences.* New York: State University of New York Press.

Mills, G. (2017). *Action research: A guide for the teacher researcher* (6th ed.). NY: Pearson Education.

Mirra, N., Filipiak, D., & Garcia, A. (2015). Revolutionizing inquiry in urban English classrooms: Pursuing voice and justice through youth participatory action research. *English Journal, 105*(2), 49–57.

Mitchell, K., & Elwood, S. (2012). From redlining to benevolent societies: The emancipatory power of spatial thinking. *Theory & Research in Social Education, 40*, 134–163.

Mostofo, J. (2014). The impact of using lesson study with pre-service mathematics teachers. *Journal of Instructional Research, 3*, 55–63.

Muir, T., & Beswick, K. (2007). Stimulating reflection on practice: Using the supportive classroom reflection process. *Mathematics Teacher Education and Development, 8*, 74–93.

National Council of Teachers of Mathematics. (2012). *Linking mathematics education research and practice.* Retrieved from https://www.nctm.org/Standards-and-Positions/Position-Statements/Linking-Mathematics-Education-Research-and-Practice/

National Council of Teachers of Mathematics Linking Research and Practice Task Force. (2005). *Harnessing the power of research for practice.* Retrieved from http://www.nctm.org/uploadedFiles/About_NCTM/Board_and_Committess/research_practice.pdf

National Writing Project. (2008). *Writing project professional development for teachers yields gains in student writing achievement.* Retrieved from https://www.nwp.org/cs/public/download/nwp_file/10683/NWP_Research_Brief_2008.pdf

Noffke, S. E., Clark, B. G., Palmeri-Santiago, J., Sadler, J., & Shujaa, M. (1996). Conflict, learning, and change in a school/university partnership: Different worlds of sharing. *Theory Into Practice, 35*, 165–172.

Noffke, S. E., & Somekh, B. (Eds.). (2009). *The Sage handbook of educational action research.* Thousand Oaks, CA: Sage.

Olson, C. B., & Land, R. (2007). A cognitive strategies approach to reading and writing instruction for English language learners in secondary school. *Research in the Teaching of English, 41*, 269–303.

Pella, S. (2015). Pedagogical reasoning and action: Affordances of practice-based teacher professional development. *Teacher Education Quarterly, 42*(3), 81–101.

Phillips, D. K., & Carr, K. (2009). Dilemmas of trustworthiness in preservice teacher action research. *Action Research, 7*, 207–226.

Price, J. N. (2001). Action research, pedagogy and change: The transformative potential of action research in pre-service teacher education. *Journal of Curriculum Studies, 33*(1), 43–74.

Price, J. N., & Valli, L. (2005). Preservice teachers becoming agents of change: Pedagogical implications for action research. *Journal of Teacher Education, 56*(1), 55–72.

Putnam, R. T., & Borko, H. (2000). What do new views of knowledge and thinking have to say about research on teacher learning? *Educational Researcher, 29*(1), 4–15.

Raygoza, M. C. (2016). Striving toward transformational resistance: Youth participatory action research in the mathematics classroom. *Journal of Urban Mathematics Education, 9*, 122–152.

Reason, P., & Bradbury, H. (Eds.). (2008). *The Sage handbook of action research* (2nd ed.). Thousand Oaks, CA: Sage.

Reason, P., & Torbert, W. (2001). The action turn: Toward a transformational action science. *Concepts and Transformation, 6*(1), 36–52.

Reidel, M., & Salinas, C. (2011). The role of emotion in democratic dialogue: A self study. *Social Studies Research and Practice, 6*(1), 2–20.

Resnick, M. (1996). Making connections between families and schools. In H. Banford, M. Berkman, C. Chin, C. Cziko, B. Fecho, D. Jumpp, . . . M. Resnick, *Cityscapes: Eight views from the urban classroom* (pp. 115–132). Berkeley, CA: National Writing Project.

Roth, K. (2007). Science teachers as researchers. In S. K. Abell & N. G. Lederman (Eds.), *Handbook of research on science education* (pp. 1203–1260). Mahwah, NJ: Lawrence Erlbaum.

Russ, R. S., Sherin, B. L., & Sherin, M. G. (2016). What constitutes teacher learning? In D. H. Gitmoer & C. A. Bell (Eds.), Handbook of research on teaching (5th ed., pp. 391–438). Washington, DC: American Educational Research Association.

Rust, E., & Meyer, F. (2006). The bright side: Teacher research in the context of educational reform and policy-making. *Teachers and Teaching Theory and Practice, 12*(1), 69–86.

Sánchez, R. M. (2007). Music and poetry as social justice texts in the secondary classroom. *Theory & Research in Social Education, 35*, 646–666.

Sayer, P. (2005). An intensive approach to building conversation skills. *ELT Journal, 59*(1), 14–22.

Scherff, L. (2012). "This project has personally affected me": Developing a critical stance in preservice English teachers. *Journal of Literacy Research, 44*, 200–236.

Scott, A., Clarkson, P., & McDonough, A. (2012). Professional learning and action research: Early career teachers reflect on their practice. *Mathematics Education Research Journal, 24*, 129–151.

Sherin, M. G. (2002). When teaching becomes learning. *Cognition and Instruction, 20*, 119–150.

Shulman, L. S. (1987). Knowledge and teaching: Foundations of the new reform. *Harvard Educational Review 57*(1), 1–22.

Shulman, L. S. (1999). Professing educational scholarship. In E. C. Lagemann & L. S. Shulman (Eds.), *Issues in education research: Problems and possibilities* (pp. 159–165). San Francisco, CA: Jossey-Bass.

Silvers, P. (2001). Critical reflection in the elementary grades: A new dimension in literature discussions. *Language Arts, 78*, 556–563.

Smith, M. W., & Connolly, W. (2005). The effects of interpretive authority on classroom discussions of poetry: Lessons from one teacher. *Communication Education, 54*, 271–288. doi:10.1080/03634520500442145

Sparks, S. D. (2016). NCLB rewrite sets new path on school research. *Education Week, 35*(15), 18.

Stanley, W., & Nelson, J. L. (1986). Social education for social transformation. *Social Education, 50*, 528–530.

Stenhouse, L. (1985). *Research as a basis for teaching.* London, England: Heinemann.

Stenhouse, L., Verma, G. K., Wild, R. D., & Nixon, J. (1982). *Teaching about race relations: Problems and effects.* London, England: Routledge/Kegan Paul.

St. John, M., & Stokes, L. (2008). *Investing in the improvement of education: Lessons to be learned from the National Writing Project* (Inverness Research report). Retrieved from http://inverness-research.org/reports/2008-12_Rpt_NWP-Improvement-Infrastructure.pdf

Stock, P. L. (1993). The function of anecdote in teacher research. *English Education, 25,* 173–187.

Storms, S. B. (2013). Preparing teachers for social justice advocacy. *Multicultural Education, 20*(2), 33–39.

Sturk, A. (1992). Developing a community of learners inside and outside the classroom. In P. Shannon (Ed.), *Becoming political: Readings and writings in the politics of literacy education* (pp. 263–273). Portsmouth, NH: Heinemann.

Tendero, J. (1998). Worth waiting for: Girls writing for their lives in the Bronx. *Teacher Research, 5*(2), 10–25.

The Linking Research and Practice Task Force. (2005). *Harnessing the power of research for practice* (Report to the National Council of Teachers of Mathematics). Retrieved from https://www.nctm.org/uploadedFiles/About/President,_Board_and_Committees/Report-LinkingResearchAndPractice.pdf

Thomas-Brown, K. (2010). Using "When the levees broke/teaching the levees" to teach middle school students about empathy and social justice. *Social Studies Research and Practice, 5*(2), 76–90.

Tobin, K. (1987). The role of wait time in higher cognitive level learning. *Review of Educational Research, 57*(1), 69–95.

Treagust, D. F., Won, M., & Dutt, R. (2014). Paradigms in science education research. In N. G. Lederman & S. K. Abell (Eds.), *Handbook of research on science education* (Vol. 2, pp. 3–17). New York, NY: Routledge

Van Driel, J. H, & Berry, A. (2012). Teacher professional development focusing on pedagogical content knowledge. *Educational Researcher, 41,* 26–28.

Van Driel, J. H., Berry, A., & Meirink, J. (2014). Research on science teacher knowledge. In N. G. Lederman & S. K. Abell (Eds.), *Handbook of research on science education* (Vol. 2, pp. 848–870). New York, NY: Routledge.

van Manen, M. (1990). Beyond assumptions: Shifting the limits of action research. *Theory Into Practice, 29,* 152–157.

VanSledright, B. (2002). *In search of America's past: Learning to read history in elementary school.* New York, NY: Teachers College Press.

VanSledright, B. (2004). What does it mean to think historically . . . and how do you teach it? *Social Education, 68,* 230–233.

Vaughan, M., & Burnaford, G. (2015). Action research in graduate teacher education: A review of the literature, 2005-2015. *Educational Action Research, 24,* 280–299.

Viadero, D. (2004). Education department issues practical guide to research-based practice. *Education Week, 23*(16), 12.

Volk, K. S. (2010). Action research as a sustainable endeavor for teachers. Does initial training lead to further action? *Action Research, 8,* 315–332.

Wade, R. C. (1999). Voice and choice in a university seminar: The struggle to teach democratically. *Theory & Research in Social Education, 27,* 70–92.

Warren, S., Doorn, D., & Green, J. (2008). Changes in vision: Teachers engaging in action research. *Educational Forum, 72,* 260–270.

Wenger, E. (1998). *Communities of practice: Learning, meaning, and identity.* Cambridge, England: Cambridge University Press.

Wittrock, M. C. (2005). Contemporary methodological issues and future directions in research on teaching English. In D. Lapp, D. Fischer, J. Flood, J. Jensen, & J. R. Squire (Eds.), *Handbook of research on teaching the English language arts* (2nd ed., pp. 301–320). New York, NY: Routledge.

Zagora, V. M. (2011). An approach to integrating writing skills into the social studies classroom. *Social Education, 75*, 17–21.

Zeichner, K. (1993). Action research: Personal renewal and social reconstruction. *Educational Action Research, 1*, 199–219.

Zeichner, K. (1994). Personal transformation and social reconstruction through action research. In S. Hollingsworth & H. Sockett (Eds.), *Teacher research and educational reform* (pp. 66–85). Chicago, IL: University of Chicago Press.

Zeichner, K. (2001). Educational action research. In P. Reason & H. Bradbury (Eds.), *Handbook of action research: Participative inquiry and practice* (pp. 273–283). Thousand Oaks, CA: Sage.

Zeichner, K. M., & Noffke, S. E. (2001). Practitioner research. In V. Richardson (Ed.), *Handbook of research on teaching* (pp. 298–330). Washington, DC: American Educational Research Association.

Zevenbergen, R. (2001). Peer assessment of student constructed posters: Assessment alternatives in preservice mathematics education. *Journal of Mathematics Teacher Education, 4,* 95–113.

Chapter 7

(Re)framing Resistance to Culturally Relevant Education as a Multilevel Learning Problem

REBECCA COLINA NERI
University of California, Los Angeles

MARITZA LOZANO
California State University, Fullerton

LOUIS M. GOMEZ
University of California, Los Angeles

Despite evidence of promise, the adoption of culturally relevant educational (CRE) approaches to teaching and learning remains sporadic and underwhelming. In this chapter, we question this state of affairs by investigating teacher resistance to CRE. Through our examination of the literature, we have come to understand teacher resistance to CRE as a multilevel learning problem that stems from (a) limited understanding and belief in the efficacy of CRE and (b) a lack of know-how needed to execute it. We therefore characterize resistance as a learning problem, rather than a problem of individual compliance, and view contextual variation in its take up as an opportunity to learn. Framing teacher resistance to CRE as a multilevel learning problem provides a way forward by shifting the perception of resistance as simply negative to an understanding of resistance as a diagnostic tool, or warning signal about when, where, for whom, and why a change can be particularly difficult. By representing our review of the literature as a problem space map, we offer a tool that can be used to pinpoint, anticipate, and preemptively address the multilevel factors that contribute to teachers' resistance to CRE.

RESISTANCE AND CULTURALLY RELEVANT EDUCATION

It is not even mildly controversial to suggest that in order to successfully teach nondominant students all their teachers should possess practical pedagogies that effectively draw on the racial, ethnic, linguistic, and cultural assets that these learners bring to school. Beginning over 30 years ago, practitioners and

Review of Research in Education
March 2019, Vol. 43, pp. 197–226
DOI: 10.3102/0091732X18821120
Chapter reuse guidelines: sagepub.com/journals-permissions
© 2019 AERA. http://rre.aera.net

researchers began to invent a new class of culturally relevant education (CRE) practices and pedagogies to help educators work effectively in diverse classrooms (Gay, 1975, 1980; Ladson-Billings, 1992). Here, CRE (Aronson & Laughter, 2016; Dover, 2013) refers to a collection of representative approaches that center the core tenets of culturally responsive teaching (Gay, 1975, 1980) and culturally relevant pedagogy (Ladson-Billings, 1994). Culturally responsive teaching focuses on competency and methods and describes what teachers should do to be culturally responsive. Culturally relevant pedagogy centers attitudes and dispositions, "describing a posture a teacher might adopt that, when fully embodied, would determine planning, instruction, and assessment" (Aronson & Laughter, 2016, p. 167). While these two approaches differ in that one centers instruction and the other pedagogy, they also share a common commitment to pursuing social justice education and a strong belief in the power of the "classroom as a site for social change" (Aronson & Laughter, 2016, p. 164). Aligning the key tenets of each of these approaches to the four markers of CRE (Dover, 2013), Aronson and Laughter (2016) describe culturally relevant educators as teachers, who in their pursuit of social justice,

1. use constructivist methods to develop bridges connecting students' cultural references to academic skills and concepts while also building on the knowledges and cultural assets students bring with them into the classroom;
2. engage students in critical reflection about their own lives and societies and using inclusive curricula and activities to support analysis of all the cultures represented;
3. facilitate students' cultural competence and construct a classroom learning environment in which students both learn about their own and others' cultures and develop pride in their own and others' cultures; and
4. explicitly unmask and unmake oppressive systems through the critique of discourses of power, extending their work beyond the classroom in active pursuit of social justice for all members of society. (p. 167)

Despite evidence of promise, the adoption of CRE approaches remains sporadic and underwhelming. In this chapter, we question this state of affairs, exploring why the field, as a whole, has offered a muted response to spreading CRE. Two rather large criteria disciplined our review. First, we considered articles from the published literature concerning in-service teaching. While issues of resistance are considered in the preservice literature (e.g., Cockrell, Placier, Cockrell, & Middleton, 1999), the preponderance of the work concerns how teachers-to-be react to diversity and multiculturalism when they encounter students in the higher education classroom rather than how they react to students, in practice. Second, we considered a broad set of empirical results ranging from large sample survey data to single cases of teachers reporting their experiences with, conceptualizations of, and reactions to CRE.

Framing Resistance

Resistance has been taken up across myriad fields and disciplines in different ways. While some argue that resistance stems from the individual, others contend that resistance is produced by the organizational context in which a proposed change takes place. And, while many understand resistance as a negative part of organizational life, others remind us that change is not always positive, and therefore, resistance plays an essential role in the healthy development of an organization. There are also many scholars who have used the notion of resistance to describe "how oppositional behavior may be an impetus towards social justice" (Solorzano & Delgado Bernal, 2001, p. 310) and who would argue that implementing CRE is, in and of itself, a form of resisting the status quo. We suspect that there are elements of insight to each of these characterizations that together demonstrate the complexity of resistance as a multilevel and multidimensional problem. We, for example, take it as axiomatic that most teachers want to do a good job and want their students to learn. However, a long history of education research and reform efforts has proven, perhaps above all else, that the practice of teaching is anything but straightforward or simple. Teachers have a responsibility to make sense of a plethora of often short-lived and conflicting interventions, prioritizing those that improve teaching and learning and resisting those that do not. How and why teachers make the decision to adopt or resist a proposed change is contingent upon a complex system of beliefs, knowledge, and know-how. In this effort, we aim to further problematize the notion of resistance rather than accepting it as a terminal explanation in characterizing why CRE has failed to reach widespread implementation.

CRE for most schooling organizations and individuals represents a change. They are moving from some other, perhaps older, form of pedagogy to CRE, which is probably new to them. Rogers (2003) explains that when faced with an innovation, individuals engage in an innovation-decision process, or "an information-seeking and information-processing activity, where an individual is motivated to reduce uncertainty about the advantages and disadvantages of an innovation" (p. 172). He names five stages that occur throughout this process. During the *knowledge* stage, an individual becomes aware of a proposed change, learns what it is, how to use it correctly, and the principles behind how and why it works. The *persuasion* stage is more affective, or feeling-centered. After gaining knowledge about the proposed change, individuals develop a positive or negative attitude toward the change that may influence their adoption of or resistance to the innovation. The *decision* stage occurs when an individual chooses to adopt or resist the proposed change. While an individual may have already developed resistance toward the innovation, it is during this stage that they make a decision to, actively or passively, resist the change. In the *implementation* stage, an individual would put the proposed change into practice. Here, the innovation goes through a process of reinvention as individuals modify and adapt it during the process of implementation. Finally, in the *confirmation* stage, individuals seek approval or support for their decision. The confirmation, or lack thereof, individuals receive influences their decision to sustain the innovation. However, many will seek confirmation from individuals they believe will support their decision.

Across these stages, there are various attributes of innovation that influence if, and how quickly, an innovation is adopted. Rogers (2003) has found the most powerful of these attributes to be the *relative advantage* of the proposed change, or the extent to which it is perceived as better than existing practices. The adoption of an innovation is also affected by (a) its *compatibility* with the values, past experiences, and needs of individual adopters; (b) its *complexity*, or how difficult it is to understand and use; (c) *triability*, or the degree to which it can be engaged in experimentation; and (d) its *observability* or visibility to others. The innovation-decision process is further nuanced by differences in the speed at which individuals adopt the innovation. *Early adopters* tend to be gatekeepers for an innovation, hold leadership roles or are respected as leaders in their context, and have good interactions with other members of the social system. As such early adopters are essential to the implementation of an innovation, but must also learn to navigate varied levels of critique and pushback for bringing a particular innovation into an existing context. *Late adopters* tend to be more skeptical about the value and efficacy of an innovation. Their willingness to implement the innovation is often motivated by peer pressure or economic necessity. Late adopters will often wait until they know an innovation works before taking it up.

The resistance to change literature offers important insight into individual- and organizational-level factors that influence if, and how quickly, individuals adopt an innovation. The majority of this literature focuses on the individual-level factors that contribute to resistance. The theory of cognitive dissonance argues that people strive to keep their attitudes and behaviors consistent (Burnes & Jackson, 2011; Festinger, 1957; Jones, 1990; Peters, 2012). When encountering changes, or paradoxes, that expose an inconsistency within or between their attitudes and behaviors, people will attempt to reestablish consistency by lessening the strength of the driving or restraining forces. The intensity of the misalignment between people's attitudes and behaviors and the proposed change determines the level of resistance. The lower the intensity, the less likely it will be met with resistance. The higher the intensity, the more likely individuals will be able to reduce the dissonance through changing their behaviors and/or attitudes or resisting the paradoxical change altogether. In addition to its alignment with individuals' attitudes and behaviors, the depth of an intervention, or the magnitude of its impact on the psychological makeup and personality of individuals, can contribute to resistance as it determines the level of participation needed from individuals in order for the change to be effectively implemented (Cummings & Worley, 2009; Huse, 1980; Schmuck & Miles, 1971). Finally, an individual's level of resistance can be affected by the interaction between a proposed change and the psychological contract of an organization, or the unwritten set of expectations between members in the organization (Argyris, 1960; D. M. Rousseau, 1989). Individuals who perceive the proposed change as a breach to their organization's psychological contract will be more likely to find it unfair and resistant to take it up.

While the majority of the resistance to change literature centers on individual-/ employee-level factors, the foundational underpinnings of resistance to change (Lewin, 1943, 1946, 1947) focus more heavily on the context in which a proposed change takes place. Lewin argued that individual and group behavior is produced in a complex system or field of restraining and driving forces. These forces have been found to include leadership style and behavior; a leader's willingness to change their behavior; incompatible goals in the system; various elements related to organizational culture; and the extent to which employees have genuine choice and opportunities to participate in the proposed changes and how they are managed (Burnes, 2014; Coch & French, 1948; Cummings & Worley, 2009; Dent & Goldberg, 1999; Lewin, 1947; Senge, 1990). Here, scholars posit that efforts to redress resistance and change behavior are best achieved through the engagement of participative decision-making rather than top-down imposition of change.

In Figure 1, we demonstrate how the various approaches described above work together to influence resistance to a proposed change or innovation. While this framework addresses resistance to change broadly, it is also helpful for understanding how issues related to race and culture make resistance to CRE a unique problem. Rogers (2003) explains that the *relative advantage* of an innovation (i.e., if it is perceived as better than existing practices) is the strongest predictor of how quickly it will be adopted. As we discuss in this chapter, restraining forces like standardization and accountability policies and practices prioritize achievement measures and curriculum that homogenize educators and students. Therefore, teachers are often faced with the difficult challenge of navigating conflicting responsibilities and standards, which greatly affects their willingness to adopt CRE during the decision stage of the innovation-diffusion process. If teachers do still decide to implement CRE, their efforts can be further thwarted during the confirmation stage when they seek approval from their colleagues. The literature (Esposito & Swain, 2009; Kohli & Pizarro, 2016; Underwood & Mensah, 2018) reports that when teachers take up CRE, they are often isolated and excluded by their colleagues who perceive CRE and issues of race and culture as irrelevant, unimportant, or even a direct threat to the psychological contract of their schooling organization.

Furthermore, there remains a pervasive mismatch between teachers' cultural frames of reference and those of their students, which often results in a lack of sufficient racial/cultural knowledge and know-how. Therefore, during the knowledge stage of the CRE innovation-diffusion process, it can require a greater amount of effort for teachers to learn what CRE is, how to make it work effectively, and the principles behind how and why it works. During the persuasion and decision stages, when teachers are forming attitudes and beliefs about CRE and deciding whether to adopt or resist it, issues related to race and culture can influence how compatible and complex teachers perceive the change to be. Here, issues related to race and culture can further exacerbate CRE's misalignment to teachers' behaviors and attitudes (i.e.,

FIGURE 1
Resistance to Change Framework

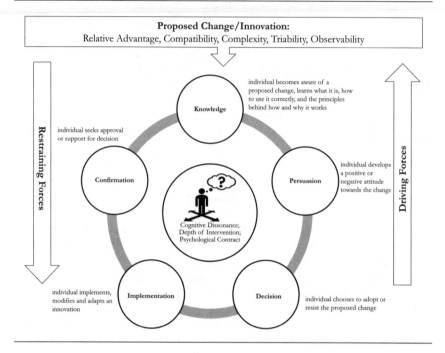

Note. This figure characterizes how myriad individual- and system-level forces work together to influence resistance to a proposed change or innovation.

cognitive dissonance) and quite possibly more deeply affect their psychological makeup requiring a greater amount of their participation (i.e., depth of intervention). We suggest how racial/cultural beliefs, knowledge, and know-how contribute to our characterization of teacher resistance to CRE as a unique, multilevel learning problem in more detail throughout this chapter.

Teacher Resistance to CRE as a Multilevel Learning Problem

Through our examination of the literature, we have come to understand teacher resistance to CRE as a multilevel problem that stems from (a) limited understanding, and belief in the efficacy, of CRE and (b) a lack of know-how needed to execute it. The multilevel nature of resistance becomes evident when considering that even when teachers are philosophically aligned with CRE, they struggle with its execution. While this is in part due to their own level of content, pedagogical, and racial/cultural knowledge and know-how, it is also largely influenced by the quality of organizational- and institutional-level supports teachers have access to.

Unfortunately, high-quality supports for implementing CRE are few and far between, if available at all. The majority of schools, districts, and government-level organizations have not learned why they should, nor how to, create these supports. We therefore characterize resistance to CRE as a multilevel learning problem, rather than a problem of individual compliance, and view contextual variation in its take up as an opportunity to learn. Framing resistance as a learning problem provides a way forward by shifting the perception of resistance as simply negative to an understanding of resistance as a diagnostic tool, or warning signal about when, where, for whom, and why a change can be particularly difficult (Waddell & Sohal, 1998). This approach to investigating resistance enables individuals, school leaders, and district- and government-level administration to be more planful about the introduction and management of CRE as an innovation. Returning to our foundational assumption, that most teachers want to do a good job, resistance, then, might offer telltale markers about how to apply resources to make it possible for more people to engage in an anticipated positive behavior like CRE. To support these efforts, we adapted our review of the literature into a visual problem space, represented in Figure 2, that can be used to pinpoint, anticipate, and preemptively address the multilevel factors that contribute to teachers' resistance to implementing CRE.

Beginning with individual-level factors that contribute to teacher resistance to CRE, we first describe how teachers' willingness and ability to take up CRE is contingent upon their beliefs about the validity, efficacy, and utility of CRE; knowledge about what it is; and know-how to execute. A great deal of what we know from teachers' commentary about CRE, when they find it difficult, has to do with a general lack of understanding of what to do and an uncertainty that it works. If teachers do not think CRE is going to be efficacious, which is greatly dependent on knowing how to make it work, they are not likely to create learning environments that are hospitable to its practices. The next element of our framework explores the institutional- and organizational-level factors that contribute to teacher resistance to CRE. Teachers overwhelmingly report that their work settings are not socially fertile places for CRE (Borrero, Flores, & de la Cruz, 2016; Esposito & Swain, 2009; Kohli & Pizarro, 2016). Here, teachers' willingness and ability to implement CRE is often diminished by conflicting mandates, standards, and responsibilities and a lack of resources, materials, and support from colleagues and leadership. In this section of the chapter, we also highlight some of the ways schooling organizations, districts, and government entities might overcome these challenges by developing the know-how to support teachers in their efforts to implement CRE approaches. Our aim, as we go forward in this examination, is to suggest how each of the multilevel dimensions of this framing, either individually or in concert, limit teachers' decision-making and heighten their sense of vulnerability in relation to CRE. We posit that learning to see teacher resistance to CRE as a multilevel learning problem might offer useable and actionable insights that support its widespread implementation.

FIGURE 2
Teacher Resistance to CRE as a Multilevel Learning Problem Space

Institutional-Level

Building Coherence & Alignment:
- Conflicting Standards, Objectives, and Pacing
- Competing vs. Coalescing Interventions & PD
- Time to get it right
- Commitment to long-term change

Accountability Practices:
- Admin support vs. pressure
- Evaluation measures/routines
- Unsupported mandates

Differentiating Curriculum & Pedagogy:
- Overly homogenized
- Diversifying curriculum
- Pedagogical Models/Replicable Strategies
- Multiple forms of assessment
- Value of process-oriented measures

Organizational-Level

School Leadership:
- Navigating district- and state-level mandates
- Coherence b/w conflicting priorities
- Time to get it right
- Distributing authority
- Differentiating teacher learning
- Punitive vs. Constructive evaluation practices

Shared Vision:
- Commitment to long-term change
- Common Language
- School-community relationships

Professional Learning:
- Professional collaboration vs. isolation
- Common Language
- Brave Spaces to talk about CRE
- PD and Leadership Opportunities

Resources & Training:
- Aligned, high-quality, coalesced PD & time to get it right in practice
- Diversified curriculum, pedagogical models, and assessment
- Differentiation
- Commitment to sociopolitical issues
- Process-oriented measures

Teacher-Level

Beliefs:
- Limiting CRE's value to motivation/engagement
- Value CRE for academic achievement
- Value CRE for content mastery
- Subject-specific race-neutrality
- Question developmental appropriateness
- Measuring efficacy of CRE

- Blame students, families, communities: *"They don't care enough"*
- Question student capabilities: *"Students can't handle it"*
- Question CRE for all students: *"Students best served in own community"*
- Minimize the importance of race and culture: *"Kids want to be kids"*
- Meritocratic ideals: *"All students can succeed if they just work hard."*
- Unwillingness to own one's role: *"But I'm not racist." "My way works best."*

Building Empowering Learning Communities:
- Distributing authority/autonomy
- Differentiation
- Facilitating groupwork, projects, inquiry, talk
- Maintaining high expectations
- Mutually constructive relationships w/students/families/communities
- (In)congruence b/w teachers' and students' cultural frames of reference

Diversifying Curriculum and Pedagogy:
- Access to high-quality materials and curriculum
- Access to pedagogical models & replicable strategies
- Content knowledge to diversify curriculum
- Multiple forms of assessment/process-oriented measures
- Managing conversations about race & culture

Note. This visual problem space can be used to pinpoint, anticipate, and preemptively address the multilevel factors that contribute to teachers' resistance to implementing CRE.

TEACHER BELIEFS AND KNOW-HOW AS SOURCES OF RESISTANCE TO CRE

Resistance to CRE in many ways begins with teachers questioning: Is this my responsibility? Is this important enough to revise my practice? And if so, is this a priority? The literature often frames teachers' answers to these questions as a matter of beliefs and know-how. Teachers' beliefs about the efficacy, utility, and validity of CRE are greatly influenced by their knowledge of what CRE is and their know-how to execute. The dialectical relationship between beliefs and know-how is foundational to our notion of resistance to CRE. In the section that follows, we describe individual-level factors—beliefs, attitudes, knowledge, and know-how—that contribute to teacher resistance to CRE. Later sections take up the ways teacher beliefs and know-how are affected by organizational- and institutional-level support and demands.

Doubts About the Validity/Utility/Efficacy of CRE: *Is This My Responsibility? Is This Important Enough to Revise My Practice? Is This a Priority?*

Extant literature reports teachers' doubts about the validity, efficacy, and utility of CRE stem from the myth of subject-specific race-neutrality and teachers' own problematic and unrealistic ideas about race and culture. These doubts can result in outright resistance to CRE. However, most often they result in teachers' limiting their perceptions of the usefulness, value, and relevance of CRE to issues of student motivation or engagement rather than seeing it as valuable for academic achievement and rigorous student learning (Aronson & Laughter, 2016; Bianchini & Brenner, 2010; Ebersole, Kanahele-Mossman, & Kawakami, 2016; Farmer, Hauk, & Neumann, 2005). Through her work with administrators and teachers, Young (2010) has found that when defining CRE, teachers rarely make any reference to academic success. She explains that students' cultural capital is most often regarded as "the means to build learning on their personal experiences and to make the curriculum meaningful to them but not necessarily as a way to promote rigorous academic learning" (p. 252). Redman (2014) reported similar findings in relation to content mastery in her work with novice science teachers who displayed "attitudes that culturally relevant pedagogy is valuable more for its ability to motivate and engage students than actually help them to understand science" (p. 157). Reflecting on their efforts to implement CRE, the teachers in her study reported an incongruence between learning content standards and enacting CRE as they found it challenging "to 'juggle' the need to teach 'rigorous science curriculum' and 'make it culturally relevant'" (p. 159). When teachers doubt the value of CRE for rigorous academic learning, issues of race and culture are often minimized, ignored, pushed to the background, or treated as an add-on, if time permits, after attending to content standards and academic achievement measures. In this section, we describe how the myth of subject-specific race-neutrality and colorblindness contribute to teachers' doubts about the appropriateness, usefulness, and value of CRE approaches to teaching and learning.

Subject-Specific Race-Neutrality

Studies in both mathematics and science education demonstrate that while teachers may believe issues of race and culture are appropriate for other subjects like the arts or humanities, they often question their relevance to the hard sciences (Barton, 2003; R. Gutiérrez, 2013; Laughter & Adams, 2012; Martin, 2010; Nasir, 2016; C. Rousseau & Tate, 2003; Shah, 2017). In their work with mathematics educators, C. Rousseau and Tate (2003) found that teachers are often resistant to issues related to race and culture because these issues "didn't really come up" in their courses (p. 214). Similarly, Barton (2003) has found that science educators often question their responsibility to focus on issues of race and culture because they believe cultural relevance and social justice are more appropriate and relevant to the arts or humanities, but not their own subject matter.

The myth that race and culture are not relevant to content mastery and academic achievement can also result in the (re)production of stereotypes about students of color and affect teachers' willingness to own up to their responsibility to implement CRE (Bobo & Hutchings, 1996; Diversity in Mathematics Education Center for Learning and Teaching, 2007; Martin, 2009). Take mathematics as a content-specific example. Studies in mathematics education have found that teachers of Black and Latinx students place an overemphasis on monitoring behavior, frequently isolate students from their peers or classroom learning environment, and often resort to exclusionary discipline practices (Battey & Stark, 2009; Nasir, 2011; Nasir, Snyder, Shah, & Ross, 2013). Furthermore, students of color lack access to key educational resources, most notably high-quality instruction (Anyon, 1980; Haberman, 1991; Ladson-Billings, 1997), teachers with a high level of Mathematical Knowledge for Teaching (MKT; Hill, 2007; Hill, Rowan, & Ball, 2005), and college-preparatory mathematics courses, including AP courses (Darling-Hammond, 2010; Noguera, 2004; Oakes, 2005). In these ways, mathematics classrooms become racialized spaces wherein "racial storylines" act as barriers that shape not only the way "we collectively make sense of (and reproduce) achievement patterns" (Nasir, 2016, p. 12) but also students' perceptions of their ability to do mathematics (Martin, 2013; Nasir, 2011; Nasir et al., 2013). Without critical analyses of how issues of race and culture, like those described above, shape access and opportunity, racial gaps in mathematics achievement can lead to stereotypes of Black and Latinx students as non-math people. R. Gutiérrez (2013) argues further that as our society has traditionally used mathematics achievement as a proxy for intelligence, these stereotypes of Black and Latinx students as non-math people can also result in stereotypes about their intelligence. If left unchallenged, these stereotypes can further impede teachers' willingness to take ownership for CRE.

Problematic and Unrealistic Ideas About Race and Culture

Teachers often hold problematic and unrealistic ideas about race and culture that contribute to their doubts about the validity, utility, and efficacy of CRE for teaching and learning. Bonilla-Silva (2006) offers four frames that are helpful for understanding how ideas and beliefs rooted in colorblindness (re)produce status quo and deficit approaches to teaching and learning. We use these frames to organize our examination of the literature related to teachers' doubts about the usefulness, value, and appropriateness of CRE. In what follows, we first describe each frame and then provide example(s) from the literature that demonstrate how colorblind ideology produces beliefs and doubts that contribute to teacher resistance to CRE.

1. *Naturalization*: Makes sense of racial phenomena as a natural occurrence (i.e., schools are segregated because people "gravitate toward likeness").
     For example, "ELs would be better served in their own community" (Argumedo, 2016, p. 46).
2. *Cultural racism*: Makes sense of the social standing of minorities through culturally based arguments (i.e., the blame game).
     For example, "these students don't care about school" (C. C. Johnson, 2011; Liou, Marsh, & Antrop-González, 2017); "these kids can't handle it" (Coffey & Farinde-Wu, 2016); "they are not prepared to engage in inquiry"

(Bianchini & Brenner, 2010; Bryan & Atwater, 2002); and "they just need to learn the basics" (Diamond, Randolph, & Spillane, 2004; Evans, 2007).

3. *Minimization of racism*: Decentralizes discrimination and therefore minimizes issues of race and culture.

For example, "kids just want to be kids; they don't want to think about race and culture" (Freire & Valdez, 2017; Harris Russell, McDonald, Jones, & Weaver, 2016); "we don't have those kids, or this is only for students of color" (Argumedo, 2016; Mette, Nieuwenhuizen, & Hvidston, 2016); "race is too controversial and will cause more problems than it solves" (Buehler, Gere, Dallavis, & Haviland, 2009; Evans, 2007).

4. *Abstract liberalism*: Holds strong commitments to abstract notions of meritocracy and equality, without consideration of what it takes to achieve equity.

For example, "all students should be treated the same" (Brown & Crippen, 2017; Warren, 2013); "it's not a race thing, but rather an issue of motivation and hard work" (Argumedo, 2016).

Through these frames, we can begin to understand how teachers' problematic and unrealistic ideas about race and culture can contribute to their resistance to implement CRE. However, schools have increasingly become spaces in which race is salient and expressions of colorblindness are becoming less socially acceptable. Jayakumar and Adamian (2017) developed a fifth frame of colorblindness—*the disconnected power analysis frame*—to explain that as schools and organizations become increasingly race-conscious, people tend to draw on new understandings of racism that allow them "to believe they are racially progressive and committed to eradicating structural inequities while maintaining, if not bolstering, their white privilege" (p. 931). This frame is particularly helpful for understanding teaching in urban settings where educators have a growing responsibility for addressing issues of disparity and unequal access. Here, we see an increased amount of sympathy for students of color, but a lack of reflection on one's own privilege and an unwillingness to distribute one's power in ways that are necessary for facilitating highly interactive and dialogic instructional forms, often contributing to: (a) an overreliance on direct instruction (Borrero & Sanchez, 2017; Coffey & Farinde-Wu, 2016; Patchen & Cox-Petersen, 2008) and (b) teacher beliefs such as, *my* practice and *my* students are fine (Evans, 2007; McKenzie & Scheurich, 2008) and I do not need to do this work because I am not racist (Vaught & Castagno, 2008).

Resistance to CRE is rarely a direct product of teacher beliefs; rather, it is produced through the interaction between beliefs, know-how, and the diffusion of CRE as an innovation. If, and how quickly, teachers adopt CRE is influenced by CRE's alignment, or compatibility, with their attitudes and beliefs (i.e., cognitive dissonance) as well as the magnitude of CRE's impact on their psychological makeup (i.e., depth of intervention). However, as we explain in the section that follows, how teachers perceive the alignment of CRE to their practice, beliefs, and attitudes and its demand on their participation and effort is heavily influenced by their level of content, pedagogical, and racial/cultural knowledge and know-how.

Knowledge and Know-How: *What Is This? How Do I Do This? When Do I Do This?*

How do you do [culturally relevant pedagogy] without deviating too far from the curriculum? Are our kids really mature enough to address such deep inequalities? Do they even know how? Do we as teachers? . . . It's a great idea . . . [but] how do we do it? (Teacher; Young, 2010, p. 258)

Building Empowering Learning Communities . . . Lost in Translation

An essential element of CRE is building an empowering learning community. Here, we define empowering learning communities as organizational settings wherein both teachers and their students feel safe and empowered to take risks, share power and authority, engage in critical conversations about oppression and social inequity, and critically reflect upon teaching and learning. Teachers face many challenges when attempting to build empowering learning communities with and for their students that include (a) (mis)recognizing students' diverse ways of knowing, communicating, and participating; (b) diversifying curriculum and pedagogy; and (c) integrating and managing sociopolitical inquiry. In this section, we discuss the most cited challenges teachers face when attempting to plan, execute, and reflect upon CRE.

(Mis)recognizing Students' Diverse Ways of Knowing, Communicating, and Participating

G. R. Howard (2006) argues that knowing one's students requires knowing oneself. Often, teachers' cultural frames of reference are not only (in)congruent with those of their students but also privileged in society. While this argument is applicable to all teachers, regardless of race and culture, it takes on heightened meaning for White teachers whose conceptions of cultural capital are congruent with and reinforced by dominant narratives. Conversely, teachers of color are more likely to share cultural frames of reference with their students, but here it is important to remember that identity is intersectional, fluid, and rooted in context. Studies have suggested that prior educational experience, age, socioeconomic status, language, and religion can lead to incongruencies between students' cultural frames of reference and those of their teachers of color (Coffey & Farinde-Wu, 2016; Freire & Valdez, 2017; Philip, 2011). When teachers' cultural frames of reference are incongruent to those of their students they can misconstrue students' ways of knowing and participating as behavior issues or defiance and fail to recognize, value, and incorporate their learning and insights into the classroom (Brown & Crippen, 2017; Coffey & Farinde-Wu, 2016; Gregory & Mosely, 2004; K. Gutiérrez, Rymes, & Larson, 1995; Philip, 2011). Additional tensions arise when teachers' cultural frames of reference inhibit their ability to recognize the role of power in teacher–student relationships. When teachers fail to recognize the power they exert in relationships with their students and the communities they serve, the results could be damaging. The lack of recognition of power manifests in a number of ways, including teachers' expressions of prejudice toward their students (Hyland, 2005), diminished opportunities to foster student identity and voice (Arce, 2004), and a failure to foster relationships based on mutual vulnerability (Borrero & Sanchez, 2017; Zembylas, 2003).

The ability to recognize students' diverse ways of knowing, communicating, and participating as valid, useful, and powerful forms of learning is a type of know-how that teachers often struggle to cultivate. It requires that teachers develop cultural competence; utilize various forms of assessment to reflect upon their instruction and the types of knowledge and participation it privileges and constrains; and structure learning opportunities that validate and integrate students' funds of knowledge. However, if teachers are not provided time and practical support, the process of developing racial and cultural know-how can often feel aimless, inaccessible, and unattainable. Warren's (2014) work on teacher empathy and K. Gutiérrez et al.'s (1995) work on script and counterscript may offer the field replicable, adaptable, and practical strategies to support teachers in the development of racial and cultural know-how that could serve as a way forward.

Warren (2014) explains that student feedback, or concrete behavioral information, can and should inform how the teacher adjusts or modifies future interactions with students. Here, he offers teachers a practical strategy for utilizing student behavior as concrete data to rethink instruction. The interpretation of student feedback is very subjective; therefore, as teachers reflect upon and plan a response to a specific behavior, they also learn to critically consider a variety of antecedents, including "the present state of the student–teacher relationship, perception of student confidence level with instructional content, teacher bias or stereotypes, and personal knowledge of student learning disability" (p. 414). Take as example a newcomer EL student putting her head down in a math class. Too often, this behavior is perceived as the student not understanding the content. However, as the teacher reflects upon and questions this behavior as a form of concrete data to inform instruction, she learns that this student is actually bored because she was taking advanced math at her old school. Through engaging in this process, the teacher learns to develop an "imagine other" form of perspective and question her own assumptions and biases.

K. Gutiérrez et al. (1995) describe how teachers can analyze teacher script and student counterscript to identify moments when, in their facilitation of classroom discussion, they privilege their own internal cultural understandings and fail to recognize, or even actively silence, their students' ways of knowing, participating, and communicating. In their microanalysis of a classroom discussion, they explain how the teacher continuously imposes his own internalized cultural understandings on the students through "a form of monologism that attempted to stifle dialogue and interaction and the potential for taking up a critical stance" (p. 446). The teacher used language, such as "Don't shout out because you'll be giving it away to someone who didn't know to start with," that not only conveys the message that there is only one right answer but also that the students who do not raise their hands do not know the answer. In response, the students began having conversations and making references of their own that were largely ignored by the teacher as he continued to push the conversation forward. It is here, in what the authors refer to as the underlife of the classroom, that the teacher misses an opportunity to reflect on and revise his instruction to make it more culturally relevant and engaging. The comments students were making, while often falsely construed as misbehavior, were actually resistance to a classroom discussion they did not feel included, nor valued in and that actively silenced their cultural ways of knowing, participating, and communicating. Analyzing the students' comments further revealed that the side comments students were making, although dismissed by the teacher as irrelevant, were actually related to the topic of discussion and demonstrated that students were constructing their own learning space in the underlife of the classroom. In this example, the teacher might have responded differently if he was better supported in developing the know-how to recognize and build on students' cultural and linguistic repertoires.

Diversifying Curriculum and Pedagogy

Conceptual clarity around CRE is important for its implementation. Teachers report that their hesitancy to take up CRE often stems from confusion about its conceptual underpinnings (Borrero & Sanchez, 2017; Kohli & Pizarro, 2016). Essential to teachers' development of conceptual clarity around CRE is having access to culturally relevant curriculum and pedagogical models. These resources not only provide teachers with adaptable roadmaps to plan for CRE, they also provide a foundation upon which teachers can learn by doing and reflect upon their practice. However, studies demonstrate that teachers' know-how to execute CRE is greatly hampered by a lack of high-quality, culturally relevant curriculum and resources; the absence of consensus around pedagogical models of instruction that support CRE; and a scarcity of successful examples of this work in varied settings (Aronson & Laughter, 2016; Bianchirli & Cavazos, 2001; Borrero, Ziauddin, & Ahn, 2018; Esposito, Davis, & Swain, 2012; Montalvo, Combes, & Kea, 2014; Underwood & Mensah, 2018). Here, teachers are often charged with the task of "making it up as they go along," by finding, choosing, or developing their own materials. Diversifying curriculum and pedagogy requires a great amount of content mastery and knowing one's students well enough to make rigorous learning connections that can then be used to design and facilitate CRE. Teachers have reported this task to be very challenging especially when the resources available to them homogenize educators and students (Borrero et al., 2016; Esposito et al., 2012; Freire & Valdez, 2017; Royal & Gibson, 2017). Furthermore, the process of identifying cultural capital in a classroom is very ambiguous, as there is no, and nor should there be, "specific list of cultural characteristics to look for or a rulebook for deciding what is or is not culture" (Goldenberg, 2014, p. 122). As a result, teacher resistance to CRE is exacerbated by a lack of adaptable strategies for acquiring student funds of knowledge (Goldenberg, 2014; Warren, 2014), access to multiple forms of assessment (Bianchini & Brenner, 2010; Farmer et al., 2005; T. C. Howard & Rodriguez-Minkoff, 2017; Sleeter, 2012), and a lack of time, resources, support, and training that are necessary for designing instruction that is relevant to *all* students in their classroom (Brown & Crippen, 2017; Ebersole et al., 2016; Mette et al., 2016; Stillman, 2011; Vaught & Castagno, 2008).

Integrating and Managing Sociopolitical Inquiry

Ladson-Billings (2014) explains that even when teachers embraced culturally relevant pedagogy and "searched for cultural examples and analogues as they taught prescribed curricula . . . they rarely pushed students to consider critical perspectives on policies and practices that may have direct impact on their lives and communities" (p. 78). In order to facilitate contextualized, relevant, and rigorous instruction, teachers must be aware of the types of sociopolitical issues that their students face, in their communities and in their families. This keen awareness is crucial for creating curriculum, lessons, and tasks that support students in working through, responding, and taking concrete action on critical issues that directly affect their lives. However, the literature demonstrates that teachers often lack the knowledge and know-how needed to facilitate discussions and student learning around sociopolitical inquiry (Aronson & Laughter, 2016; Borrero et al., 2016; C. C. Johnson, 2011). Resistance to CRE can be influenced by teacher knowledge, including their level of cultural competence; their understanding of problems that are relevant to the lives and communities of their students; and their ability to meaningfully integrate sociopolitical issues into content learning. On the other hand, resistance to CRE based in know-how can result from teachers' ability to facilitate respectful and constructive dialogue between students; adapt sociopolitical inquiry to specific grade levels and disciplines; and utilize productive discussion strategies when they do not have answers for students' questions. Studies show that lacking the knowledge and know-how needed to facilitate sociopolitical discussions and learning produces doubts about the appropriateness and value of CRE (Freire & Valdez, 2017; Young, 2010) and the fear of being labeled racist (Bell, 2002; Buehler et al., 2009; Evans, 2007; Gregory & Mosely, 2004).

Section Summary

The absence of a range of practical know-how, usable pedagogical models, and high-quality resources exacerbates teachers' resistance to CRE. Teachers are increasingly tasked with making sense of changing expectations while their time to engage in problem solving is diminished. When teachers view the road ahead of them as uncharted and uncertain, with little support in the form of concrete examples and resources to implement CRE, the level of uncertainty and associated anxiety is elevated. Such feelings of uncertainty give way to low-risk learning communities and one-size-fits-all curricula and pedagogical strategies that will not meet the demands of pushing through the uncharted waters of CRE. Broadly, teachers fear the repercussions of exposing their limitations. Thus, whether teachers have limited conceptions of culture or limited understanding of CRE teaching practices (Underwood & Mensah, 2018), in these cases what matters most is that teachers feel vulnerable and fear facing or owning these limitations. The extent to which teachers are supported in developing sociopolitical consciousness, acquiring cultural competence, and have access to a range of workable pedagogical models and quality resources that support their understanding of why and how to do this work well will determine the likelihood that teachers take up CRE.

INSTITUTIONAL FACTORS: FEDERAL POLICY, EDUCATION AGENCIES, DISTRICTS, AND SCHOOLS

Institutionally, policy initiatives and district mandates work together to promote change and improvement in schools. However, the translation of policy to practice may create environments that are hostile to experimentation and innovation. Because policy is intent on promoting good for the many, oftentimes it falls short in its attention to ethnic, cultural, racial, or linguistic differences. Here, we describe the ways that institutional factors can derail innovation efforts and divert resources that could be used to support CRE implementation.

Building Coherence and Alignment

In this discussion, we cannot ignore the role of federal policy in shaping institutional contexts that contribute to the homogenization of educational practice (Anyon, 2005). Under the guise of coherence and alignment, federal policy mandates and current reform agendas have increasingly coupled standardized measures of student achievement with punitive evaluation systems (Braun, Chapman, & Vezzu, 2010; Coburn, 2004; DeBray-Pelot & McGuin, 2009). Here, these policy initiatives work to normalize standardized instructional practices by funding initiatives that, in practice, often discourage innovation. The field is full of policy examples that advocate for the "fidelity of implementation" of one-size-fits-all programs and approaches to achievement. Take, as example, the No Child Left Behind Act (NCLB; 2003). We use this example to highlight how policy initiatives are filtered through multiple levels of the education system in ways that contribute to teacher resistance to CRE.

In the early 2000s, NCLB and the accompanying Reading First program (Reading First Program of the No Child Left Behind Act of 2001) were two heavily funded policy initiatives that purported to address the growing literacy achievement gaps between diverse groups of students. This set of initiatives created accountability mandates that forced school systems to adhere to a set of norms, rules, and procedures in ways that both changed and came to characterize the nature of work in schools (Hamilton, 2003). Their stated goal was the achievement of proficiency on standardized measures of performance for all students by 2014. To support the attainment of this goal, NCLB and Reading First promoted the use of five specific instructional literacy practices: phonemic awareness, phonics, fluency, vocabulary, and reading comprehension. The practices, based on findings from the National Reading Panel (National Institute of Child Health and Human Development, 2000a, 2000b), were identified as essential for addressing gaps in reading achievement. Federal funding was disseminated nationally to state education agencies (SEAs) to support the implementation of these literacy practices in K–3 classrooms across local education agencies (LEAs) and districts.

Despite the National Reading Panel's acknowledgement that it did not investigate all possible topics essential to learning to read nor take up "issues relevant to second language learning," these five practices were taken as the essential building blocks in learning to read. A significant amount of available funding was diverted to resources and training that supported these practices. Low-performing schools were offered additional training and resources through Reading First in exchange for additional commitments tied to funding. For example, school leaders were required to attend monthly district-mandated literacy-focused training sessions while their teachers were required to attend annual reading institutes offered by the LEAs and ongoing professional development sessions offered through their districts. In addition, funding was made available to create instructional literacy coach positions (Deussen, Coskie, Robinson, & Autio, 2007). Yet these narrow literacy-focused supports failed to acknowledge the complexity of teaching (Cochran-Smith & Lytle, 2006) or support the needs of racially, ethnically, and linguistically minoritized students (Gándara & Baca, 2008; Gándara, Rumberger, Maxwell-Jolly, & Callahan, 2003; Wiley & Wright, 2004; Wright & Choi, 2006). These policy initiatives poured funding into LEAs, districts, and schools, especially those identified as low-achieving, specifically targeting the implementation of the five instructional literacy practices but did not acknowledge the value of differentiating or diversifying curriculum, pedagogy, or instructional strategies (Gerstl-Pepin & Woodside-Jiron, 2005). All funding was devoted to the homogenization of instructional practices that were aligned with heightened levels of accountability (Gándara & Rumberger, 2009; Pacheco, 2010). As the policy initiative traveled through each level of the system, it was translated into mandates and practices; those charged with mandate implementation made sense of the initiative using their knowledge, expertise, and understandings. Sensemaking across the system contributed to the application of differential meanings (Coburn, 2001). As people applied their own interpretations to the policy, degrees of support offered to SEAs, LEAs, districts, and ultimately schools varied greatly. In Reading First we see an example of the manner in which policy initiatives contribute to the neglect of race, culture, and language in the institutional landscape. Policy initiatives like these heighten attention to standardization and accountability, diverting resources that would best support investments in the know-how required for widespread implementation of CRE.

The Effects of Accountability Practices on Differentiation

The adoption and implementation of standardized instructional practices have adverse results for nondominant groups of students. Even for teachers aligned philosophically with the core tenets of CRE, the organizational climate in these contexts makes it virtually impossible to recognize, much less value, the importance of these approaches in practice. Research findings suggest that high-stakes accountability policies, coupled with a school's level of performance, have negative effects on classroom instruction (Cuban, 1984; Tyack & Tobin, 1994), reify social stratification (Diamond & Spillane, 2004; Meyer & Rowan, 1992; Noguera, 2001), and dramatically limit power and autonomy of individuals (Malen & Cochran, 2008). In her research, Pacheco (2010) examined the reach of language and literacy accountability policies on the practice of reading in bilingual classrooms. Findings revealed that despite strong espoused beliefs in the value of biliteracy and bicultural practices, teachers and school leaders internalized and implemented the "reductive notions of English literacy" (p. 301) that were reflected in accountability policies. Because success was defined by narrow definitions of performance, learners were provided with limited opportunities to engage in high quality tasks. Like Pacheco, other scholars demonstrate that alignment of policy and practice has resulted in unequal educational opportunities for students from nondominant communities (Diamond & Spillane, 2004; Lee, 2006). A study by Diamond and Spillane (2004) that compared the ways that low-performing and high-performing schools made sense of high-stakes outcomes found that while low-performing schools emphasize reductive pedagogical approaches, high-performing schools complexified the curriculum. These findings illustrate the potential exacerbation of the issue of resistance to CRE. High-accountability contexts may privilege the standardization of instructional practices. Teachers that work in these contexts face the pressures of low performance, ultimately implementing overly simplified pedagogical practices.

Implications for Districts, LEAs, and SEAs

In the current era of accountability, it is increasingly important to understand the ways in which accountability mandates negatively affect educational outcomes for students in urban school contexts. Accountability measures that attach punitive actions to persistent underachievement on student outcome measures have been shown to promote "an ideology of remediation" (Pacheco, 2010, p. 295), "overemphasize 'lower-level' skills" (Pacheco, 2010, p. 294), and constrain professional autonomy and decision making (Malen & Cochran, 2008). The example above illustrates the incomplete nature of reform efforts to meet the needs of diverse students. Essential to the implementation of CRE is the recognition of the value and richness of students' social, cultural, and linguistic repertoires. Policy should expect variation. With the expectation of variation, teachers and schools inclined to implement CRE might fare better in attending to the richness that students from nondominant backgrounds bring to school settings. The literature suggests that districts should attend to the diversity that exists within their boundaries and seek to build on the variation rather than obliterate it. Districts have the power to structure school-based systems of support in ways that prioritize the differentiation of curriculum, pedagogical models, and adaptable strategies. The literature also suggests that districts should leverage their resources to invest in commitments to develop cohesive, actionable, and practice-oriented professional development and learning opportunities that might leverage the implementation of CRE. District leaders might discover that they themselves are learners in the work of implementing CRE who lack sufficient know-how to make decisions about what works best, for whom, and under what conditions.

ORGANIZATIONAL CLIMATE: TAKING THE PATH OF MOST RESISTANCE

Am I Allowed to Do This? Will There Be Repercussions If I Do? Do I Have Support?

The organizational climate in schools can greatly contribute to resistance to CRE implementation. While some school leaders have found success in shielding their teachers from district mandates, punitive evaluations, and conflicting standards, teachers overwhelmingly report that hyper-accountability and hyper-standardization produce an unsupportive ethos of schooling and escalate the homogenization of curricula, teaching, and learning. In this section, we discuss key organizational factors that can help us reframe the problem of resistance to CRE implementation as a multilevel learning problem.

School Leadership and Vision

Several studies suggest that teachers' willingness and ability to implement CRE is often contingent upon the ethos of their school. School leaders play a major role in determining the types of relationships, teaching, and learning that are valued, setting the school's goals and priorities. Leaders also exercise their power to make decisions about the structures, resources, and training opportunities that best support teachers in achieving the school's collective vision (L. Johnson, 2007). The school leader also sets the tone for the promotion and establishment of relationships between the school and broader community (Bertrand & Rodela, 2017). While school leaders have the power to develop and implement practices that prioritize schoolwide learning and privilege process-oriented approaches, they must also respond to district mandates and externally imposed measures of performance. In response to external pressures of performance, school structures are often set up to embrace quick-fix solutions rather than make long-term commitments and investments in time to get it right. In such contexts, the spirit of experimentation is lost and instead gives way to the fears of uncertainty and failure. Imbued with the pressure to reach target measures, school leaders, along with teachers, find themselves under increased surveillance, feeding personal and professional vulnerabilities. Even school leaders with the best of intentions can struggle to shield their teachers from the pressures of accountability and standardization (Liou et al., 2017).

Shared Vision and Professional Learning

The nature of CRE teaching requires an inquiry-based professional learning environment (Esposito et al., 2012; Ryoo, Goode, & Margolis, 2015) that encourages teachers to explore innovative practices through experimentation (Elmore, 1996; Gay, 2013; Taba, 1962); make requests for support (Drago-Severson & Blum-DeStefano, 2017); and engage critical concepts of belief and know-how related to race and racism (Philip, 2011). However, in the face of increased scrutiny, schools often succumb to the pressures of standardization and hyper-accountability, emphasizing standardized teaching and assessment practices (Bianchini & Brenner, 2010; Flores, 2007) and punitive evaluation (Cramer, Little, & McHatton, 2018; Stillman, 2011). School cultures like these not only do little to promote inquiry-based teacher learning, they also heighten levels of professional vulnerability and isolation that make it challenging for teachers to engage in innovative efforts like implementing CRE.

As the literature reveals, teachers who express interest in enacting CRE often feel isolated in their efforts to counter deficit perspectives of students and perceive their work in direct opposition to school goals (Borrero et al., 2016; Buehler et al., 2009; Hyland, 2009). Teachers report that their efforts to engage colleagues in conversations about race, culture, and CRE are overwhelmingly perceived as threatening (Arce, 2004; Drago-Severson & Blum-DeStefano, 2017) and are often subject to critique (McKenzie & Scheurich, 2008), amplifying their feelings of vulnerability and isolation. Furthermore, multiple examples reveal that teachers who are interested and actively engaged in CRE efforts are often subjected to professional isolation by leadership and colleagues through open reprimands (Underwood & Mensah, 2018) and being blatantly overlooked for leadership and professional development opportunities (Kohli & Pizarro, 2016). When teachers are embedded in spaces where school leaders and colleagues do not value CRE and, at times, actively disrupt these efforts through exclusionary practices, sustaining the work is increasingly challenging (Gay, 2014; McIntyre, 1997). As feelings of isolation grow, some teachers develop a fear of blame from colleagues (Esposito & Swain, 2009) while others experience fatigue about being the only ones willing to challenge the status quo. In the face of increased scrutiny, teachers are more likely to altogether abandon efforts like CRE that fall outside the purview of district- or state-level policy mandates and are perceived to have limited instructional value in support of school priorities (Mette et al., 2016; Sleeter, 2012).

Implications for Schools

In effect, school contexts can perpetuate professional isolation, misalignment, and incoherence. The failure to recognize teachers' need for differentiated knowledge and know-how amplifies incoherence within and across the school. When teachers' efforts to implement CRE are met with passive resistance from their colleagues, and active resistance from their school leaders, teachers resort to hiding their efforts from administration (Esposito et al., 2009) or abandon these altogether. To combat professional isolation school leaders must focus their efforts on the design of learning environments that develop localized knowledge coupled with an emphasis on processes, coherence, and alignment. Social justice–oriented school leaders in such contexts prioritize the importance of relationships within and across their school communities, recognizing the importance of partnership and shared decision making—a crucial first step in building empowering learning communities. By recognizing the centrality of CRE to learning, school systems can develop enhanced structures to support teachers in developing the knowledge and know-how required to successfully implement and adapt CRE to meet the needs of their students and broader communities.

FRAMEWORK IN ACTION: FUNDS OF KNOWLEDGE TEACHER PEDAGOGY GROUPS

In this review of literature, we explore teacher resistance to CRE as a multilevel learning problem. We adapted our framework into a visual problem space (see Figure 2) that can be used to more comprehensively pinpoint, anticipate, and preemptively address the multilevel factors that contribute to teachers' resistance to implementing CRE approaches for teaching and learning. In this section, we describe how this visualization of the problem space can be used as a diagnostic and conversational tool to guide the planning and implementation of interventions that support the widespread take up of CRE. To focus our efforts, we center our exploration in the commonly known and widespread approach of Funds of Knowledge (FK; Moll, Amanti, Neff, & Gonzalez, 1992). We take FK to be an instantiation of CRE. FK is an approach to educational praxis that has gained traction in schools and achieved success in improving the teaching and learning of racially, ethnically, and linguistically minoritized students. Perhaps the greatest contributor to FK's success is its pragmatic toolkit for developing teachers' know-how to recognize, validate, and integrate the historically accumulated skills and cultural resources that students use to navigate their daily lives. Stemming from Vygotskian learning theory, FK engages teachers in a process wherein they interview students' households to identify and gather students' FK and utilize this data in teacher pedagogy groups to challenge deficit assumptions and revise their instruction to be more culturally relevant. As an actionable and practice-oriented intervention, FK has achieved widespread implementation, traveling across educational sectors and international borders. As a result of its widespread take up, education researchers and practitioners who utilize the FK approach have begun to (re)contextualize its original unit of analysis (i.e., students' households) and methods (i.e., teacher pedagogy groups) in relation to context-specific affordances, demands, and constraints. In the example below, we explain how our Teacher Resistance to CRE Problem Space (see Figure 2) can be used as a diagnostic tool to support the implementation and (re)contextualization of FK. While we lack the space here to do this work comprehensively, we believe starting this exercise can provide insight into how our framework can be used in action to anticipate, and preemptively address, various forms of resistance to interventions, like FK, that hold promise for supporting the widespread implementation of CRE.

To focus these efforts, we explore a practice-based example of utilizing FK to improve the teaching and learning of mathematics at a large urban high school we will name Vision Academy. Vision Academy has been trying, with limited success, to implement FK over the past 2 years. Only a few teachers in the math department have attempted to implement a FK approach to instruction, but even these efforts have been sporadic and lack integration with content-specific learning. Why might this happen? Simplistic responses might limit the characterizations of this problem solely to a matter of teacher beliefs or know-how and, in doing so, lessen the chance for the FK approach to be meaningfully taken up across the math department. Conversely, investigating teacher resistance to FK as a multilevel learning problem can provide insights for how to plan for and execute the sustainable and widespread implementation of FK. Here, it is important to consider how institutional-, organizational-, and individual-level factors work together to infringe on teachers' decision making and heighten their level of vulnerability to implement FK.

At an institutional level, it would be important to know if policy initiatives, district mandates, standards, and curriculum reflect students' diverse forms of cultural knowledge or further homogenize educators and students as it would determine the types of materials and resources teachers have access to. If teachers lack access to culturally relevant curriculum, then on an individual level it would be essential to cultivate their know-how to diversify curriculum and materials. Without this know-how, implementing FK in practice would be extremely challenging. This institutional-level factor would also determine the types of outcomes and measures that schools, and specifically School Leaders, are held accountable to. Successful efforts to implement FK will largely depend on how schools are charged with improving standardized measures of academic achievement. Punitive evaluation practices can potentially threaten a teachers' professional well-being and impact the take up of FK.

On an organizational level, it might be important to consider whether the math department at Vision Academy shares a commitment to and common language for designing, executing, and reflecting upon FK. Not having a shared commitment and common language can result in the professional isolation and exclusion of teachers who move forward in their efforts to implement FK. Here, it also important to consider whether the math department is provided with time to engage in teacher pedagogy groups. As teachers are challenged by myriad conflicting responsibilities, a lack of time will often result in sporadic and fleeting efforts to implement FK. Also important to consider on an organizational level is the state of school–family –community relationships. If the school does not meaningfully engage nor have clear channels of communication with families and communities, teachers' willingness and ability to gather students' FK through interviewing their households will be greatly diminished.

Finally, on an individual level, it would be essential to know if teachers believe issues of race and culture are related to and important for the teaching and learning of mathematics. If teachers understand mathematics as race-neutral, their efforts to implement FK would most likely be limited to motivation and engagement, instead of promoting rigorous content-specific learning. Here, the types of training and professional development teachers have access to become essential. These are only some of the ways that multilevel factors might interact to produce teacher resistance to implement FK. However, they demonstrate that, in order to be successful, innovations and interventions aimed at promoting the widespread take up of CRE must learn to see teacher resistance as a multilevel learning problem and, ideally, support the development of institutional and organizational know-how necessary for providing teachers with effective resources, training, and support.

SUMMARY

In this review, we have argued against the notion that teacher resistance to CRE implementation stems solely from the beliefs and doubts of the individual. To explain resistance in such a way is far too simplistic. While we recognize the importance of individuals' beliefs and doubts in taking up change initiatives and fueling deficit-based perspectives about students and communities from nondominant backgrounds, we advance the notion that resistance is first and foremost a multilevel problem of learning. Learning is reflected in the limited knowledge and know-how evident through standardization efforts, accountability practices, and policy-induced mandates across multiple levels in systems of education. We have purposely centered our analysis on teacher resistance, providing an amplified view of the complex intersection of beliefs, doubts, knowledge, and know-how. Our aim in this analysis has been to showcase the ways that all teachers, regardless of their predispositions to the adoption of innovation change efforts, are frequently ill-supported in the pursuit of CRE implementation. A focus on shared learning within and across system spaces has been recently taken up in the literature. In their work, Bryk, Gomez, Grunow, and LeMahieu (2015) argue that the reasons most innovations and change strategies result in limited success is due to the lack of support educators receive to learn their way through change and improvement. In such contexts, educators are rarely given the time, resources, and support needed to experiment and learn. Similarly, in his work, Mintrop (2016) describes the importance of investing long term in commitments to change. Here, time must be afforded to work through the management of change in an effort to get it right. As a field, we must remain vigilant in our efforts to build multilevel know-how for disrupting resistance to CRE. The establishment of supportive learning contexts will require a multilevel perspective that explicitly attends to context-specific knowledge and know-how, both within schools and across districts. We adapted our framework into a problem space map for diagnosing potential challenges in the adoption of CRE-aligned interventions. We believe that this problem space can be used by schools, districts, and LEAs as a tool for learning how to locate themselves, identify blind spots, and assess the level of know-how required to support teachers with CRE implementation.

REFERENCES

Anyon, J. (1980). Social class and the hidden curriculum of work. *Journal of Education, 162*(1), 67–92.

Anyon, J. (2005). What "counts" as educational policy? Notes toward a new paradigm. *Harvard Educational Review, 75,* 65–88.

Arce, J. (2004). Latino bilingual teachers: The struggle to sustain an emancipatory pedagogy in public schools. *International Journal of Qualitative Studies in Education, 17,* 227–246. doi:10.1080/09518390310001653880

Argumedo, J. J. (2016). *Responding to disproportionality of students of color through addressing teacher practice* (Unpublished doctoral dissertation). Retrieved from https://escholarship .org/uc/item/53z97947

Argyris, C. (1960). *Understanding organizational behavior.* Oxford, England: Dorsey.

Aronson, B., & Laughter, J. (2016). The theory and practice of culturally relevant education. *Review of Educational Research, 86,* 163–206. doi:10.3102/0034654315582066

Barton, A. C. (2003). *Teaching science for social justice.* New York, NY: Teachers College Press.

Battey, D., & Stark, M. (2009). Inequitable classroom practices: Avoiding ability attributions from misconceptions in mathematics. In C. Malloy (Ed.), *Mathematics for all: Instructional strategies for diverse classrooms* (pp. 167–177). Reston, VA: National Council of Teachers of Mathematics.

Bell, L. A. (2002). Sincere fictions: The pedagogical challenges of preparing white teachers for multicultural classrooms. *Equity & Excellence in Education, 35,* 236–244. doi:10.1080/713845317

Bertrand, M., & Rodela, K. C. (2017). A framework for rethinking educational leadership in the margins: Implications for social justice leadership preparation. *Journal of Research on Leadership Education.* Advance online publication. doi:10.1177/1942775117739414

Bianchini, J. A., & Brenner, M. E. (2010). The role of induction in learning to teach toward equity: A study of beginning science and mathematics teachers. *Science Education, 94,* 164–195. doi:10.1002/sce.20353

Bianchirli, J. A., & Cavazos, L. M. (2001). Challenges faced in transforming content and pedagogy. *Counterpoints, 150,* 259–293.

Bobo, L., & Hutchings, V. L. (1996). Perceptions of racial group competition: Extending Blumer's theory of group position to a multiracial social context. *American Sociological Review, 61,* 951–972.

Bonilla-Silva, E. (2006). What is racism? The racialized social system framework. In M. Durr & S. A. Hill (Eds.), *Race, work, and family in the lives of African Americans* (pp. 13–43). Lanham, MD: Rowman & Littlefield.

Borrero, N. E., Flores, E., & de la Cruz, G. (2016). Developing and enacting culturally relevant pedagogy: Voices of new teachers of color. *Equity & Excellence in Education, 49*(1), 27–40. doi:10.1080/10665684.2015.1119914

Borrero, N. E., & Sanchez, G. (2017). Enacting culturally relevant pedagogy: Asset mapping in urban classrooms. *Teaching Education, 28*, 279–295. doi:10.1080/10476210.2017.1 296827

Borrero, N. E., Ziauddin, A., & Ahn, A. (2018). Teaching for change: New teachers' experiences with and visions for culturally relevant pedagogy. *Critical Questions in Education, 9*(1), 22–39.

Braun, H., Chapman, L., & Vezzu, S. (2010). The Black-White achievement gap revisited. *Education Policy Analysis Archives, 18*(21). Retrieved from https://epaa.asu.edu/ojs/article /view/772

Brown, J. C., & Crippen, K. J. (2017). The knowledge and practices of high school science teachers in pursuit of cultural responsiveness. *Science Education, 101*, 99–133. doi:10.1002/sce.21250

Bryan, L. A., & Atwater, M. M. (2002). Teacher beliefs and cultural models: A challenge for science teacher preparation programs. *Science Education, 86*, 821–839. doi:10.1002/ sce.10043

Bryk, A. S., Gomez, L. M., Grunow, A., & LeMahieu, P. G. (2015). *Learning to improve: How America's schools can get better at getting better.* Cambridge, MA: Harvard Education Press.

Buehler, J., Gere, A. R., Dallavis, C., & Haviland, V. S. (2009). Normalizing the fraughtness: How emotion, race, and school context complicate cultural competence. *Journal of Teacher Education, 60*, 408–418. doi:10.1177/0022487109339905

Burnes, B. (2014). *Managing change* (6th ed.). Harlow, England: Pearson.

Burnes, B., & Jackson, P. (2011). Success and failure in organizational change: An exploration of the role of values. *Journal of Change Management, 11*(2), 133–162.

Coburn, C. E. (2001). Collective sensemaking about reading: How teachers mediate reading policy in their professional communities. *Educational Evaluation and Policy Analysis, 23*, 145–170.

Coburn, C. E. (2004). Beyond decoupling: Rethinking the relationship between the institutional environment and the classroom. *Sociology of Education, 77*, 211–244.

Coch, L., & French, J. R., Jr. (1948). Overcoming resistance to change. *Human Relations, 1*, 512–532.

Cochran-Smith, M., & Lytle, S. (2006). Troubling images of teaching in No Child Left Behind. *Harvard Educational Review, 76*, 668–697.

Cockrell, K. S., Placier, P. L., Cockrell, D. H., & Middleton, J. N. (1999). Coming to terms with "diversity" and "multiculturalism" in teacher education: Learning about our students, changing our practice. *Teaching and Teacher Education, 15*, 351–366. doi:10.1016/ S0742-051X(98)00050-X

Coffey, H., & Farinde-Wu, A. (2016). Navigating the journey to culturally responsive teaching: Lessons from the success and struggles of one first-year, Black female teacher of Black students in an urban school. *Teaching and Teacher Education, 60*, 24–33. doi:10.1016/j. tate.2016.07.021

Cramer, E., Little, M. E., & McHatton, P. A. (2018). Equity, equality, and standardization: Expanding the conversations. *Education and Urban Society, 50*, 483–501. doi:10.1177/0013124517713249

Cuban, L. (1984). *How teachers taught: Constancy and change in American classrooms, 1890– 1980.* New York, NY: Longman.

Cummings, T. G., & Worley, C. G. (2009). *Organization development and change* (9th ed.). Cincinnati, OH: South-Western.

Darling-Hammond, L. (2010). Teacher education and the American future. *Journal of Teacher Education, 61*(1–2), 35–47. doi:10.1177/0022487109348024

DeBray-Pelot, E., & McGuin, P. (2009). The new politics of education: Analyzing the federal education policy landscape in the post-NCLB era. *Educational Policy, 23*(1), 15–42.

Dent, E. B., & Goldberg, S. G. (1999). Challenging "resistance to change". *Journal of Applied Behavioral Science, 35*(1), 25–41.

Deussen, T., Coskie, T., Robinson, L., & Autio, E. (2007). *"Coach" can mean many things: Five categories of literacy coaches in reading first* (Issues & Answers Report, REL 2007-No. 005). Washington, DC: U.S. Department of Education, Institute of Education Sciences, National Center for Education Evaluation and Regional Assistance, Regional Educational Laboratory Northwest.

Diamond, J. B., Randolph, A., & Spillane, J. P. (2004). Teachers' expectations and sense of responsibility for student learning: The importance of race, class, and organizational habitus. *Anthropology & Education Quarterly, 35*(1), 75–98. doi:10.1525/aeq.2004.35.1.75

Diamond, J. B., & Spillane, J. P. (2004). High-stakes accountability in urban elementary schools: Challenging or reproducing inequality. *Teachers College Record, 106*, 1145–1176.

Diversity in Mathematics Education Center for Learning and Teaching. (2007). Culture, race, power, and mathematics education. In F. K. Lester (Ed.), *Second handbook of research on mathematics teaching and learning* (pp. 405–433). Charlotte, NC: Information Age.

Dover, A. G. (2013). Teaching for social justice: From conceptual frameworks to classroom practices. *Multicultural Education, 15*(1), 3–11.

Drago-Severson, E., & Blum-DeStefano, J. (2017). The self in social justice: A developmental lens on race, identity, and transformation. *Harvard Educational Review, 87*, 457–482. doi:10.17763/1943-5045-87.4.457

Ebersole, M., Kanahele-Mossman, H., & Kawakami, A. (2016). Culturally responsive teaching: Examining teachers' understandings and perspectives. *Journal of Education and Training Studies, 4*, 97–104. doi:10.11114/jets.v4i2.1136

Elmore, R. (1996). Getting to scale with good educational practice. *Harvard Educational Review, 66*, 1–27. doi:10.17763/haer.66.1.g73266758j348t33

Esposito, J., Davis, C. L., & Swain, A. N. (2012). Urban educators' perceptions of culturally relevant pedagogy and school reform mandates. *Journal of Educational Change, 13*, 235–258. doi:10.1007/s10833-011-9178-6

Esposito, J., & Swain, A. N. (2009). Pathways to social justice: Urban teachers' uses of culturally relevant pedagogy as a conduit for teaching for social justice. *Penn GSE Perspectives on Urban Education, 6*(1), 38–48.

Evans, A. E. (2007). School leaders and their sensemaking about race and demographic change. *Educational Administration Quarterly, 43*, 159–188. doi:10.1177/0013161X06294575

Farmer, J., Hauk, S., & Neumann, A. M. (2005). Negotiating reform: Implementing process standards in culturally responsive professional development. *High School Journal, 88*(4), 59–71. doi:10.1353/hsj.2005.0008

Festinger, L. (1957). *A theory of cognitive dissonance.* Redwood City, CA: Stanford University Press.

Flores, M. T. (2007). Navigating contradictory communities of practice in learning to teach for social justice. *Anthropology & Education Quarterly, 38*, 380–404. doi:10.1525/aeq.2007.38.4.380

Freire, J. A., & Valdez, V. E. (2017). Dual language teachers' stated barriers to implementation of culturally relevant pedagogy. *Bilingual Research Journal, 40*(1), 55–69. doi:10.1080/15235882.2016.1272504

Gándara, P., & Baca, G. (2008). NCLB and California's English language learners: The perfect storm. *Language Policy, 7*, 201–216.

Gándara, P., & Rumberger, R. W. (2009). Immigration, language, and education: How does language policy structure opportunity? *Teachers College Record, 111*, 750–782.

Gándara, P., Rumberger, R. W., Maxwell-Jolly, J., & Callahan, R. (2003). English learners in California schools: Unequal resources, unequal outcomes. *Education Policy Analysis Archives, 11*, 36.

Gay, G. (1975). Organizing and designing culturally pluralistic curriculum. *Educational Leadership, 33*, 176–183.

Gay, G. (1980). Ethnic pluralism in social studies education: Where to from here? *Social Education, 44*, 52–55.

Gay, G. (2013). Teaching to and through cultural diversity. *Curriculum Inquiry, 43*(1), 48–70. doi:10.1111/curi.12002

Gay, G. (2014). Teachers' beliefs about cultural diversity. In H. Fives & M. G. Gill (Eds.), *International handbook of research on teachers' beliefs* (pp. 436–452). London, England: Routledge. doi:10.4324/9780203108437.ch25

Gerstl-Pepin, C. I., & Woodside-Jiron, H. (2005). Tensions between the "science" of reading and a "love of learning": One high-poverty school's struggle with NCLB. *Equity & Excellence in Education, 38*, 232–241.

Goldenberg, B. M. (2014). White teachers in urban classrooms. *Urban Education, 49*, 111–144. doi:10.1177/0042085912472510

Gregory, A., & Mosely, P. M. (2004). The discipline gap: Teachers' views on the over-representation of African American students in the discipline system. *Equity & Excellence in Education, 37*, 18–30. doi:10.1080/10665680490429280

Gutiérrez, K., Rymes, B., & Larson, J. (1995). Script, counterscript, and underlife in the classroom. *Harvard Educational Review, 65*, 445–471.

Gutiérrez, R. (2013). Why (urban) mathematics teachers need political knowledge. *Journal of Urban Mathematics Education, 6*(2), 7–19.

Haberman, M. (1991). Can cultural awareness be taught in teacher education programs? *Teaching Education, 4*(1), 25–31.

Hamilton, L. (2003). Assessment as a policy tool. *Review of Research in Education, 27*, 25–68.

Harris Russell, C., McDonald, D., Jones, L. A., & Weaver, L. (2016). The continuum of lens through which teachers view cultural differences: How perceptions impact pedagogy. *Journal of Family Strengths, 16*(1), 5.

Hill, H. C. (2007). Learning in the teaching workforce. *Future of Children, 17*(1), 111–127. doi:10.1353/foc.2007.0004

Hill, H. C., Rowan, B., & Ball, D. L. (2005). Effects of teachers' mathematical knowledge for teaching on student achievement. *American Educational Research Journal, 42*, 371–406. doi:10.3102/00028312042002371

Howard, G. R. (2006). *We can't teach what we don't know: White teachers, multiracial schools.* New York, NY: Teachers College Press.

Howard, T. C., & Rodriguez-Minkoff, A. C. (2017). Culturally relevant pedagogy 20 years later: Progress or pontificating? What have we learned, and where do we go? *Teachers College Record, 119*, 1–32.

Huse, E. F. (1980). *Organization development and change* (2nd ed.). St. Paul, MN: West.

Hyland, N. E. (2005). Being a good teacher of Black students? White teachers and unintentional racism. *Curriculum Inquiry, 35*, 429–459.

Hyland, N. E. (2009). One white teacher's struggle for culturally relevant pedagogy: The problem of the community. *New Educator, 5*(2), 95–112. doi:10.1080/15476 88X.2009.10399567

Jayakumar, U. M., & Adamian, A. S. (2017). The fifth frame of colorblind ideology: Maintaining the comforts of colorblindness in the context of white fragility. *Sociological Perspectives, 60*, 912–936.

Johnson, C. C. (2011). The road to culturally relevant science: Exploring how teachers navigate change in pedagogy. *Journal of Research in Science Teaching, 48,* 170–198. doi:10.1002/tea.20405

Johnson, L. (2007). Rethinking successful school leadership in challenging U.S. schools: Culturally responsive practices in school-community relationships. *International Studies in Educational Administration, 35*(3), 49–58.

Jones, E. E. (1990). *Interpersonal perception.* New York, NY: Freeman.

Kohli, R., & Pizarro, M. (2016). Fighting to educate our own: Teachers of color, relational accountability, and the struggle for racial justice. *Equity & Excellence in Education, 49,* 72–84. doi:10.1080/10665684.2015.1121457

Ladson-Billings, G. (1992). Reading between the lines and beyond the pages: A culturally relevant approach to literacy teaching. *Theory Into Practice, 31,* 312–320.

Ladson-Billings, G. (1994). *The dreamkeepers: Successful teachers of African American children.* San Francisco, CA: Jossey-Bass.

Ladson-Billings, G. (1997). It doesn't add up: African American students' mathematics achievement. *Journal for Research in Mathematics Education, 28,* 697–708.

Ladson-Billings, G. (2014). Culturally relevant pedagogy 2.0: a.k.a. the remix. *Harvard Educational Review, 84,* 74–84. doi:10.17763/haer.84.1.p2rj131485484751

Laughter, J. C., & Adams, A. D. (2012). Culturally relevant science teaching in middle school. *Urban Education, 47,* 1106–1134. doi:10.1177/0042085912454443

Lee, J. (2006). *Tracking achievement gaps and assessing the impact of NCLB on the gaps: An in-depth look into national and state reading and math outcome trends.* Cambridge, MA: Civil Rights Project at Harvard University.

Lewin, K. (1943). Forces behind food habits and methods of change. *Bulletin of the National Research Council, 108,* 35–65.

Lewin, K. (1946). Action research and minority problems. In G. W. Lewin (Ed.), *Resolving social conflict* (pp. 201–216). London, England: Harper & Row.

Lewin, K. (1947). Frontiers in group dynamics: Concept, method and reality in social science; social equilibria and social change. *Human Relations, 1*(1), 5–41.

Liou, D. D., Marsh, T. E. J., & Antrop-González, R. (2017). Urban sanctuary schools for diverse populations- Examining curricular expectations and school effectiveness for student learning. *Equity & Excellence in Education, 50,* 68–83. doi:10.1080/10665684.2016.1250237

Malen, B., & Cochran, M. (2008). Beyond pluralistic patterns of power: Research on the micropolitics of schools. In B. Cooper, J. Cibulka, & L. Fusarelli (Eds.), *Handbook of education politics and policy* (pp. 148–178). New York, NY: Routledge.

Martin, D. B. (2009). Researching race in mathematics education. *Teachers College Record, 111,* 295–338.

Martin, D. B. (2010). Not-so-strange bedfellows: Racial projects and the mathematics education enterprise. In U. Gellert, E. Jablonka, & C. Morgan (Eds.), *Proceedings of the sixth mathematics education and society conference* (pp. 57–79). Berlin, Germany: Freie Universität Berlin.

Martin, D. B. (2013). Race, racial projects, and mathematics education. *Journal for Research in Mathematics Education, 44,* 316–333.

McIntyre, A. (1997). *Making meaning of whiteness: Exploring racial identity with white teachers.* Albany: State University of New York Press.

McKenzie, K. B., & Scheurich, J. J. (2008). Teacher resistance to improvement of schools with diverse students. *International Journal of Leadership in Education, 11,* 117–133. doi:10.1080/13603120801950122

Mette, I. M., Nieuwenhuizen, L., & Hvidston, D. J. (2016). Teachers' perceptions of culturally responsive pedagogy and the impact on leadership preparation: Lessons for future reform efforts. *NCPEA International Journal of Educational Leadership Preparation, 11*(1). Retrieved from https://files.eric.ed.gov/fulltext/EJ1103652.pdf

Meyer, J. W., & Rowan, B. (1992). The structure of educational organizations. In J. W. Meyer & W. R. Scott (Eds.), *Organizational environments: Ritual and rationality* (pp. 71–97). Newbury Park, CA: Sage.

Mintrop, R. (2016). *Design-based school improvement: A practical guide for education leaders.* Cambridge, MA: Harvard Education Press.

Moll, L. C., Amanti, C., Neff, D., & Gonzalez, N. (1992). Funds of knowledge for teaching: Using a qualitative approach to connect homes and classrooms. *Theory Into Practice, 31,* 132–141.

Montalvo, R., Combes, B. H., & Kea, C. D. (2014). Perspectives on culturally and linguistically responsive RtI pedagogics through a cultural and linguistic lens. *Interdisciplinary Journal of Teaching and Learning, 4,* 203–219.

Nasir, N. S. (2011). *Racialized identities: Race and achievement among African American youth.* Stanford, CA: Stanford University Press.

Nasir, N. S. (2016). Why should mathematics educators care about race and culture? Why mathematics education does not attend to race and culture. *Journal of Urban Mathematics Education, 9*(1), 7–18.

Nasir, N. S., Snyder, C. R., Shah, N., & Ross, K. M. (2013). Racial storylines and implications for learning. *Human Development, 55,* 285–301. doi:10.1159/000345318

National Institute of Child Health and Human Development. (2000a). *Report of the national reading panel. Teaching children to read: An evidence-based assessment of the scientific research literature on reading and its implications for reading instruction* (NIH Publication No. 00-4769). Washington, DC: U.S. Government Printing Office.

National Institute of Child Health and Human Development. (2000b). *Report of the national reading panel. Teaching children to read: An evidence-based assessment of the scientific research literature on reading and its implications for reading instruction: Reports of the subgroups* (NIH Publication No. 00-4754). Washington, DC: U.S. Government Printing Office.

No Child Left Behind (NCLB) Act of 2001, 20 U.S.C.A. § 6301 et seq. (West 2003).

Noguera, P. (2001). Racial politics and the elusive quest for excellence and equity in education. *Education and Urban Society, 34*(1), 18–41.

Noguera, P. A. (2004). Social capital and the education of immigrant students: Categories and generalizations. *Sociology of Education, 77,* 180–183.

Oakes, J. (2005). *Keeping track.* New Haven, CT: Yale University Press.

Pacheco, M. (2010). English-language learners' reading achievement: Dialectical relationships between policy and practices. *Reading Research Quarterly, 45,* 292–317.

Patchen, T., & Cox-Petersen, A. (2008). Constructing cultural relevance in science: A case study of two elementary teachers. *Science Education, 92,* 994–1014.

Peters, L. (2012). The rhythm of leading change. *Journal of Management Inquiry, 21,* 405–411.

Philip, T. M. (2011). An "ideology in pieces" Approach to studying change in teachers' sensemaking about race, racism, and racial justice. *Cognition and Instruction, 29,* 297–329. doi:10.1080/07370008.2011.583369

Reading First Program of the No Child Left Behind Act of 2001 (PL 107-110, 115 Stat. 1425).

Redman, E. H. (2014). *A study of novice science teachers' conceptualizations of culturally relevant pedagogy.* Retrieved from https://escholarship.org/uc/item/5sz9c5jm

Rogers, E. M. (2003). *Diffusion of innovations* (5th ed.). New York, NY: Free Press.

Rousseau, C., & Tate, W. F. (2003). No time like the present: Reflecting on equity in school mathematics. *Theory Into Practice, 42,* 210–216. doi:10.1207/s15430421tip4203

Rousseau, D. M. (1989). Psychological and implied contracts in organizations. *Employee Responsibilities and Rights Journal, 2,* 121–139.

Royal, C., & Gibson, S. (2017). They schools: Culturally relevant pedagogy under siege. *Teachers College Record, 119*, 1–25.

Ryoo, J., Goode, J., & Margolis, J. (2015). It takes a village: Supporting inquiry- and equity-oriented computer science pedagogy through a professional learning community. *Computer Science Education, 25*, 351–370. doi:10.1080/08993408.2015.1130952

Schmuck, R., & Miles, M. B. (1971). *Organization development in schools.* Palo Alto, CA: National Press Books.

Senge, P. (1990). *The fifth discipline: The art and science of the learning organization.* New York, NY: Doubleday Currency.

Shah, N. (2017). Race, ideology, and academic ability: A relational analysis of racial narratives in mathematics. *Teacher College Record, 119*(7), 1–42.

Sleeter, C. E. (2012). Confronting the marginalization of culturally responsive pedagogy. *Urban Education, 47*, 562–584. doi:10.1177/0042085911431472

Solorzano, D. G., & Bernal, D. D. (2001). Examining transformational resistance through a critical race and LatCrit theory framework: Chicana and Chicano students in an urban context. *Urban Education, 36*, 308–342.

Stillman, J. (2011). Teacher learning in an era of high-stakes accountability: Productive tension and critical professional practice. *Teachers College Record, 113*, 133–180.

Taba, H. (1962). *Curriculum development: Theory and practice.* New York, NY: Harcourt, Brace & World.

Tyack, D., & Tobin, W. (1994). The "grammar" of schooling: Why has it been so hard to change? *American Educational Research Journal, 31*, 453–479.

Underwood, J. B., & Mensah, F. M. (2018). An investigation of science teacher educators' perceptions of culturally relevant pedagogy. *Journal of Science Teacher Education, 29*(1), 46–64. doi:10.1080/1046560X.2017.1423457

Vaught, S. E., & Castagno, A. E. (2008). "I don't think I'm a racist": Critical race theory, teacher attitudes, and structural racism. *Race Ethnicity and Education, 11*, 95–113. doi:10.1080/13613320802110217

Waddell, D., & Sohal, A. S. (1998). Resistance: A constructive tool for change management. *Management Decision, 36*, 543–548. doi:10.1108/00251749810232628

Warren, C. A. (2013). The utility of empathy for white female teachers' culturally responsive interactions with black male students. *Interdisciplinary Journal of Teaching and Learning, 3*, 175–200.

Warren, C. A. (2014). Towards a pedagogy for the application of empathy in culturally diverse classrooms. *Urban Review, 46*, 395–419. doi:10.1007/s11256-013-0262-5

Wiley, T. G., & Wright, W. E. (2004). Against the undertow: Language-minority education policy and politics in the "age of accountability". *Educational Policy, 18*, 142–168.

Wright, W. E., & Choi, D. (2006). The impact of language and high-stakes testing policies on elementary school English language learners in Arizona. *Education Policy Analysis Archives, 14*, 13.

Young, E. (2010). Challenges to conceptualizing and actualizing culturally relevant pedagogy: How viable is the theory in classroom practice? *Journal of Teacher Education, 61*, 248–260. doi:10.1177/0022487109359775

Zembylas, M. (2003). Interrogating teacher identity: Emotion, resistance, and self-formation. *Educational Theory, 53*(1), 107–127.

Chapter 8

Teaching Practices That Support Student Sensemaking Across Grades and Disciplines: A Conceptual Review

MIRANDA SUZANNE FITZGERALD
ANNEMARIE SULLIVAN PALINCSAR
University of Michigan

Sensemaking entails being active, self-conscious, motivated, and purposeful in the world. It is an activity that is always situated within the cultural and historical contexts in which we interact with others and with the aid of tools. In this chapter, we contrast everyday sensemaking with academic sensemaking and treat academic sensemaking in a disciplinary-specific manner, exploring how teachers engage students in academic sensemaking within the domains of mathematics, science, history, and literature. Consistent with the focus of this volume, which is designed to feature teacher practice, the goal of our chapter is to explore the practices in which teachers engage when the purpose is to position students as sensemakers and create a classroom culture that provides the resources and contexts to develop skill with academic sensemaking. Our analyses revealed the broad range of practices necessary to characterize the enactment of instruction that is designed to teach and promote sensemaking, as well as the multitude of purposes those practices served. To explicate the domain-specific nature of teacher practice, we analyzed selected studies in which the researchers provided significant detail regarding teachers' practices. We conclude that sensemaking is a productive lens for investigating and characterizing great teaching.

Observing a row of sunflowers, one shorter than the next, a 4-year-old commented, "I think I know how this happened. The first flower got more sun and grew very tall; it made shade for the next flower, which grew tall, but not as big. Each flower made shade for the next flower." In a conversation about how we have day and night, one 5-year-old suggested, "At night the sun goes down into the water and the

Review of Research in Education
March 2019, Vol. 43, pp. 227–248
DOI: 10.3102/0091732X18821115
Chapter reuse guidelines: sagepub.com/journals-permissions
© 2019 AERA. http://rre.aera.net

stars come up in the sky," while another proposed, "God makes day and night." Each of these illustrates young children engaged in sensemaking. While we elaborate on a definition of sensemaking below, the general features of sensemaking include being active, self-conscious, motivated, and purposeful in the world. It is possible to "learn" without making sense; we overhear our university students alluding to this when they muse about "learning for the test," and hoping that the learning "sticks" for the next 24 hours.

"Sensemaking" figures prominently in several literatures. It has a long history in organizational studies where it was introduced by organizational theorist, Karl Weick. Weick appealed to sensemaking to explain how the meanings that both inform and constrain identity and action in organizations come to be. He wrote, "Sensemaking is what it says it is, namely, making something sensible" (Weick, 1995, p. 16). Weick and his colleagues (Weick, Sutcliffe, & Obstfeld, 2005) propose that people organize to make sense of equivocal inputs and "enact this sense back into the world to make that world more orderly" (p. 410). The child who explains the day/night cycle in terms of the "sun goes into the water" may well be drawing upon experience watching the sun appear to disappear on the horizon of a body of water, or hearing her parents say, "Be sure you are back before the sun sets," and a "setting sun" probably seems far more orderly—and believable—than the earth spinning at 1,000 miles per hour, always half in and half out of the sun's rays.

Klein, Moon, and Hoffman (2006) distinguish sensemaking from creativity and curiosity, both of which—they argue—are aspects of sensemaking to the extent that creativity and curiosity can drive sensemaking but are not synonymous with sensemaking. Furthermore, they distinguish sensemaking from comprehension, proposing that comprehension relates to understanding specific stimuli (such as words and chunks of text), while sensemaking pertains to complex events (such as plant growth and the day/night cycle, mathematical problems, multiple accounts of historical events, or literary works). Klein et al. conclude that mental modeling is perhaps closest to sensemaking since mental models can be used to explain events.

We were motivated to prepare this review because we believe that an important orientation that successful teachers bring to their work is the presumption that their students are constantly engaged in making sense of the world. While student sensemaking may not always lead to canonical explanations (e.g., for the day/night cycle), humans use what they observe and experience to make sense of their worlds, the past, and literature. We further maintain that *making sense is a social process*, that is, sensemaking is an activity that is always situated within the cultural and historical contexts in which we interact with others and with the aid of tools. As Bruner and Haste (1987), in their volume, *Making Sense*, explain,

The set of frameworks for interpretation available to the growing individual reflects the *organizing consciousness of the whole culture*—in other words, it is difficult, if not impossible, for a child to develop a concept that does not have an expression within her culture of origin . . . the development of concepts will depend on the available resources within the culture. (p. 9)

Vygotsky, in *Thinking and Speech* (1934/1987), made a helpful distinction between the everyday, or spontaneous, concepts that arise from individuals' sensemaking as they interact with the world and those that are promoted in the context of school instruction. School instruction is typically designed to foster a mode of thinking that is characterized by generality, systemic organization, conscious awareness, and voluntary control. Vygotsky (1934/1987) further argued that, while everyday concepts are spontaneously appropriated as the learner engages in social interaction in the context of joint activity experienced in one's immediate community (e.g., family), "scientific" or formal concepts result from the deliberate and systematic instruction typical of educational settings. For the remainder of this chapter, we will contrast *everyday sensemaking* with *academic sensemaking*. Furthermore, we will treat academic sensemaking in a disciplinary-specific manner, exploring how teachers engage students in academic sensemaking within the domains of mathematics, science, history, and literature.

Consistent with the focus of this volume, which is designed to feature *teacher practice*, the goal of our chapter is to explore the practices in which teachers engage when the purpose is to position students as sensemakers and create a classroom culture that provides the resources and contexts to develop skill with academic sensemaking. One intriguing feature of this problem space is that learners do not leave their everyday sensemaking at the school door. Hence, teachers negotiate the everyday sensemaking in which learners engage—which may be more or less continuous with the formal sensemaking to which they are introducing students—with academic sensemaking. Our review was designed to explore what we know about the specific ways in which teachers engage in this negotiation and how it compares and contrasts as they teach within specific domains.

METHOD

To prepare this chapter, we undertook a conceptual review of the literature. Kennedy (2007) made a useful distinction between a *systematic review* and a *conceptual review* of the literature. A systematic review typically focuses on a specific empirical issue that is often framed as a cause and effect question; examples might be the following: What effect(s) does collaborating with other learners have on students' sensemaking? What effect(s) does prior knowledge have on sensemaking? In pursuit of specific answers, researchers conduct an exhaustive review of the literature seeking evidence that might speak to the question(s) guiding the review. A *conceptual review*, in contrast, is designed to yield new insights; exploring, for example, how the study of a topic has been represented in the literature; what approaches have been used in its study; what areas of contest are emerging. This is the approach that we have taken in our review; we cast a broad net, beginning with programs of research with which we were familiar, as well as using search terms related to sensemaking, consulting Google Scholar, and doing ancestry searches of reference lists. We searched for programs of research that investigated *how teachers support learners to engage in sensemaking*. We purposefully sampled across research in the teaching of science, mathematics, history, and literature since one of the questions guiding our review is how sensemaking is construed and supported by particular teacher practices across disciplines. To be included in our review, the research had to attend to both the teacher and learner. This means that a large literature that focuses exclusively on learners as sensemakers was not included in our review. We analyzed each article to identify (a) what sensemaking looks like in the research, (b) the context of the research, (c) what the researcher studied about the relationship(s) between teacher practice and student sensemaking, (d) the methods used, (e) the codes/rubrics for characterizing teacher practice, (f) the findings, (g) the implications for teacher learning/teacher development, and (h) implications for future research.

HOW IS ACADEMIC SENSEMAKING REPRESENTED IN THE EDUCATION LITERATURE ON DISCIPLINARY TEACHING AND LEARNING?

From a disciplinary perspective, the purpose of schooling is to apprentice students into the ways of thinking, knowing, talking, and engaging in inquiry that are consistent with the disciplines. In their conceptual meta-analysis, Goldman et al. (2016) identified five core constructs useful to characterizing knowledge across disciplines: (a) epistemology—that is, beliefs about the nature of knowledge and the nature of knowing; (b) inquiry practices/strategies of reasoning; (c) overarching concepts, themes, and frameworks; (d) forms of information representation/types of texts; and (e) discourse practices, including the oral and written language used to convey information.

To illustrate, when learning history in a discipline-specific manner, students are supported to experience history as a process of investigation. Students construct interpretations and arguments of historical events as they read primary, secondary, and/or tertiary texts, attending to the perspective of the authors, the contexts in which the texts were generated, and the ways in which the texts corroborate, or fail to corroborate one another (Bain, 2006; Lee, 2006).

Similar to history, argumentation is core to scientific inquiry. Investigations in which one collects and analyzes data, or interprets data that have been collected by others, are used to generate and test explanations for scientific phenomena (Chin & Osborne, 2010).

Kilpatrick (2001) identified five strands of mathematical literacy that support sensemaking

(a) conceptual understanding, which refers to the student's comprehension of mathematical concepts, operations, and relations; (b) procedural fluency, or the student's skill in carrying out mathematical procedures flexibly, accurately, efficiently, and appropriately; (c) strategic competence, the student's ability to formulate, represent, and solve mathematical problems; (d) adaptive reasoning, the capacity for logical thought and for reflection on, explanation of, and justification of mathematical arguments; and (e) productive disposition, which includes the student's habitual inclination to see mathematics as a sensible, useful, and worthwhile subject to be learned, coupled with a belief in the value of diligent work and in one's own efficacy as a doer of mathematics. (p. 107)

Finally, in literary reasoning, readers draw upon a repertoire of beliefs, experiences, rhetorical knowledge, and knowledge of literature to engage in argumentation about the meanings of literary texts (Lee, Goldman, Levine, & Magliano, 2016). With these brief characterizations reflecting academic sensemaking in a broad sense, we turn to specific studies of academic sensemaking within each discipline.

Sensemaking in the Teaching of Science

Sensemaking in the natural sciences has a significant kinship with sensemaking more generally. In contemporary discussions regarding the conduct of science, philosophers of science acknowledge that what is observed is influenced by what the observer *knows* and *how the observer chooses to look*. Consistent with the characterization of Goldman et al. (2016), Duschl (2008) urged that science instruction focus on

the *conceptual structures* and *cognitive processes* used when reasoning scientifically, the *epistemic* frameworks used when developing and evaluating scientific knowledge, and the *social* processes that shape how knowledge is communicated, represented, argued, and debated. (p. 277)

The literature that we reviewed specific to research in science was consistent with this call. Hogan, Nastasi, and Pressley (1999) studied eighth-grade students constructing mental models specific to the nature of matter and phase changes, as well as building explanations from evidence. In fact, explanations and argumentation were integral to all of the research that we reviewed in science. For example, Engle and Conant (2002) traced the development of an argument as a reflection of disciplinary engagement with a class of fifth graders, investigating how animals survive, in a Fostering a Community of Learners classroom (Brown & Campione, 1994). McNeill and Pimentel (2009) focused on the dialogic process by which students made sense of data for the purpose of generating claims and critiquing those claims and justifications. Their research, conducted with secondary students, focused on evaluating claims specific to climate change. Manz (2016) studied the activity of third-grade students constructing and critiquing claims and the evidence that supports those claims; one of her goals was that students see evidence as open to interpretation. Specifically, the students were investigating the influence of environmental conditions on plant growth. Herrenkohl and Cornelius (2013) investigated the implementation and outcomes of an application called SenseMaker, which was designed to support fifth-grade students' engagement in scientific and historical argumentation. Specific to science, the students were supported to understand the relationship among predictions, evidence, and theories; furthermore, they were supported to develop and revise theory in the service of providing an explanation for a scientific question (i.e., Why do objects sink or float?). Their goal was to communicate that sensemaking in science is undergirded by creating sound arguments.

In each of these examples, sensemaking was a social process; the purpose of which was to engage students in generating and evaluating claims that explain scientific phenomena.

Sensemaking in the Teaching of Mathematics

A review of the instructional literature in mathematics reveals not only areas of overlap with teaching and learning in science but also distinctive features. One of the areas of overlap is the expectation that students assume an exploratory stance toward the subject matter. For example, Silver and Stein (1996), in an effort to move away from drill and practice in mathematics teaching, designed tasks that would engage students in constructing meaning through the application of important mathematical concepts, symbols, and rules. Similar to explanatory work in science, middle school students in their research were expected to explain and justify their solutions to mathematical problems to others. An extension of this research in Stein, Engle, Smith, and Hughes (2008) documented teacher mediation of mathematical discussions in which students constructed and evaluated their own and others' mathematical ideas. Similarly, Pape, Bell, and Yetkin (2003) designed instruction in which middle school students analyzed mathematical problems (e.g., using multiple representations of algebraic equations), critically examined and justified their own mathematical reasoning, compared it with their classmates, and justified (or modified) their own reasoning. Distinguishing the instruction designed by Pape and colleagues was attention to what the researchers referred to as *self-regulating behaviors and attributions*, in which students named and described the strategies in which they were engaged that were critical to accomplishing the mathematical task; these strategies were documented and discussed. In this example, the teacher communicated to the students that the processes used in mathematical sensemaking are as important as the solutions themselves. Maher and her colleagues have conducted a program of research designed to explore how mathematical reasoning develops over time, with a particular focus on the features of the context, including the problems and discourse patterns, that engage students in mathematical sensemaking (e.g., Maher, 2005; Mueller, Yankelewitz, & Maher, 2014; Powell, Francisco, & Maher, 2003). In their research, sensemaking entails using reasoning to compare fractions, find equivalent fractions, and use Cuisenaire rods to perform operations on fractions. While the science community focuses on practices, such as making evidence-based claims, analyzing data, and explaining phenomena, the focus of the mathematics community appears to be on the processes of mathematical sensemaking.

Sensemaking in the Teaching of History

To illustrate the features of sensemaking in history instruction, we drew heavily from the program of research by Monte-Sano and her colleagues with middle and high school students (e.g., Monte-Sano, 2008, 2011; Monte-Sano, De La Paz, &

Felton, 2014). In this program of research, the focus was on historical reasoning through the activity of reading and interpreting historical text in order to construct written historical arguments. Drawing on Wineburg's (1991) study of expert historians, Monte-Sano and her colleagues emphasized the following processes: (a) sourcing (i.e., noting authors of historical documents, as well as their intentions and assumptions), (b) corroborating (i.e., comparing multiple historical documents), and (c) contextualizing (i.e., situating the historical document in the time and place in which it was created). Particularly important to this review is the emphasis that Monte-Sano, referencing Bereiter and Scardamalia (1987), placed on writing as an opportunity for learners to transform knowledge already in the mind; in other words, to make sense of what is "known." Monte-Sano argued that writing is integral to sensemaking in history because as learners write, they learn how to use and frame evidence; they have the opportunity to explore biases in sources, compare and situate evidence, and take into account different perspectives on events.

Investigating a curriculum called *Reading Like a Historian*, which was designed to support secondary students to read and interpret historical documents, Reisman (2012) similarly drew upon the disciplinary-specific practices identified above. One contribution that Reisman made to the sensemaking literature is her application of Wineburg's (1994) expansion of the Kintsch situation model framework (Kintsch, 1986). Rather than a single representation, Wineburg (1994) explains that historians construct three representations: the representation of the text, which is historically contextualized and can prove "slippery" given the nature of language; the representation of the event, which includes the actors and their motivations; and the representation of the subtext, which enables the reader to make judgments about the authors' intents and biases. Reisman's curriculum calls attention to the intertextual nature of historical reading and the constructed nature of historical accounts. Students were expected to engage in historical inquiry by (a) building background knowledge to contextualize and make sense of historical documents, (b) reading and interrogating multiple historical accounts, and (c) constructing knowledge by reconciling those accounts. The students were supported to construct multiple representations of texts through explicit strategy instruction in historical reading strategies (sourcing, contextualization, close reading, corroboration) and by responding to guiding questions related to the strategies to interrogate the historical accounts. For example, students used a *historical reading strategies* chart, which posed questions such as the following: What words or phrases does the author use to convince me that he/she is right? How does this document make me feel? What is the author's point of view? What else was going on at that time when this was written? What do other pieces of evidence say? The questions on the chart were designed to support students to construct representations of the text, event, and subtext as they engaged in historical inquiry. In this manner, historical sensemaking is both a layered and recursive process in which the reader modifies their model of the historical event as they encounter different documents. Recall that

Herrenkohl and Cornelius (2013) studied both scientific and historical sensemaking. The SenseMaker app for history (in contrast to science) engaged students in critically considering the sources of historical accounts, cross-checking of sources, and being open to uncertainty as they engaged in historical inquiry.

Sensemaking in the Teaching of Literature

As one might anticipate, there is a broad literature that we could draw upon when considering sensemaking in the teaching of literature, given the parallels between comprehension and sensemaking. We limited ourselves to four programs of research that make unique contributions to this literature, beginning with the work of Aukerman. Aukerman (2007, 2013) distinguished three forms of comprehension pedagogy. The first she referred to as *comprehension-as-outcome* pedagogy, which she proposed emphasizes getting the meaning "right." The second she called *comprehension-as-procedure* pedagogy, which she characterized as teaching students to do the "right" things while reading; for example, engage the use of strategies such as inferring, summarizing, and visualizing. She identified the third as *comprehension-as-sensemaking* pedagogy, which is pedagogy that values the actual meanings readers make of text, regardless of "rightness."

Consistent with the definitions of sensemaking that we explored in the introduction, comprehension-as-sensemaking acknowledges the active exploration of possibilities for meaning and is a creative process. Consistent with contemporary definitions of comprehension (e.g., "the process of simultaneously extracting and constructing meaning through interaction and involvement with written language," RAND Reading Study Group, 2002, p. 11), Aukerman maintained that sensemaking is something that all readers do, but that teachers do not always treat this intellectual activity as generative if they are not teaching from a *comprehension-as-sensemaking* orientation. Aukerman further distinguished two forms of comprehension-as-sensemaking pedagogy, *expressivist*, which emphasizes surfacing student interpretations, and *dialogic*, which seeks to juxtapose and engage with students' varying understandings through dialogue. Aukerman (2013) elaborated,

Dialogic comprehension-as-sensemaking pedagogy is not a matter of simply nurturing and celebrating student understandings, but rather of engaging students in dialogue about text in which understandings are transformed through encountering the understandings of others; even when students read alone, they will be engaging with a plethora of possibilities as they make sense of text. From a dialogic perspective on comprehension-as-sensemaking, then, neither a text's meaning, nor the way in which a student arrives at meaning for a text, are predetermined: they are surprises, to use Matusov's (2009) term, that unfold in refraction with other voices that are also working at sensemaking (Bakhtin, 1981). (p. 7)

The dialogic nature of teaching comprehension as a sensemaking process is also featured in the research of Lee (2006), whose orientation to the teaching of literary interpretation is referred to as *cultural modeling*. In her instruction, Lee drew heavily on the cultural resources (including language, cultural referents, and cultural values) of the secondary students she was teaching. The focus of the dialogic instruction was on the reasoning in which the students engaged as they collectively interpreted text. Among her contributions to the literature is her elaboration on the cultural and linguistic tools that students bring to sensemaking with text.

The research of Grossman, Loeb, Cohen, and Wyckoff (2013) and Wolf, Crosson, and Resnick (2006) is illustrative of sensemaking instruction that focused on *sensemaking processes*. Grossman et al. (2013) sought to identify the teaching practices that were characteristic of teachers who were more effective at supporting literary reasoning and literacy analysis. Drawing upon the Protocol for Language Arts Teaching Observation (PLATO), they discerned that explicit strategy instruction distinguished the practice of more effective teachers. These teachers modeled and provided guided practice in the use of approaches to engaging in sophisticated literary analysis, reading comprehension, and writing. Similarly, Wolf et al. (2006) investigated pedagogy that made explicit the high-level thinking that facilitates sensemaking with the active use of prior knowledge and engagement in activity that promotes getting to the underlying meaning of text.

Thus far, we have examined the ways in which sensemaking is represented as the focus and means of instruction across the teaching of science, mathematics, history, and literature. While there are many features that overlap, there are unique features as well that reflect the tools and norms of the respective disciplines, as well as the pedagogical orientation of the researcher. In the next section of this chapter, we turn to investigations of teachers' practices in these instructional contexts and what they reveal about the efficacy of teacher practices specific to supporting student sensemaking.

EXPLORING SPECIFIC TEACHER PRACTICES IN SENSEMAKING INSTRUCTION

Lampert (2010) defined teaching practice by drawing a distinction between *having an idea* and *carrying out that idea*; the carrying out of the idea being integral to practice. An important caveat in our discussion of instructional practice is that—as Bruner (1966) noted—any discussion of instruction is, in fact, a discussion of both curriculum and pedagogy. As the descriptions above suggest, the curricula that were being investigated were intended to engage students in sensemaking. Given that the role of teachers is to enact the instructional discourse, as well as mediate the environment in which instruction occurs (Cohen & Ball, 2001), it is important to examine the teachers' practices in the context of the sensemaking curricula.

Before exploring the specific practices, we want to note the general character of the research methods used across the studies we reviewed. With few exceptions, the research was qualitative in nature and typically conducted with a single teacher or a small set of teachers; one exception is the research by Grossman et al. (2013), in which the participants were 24 teachers in 9 middle schools; another exception is the quasi-experimental research by Reisman (2012), in which the participants included five treatment teachers. Typically, the data were gathered with the use of classroom observations and video (e.g., Herrenkohl & Cornelius, 2013; Hogan et al., 1999), which was transcribed and coded, drawing upon extant and new schemes (e.g., Manz, 2016; McNeill & Pimentel, 2009). In a few instances the data were used descriptively to construct case studies (e.g., Warren, Ballenger, Ogonowski, Rosebery, & Hudicourt-Barnes, 2001) or comparative case studies (Herrenkohl & Cornelius, 2013; Monte-Sano, 2008). Researchers occasionally engaged in microanalyses of classroom conversation and linguistic practices (e.g., Aukerman, 2007; Lee, 2006). Observations were frequently supplemented by interviews (e.g., Cervetti, DiPardo, & Staley, 2014) and, occasionally, teacher artifacts (such as the planning documents used in Pape et al., 2003) or student artifacts (e.g., Monte-Sano, 2011; Silver & Stein, 1996). In most cases, the researchers worked very closely with the teacher(s), or were, themselves, the teacher.

While we refer to teacher "practice," the overarching practice across all of these studies was *engaging in discussion*; hence, many of the findings were reported in terms of discourse moves. This is consistent with the theoretical orientation with which we began this chapter; language plays a pivotal role in sensemaking instruction because it provides the means for learners to interact with others, to compare and contrast their thinking, and to negotiate meaning making.

However, there were additional practices that cannot be captured in terms of discourse; for example, making decisions about what resources to provide the students or making decisions about the sequencing of the problems presented to the students, or presenting multiple representations of a problem.

We begin with a characterization of teacher practices across the broad literature for the purpose of identifying commonalities in teachers' practices that can be discerned by looking across the studies. Then, because it was not possible to do justice to the full range of teacher practices using a generic approach, we consider the disciplinary-specific nature of the practices.

General Teaching Practices Associated With Supporting Sensemaking

To answer the question, "What are the general teaching practices associated with supporting sensemaking?" we constructed a table in which we arrayed the findings from each of the 24 instructional studies that we analyzed. We then examined those findings for patterns in the five major categories that emerged from this analysis.

The most frequent category of practice was *teacher questioning*; however, the features of questions that were determined to be relevant to describing teacher practice varied in significant ways. For example, teacher questions served a broad range of purposes, including extending and clarifying student thinking (e.g., Hogan et al., 1999) and requesting additional information (e.g., eliciting reasoning and justification for responses, e.g., Pumtembeker, Stylianou, & Goldstein, 2007). Teacher questions were characterized as having different features within and across studies; for example, they were described in terms of their "openness" with more open questions yielding more productive discussion (e.g., McNeill & Pimentel, 2009). They were described in terms of their degree of refinement, with productive questions moving toward greater refinement (e.g., Manz, 2016) and being driven by specific conceptual goals (e.g., Pumtembeker et al., 2007). They were also described in terms of how the questions were informed by student contributions, with more productive questions building from student contributions (e.g., Cervetti et al., 2014).

The second category of practice was *making connections*. This seems especially appropriate to the activity of sensemaking if one subscribes to the notion that—in the activity of sensemaking—we bring sense to ideas that we already know at some level. The purposes making connections served included making connections between activities and concepts (e.g., Monte-Sano et al., 2014; Pumtembeker et al., 2007), making connections among students' ideas (Stein et al., 2008), making connections among ideas that emerged over time (e.g., Silver & Stein, 1996), and making connections among epistemic levels (Manz, 2016). In order to engage in the practice of making connections, teachers in these sensemaking studies were also observed to track knowledge development, monitoring for evidence of required knowledge (e.g., Hogan et al., 1999), and supporting students to build background knowledge to support sensemaking (Monte-Sano et al., 2014). Tucked within this category is the practice of revoicing (O'Connor & Michaels, 1993). Revoicing has been used to characterize the discourse moves that teachers make in which they make an inference about a student's contribution to the discussion that serves to bring that student's contributions into alignment with the academic task and, in the process, serves to position the student as a contributor to the academic discourse.

The third most frequent category of practice was *increasing challenge*. This was accomplished in multiple ways, some of which were represented in the teachers' talk, for example, pressing students to elaborate on their responses (Henningsen & Stein, 1997), promoting higher levels of reasoning (e.g., Lee, 2006), or sustaining pressure for students to continue their exploration of a context or problem (e.g., Aukerman, 2007). This practice was also demonstrated when teachers progressed to more challenging tasks or sequenced the problems or tasks in the curriculum with an eye to the intellectual demands (e.g., Monte-Sano, 2011).

There were a number of practices that served to *enculturate* students into the activity of engaging in sensemaking conversations. For example, establishing the norms and conditions that would be necessary for productive classroom conversation (e.g., Engle & Conant, 2002), communicating the disciplinary-specific standards by which knowledge claims are made (we elaborate on this below), and giving authority to students, which in some cases, was associated with the teacher refraining from assuming the role of evaluator (e.g., Aukerman, 2007).

A final category of practice was *differentiating instruction*. This practice was enacted in an array of ways. Examples include spending additional time with students who were struggling, alternating whole-class instruction with working in small groups or individually (Grossman et al., 2013), providing additional support (e.g., Monte-Sano et al., 2014), and increasing explicitness (e.g., Silver & Stein, 1996).

As we analyzed the studies we reviewed, we were struck by the broad range of practices necessary to characterize the enactment of instruction that is designed to teach and promote sensemaking, as well as the multitude of purposes those practices served. However, we were also dissatisfied with how incomplete a picture these broad categories provided. Our conclusion was that, while these appeared to be "necessary" practices, they were insufficient to capturing the domain-specific nature of teacher practice in sensemaking contexts. For that reason, in the next section, we look closely at four studies, one for each of the disciplines we review, for the purpose of explicating the domain-specific nature of teacher practice. We selected studies in which the researchers provided significant detail regarding teachers' practices.

Domain-Specific Teaching Practices

Science

Recall that in the study by Manz (2016), the researcher was interested in how the teacher framed and supported the construction of evidence and how (third-grade) students' roles shifted over time in this sensemaking activity. Consistent with the sensemaking literature, the construction of evidence was conceived of as a process of transformation. As we read Manz's description of the instruction core to her research, we were reminded of the writing of Marcello Pera, a philosopher of science. Pera (1994) characterized *traditional* science in terms of a *methodological model* in which scientific research is a game with two players—the scientist whose inquiry raises questions and nature that provides the answers. The impartial arbiter in this game is method, ascertaining whether the game was conducted well and determining when it is over. Pera (1994) noted, "As it is guided or forced by the rules of the arbiter, nature speaks out. And 'knowing' amounts to the scientist's recording of nature's true voice, or mirroring its real structure" (p. ix). In contrast, presenting a more contemporary view, consistent with a sensemaking perspective, Pera presented a *dialectical model*, in which there are three players: an individual or group of individuals, nature, and another group of individuals that debates with the first according to the features of scientific dialectics. From this perspective, there is no impartial arbiter, nature responds to a "cross-examination," and knowing emerges from the *community's agreement* upon nature's correct answer. Furthermore, as Pera noted, agreement among the members of a community is not merely conversational because it is constrained by nature. For the dialectical process described above to be at play in classrooms, there must be opportunities for students as community members to express disagreement and skepticism.

Manz (2016) documented this dialogic process, tracing how the participating teacher and students constructed and negotiated evidence. She labeled talk in terms of "epistemic levels" (such as noticing, claims, and facts) with each level representing a shift in sophistication and a move toward identifying generalizable facts. Manz (2016) documents how, when the instructional dialogue was initiated, the teacher assumed a primary role in the evidence construction process by making connections among the epistemic levels, rendering the relationships among comparison, evidence, and claim transparent to the class, and purposefully "shifting the level of conversation from one level to another" (p. 1124). As instruction proceeded, there was evidence that the students assumed a greater role in the evidence construction and the teacher's role shifted to include revoicing student contributions, prompting for connections among the epistemic levels, and problematizing particular ideas contributed by the students. Manz (2016) concludes that the most noteworthy aspect of the teacher's practice was the manner in which the teacher made visible the relationships among the epistemic levels.

This study illustrates the value of investigating teacher practice over the course of time (in this case, over 18 lessons). Furthermore, the richness of the findings was enhanced by the contribution of the discipline-specific framework that represented evidence construction as transformation and provided a useful tool for characterizing shifts in the teachers' practice over time, in response to what the students were increasingly able to do independently. Finally, this study reveals the role that the teacher's content knowledge for teaching (Ball, Thames, & Phelps, 2008) played in the teacher's practice.

Mathematics

To illustrate the close study of teacher practice in the context of mathematics teaching, we selected the research reported by Mueller et al. (2014), who studied one teacher's practices as she supported her (sixth-grade) students who were participating in an after-school program for 12 two-hour sessions. The teacher was a participant in an intervention titled the Informal Mathematics Learning Program, which supported teachers to constitute a community of mathematical learners co-constructing arguments, justifying solutions, and engaging in mathematical reasoning. Similar to the study by Manz (reviewed above), the researchers brought a clear theoretical stance to the design of the intervention. For example, they conceive of the teacher playing a minimal role during the initial exploration of a mathematical problem to "encourage students to engage in mathematical discourse, share representations, co-construct ideas and justifications, and ultimately take a more active role in their own learning" (p. 2). However, they also note the important role that teacher questioning plays in inducing learners to engage in elaborated forms of reasoning that are likely to lead to deeper understanding. As we suggested earlier in this review, these authors identified task design as playing a critical role in establishing sensemaking opportunities, as does listening carefully to students.

Using video data from which the researchers identified critical events, they transcribed and coded the data, which enabled them to construct a storyline and compose a narrative (described in Powell et al., 2003). The goal of this approach to analysis was to investigate the effects of the teacher's moves on learners as evidenced by their ideas, arguments, and solutions.

Mueller et al. (2014) identified three categories of moves that were salient in accounting for student engagement in mathematical sensemaking. The first were those moves that served to make students' ideas public; these moves were especially prominent in the first two of the five sessions analyzed. The second and third categories of moves were those that elicited and extended students' ideas and encouraged explanations and justifications; these moves were in play particularly when the tasks were more challenging for the students. These moves encouraged persistence and provided an occasion for emphasizing the importance of collective problem solving. Interestingly, the researchers observed that students began to appropriate these moves in their own exchanges with one another. Furthermore, there was more evidence of these moves when the mathematical problem encouraged multiple solutions. One interesting pattern that the researchers characterize is the relationship between teacher moves, such as considering the reasonableness of a proposed solution and the opportunities for students to attain increased mathematical autonomy.

Similar to the study by Manz (2016), this study illustrates the value of investigating teacher practice across time; practices that were more or less ideal for supporting sensemaking looked different across the sequence of lessons. The rich, qualitative data that these researchers collected enabled them to make claims about the different purposes that various teacher practices served and the relationship between those moves and features of the task. In fact, one of the most interesting insights from this study was the important role that choosing and analyzing mathematical tasks plays in determining the usefulness of various teacher practices. This finding speaks to the role of content knowledge for teaching in mathematics as well.

History

To explore practice specific to the teaching of history, we selected the study reported by Monte-Sano et al. (2014). Recall that these authors were committed to integrating the teaching of history with the teaching of reading and writing. They studied two expert eighth-grade history teachers implementing a curriculum that integrated the disciplinary use of evidence in writing historical arguments from multiple historical sources. The "disciplinary use of evidence" includes recognizing bias in sources, comparing evidence across sources, situating evidence in its context and taking into account different perspectives and multiple causes (p. 543). To support teachers in this activity of historical sensemaking, the researchers introduced two disciplinary-literacy tools: a mnemonic device, IREAD, which prompts students to read the whole document once, annotate to connect ideas in the text to the question(s) the reader is pursuing, and reflect on the source and context. The second tool, H2W (How to Write Your Essay), proposed a five-paragraph essay that contained an introduction, two supporting paragraphs, a rebuttal paragraph, and a conclusion (all of which were framed in historically specific ways).

It is not possible to do justice to all of the observations that Monte-Sano and her colleagues made regarding the teaching practices they observed as the two teachers enacted this intervention; we present the highlights. Thinking aloud was prominent in their practice, particularly in the initial phase of instruction, followed by guided practice. When introducing the texts with which the students would work, the teachers framed these texts as arguments that would be used to support the students to construct their own arguments. There were important differences between the two teachers. For example, the teacher who had more struggling readers provided more explicit support, modeled longer, and more actively paced the students' work. Both teachers, who revealed strong content knowledge, encouraged more complex forms of reasoning with the texts, supporting the students to use context to interpret the authors' meanings. In addition, and particularly relevant to teaching for sensemaking, both teachers were attentive to building the relevant background knowledge that would facilitate making sense of historical controversies and primary sources so that the students could, in fact, evaluate those sources.

There are interesting parallels between the interventions studied by Manz, Mueller et al., and Monte-Sano et al. Making thinking public (regarding scientific, mathematical, and historical thinking) was integral to instruction in each of these studies. While, once again, studying practice over time made it possible for the researchers to document how the practice changed over time, studying the practice of two teachers who had students with different levels of literacy proficiency made it possible to see how the practices took these differences into account. Once again, the enabling role of teachers' content knowledge for teaching was salient in this research.

Literature

We conclude our investigation of disciplinary-specific practice by looking closely at the research of Aukerman (2013). What distinguishes Aukerman's research is the salience of sensemaking in her instructional orientation; she does, after all, label her approach *comprehension-as-sensemaking*. As described earlier, she distinguishes this approach to the teaching of literature from *comprehension-as-outcome*, with its focus on leading students to "correct" readings of text and *comprehension-as-procedure*, with its focus on engaging students in particular ways/routines/strategies while reading. What distinguishes *comprehension-as-sensemaking* is its acknowledgment that sensemaking is something that readers must do; the difference is that, when one brings this orientation to the teaching of comprehension, there is an openness to the understandings that students achieve through their intellectual work, even if that understanding and the ways of arriving at that understanding do not align with the teacher's.

What are the practices associated with teaching reading comprehension-as-sensemaking? Aukerman (2013) has enumerated these practices. They include (a) inviting students to read texts where divergent understandings are likely to become visible, ones that will challenge but not overwhelm the students who will be making sense of them; (b) putting students in situations where they exercise their own textual authority rather than consistently positioning the teacher as the only textual authority (e.g., by withholding evaluation of student responses, whether these lie within or outside perceived institutional bounds); (c) expecting that all classroom participants take the sensemaking of others, within and beyond the classroom, seriously (e.g., by asking students to consider closely the contributions of a low-status student; or by asking them to engage with a published critique of a text being studied); (d) facilitating frequent opportunities where students' sensemaking and resolved meanings become visible, develop, and intermingle (e.g., by facilitating dialogue rich with teacher uptake and open discussion among students, particularly when divergent under-standings begin to become visible); (e) encouraging students' awareness of how others respond to the meanings they resolve, and also of how these responses might matter given the purposes that are at stake for them (e.g., by pointing out disagreements or places where a course of action chosen on the basis of one's sensemaking—such as following a written series of steps to conduct an experiment—might be rewarding or disappointing to the reader); (f) making additional social, cultural, and semiotic resources available for the reader to do her/his work, and encouraging students to make creative use of such resources (e.g., by supporting students' decoding profi-ciency or vocabulary knowledge; or by pointing out how her/his own cultural blind-ers might have made her/him initially unaware of certain textual possibilities); and (g) inviting students to consider potential new purposes and interests as they engage with text (e.g., by inviting students who are particularly drawn toward pictures in the text to consider how engagement with the words might open different doors for them as readers; or by suggesting that stories can be read with a feminist or critical lens, as well as for the content of the story). Aukerman is careful to add that students' under-standings are not beyond critique; the expectation is that, sensemaking is transformed through dialogue.

The social nature of sensemaking is salient in each of the four studies that we reviewed; in each case, the teacher and students are encouraged to make their think-ing "public." With the exception of Aukerman (2013), the teacher's use of public thinking provides learners access to expert sensemaking (scientifically, mathemati-cally, historically) and provides students access to heuristics, resources, and tools that will advance productive sensemaking in disciplinary-specific ways. Construction, co-construction, and transformation are synonymous with sensemaking across these contexts. The context features phenomena, problems, and/or texts that serve as grist for sensemaking. Finally, both teachers and students play prominent roles in the instructional contexts, with teachers' moves responsive to student engagement.

In the next section, we look across the studies reviewed for the purpose of identify-ing implications for teacher learning/development and for research.

IMPLICATIONS FOR TEACHER LEARNING AND TEACHER DEVELOPMENT

To answer the question "What are the implications for teacher learning/teacher development?" we constructed a table in which we arrayed the implications for teacher learning and development identified by each of the 24 instructional studies that we analyzed. We then examined those implications for patterns in the categories that emerged. Four categories emerged from this analysis.

The most frequent category of implications for teacher learning and development was a category that we describe as *framing and enacting opportunities* for students to engage in sensemaking. Referring to sensemaking with text, Aukerman (2013) proposed that "reading comprehension pedagogy should shift from its current focus on institutional understandings to a primary emphasis on eliciting, illuminating, and juxtaposing students' sensemaking" (p. 20). Doing so requires teachers to provide opportunities for students to engage in the work of sensemaking in the classroom. Across disciplines, the studies that we analyzed identified implications for practice related to the ways in which teachers provide and represent opportunities for students to make sense of the world. For example, these studies called for teachers to provide students with opportunities to (a) engage in disciplinary thinking (Monte-Sano, 2011); (b) inquire, reason, and argue about historical events and scientific phenomena (Manz, 2016; Monte-Sano, 2008); (c) see history as an interpretive discipline (Monte-Sano, 2008); (d) exercise interpretive authority in evaluating text and talk (Aukerman, 2007, 2013); (e) make connections between and draw upon prior knowledge, everyday experiences, cultural practices, and new learning (Lee, 2006; McNeill & Pimentel, 2009); and (f) elaborate on their knowledge and reasoning (Wolf et al., 2006).

The second category of implications for teacher learning and development is related to the opportunities that teachers frame and provide for students to engage in sensemaking through a focus on *teacher education* and *professional development*. Multiple studies that we reviewed proposed that instructional practices are teachable; hence, teachers can be supported to use instructional moves—including discourse moves—in ways that foster students' sensemaking (Grossman et al., 2013; Manz, 2016). Thus, if research and observation protocols can identify instructional practices that support sensemaking, teacher education and professional development can be designed to focus on enhancing teachers' instruction. While it is important to initiate this kind of training in teacher education programs (Cervetti et al., 2014), research also points to the importance of providing teachers with professional development opportunities that are supportive and sustained over time (De La Paz et al., 2017). Professional development for teachers focused on creating opportunities for and fostering students' sensemaking might target creating knowledge-centered learning environments (Pumtembeker et al., 2007); examining exemplary interactions among teachers and students during sensemaking activity (Hogan et al., 1999); and providing classroom supports for teachers to engage students in sensemaking, such as the use of tasks that build on students' prior knowledge and experiences (Silver & Stein, 1996).

The third category of implications for teacher learning and development was the importance of teachers' knowledge, including both *disciplinary knowledge* and *knowledge of students*. Multiple studies emphasized the importance of teachers' disciplinary knowledge—including but not limited to knowledge of disciplinary content—in fostering students' sensemaking. For instance, facilitating sensemaking discussions requires deep content knowledge on the part of the teacher and allows them to notice and respond to students' ideas (e.g., Cervetti et al., 2014; Monte-Sano et al., 2014). In addition to content knowledge, the studies that we analyzed called attention to the importance of teachers' knowledge of their discipline (e.g., Herrenkohl & Cornelius, 2013; Monte-Sano, 2008). Recall that, in the majority of the studies we reviewed, the students were engaged in sensemaking in the context of disciplinary tasks, such as developing scientific or written historical arguments and interpreting literature. To engage students in disciplinary work, teachers must understand and be able to support students to engage in the practices of their discipline to make sense of the world in disciplinary-specific ways. Extending these ideas, Monte-Sano et al. (2014) described the ways in which it is necessary for teachers to use both their knowledge of the discipline and knowledge of their students in order to press student thinking and respond to students' ideas.

The fourth and final category of implications for teacher learning and development is the need for *high-quality curriculum materials* to support instruction. Connecting to a point that we made earlier in this chapter, teachers' instructional practices are always in interplay with the curriculum materials to which they have access. In other words, for teachers to productively engage students in making sense of the world, they must have access to curriculum materials that are rich enough to support this complex work. For instance, Hogan et al. (1999) pointed to the importance of a curriculum that encourages students to engage in knowledge construction. Other studies that we reviewed emphasized the importance of providing teachers with tools and materials that foster disciplinary teaching and learning—such as primary source documents in history—that can be used to encourage students to engage in disciplinary thinking and reasoning (Monte-Sano et al., 2014). To this end, Reisman (2012) argued for providing teachers with curriculum materials and lessons that focus on using discipline-specific strategies to make sense of the world. To support teachers to engage in the work of fostering students' sensemaking, they need access to high-quality curriculum materials that align with and facilitate this process.

DIRECTIONS FOR FUTURE RESEARCH

The complexity of supporting students' academic sensemaking translates to a rich, multipronged research agenda. Specific to instructional practices, given the prominence of discourse moves, there is much to be learned about the efficacy of particular discourse moves in particular contexts, within and across particular disciplines, and at particular grade levels. Lee (2006), for example, advocated for research on instructional practices in order to determine not only what is *possible* but what is *generative*.

The field needs research exploring *teacher learning and professional development* in relationship to supporting students' sensemaking. For example, we might ask about the use of particular experiences and strategies—such as the use of video or transcript analysis, or the use of software (such as SenseMaker; Herrenkohl & Cornelius, 2013)—to support teachers who vary in their experience and expertise engaging in sensemaking instruction. Specific to the study of teachers, we might ask how teachers' beliefs about how students learn, the assumptions they make about their students as sensemakers, and teachers' own epistemic commitments influence their teaching practices and with what consequences.

There is the need for research that expands and diversifies the research contexts in which sensemaking instruction in conducted. As described previously, the majority of the research that we reviewed was small-scale qualitative research, focusing on one or a small set of classroom teachers. The effectiveness of identified instructional approaches and practices emerging from the research to date needs to be investigated in more diverse educational contexts.

Given the role that assessment plays in driving instruction, and given the challenge of designing assessment instruments that place a premium on sensemaking, we propose that research on assessment of sensemaking to inform curriculum and instruction would be valuable. Finally, we imagine that the next review of the sensemaking literature will find technology playing a prominent role in curriculum and instruction designed to promote academic sensemaking.

CONCLUSION

There is general agreement that, in order to develop, retain, and reward great teachers, there have to be effective ways of understanding and representing great teaching, but this is an area that is fraught with challenges (Baker et al., 2010; Darling-Hammond, Amrein-Beardsley, Haertel, & Rothstein, 2012). Our review of the sensemaking literature suggested that using the lens of sensemaking offers rich potential for investigating and characterizing great teaching. Sensemaking is easily apprehended as an idea and it is resonant with our everyday ways of being in the world. We found remarkable consistency and specificity in the major categories of teaching practices across four disciplinary areas, and those that were unique to the disciplines offered important insights into the language, tools, and ways of reasoning that are valued within disciplinary communities. From a sensemaking perspective, teachers are advantaged when they value the experiences and knowledge that students bring with them into academic contexts. Such a perspective positions teachers to be respectful of students' ideas and to approach curriculum and teaching mindful of students' assets, an increasingly valuable stance in our increasingly diverse schools.

REFERENCES

Aukerman, M. S. (2007). When reading it wrong is getting it right: Shared evaluation pedagogy among struggling fifth grade readers. *Research in the Teaching of English, 42*(1), 56–103.

Aukerman, M. (2013). Rereading comprehension pedagogies: Toward a dialogic teaching ethic that honors student sensemaking. *Dialogic Pedagogy: An International Online Journal, 1*. Retrieved from https://dpj.pitt.edu/ojs/index.php/dpj1/article/view/9/17

Bain, R. (2006). Rounding up unusual suspects: Facing the authority hidden in the history curriculum. *Teachers College Record, 108*(10), 2080–2114.

Baker, E. L., Barton, P. E., Darling-Hammond, L., Haertel, E., Ladd, H. F., Linn, R. L., . . . Shepard, L. (2010). *Problems with the use of student test scores to evaluate teachers.* Washington, DC: Economic Policy Institute.

Bakhtin, M. (1981). Discourse in the novel. In M. Holquist (Ed.), *The dialogic imagination* (pp. 259–492). Austin: University of Texas Press.

Ball, D. L., Thames, M. H., & Phelps, G. (2008). Content knowledge for teaching: What makes it special? *Journal of Teacher Education, 59*, 389–407.

Bereiter, C., & Scardamalia, M. (1987). *The psychology of written composition.* Hillsdale, NJ: Lawrence Erlbaum.

Brown, A., & Campione, J. (1994). Guided discovery in a community of learners. In K. McGill (Ed.), *Classroom lessons: Integrating cognitive theory and classroom practice* (pp. 229–270). Cambridge: MIT Press.

Bruner, J. S. (1966). *Toward a theory of instruction.* Cambridge, MA: Belknap Press of Harvard University Press.

Bruner, J., & Haste, H. (1987). *Making sense: The child's construction of reality.* New York, NY: Methuen.

Cervetti, G. N., DiPardo, A. L., & Staley, S. J. (2014). Entering the conversation: Exploratory talk in middle school science. *Elementary School Journal, 114*, 547–572.

Chin, C., & Osborne, J. (2010). Supporting argumentation through students' questions: Case studies in science classrooms. *Journal of the Learning Sciences, 19*, 230–284.

Cohen, D. K., & Ball, D. L. (2001). Making change: Instruction and its improvement. *Phi Delta Kappan, 83*(1), 73–77.

Darling-Hammond, L., Amrein-Beardsley, A., Haertel, E., & Rothstein, J. (2012). Evaluating teacher evaluation. *Phi Delta Kappa, 93*(6), 8–15.

De La Paz, S., Monte-Sano, C., Felton, M., Croninger, R., Jackson, C., & Piantedosi, K. W. (2017). A historical writing apprenticeship for adolescents: Integrating disciplinary learning with cognitive strategies. *Reading Research Quarterly, 52*(1), 31–52.

Duschl, R. A. (2008). Science education in three part harmony: Balancing conceptual, epistemic and social learning goals. *Review of Research in Education, 32*, 268–291.

Engle, R. A., & Conant, F. R. (2002). Guiding principles for fostering productive disciplinary engagement: Explaining an emergent argument in a community of learners classroom. *Cognition and Instruction, 20*, 399–483.

Goldman, S. R., Britt, M. A., Brown, W., Cribb, G., George, M., & Greenleaf, C., . . . Project READI. (2016). Disciplinary literacies and learning to read for understanding: A conceptual framework for disciplinary literacy. *Educational Psychologist, 51*, 219–246.

Grossman, P., Loeb, S., Cohen, J., & Wyckoff, J. (2013). Measure for measure: The relationship between measures of instructional practice in middle school English language arts and teachers' value-added scores. *American Journal of Education, 119*, 445–470.

Henningsen, M., & Stein, M. K. (1997). Mathematical tasks and student cognition: Classroom-based factors that support and inhibit high-level mathematical thinking and reasoning. *Journal for Research in Mathematics Education, 28*, 524–549.

Herrenkohl, L. R., & Cornelius, L. (2013). Investigating elementary students' scientific and historical argumentation. *Journal of the Learning Sciences, 22*, 413–461.

Hogan, K., Nastasi, B. K., & Pressley, M. (1999). Discourse patterns and collaborative scientific reasoning in peer and teacher-guided discussions. *Cognition and Instruction, 17*, 379–432.

Kennedy, M. M. (2007). Defining a literature. *Educational Researcher, 36*, 139–147.

Kilpatrick, J. (2001). Understanding mathematical literacy: The contribution of research. *Educational Studies in Mathematics, 47*, 101–116.

Kintsch, W. (1986). Learning from text. *Cognition and Instruction, 3*(2), 87–108.

Klein, G., Moon, B., & Hoffman, R. R. (2006). Making sense of sensemaking 1: Alternative perspectives. *IEEE Intelligent Systems, 21*(4), 70–73.

Lampert, M. (2010). Learning teaching in, from, and for practice: What do we mean? *Journal of Teacher Education, 61*(1–2), 21–34.

Lee, C. D. (2006). "Every good-bye ain't gone": Analyzing the cultural underpinnings of classroom talk. *International Journal of Qualitative Studies in Education, 19*, 305–327.

Lee, C. D., Goldman, S. R., Levine, S., & Magliano, J. (2016). Epistemic cognition in literary reasoning. In J. A. Greene, W. A. Sandoval, & I. Braten (Eds.), *Handbook of epistemic cognition* (pp. 165–183). New York, NY: Routledge.

Maher, C. A. (2005). How students structure their investigations and learning mathematics: Insights from a long-term study. *Journal of Mathematical Behavior, 24*(1), 1–14.

Manz, E. (2016). Examining evidence construction as the transformation of the material world into community knowledge. *Journal of Research in Science Teaching, 53*, 1113–1140.

Matusov, E. (2009). *Journey into dialogic pedagogy.* Hauppauge, NY: Nova.

McNeill, K. L., & Pimentel, D. S. (2009). Scientific discourse in three urban classrooms: The role of the teacher in engaging high school students in argumentation. *Science Education, 94*, 203–229.

Monte-Sano, C. (2008). Qualities of historical writing instruction: A comparative case study of two teachers' practices. *American Educational Research Journal, 45*, 1045–1079.

Monte-Sano, C. (2011). Beyond reading comprehension and summary: Learning to read and write in history by focusing on evidence, perspective, and interpretation. *Curriculum Inquiry, 42*, 212–249.

Monte-Sano, C., De La Paz, S., & Felton, M. (2014). Implementing disciplinary-literacy curriculum for US history: Learning from expert middle school teachers in diverse classrooms. *Journal of Curriculum Studies, 46*, 540–575.

Mueller, M., Yankelewitz, D., & Maher, C. (2014). Teachers promoting student mathematical reasoning. *Investigations in Mathematics Learning, 7*(2), 1–20.

O'Connor, M. C., & Michaels, S. (1993). Aligning academic task and participation status through revoicing: Analysis of a classroom discourse strategy. *Anthropology & Education Quarterly, 24*, 318–335.

Pape, S. J., Bell, C. V., & Yetkin, I. E. (2003). Developing mathematical thinking and self-regulated learning: A teaching experiment in a seventh-grade mathematics classroom. *Educational Studies in Mathematics, 53*, 179–202.

Pera, M. (1994). *The discourses of science.* Chicago, IL: University of Chicago Press.

Powell, A., Francisco, J. M., & Maher, C. A. (2003). An analytical model for studying the development of learners' mathematical ideas and reasoning using videotape data. *Journal of Mathematical Behavior, 22*, 405–435.

Pumtembeker, S., Stylianou, A., & Goldstein, J. (2007). Comparing classroom enactments of an inquiry curriculum: Lessons learned from two teachers. *Journal of the Learning Sciences, 16*, 81–130.

RAND Reading Study Group. (2002). *Reading for understanding: Toward an R & D program in reading.* Santa Monica, CA: Author.

Reisman, A. (2012). Reading like a historian: A document-based history curriculum intervention in urban high schools. *Cognition and Instruction, 30*, 86–112.

Silver, E. A., & Stein, M. K. (1996). The QUASAR project: The "revolution of the possible" in mathematics instructional reform in urban middle schools. *Urban Education, 30*, 476–521.

Stein, M. K., Engle, R. A., Smith, M. S., & Hughes, E. K. (2008). Orchestrating productive mathematical discussions: Five practices for helping teachers move beyond show and tell. *Mathematical Thinking and Learning, 10,* 313–340.

Vygotsky, L. S. (1987). Thinking and speech. In R. W. Rieber, & A. S. Carton (Eds.), *The collected works of LS Vygotsky: Problems of general psychology* (Vol. 1, pp. 39–285). New York, NY: Plenum Press. (Original work published 1934)

Warren, B., Ballenger, C., Ogonowski, M., Rosebery, A. S., & Hudicourt-Barnes, J. (2001). Rethinking diversity in learning science: The logic of everyday sense-making. *Journal of Research in Science Teaching, 38,* 529–552.

Weick, K. E. (1995). *Sensemaking in organizations.* Thousand Oaks, CA: Sage.

Weick, K. E., Sutcliffe, K. M., & Obstfeld, D. (2005). Organizing and the process of sense-making. *Organization Science, 16,* 409–421.

Wineburg, S. S. (1991). Historical problem solving: A study of the cognitive processes used in the evaluation of documentary and pictorial evidence. *Journal of Educational Psychology, 83*(1), 72–87.

Wineburg, S. S. (1994). The cognitive representation of historical texts. In G. Leinhardt, I. Beck, & C. Stainton (Eds.), *Teaching and learning in history* (pp. 85–135). Hillsdale, NJ: Lawrence Erlbaum.

Wolf, M. K., Crosson, A., & Resnick, L. B. (2006). Classroom talk for rigorous reading comprehension instruction. *Reading Psychology, 26*(1), 27–53.

Chapter 9

A Transdisciplinary Approach to Equitable Teaching in Early Childhood Education

Mariana Souto-Manning
Teachers College, Columbia University

Beverly Falk
Dina López
The City College of New York, City University of New York

Lívia Barros Cruz
Nancy Bradt
Teachers College, Columbia University

Nancy Cardwell
The City College of New York, City University of New York

Nicole McGowan
Aura Perez
Ayesha Rabadi-Raol
Elizabeth Rollins
Teachers College, Columbia University

In this review of research, we offer a meta-analysis of young children's learning and development within and across psychology, education, and linguistics. Engaging with Soja's concept of Thirdspace, we mapped young children's learning and development transdisciplinarily, seeking to (re)conceptualize early childhood teaching in ways that are answerable to intersectionally minoritized children, families, and communities of color—those whose voices, values, perspectives, and knowledges have been historically and continue to be contemporarily marginalized. To do so, we identified seven principles with the potential to transform early childhood teaching practice. We posit that together these principles can shift the architecture of early childhood teaching, offering promising possibilities for fostering equity by allowing us to move toward emancipatory praxis and negotiate practical solutions to education's long history of inequities and oppressions.

Review of Research in Education
March 2019, Vol. 43, pp. 249–276
DOI: 10.3102/0091732X18821122
Chapter reuse guidelines: sagepub.com/journals-permissions

Within a landscape where intersectionally minoritized[1] children of color are the growing demographic majority in early childhood classrooms, where research from multiple disciplines confirms that the early years of life are a critical time for learning and development, and where major investments have been made in early childhood education throughout the country (Barnett, 2017; Hustedt, Friedman, & Barnett, 2012; U.S. Department of Education, 2016), this review of research seeks to identify key ideas across disciplines to deepen our understandings of how early childhood teaching in the United States has changed historically and can change in response to shifting demographics across time in coordinated and responsive ways. Rejecting fragmented attempts to address early childhood education "best practice" for specific populations (e.g., English language learners, children with disabilities), in this review we ask,

How can a transdisciplinary meta-analysis of young children's learning within and across psychology, education, and linguistics help us foster a more equitable framework for changing early childhood teaching in ways that account for intersectionally-minoritized young children?

Our review of research is especially important given the ways in which societal practices and policies have historically and contemporarily disproportionally disadvantaged intersectionally minoritized people of color, contributing to the reproduction of inequities in and through teaching (Nieto & Bode, 2018; Pérez & Saavedra, 2017; Souto-Manning & Rabadi-Raol, 2018).

THE TRIALECTICS OF SPATIALITY AS THEORETICAL FRAMEWORK

Actuating the belief that spatial dimensions have great practical and political significance, we engage with the concepts of Firstspace, Secondspace, and Thirdspace (Soja, 1996) to interrupt the ways in which knowledge has been traditionally conceptualized. According to Soja (1996), "a Firstspace perspective . . . focuses on the 'real' material world," in contrast to "a Secondspace perspective that interprets this reality through 'imagined' representations of spatiality" (p. 6). Building on Firstspace and Secondspace perspectives, Thirdspace "can be described as a creative recombination and extension" (p. 6). It is this creative recombination and extension that guides our transdisciplinary review of research, whereby we seek to map, (re)imagine, and (re)envision teaching practices in early childhood education in ways that are answerable to children and families who have been traditionally minoritized. Thus, our review takes up and is organized according to Firstspace, Secondspace, and Thirdspace perspectives.

A *Firstspace* perspective is "explored primarily through its readable texts and contexts" (Soja, 1996, p. 22). It prioritizes and seeks to ensure continuity, mapping the traditional within existing disciplines and disciplinary boundaries. Firstspace comprises the materiality of dominant discourses. In this review, the Firstspace maps out the big ideas in early childhood education, assets-based pedagogies, and bilingual education.

In the *Secondspace*, we identify the limitations of each of these fields in isolation. Noting how social and racial inequities have affected educational practices for historically minoritized young children, families, and communities, we also consider the limitations of the other reviewed fields as they apply to the education of young children. Doing so affords us a new conceptual understanding of the need to interrupt inequity and foster equity in early childhood education by combining the strengths of each disciplinary field through a transdisciplinary approach.

While a Secondspace perspective allows us to move beyond traditionally delineated disciplinary lines, it is composed primarily of "representational discourses" (Soja, 1996, p. 22), not affording "the translation of knowledge into action in a conscious—and consciously spatial—effort to improve the world" (Soja, 1996, p. 22). This is why after reading and mapping research in distinct fields of study (Firstspace perspective) and critiquing them for their limitations (Secondspace perspective), we then offer insights into how to move early childhood teaching toward a Thirdspace, which combines the "real" and the "imagined."

Everything comes together in *Thirdspace*: subjectivity and objectivity, the abstract and the concrete, the real and the imagined, the knowable and the unimaginable, the repetitive and the differential, structure and agency, mind and body, consciousness and the unconscious, the disciplined and the transdisciplinary, everyday life and unending history. . . . This all-inclusive simultaneity opens up endless worlds to explore and, at the same time, presents daunting challenges. (Soja, 1996, pp. 56–57)

A Thirdspace perspective is particularly apt for the transdisciplinary reimagination of early childhood teaching. It rejects simplistic or single definitions of what counts as quality early childhood teaching and the societal positioning of culturally and linguistically minoritized children of color as "Other." It deconstructs status quo power hierarchies and centers multiple ways of knowing. Thirdspace is where real and imagined realities, illusions and allusions, the known and the unknown, coexist and co-construct meaning and experience. A Thirdspace epistemology pays attention to the "multiple spaces that difference makes around" (Soja, 1996, p. 86) issues pertaining to racism and entangled forms of bigotry (Kendi, 2016). It acknowledges and intentionally (re)positions difference and multiplicity as levers for transformation. Thirdspace calls us "to build further, to move on, to continuously expand the production of knowledge beyond what is presently known" (Soja, 1996, p. 61) in emancipatory and transformative ways, in ways that interrupt the marginalization of certain knowledges, perspectives, voices, and values.

Instead of focusing on the well-known practice of "Othering," a Thirdspace perspective demands thinking of thirding, "the creation of another mode of thinking about space that draws upon the material and mental spaces of the traditional dualism but extends well beyond them in scope, substance, and meaning" (Soja, 1996, p. 11), reimagining places and practices, shifting how we perceive realities, and calling for the recentering of knowledge formation, which fosters transformative understandings. Engaging in thirding, we refute the common practice of marginalizing or "Othering" intersectionally minoritized children and instead engage in centering their practices, voices, values, and knowledges in reimagining and transforming early childhood teaching (as shown by Goodwin, Cheruvu, & Genishi, 2008; Pérez & Saavedra, 2017; Souto-Manning & Rabadi-Raol, 2018).

Thirdspace invites us to position multiple ways of knowing as powerful opportunities for challenging "the existing power relations in their sources" (Soja, 1996, p. 89) and to engage in "emancipatory praxis . . . the search for practical solutions to the problems of race, class, gender, and other, often closely associated, forms of human inequality and oppression" (Soja, 1996, p. 22). This is what we seek to do in this review of research.

TRANSDISCIPLINARY METHODS

Engaging with Soja's (1996) concept of Thirdspace, our review of research is framed from a transdisciplinary perspective. Like Artiles, Dorn, and Bal (2016),

[w]e did not craft the chapter in a traditional literature review genre in which systematic searches are conducted covering a time period with specific criteria to select and code research studies. Rather, we drew from our extensive expertise and experience conducting research and synthesizing the empirical literature on the topic [of early childhood education]. (p. 780)

In doing so, we sought to develop a (re)conceptualization of early childhood teaching that is answerable to children, families, and communities of color, whose voices, values, perspectives, and knowledges have too often been missing.

Procedurally, we first reviewed literature that outlined the history of the big ideas shaping early childhood education. This initial review unveiled how early childhood education reflects society's historical deficit positioning and marginalizing of intersectionally minoritized children, families, and communities—for example, the "achievement gap" versus the "education debt" (Ladson-Billings, 2006). Mapping from the margins, we identified race, culture, and language (and their interconnections) as the key areas marginalized and invisiblized in dominant conceptualizations of early childhood teaching. Given the interconnections between culture and race (as unveiled by researchers such as Gay, 2002; Ladson-Billings, 1995; Nieto & Bode, 2018), between language and race (as identified by Alim, Rickford, & Ball, 2016; Flores & Rosa, 2015), and the knowledge that it is not race biologically but how race is codified socially that incurs inequities, we reviewed key areas related to the intersections of race and culture as they pertain to teaching (culturally responsive teaching, culturally relevant pedagogy, and culturally sustaining pedagogy) as well as key areas related to the intersections of race and language (namely, multilingualism and translanguaging).

From a Firstspace perspective, we reviewed research in child development (in psychology and health professions), assets-based pedagogies (in education), and bilingualism (in applied linguistics). In groups led by researchers in each of the afore-mentioned areas, through a constant comparative method of qualitative analysis (Glaser, 1965), we identified key principles in each of these fields of study. After developing a cartography for each of these fields, identifying the major topographies of each, we unveil what is not represented on the maps, especially attending to early childhood teaching (Secondspace). We then take a transdisciplinary approach, expanding our understanding by mapping across child development, assets-based pedagogies, and bilingualism, specifically seeking to reconceptualize early childhood teaching in ways that foundationally reposition intersectionally minoritized young children, families, and communities. That is, we move toward a reconceptualized, transdisciplinary Thirdspace for changing early childhood teaching, transcending the traditionally delineated disciplinary fields we studied. In doing so, we identify principles for changing teaching practice in early childhood education that account for the brilliance of intersectionally minoritized young children while purposefully and intentionally rejecting deficit approaches. Our focus on young intersectionally minoritized children is informed by our commitment to equity and by their dispro-portional representation in special education and disciplinary actions from preschool onward (Gilliam, 2005; Howard, 2016).

In alignment with the objective of transdisciplinary approaches, through our review, we have sought to address real-world issues—the historic and contemporary failing of intersectionally minoritized children who have been framed through deficit lenses over time. Seeking to attend to extant fragmentations in the field of teaching, such as theory and practice and interest and knowledge (Britzman, 2003), through this review, we aim to disprivilege knowledges that perpetuate inequities. We thus offer a set of principles with the potential to transform early childhood teaching—at once developmentally appropriate, culturally relevant, and linguistically sustaining. Our intention in doing so is to transform the field's understanding of early childhood teaching in ways that prioritize equity and justice.

FIRSTSPACE REVIEW: READING EXISTING TEXTS AND TRADITIONALLY DELINEATED DISCIPLINES

In this section, we offer our Firstspace mapping, reading the text and context of each of the following disciplinary fields: child development, assets-based pedagogies, and bilingualism. Each subsection below attends to these distinct cartographies. While our Firstspace cartography resulting from our review of literature is not exhaustive, it is intended to identify key topographies in the cartography of each of these disciplines.

Child Development[2]

A review of the child development literature offers key understandings that have evolved since the origins of the field. Drawing on work in psychology and the health professions and aided by philosophy and traditional conceptualizations of early education, we identify principles and practices that pertain to young children's learning and development. We begin by pointing out that the concepts identified here originated in a context that historically privileged Eurocentrism, thus establishing and perpetuating Whiteness as the norm. From this perspective, we identify major topographies in our mapping of child development and early childhood education.

All Children Have an Innate Drive to Learn

The notion of early childhood as a distinct period of development was established in the 18th century with the philosophies of Jean Jacques Rousseau and then enacted in the 19th century by Frederich Froebel, who established the first kindergarten. Central to this work were the beliefs that children have an inherent drive to learn, that learning is propelled by interest and internal motivation, and that children learn through active exploration (Feeney, Christensen, & Moravick, 1983).

Over the course of the 20th century, ideas about children and the need for a special kind of education for young children continued to develop in direct contrast to the philosophy of behaviorism, an outgrowth of earlier European philosophies that were and remain dominant in U.S. education. Child-centered approaches pushed back at behaviorism's view that the learner is an empty vessel in need of filling and that learning is an incremental process of mastering increasingly complex skills through direct instruction and repetition of skills reinforced by punishments or rewards (Lascaredes & Hinitz, 2000).

Prevalent in the emerging discipline of psychology, started by G. Stanley Hall, behaviorism led to the Child Study Movement of the early 20th century, which launched the practice of observing children as a way of learning about their thinking and growth (Cohen, Stern, Balaban, & Gropper, 2015). Further developed by B. F. Skinner (1953), behaviorism was the basis of the reductive practices of Bereiter and Englemann's DISTAR program used in some of Head Start's deficit models and other public education initiatives launched in the 1960s for no- and low-income children (Zigler & Styfco, 2010).

Young Children Learn Through Active Inquiry

Challenging behaviorism, John Dewey, an early 20th-century philosopher, theorized that learning takes place through active experiences not passive reception. He argued that education should support children's continuous progress for the purpose of nurturing democracy (Dewey, 1938/1997, 2001).

These theories were supported by the work of Jean Piaget, a Swiss psychologist, whose observational studies of young children documented how children construct understandings through activities that build on prior knowledge and experiences. As a result of his close observations, Piaget (1973) noted that young children learn best through active engagement and inquiry. He proposed stages through which all children progress.

Children's Learning Is Varied

While Piaget's theories helped establish appreciation for the uniqueness of childhood and active learning in "child-centered" classrooms, his theories of stages of development have been widely critiqued. One critique is that his theories were Eurocentric—he only observed White, middle-class, European children. Another critique is that because of the limited sample of his study, his theories did not sufficiently take into account children's prior knowledge and varying social and cultural contexts (experiences, funds of knowledge, linguistic repertoires, and cultural practices), which account for variation in their development of concrete and abstract conceptual understandings (Genishi & Dyson, 2009). These critiques were based on research showing that young children do not always follow the specific stages of development identified by Piaget, which, in turn, led to an underestimation of their capabilities (e.g., Borke, 1975; Gobbo & Chi, 1986; Nunes, Schliemann, & Carraher, 1993; Pascual-Leone, 1988; Weiten, 2017). Acknowledging these limitations, subsequent research confirmed that young children's learning is active, multimodal, and develops along unique trajectories and timelines (Genishi & Dyson, 2009, 2012; see also National Research Council, 2000; Shonkoff, 2017; Spodek & Saracho, 2013).

Sociocultural Contexts Affect Learning

In addition to theories that children learn through active experiences along unique trajectories, other studies of development have affirmed that learning results from a dynamic interaction between individuals and their sociocultural contexts and that learning takes place with assistance from "more knowledgeable" others who help children develop mental tools en route to higher order functions (Bodrova & Leong, 2006; Vygotsky, 1978). Many researchers have expanded on these ideas while also emphasizing the impact that families, communities, and cultural practices have on children's cognitive, socioemotional, and language development (e.g., Bruner, 1996; Cazden, 1981; Heath, 1983; Moll, Amanti, Neff, & Gonzalez, 1992; Rogoff, 2003). This recognition has exposed how theories that do not acknowledge sociocultural contexts stigmatize and disadvantage minoritized children, families, and communities (Goodwin et al., 2008).

Caring and Reciprocal Relationships Are Essential to Development

Cognition and emotions are integrally connected (Tronick, 1989), and thus caring and reciprocal relationships are key to children's development and learning. While this understanding emanates from Freud's psychosexual theories and Bowlby's (1969) theories of attachment, more recent research emphasizes the importance of networks of trusting and reciprocal relationships to ensure children's optimal growth and development (e.g., Greenfield & Suzuki, 1998).

Neuroscience has afforded renewed understandings about the interconnection of cognitive, socioemotional, and physical development. For example, Shonkoff and Phillips (2000) have employed neuroimaging technologies to reveal how interactions and experiences build the brain's architecture in the early years of life, laying a foundation for critical competencies influencing future capacities to learn. These findings confirm that learners build from prior knowledge to actively construct understandings of the world (Immordino-Yang, 2017).

Furthermore, research in neuroscience confirms sociocultural constructivist theories that demonstrate individuals' power to transcend and heal from adverse experiences through the protective factors of reciprocal, supportive relationships with caring adults and within families, schools, neighborhoods, and communities (Brown & Reeve, 1987; Grindal, Hinton, & Shonkoff, 2012; Rogoff, 2003). This suggests that no matter how protective factors are operationalized across cultures and contexts, care and support from families and communities can reduce the negative impact of inequity and oppression in children's lives (Lally & Mangione, 2017; Nelson & Sheridan, 2011).

These findings are significant because they challenge society's negative positioning of minoritized peoples as having deficits and genetic flaws, and instead point to the damaging consequences of societal inequities and injustices (Bloch, 1992; Delpit, 1988; Gabarino, Dubrow, Kostelny, & Pardo, 1998; Goodwin et al., 2008; Pérez & Saavedra, 2017; Polakow, 2012; Souto-Manning & Rabadi-Raol, 2018). They also challenge the notion of a singular "best practice" that does not take into account the range of life contexts and knowledges experienced by children from culturally, racially, and linguistically minoritized communities and contexts. In this way, neuroscientific findings affirm the need to value and support the varied practices, ideas, and ways of being across diverse cultures, language practices, belief structures, and life conditions (Cannella, 1997).

Summary

Research on development generally agrees that early childhood is a distinct and important time, that children learn through active and multimodal engagement with relationships and experiences, that social and emotional development are integrally connected to cognitive development, and that development is varied and is affected by children's sociocultural contexts.

While the field has developed important understandings, more insight is needed about how children are situated in diverse and complex sociocultural contexts. To do this, we turn to assets-based pedagogies and bilingual education to more fully account for the strengths and assets of diversities in people, ideas, and ways of being. We are compelled to do this because within the context of rapidly shifting demographics in the United States, we acknowledge "the extraordinary social justice mandate [. . .] to find teaching approaches that ensure all children's success" (Morrison, Robbins, & Rose, 2008, p. 433).

Assets-Based Pedagogies: Culturally Relevant, Responsive, and Sustaining Pedagogies[3]

Seeking to interrupt inequity and foster equity, a number of assets-based pedagogical approaches have been identified as possible pathways for ensuring the academic success of an increasingly diverse population of students. Notable for honoring, leveraging, building upon, and/or sustaining the cultural practices and legacies of intersectionally minoritized people of color are the following approaches: culturally responsive teaching (CRT; Gay, 2010), culturally relevant pedagogy (CRP; Ladson-Billings, 1995), and culturally sustaining pedagogy (Paris, 2012).

"Culturally responsive teaching is defined as using the cultural characteristics, experiences, and perspectives of ethnically diverse students as conduits for teaching them more effectively" (Gay, 2002, p. 106). Gay (2013) argued that "the education of racially, ethnically, and culturally diverse students should connect in-school learning to out-of-school living; promote educational equity and excellence; create community among individuals from different cultural, social, and ethnic backgrounds; and develop students' agency, efficacy, and empowerment" (p. 49). CRT calls for teachers to (a) develop a knowledge base about cultural diversity, replacing pathological perceptions of students and communities of color with strengths-based ones and learning from their families and communities; (b) include ethnic and cultural diversity content within the curriculum with the understanding that the social and cultural practices of their students are context specific; (c) build caring learning communities through "cultural scaffolding . . . using their own cultures and experiences to expand their intellectual horizons and academic achievement" (Gay, 2002, p. 109); (d) learn about what their students know and are capable of doing and engage these knowledges and abilities in communicating with students; and (e) establish a congruence between the methods of instruction and the learning styles, backgrounds, and experiences of diverse students.

Culturally relevant pedagogy is a framework comprised of three tenets: "(a) Students must experience academic success; (b) students must develop and/or maintain cultural competence; and (c) students must develop a critical consciousness through which they challenge the status quo of the current social order" (Ladson-Billings, 1995, p. 160). These tenets prioritize collective empowerment as opposed to the success of individuals, thus rejecting Eurocentrism and instead centering the ways and systems of knowing of people of color (Ladson-Billings, 2000). Instead of the academic success of students of color coming at the expense of compromising their psychosocial and cultural well-being (e.g., Fine, 1986; Fordham, 1988), CRP is predicated on the simultaneous development of academic success and maintenance of cultural integrity (Ladson-Billings, 1995). It upholds high expectations for students of color, promotes cultural competence, and supports students in developing "a broader sociopolitical consciousness that allows them to critique social norms, values, mores, and institutions that produce and maintain social inequities" (Ladson-Billings, 1995, p. 162). Thus, rather than merely accepting social inequities, culturally relevant teachers expect students to challenge norms.

In their review of research, Aronson and Laughter (2016), who reviewed more than 40 empirical studies of assets-based pedagogy, offered a helpful conceptual distinction between CRT (Gay, 2010) and CRP (Ladson-Billings, 1995): CRT focuses on teaching practice, whereas CRP prioritizes teachers' mindsets. CRT seeks "to influence competency and methods, describing what a teacher should be doing in the classroom to be culturally responsive," whereas CRP "primarily seeks to influence attitudes and dispositions, describing a posture a teacher might adopt that, when fully embodied, would determine planning, instruction, and assessment" (Aronson & Laughter, 2016, pp. 166–167). Both prioritize "social justice and the classroom as a site for social change" (Aronson & Laughter, 2016, p. 163).

Although CRT and CRP both fiercely reject deficit paradigms and go beyond diversity as difference, making important contributions to the development and understanding of assets-based pedagogies, in 2012, Paris called for a "change in stance, terminology, and practice" (p. 93). He argued that the terms CRP and CRT may not "go far enough in their orientation to the languages and literacies and other cultural practices of students and communities to ensure the valuing and maintenance of our increasingly multiethnic and multilingual society" (p. 94). Paris (2012) explained that culturally sustaining pedagogy demands "support[ing] young people in sustaining the cultural and linguistic competence of their communities while simultaneously offering access to dominant cultural competence" (p. 95). Culturally sustaining pedagogy is predicated on "a critical centering on dynamic community languages, valued practices and knowledges, student and community agency and input, historicized content and instruction, a capacity to contend with internalized oppressions, and an ability to curricularize all of this in learning settings" (Paris & Alim, 2017, p. 14). It demands revisioning the goal and purpose of teaching and learning, moving away from the performance of "White middle-class norms" and moving purposefully and deliberately toward exploring, critically problematizing, honoring, and extending "their heritage and community practices" (Paris & Alim, 2017, p. 86). Extending prior conceptualizations of assets-based pedagogies—that is, CRT and CRP—in important ways, culturally sustaining pedagogy "has as its explicit goal supporting multilingualism and multiculturalism in practice and perspective for students and teachers" (Paris, 2012, p. 95).

Morrison et al.'s (2008) review of 45 empirical research studies found that teachers engaging in assets-based teaching effectively supported student learning through the enactment of high expectations. Aronson and Laughter (2016), who reviewed more than 40 empirical studies of assets-based pedagogies, noted the effectiveness of such approaches to teaching:

Students in every content area made connections to academic cultures and gained pride in their home cultures through developing connections between the two. In math, students gained power and agency to solve problems. In science, students came to value multiple ways of creating knowledge. In history/social studies, students upended discourses of invisibility. In ELA, students saw language as a medium for connecting across cultures. In ESL, students overcame the misalignment of cultural expectations and practices. (p. 198)

It is clear that assets-based pedagogical "approaches contribute to positive racial identity, resiliency and achievement" (Hanley & Noblit, 2009, p. 52).

Drawing on Souto-Manning, Llerena, Martell, Maguire, and Arce-Boardman (2018), below we review empirical studies employing the assets-based pedagogies we identified above, which show the impact of supporting student learning through upholding high expectations and high levels of support, (re)positioning students' strengths centrally in teaching, taking responsibility for students' success, and cultivating a collaborative learning community.

Upholding High Expectations and Offering High Levels of Support

To support student learning while upholding high expectations, researchers have documented the benefits of clarifying, modeling, and scaffolding curricular expectations (Cahnmann & Remillard, 2002; Morrison et al., 2008). Cahnmann and Remillard's (2002) study of two third grade teachers in an urban setting, focusing on culturally, linguistically, and socioeconomically diverse students, shows us how modeling metacognitive strategies, collaboration, and scaffolding improved students' mathematical achievement. While having high expectations, the teachers offered high levels of support, making cultural connections with students and offering meaningful and complex mathematics problems.

(Re)positioning Students' Strengths Centrally in Teaching

Researchers have documented the need for students of color to see themselves in the texts that they read and in their teachers, which effectively position their strengths and experiences as relevant and integral (Bell & Clark, 1998; Morrison et al., 2008; Souto-Manning & Martell, 2016). For example, Bell and Clark (1998) conducted a quantitative study identifying the positive effects of using culturally relevant texts and making expectations clear to African American students; researchers examined the effects of racial images and cultural themes on the reading comprehension of African American children in first to second grades and third to fourth grades. They found that "comprehension was significantly more efficient for stories depicting both Black imagery and culturally related themes than for stories depicting both White imagery and culturally distant themes" (p. 470).

Taking Responsibility for Students' Success

High expectations can be communicated pedagogically through investments in student learning (Ladson-Billings, 1995). Bridging home and school communicative practices is an important component in taking responsibility for students' success. For example, Jiménez and Gertsen (1999) conducted a qualitative study (drawing on extensive observations and interviews) that documented student learning, with a focus on how two Latinx teachers' influences on instruction (including rapport, language, and culture) positively influenced the academic achievement of Latinx students in the elementary grades. They affirmed that "it is not so much shared ethnicity as shared cultural and social norms that influence the educational success" (p. 296) of minoritized students.

Cultivating a Collaborative Learning Community

Collaborative learning communities, which reflect students' cultural values, are important in supporting student learning (Morrison et al., 2008; Stuart & Volk, 2002). Stuart and Volk (2002) conducted a qualitative study of peer collaboration and the use of culturally relevant texts in a summer literacy program for 6- to 8-year-olds (most of whom were bilingual), documenting literacy gains. The curriculum was built on children's home experiences. The children collaborated in discussion, reading, writing, and project extensions (e.g., acting out stories). By fostering collaboration, teachers acknowledged that there was more expertise distributed in the learning community than in any individual.

Summary

The studies reviewed highlight how assets-based pedagogies are predicated on teachers enacting high expectations and high levels of support as well as taking responsibility for students' learning and development. They affirm assets-based pedagogies as effective, influencing learning. In situated ways, they show how such pedagogies come to life as teachers become learners and work to critically reshape curriculum, intentionally centering minoritized perspectives and experiences within the context of authentic relationships and collaborative communities.

Bilingualism[4]

Scholarship on bilingualism has highlighted the dynamic and complex nature of language practices. In this section, we examine recent literature that challenges long-held conceptualizations of bilingualism and consider empirical studies that focus specifically on young emergent bilinguals.

From Monoglossic to Heteroglossic Conceptualizations of Bilingualism

Once conceptualized as the possession of two separate and bound language systems, bilingualism is increasingly recognized as a dynamic and complex practice that draws on individuals' entire linguistic repertoires. García's (2009) concept of dynamic bilingualism takes us from a monoglossic perspective to a heteroglossic one. A monolingual perspective of bilingualism views languages as separate and discrete, regarding only individuals who possess equal abilities in two languages—essentially two monolingual people in one—as true bilinguals. In contrast, dynamic bilingualism suggests the "language practices of bilinguals are complex and interrelated" and "do not emerge in a linear way or function separately" (García & Wei, 2014, pp. 13–14). Hopewell and Escamilla (2015) proposed a similar concept of *holistic bilingualism* "grounded in the idea that what is known and understood in one language contributes to what is known and understood in the other, and that all languages contribute to a single and universally accessible linguistic and cognitive system" (p. 39). These theories of dynamic and holistic bilingualism have important implications for how the linguistic and discursive practices of emergent bilinguals are perceived. Within these perspectives, bilinguals do not simply switch codes or move from one language to another, but they draw on the particular linguistic resources that specific sociocultural contexts require. Thus, these practices represent less of a duality but rather "language practices [that] are multiple and ever adjusting to the multilingual multimodal terrain of the communicative act" (García, Flores, & Woodley, 2012, p. 50). As part of the theory of dynamic bilingualism, García (2009) extended the work of the Welsh scholar Cen Williams on *translanguaging* as a pedagogical practice to an understanding of *translanguaging* as the fluid and dynamic ways in which bilinguals use their linguistic resources to make sense, make meaning, and communicate with others.

Despite prevailing monolingual ideologies and policies in the United States, there are increasing numbers of children who speak languages other than dominant American English at home (Arreguín-Anderson, Salinas-Gonzalez, & Alanis, 2018; Castro, 2014; Espinosa, 2015). However, the bilingualism of young children—of indigenous and immigrant families—has historically been perceived as a major disadvantage and problem to be overcome (Flores & Rosa, 2015; Souto-Manning, 2016). For example, the notion of a "language gap" positions raciolinguistically minoritized children as limited language users and effectively places the blame on families rather than on institutions (García & Otheguy, 2016; Souto-Manning & Yoon, 2018). Bilingual children have been assigned a variety of deficit-oriented labels: "Limited English Proficient," "English as a Second Language," and "English Language Learners" (Kleyn & Stern, 2018). In contrast, the terms emergent bilingual learner and, more recently, emergent multilingual learner acknowledge children's existing home language resources as they become bilingual (García, Kleifgen, & Falchi, 2008; Kleyn & Stern, 2018).

In early childhood education, Gort and Pontier (2012) have developed a dynamic understanding of bilingual development and put forth the terms emergent bilingualism and biliteracy, which take into account a developmental perspective of young children's bilingualism. Below, we review recent empirical studies that examine the language practices of emergent bilinguals in early childhood settings organized along three themes: language practices as flexible and fluid, language development as a nonlinear and dynamic process, and bilingualism as a resource for learning.

Language Practices as Flexible and Fluid

Recent empirical studies have demonstrated that young emergent bilinguals use their language repertoires in more flexible and fluid ways than their monolingual peers (e.g., Arreguín-Anderson et al., 2018; Axelrod, 2014; Espinosa, 2015; Genishi & Dyson, 2009; Soltero-González, 2009; Souto-Manning & Martell, 2016).

Although there is still debate within the literature about the complexity and multi-plicity of language learning processes and their effect on children's development, there is growing consensus that speaking more than one language from an early age changes how the brain functions and develops (Espinosa, 2015). In a brief overview of recent neuroscience studies, Espinosa (2015) highlights that children who are exposed to more than one language from an early age develop two interconnected linguistic systems; this not only influences the general organization of the brain but also improves the brain's plasticity. Additionally, research confirms that bilingualism does not lead to confusion or language delays or disorders (Conboy, 2013; Espinosa, 2015; Hoff & Core, 2015). Furthermore, studies with young emergent bilinguals suggest that play serves as a significant tool to support bilingual language develop-ment (Arreguín-Anderson et al., 2018; Axelrod, 2014). Axelrod (2014) suggested that when students can freely experiment with and experience their full language repertoires, they use play to expand their use and knowledge of languages. Instead of perceiving the "mixing" of languages negatively, research indicates that teachers can build on students' translanguaging practices to enrich and nurture learning (Arreguín-Anderson et al., 2018; Axelrod, 2014; Genishi & Dyson, 2009; Soltero-González, 2009; Souto-Manning & Martell, 2016).

Language Development as a Nonlinear and Dynamic Process

Recent literature also highlights that in the process of learning languages, students develop awareness and domain of languages through active and dynamic experiences which often do not follow a predictable sequence (e.g., Cho, 2016; Durán, 2016; Genishi & Dyson, 2009; Guzman-Orth, Lopez, & Tolentino, 2017; Souto-Manning & Yoon, 2018). Guzman-Orth et al. (2017) highlighted translanguaging as one defining characteristic of how language is dynamic and nonlinear. Durán (2016) found that bilingual first-grade children's awareness and understanding of their audi-ence's language practices affected their written language choices. Specifically, they used both English and Spanish to write for bilingual audiences, developing "sponta-neous biliteracy," the ability to write in Spanish without formal instruction (Durán, 2016, p. 109). Furthermore, academic socialization, the values and norms of an aca-demic community, affects children's dynamic language development (Cho, 2016; García-Sánchez, 2010). A bilingual child can be perceived as high achieving in one language context but not in another, depending on the differing social, cultural, and academic expectations (Souto-Manning & Martell, 2016; Souto-Manning & Yoon, 2018). Thus, academic socialization, including learning and teaching and adult per-ceptions of language, can affect bilingual children's success in learning (Cho, 2016).

Bilingualism as a Resource for Learning

The literature also points to the importance of using children's bilingualism as a resource for learning (e.g., Durán, Roseth, Hoffman, & Robertshaw, 2013; Gort & Sembiante, 2015; Soltero-González, 2009; Souto-Manning & Martell, 2016;

Souto-Manning & Yoon, 2018). Durán et al. (2013) found that preschool students in Transitional Bilingual Education, when compared to peers in English monolingual classrooms, experienced more benefits in Spanish-language development without hindering English-language development. But research has also shown that bilingual development can happen in classrooms and programs deemed to be monolingual. Specifically, Soltero-González (2009) showed that even under Arizona's English-only mandate, bilingual children found opportunities to "draw on hybrid practices and multiple literacies . . . in student-centered social space" (p. 75), through translanguaging and referring to multiple items in both Spanish and English, for example. Simon-Cereijido and Gutiérrez-Clellen (2014) reinforced the importance of leveraging children's existing language abilities and practices for further development. Their study found that children in bilingual classrooms showed significantly increased vocabulary in both languages, compared with children in monolingual preschool classrooms. Moving from a monoglossic to a heteroglossic perspective allows bilinguals to be perceived from a strengths-based perspective and thus provides the opportunity to transform the classroom into a rich place for individual and collective learning (Gort & Sembiante, 2015).

Summary

Taken collectively, the empirical evidence supports the most recent theoretical contributions of sociolinguistics, language studies, and bilingual education. The studies reviewed highlight the ways in which young emergent bilinguals draw on their entire linguistic repertoires to make meaning and communicate in early childhood settings, how new language practices emerge in relation to existing language practices, and the ways in which bilingualism is a crucial resource for learning.

SECONDSPACE: CRITICAL INTERPRETATIONS AND REPRESENTATIONAL DISCOURSES

In this section, we take up a Secondspace perspective, attending to "representational discourses" (Soja, 1996, p. 22). Specifically, we offer critical interpretations and distinct analyses of Firstspace literatures to articulate conceptual understandings that help elucidate the gaps in each field as they pertain to the (mis)education of culturally and linguistically minoritized young children of color. While it is beyond the scope of our review to delve comprehensively into this discussion, in this section we identify some of the key silences and limitations of each disciplinary field in isolation and present a rationale for their productive synthesis and "recombination" moving toward mapping a Thirdspace (Soja, 1996) for transforming early childhood teaching.

Some Limitations of Child Development Theories

Although early conceptions of child development grounded in developmental psychology have importantly identified childhood as a distinct period of human development, the theories that evolved had significant limitations. As discussed earlier, one limitation is their (over)reliance on a White, European, middle-class perspective, as noted in the earliest critiques of Piaget's stage theories. Subsequent research and critiques from neuroscience, sociocultural, and linguistic theories continued to reframe child development as a dynamic social process, in which relationships are embedded in multiple cultural and linguistic contexts and language functions as a conduit of culture (Bruner, 1996; Cazden, 1981; Genishi & Dyson, 2009, 2012; Genishi, Dyson, & Fassler, 1994; Heath, 1983; National Research Council, 2000). More recent critiques push for a conception of child development that de-centers Whiteness, monolingualism, and monoculturalism in favor of centering the values, voices, and experiences of intersectionally minoritized communities as a matter of equity and justice (e.g., Mallory & New, 1994; Pérez & Saavedra, 2017; Souto-Manning & Rabadi-Raol, 2018). These critiques and related findings point to the need for the field of child development to more fully interrogate the theoretical centrality of Whiteness to its conceptualizations of developmental appropriateness or quality teaching practices and to (re)position the linguistic and cultural assets of intersectionally minoritized communities foundationally in and through early childhood teaching.

Some Limitations of Assets-Based Pedagogies

Culturally responsive (Gay, 2002), relevant (Ladson-Billings, 1995), and sustaining (Paris, 2012) pedagogies are promising assets-based pedagogies that seek to disrupt "the overwhelming presence of Whiteness" (Sleeter, 2001, p. 94) sponsored by traditional approaches to teaching and learning. They importantly recognize the schooling needs and assets of children of color. Three limitations pertain to their roots, applications, and positioning of early childhood education. Assets-based pedagogies are firmly rooted in the U.S. context and could benefit from further engagement with global south onto-epistemologies. As explained by Pérez and Saavedra (2017), "Global south onto-epistemologies decolonize and disrupt global north dominance by centering the lived ways of knowing and being of minoritized peoples . . . [and] have great promise to transform early childhood education" (p. 2). In terms of applications, there have been misinterpretations of these assets-based pedagogies, such as regarding culturally responsive as meaning to be responsive to culture, and culturally relevant to be relevant to cultures, which make up the classroom community, apart from the frameworks and tenets undergirding these approaches. Thus, teachers attempting to engage in CRT (Gay, 2013) by incorporating culturally specific content into the curriculum may, in effect, do so in stereotyped ways. This is visible in "heroes and holidays" approaches (described in Lee, Menkart, & Okazawa-Rey, 2002). Finally, while some research on assets-based approaches to teaching young children has been published (e.g., Souto-Manning, 2009, 2013; Souto-Manning et al., 2018; Souto-Manning & Martell, 2016), much research on these approaches examines the experiences of older children (as visible in the following reviews of empirical research; Aronson & Laughter, 2016; Morrison et al., 2008). Thus, early childhood education has often been positioned marginally in assets-based pedagogies. Given these limitations, it is useful to consider how child development and bilingualism might productively inform assets-based pedagogies, specifically attending to the education of young children.

Some Limitations of Bilingualism Research

While recent contributions in bilingualism research offer important insights about the dynamic and flexible language practices of bilingual individuals and communities, there are gaps regarding bilingualism research and the teaching of young bilingual children. Here we identify three. First, while theories of dynamic bilingualism and translanguaging help us understand languaging and language practices, they are often not specific to young children's development. The work of Gort and Pontier (2012) on emergent bilingualism and biliteracy begins to address this gap, but further research is needed to understand how young bilinguals develop and engage their linguistic repertoires. Second, while there has been research on understanding instructional models such as dual language bilingual programs and the "effectiveness" of their language allocation policies (e.g., Baker & Wright, 2017), these studies address the academic and educational outcomes associated with varying bilingual models but less so the cognitive and socioemotional development of bilingual children, thus not undertaking a whole child perspective (Siddle Walker, 1996). The scarce but growing literature that brings together play, socially mediated language practices, and bilingual development is beginning to address this limitation (e.g., Arreguín-Anderson et al., 2018; Axelrod, 2014). Finally, while dynamic bilingualism attempts to move away from understanding languages as bound systems and toward how people use languages, there has been less emphasis on understanding (a) languages as conduits of cultural practices and (b) cultures as dynamic, rather than fixed (Paris & Alim, 2017).

Our transdisciplinary analysis is predicated on our belief that these three disciplinary fields of study can be strengthened and informed by one another, addressing the limitations identified by our review informed by a Secondspace perspective. Seeking to move from real or imagined realities toward a Thirdspace perspective, we reenvision early childhood teaching transdisciplinarily, in ways that interrupt inequities and foster equity and justice.

TOWARD A THIRDSPACE FOR EARLY CHILDHOOD TEACHING

The seven principles we identify below offer promising possibilities for changing inequitable teaching practices and fostering equity in and through teaching in early childhood education, thereby helping the field move toward a Thirdspace for transforming early childhood teaching. Although we do not include all the literature we reviewed in the identification of these principles due to length restrictions, they are rooted in topographies across the cartographies of child development, assets-based

pedagogies, and bilingualism. We posit that such principles (see Figure 1) can contribute to changing early childhood teaching practices in ways that foundationally
account for racial, cultural, linguistic, and developmental diversities—an important
contribution to the field in light of early childhood education's shifting demographics
and persistent racial disproportionality, which demand a change in teaching
practices.

Below, we briefly describe each of these foundational principles, which are manifested in three aspects of curriculum: formal, symbolic, and societal. Formal classroom and school contexts comprise what is studied and how it is taught. Symbolic
curriculum—classroom organization, semiotics, and materials— encompasses what
is displayed on the walls, what materials are made available, how the diverse ways that
individual children learn are built into the structure of the classroom. Societal curriculum accounts for the quality of the relationships that adults in the school/class-
room have with children, families, communities, as well as with each other, and their
perceptions of and interactions with children and families (Gay, 2002).

All Children Can Learn

The first principle is the foundational belief that all children can learn. While the
history of early childhood education was founded on the notion that "all" children
have an inherent drive to learn (Feeney et al., 1983), because this thinking emanated
from Eurocentric philosophies and epistemologies (Ladson-Billings, 2000), our
transdisciplinary review and analysis of research unveiled how "all" did not sufficiently represent or include children from minoritized backgrounds (Siddle Walker,
1996). This principle is predicated on viewing intersectionally minoritized young
children's and families' cultural repertoires and language practices as assets, while
challenging and troubling deficit assumptions and stereotypes about minoritized
children and their families. It also involves adults ensuring equitable opportunities
for learning, taking responsibility for children's progress, and holding high expectations for young children across racial, cultural, linguistic, and socioeconomic backgrounds as well as dis/abilities.

Young Children's Learning Is Varied

Closely connected to the notion that all children can learn is the understanding
that children's learning is varied (Genishi & Dyson, 2009, 2012; National Research
Council, 2000). Transdisciplinary research acknowledges young children's progress
along different trajectories and timelines. This principle requires that educators
recognize, affirm, and support children's differing strengths, needs, experiences,
and interests; their different paces and styles of learning and development; their
diverse ways of expression and varied paces in emotional and social development;
and the variations in their learning and development stemming from sociocultural
contexts, practices, and experiences. It requires understanding the cultural nature
of learning and of child development (Rogoff, 2003).

FIGURE 1
Foundational Principles for Equitable Teaching in Early Childhood Education

All children can learn.
Curriculum and teaching challenge and support all children
Adults take responsibility for progress and growth of children
Interests, cultural and language backgrounds are seen as assets
Opportunities for learning are varied regardless of age, culture, dis/ability
Home languages and cultural knowledges are validated and leveraged
Assumptions and stereotypes are challenged/troubled
Adults access multiple available resources

Young children's learning is varied.
Strengths, needs, and interests (... are acknowledged, valued, supported)
Pace, trajectory, and style
Ways of expression and social-emotional development
Sociocultural contexts and experiences

Young children are active and multimodal meaning makers.
Children are actively engaged as doers through multiple modalities
Children are supported to use multiple communicative repertoires
Children have opportunities to self-initiate and make choices
Opportunities exist for engagement in child-initiated and child-led play
Multiple cultural influences on children's development are sustained
Interdisciplinary approaches to learning are supported

Young children's sociocultural contexts are valuable assets for learning.
Multiple cultural and language referents and bodies of knowledge are used
Practices/policies are culturally relevant, supportive, and responsive to children and families
Family funds of knowledge and community resources are recognized, valued, included
Children are supported to develop/have a positive sense of identity
Families and communities are positioned and included as partners in learning

Young children's languaging practices are diverse, fluid, and flexible.
Language practices are recognized, valued, supported as fluid and flexible
Language development is seen as a non-linear and dynamic process
Children's existing language practices are valued and built upon in/through teaching
Multiple languages are honored and leveraged as resources
Efforts are made to include, communicate with, and learn from and with families

(continued)

FIGURE 1 (CONTINUED)

Young children learn and develop within the context of caring and reciprocal relationships.
Caring and reciprocal relationships are cultivated, developed, and enacted
Children's questions and concerns are acknowledged and addressed
Children's understandings, interests, experiences are acknowledged and honored in curriculum
Children are supported to develop agency – advocacy, independence, self-regulation
Children are encouraged and supported to be inclusive and empathetic
Practices and policies are centered on the whole child
Young children are critical thinkers and inquirers.
Critical thinking and questioning are promoted and fostered
Controversies and stereotypes are dealt with directly
Social norms are interrogated (rather than accepted as truths)
Curriculum and teaching make space for children and teachers to problematize social inequities
Multiple perspectives are promoted and fostered
Issues of fairness and inclusivity are welcomed, fostered, promoted, and incorporated

Young Children Are Active and Multimodal Meaning Makers

Acknowledging that all children's learning and development is varied and that all children can learn, this principle attends to how young children learn. Considering young children's purposeful and reciprocal engagements and interactions, transdisciplinary research findings support the understanding that young children are active and multimodal meaning makers. Engaging with a Thirdspace perspective for reimagining and transforming early childhood teaching requires acknowledging and supporting a range of timelines (Genishi & Dyson, 2009, 2012), facilitating a range of learning experiences (e.g., individual, small group, whole class) that actively engage young children as doers, and supporting their multimodal meaning making and sophisticated communicative repertoires (e.g., Arreguín-Anderson et al., 2018; Axelrod, 2014; Genishi & Dyson, 2009; Soltero-González, 2009; Souto-Manning et al., 2018; Souto-Manning & Martell, 2016; Souto-Manning & Yoon, 2018). This view of teaching also requires educators to provide children with opportunities to self-initiate and make choices, engage in child-initiated and child-led play, as well as interdisciplinary approaches to learning (National Research Council, 2000). In doing so, early childhood teaching engages in the systematic and purposeful recognition, leveraging, and support of multiple cultural and linguistic practices and legacies.

Young Children's Sociocultural Contexts Are Valuable Assets for Learning

Our transdisciplinary review and analysis of research revealed that another key principle is recognizing and valuing young children's sociocultural contexts as assets foundational for learning and development (e.g., Axelrod, 2014; Moll et al., 1992; Souto-Manning et al., 2018; Souto-Manning & Martell, 2016; Souto-Manning & Yoon, 2018; Vygotsky, 1978). This principle calls for practices and policies to centrally account for multiple cultural and language referents and bodies of knowledge, paying particular attention to those that have been historically minoritized. This means that families' funds of knowledge (Moll et al., 1992) and community resources (Souto-Manning, 2013) need to be identified, recognized, valued, leveraged, and sustained and that intersectionally minoritized families and communities must be positioned as full partners in teaching and learning. Research across disciplines underscores how such learning environments support children in developing positive self-identity and empathy across cultures, languages, and socioeconomics, while simultaneously ensuring that children do not "grow up with an exaggerated sense of their own importance and value in the world—a dangerous ethnocentrism" (Bishop, 1990, p. x).

Young Children's Languaging Practices Are Diverse, Fluid, and Flexible

This principle requires teachers to support linguistic diversity as a norm (Genishi & Dyson, 2009) in and through their teaching practices. According to our review and analysis of research across disciplines, support for linguistic diversity involves the need for teachers to learn about their students' communicative practices and to intentionally and strategically engage in translanguaging to support learning (e.g., Arreguín-Anderson et al., 2018; Axelrod, 2014; Genishi & Dyson, 2009; Soltero-González, 2009; Souto-Manning & Martell, 2016; Souto-Manning & Yoon, 2018), develop cultural competence (Ladson-Billings, 1995), and sustain young children's rich languaging repertoires (Paris, 2012; Paris & Alim, 2017). Doing so decenters dominant American English so that multilingualism—in all its forms—can be fully embraced and sustained. Embracing multilingualism includes ensuring that young children's multiple languaging practices be recognized, valued, and leveraged as resources in learning, and that the classroom landscape (including tools, materials, and artifacts) reflects the full range of their linguistic repertoires as well as the linguistic repertoires of their families and communities. It also involves teachers acknowledging the varied processes by which multilingual children develop their linguistic repertoires, not stigmatizing or characterizing children as deficient as a result of the pace of their language learning processes, and making efforts to communicate with, include, and learn from and with families in their home languages.

Young Children Learn and Develop Within the Context of Caring and Reciprocal Relationships

Teaching and learning are relational endeavors (Freire, 2000, 2005; Souto-Manning & Yoon, 2018), and young children learn within the context of caring and reciprocal relationships (with families, community members, teachers, and peers). As it relates to classroom communities, this principle stresses ensuring that children's thoughts, ideas, and voices are heard; that their questions and concerns are acknowledged and addressed; and that their understandings, interests, and experiences are honored and used to create, revise, or adapt learning experiences. Additionally, this principle demands that young children are supported to develop agency (advocacy, independence, and self-regulation) and are encouraged to be inclusive and empathetic with each other. Our review and analyses of research point toward the importance of teaching practices and policies (of the classroom and school) centered on the whole child (Siddle Walker, 1996).

Young Children Are Critical Thinkers and Inquirers

Rooted in literature that affirms young children as active inquirers who are aware of inequities and competent in understanding and/or discussing issues of fairness (e.g., Derman-Sparks & Phillips, 1997; Paley, 1986; Ramsey, 2015; Souto-Manning, 2013; Souto-Manning et al., 2018; Souto-Manning & Martell, 2016), this principle requires fostering critical thinking and questioning—engaging with controversies, interrupting, and interrogating social norms as truths in and through early childhood teaching, from infancy on (Souto-Manning, 2013; Souto-Manning & Yoon, 2018). Curriculum and teaching make space for children and teachers to problematize social inequities while multiple perspectives and issues of fairness and inclusivity are welcomed and nurtured. The development of cultural competence and critical consciousness (Ladson-Billings, 1995) are centered. At the same time that these critical skills are supported and children's linguistic and cultural practices are affirmed and sustained, attention is paid to ensuring that they simultaneously develop the skills and knowledges needed to successfully navigate—and to eventually work to interrupt and dismantle—the culture of power (Delpit, 1988). This principle "seeks to perpetuate and foster—to sustain—linguistic, literate, and cultural pluralism as part of the democratic project of schooling" (Paris, 2012, p. 95).

Taken together, these seven principles reconceptualize early childhood teaching in ways that are answerable to minoritized young children and communities who have historically been underserved, marginalized, and invisiblized in and through education systems (Pérez & Saavedra, 2017; Souto-Manning & Rabadi-Raol, 2018). Thus, they afford us pathways for transforming the architecture of early childhood education (Teacher Education Exchange, 2017) in ways that center assets-based pedagogies and honor multilingualism and translanguaging in integral ways.

CONCLUSION AND IMPLICATIONS FOR THE FIELD

Our transdisciplinary review of research resulted in seven principles for shifting the architecture of early childhood teaching, for changing teaching in ways that foster equity in and through teaching in early childhood education across formal, symbolic, and societal contexts (Gay, 2002). Rooted in key findings from our qualitative transdisciplinary analysis, we offer them as guidelines that can be used for transforming early childhood teaching practices in ways that foundationally account for racial, cultural, and linguistic diversities.

Moving forward, we encourage our early childhood education colleagues to reflect on teaching in relation to these principles. And we encourage researchers as well as educators to document teaching and learning environments that embody these principles. After all, we need more situated representations of what equitable teaching looks like in early childhood education in order to educate and inspire our profession and better support the learning and development of the young children we serve.

Early childhood education's shifting demographics, diversities, and enduring racial disproportionality urgently call for a transformation in teaching practices, one that moves away from Eurocentric notions of teaching practices and instead fully honors, leverages, develops, and sustains the strengths and assets of intersectionally minoritized peoples—their ideas, ways of being, and systems of knowing. We posit that the principles we identify in our transdisciplinary review of research are starting points for this much-needed transformation, allowing us to move toward emancipatory praxis; toward practical solutions to the long history of racism and closely associated inequities and oppressions that are manifested in U.S. education—from early childhood onward. These principles address a real problem as they offer a possible pathway toward realizing more equitable and just teaching practices in early childhood education.

ACKNOWLEDGMENTS

This review of research is the product of collective work completed as part of a study supported by a grant from the Foundation for Child Development. Mariana Souto-Manning and Beverly Falk are the co–principal investigators of the study resulting in the work reflected in this chapter. Mariana Souto-Manning took the lead conceptualizing and writing the first draft of this chapter. Along with Mariana Souto-Manning, Beverly Falk and Dina López led the review of research in particular disciplines (resulting in Firstspace reviews of Child Development and Bilingualism, respectively). The ordering of other authors' names is alphabetical; although imperfect, it signals equal co-authorship.

NOTES

[1] We employ the term intersectionally minoritized instead of minority because "it more accurately conveys the power relations and processes by which certain groups are socially, economically, and politically marginalized within the larger society" (McCarty, 2002, p. xv). Combining minoritized with intersectional acknowledges "prejudice stemming from the intersections of racist ideas and other forms of bigotry" (Kendi, 2016, p. 5).

[2] This subsection was developed under the leadership of Beverly Falk.

[3] This subsection was developed under the leadership of Mariana Souto-Manning.

[4] This subsection was developed under the leadership of Dina López.

REFERENCES

Alim, H. S., Rickford, J. R., & Ball, A. (Eds.). (2016). *Raciolinguistics: How language shapes our ideas about race.* New York, NY: Oxford University Press.

Aronson, B., & Laughter, J. (2016). The theory and practice of culturally relevant education: A synthesis of research across content areas. *Review of Educational Research, 86,* 163–206.

Arreguín-Anderson, M. G., Salinas-Gonzalez, I., & Alanis, I. (2018). Translingual play that promotes cultural connections, invention, and regulation: A LatCrit perspective. *International Multilingual Research Journal, 12,* 273–287. doi:10.1080/19313152.2018 .1470434

Artiles, A., Dorn, S., & Bal, A. (2016). Objects of protection, enduring nodes of difference: Disability intersections with "other" differences, 1916 to 2016. *Review of Research in Education, 40,* 777–820. doi:10.3102/0091732X16680606

Axelrod, Y. (2014). "Todos vamos a jugar, even the teachers": Everyone playing together. *Young Children, 69*(2), 24–31.

Baker, C., & Wright, W. (2017). *Foundations of bilingual education and bilingualism* (6th ed.). Bristol, England: Multilingual Matters.

Barnett, W. S. (2017). *Getting the facts right on pre-k and the president's prek-k proposal.* New Brunswick, NJ: NIEER.

Bell, Y., & Clark, T. (1998). Culturally relevant reading material as related to comprehension and recall in African American children. *Journal of Black Psychology, 24,* 455–475.

Bishop, R. S. (1990). Mirrors, windows, and sliding glass doors. *Perspectives, 6*(3), ix–xi.

Bloch, M. (1992). Critical perspectives on the historical relationship between child development and early childhood education research. In S. Kessler & E. B. Swadener (Eds.), *Reconceptualizing the early childhood curriculum: Beginning the dialogue* (pp. 3–20). New York, NY: Teachers College Press.

Bodrova, E., & Leong, D. (2006). *Tools of the mind.* New York, NY: Pearson.

Borke, H. (1975). Piaget's mountains revisited: Changes in the egocentric landscape. *Developmental Psychology, 11,* 240–243.

Bowlby, J. (1969). *Attachment and loss.* New York, NY: Basic Books.

Britzman, D. (2003). *Practice makes practice: A critical study of learning to teach* (Rev. ed.). Albany: State University of New York Press.

Brown, A. L., & Reeve, R. A. (1987). Bandwidths of competence: The role of supportive contexts in learning and development. In L. S. Liben (Ed.), *Development and learning: Conflict or congruence?* (pp. 173–223). Hillsdale, NJ: Erlbaum.

Bruner, J. (1996). *The culture of education.* Cambridge, MA: Harvard University Press.

Cahnmann, M. S., & Remillard, J. T. (2002). What counts and how: Mathematics teaching in culturally, linguistically, and socioeconomically diverse urban settings. *Urban Review, 34,* 179–204.

Cannella, G. S. (1997). *Deconstructing early childhood education: Social justice and revolution.* New York, NY: Peter Lang.

Castro, D. (2014). The development and early care and education of dual language learners: Examining the state of knowledge. *Early Childhood Research Quarterly, 29,* 693–698.

Cazden, C. B. (1981). *Language in early childhood education.* Washington, DC: National Association for the Education of Young Children.

Cho, H. (2016). Formal and informal academic language socialization of a bilingual child. *International Journal of Bilingual Education and Bilingualism, 19,* 387–407.

Cohen, D., Stern, S., Balaban, N., & Gropper, N. (2015). *Observing and recording the behavior of young children.* New York, NY: Teachers College Press.

Conboy, B. (2013). Neuroscience research: How experience with one or multiple languages affects the developing brain. In State Advisory Council on Early Learning and Care (Ed.), *California's best practices for young dual language learners: Research overview papers* (pp. 1–37). Sacramento: California Department of Education. Retrieved from https://www.cde.ca.gov/sp/cd/ce/documents/dllresearchpapers.pdf

Delpit, L. (1988). The silenced dialogue: Power and pedagogy in educating other people's children. *Harvard Educational Review, 58,* 280–298.

Derman-Sparks, L., & Phillips, C. B. (1997). *Teaching/learning anti-racism: A developmental approach.* New York, NY: Teachers College Press.

Dewey, J. (1997). *Experience and education.* New York, NY: Touchstone. (Original work published 1938)

Dewey, J. (2001). *The school and society.* New York, NY: Dover.

Durán, L. (2016). Audience and young bilingual writers: Building on strengths. *Journal of Literacy Research, 49*(1), 92–114.

Durán, L., Roseth, C., Hoffman, P., & Robertshaw, B. (2013). Spanish-Speaking preschoolers' early literacy development: A longitudinal experimental comparison of predominantly English and transitional bilingual education. *Bilingual Research Journal, 36*(1), 6–34.

Espinosa, L. M. (2015). Challenges and benefits of early bilingualism in the U.S. context. *Global Education Review, 2*(1), 40–53.

Feeney, S., Christensen, D., & Moravick, E. (1983). *Who am I in the lives of children? An introduction to teaching young children.* Columbus, OH: Charles E. Merrill.

Fine, M. (1986). Why urban adolescents drop into and out of high school. *Teachers College Record, 87,* 393–409.

Flores, N., & Rosa, J. (2015). Undoing appropriateness: Raciolinguistic ideologies and language diversity in education. *Harvard Educational Review, 85,* 149–171.

Fordham, S. (1988). Racelessness as a factor in Black student's school success: Pragmatic strategy or pyrrhic victory? *Harvard Educational Review, 58,* 54–84.

Freire, P. (2000). *Pedagogy of the oppressed* (30th anniversary ed.). New York, NY: Continuum.

Freire, P. (2005). *Teachers as cultural workers: Letters to those who dare teach.* Boulder, CO: Westview Press.

Gabarino, J., Dubrow, N., Kostelny, K., & Pardo, C. (1998). *Children in danger: Coping with the consequences of community violence.* San Francisco, CA: Jossey-Bass.

García, O. (2009). *Bilingual education in the 21st century: A global perspective.* West Sussex, England: Wiley-Blackwell.

García, O., Flores, N., & Woodley, H. (2012). Transgressing monolingualism and bilingual dualities: Translanguaging pedagogies. In A. Yiakoumetti (Ed.), *Harnessing linguistic variation to improve education* (pp. 45–75). Oxford, England: Peter Lang.

García, O., Kleifgen, J. A., & Falchi, L. (2008). *From English language learners to emergent bilinguals.* New York, NY: Campaign for Educational Equity.

García, O., & Otheguy, R. (2016). Interrogating the language gap of young bilingual and bidialectal students. *International Multilingual Research Journal, 11*(1), 52–65.

García, O., & Wei, L. (2014). *Translanguaging: Language, bilingualism and education.* New York, NY: Palgrave Macmillan.

García-Sánchez, I. M. (2010). The politics of Arabic language education: Moroccan immigrant children's socialization into ethnic and religious identities. *Linguistics and Education, 21,* 171–196.

Gay, G. (2002). Preparing for culturally responsive teaching. *Journal of Teacher Education, 53,* 106–116.

Gay, G. (2010). *Culturally responsive teaching: Theory, research, and practice.* New York, NY: Teachers College Press.

Gay, G. (2013). Teaching to and through cultural diversity. *Curriculum Inquiry, 43*(1), 48–70.

Genishi, C., & Dyson, A. H. (2009). *Children, language, and literacy: Diverse learners in diverse times.* New York, NY: Teachers College Press.

Genishi, C., & Dyson, A. H. (2012). Racing to the top: Who's accounting for the children? *Bank Street Occasional Papers, 27,* 18–20.

Genishi, C., Dyson, A. H., & Fassler, R. (1994). Language and diversity in early childhood: Whose voices are appropriate? In B. Mallory & R. New (Eds.), *Diversity and developmentally appropriate practices: Challenges for early childhood education* (pp. 250–268). New York, NY: Teachers College Press.

Gilliam, W. (2005). *Prekindergarteners left behind: Expulsion rates in state prekindergarten programs.* New York, NY: Foundation for Child Development.

Glaser, B. G. (1965). The constant comparative method of qualitative analysis. *Social Problems, 12*, 436–445.

Gobbo, C., & Chi, M. (1986). How knowledge is structured and used by expert and novice children. *Cognitive Development, 1*, 221–237.

Goodwin, A. L., Cheruvu, R., & Genishi, C. (2008). Responding to multiple diversities in early childhood education. In C. Genishi & A. L. Goodwin (Eds.), *Diversities in early childhood education: Rethinking and doing* (pp. 3–10). New York, NY: Routledge.

Gort, M., & Pontier, R. (2012). Exploring bilingual pedagogies in dual language preschool classrooms. *Language and Education, 27*, 223–245.

Gort, M., & Sembiante, S. F. (2015). Navigating hybridized language learning spaces through translanguaging pedagogy: Dual language preschool teachers' languaging practices in support of emergent bilingual children's performance of academic discourse. *International Multilingual Research Journal, 9*(1), 7–25.

Greenfield, P. M., & Suzuki, L. K. (1998). Culture and human development: Implications for parenting, education, pediatrics, and mental health. In I. E. Sigel & K. A. Renninger (Eds.), *Handbook of social psychology: Child psychology in practice* (pp. 1059–1109). New York, NY: Wiley.

Grindal, T. A., Hinton, C., & Shonkoff, J. P. (2012). The science of early childhood development: Lessons for teachers and caregivers. In B. Falk (Ed.), *Defending childhood: Keeping the promise of early education* (pp. 13–23). New York, NY: Teachers College Press.

Guzman-Orth, D., Lopez, A. A., & Tolentino, F. (2017). *A framework for the dual language assessment of young dual language learners in the United States.* Retrieved from https://files.eric.ed.gov/fulltext/EJ1168394.pdf

Hanley, M. S., & Noblit, G. (2009). *Cultural responsiveness, racial identity, and academic success: A review of literature.* Retrieved from http://www.heinz.org/userfiles/library/culture-report_final.pdf

Heath, S. B. (1983). *Ways with words: Language, life and work in communities and classrooms.* New York, NY: Cambridge University Press.

Hoff, E., & Core, C. (2015). What clinicians need to know about bilingual development. *Seminars in Speech and Language, 36*(2), 89–99.

Hopewell, S., & Escamilla, K. (2015). How does a holistic perspective on bi/multiliteracy help educators address the demands of Common Core State Standards for ELLs/emergent bilinguals? In G. Valdés, K. Menken, & M. Castro (Eds.), *Common Core and English language learners/emergent bilinguals: A guide for all educators* (pp. 39–40). Philadelphia, PA: Caslon.

Howard, T. (2016). Why black lives (and minds) matter: Race, freedom schools and the quest for educational equity. *Journal of Negro Education, 85*, 101–113.

Hustedt, J. T., Friedman, A. H., & Barnett, W. S. (2012). Investments in early education: Resources at the federal and state levels. In R. Pianta & S. Sheridan (Eds.), *Handbook of early childhood education* (pp. 48–72). New York, NY: Guilford Press.

Immordino-Yang, M. H. (2017). *Emotions, learning and the brain.* New York, NY: Norton.

Jiménez, R., & Gertsen, R. (1999). Lessons and dilemmas derived from the literacy instruction of two Latina/o teachers. *American Educational Research Journal, 36*, 265–301.

Kendi, I. (2016). *Stamped from the beginning: The definitive history of racist ideas in America.* New York, NY: Nation Books.

Kleyn, T., & Stern, N. (2018). Labels as limitations. *MinneTESOL Journal, 34,* 1–9.

Ladson-Billings, G. (1995). But that's just good teaching! The case for culturally relevant pedagogy. *Theory into Practice, 34,* 159–165.

Ladson-Billings, G. (2000). Racialized discourses and ethnic epistemologies. In N. Denzin & Y. S. Lincoln (Eds.), *The Sage handbook of qualitative research* (2nd ed., pp. 257–277). Thousand Oaks, CA: Sage.

Ladson-Billings, G. (2006). From the achievement gap to the education debt: Understanding achievement in U.S. schools. *Educational Researcher, 35*(7), 3–12.

Lally, J. R., & Mangione, P. (2017). *Caring relationships: The heart of early brain development.* Retrieved from https://www.naeyc.org/resources/pubs/yc/may2017/caring-relationships-heart-early-brain-development

Lascaredes, V. C., & Hinitz, B. F. (2000). *The history of early childhood education.* New York, NY: Falmer Press.

Lee, E., Menkart, D., & Okazawa-Rey, M. (Eds.). (2002). *Beyond heroes and holidays: A practical guide to K–12 anti-racist, multicultural education and staff development.* Washington, DC: Teaching for Change.

Mallory, B., & New, R. (Eds.). (1994). *Diversity and developmentally appropriate practices: Challenges for early childhood curriculum.* New York, NY: Teachers College Press.

McCarty, T. (2002). *A place to be Navajo: Rough Rock and the struggle for self-determination in Indigenous schooling.* New York, NY: Routledge.

Moll, L., Amanti, C., Neff, D., & Gonzalez, N. (1992). Funds of knowledge for teaching: Using a qualitative approach to connect homes and classrooms. *Theory into Practice, 31,* 132–141.

Morrison, K., Robbins, H., & Rose, D. (2008). Operationalizing culturally relevant pedagogy: A synthesis of classroom-based research. *Equity and Excellence in Education, 41,* 433–452.

National Research Council. (2000). *Eager to learn: Educating our preschoolers.* Washington, DC: National Academy Press.

Nelson, C. A., & Sheridan, M. A. (2011). Lesson from neuroscience research for understanding causal links between family and neighborhood characteristics and educational outcomes. In G. J. Duncan & R. J. Murnane (Eds.), *Whither opportunity* (pp. 27–46). New York, NY: Russell Sage Foundation.

Nieto, S., & Bode, P. (2018). *Affirming diversity: The sociopolitical context of multicultural education* (7th ed.). New York, NY: Teachers College Press.

Nunes, T., Schliemann, A., & Carraher, D. (1993). *Street mathematics and school mathematics.* Cambridge, England: Cambridge University Press.

Paley, V. G. (1986). On listening to what children say. *Harvard Educational Review, 56,* 122–132.

Paris, D. (2012). Culturally sustaining pedagogy: A needed change in stance, terminology, and practice. *Educational Researcher, 41*(3), 93–97.

Paris, D., & Alim, H. S. (Eds.). (2017). *Culturally sustaining pedagogies: Teaching and learning for justice in a changing world.* New York, NY: Teachers College Press.

Pascual-Leone, J. (1988). Affirmations and negotiations, disturbances and contradictions in understanding Piaget: Is his later theory causal? *Contemporary Psychology, 33,* 420–421.

Pérez, M. S., & Saavedra, C. (2017). A call for onto-epistemological diversity in early childhood education and care: Centering global South conceptualizations of childhood/s. *Review of Research in Education, 41,* 1–29. doi:10.3102/0091732X16688621

Piaget, J. (1973). *To understand is to invent: The future of education.* New York, NY: Grossman.

Polakow, V. (2012). Foreclosed childhoods: Poverty, inequality, and discarding the young. In B. Falk (Ed.), *Defending childhood: Keeping the promise of early education* (pp. 89–113). New York, NY: Teachers College Press.

Ramsey, P. (2015). *Teaching and learning in a diverse world: Multicultural education for young children* (4th ed.). New York, NY: Teachers College Press.

Rogoff, B. (2003). *The cultural nature of human development.* New York, NY: Oxford University Press.

Shonkoff, J. (2017). Breakthrough impacts: What science tells us about supporting early childhood development. *Young Children, 72*(2), 8–16.

Shonkoff, J., & Phillips, D. (Eds.). (2000). *From neurons to neighborhoods: The science of early childhood development.* Washington, DC: National Academies Press.

Siddle Walker, V. (1996). *Their highest potential: An African American school community in the segregated south.* Chapel Hill: University of North Carolina Press.

Simon-Cereijido, G., & Gutiérrez-Clellen, V. (2014). Bilingual education for all: Latino dual language learners with language disabilities. *International Journal of Bilingual Education and Bilingualism, 17*, 235–254.

Skinner, B. F. (1953). *Science and human behavior.* New York, NY: Macmillan.

Sleeter, C. (2001). Preparing teachers for culturally diverse schools: Research and the overwhelming presence of whiteness. *Journal of Teacher Education, 52*(2), 94–106.

Soja, E. (1996). *Thirdspace: Journeys to Los Angeles and other real-and-imagined places.* Malden, MA: Blackwell.

Soltero-González, L. (2009). The hybrid literacy practices of young immigrant children: Lessons learned from an English-only preschool classroom. *Bilingual Research Journal, 31*(1–2), 75–93.

Souto-Manning, M. (2009). Negotiating culturally responsive pedagogy through multicultural children's literature: Towards critical democratic literacy practices in a first grade classroom. *Journal of Early Childhood Literacy, 9*(1), 53–77.

Souto-Manning, M. (2013). *Multicultural teaching in the early childhood classroom: Strategies, tools, and approaches, preschool–2nd grade.* New York, NY: Teachers College Press.

Souto-Manning, M. (2016). Honoring and building on the rich literacy practices of young bilingual and multilingual learners. *Reading Teacher, 70*, 263–271.

Souto-Manning, M., Llerena, C. L., Martell, J., Maguire, A. S., & Arce-Boardman, A. (2018). *No more culturally irrelevant teaching.* Portsmouth, NH: Heinemann.

Souto-Manning, M., & Martell, J. (2016). *Reading, writing, and talk: Inclusive teaching strategies for diverse learners, K–2.* New York, NY: Teachers College Press.

Souto-Manning, M., & Rabadi-Raol, A. (2018). (Re)centering quality in early childhood education: Toward intersectional justice for minoritized children. *Review of Research in Education, 42*, 203–225. doi:10.3102/0091732X18759550

Souto-Manning, M., & Yoon, H. S. (2018). *Reading and rewriting worlds: Rethinking early literacies.* London, England: Routledge.

Spodek, B., & Saracho, O. N. (Eds.). (2013). *Handbook of research on the education of young children* (3rd ed.). New York, NY: Routledge.

Stuart, D., & Volk, D. (2002). Collaboration in a culturally responsive literacy pedagogy: Educating teachers and Latino children. *Reading: Literacy and Language, 36*, 127–134.

Teacher Education Exchange. (2017). *Teacher development 3.0: How we can transform the professional education of teachers.* Retrieved from http://eprints.brighton.ac.uk/17956/1/teacherdevelopmentthreepointzero.pdf

Tronick, E. (1989). Emotions and emotional communication in infants. *American Psychologist, 44*, 112–119.

U.S. Department of Education. (2016). *The state of racial diversity in the educator workforce.* Washington, DC: Office of Planning, Evaluation and Policy Development.

Vygotsky, L. (1978). *Mind in society.* Cambridge, MA: Harvard University Press.

Weiten, W. (2017). *Psychology: Themes and variations* (10th ed.). Boston, MA: Cengage Learning.

Zigler, E., & Styfco, S. (2010). *The hidden history of Head Start.* New York, NY: Oxford University Press.

Chapter 10

Changing How Writing Is Taught

STEVE GRAHAM
Arizona State University

If students are to be successful in school, at work, and in their personal lives, they must learn to write. This requires that they receive adequate practice and instruction in writing, as this complex skill does not develop naturally. A basic goal of schooling then is to teach students to use this versatile tool effectively and flexibly. Many schools across the world do not achieve this objective, as an inordinate number of students do not acquire the writing skills needed for success in society today. One reason why this is the case is that many students do not receive the writing instruction they need or deserve. This chapter identifies factors that inhibit good writing instruction, including instructional time; teachers' preparation and beliefs about writing; national, state, district, and school policies; and historical, social, cultural, and political influences. It then examines how we can address these factors and change classroom writing practices for the better across the world by increasing pertinent stakeholders' knowledge about writing, with the goal of developing and actualizing visions for writing instruction at the policy, school, and classroom levels. This includes specific recommendations for helping politicians, school administrators, teachers, and the public acquire the needed know-how to make this a reality.

Writing is a fundamental skill. More than 85% of the population of the world can now write (Swedlow, 1999). Writers use this versatile skill to learn new ideas, persuade others, record information, create imaginary worlds, express feelings, entertain others, heal psychological wounds, chronicle experiences, and explore the meaning of events and situations (Graham, 2018a). In school, students write about the materials read or presented in class to enhance their understanding (Bangert-Drowns, Hurley, & Wilkinson, 2004; Graham & Hebert, 2011). At work, white- and blue-collar workers commonly use writing to perform their jobs (Light, 2001).

Review of Research in Education
March 2019, Vol. 43, pp. 277–303
DOI: 10.3102/0091732X18821125
Chapter reuse guidelines: sagepub.com/journals-permissions

At home, writing provides a means for initiating and maintaining personal connections, as we tweet, text, email, and "friend" each other using a variety of social networks and media (Freedman, Hull, Higgs, & Booten, 2016).

The importance, versatility, and pervasiveness of writing exacts a toll on those who do not learn to write well, as this can limit academic, occupational, and personal attainments (Graham, 2006). While children typically begin learning how to write at home (Tolchinsky, 2016), a basic aim of schooling is to teach students to become competent writers. Do schools successfully meet this obligation? The available evidence indicates that this objective is met for some students but not all. Take, for instance, the United States, where approximately two thirds of 8th- and 12th-grade students scored at or below the basic level (denoting only partial mastery of grade-level writing skills) on the most recent Writing Test administered by the National Assessment of Educational Progress (National Center for Educational Statistics, 2012). The relatively poor performance over time on this and other indicators of students' writing skills led the National Commission on Writing (NCOW, 2003) to label writing a neglected skill in American schools.

Unfortunately, concerns about students' writing development are not limited to the United States but are common across the globe (see Graham & Rijlaarsdam, 2016). While there are many factors that influence children's development as writers, including poverty, genetics, and biological functioning (Graham, 2018a), many children do not receive the writing instruction at school that they deserve or need. The current chapter examines how this situation can be productively changed. We begin this exploration by examining how writing is currently taught in elementary and secondary schools. Without such background information, it is difficult to craft effective solutions. We then consider how writing practices in schools can be changed to make them more effective.

WRITING INSTRUCTION AT SCHOOL: HOW IS WRITING TAUGHT?

Most of what we know about how writing is currently taught in school settings comes from surveys asking teachers about their instructional practices in writing (e.g., Gilbert & Graham, 2010; Tse & Hui, 2016), observational studies designed to describe how writing is taught at school (e.g., Applebee & Langer, 2011; Rietdijk, van Weijen, Jassen, van den Bergh, & Rijlaarsdam, 2018), and mixed method investigations designed to provide a rich description of writing instruction through both interviews and observations (e.g., Hertzberg & Roe, 2016; McCarthy & Ro, 2011). Findings from 28 survey, observation, and mixed method studies involving the writing practices of more than 7,000 teachers are summarized in this section.[1] While two thirds of these studies were conducted in the United States, the other investigations provided information on writing instruction in Europe (e.g., De Smedt, van Keer, & Merchie, 2016), China (e.g., Hsiang, Graham, & Wong, 2018), South America (Margarida, Simao, Malpique, Frison, & Marques, 2016), and New Zealand (Parr & Jesson, 2016). Even though the findings from these studies do not cover all aspects of writing instruction in schools across the globe, they do provide an up-to-date (if incomplete) picture of how writing is now taught in schools (all the studies were published in the past 15 years).

There were two basic overall findings from the 28 studies that examined how writing is taught in contemporary classrooms. One, some teachers provide students with a solid writing program, and in some classrooms this instruction is exemplary (e.g., Wilcox, Jeffrey, & Gardner-Bixler, 2016). Two, this is not typically the case, as writing and writing instruction in most classrooms are inadequate. These findings were generally universal, applying across countries and grades.

In terms of providing students with a solid writing program, it was consistently the case that in each study reviewed (e.g., Cutler & Graham, 2008; Dockrell, Marshall, & Wyse, 2016; Hsiang & Graham, 2016), there were teachers who committed a considerable amount of time to teaching writing. This included elementary grade teachers who devoted 1 hour a day to writing and writing instruction (as recommended by the *What Works Practice Guide* for elementary writing instruction; Graham et al., 2012) and who used a variety of instructional practices to promote students' writing success and growth, including applying evidence-based practices. In the elementary grades, these evidence-based practices included writing for different purposes, teaching strategies for carrying out writing processes such as planning and revising, conducting formative assessments to guide writing instruction, and teaching students foundational writing skills like handwriting, spelling, and sentence construction. At the secondary level, this included the same instructional practices (except that handwriting and spelling were not typically taught) as well as using writing as a way to support reading and learning. As Applebee and Langer (2011) observed, some teachers create rich and engaging writing programs, using instructional practices with a proven record of success (as identified in recent reports and meta-analyses: Graham, Bruch, et al., 2016; Graham & Perin, 2007).

It is also important to note that there were several studies (e.g., Cutler & Graham, 2008; Parr & Jesson, 2016) where the majority of teachers devoted considerable time to writing instruction and used a variety of evidence-based and other instructional practices to teach writing (e.g., conferencing). Likewise, several survey studies found that (a) middle and high school teachers across disciplines reported using writing to support student learning (Gillespie, Graham, Kiuhara, & Hebert, 2014; Ray, Graham, Houston, & Harris, 2016), (b) primary grade teachers indicated that they taught handwriting or spelling using evidence-based practices (Graham, Harris, et al., 2008; Graham, Morphy, et al., 2008), and (c) elementary and middle school teachers commonly made a variety of adaptations for struggling writers in their class (Troia & Graham, 2017).

Some of the positive findings from these studies must be tempered by other issues that emerged in these and other investigations. For example, in Parr and Jesson (2016), teachers placed little emphasis on two important types of writing: persuasive and expository writing. Primary grade teachers in the Cutler and Graham (2008) study overemphasized teaching basic writing skills (grammar, handwriting, and spelling) while placing little emphasis on teaching students how to carry out critical writing processes such as planning and revising. This lack of attention to teaching students how to plan and revise was also a common theme in other studies (e.g., Dockrell et al., 2016; Rietdijk et al., 2018). While a majority of the middle and high school teachers in the investigations conducted by Gillespie et al. (2014) and Ray et al. (2016) frequently used writing to support learning across the disciplines, most of the writing activities applied for this purpose involved writing without composing (e.g., filling in blanks on a work sheet, note taking, and one-sentence responses to questions). Writing without composing was also quite common in other studies examining writing practices in both English and content classes at the secondary level (e.g., Applebee & Langer, 2011; Graham, Cappizi, Harris, Hebert, & Morphy, 2014; Kiuhara, Graham, & Hawken, 2009).

While it is essential to recognize that many teachers provide their students with strong, even exemplary writing instruction, it is equally important to draw a picture of common classroom practices. Unfortunately, the overall picture that emerged from the 28 studies reviewed was that writing instruction in most classrooms is not sufficient. One indicator of this inadequacy was that a majority of teachers did not devote enough time to teaching writing (e.g., Brindle, Harris, Graham, & Hebert, 2016; Graham et al., 2014; Kiuhara et al., 2009). Writing is a complex and challenging task, requiring a considerable amount of instructional time to master (Graham, 2018a). At both the elementary and the secondary level, the typical teacher devoted much less than 1 hour a day to teaching writing (e.g., Coker et al., 2016; Drew, Olinghouse, Luby-Faggella, & Welsh, 2017). In some instances, the amount of time committed to teaching writing was severely limited. Typical elementary grade teachers in the Netherlands, for example, reported that they conducted a writing lesson once a week or less often (Rietdijk et al., 2018). In China, elementary and middle school teachers held a writing lesson just once every 2 to 3 weeks (e.g., Hsiang et al., 2018; Hsiang & Graham, 2016).

A second indicator of insufficient writing instruction was that students in a typical class did not write frequently. While teachers commonly assigned a variety of different types of writing over the course of a year, students engaged in most of these activities no more than once or twice during the year (e.g., Brindle et al., 2016; Kiuhara et al., 2009; Koko, 2016). The writing activities most commonly assigned to students involved very little extended writing, as students were seldom asked to write text that was a paragraph or longer (e.g., Gilbert & Graham, 2010).

A third indicator of insufficient writing instruction involved the use of teaching procedures. While the typical teacher applied a variety of different instructional practices (e.g., McCarthy & Ro, 2011; Tse & Hu, 2016) and made many different instructional adaptations over the course of the school year (e.g., Troia & Graham, 2017), most of these teaching procedures were applied infrequently, often less than once a month (e.g., Graham et al., 2014; Graham, Harris, MacArthur, & Fink-Chorzempa, 2003; Hertzberg & Roe, 2016). This included teachers' use of evidence-based practices for teaching writing (e.g., Drew et al., 2017; Gilbert & Graham,

2010). Undoubtedly, how frequently teachers applied specific instructional practices, made particular instructional adaptations, or assigned different types of writing was related to the time they devoted to teaching writing. Even so, these findings draw into question the depth and intensity of writing instruction in the typical classroom.

A fourth indicator of the insufficiency of writing instruction in the typical classroom was the notable absence of the use of digital tools for writing. While most writing outside of school today is done digitally (Freedman et al., 2016), the use of digital tools for writing or writing instruction was notably absent in the typical classroom (e.g., Applebee & Langer, 2011; Coker et al., 2016; Simmerman et al., 2012).

Finally, a variety of specific issues involving classroom writing practices emerged within the context of individual studies. This included concerns that the primary audience for students' writing was the teacher (Applebee & Langer, 2011), writing involved little collaboration among students (De Smedt et al., 2016), the time spent in preparing for high-stakes writing tests was excessive (Applebee & Langer, 2011), classroom resources for teaching writing were inadequate (Dockrell et al., 2016), formative evaluation occurred infrequently (Rietdijk et al., 2018), motivation for writing was largely ignored (Cutler & Graham, 2008; Wilcox et al., 2016), and the writing needs of students with a disability or who were learning a second language were not sufficiently addressed (Dockrell et al., 2016). It is possible that these issues are prevalent in most classrooms, but they were not widely examined in the studies reviewed.

In summary, it is evident that teachers can, and some do, devote considerable time and effort to teaching writing. Most teachers are also familiar with a broad array of instructional methods, activities for composing, and possible adaptations for struggling writers. Nevertheless, the typical teacher does not devote enough time to writing and writing instruction. Students do not write often enough, and they are seldom asked to write longer papers that involve analysis and interpretation. Teachers apply the instructional procedures they are familiar with infrequently, including evidence-based practices and adaptations for struggling writers. Digital technology, including word processors and computers, are not an integral part of most writing instruction in schools. For many students worldwide, the NCOW (2003) report was correct: Writing is a neglected skill.

CHANGING WRITING PRACTICES IN SCHOOLS

If writing practices in schools are to change, it is important to identify the factors that inhibit good writing instruction. One critical contributor to quality writing instruction is time.

Writing is an extremely complex skill (Hayes, 2012), and learning how to write requires time and good instruction (Graham et al., 2012). Concerns about how much time is devoted to teaching writing led the NCOW (2003) report to assert that "in today's schools, writing is a prisoner of time" (p. 20). This position is supported by the consistently replicated finding that teachers who devote more time to teaching writing apply more instructional writing practices more often (e.g., Coker et al., 2016; Hsiang et al., 2018; Koko, 2016).

The composition of the classroom is also a contributing factor in how writing is taught. As NCOW (2003) noted, it becomes increasingly difficult to provide writing instruction responsive to students' needs as the number of students in a classroom increases. I am not implying that teachers do not try to meet such challenges, as illustrated by findings that they apply more writing instructional practices when their class contains more students experiencing difficulties learning to write (e.g., Gilbert & Graham, 2010; Gillespie et al., 2014).

Classroom writing practices are further influenced by teachers' beliefs and knowledge (Graham & Harris, 2018). Teachers devote more time and attention to teaching writing if they are better prepared to teach it, feel more confident in their capabilities to teach it, derive greater pleasure from teaching it, and consider it an important skill (e.g., Brindle et al., 2016; De Smedt et al., 2016; Hsiang & Graham, 2016; Kiuhara et al., 2009; Rietdijk et al., 2018; Troia & Graham, 2016). They are also more likely to apply specific writing practices they view as acceptable (e.g., Troia & Graham, 2017).

Factors that contribute to how writing is taught go well beyond the classroom and teacher determinants identified above. For instance, how much time is devoted to writing and the number and type of students in a classroom are related to national, state, district, and school policies. In the Netherlands, for instance, teachers can meet the expectations established by the Dutch Inspectorate by teaching writing just two times a month (Rietdijk et al., 2018). Similarly, the importance placed on teaching writing and preparing teachers to do so depends on a complex mix of historical, social, cultural, political, and institutional influences (Graham, 2018a). For example, writing and reading are both valued historically, socially, and culturally in China, but reading enjoys primacy over writing in schools because reading is valued more than writing and it is commonly believed that students learn to write through reading (see Hsiang et al., 2018). Moreover, writing instruction in schools involves a complex interaction between teachers and factors outside their control. Take, for instance, preparation to teach writing. Teachers can and do learn how to teach writing through their own efforts and experiences, but their preparation also rests on institutional programs such as the preservice and in-service training they receive at college and as a teacher, respectively. Such institutional preparation is often viewed by teachers and those who deliver such instruction as inadequate (e.g., Brindle et al., 2016; Myers et al., 2016), potentially undercutting teachers' own personal efforts to become good writing teachers.

Consequently, changing classroom writing practices involves more than changing teachers. As Bransford, Darling-Hammond, & LePage (2005) argued, dramatic educational change is not possible without addressing "both sides of the reform coin: better teachers and better systems" (p. 38). I suggest that efforts to change writing instruction in the United States and beyond need to be even broader. If writing and writing instruction are not valued and understood by society at large, as well as policymakers and school personnel more specifically, the potential impact of changing writing instruction for the better will be restricted.

Particularly important to changing classroom writing practices is to enhance teachers', principals', and policymakers' knowledge about writing. Each of these stakeholders need to acquire specific know-how, which includes knowledge about writing, a vision for teaching writing, and professional commitment. In addition, the success of efforts to increase their know-how rests in part on society's knowledge about writing, its importance, and the need to teach it.

A pertinent question at this point is why I am emphasizing knowledge about writing as a lever for changing classroom writing practices. In terms of teaching writing, good instruction requires rich and interconnected knowledge about subject matter and content, students' learning and diversity, and subject-specific as well as general pedagogical methods (Feltovich, Prietula, & Ericsson, 2018; Grossman & McDonald, 2008; Russ, Sherin, & Sherin, 2016; Schoenfeld, 1998; Shulman, 1987); a professional vision of teaching as well as adaptive skills for applying this knowledge productively, strategically, and effectively (Ball & Cohen, 1999; Stigler & Miller, 2018); and a professional commitment to ensure that this knowledge and needed actions are applied day in and day out (Bransford et al., 2005). If teachers acquire the needed knowledge, vision, and commitment, they are more likely to become masterful, efficacious, and motivated writing teachers, devoting more time to teaching it. This is a necessary but not a sufficient solution for improving writing instruction in classrooms worldwide. Policymakers, district personnel, and principals also need to acquire specific know-how about writing in order to make writing instruction an educational priority so that teachers' efforts are valued and supported. In addition, society needs to view writing as valuable, as this lays the framework for more general expectations that writing must be emphasized and taught.

In the next section, I examine the types of knowledge needed to change how writing is typically taught worldwide. The most critical aspects of knowledge in this section are italicized. Once these different forms of knowledge are presented, I consider how this knowledge can be actualized through the development and actualization of visions for writing instruction, emphasizing that it is advantageous if visions for teaching writing are coherent, well constructed, and consistent across all levels (i.e., national, state, district, school, and classroom) or as many levels as possible. To change how writing is taught, either locally or more broadly, pertinent stakeholders need to acquire the needed knowledge about writing, so recommendations for helping policymakers, school administrators, teachers, and the public to acquire the needed know-how are offered.

WRITING KNOWLEDGE

Knowledge includes all mental structures in long-term memory, including facts, opinions, concepts, theories, beliefs, attitudes, and orientations (Graham, 2018b). If teaching practices in elementary and secondary schools are to be transformed, relevant stakeholders need to acquire knowledge about the subject of writing, how students learn and develop as writers, and effective practices for teaching writing.

Knowledge About Writing

Writing instruction may receive little emphasis in most schools because it is not valued. In a school curriculum that is overcrowded, those subjects that are viewed as most important to students' current and future success are likely to receive the greatest attention. As a result, society, policymakers, school administrators, and teachers *need to know why writing is important* and why it must be included as a central and prized component of the school curriculum (NCOW, 2003).

One reason why schools need to place more emphasis on writing is that it *enhances students' performance in other important school subjects*. Students understand and retain material read or presented in science, social studies, and mathematics when they are asked to write about it (Bangert-Drowns et al., 2004; Graham & Hebert, 2011; Graham & Perin, 2007). Increasing how much they write and teaching writing improves reading skills (Graham & Hebert, 2011). Making writing a part of reading instruction further enhances how well students read (Graham, Liu, Aitken, et al., 2018). In essence, students are unlikely to maximize their growth in other school subjects if writing is notably absent.

Writing is equally *important to students' future success*. Students who graduate from high school with weak writing skills are at a disadvantage in college and the world of work. For instance, writing competence is used by employers to make decisions about hiring and promotion in white-collar jobs, and approximately 90% of blue-collar jobs require some form of writing (NCOW, 2004, 2005). Furthermore, writing is now a central feature of social life, as it is used to communicate, share ideas, persuade, chronicle experiences, and entertain others (Freedman et al., 2016).

The value attributed to writing depends on understanding not only why it is important but also *how writing achieves its effects*. For example, writing about something read can facilitate comprehension because writing "provides students with a tool for visibly and permanently recording, connecting, analyzing, personalizing, and manipulating key ideas in text" (Graham & Hebert, 2011, p. 712). Likewise, writing instruction enhances students' skills as readers because writing and reading share a close and reciprocal relation, relying on common knowledge and processes (Shanahan, 2006). Instruction that improves writing skills and processes should improve reading skills and processes, and vice versa.

As this discussion implies, knowledge of writing involves knowing about other related skills. This includes *how writing and reading are connected* (see Fitzgerald & Shanahan, 2000). For instance, writing and reading can be used together to accomplish specific learning goals (e.g., reading source material to write a paper about the impact of plastics on wildlife), and engaging in the act of writing can provide insight into reading, and vice versa (e.g., writers need to make premises explicit and observe the rules of logic when composing text, so this should make them aware of the same issues when reading). In addition to reading, it is *important to know how writing and language are connected*, because oral language serves as a foundation for writing, as writers draw on their knowledge of phonological awareness, vocabulary, syntactic structures, discourse organizations and structures, and pragmatics (Shanahan, 2006).

Although writing draws on knowledge gained through language development, *writing requires the development of specialized knowledge* too (Graham, 2018b). Writers must learn the purposes and features of different types of texts (e.g., how writing is used to accomplish different purposes, the features of different types of text, attributes of strong writing, specialized vocabulary for specific types of text, and rhetorical devices for creating a specific mood) as well as how to transcribe ideas into text (e.g., spelling, handwriting, typing, and keyboarding), construct written sentences (e.g., punctuation, capitalization, more frequent use of subordinate clauses when writing specific types of text), carry out processes for creating and revising text (e.g., schemas for text construction and strategies for setting goals, gathering and organizing possible writing content, and drafting text, as well as monitoring, evaluating, and revising plans and text), use the tools of writing (e.g., paper and pencil, word processing), and respond to an absent audience (e.g., consider what an audience knows about the topic).

Four other forms of knowledge about writing are important to designing better writing instruction. One, it is important to realize that *writing is not a single unitary skill* (Bazerman et al., 2017). It involves many different forms, and how well a student writes varies across forms (Rijlaarsdam et al., 2012). Even within a single form of writing, the quality of students' writing may differ from one assignment to the next depending on a variety of factors, including their knowledge of the topic (Olinghouse, Graham, & Gillespie, 2015) or their motivation to write (Knudson, 1995).

Two, a basic assumption behind school-based writing instruction is that it prepares students for the writing they will do outside school. This assumption has been challenged repeatedly (e.g., Hull & Schultz, 2001), and consequently, *knowing what types of writing students do at home, in college, and at work is important* to deciding what types of writing should be emphasized in school. In addition, knowing what types of writing students do outside school is essential if such writing is to be integrated into school activities. This may increase the value of school-based writing in students' views (Freedman et al., 2016).

Three, one's *beliefs about writing can foster or hinder writing* in various ways. Such beliefs influence whether one engages in writing, how much effort is committed, and what resources are applied (Graham, 2018a). They include judgments about the value and utility of writing, the attractiveness of writing as an activity, why one engages in writing, one's competence as a writer, and why one is or is not successful when writing. They also include beliefs about one's identity as a writer, which can differ from one writing community to the next.

Four, *writing is a social activity*, situated within specific contexts (Bazerman, 2016; Graham, 2018a), such as classrooms, places of work, or online communities. Within these communities, what is written is accomplished by writers (and possibly collaborators) for specific audiences. As a result, writing involves an interaction between the context in which it occurs and the mental and physical resources writers and their collaborators (including teachers and mentors) bring to the task of writing (Graham, 2018b). Efforts to change writing instruction in schools must take into account both the social and the individual aspects of writing.

The importance of knowledge about how to write, as represented by a teacher's capabilities as a writer, to changing school-based writing practices is unclear. While skilled writers can describe some of the things they do when writing, their descriptions are incomplete (Hayes & Flower, 1980). It is probably more important for relevant stakeholders to have a *positive identity as a writer* (Woodward, 2013). This increases the likelihood that they will write, enjoy writing, and see the value of writing and teaching it.

Knowledge About How Writing Develops

Earlier it was established that many students spend little time writing or learning how to write in school. This situation is inconsistent with what we know about how writing develops. *Writing develops across the life span, some forms of writing take many years to master, and writing growth is a consequence of writing and deliberate practice* (Bazerman et al., 2017; Graham, Harris, & Chambers, 2016; Kellogg & Whiteford, 2009).

The factors that shape writing development are multifaceted and overlapping. For example, *writing development is shaped by participation in various writing communities* (Bazerman, 2016; Graham, 2018b). For instance, as students participate in a 10th-grade English class, they acquire one or more identities as a writer, learn more about the audiences and the particular purposes for writing in that context (including goals, norms, values, and stances), and obtain typified actions (routines or schemas) for carrying out writing tasks. In many instances, learning acquired in one writing community can be useful in other writing communities, as when young children use writing skills learned at home in school.

Writing development is further shaped by a variety of processes operating at the individual level (see Graham, 2018b). It includes learning as a consequence of action. Students acquire knowledge and beliefs about the cognitive and physical actions they use when writing by evaluating the effectiveness of these operations. It involves learning by expansion. Students acquire writing knowledge and confidence through nonwriting activities, as when insight into writing is obtained through reading (e.g., Graham, Liu, Bartlett, et al., 2018). It entails learning by observing. Students acquire knowledge and specific dispositions by observing others engage in the act of writing. It includes learning through deliberate agency. Students make conscious decisions to apply a previously learned writing skill to new situations. It involves learning through accumulated capital. Writing growth serves as a catalyst for additional growth (e.g., increased knowledge about how to write enhances motivation to write).

Writing development is also shaped through instruction (Graham, Harris, et al., 2016). Students acquire knowledge and beliefs about how to write through mentoring, feedback, collaboration, and instruction. This can be provided by a teacher, another adult such as a parent or peer, or even a machine (Graham, Harris, & Santangelo, 2015; Graham, Hebert, & Harris, 2015). Moreover, teachers can arrange the writing environment to facilitate student growth, as happens when students are asked to evaluate what actions worked best while writing (learning as a consequence of action).

Regardless of the processes that shape students' growth as writers, *writing development is variable*, with no single path or end point (Bazerman et al., 2017). It is uneven, as students are better at some writing tasks than at others (Graham, Hebert, Sandbank, & Harris, 2016). It does not follow a steady progression from point A to point B, as students' growth can accelerate, plateau, or regress. It varies from one student to the next, because students' experiences as writers differ, as does their genetic and neurological makeup (Graham, 2018a). There is no prespecified sequence of normal development in writing, just social norms of what might be expected, as is the case with the *Common Core State Standards* (CCSS; National Governors Association & Council of Chief School Officers, 2010).

Even though students' path to writing competence is variable and uncertain, this does not mean that it is without form. For example, instruction designed to enhance specific aspects of writing (e.g., writing knowledge, strategies, and motivation) results in students' writing growth (Graham, 2006). Increasing young writers' facility with foundational writing skills such as handwriting, spelling, typing, and sentence construction reduces cognitive overload, freeing up mental resources for other important aspects of writing. Additionally, growth does not occur in a vacuum; *writing development influences and is influenced by development in speech, reading, learning, emotions, identity, a sense of efficacy, and collective actions* (Bazerman et al., 2017).

Finally, *writing development is influenced by gender, family wealth, culture, neurological functioning, and genetic factors* (Graham, 2018a). This does not mean that an individual child's future growth as a writer is somehow fixed and nothing can be done to change this path. For instance, students with disabilities experience difficulty learning to write, but there is evidence that their writing development can be accelerated through explicit and systematic instruction (e.g., Gillespie & Graham, 2014). If the writing development of all students is to be maximized, knowledge is needed about the writing experiences, interests, characteristics, and development of students whose backgrounds differ by gender, class, culture, race, ethnicity, language, and disability status. *Equally important is the belief that all children can learn to write well.*

Knowledge About Teaching Writing

At the most basic level, effective writing instruction depends on time (NCOW, 2003). Teachers who devote more time to writing instruction apply multiple methods more often to promote writing growth (e.g., Gilbert & Graham, 2010; Hsiang et al., 2018). In effect, *quality writing instruction cannot occur if sufficient time is not available.*

Time alone is not sufficient to ensure that students receive strong writing instruction. In addition, *goals for instruction must be identified, the curriculum content specified, and effective instructional practices applied* (Bransford et al., 2005). If high-stakes assessments used to measure students' writing were used as a guide, the primary goal for writing at national, state, and local levels would be to capably write specific kinds of text, for no real audience or purpose (other than testing), using information held in long-term memory (Mo & Troia, 2017). If writing instruction is to be changed for the better, *goals for writing need to focus on using writing for real purposes and writing in a more realistic fashion* (e.g., access to source material, engaging in critical thinking). Moreover, goals need to address motivation (e.g., writers who are efficacious, value writing, and develop a positive identity as a writer), knowledge (e.g., writers who know how to use a variety of writing tools to meet their writing objectives), process (e.g., writers who can flexibly use writing skills and strategies to meet different writing demands), and social contexts (e.g., writers who can adjust their writing to fit the context).

In terms of writing curriculum, *there is no single agreed-on set of skills, knowledge, processes, or dispositions for teaching writing.* Recent efforts like the CCSS (National Governors Association & Council of Chief School Officers, 2010) represent an ambitious attempt to identify what needs to be taught at a minimal level, but they do not address all of the goals for writing identified above, nor do they align well with many procedures shown to improve students' writing (Troia et al., 2015). *Writing instruction is likely to be more effective when goals, curriculum, instructional methods, and assessment are aligned.*

Recent work by Graham and his colleagues to identify evidence-based practices in writing (Graham, Harris, et al., 2016; Graham, Harris, et al., 2015; Graham, Hebert, et al., 2015; Graham, Liu, Aitken, et al., 2018; Graham, Liu, Bartlett, et al., 2018) provides insight into writing curriculum and instruction. Their work draws on empirical intervention studies and qualitative investigations with exceptional literacy teachers. At a macro-level, they found that *effective writing instruction involves (a) writing frequently for real and different purposes; (b) supporting students as they write; (c) teaching the needed writing skills, knowledge, and processes; (4) creating a supportive and motivating writing environment; and (5) connecting writing, reading, and learning.* At a more micro-level, this work provides a partial (not complete) frame for identifying curricular objectives in writing (and instructional procedures for addressing them). Based on this framework, curricular objectives should address basic foundational skills (handwriting, spelling, and typing), sentence construction skills, knowledge about different types of text, the characteristics of good writing, vocabulary for writing, and processes for planning, drafting, evaluating, and revising text. Curricular objectives should further focus on establishing classroom routines where students' writing is supported (e.g., peers work together, students receive useful and timely feedback), students act in a self-regulated fashion (e.g., taking ownership of their writing, doing as much as they can on their own), writing is used to support students' learning and reading in multiple disciplines, and students learn to apply traditional as well as 21st-century writing tools (e.g., digital tools that allow for multimodal writing).

Beyond the principles established by Graham and colleagues above, instructional practices in writing need to address the following: applying effective strategies for managing the classroom and student behavior (Bransford et al., 2005), connecting writing within and outside school (Freedman et al., 2016), using formative assessment to improve learning and instruction (Graham, Hebert, et al., 2015), and implementing experiences that help students grow as writers. In addition, attention needs to be aimed at ensuring that students use correct grammar and usage in their writing. A meta-analysis by Graham, Harris, and Hebert (2011) found that grammar miscues negatively influence readers' perceptions about the writer's message.

While many of the instructional procedures in writing that are effective with students in general are also effective for students whose backgrounds differ by gender, class, culture, race, ethnicity, language, and disability status (e.g., Gillespie & Graham, 2014; Graham, Harris, & Beard, in press), *improving how writing is taught in schools requires that instruction is differentiated to meet students' needs.* This includes designing instructional lessons so that they are tailored to address the needs of different students (e.g., incorporating culturally responsive instruction), using instructional methods that are particularly effective with these students (e.g., feedback and progress monitoring, cooperative learning, and tutoring students of low socioeconomic status; Dietrichson, Bog, Filges, & Jorgensen, 2017), making adaptations in writing assignments and instruction for particular students (e.g., providing additional time for writing), providing accommodations to address particular challenges (e.g., allowing a student with a physical disability to use a word prediction word processor program), identifying and addressing roadblocks to learning (e.g., frequent absences), and expecting that each child will learn to write well (Graham, Harris, & Larsen, 2001).

Finally, *teachers' disposition toward teaching writing is an important ingredient in delivering high-quality writing instruction.* Teachers who are more self-efficacious about their instructional capabilities, enjoy teaching writing, and view instructional practices as acceptable are more likely to teach writing (e.g., Brindle et al., 2016; Troia & Graham, 2016, 2017).

DEVELOPMENT AND ACTUALIZATION OF VISIONS FOR TEACHING WRITING

Developing a Vision for Teaching Writing

Imagine asking teachers, principals, district superintendents, or policymakers involved in crafting educational goals for writing to describe their vision for teaching writing, and they were unable to answer this question or each had different answers! If students are to receive the writing instruction they need and deserve, there must be a coherent vision for how writing is taught in the classroom, across classrooms and grades in a school, within the district and across districts within a state, across states, and within the nation. While I realize that this may not be possible in all situations, the goal should be to have a coherent, well-constructed, and consistent vision for teaching writing on as many levels as possible.

Developing such a vision for writing instruction does not mean that each teacher, school, or district has to do the same thing but that everyone is rowing together in the same direction. This requires a set of common goals for writing (as is the case with the CCSS in the United States) and decisions about what will be taught and who will be responsible for what aspects of writing instruction. It should not be limited to just writing but should also address how the teaching of writing, reading, and learning are integrated and used to support one another. Furthermore, it should go beyond the classroom, connecting writing in and out of school.

The development of such a plan is likely to be more effective if it is (a) informed by the types of knowledge about writing, development, and teaching presented in the previous section; (b) developed with the help of teachers; and (c) supported by those who implement it (including principals and teachers). There is an important caution in developing specific visions for teaching writing that must be acknowledged. While specific visions can provide districts, schools, and individual teachers with a valuable road map, they can become a straightjacket, needlessly constraining how writing is taught. They are never complete, nor should they be viewed that way. Teachers and schools need the flexibility to apply their professional knowledge to develop a vision for teaching writing that is responsive to their students and situation. Moreover, visions for teaching writing at any level should not be viewed as set in concrete but are subject to change as needed.

Even when goals for writing and decisions about what to teach and who teaches what are made collectively (at any level), each teacher must still make a host of other decisions before or after instruction starts that shape the actualized vision for teaching writing. This includes deciding the value placed on writing, what kinds of writing are assigned, who serves as the audience, classroom norms for writing, and the writing identity of the class (Graham, 2018b). Teachers must further make decisions about the roles and responsibilities of students, methods for fostering positive social interactions, the amount of power students exercise, the physical arrangement of the class, the tools used for writing, typified routines for accomplishing writing and classroom goals, and instructional procedures for teaching writing. These decisions should take into account the characteristics of the students in the class and are influenced by teachers' beliefs about how students learn to write.

Putting Visions for Teaching Writing Into Action

It is not enough to know what to do; knowledge and vision must be enacted if meaningful change is to take place. To illustrate, school districts need to engage in a number of processes in order to enact their visions of writing instruction. This includes developing an implementation plan, making decisions and judgments about what to do and who is responsible, monitoring and evaluating the plan as it is enacted, reflecting on what did and did not work, and engaging in problem solving throughout (these same processes apply, often at a more abstract level, for visions enacted by states and nations). Teachers must also engage in the same processes as they translate their vision for teaching writing into daily lessons and longer units or put into place procedures for differentiating instruction, to provide two examples.

Because teaching writing is a complex process and the actions and reactions of those providing and receiving instruction are not fully predictable, schools and teachers develop schemas for operationalizing their visions (Feltovich et al., 2018). For example, a teacher may apply a commonly used routine where students are expected to plan, draft, edit, revise, and publish their compositions. The advantage of such an approach is that these are important components of the writing process and uncertainty is reduced as students know what they are to do. The disadvantage is that writing does not always follow such a linear progression. Thus, the routines created by schools and teachers should be viewed as permeable and flexible, with schools and teachers monitoring, evaluating, and modifying their use to ensure effectiveness.

An important ingredient in operationalizing a vision for teaching writing is to apply methods with a proven track record of success (Graham, Bruch, et al., 2016). A number of evidence-based writing practices were identified earlier that have been applied effectively in multiple settings. The use of such practices may have a "wanted" side effect. They should enhance teachers' efficacy and attitude toward teaching writing as there is a good chance they will work. Even so, caution must be exercised when applying these procedures as there is no guarantee that they will be successful. As a result, the implementation of an evidence-based practice involves the same analytic problem-solving processes identified above—planning, implementing, observing, evaluating, and reflection, leading to decisions about whether to continue using the practice, modify it, or drop it. Again, the same processes should be used when schools or teachers apply other instructional writing practices, such as the ones they create through their own experiences.

While individual teachers do make a difference (Ball & Cohen, 1999), this is not enough. Students need to receive high-quality writing instruction from one class to the next. This requires a system approach, as noted earlier. Enacting visions for teaching writing will be best served through an approach where the knowledge acquired at each level is used to improve practice at all levels. This means that teachers and principals within schools as well as principals and district personnel need to establish lines of communications and trust so that acquired knowledge, observations, critical feedback, and possible solutions can flow easily from teacher to teacher, teachers to administrators, and administrators to district leaders. The same premise applies to communication between school districts and policymakers at the state level as well as between policymakers at the state and national levels.

MAKING SURE RELEVANT STAKEHOLDERS ACQUIRE THE NEEDED WRITING KNOW-HOW

The task proposed here is no small undertaking. Writing instruction is not adequate in many classrooms across the globe. Changing this situation requires considerable engagement, effort, fortitude, and professionalism from all relevant stakeholders:

policymakers, school administrators, and teachers. Furthermore, the success of their efforts will be constrained if society does not value writing or view it as important. Recommendations for helping these stakeholders acquire the knowledge about writing each needs to accomplish this task are presented next, with a particular focus on how this might be done in the United States. Many of the proffered suggestions can be applied in other countries too.

Policymakers

The level of know-how needed by specific stakeholders differs. At a minimal level, policymakers need to know that (a) writing is important; (b) writing and writing instruction promote writing, reading, and successful learning; (c) writing in and outside school is connected; (d) the time spent writing and teaching writing is not sufficient in most classrooms; and (e) many students (especially in their district or state) are not developing the writing skills needed for success in school, college, or work.

How can policymakers' knowledge be increased? One way is for organizations like the National Writing Project (NWP), American Federation of Teachers, National Council of Teachers of English (NCTE), and International Literacy Association (ILA) to band together and coordinate an informational campaign (involving print material, television, radio, and personal contacts) directed at policymakers (as well as the public at large). These organizations can further encourage their members, especially teachers, to contact politicians and policymakers (by email, letter, or meeting in person) to advocate on behalf of writing. In turn, teachers can encourage parents to do the same. This last recommendation will likely be more successful if teachers help parents understand why writing is so critical.

Organizations like the ones above can also form working coalitions with organizations like the Carnegie Foundation for the Advancement of Teaching, Bill and Melinda Gates Foundation, and Chan Zuckerberg Initiative, as well as local private and corporate foundations. This can increase the impact and broaden the scope of organizations like NCTE and ILA to advocate for writing and inform policymakers and the public about why it is so important and how we can do a better job of teaching it (e.g., solicit funds to hire lobbyists to promote more and better writing instruction). In any event, it will take a coordinated and substantive effort to make strong writing instruction a priority with policymakers at the local, state, and national levels. We need to create and take advantage of every "opportunity to call attention to the urgent need to improve writing" (Graham, Heller, Applebee, Olson, & Collins, 2013, p. 16).

If a policymaker is directly involved in creating the actual vision for teaching writing at the local, state, or national level, then greater know-how about writing is needed. One way to ensure that the needed know-how is available when such work takes place is to include representation from professional organizations focused on writing, teachers and school administrators knowledgeable about teaching writing, and scholars of writing and writing instruction. The direct participation of these parties in the vision-crafting process will provide policymakers with external pools of knowledge about writing, increasing the likelihood they create a vision for writing instruction that is well-informed and viewed as acceptable by those charged with enacting it. Regardless, it is critical that state and district academic standards assign clear, coherent, and realistic responsibilities for writing instruction in all subject areas. Moreover, policymakers need to identify levers for encouraging schools and teachers in each discipline to take responsibility for teaching writing.

Teachers and School Administrators

Those who teach writing and reading, or use writing to support learning need to be knowledgeable about writing, its development, and writing instruction. They also need to learn how to apply this knowledge to create, enact, sustain, and modify (as needed) a vision for teaching writing in their particular class and context that is reasonably consistent with any school, district, state, or national goals that are applicable to their situation and context. Such knowledge is needed by virtually every teacher in a school (if not all), as writing can facilitate reading and content learning (Bangert-Drowns et al., 2004; Graham & Hebert, 2011). School principals, and to a lesser degree district administrators, also need to acquire the same types of knowledge and expertise. However, instead of learning how to implement the constructed vision in a classroom (although such knowledge would be advantageous), they need to learn how to successfully shepherd it through a school or district, respectively. To illustrate, principals who have strong knowledge and beliefs about effective writing practices act in ways that help teachers do their best work (McGhee & Lew, 2007).

A traditional partner in preparing teachers (and school administrators) are universities. As noted earlier, these programs are not viewed positively by a majority of their clientele. As an example, 76% of third- and fourth-grade teachers in Brindle et al. (2016) rated their college preparation as inadequate and indicated that they were less prepared to teach writing than any other subject. Only 17% of teachers took at least one writing course, 68% took one or two courses that included some writing instructional content, and just 20% taught writing as part of their field experience. Furthermore, faculty focused on literacy instruction in universities (the ones who are most likely to teach writing know-how) report that there is a lack of time for writing in their educational programs, and they are only moderately positive about their success in teaching writing to preservice teachers (Myers et al., 2016). While there are clearly some universities that do a good job of preparing students to teach writing, this is not typically the case, making them an unreliable partner in changing classroom writing practices. This situation cannot be easily changed, and it requires both bottom-up and top-down approaches if change is to occur broadly, with faculty interested in writing constantly pushing for greater emphasis on methods for teaching writing in their programs, as well as changes in state certifications that require universities to place greater emphasis on teaching writing.

This situation places much of the load on school districts for ensuring that teachers and school administrators acquire the needed writing know-how. Changing teaching practices in writing will require a systematic and extended effort on the part of schools and school districts. This can be facilitated with greater funding from state and national governments, which accentuates the need to lobby these entities by all parties interested in improving writing instruction. The good news is that principles for providing high-quality and effective professional development (PD) are available (e.g., Ball & Cohen, 1999; Darling-Hammond & Bransford, 2005), and a small but growing body of research demonstrates that basing PD on these principles can change teachers' writing practices and improve students' writing performance (e.g., Gallagher, Arshan, & Woodworth, 2017; Harris et al., 2012; Wolbers, Dostal, Skerrit, & Stephenson, 2017). The elements of such PD for writing are described below. The identified principles address both system-level and classroom change.

- Redesign the school schedule so that there is adequate time for PD and ongoing learning efforts by teachers and principals.
- Ensure that PD aligns with the district's learning standards and vision for teaching writing (strong alignment with the school's and teachers' visions is highly preferred).
- Design PD to improve writing instruction within and across grades as well as to support reading and learning, providing a set of shared expectations among teachers and administrators.
- Ensure that writing PD complements other ongoing reform efforts.
- Conduct needs assessments to determine content and the pedagogical needs of teachers and principals as well as the characteristics, strengths, and needs of students (paying special attention to students who may be most vulnerable). Such assessments can involve input from parents and students.
- Pay particular attention to the needs of new teachers or teachers new to the school system.
- Seek active participation from teachers and principals in designing and delivering PD.
- Focus PD on changing classroom practices to ultimately promote students' growth as writers, increase the value students place on writing, and improve their ability to use writing flexibly for different purposes.
- Deliver PD that is intensive and sustained over time.
- Create a trusting and respectful PD environment for teachers and principals, where they can freely voice their opinion, collaborate, take risks, reflect, question, engage in discourse around the targeted instructional practices, and solve problems.
- Provide teachers and principals the opportunity to see and analyze the methods to be learned, engage in active and deliberate practice with feedback to apply these methods while learning, and receive long-term support and feedback as they are applied in class or school.
- Use the same instructional materials during PD that are to be applied in the classroom.

- Use technological tools to support PD, such as podcasts, blogs, or digital spaces where teachers or principals can share their successes and seek assistance.
- Collect data on whether the instructional practices presented in PD achieve the intended effects; readjust and modify as needed.

Another avenue for advancing writing instruction know-how for teachers and school administrators involves their own personal efforts. For example, many teachers are positive about their own efforts to become better-prepared writing teachers (e.g., Gilbert & Graham, 2010). This path to stronger competence should be encouraged and rewarded. One way of doing this is to provide school time for principals and teachers to share new ideas and skills learned through personal activities like reading professional material, attending conferences, observing colleagues, and so forth. School personnel can be encouraged to create learning communities where they meet and share new ideas. This can be done in person, online, or both. Teachers and principals can coach one another (Kraft, Blazar, & Hogan, 2018). These kinds of activities should enhance teaching skills, efficacy, and attitudes toward teaching writing.

School personnel can also improve writing knowledge and skills by taking advantage of services offered by professional organizations, the most notable of which is the NWP (https://www.nwp.org/). It has sites in every state in the United States and provides services through summer institutes and ongoing, school-based in-service programs. A notable feature of the NWP is that it emphasizes teachers teaching teachers. Other professional organizations, like NCTE and ILA, offer a range of resources for teaching writing, such as conferences, books, research and teacher-oriented journals, and position papers. While such organizations provide invaluable services to teachers and schools, they reach a relatively small proportion of teachers in schools. There is a need for a professional organization in writing that reaches even more teachers.

Teachers and school administrators can also benefit from programs that offer one or more forms of in-service for teaching writing. For instance, two organizations, SRSD Online and thinkSRSD, offer programs on how to implement self-regulated strategy development (Harris, Graham, Mason, & Freidlander, 2008), an evidence-based practice that has been scientifically tested in more than 100 investigations and shown to be effective with a broad range of students (Graham, Harris, & McKeown, 2013). There are a variety of such programs available, with some focusing on digital writing tools and others that provide in-service centered on specific materials or methods (Calkins, 2014). Those who use such programs need to apply due diligence, making sure that the program selected is a good match to their vision for teaching writing and there is solid evidence (not testimonials) that they work.

Another avenue for changing writing practices is university and school partnerships. To illustrate, West and Saine (2016) described a project where secondary students received writing feedback from virtual writing mentors who were preservice teacher candidates. There are many forms that such partnerships can take, ranging from tightly focused partnerships such as the one above to ones aimed at broadly changing how writing is taught. Such partnerships can potentially provide a useful and collaborative means for improving writing instruction.

Society at Large

I have repeatedly noted that the public needs to value writing if efforts to change writing practices are to be successful. This includes knowing that writing is important, it needs to be taught, schools must devote time to teaching it, and many students do not acquire the needed writing skills. For parents of school-age children, it is also beneficial if they know the value of sharing their writing with their children, demonstrating a positive attitude toward writing, acting as a positive and constructive sounding board for their children's writing, and serving as both partner and instructor (when appropriate) in the child's journey as a writer. The more people acquire such knowledge, the more likely the public will view writing as valuable and indispensable, demanding and supporting both local and broader efforts to improve writing instruction in schools.

As noted earlier, public campaigns designed to inform policymakers and the public about the importance of writing is one way of increasing society's relevant knowhow. Such endeavors are likely to be most successful when they combine a variety of different formats: television and radio advertisements, print and online materials, and local forums. Teachers and school administrators are another important source for increasing the public's knowledge about writing. Schools should make sure that parents know why writing is critical and how they can help their children become better writers. This can include bringing some aspect of school writing instruction into the home (e.g., asking parents to read and respond positively to what their children write) or some aspect of writing at home into the school (e.g., asking students to share at school something written at home).

Other potential sources of information about writing and its importance are parent organizations concerned with some aspect of education or child development. For example, the Learning Disabilities Association provides parents with information about the importance of reading and writing, the challenges faced by students who have difficulty mastering these literacy skills, and the consequences of not doing so (https://ldaamerica.org/parents/). I am not familiar with any similar parent organization focused on writing, but the creation of such groups would enhance public knowledge about writing and its importance.

FUTURE DIRECTIONS

Changing classroom writing practices on a broad scale as advocated here is a formidable challenge. It requires that relevant stakeholders pull together in their efforts rather than work at cross-purposes. This necessitates keeping an open mind about different approaches to teaching writing, views on how it develops, and ways to promote better classroom instruction. This may be more of an obstacle for scholars in writing (e.g., Prior, 2017) than for school personnel, as teachers have demonstrated a capacity to be flexible in their orientation to teaching writing (Brindle et al., 2016; Graham, Harris, Fink, & MacArthur, 2002).

As the field of writing and its many supporters move toward the future, it is essential to realize that all changes leading to better writing instruction, no matter how small, are a move toward the goal of changing classroom practices broadly. As a result, the efforts of individual teachers contribute significantly to the more collective efforts of groups of teachers, schools, school districts, states, nations, and so forth.

It is relatively easy to envision how one or more entities (e.g., teacher, school, or school district) might take up the ideas presented here to change and improve writing instruction. The real challenge is how to put into action the forces needed to develop and successfully implement a coherent, well-constructed, and consistent vision of writing instruction that cuts across multiple levels (moving from national goals to teacher goals, or vice versa). While I offer a set of ideas and recommendations for accomplishing this task, many different parties would need to step forward to accomplish this objective. Other approaches for broadly changing writing classroom practices are also possible, and I am hopeful that my ideas serve as a springboard for action on the part of many different stakeholders as well as the development of even better recommendations for improving classroom writing instruction.

Future efforts to improve writing instruction will emanate from multiple sources, ranging from more organic actions that emerge at the grassroots level to highly systematic and planned actions undertaken by organizations and governments. Scholars need to study these efforts to determine if and how writing practices in the classroom are changed. Moreover, complex problems like learning to write are not just the responsibility of schools (Harris, 2018), as there are many aspects of writing acquired outside school in a variety of writing communities (Graham, 2018b). We need to develop a science that integrates in-school and out-of-school learning so that we take a broader, systems approach to the study of writing, the acquisition of writing skills, and the promotion of writing instruction.

For the particular set of ideas and actions recommended in this chapter, research is needed to expand what is known about writing and its acquisition. While significant strides toward understanding writing, in and out of school, were made in the past 50 years (see MacArthur, Graham, & Fitzgerald, 2016), this knowledge is incomplete. Furthermore, we know virtually nothing about how teachers, school administrators, and policymakers construct their visions for writing; the types of knowledge needed to do so; and how to put the resulting plans into action. Moving forward, it is critical to understand these processes so that such efforts can be better facilitated and evaluated.

Last, there is a need to test new as well as old methods for helping relevant stakeholders acquire the needed writing know-how. For instance, we are not well-informed about how to provide PD effectively at scale. Just as worrying, practitioners generally view their college preparation of teaching writing as inadequate (e.g., Kiuhara et al., 2009). We need to explore how to change this so that colleges can become a reliable and trusted partner in improving writing instruction in the future.

NOTE

[1] A table summarizing these studies is available from the author: steve.graham@asu.edu.

REFERENCES

Applebee, A., & Langer, J. (2011). A snapshot of writing instruction in middle schools and high schools. *English Journal, 100*, 14–27.

Ball, D. L., & Cohen, D. K. (1999). Developing practice, developing practitioners: Toward a practice-based theory of professional education. In L. Darling-Hammond & G. Sykes (Eds.), *Teaching as a learning profession: Handbook for policy and practice* (pp. 3–31). San Francisco, CA: Jossey-Boss.

Bangert-Drowns, R., Hurley, M., & Wilkinson, B. (2004). The effects of school-based writing-to-learn interventions on academic achievement: A meta-analysis. *Review of Educational Research, 74*, 29–58.

Bazerman, C. (2016). What do sociocultural studies of writing tell us about learning to write? In C. A. MacArthur, S. Graham, & J. Fitzgerald (Eds.), *Handbook of writing research* (2nd ed., pp. 11–23). New York, NY: Guilford Press.

Bazerman, C., Applebee, A. N., Berninger, V. W., Brandt, D., Graham, S., Matsuda, P. K., . . . Schleppegrell, M. (2017). Taking the long view on writing development. *Research in the Teaching of English, 51*, 351–360.

Bransford, J., Darling-Hammond, L., & LePage, P. (2005). Introduction. In L. Darling-Hammond & J. Bransford (Eds.), *Preparing teachers for a changing world: What teachers should learn and be able to do* (pp. 35–117). New York, NY: Wiley.

Brindle, M., Harris, K. R., Graham, S., & Hebert, M. (2016). Third and fourth grade teachers' classroom practices in writing: A national survey. *Reading & Writing: An Interdisciplinary Journal, 29*, 929–954.

Calkins, L. (2014). *Units of study in argument, information, and narrative writing middle school series bundle, Grades 6–8.* Portsmouth, NH: Heinemann.

Coker, D., Farley-Ripley, E., Jackson, A., Wen, H., MacArthur, C., & Jennings, A. (2016). Writing instruction in first grade: An observational study. *Reading & Writing: An Interdisciplinary Journal, 29*, 793–832.

Cutler, L., & Graham, S. (2008). Primary grade writing instruction: A national survey. *Journal of Educational Psychology, 100*, 907–919.

Darling-Hammond, L., & Bransford, J. (2015). *Preparing teachers for a changing world: What teachers should learn and be able to do.* New York, NY: Wiley.

De Smedt, F., van Keer, H., & Merchie, E. (2016). Student, teacher, and class-level correlates of Flemish late elementary school children's writing performance. *Reading & Writing: An Interdisciplinary Journal, 29*, 833–868.

Dietrichson, J., Bog, M., Filges, T., & Jorgensen, A. (2017). Academic interventions for elementary and middle school students with low socioeconomic status: A systematic review and meta-analysis. *Review of Educational Research, 87*, 243–282.

Dockrell, J., Marshall, C., & Wyse, D. (2016). Teachers' reported practices for teaching writing in England. *Reading & Writing: An Interdisciplinary Journal, 29*, 409–434.

Drew, S., Olinghouse, N., Luby-Faggella, M., & Welsh, M. (2017). Framework for disciplinary writing in science Grades 6–12: A national survey. *Journal of Educational Psychology, 109*, 935–955.

Feltovich, P., Prietula, M., & Ericsson, A. (2018). Studies of expertise from psychological perspectives: Historical foundations and recurrent themes. In A. Ericsson, R. Hoffman, A. Kozbelt, & M. Williams (Eds.), *The Cambridge handbook of expertise and expert performance* (2nd ed., pp. 59–83). Cambridge, England: Cambridge University Press.

Fitzgerald, J., & Shanahan, T. (2000). Reading and writing relations and their development. *Educational Psychologist, 35,* 39–50.

Freedman, S. W., Hull, G. A., Higgs, J. M., & Booten, K. P. (2016). Teaching writing in a digital and global age: Toward access, learning, and development for all. In D. H. Gitomer & C. A. Bell (Eds.), *Handbook of research on teaching* (5th ed., pp. 1389–1450). Washington, DC: American Educational Research Association.

Gallagher, A., Arshan, N., & Woodworth, K. (2017). Impact of the National Writing Project's College-Ready Writers Program in high-need rural districts. *Journal of Research on Educational Effectiveness, 10,* 570–595.

Gilbert, J., & Graham, S. (2010). Teaching writing to elementary students in Grades 4 to 6: A national survey. *Elementary School Journal, 110,* 494–518.

Gillespie, A., & Graham, S. (2014). A meta-analysis of writing interventions for students with learning disabilities. *Exceptional Children, 80,* 454–473.

Gillespie, A., Graham, S., Kiuhara, S., & Hebert, M. (2014). High school teachers' use of writing to support students' learning: A national survey. *Reading & Writing: An Interdisciplinary Journal, 27,* 1043–1072.

Graham, S. (2006). Writing. In P. Alexander & P. Winne (Eds.), *Handbook of educational psychology* (pp. 457–478). Mahwah, NJ: Lawrence Erlbaum.

Graham, S. (2018a). A revised writer(s)-within-community model of writing. *Educational Psychologist, 53,* 258–279.

Graham, S. (2018b). A writer(s) within community model of writing. In C. Bazerman, V. Berninger, D. Brandt, S. Graham, J. Langer, S. Murphy, . . . M. Schleppegrell (Eds.), *The lifespan development of writing* (pp. 271–325). Urbana, IL: National Council of English.

Graham, S., Bollinger, A., Booth Olson, C., D'Aoust, C., MacArthur, C., McCutchen, D., & Olinghouse, N. (2012). *Teaching elementary school students to be effective writers: A practice guide.* Washington, DC: U.S. Department of Education, Institute of Education Sciences, National Center for Education Evaluation and Regional Assistance.

Graham, S., Bruch, J., Fitzgerald, J., Friedrich, L., Furgeson, J., Greene, K., . . . Smither Wulsin, C. (2016). *Teaching secondary students to write effectively* (NCEE 2017-4002). Washington, DC: U.S. Department of Education, Institute of Education Sciences, National Center for Education Evaluation and Regional Assistance.

Graham, S., Cappizi, A., Harris, K. R., Hebert, M., & Morphy, P. (2014). Teaching writing to middle school students: A national survey. *Reading & Writing: An Interdisciplinary Journal, 27,* 1015–1042.

Graham, S., & Harris, K. R. (2018). An examination of the design principles underlying a self-regulated strategy development study based on the writers in community model. *Journal of Writing Research, 10,* 139–187.

Graham, S., Harris, K. R., & Beard, K. (2018). Teaching writing to young African American male students using evidence-based practices. *Reading & Writing Quarterly.* Advance online publication. doi:10.1080/10573569.2018.1535775

Graham, S., Harris, K. R., & Chambers, A. (2016). Evidence-based practice and writing instruction. In C. MacArthur, S. Graham, & J. Fitzgerald (Eds.), *Handbook of writing research* (Vol. 2, pp. 211–226). New York, NY: Guilford Press.

Graham, S., Harris, K. R., Fink, B., & MacArthur, C. (2002). Primary grade teachers' theoretical orientations concerning writing instruction: Construct validation and a nationwide survey. *Contemporary Educational Psychology, 27,* 147–166.

Graham, S., Harris, K. R., & Hebert, M. (2011). It is more than just the message: Analysis of presentation effects in scoring writing. *Focus on Exceptional Children, 44*(4), 1–12.

Graham, S., Harris, K. R., & Larsen, L. (2001). Prevention and intervention of writing difficulties for students with learning disabilities. *Learning Disability Research & Practice, 16,* 74–84.

Graham, S., Harris, K. R., MacArthur, C., & Fink-Chorzempa, B. (2003). Primary grade teachers' instructional adaptations for weaker writers: A national survey. *Journal of Educational Psychology, 95,* 279–293.

Graham, S., Harris, K. R., Mason, L., Fink-Chorzempa, B., Moran, S., & Saddler, B. (2008). How do primary grade teachers teach handwriting? A national survey. *Reading & Writing: An Interdisciplinary Journal, 21,* 49–69.

Graham, S., Harris, K. R., & McKeown, D. (2013). The writing of students with LD and a meta-analysis of SRSD writing intervention studies: Redux. In L. Swanson, K. R. Harris, & S. Graham (Eds.), *Handbook of learning disabilities* (2nd ed., pp. 405–438). New York, NY: Guilford Press.

Graham, S., Harris, K. R., & Santangelo, T. (2015). Research-based writing practices and the Common Core: Meta-analysis and meta-synthesis. *Elementary School Journal, 115,* 498–522.

Graham, S., & Hebert, M. (2011). Writing-to-read: A meta-analysis of the impact of writing and writing instruction on reading. *Harvard Educational Review, 81,* 710–744.

Graham, S., Hebert, M., & Harris, K. R. (2015). Formative assessment and writing: A meta-analysis. *Elementary School Journal, 115,* 524–547.

Graham, S., Hebert, M., Sandbank, M., & Harris, K. R. (2016). Credibly assessing the writing achievement of young struggling writers: Application of generalizability theory. *Learning Disability Quarterly, 39,* 72–82.

Graham, S., Heller, R., Applebee, A., Olson, C., & Collins, J. (2013). *Get it in writing: Making adolescent writing an immediate priority in Texas.* Atlanta, GA: Southern Regional Educational Board.

Graham, S., Liu, K., Aitken, A., Ng, C., Bartlett, B., Harris, K. R., & Holzapel, J. (2018). Balancing reading and writing instruction: A meta-analysis. *Reading Research Quarterly, 53,* 279–304.

Graham, S., Liu, K., Bartlett, B., Ng, C., Harris, K. R., Aitken, A., . . . Talukdar, J. (2018). Reading for writing: A meta-analysis of the impact of reading and reading instruction on writing. *Review of Educational Research, 88,* 243–284.

Graham, S., Morphy, P., Harris, K., Fink-Chorzempa, B., Saddler, B., Moran, S., & Mason, L. (2008). Teaching spelling in the primary grades: A national survey of instructional practices and adaptations. *American Educational Research Journal, 45,* 796–825.

Graham, S., & Perin, D. (2007). *Writing next: Effective strategies to improve writing of adolescent middle and high school.* Washington, DC: Alliance for Excellence in Education.

Graham, S., & Rijlaarsdam, G. (2016). Writing education around the globe. *Reading & Writing: An Interdisciplinary Journal, 29,* 781–792.

Grossman, P., & McDonald, M. (2008). Back to the future: Directions for research in teaching and teacher education. *American Educational Research Journal, 45,* 184–205.

Harris, K. R. (2018). Educational psychology: A future retrospective. *Journal of Educational Psychology, 110,* 163–173.

Harris, K. R., Graham, S., Mason, L., & Friedlander, B. (2008). *Powerful writing strategies for all students.* Baltimore, MD: Brookes.

Harris, K. R., Lane, K., Graham, S., Driscoll, S., Sandmel, K., Brindle, M., & Schatschneider, C. (2012). Practice-based professional development for self-regulated strategy development in writing: A randomized control study. *Journal of Teacher Education, 63,* 103–119.

Hayes, J., & Flower, L. (1980). Identifying the organization of writing processes. In L. Gregg & E. Steinberg (Eds.), *Cognitive processes in writing* (pp. 3–30). Hillsdale, NJ: Lawrence Erlbaum.

Hayes, J. R. (2012). Modeling and remodeling writing. *Written Communication, 29,* 369–388.

Hertzberg, F., & Roe, A. (2016). Writing in the content areas: A Norwegian case study. *Reading & Writing: An Interdisciplinary Journal, 29,* 555–576.

Hsiang, T., Graham, S., & Wong, P. (2018). Teaching writing in Grades 7–9 in urban schools in the Greater China Region. *Reading Research Quarterly, 53,* 473–507.

Hsiang, T. P., & Graham, S. (2016). Teaching writing in Grades 4–6 in urban schools in the Greater China Region. *Reading and Writing: An Interdisciplinary Journal, 29,* 869–902.

Hull, G., & Schultz, K. (2001). Literacy and learning out of school: A review of theory and research. *Review of Educational Research, 71,* 575–611.

Kellogg, R., & Whiteford, A. (2009). Training advanced writing skills: The case for deliberate practice. *Educational Psychologist, 44,* 250–266.

Kiuhara, S., Graham, S., & Hawken, L. (2009). Teaching writing to high school students: A national survey. *Journal of Educational Psychology, 101,* 136–160.

Koko, K. (2016). Writing in mathematics: A survey of K–12 teachers' reported frequency in the classroom. *School Science & Mathematics, 116,* 276–285.

Knudson, R. (1995). Writing experiences, attitudes, and achievement of first to sixth graders. *Journal of Educational Research, 89,* 90–97.

Kraft, M., Blazar, D., & Hogan, D. (2018). The effects of teacher coaching on instruction and achievement: A meta-analysis of the causal evidence. *Review of Educational Research, 88,* 547–588.

Light, R. (2001). *Making the most of college.* Cambridge, MA: Harvard University Press.

MacArthur, C., Graham, S., & Fitzgerald, J. (2016). *Handbook of research on writing* (2nd ed.). New York, NY: Guilford Press.

Margarida, A., Simao, V., Malpique, A., Frison, L., & Marques, A. (2016). Teaching writing to middle school students in Portugal and in Brazil: An exploratory study. *Reading & Writing: An Interdisciplinary Journal, 29,* 955–979.

McCarthy, S., & Ro, Y. (2011). Approaches to writing instruction. *Pedagogies: An International Journal, 6,* 273–295.

McGhee, M., & Lew, C. (2007). Leadership and writing: How principals' knowledge, beliefs, and interventions affect writing instruction in elementary and secondary schools. *Educational Administration Quarterly, 43,* 358–380.

Mo, Y., & Troia, G. (2017). Similarities and differences in constructs represented by U.S. middle school writing tests and the 2007 national assessment of educational progress writing assessment. *Assessing Writing, 33,* 48–67.

Myers, J., Scales, R. Q., Grisham, D. L., Wolsey, T. D., Dismuke, S., Smetana, L., . . . Martin, S. (2016). What about writing: A national exploratory study of writing instruction in teacher preparation programs. *Literacy Research & Instruction, 55,* 309–330.

National Center for Educational Statistics. (2012). *The nation's report card: Writing 2011* (NCES 2012-470). Washington, DC: U.S. Department of Education, Institute of Educational Sciences.

National Commission on Writing. (2003). *The neglected "R": The need for a writing revolution.* Washington DC: College Board.

National Commission on Writing. (2004, September). *Writing: A ticket to work or a ticket out: A survey of business leaders* (National Writing Project). Retrieved from https://www.nwp.org/cs/public/print/resource/2540

National Commission on Writing. (2005). *Writing: A powerful message from state government.* New York, NY: College Board.

National Governors Association & Council of Chief School Officers. (2010). *Common core state standards*. Retrieved from http://www.corestandards.org/

Olinghouse, N. G., Graham, S., & Gillespie, A. (2015). The relationship of discourse and topic knowledge to fifth graders' writing performance. *Journal of Educational Psychology, 107*, 391–406.

Parr, J., & Jesson, R. (2016). Mapping the landscape of writing instruction in New Zealand. *Reading & Writing: An Interdisciplinary Journal, 29*, 981–1011.

Prior, P. (2017). Setting a research agenda for writing development: The long view from where. *Research in the Teaching of English, 52*, 211–219.

Ray, A., Graham, S., Houston, J., & Harris, K. R. (2016). Teachers' use of writing to support students' learning in middle school: A national survey in the United States. *Reading & Writing: An International Journal, 29*, 1039–1068.

Rietdijk, S., van Weijen, D., Jassen, T, van den Bergh, H., & Rijlaarsdam, G. (2018). Teaching writing in primary education: Classroom practice, time, teachers' beliefs and skills. *Journal of Educational Psychology, 110*, 640–663.

Rijlaarsdam, G., Van den Bergh, H., Couzijn, M., Janssen, T., Braaksma, M., Tillema, M., . . . Raedts, M. (2012). Writing. In K. R. Harris, S. Graham, & T. Urdan (Eds.), *APA educational psychology handbook* (Vol. 3, pp. 189–227). Washington, DC: American Psychological Association.

Russ, R., Sherin, B., & Sherin, M. (2016). What constitutes teacher learning? In D. Gitomer & C. Bell (Eds.), *Handbook of research on teaching* (2nd ed., pp. 391–438). Washington, DC: American Educational Research Association.

Schoenfeld, A. (1998). Toward a theory of teaching-in-context. *Issues in Education, 4*(1), 1–94.

Shanahan, T. (2006). Relations among oral language, reading, and writing development. In C. A. MacArthur, S. Graham, & J. Fitzgerald (Eds.), *Handbook of writing research* (pp. 171–183). New York, NY: Guilford Press.

Shulman, L. (1987). Knowledge and teaching: Foundations of the new reform. *Harvard Educational Review, 57*(1), 1–23.

Simmerman, S., Harward, S., Pierce, L., Peterson, N., Morrison, T. G., Korth, B., . . . Shumway, J. (2012). Elementary teachers' perceptions of process writing. *Literacy Research & Instruction, 51*, 292–307.

Stigler, J., & Miller, K. (2018). Expertise and expert performance in teaching. In A. Ericsson, R. Hoffman, A. Kozbelt, & M. Williams (Eds.), *The Cambridge handbook of expertise and expert performance* (2nd ed., pp. 431–454). Cambridge, England: Cambridge University Press.

Swedlow, J. (1999). The power of writing. *National Geographic, 196*, 110–132.

Tolchinsky, L. (2016). From text to language and back again: The emergence of written language. In C. A. MacArthur, S. Graham, & J. Fitzgerald (Eds.), *Handbook of writing research* (2nd ed., pp. 144–159). New York, NY: Guilford Press.

Troia, G., & Graham, S. (2016). Common Core Writing and Language Standards and aligned state assessments: A national survey of teacher beliefs and attitudes. *Reading & Writing: An Interdisciplinary Journal, 29*, 1719–1743.

Troia, G., & Graham, S. (2017). Use and acceptability of adaptations to classroom writing instruction and assessment practices for students with disabilities: A survey of Grade 3–8 teachers. *Learning Disabilities Research & Practice, 32*, 257–269.

Troia, G., Olinghouse, N., Hawkins, L., Kioke, R., Cen, A., Wilson, J., & Stewart, K. (2015). Academic standards for writing. *Elementary School Journal, 116*, 291–321.

Tse, S., & Hui, S. (2016). Chinese writing curriculum reforms in Hong Kong in recent years and their impact on teaching and learning. *Reading & Writing: An Interdisciplinary Journal, 29*, 1013–1037.

West, J., & Saine, P. (2016). The mentored multigenre project: Fostering authentic writing interactions between high school writers and teacher candidates. *Journal of Adolescent & Adult Literacy, 60*, 629–641.

Wilcox, K., Jeffrey, J., & Gardner-Bixler, A. (2016). Writing to the Common Core: Teachers' response to changes in standards and assessments for writing in elementary schools. *Reading & Writing: An Interdisciplinary Journal, 29*, 903–928.

Wolbers, K., Dostal, H., Skerrit, P., & Stephenson, B. (2017). The impact of three years of professional development on knowledge and implementation. *Journal of Educational Research, 110*, 61–71.

Woodward, R. (2013). Complicating "writing teachers must write": Tensions between teachers' literate and instructional practices. In P. Dunston, L. Gambrell, K. Headley, S. Fullerton, & P. Stecker (Eds.), *62nd yearbook of the Literacy Research Association*. Altamonte Springs, FL: Literacy Research Association.

Chapter 11

Developing a Complex Portrait of Content Teaching for Multilingual Learners via Nonlinear Theoretical Understandings

KARA MITCHELL VIESCA
University of Nebraska-Lincoln

KATHRYN STROM
California State University, East Bay

SVENJA HAMMER
Leuphana University Lüneburg

JESSICA MASTERSON
CINDY HAMMER LINZELL
JESSICA MITCHELL-MCCOLLOUGH
University of Nebraska-Lincoln

NAOMI FLYNN
University of Reading

Utilizing a complex theory of teacher learning and practice, this chapter analyzes ~120 empirical studies of content teacher development (both preservice and in-service) for working with multilingual learners as well as research on content teaching for multilingual students. Our analysis identified three dimensions of quality content teaching for multilingual learners that are complex and intricately connected: context, orientations, and pedagogy. This chapter explores the results of our literature analysis and argues for improving content teaching for multilingual students through improved theoretically grounded research that embraces, explores, and accounts for the expansive complexities inherent in teacher learning and practice.

The underpreparation of content teachers to work with multilingual students[1] is a well-documented issue (Faltis & Valdés, 2016; Freeman & Freeman, 2014). However, as Faltis and Valdés (2016) argue, there is little consensus

Review of Research in Education
March 2019, Vol. 43, pp. 304–335
DOI: 10.3102/0091732X18820910
Chapter reuse guidelines: sagepub.com/journals-permissions

among teacher educators regarding what knowledge, skills, and inclinations content teachers of multilingual students should have to be "good" and "effective." They also highlight the variety of research that exists on the topic—some empirical, some informed by nonempirical work—and suggest that "more and better research is needed if teacher educators are to be better informed about how to most effectively prepare preservice teachers for teaching in linguistically diverse classrooms" (p. 551).

Building on this argument of needing more and better research, specifically regarding how it may affect content classroom teaching with multilingual students, we examined existing research that might inform improved teacher learning and practice. From our review, we argue that future research needs to be strengthened through more theoretically guided, grounded, and reasoned research. Particularly, our analysis of the current, mainly U.S.-based, English-medium literature illustrates how understanding and reasoning through a contemporary body of empirical research with an ontologically different theoretical perspective of teacher learning and practice can offer forward directions for developing a complex portrait of content teaching for multilingual learners. We posit that such a complex portrait can positively affect content teaching practices in educational settings with multilingual students via improved research and practice grounded in the reality of the highly situated constellations of relationships and interconnections of teaching, learning, and practice. Complexifying our understandings of teacher learning, quality practice, and their relationships provides the field with necessary tools to reconceptualize change in practice, as well as how it is evidenced and analyzed, for content teachers of multilingual learners and beyond.

THEORETICAL FOUNDATIONS

Despite the immense complexity of teacher development, dominant research and policy perspectives in this area largely remain reductionist and transactional, positioning the teacher as an autonomous actor/empty vessel who takes her learning from her preservice instruction or a professional development (PD) activity and merely transfers it into classroom practice (Opfer & Pedder, 2011; Strom, 2015). However, an emerging body of literature in teacher education reframes teacher learning and practice as emergent phenomena (Ell et al., 2017; Strom, Martin, & Villegas, 2018) that are jointly constructed from the negotiations of multiple situated elements (Anderson & Stillman, 2010; Gatti, 2016), which include not just the teacher and her students but also other classroom-, school-, district-, and policy-level factors (Strom, 2015; Strom & Martin, 2017). To frame and interpret this review of literature, we draw on insights from rhizomatics (Deleuze & Guattari, 1987; Strom, 2015), a critical theory of complexity that provides important conceptual tools for developing a different ontological perspective of teaching and learning about teaching (and the relationship between the two). Rhizomatics, which is based on the figuration of the rhizome, offers an alternative worldview that critiques linear, binary Western thinking patterns and instead emphasizes heterogeneity, connection, multiplicity, and flux (Deleuze & Guattari, 1987).

One of the key concepts of rhizomatics, *assemblage*, provides an analytic apparatus to examine teaching phenomena from a complex, critical lens (Strom, 2015; Strom & Martin, 2017). An assemblage is a multiplicity, or a constellation of elements that includes people, things, spaces, ideas, sets of circumstances, histories, power relations, and so on. An assemblage is both a substantive (a noun) and a process (a doing; Deleuze & Guattari, 1987). It is the constellation of the things and forces that comprise it, and it also refers to the ways that the components of a particular assemblage work together to do something. Applied to teaching, then, we could consider the teacher as part of a situated assemblage, together with her students, the content and pedagogy, her classroom space and materials, people and other elements in the larger school context, sociocultural/historic conditions, current educational policies and other political elements, and so on (Strom, 2015; Strom & Martin, 2017). These elements, both human and nonhuman, all collectively shape the functioning of a teaching assemblage (Strom, 2015).

Overall, we argue that the concept of assemblage helps bridge multiple ontological shifts that we suggest better attend to the complexity of teaching (Strom & Martin, 2017). Specifically, an assemblage view moves the central referent in studying teaching from the *teacher* to the *teaching multiplicity*. It also provides a collective or distributed view of agency—that is, teaching is not done by an autonomous teacher but is the joint product of the entire assemblage. Thus, the agency is distributed, though not always equally. Moreover, this agency is shared by both human and material factors including the dimensions that we outline in the review of literature that follows. These teaching-assemblages are also *mobile*—teaching and all the elements that comprise it are not static but are vital and dynamic. Furthermore, they not only morph from moment to moment but are also interdependent and change in relation to the rest of the assemblage. Thus, teaching is an emergent, situated, temporal phenomenon in continual flux. Finally, assemblages are defined by their heterogeneity (Deleuze & Guattari, 1987).

From an assemblage perspective, *difference* is the reigning characteristic of educational activity. Because teaching activity is produced by heterogeneous assemblages (specific sets of actors, materials, and conditions/forces that, together, are continually differentiating in relation to each other), the teaching (and teacher) "becomes different" depending on the situated functioning of that specific teaching-assemblage. The "products" (e.g., teaching practices and learning) are jointly constructed by these continually differentiating elements, which means that the teaching practices are always hybrid. Moreover, from a rhizomatic perspective, difference is a creative, generative force—more heterogeneity introduced into an assemblage means the possibilities for new forms of teaching and learning are expanded (Strom & Martin, 2017). This last shift concerning difference and hybridity is particularly significant in the context of the education of multilingual learners, who bring with them a profusion of difference in terms of linguistic resources, background experiences, and cultural funds of knowledge. Thus, a rhizomatic perspective and the concept of assemblage not only offers ways to analyze the multiple dimensions of teaching of multilingual learners that we discuss in this chapter, but they also provide an ontologically different, and fundamentally assets-based, way to view multilingual learners and their contributions to classrooms.

A rhizomatic perspective is also compatible with, and expands on, commonly accepted understandings regarding language learning, including the sociomaterial and mediated nature of learning (Martin & Strom, 2015; Vygotsky, 1978) and the importance of translanguaging (García, 2009). For example, translanguaging, a term that Orellana and García (2014) define as "the ways bilinguals draw on their full linguistic toolkits in order to process information, make meaning, and convey it to others" (p. 386), focuses on language as *process* (rather than a fully formed object) that materializes in practice—thus aligning with a rhizomatic emphasis on becoming over being (Deleuze & Guattari, 1987). Moreover, translanguaging is an assemblaging activity: It brings together heterogeneous elements in a particular situation and produces something new—not additive, but qualitatively different—as a result of its interactions. García and Leiva (2014) draw their understanding of translanguaging from Maturana and Varela's (1973) notion of "autopoiesis," or creation within a self-organizing system. A rhizomatic perspective expands this notion to "sympoiesis," or co-organizing (Haraway, 2016). From a critically complex viewpoint, there is no such thing as a self-organizing system; every assemblage or activity system is connected to others. Instead, processes like translanguaging are *sympoietic*: All the elements of language, context, and learner are being produced in relation to each other—they are made collaboratively.

As a final note, while rhizomatics and the notion of teaching as an assemblage have not yet intersected significantly with various bodies of critical theory-informed literature in education research, we argue that an understanding of a teaching assemblage is incomplete without attending to the human and nonhuman factors that have been identified and researched within expansive and important bodies of research, such as culturally sustaining/relevant/responsive pedagogies (e.g., Gay, 2002; Ladson-Billings, 1995; Paris, 2012), critical race/critical Whiteness (e.g., Ladson-Billings & Tate, 1995; Howard & Navarro, 2016; Matias, 2013), intersectional work with critical race and critical disability studies (e.g., Annamma, Jackson, & Morrison, 2017), and so on. While it is not within the scope of this chapter to describe, explore, and interact with those important connections, the theoretical perspective we employ is a critical one focused on equity and justice that attends to power and privilege in ways that meaningfully connect with the important work already occurring in education research around race, gender, sexual orientation, culture, language, ability, and other dimensions of justice. In the sections that follow, we further discuss critically oriented rhizomatic ideas alongside an analysis of literature regarding teacher development and practices for teaching multilingual learners in mainstream settings.

BODY OF LITERATURE ANALYZED

We defined (and continually refined) the scope of the literature we analyzed, which was broadly concerned with research on content teacher development and content teaching for multilingual students in general content classroom settings (thus excluding studies with a specific focus on bilingual education or English as a second language [ESL] efforts). We included only peer-reviewed, empirical academic journal articles published between 2008 and early 2018 on this topic. To maintain a manageable number of studies, we did not include empirical work published in books, though we acknowledge strong research is published in such outlets as well. We bounded our review with the year 2008, which is significant in our minds, as this was when Lucas and Grinberg (2008) published a first-of-its-kind literature review on the preparation of content teachers of multilingual students.

To source articles for the chapter, we first conducted database searches (e.g., ERIC, EBSCO, etc.) of English-language journals with various combinations of general key words and phrases, including "English language learners," "mainstream classes," and "linguistically responsive." We then proceeded with hand searches of relevant journals, for which we sifted through each volume beginning in 2008, looking for studies that met the aforementioned criteria. In total, we ended with 122 articles on which the following analysis is based. This literature was all published in English and mostly conducted in the United States, but not exclusively. However, the focus of this body of research was on multilingual students attending English medium classrooms and learning English along with content in those classrooms, mostly in the United States.

As we read and analyzed the literature, we attended to main results found, the questions asked, theories used, and assumptions made by researchers. Via this iterative, collaborative process of reading, analysis, discussion, and memoing, our team identified three major dimensions of quality content teaching for multilingual students, which are supported by both the current empirical literature and our theoretical perspective: pedagogy, context, and orientations. These dimensions are described below with our synthesis of current research results, followed by an analysis of these results from our theoretical perspective that then expands and complexifies the components and relationships within each dimension, as well as provides forward thinking possibilities for teacher learning and practice within and across these dimensions. In the end, our work presents a complex portrait of content teaching with multilingual students, a foundational tool for future research, policy, and practice that can produce and co-construct improved teacher learning and practice.

As we discuss these dimensions below, we focus particularly on the phenomenon of teacher learning and practice as a complex assemblage of teaching, learning, students, context, resources, policies, histories, and so on. While the currently available research was not conducted from the theoretical perspective we employ here, this body of literature offers important insights to consider. This belief aligns with the ontologically different perspective we are seeking to employ, which shifts us away from binaries like either/or. In other words, we do not seek to argue that research done from our theoretical perspective is right and research using from other perspectives is wrong. We both find value in the work that has been done *and* we argue that there is room to grow and expand from what we know and are currently doing into more complex ways of conceptualizing, investigating, and understanding teacher learning and practice. In particular, we argue for attention to process rather than product (on becoming rather than being), for teaching to be understood as an assemblage, and for recognizing, embracing, and working within the reality of *difference* as both a constant and as productive (i.e., as a creative force). The analysis below presents current research findings with an interpretation attending to the possibilities of what a complex, nonlinear perspective of teacher learning and practice offers.

A COMPLEX PORTRAIT: QUALITY CONTENT TEACHING FOR MULTILINGUAL STUDENTS

Our analysis provided important insights into understanding quality teaching for multilingual learners in content-area classrooms, especially when considered as an assemblage, or a set of complex, dynamic interactions, and interdependent relationships between teachers, students, and available resources (e.g., teacher expertise, curricula, technology). The three dimensions of quality teaching identified via our investigation are described below: pedagogy, context, and orientations.

Pedagogy

The research results centered on pedagogy illustrate the value of sociocultural, inquiry-based, and culturally sustaining pedagogies; the connections between content and language instruction; the complexity of assessment; the value of home languages and bilingual supports; and a variety of language development approaches. We provide a brief overview of these research findings corresponding to these identified topics and then an analysis and critique of these studies from our theoretical perspective to illustrate the multifaceted dimension of pedagogy in relation to a complex portrait, or what we argue is a multifaceted assemblage, of content teaching for multilingual students.

Sociocultural, Inquiry-Based, and Culturally Sustaining Pedagogies

Several identified studies examined sociocultural instructional practices and their positive impact on multilingual student learning (e.g., Shaw, Lyon, Stoddart, Mosqueda, & Menon, 2014; Swanson, Bianchini, & Lee, 2014; Teemant &

Hausman, 2013). Other research focused on the ways specific aspects of sociocultural pedagogy, such as collaboration, dialogue, and other forms of social interaction, affected learning (Brooks & Thurston, 2010; Cole, 2013; Garrett & Hong, 2016; Moore & Schleppegrell, 2014; Turner, Dominguez, Empson, & Maldonado, 2013). A further subset of studies examined the types of interactions in the classroom that supported multilingual student learning (Hoffman, Villarreal, DeJulio, Taylor, & Shin, 2017; Im & Martin, 2015; Kibler, 2010) and the types of inquiry-based pedagogies that also supported positive learning gains for multilingual students (Jackson & Ash, 2012; Johnson, Bolshakova, & Waldron, 2016; Manzo, Cruz, Faltis, & de la Torre, 2011; Santau, Maerten-Rivera, & Huggins, 2011). Furthermore, the work of Huerta (2011), Pawan (2008), Macleroy (2013), Carbone and Orellana (2010), and Johnson et al. (2016) illustrated the value of what Paris (2012) calls culturally sustaining pedagogies that attend to culture and community (both inside and outside the classroom) in complex ways. Overall and in combination, these studies suggest the possibilities of a quality teaching-assemblage via attention to pedagogy in complex, interconnected ways. Specifically, together these studies offer a portrait of a suggested pedagogy in content classrooms for multilingual students that is complex and attends to inquiry, interaction, context, culture, discourse, and the tangible and intangible resources inside and outside of the classroom. These studies suggest pedagogical approaches to support multilingual student learning in content classrooms is deeply active, connected, engaging for students, and relevant to their lives outside of school. Yet, individually, some of these studies employ methods that a rhizomatics perspective calls into question, such as posing a teacher learning research question and answering it with student standardized test scores. This issue is taken up further below.

The Connections Between Content and Language

Multiple studies examined approaches to teaching content and language, with many providing evidence of a strong relationship between the two, as well as specific ways to combine them (Beal, Adams, & Cohen, 2010; Brown, Ryoo, & Rodriguez, 2010; Carrejo & Reinhartz, 2012; Echevarria, Richards-Tutor, Canges, & Francis, 2011; Echevarria, Richards-Tutor, Chinn, & Ratleff, 2011; Jackson & Ash, 2012; Lara-Alecio et al., 2012; Lee, Penfield, & Buxton, 2011). Moreover, the findings across these studies show evidence for a strong relationship across content areas such as science, mathematics, and literacy. For instance, Alt, Arizmendi, and Beal (2014) found that math difficulties in multilingual students appear to be related to the language demands of math tasks. In total, these studies illustrate both the opportunity and challenges inherent in integrating language and content teaching for multilingual students.

Pass and Mantero (2009) illustrate some of the challenges in integrating language and content, specifically within the structural inequalities and larger issues across a school. They suggest that quality pedagogy may occur when teachers make content comprehensible and work flexibly with students to not only build on the linguistic and cultural assets they bring to the classroom but also be limited by larger contextual issues. This research illustrates also the interconnected nature of the dimensions of quality teaching we identified in our analysis of the literature—pedagogy, context, and orientations. We do not suggest that they exist as separate and distinct dimensions, rather, as suggested by Pass and Mantero, in interconnected ways that affect and influence one another. Similarly, as Brown et al. (2010) suggest, we offer that attending to all of the dimensions is important, yet at times, we may focus more on one or the other to improve teacher learning and practice or to simply discuss and clarify meaning (such as in this section). Overall, the studies focusing on teaching content and language suggest an important yet nonlinear relationship between the development of language and content in content classrooms for multilingual students that are affected by context.

The Complexity of Assessment

Assessment can be an incredibly complex act that is performed in overly simplistic ways (e.g., assessing students only in English on tests created, normed, and standardized for monolingual/highly proficient speakers of English). The research we analyzed emphasized this issue attending to the necessary accommodations for students (Clark-Gareca, 2016) and the opportunity for teachers, when given time and support, to learn from student assessments in order to better understand their students' strengths and struggles, which also resulted in changes in teaching practice (Buxton, Allexsaht-Snider, et al., 2013). Alt, Arizmendi, Beal, and Hurtado (2013) investigated the complexity of multilingual assessments by studying a Spanish-enhanced standardized mathematical test and found that the Spanish enhancement was beneficial for Spanish-speaking students learning English, although the amount of benefit students received was predicted by the level of the child's language dominance in Spanish. While a smaller constellation of studies, together, they suggest the importance of attending to the complexity of assessing multilingual students as well as the possibilities and opportunities of thoughtful accommodations, multilingual assessments, and an emphasis on teachers learning from assessments about student strengths and abilities.

The Value of Home Languages and Bilingual Supports

The power of bilingualism and home language supports in the classrooms for multilingual students was illustrated by several studies. In a value-added-model study examining features of teacher effectiveness, Loeb, Soland, and Fox (2014) found that teachers who were found effective with multilingual students were also found to be effective with other students, or vice versa. However, researchers reported that teachers who were fluent in the students' home language and/or had a bilingual teaching certificate were more effective with multilingual students than non-multilingual students. Two studies looked at students' language choices in instructional environments (Martínez, 2010; Van Laere, Agirdag, & van Braak, 2016) and found complex choices and relationships between content, pedagogy, and expansive student linguistic repertoires. Kibler (2014) found that bilingual practices in an English-medium high school supported strong learning outcomes for the student she followed. From this research, we suggest that part of the complex portrait of quality content teaching for multilingual students attends to languages other than English and their use by teachers and students in classrooms.

Variety of Language Development Approaches

Specific language development strategies were the foci of a group of studies. For instance, Ajayi (2015) documented benefit in explicit vocabulary instruction. Kieffer and Lesaux (2012) examined an academic language intervention intended to affect morphological awareness and found a positive impact. Similarly, Lesaux, Kieffer, Kelley, and Harris (2014) looked at the outcomes of an academic language intervention focused on vocabulary, reading comprehension, and writing development and instruction. They found the intervention had an impact, but varied in significance and meaningfulness, and they did not find an impact on reading comprehension based on the vocabulary work. Vaughn et al. (2009) found value in instructional practices like structured pairing, vocabulary instruction, graphic organizers, and written responses, connecting these practices to multilingual student test scores. Two studies found positive benefit in teaching multilingual students cognitive strategies (Kim et al., 2011; Olson et al., 2012). Finally, Bunch (2009) suggests attending to the ways students modify their language for audience and purpose in classroom speech events to disrupt the unhelpful focus on either academic language or social language. In combination, these studies illustrate a variety of potentially beneficial approaches that likely could be integrated into varying teaching assemblages in myriad ways across a variety of locations. Particularly, these studies illustrate the value of language development strategies, but none of them alone or collectively suggest there is only one way to do this work well.

Pedagogy as a Dimension in a Complex Teaching Assemblage

The research we analyzed provides valuable and interesting findings, particularly when viewed as a whole body of research that illustrates the varied complexities, relationships, and productivity of teacher learning and practice in process, as well as in relation to the education of multilingual students. However, there are some notable and important critiques as well as gaps to note that provide forward thinking possibilities for changing teacher practice. We particularly emphasize the assumptions made across various studies that have implications for how teacher learning and practice is understood, researched, and resourced.

A major issue that emerged from the literature we examined is the use of student test scores in the studies. First, several studies assume that student test scores are accurate representations of multilingual student knowledge (e.g., Beal et al., 2010; Lesaux et al., 2014, Santau et al., 2011). However, we know that, due to the complexity of bilingual language development that includes varied student cultural and linguistic experiences and repertoires, tests are often indicators of varied linguistic and cultural knowledge rather than knowledge of mathematics, science, and so on (Alt et al., 2013; Basterra, Trumbull, & Solano-Flores, 2011).

Second, multiple studies asked questions about teacher learning, and then answered those questions with data drawn from student standardized test scores (e.g., Olson et al., 2012; Shaw et al., 2014). This is something that occurred across the studies discussed in all three of our dimensions (pedagogy, context, and orientations) but was especially prevalent in pedagogy. While we agree that student test scores are part of a complex portrait of quality teaching, we question the linear connections that are drawn quite extensively between teacher learning and practice to student test scores. We suggest that the opportunity exists to disrupt a "representational" view of reality—that something like student test scores can accurately reflect complex, relationship, multiplistic, highly mediated phenomena like teacher learning and practice. Instead, there are multiple processes of transformation implicated on the nomadic path to those test scores, including negotiations with/among/between teachers, learning, activity, resources, context, students, policies, curriculum, and other actors. Instead of focusing on the product of test scores as indicators of teacher learning, we suggest adopting a process-oriented view that attends to the complexities and productivity of these complex, varied, and multifaceted negotiations. Certainly test scores may tell us *something*, particularly when those tests account for the complexity of multilingual and multicultural assessment. However, the use of student test scores as the definitive answer to questions of teacher learning is problematic.

Additional problematic assumptions about what student test scores can do were also found throughout this body of literature. For example, Loeb et al. (2014) assume student test scores are a valuable way to measure teacher effectiveness using a value-added model, and Llosa et al. (2016) assume that curriculum and PD effectiveness is possible to ascertain with student test scores. Yet Llosa et al. (2016) do examine test scores from a more complex perspective by disaggregating data along English proficiency levels, something that is often overlooked in multilingual student test score use and analyses. Similarly, Olson et al. (2012) use tests in Spanish as well as English for a slightly more complex set of data, but still assume that standardized test scores for students can indicate teacher learning. Overall, the dominant role that student test scores played in research regarding pedagogy illustrates an overly simplistic sense of how quality pedagogy is constructed and enacted.

Similarly, studies made reductive assumptions by suggesting that teacher learning is observable in teacher practices via a rubric (e.g., Hoffman et al., 2017; Manzo et al., 2011). We see two major theoretical implications here. First, this assumes a linear, one-to-one correspondence between learning and practice (similar to the issues described above with the use of student test scores). Second, such an assumption illustrates the desire to reproduce sameness (e.g., with an observation "checklist"). In the complexity of teaching and learning in content classrooms with multilingual students, these simplistic assumptions are problematic and further explored below.

In total, the research examining the dimension of pedagogy for multilingual students in content classrooms offers promising opportunities via sociocultural instructional practices that are inquiry-based and dialogic, in integrating language and content, and in using assessment in thoughtful ways, as well as in attending to bilingualism and home languages in classroom practices. We also see the possibilities and opportunities for future research to move into more nonlinear spaces—to emphasize a process-oriented perspective of pedagogy that embraces the varied components of the entire assemblage of quality teaching, learning, and practice for both teachers and multilingual students in content classrooms. Specifically, in moving away from a focus on overly linear relationships between teacher learning and student test scores and between teacher learning and teacher practice, pedagogy can be conceived, researched, and enacted as a complex assemblage that varies in time, space, location, and among the variety of actors, discourses, and resources with which it is constructed. Thus, we also can embrace the productive possibilities of difference across pedagogical approaches and in the variety of contexts and with the variety of teachers, students, and learning spaces where quality content teaching can occur. This is not to say that a quality pedagogy for content teaching for multilingual students is a pedagogy where anything goes. We do suggest, however, that, guided by the principles and findings from this research, an approach that moves toward improving teaching and learning in content classrooms is one that embraces that complexity and shifts away from a focus on linear relationships (e.g., teacher learning tied directly to student learning) and toward understanding and embracing the entire complex assemblage of teaching, learning, and practice. On the one hand, we realize that the incredible complexity that characterizes teaching, learning, and practice cannot be fully analyzed and researched in every study and peer-reviewed journal article. On the other, however, theoretical and methodological approaches that embrace, connect with, and build on the inherent complexity in this work will move our understandings of quality pedagogy in content classrooms forward.

Context

From an assemblage perspective, and as demonstrated by multiple studies in this review, the dimension of *context* plays an important role in quality teaching of multilingual learners, though it is not always the explicit focus of study. While "context" might denote a range of elements, the literature we examined interpreted context almost solely as educational policy, although elements of historical context and culture are implicated therein. Mainly, the studies we analyzed described "top-down" or formal policies, which routinely focused on local, state, and/or national educational policies and how their enactment affected achievement outcomes for multilingual learners (e.g., Battey et al., 2013; Enright & Gilliland, 2011; López, Scanlan, & Gundrum, 2013; Pease-Alvarez, Samway, & Cifka-Herrera, 2010).

However, some studies also looked at policies within the classroom or building level (e.g., Kanno & Kangas, 2014; Mitchell, 2012). As they highlight the power of educational policy initiatives across varying levels, together these studies also underscore the necessity of a cautious and thoughtful approach to policy development and implementation.

In terms of the results of the research a variety of findings are important to highlight. The majority of studies we identified as contributing to the dimension of context described mandated, or top-down, policies and their impacts on students and/or teachers. Enright and Gilliland (2011) looked at the 2001 No Child Left Behind Act, finding that students in content classrooms learned that the *performance* or *display* of their knowledge and skills was more important than their actual proficiencies. López et al. (2013) examined course requirements for U.S. teachers of multilingual learners and connected those to student test scores, suggesting a complex relationship between policy requirements and outcomes on standardized tests. At the state level, Battey et al. (2013) describe the relatively minor impact of Arizona's HB 2064 (mandating tracking and separation of English language instruction from content instruction for multilingual learners) on math teachers' classroom practices. Pease-Alvarez et al. (2010) found that 63% of the teachers in their study viewed the mandated literacy curriculum, open court reading, negatively. While each of these studies looks at a different policy from a different angle examining different kinds of impacts, they all document and illustrate the inherent complexity of policy implementation across contexts.

Further complexities were highlighted in studies examining de facto outcomes for multilingual students of local policies, illustrating challenges such as exclusion from Advanced Placement courses (Kanno & Kangas, 2014); insufficient levels of English proficiency being attained and then multilingual students being treated as monolingual in the education system (Mitchell, 2012); limiting school-level discourses that affect roles, responsibilities, and power for teachers and multilingual students (English, 2009); and fewer opportunities to learn for multilingual students who are associated with higher student performance (Abedi & Herman, 2010). Underscoring the gravity of these issues, Mosqueda and Maldonado (2013) found that access to more rigorous coursework is a key predictor of Latinx students' academic achievement in mathematics. One study did illustrate policy successes in positive, context-specific, and locally developed PD that specialized staff support and provided access to appropriate instructional resources for teachers (Elfers, Lucero, Stritikus, & Knapp, 2013).

In total, the research we analyzed related to the dimension of context highlights the complexity of this dimension, yet largely focuses on one aspect of that dimension: policy. While studies across our review attended to context in myriad ways, the studies with a major focus on context mainly emphasized policy. However, in terms of what we consider the dimension of context to encompass, this attention to policy is important, but only a small portion of a much more complex contextual assemblage that we argue should also include attention to historical events and perspectives;

local, national, and global contexts; the material and immaterial within and across any given time and space; the context of content (e.g., mathematics, science, social studies, etc.); sociopolitical movements; and broader societal perspectives/narratives (e.g., majoritarian stories; Love, 2004), as well as culture (e.g., in schools, districts, families, communities, etc.). To date, this has not extensively been the focus in our field (as evidenced by less than 10% of the studies in our review having an overt focus on context); however, we argue that expanded, nuanced, centered, and complex investigations of context are necessary.

Context as a Dimension in a Complex Teaching Assemblage

As the studies analyzed here show, policy is a major shaping force in teaching assemblages. It acts as an agent in the teaching process, influencing teachers, for example, to focus on content to be tested (Johnson et al., 2016), to emphasize performance over learning (Enright & Gilliland, 2011), and to use materials that are out of step with research on literacy and language for multilingual learners (Pease-Alvarez et al., 2010). Policies also construct students in particular ways, whether positioning them from a deficient lens as nonproficient English speakers rather than multilingual learners (Mitchell, 2012) or by constructing multilingual learners as a homogenous group rather than one rich in difference (English, 2009).

From a rhizomatic perspective, which emphasizes the productivity of relationality and the criticality of situatedness, policies that allow adaptation to local contexts and populations of learners are required (Elfers et al., 2013; English, 2009). However, the majority of policies described in the literature reviewed were disconnected from local contexts, as well as local student needs and teacher knowledge. The studies, at times, positioned schools, students, and teachers in a passive role, with policy to be "done to" them. This position is problematic, since it ignores the agency of both teachers and students: Teachers are expected to implement the policy in their lessons, and students are expected to participate actively in them. That teachers typically have no voice in policy is especially problematic and also contradictory, since educational policy tends to position teachers as autonomous actors with complete control over their own teaching and over students' learning (as evidenced, e.g., by the use of student tests as proxies of teaching quality, a practice we critiqued above; see also Strom, 2015).

It is also problematic that, when examining the body of literature we amassed for this review, so few studies substantially investigated contextual factors (less than 10% of the studies reviewed) and those mostly focused on educational policy. Moreover, even this contextual factor was discussed largely as a neutral force rather than as one connected up to specific power relations. One of our key arguments in using a rhizomatic framework is to emphasize that the education of multilingual learners by no means occurs in isolation. It is entangled with, and produced by, historic conditions (Matsuda, Lawrence, Delgado, & Crenshaw, 1993), the current sociopolitical climate and specific related events, culture, and so on. We would argue that sociopolitical dimensions of multilingual learner education are particularly important (Lucas & Villegas, 2011). As such, researchers must take care not to treat policies as neutral but to account for them as plugged into particular flows of power that suffuse teaching-assemblages that constrain and enable teaching and learning while producing teachers and multilingual students in specific ways. Furthermore, while the studies in this review that researched dimensions attending to context that focused mainly on policy, they did also attend to other contextual factors such as classroom practices, and so on. In the end, we are seeking here to argue (and the research reviewed here suggests) that contextual elements are both complex and necessary to attend to. But we also seek to extend that argument to push research, teaching, and practice forward to pay more extensive, overt, and expansive attention to the dimension of context in improving teaching for multilingual students by attending to the variety of material and immaterial conditions across time and space that affect teaching and learning in varying geographies and assemblages. While no study can do all these things, we do suggest that more research explicitly and overtly focused on the various facets of the dimension of context in quality teaching for multilingual students in content classroom would be a welcomed, necessary, and important expansion of the research in our field.

Orientations

A substantial amount of research literature examines the attitudes,[2] beliefs, and perspectives of teachers toward students, their practices, as well as teacher preparedness to teach multilingual students. However, based on our theoretical perspective, which emphasizes that the teacher is a multiplicity that includes the experiences and knowledge from her preparation (Strom, 2015), in this section we have also included research regarding teacher learning. Not only is it clear that teacher beliefs, attitudes, and ideologies matter in terms of their relationship to multilingual students but they also work in co-construction with teacher learning opportunities as well as with practice. As Freire (2000) notes, the relationship between teacher learning and practice is also recursive: "The teacher is no longer merely the-one-who-teaches, but one who is himself taught in dialogue with the students, who in turn while being taught also teach" (p. 80). Therefore, to capture these ideas, we adopt the term *teacher-learner orientations*, which, as the research reviewed in this section shows, are of critical importance in the teaching of multilingual learners. Together, the research analyzed in this section examines teachers' perceptions toward multilingual students, teachers' perceptions of preparedness to teach multilingual learners, teacher-learner orientations, and teacher knowledge.

Teacher Perceptions Toward Multilingual Students

Several studies examined teacher perceptions regarding multilingual students. One study documented prevailing negative perspectives toward multilingual students (Vázquez-Montilla, Just, & Triscari, 2014), while another study illustrated teacher belief in a myth that math is the easiest subject for multilingual learners (Hansen-Thomas & Cavagnetto, 2010). In contrast, teachers with humanizing perspectives were found to have a positive impact on student outcomes, as shown in Lewis et al. (2012), who explored student perspectives of teachers' attitudes of care. These researchers found that caring teachers bolstered can-do attitudes in multilingual students in math, which also positively affected math test scores. There is also promising evidence that teachers can change their deficit views of multilingual students (Catalano, Reeves, & Wessels, 2017; Johnson et al., 2016; Mellom, Straubhaar, Balderas, Ariail, & Portes, 2018). Furthermore, multiple studies showed that PD opportunities regarding multilingual learners may be a powerful way to change teachers' beliefs (Kibler & Roman, 2013; Molle, 2013; Pettit, 2011). However, changes from PD do not necessarily occur in a linear manner nor are they always sufficient (Kibler & Roman, 2013; Molle, 2013). Further complicating the notion of changing beliefs, Catalano et al. (2017) found preservice teachers' changes in beliefs but also a lasting commitment to ethnocentrism. Similarly, Tandon, Viesca, Hueston, and Milbourn (2017) examined preservice teachers' perspectives regarding linguistically responsive teaching and found little change overtime. Bustos-Flores and Smith (2009) found that teachers' attitudes are influenced by multiple factors and to varying degrees. These researchers also found that teachers with some degree of bilingualism themselves may have more positive beliefs about multilingual students than those without. However, this is not always the case, as Buxton, Salinas, Mahotiere, Lee, and Secada (2013) demonstrate. They reported that even teachers from the same cultural and linguistic background are capable of holding deficit ideologies toward multilingual students, likely due to generational shifts that make teachers perceive of students as less like them. Five studies provide direct evidence for the complex relationship between teacher beliefs and practice (Bacon, 2018; Gleeson & Davison, 2016; Huerta, 2011; Pass & Mantero, 2009; Pease-Alvarez et al., 2010). Pass and Mantero (2009), for example, found a disconnect between teachers' stated beliefs and their actual classroom practices with multilingual students. Bacon (2018) also found a complex relationship between teacher ideologies and practices, and suggests the benefit of contextualizing ideologies broadly beyond individual dispositions and in relationship to practice.

Teachers' Perceptions of Preparedness to Teach Multilingual Learners

Multiple researchers found that teachers often feel underprepared to teach multilingual learners in mainstream classrooms (Coady, Harper, & de Jong, 2011; O'Neal, Ringler, & Rodriguez, 2008; Polat, 2010). Others have reported that preservice preparation may increase the sense that they are prepared, but not fully (Coady et al., 2011; Schall-Leckrone & McQuillan, 2012; Turgut, Sahin, & Huerta, 2016). Ross (2014) found a positive correlation between teachers' engagement in PD and a heightened sense of effectiveness with multilingual students. Some studies look at perceptions teachers have not just regarding students, but their learning and their role in the classroom and the relationship between beliefs and practice (Cheatham, Jimenez-Silva, Wodrich, & Kasai, 2014; Garrett & Hong, 2016). Two other studies examined teachers' perceptions of their own role in teaching multilingual learners (Ortega, Luft, & Wong, 2013; Yoon, 2008). Yoon (2008) found that teachers positioned themselves in a variety of ways: as a teacher for all students, as a teacher for regular education students, or as a teacher for a single subject. Similarly, Ortega et al. (2013) found that the focal teacher's beliefs about her role were affected by multiple student, contextual, and policy factors, including the level of participation by multilingual learners in lessons, changes in the teacher's position, and her own perception of the power and agency she had in her classroom.

Teacher-Learner Orientations

Learning formats (e.g., face-to-face, online, and/or hybrid courses) and a variety of assignments were examined for their ability to help teachers apply theory to practice as well as develop assets-based perspectives (Choi & Morrison, 2014; Lavery, Nutta, & Youngblood, 2018; Walker, Mahon, & Dray, 2017). Several studies discussed implementing specific interventions in a course or PD session or series, such as immersing participants in a foreign language (Zhang & Pelttari, 2014), modeling research-based strategies (Andrews & Weisenberg, 2013), engaging in reflection and data analysis (Li & Peters, 2016), conducting narrative inquiry (Pu, 2012), science-specific interventions focused on literacy (Lee, Adamson, et al., 2008; Lee, Maerten-Rivera, Penfield, LeRoy, & Secada, 2008), inquiry-based teaching (Adamson, Santau, & Lee, 2013), and pedagogy (Heller, Daehler, Wong, Shinohara, & Miratrix, 2012). Many of these interventions, even brief ones, affected teachers (and students) positively. However, other studies point to the complexity of teacher learning, even when in-depth opportunities are offered (Adamson et al., 2013). The impacts and outcomes of particular PD models were explored (Aguirre-Muñoz, Park, Amabisca, & Boscardin, 2008; DaSilva Iddings & Rose, 2012; Lee et al., 2016; Lys, Ringler, & O'Neal, 2009; Short, Echevarría, & Richards-Tutor, 2011) finding positive impacts on teacher and student learning. However, as Short et al. (2011) found, contextual elements also affected teachers' ability to fully implement their model, including accountability pressures and shifting teacher commitments. Addressing the complexity and nonlinearity of teacher learning, Aguirre-Muñoz et al. (2008) explored the impact of a systemic functional linguistics focused PD. Although teachers did shift in their approach to evaluating and offering feedback on student papers, and providing feedback, the authors found that teachers infused systemic functional linguistics into their practices to varying degrees, providing further evidence that what teachers learn in a PD does not necessarily transfer into practice in a linear manner (e.g., Echevarria, Richards-Tutor, Chinn, & Ratleff, 2011). As these teacher learning studies in combination illustrate, teacher learning and its relationship to practice is a complex phenomenon that may appear more or less successful in a variety of contexts and situations depending on the work done with teachers and the learning outcomes that are emphasized.

A variety of studies examined various forms of collaboration among educators and the impacts of that on content teacher learning for working with multilingual students, suggesting the value of teacher learning-practice in connection with other educators. Studies conducted with both preservice (Galguera, 2011; Jimenez-Silva & Olson, 2012) teachers, as well as in-service teachers (Brancard & Quinnwilliams, 2012) found that collaborative PD opportunities supported learning. A relatively large subset of studies found that collaborative PD between mainstream teachers and language specialists was productive in multiple ways for teacher learning, practice, and the development of a shared sense of responsibility for teaching multilingual students (Babinski, Amendum, Knotek, Sánchez, & Malone, 2018; DelliCarpini & Alonso, 2014; English, 2009; Martin-Beltrán & Peercy, 2014; Peercy & Martin-Beltrán, 2012; Peercy, Martin-Beltrán, Silverman, & Nunn, 2015; Russell, 2014, 2015; Vázquez, López, Segador, & Mohedano, 2015). Other studies highlighted the productivity of various configurations of difference and heterogeneity in partnership (Collins & Liang, 2014; Estapa, Pinnow, & Chval, 2016; Molle, 2013), illustrating the value of teachers learning to talk across difference and engage with tools and perspectives that push their thinking. Another set of studies demonstrated that teachers learn a great deal from working with students, both in preservice (Daniel, 2014; Fitts & Gross, 2012; Master, Loeb, Whitney, & Wyckoff, 2012; Mitchell, Homza, & Ngo, 2012) and in-service experiences (Sowa, 2009). Beyond working with individual teachers, students can also provide valuable information regarding frequently used pedagogical models, such as SIOP (Sheltered Instruction Observation Protocol). In a study conducted by Braden, Wassell, Scantlebury, and Grover (2016), the researchers focused on student agency and voice in the science classroom, learning that while SIOP can and does attend to some aspects of quality teaching, it does not fully recognize students' and families' funds of knowledge, nor fully develop a relationship between science and students' lives outside of school.

Teacher Knowledge Orientations

The studies addressing teacher knowledge, collectively, suggest important aspects of the knowledge base for teacher-learner orientations for teaching multilingual learners. One important dimension of this knowledge base includes knowing how to support literacy and language development in the content areas (Cho & Reich, 2008; Chval, Pinnow, & Thomas, 2015; Matuchniak, Olson, & Scarcella, 2014; Pawan, 2008; Sangster, Anderson, & O'Hara, 2013). Other work, such as a study by Schleppegrell, Greer, and Taylor (2008), suggests that metalinguistic strategies are an important part of supporting language and content development. However, knowledge of language also needs to go hand in hand with knowledge of content and students, as Turgut et al. (2016) demonstrate. Some studies examined teachers' perspectives of the knowledge required for teaching multilingual students. Interestingly, when teachers' perspectives are taken into account, they do not always agree with research literature. Faltis, Arias, and Ramírez-Marín (2010) studied both what the literature suggests the knowledge base for content teachers of multilingual learners should be and secondary teachers' perspectives of those competencies, finding some differences and tensions between the teachers' perspectives and the literature. However, Bowers, Fitts, Quirk, and Jung (2010), examining teacher perspectives of the effectiveness of various approaches in working with multilingual students, found that teachers preferred research-based instructional strategies that combined cognitive and metacognitive comprehension strategy instruction with direct instruction for academic language.

Across the studies analyzed as part of the dimension of orientation, we see a great deal of complexity and opportunity that should be accounted for. Specifically, these studies suggest the importance of teacher orientations toward students, their practice, and their learning, particularly from a critical perspective that attends to issues of power, privilege, and inequity. Furthermore, this research illustrates the value and productivity of collaborating across difference, particularly when different groups of educators work and learn together across a variety of disciplines. Finally, this research suggests that there is more work to do to help teachers feel prepared to teach multilingual students well.

Orientations as a Dimension in a Complex Teaching Assemblage

From a rhizomatic perspective, the teacher is herself an assemblage (Strom, 2015). The works we reviewed illuminated multiple possible dimensions of a teacher assemblage and the way those dimensions interacted with other human and contextual elements. The teacher is not an empty vessel—she brings with her a particular political location (Bustos-Flores & Smith, 2009), background variables such as gender (Pettit, 2011), and previous knowledge and practices learned in preservice preparation (Turgut et al., 2016) as well as PD (e.g., Bowers et al., 2010; Chval et al., 2015). Teacher's attitudes (Kibler & Roman, 2013), orientations toward multilingual learners (Huerta, 2011; Tandon et al., 2017), and beliefs (Coady et al., 2011; Pass & Mantero, 2009; Yoon, 2008) also are dimensions of the teacher multiplicity that, when coming into composition with elements such as learning activities and teaching practices, influence the teaching of multilingual learners. For instance, teachers' pre-existing attitudes about multilingual students can affect whether PD for multilingual learners results in changes in practice (Kibler & Roman, 2013), while orientations, such as having a humanizing approach, can affect student learning (Huerta, 2011). Finally, beliefs can also be a powerful shaping force of the teacher multiplicity. For instance, Yoon (2008) found that beliefs teachers held about themselves as either teachers of content or teachers of all students affected student participation levels and student perceptions of themselves as powerful or powerless. Other studies found that deficit beliefs were an influential part of the teacher multiplicity (e.g., Vázquez-Montilla et al., 2014). Multiple authors suggested that, to truly teach multilingual students in ways that would result in powerful learning, teachers must disrupt these deficit perspectives and develop affirming attitudes (e.g., Choi & Morrison 2014; Mitchell, 2012; Pawan, 2008).

Teacher multiplicities, however, are not static; they are *sympoietic*, or constantly changing in relation to the other elements to which they are connected (Haraway, 2016). For instance, interactions between elements of the teacher multiplicity and learning activities, contextual factors, teacher racialization (Matias, 2016), and students can produce new understandings about students and even change deficit mindsets over time, as shown by researchers such as Mellom et al. (2018). The notion of connection also corresponds to a shift away from binary thinking, which has characterized more traditional notions of teaching multilingual learners. However, as the literature reviewed here demonstrates, there is an emerging knowledge base about teaching multilingual learners that pursues connections, rather than separations, embracing the power of a "both/and" (rather than an "either/or") perspective. For example, studies emphasized the importance of teaching *both* content and language simultaneously (Carrejo & Reinhartz, 2012; Chval et al., 2015; Lara-Alecio et al., 2012; Lee & Maerten-Rivera, 2012) rather than seeing them as two separate instructional areas. Other examples included examining the entanglement of beliefs and practice (Huerta, 2011), bringing together language and pedagogy (Galguera, 2011), and working across content areas (Lee, Adamson, et al., 2008; Vázquez et al., 2015). Others worked across traditional teacher boundaries, bringing together mixtures of mainstream and ESL teachers (DelliCarpini & Alonso 2014; Martin-Beltrán & Peercy, 2014; Russell, 2014, 2015).

As our theoretical approach suggests, introducing difference into a multiplicity also produces conditions for growth and change. For example, Macleroy (2013) found that when teachers introduced a profusion of difference in terms of perspectives, texts, and media, as well as the space to practice, multilingual students gained more sophisticated literacy skills. This was also true for teacher learning, as Molle (2013) reported that introducing a variety of different perspectives and ideas was productive for building teacher knowledge. Furthermore, the introduction of difference into a multiplicity could also explain the productiveness of the various collaborations discussed in the studies reviewed, including between preservice teachers and young people (Fitts & Gross, 2012), mainstream and ESL teachers (e.g., DelliCarpini & Alonso, 2014), content areas (Lee, Adamson, et al., 2008), and different classrooms (Brancard & Quinnwilliams, 2012; Jimenez-Silva & Olson, 2012). These studies demonstrated that bringing different sets of knowledges, practices, and tools together produced emergent learning and practices that were supportive for multilingual learners.

There were also examples of specific elements that served as productive conditions. For instance, teachers who brought affirming orientations toward multilingual learners as part of their own orientations also were more likely to have higher student achievement (Master et al., 2012). Two other studies (Li & Peters, 2016; Sowa, 2009) showed that when teachers were active agents in their research, they co-constructed learning more meaningfully. As an illustration, Sowa (2009) demonstrated that teachers engaging in action research not only changed their practices but also their beliefs. Unfortunately, many studies examined one "slice" of the teacher multiplicity without acknowledging or connecting to other aspects of the teacher multiplicity. Some studies also reported that interactions with elements of the teacher multiplicity and target activities were shaped by contextual factors—rather than beginning with this assumption. We take up this point in the discussion.

IMPLICATIONS FOR THE FIELD: NEW DIRECTIONS FOR RESEARCH, PRACTICE, AND POLICY

As our analysis of the literature illustrates, there are many fruitful opportunities to improve teaching and learning in content classrooms for multilingual students and their teachers via complex understandings of teaching as an assemblage and students and teachers as multiplicities. This is not to argue that work done to date is without value. Rather, we argue that recognizing the complexities in teacher learning and practice is an ethical imperative, because binary, individualistic, reductionist thinking is actively harmful (Molle, 2013). Furthermore, this imperative provides a productive opportunity for theoretical work to move forward by expanding understandings of these complexities and resultant harm through interactions with strong, extant critical theoretical work (e.g., critical race theory, critical whiteness, disability crit, etc.) in more complex ways in collaboration with a rhizomatics/critical posthuman perspective. To avoid the harm of binary, individualistic and reductionist thinking in content teaching for multilingual students, our research, practice, and policies need to be informed, interact, and be co-constructed with important bodies of critical theoretical work that explore the complexities, intersectionalities, discourses, and historical contexts of teaching, learning, and practice with attention to inequitable flows of power and privilege along various axes such as race, gender, class, language, sexual orientation, ability, and so forth. As such, we suggest that another important future direction to improve content teaching and learning for multilingual students and their teachers is in accounting for the sociopolitical, cultural-historical elements of teaching multilingual students. In the studies reviewed, these elements were at times absent.

In addition to accounting for sociopolitical and cultural-historical influences, we also argue that future efforts in research, practice, and policy need to account for nonlinearity in teaching and learning. We need more holistic studies that account for expansive complexity, yet also help us understand detailed intricacies. For instance, many studies featured in this review examined only one "slice" of the issue of teaching multilingual learners—such as types of effective pedagogy for multilingual learners, beliefs of teachers toward multilingual students, or specific policies that affect teaching and learning in linguistically diverse classrooms. We argue that these are all working together, at the same time, and are inextricable from each other. Moreover, many studies leapt over the complex processes involved in teacher learning and teaching practice, attempting to draw a straight line between the learning activity or "intervention" and student test scores (e.g., Santau et al., 2011; Shaw et al., 2014). These studies ignore that, at any given time, there are multiple assemblages concurrently shaping pedagogy: The teacher herself is a multiplicity that shapes the practices that are enacted with multilingual learners, as shown by studies describing the impact of PD (e.g., Lee et al., 2016) and the impact of beliefs (e.g., Pease-Alvarez et al., 2010) on teachers' practices with multilingual learners. Moreover, multilingual students are also multiplicities who bring their background experiences, funds of knowledge, and current proficiencies (Daniel, 2014; Sowa, 2009), which shape their own learning, and in turn, influence their performance on a test.

There were also studies that made claims about teaching practice without any actual observations of teaching practice (e.g., Gleeson & Davison, 2016). If teaching is a complex phenomenon that arises from the interaction of multiple elements (Strom, 2015), researchers need to observe this phenomenon at the level of emergence—in the classroom. However, even in observations, researchers should practice caution with the use of overly simplistic checklists and reductionist protocols, since teaching and learning observed in classroom spaces is extremely dynamic and best understood with in-depth, longitudinal analyses. We are not suggesting that ethnographic research is the only research that matters for understanding teacher learning and practice, but we are suggesting that, moving forward, research that is making claims or attending to practice needs to actually observe and engage with the complexity of practice via their research methodology and approaches. Such holistic research can provide in-depth examinations of the disconnects that were present in many of the studies we analyzed, such as Master et al.'s (2012) finding that teacher performance on tests regarding content standards did not predict their ability to teach multilingual students, or Sangster et al.'s (2013) finding regarding the disconnect between teachers' beliefs about their linguistic knowledge and their actual linguistic knowledge (as captured by a standardized test). Further exploration of such complexities in a holistic, in-depth manner—such as the multimethod, in-depth examinations employed in studies such as DaSilva Iddings and Rose (2012) and Lesaux et al. (2014)—can help us move our understandings of teacher learning and practice forward in complex, comprehensive, and helpful ways for research, practice, and policy.

As we embrace complexity to improve teaching and learning for multilingual students in content classrooms, we also need to account for agency more explicitly. Teacher agency has already been discussed and identified as an important factor in our analysis, but one major gap in our analysis is attending to student agency. We argue that seeing multilingual students through a complex lens as multiplicities with their own agency is incredibly important for improving teaching and learning in content classrooms for multilingual students and their teachers. Specifically, research, practice, and policy need to attend to student agency, voice, and students' own heterogeneity and varied life experiences, as well as the various dimensions that interact when students are understood as multiplicities (particularly in the context of understanding the assemblage of content teaching for multilingual students). Furthermore, if the most powerful pedagogies for multilingual learners are ones that are interactive and hinge on social activity, student participation in teaching is necessary. How and whether students themselves choose to participate matters in both teacher and student success (Strom & Martin, 2017). The agency and complexities students bring to classroom learning are incredibly powerful facets of a complex assemblage that are woefully understudied, given their importance in the teaching-learning experience.

Finally, we suggest that there is great opportunity in accounting for teacher change from complex perspectives. We need studies that not only feature holistic methodological designs but also offer the ability to theorize the findings from complex perspectives. Certainly, multiple studies, theories, and methodologies can productively come into conversation and co-construct understandings of quality content teaching for multilingual learners. In fact, our analysis of the literature, where we have brought together varying perspectives, methodologies, and findings to explore and understand the dimensions of pedagogy, context, and orientations in content teaching for multilingual students, is an example of such opportunities. However, we contend that improved research, policy, and practice may come from researchers attending more expansively to these complexities within studies as well as across them. Rhizomatics offers one possibility for doing so, but there are multiple complex frameworks being taken up by teacher education researchers, including complexity theory (Cochran-Smith, Ell, Ludlow, Grudnoff, & Aitken, 2014; Ell et al., 2017) and cultural-historical activity theory (Anderson & Stillman, 2010; Gatti, 2016; Valencia, Martin, Place, & Grossman, 2009). Complex studies without foci on teacher learning and practice offer further models of these possibilities, such as Cochran-Smith et al.'s (2018) complex investigation into teacher education accountability and Dixon-Román's (2017) posthuman/materialism informed examination of social reproduction and quantification in education.

CONCLUSION

Moving forward, we see expansive possibilities to draw from a more critical, complex perspective of teacher learning and practice as well as the existing research literature to change and improve teaching of multilingual learners. Several possibilities were explored above, but additional next steps include expanding our research review more expansively outside of U.S. research. Many countries are working to prepare content teachers to teach multilingual students and explicitly seeking to learn from the international research literature is an opportunity for this work to grow further. We also recommend that stakeholders in efforts that affect teacher learning and practice (both in preservice and in-service initiatives) take the time to either use existing theories of teaching and learning (such as that forwarded here) or develop their own to overtly guide their work in practice, research, and policy development. We encourage all such stakeholders to also be overt regarding those theories and to make their assumptions clear through strong theoretically grounded work. Finally, we suggest the power of embracing difference. We have reviewed a wide variety of studies that have shown impact from a variety of approaches in different content, grade-level, and schooling contexts. There are overarching ideas related to *context, orientations,* and *pedagogy* that provide consistent themes and overall findings that can and should be applied to teacher learning and practice efforts in locally relevant ways. By embracing difference as productive, these locally meaningful approaches can also disrupt counterproductive efforts toward sameness or overt control over teachers' practice for the purposes of "fidelity." Including the findings of this literature review in work to promote teacher learning and practice is a positive way to look at themes, trends, and complexities and then allow stakeholders, including students, to participate in the co-construction of a locally meaningful, relevant, and impactful learning.

ACKNOWLEDGMENT

The author(s) declared the following financial support for the research, authorship, and/or publication of this article: Office of English Language Acquisition (Award No. T365Z160351).

NOTES

[1]We use the term *multilingual students* to refer to students whose daily lived realities include the use of multiple languages across home, family, friends, and community. Most often these students are labeled "English learners" at school. We reject that label for the deficit perspectives it promotes regarding multilingualism as well as the way it participates in the hegemony of English.

[2]We use the term *orientation* interchangeably with attitudes, beliefs, and perspectives here, but recognize that these terms are not always used interchangeably with agreed upon definitions.

REFERENCES

Abedi, J., & Herman, J. (2010). Assessing English language learners' opportunity to learn mathematics: Issues and limitations. *Teachers College Record, 112,* 723–746.

Adamson, K., Santau, A., & Lee, O. (2013). The impact of professional development on elementary teachers' strategies for teaching science with diverse student groups in urban elementary schools. *Journal of Science Teacher Education, 24,* 553–571. doi:10.1007/s10972-012-9306-z

Aguirre-Muñoz, Z., Park, J.-E., Amabisca, A., & Boscardin, C. K. (2008). Developing teacher capacity for serving ELLs' writing instructional needs: A case for systemic functional linguistics. *Bilingual Research Journal, 31,* 295–322. doi:10.1080/15235880802640755

Ajayi, L. (2015). Vocabulary instruction and Mexican–American bilingual students: How two high school teachers integrate multiple strategies to build word consciousness in English language arts classrooms. *International Journal of Bilingual Education and Bilingualism, 18,* 463–484. doi:10.1080/13670050.2014.924475

Alt, M., Arizmendi, G. D., & Beal, C. R. (2014). The relationship between mathematics and language: Academic implications for children with specific language impairment and English language learners. *Language, Speech, and Hearing Services in Schools, 45,* 220–233. doi:10.1044/2014_LSHSS-13-0003

Alt, M., Arizmendi, G. D., Beal, C. R., & Hurtado, J. S. (2013). The effect of test translation on the performance of second grade English learners on the KeyMath-3: Effect of test translation. *Psychology in the Schools, 50*(1), 27–36. doi:10.1002/pits.21656

Anderson, L., & Stillman, J. (2010). Opportunities to teach and learn in high-needs schools: Student teachers' experiences in urban placements. *Urban Education, 45,* 109–141.

Andrews, D., & Weisenberg, A. W. (2013). Teaching credential candidates how to adapt lessons and increase vocabulary for English learners. *NABE Journal of Research and Practice*, *4*(1). Retrieved from https://www2.nau.edu/nabej-p/ojs/index.php/njrp/article/view/19

Annamma, S. A., Jackson, D. D., & Morrison, D. (2017). Conceptualizing color-evasiveness: Using dis/ability critical race theory to expand a color-blind racial ideology in education and society. *Race Ethnicity and Education*, *20*, 147–162. doi:10.1080/13613324.2016.1 248837

Babinski, L. M., Amendum, S. J., Knotek, S. E., Sánchez, M., & Malone, P. (2018). Improving young English learners' language and literacy skills through teacher professional development: A randomized controlled trial. *American Educational Research Journal*, *55*, 117–143. doi:10.3102/0002831217732335

Bacon, C. (2018). "It's not really my job": A mixed methods framework for language ideologies, monolingualism, and teaching emergent bilingual learners. *Journal of Teacher Education*. Advance online publication. doi:10.1177/0022487118783188

Basterra, M. R., Trumbull, E., & Solano-Flores, G. (2011). *Cultural validity in assessment: A guide for educators*. New York, NY: Routledge.

Battey, D., Llamas-Flores, S., Burke, M., Guerra, P., Kang, H. J., & Kim, S. H. (2013). ELL policy and mathematics professional development colliding: Placing teacher experimentation within a sociopolitical context. *Teachers College Record*, *115*(6), 1-44. Retrieved from http://www.tcrecord.org/library/abstract.asp?contentid=16982

Beal, C. R., Adams, N. M., & Cohen, P. R. (2010). Reading proficiency and mathematics problem solving by high school English language learners. *Urban Education*, *45*(1), 58–74. doi:10.1177/0042085909352143

Bowers, E., Fitts, S., Quirk, M., & Jung, W. (2010). Effective strategies for developing academic English: Professional development and teacher practices. *Bilingual Research Journal*, *33*, 95–110. doi:10.1080/15235881003733407

Braden, S., Wassell, B. A., Scantlebury, K., & Grover, A. (2016). Supporting language learners in science classrooms: Insights from middle-school English language learner students. *Language and Education*, *30*, 438–458. doi:10.1080/09500782.2015.1134566

Brancard, R., & Quinnwilliams, J. (2012). Learning labs: Collaborations for transformative teacher learning. *TESOL Journal*, *3*, 320–349. doi:10.1002/tesj.22

Brooks, K., & Thurston, L. (2010). English language learner academic engagement and instructional grouping configurations. *American Secondary Education*, *39*(1), 45–60.

Brown, B. A., Ryoo, K., & Rodriguez, J. (2010). Pathway towards fluency: Using "disaggregate instruction" to promote science literacy. *International Journal of Science Education*, *32*, 1465–1493. doi:10.1080/09500690903117921

Bunch, G. C. (2009). "Going up there": Challenges and opportunities for language minority students during a mainstream classroom speech event. *Linguistics and Education*, *20*, 81–108. doi:10.1016/j.linged.2009.04.001

Bustos-Flores, B., & Smith, H. L. (2009). Teachers' characteristics and attitudinal beliefs about linguistic and cultural diversity. *Bilingual Research Journal*, *31*, 323–358. doi:10.1080/15235880802640789

Buxton, C. A., Allexsaht-Snider, M., Suriel, R., Kayumova, S., Choi, Y., Bouton, B., & Baker, M. (2013). Using educative assessments to support science teaching for middle school English-language learners. *Journal of Science Teacher Education*, *24*, 347–366. doi:10.1007/s10972-012-9329-5

Buxton, C. A., Salinas, A., Mahotiere, M., Lee, O., & Secada, W. G. (2013). Leveraging cultural resources through teacher pedagogical reasoning: Elementary grade teachers analyze second language learners' science problem solving. *Teaching and Teacher Education*, *32*, 31–42. doi:10.1016/j.tate.2013.01.003

Carbone, P. M., & Orellana, M. F. (2010). Developing academic identities: Persuasive writing as a tool to strengthen emergent academic identities. *Research in the Teaching of English*, *44*, 292–316.

Carrejo, D. J., & Reinhartz, J. (2012). Exploring the synergy between science literacy and language literacy with English language learners: Lessons learned within a sustained professional development program. *SRATE Journal*, *21*(2), 33–38.

Catalano, T., Reeves, J. R., & Wessels, S. (2017). "The soccer field, it has dirt": A critical analysis of teacher learners in contact with emergent multilingual students. *Critical Inquiry in Language Studies*, *15*(1), 1–20. doi:10.1080/15427587.2017.1329626

Cheatham, G. A., Jimenez-Silva, M., Wodrich, D. L., & Kasai, M. (2014). Disclosure of information about English proficiency: Preservice teachers' presumptions about English language learners. *Journal of Teacher Education*, *65*(1), 53–62. doi:10.1177/0022487113503687

Cho, S., & Reich, G. A. (2008). New immigrants, new challenges: High school social studies teachers and English language learner instruction. *Social Studies*, *99*(6), 235–242. doi:10.3200/TSSS.99.6.235-242

Choi, D. S.-Y., & Morrison, P. (2014). Learning to get it right: Understanding change processes in professional development for teachers of English learners. *Professional Development in Education*, *40*, 416–435. doi:10.1080/19415257.2013.806948

Chval, K. B., Pinnow, R. J., & Thomas, A. (2015). Learning how to focus on language while teaching mathematics to English language learners: A case study of Courtney. *Mathematics Education Research Journal*, *27*, 103–127. doi:10.1007/s13394-013-0101-8

Clark-Gareca, B. (2016). Classroom assessment and English language learners: Teachers' accommodations implementation on routine math and science tests. *Teaching and Teacher Education*, *54*, 139–148. doi:10.1016/j.tate.2015.11.003

Coady, M., Harper, C., & de Jong, E. (2011). From preservice to practice: Mainstream elementary teacher beliefs of preparation and efficacy with English language learners in the state of Florida. *Bilingual Research Journal*, *34*, 223–239. doi:10.1080/15235882.2011.597823

Cochran-Smith, M., Carney, M. C., Keefe, E. S., Burton, S., Chang, W-C., Fernández, M. B., . . . Baker, M. (2018). *Reclaiming accountability in teacher education*. New York, NY: Teachers College Press.

Cochan-Smith, M., Ell, F., Ludlow, L., Grudnoff, L., & Aitken, G. (2014). The challenge and promise of complexity theory for teacher education research. *Teachers College Record*, *116*(5), 1–38.

Cole, M. W. (2013). Rompiendo el silencio: Meta-analysis of the effectiveness of peer-mediated learning at improving language outcomes for ELLs. *Bilingual Research Journal*, *36*, 146–166. doi:10.1080/15235882.2013.814609

Collins, L. J., & Liang, X. (2014). Task relevance in the design of online professional development for teachers of ELLs: AQ methodology study. *Turkish Online Journal of Distance Education*, *15*, 268–281.

Daniel, S. M. (2014). Learning to educate English language learners in preservice elementary practicums. *Teacher Education Quarterly*, *41*(2), 5–28.

DaSilva Iddings, A. C., & Rose, B. C. (2012). Developing pedagogical practices for English-language learners: A design-based approach. *Pedagogies: An International Journal*, *7*(1), 32–51. doi:10.1080/1554480X.2012.630510

Deleuze, G., & Guattari, F. (1987). *Capitalism and schizophrenia: A thousand plateaus*. Minneapolis, MN: University of Minnesota Press.

DelliCarpini, M. E., & Alonso, O. B. (2014). Teacher education that works: Preparing secondary-level math and science teachers for success with English language learners through content-based instruction. *Global Education Review*, *1*(4), 155–178.

Dixon-Román, E. J. (2017). *Inheriting possibility: Social reproduction and quantification in education*. Minneapolis: University of Minnesota Press.

Echevarria, J., Richards-Tutor, C., Canges, R., & Francis, D. (2011). Using the SIOP model to promote the acquisition of language and science concepts with English learners. *Bilingual Research Journal, 34*, 334–351. doi:10.1080/15235882.2011.623600

Echevarria, J., Richards-Tutor, C., Chinn, V. P., & Ratleff, P. A. (2011). Did they get it? The role of fidelity in teaching English learners. *Journal of Adolescent & Adult Literacy, 54*, 425–434.

Elfers, A. M., Lucero, A., Stritikus, T., & Knapp, M. S. (2013). Building systems of support for classroom teachers working with English language learners. *International Multilingual Research Journal, 7*, 155–174. doi:10.1080/19313152.2012.665824

Ell, F., Haigh, M., Cochran-Smith, M., Grudnoff, L., Ludlow, L., & Hill, M. F. (2017). Mapping a complex system: What influences teacher learning during initial teacher education? *Asia-Pacific Journal of Teacher Education, 45*, 327–345. doi:10.1080/13598 66X.2017.1309640

English, B. (2009). Who is responsible for educating English language learners? Discursive construction of roles and responsibilities in an inquiry community. *Language and Education, 23*, 487–507. doi:10.1080/09500780902954216

Enright, K. A., & Gilliland, B. (2011). Multilingual writing in an age of accountability: From policy to practice in U.S. high school classrooms. *Journal of Second Language Writing, 20*, 182–195. doi:10.1016/j.jslw.2011.05

Estapa, A., Pinnow, R. J., & Chval, K. B. (2016). Video as a professional development tool to support novice teachers as they learn to teach English language learners. *The New Educator, 12*, 85–104. doi:10.1080/1547688X.2015.1113350

Faltis, C., Arias, M. B., & Ramírez-Marín, F. (2010). Identifying relevant competencies for secondary teachers of English learners. *Bilingual Research Journal, 33*, 307–328. doi:10.1 080/15235882.2010.529350

Faltis, C. J., & Valdés, G. (2016). Preparing teachers for teaching in and advocating for linguistically diverse classrooms: A vade mecum for teacher educators. In Gitomer & C. A. Bell (Eds.), *Handbook of research on teaching* (pp. 549–592). Washington DC: American Educational Research Association.

Fitts, S., & Gross, L. A. (2012). Teacher candidates learning from English learners: Constructing concepts of language and culture in Tuesday's Tutors after-school program. *Teacher Education Quarterly, 39*(4), 75–95.

Freeman, Y., & Freeman, D. (Eds.). (2014). *Research on preparing preservice teachers to work effectively with emergent bilinguals*. Bingley, England: Emerald.

Freire, P. (2000). *Pedagogy of the oppressed* (30th anniversary ed.). New York, NY: Bloomsbury.

Galguera, T. (2011). Participant structures as professional learning tasks and the development of pedagogical language knowledge among preservice teachers. *Teacher Education Quarterly, 38*(1), 85–106.

García, O. (2009). *Bilingual education in the 21st century: A global perspective*. Malden, MA: Wiley-Blackwell.

García, O., & Leiva, C. (2014). Theorizing and enacting translanguaging for social justice. In A. Blackledge & A. Creese (Eds.), *Heteroglossia as practice and pedagogy* (pp. 199–216). Dordrecht, Netherlands: Springer.

Garrett, R., & Hong, G. (2016). Impacts of grouping and time on the math learning of language minority kindergarteners. *Educational Evaluation and Policy Analysis, 38*, 222–244. doi:10.3102/0162373715611484

Gatti, L. (2016). Learning to teach in an urban teacher residency. *Urban Education*. Advance online publication. doi:10.1177/0042085916641171

Gay, G. (2002). Preparing for culturally responsive teaching. *Journal of Teacher Education, 53*, 106–116.

Gleeson, M., & Davison, C. (2016). A conflict between experience and professional learning: Subject teachers' beliefs about teaching English language learners. *RELC Journal, 47*(1), 43–57.

Hansen-Thomas, H., & Cavagnetto, A. (2010). What do mainstream middle school teachers think about their English language learners? A tri-state case study. *Bilingual Research Journal, 33*, 249–266. doi:10.1080/15235882.2010.502803

Haraway, D. J. (2016). *Staying with the trouble: Making kin in the Chthulucene.* Durham, NC: Duke University Press.

Heller, J. I., Daehler, K. R., Wong, N., Shinohara, M., & Miratrix, L. W. (2012). Differential effects of three professional development models on teacher knowledge and student achievement in elementary science. *Journal of Research in Science Teaching, 49*, 333–362. doi:10.1002/tea.21004

Hoffman, J. V., Villarreal, D., DeJulio, S., Taylor, L., & Shin, J. (2017). Drama in dialogic read alouds: Promoting access and opportunity for emergent bilinguals. *Journal of Pedagogy, Pluralism and Practice, 9*, 196–218.

Howard, T. C., & Navarro, O. (2016). Critical race theory 20 years later: Where do we go from here? *Urban Education, 51*, 253–273. doi:10.1177/0042085915622541

Huerta, T. M. (2011). Humanizing pedagogy: Beliefs and practices on the teaching of Latino children. *Bilingual Research Journal, 34*(1), 38–57. doi:10.1080/15235882.2011.568826

Im, S., & Martin, S. N. (2015). Using cogenerative dialogues to improve coteaching for language learner (LL) students in an inclusion science classroom. *Asia-Pacific Journal of Teacher Education, 43*, 355–369. doi:10.1080/1359866X.2015.1060295

Jackson, J. K., & Ash, G. (2012). Science achievement for all: Improving science performance and closing achievement gaps. *Journal of Science Teacher Education, 23*, 723–744. doi:10.1007/s10972-011-9238-z

Jimenez-Silva, M., & Olson, K. (2012). A community of practice in teacher education: Insights and perceptions. *International Journal of Sustainability in Higher Education, 24*, 335–348.

Johnson, C. C., Bolshakova, V. L. J., & Waldron, T. (2016). When good intentions and reality meet: Large-scale reform of science teaching in urban schools with predominantly Latino ELL students. *Urban Education, 51*, 476–513. doi:10.1177/0042085914543114

Kanno, Y., & Kangas, S. E. N. (2014). "I'm not going to be, like, for the AP": English language learners' limited access to advanced college-preparatory courses in high school. *American Educational Research Journal, 51*, 848–878. doi:10.3102/0002831214544716

Kibler, A. (2010). Writing through two languages: First language expertise in a language minority classroom. *Journal of Second Language Writing, 19*(3), 121–142. doi:10.1016/j.jslw.2010.04.001

Kibler, A. K. (2014). From high school to the noviciado: An adolescent linguistic minority student's multilingual journey in writing. *Modern Language Journal, 98*, 629–651.

Kibler, A. K., & Roman, D. (2013). Insights into professional development for teachers of English language learners: A focus on using students' native languages in the classroom. *Bilingual Research Journal, 36*, 187–207. doi:10.1080/15235882.2013.820226

Kieffer, M. J., & Lesaux, N. K. (2012). Effects of academic language instruction on relational and syntactic aspects of morphological awareness for sixth graders from linguistically diverse backgrounds. *Elementary School Journal, 112*, 519–545. doi:10.1086/663299

Kim, J. S., Olson, C. B., Scarcella, R., Kramer, J., Pearson, M., van Dyk, D., . . . Land, R. E. (2011). A randomized experiment of a cognitive strategies approach to text-based analytical writing for mainstreamed Latino English language learners in grades 6 to 12. *Journal of Research on Educational Effectiveness, 4*, 231–263. doi:10.1080/19345747.2010.523513

Ladson-Billings, G. (1995). Toward a theory of culturally relevant pedagogy. *American Educational Research Journal, 32*, 465–491.

Ladson-Billings, G., & Tate, W. F. (1995). Towards a critical race theory of education. *Teachers College Record, 97*(1), 47–68.

Lara-Alecio, R., Tong, F., Irby, B. J., Guerrero, C., Huerta, M., & Fan, Y. (2012). The effect of an instructional intervention on middle school English learners' science and English reading achievement. *Journal of Research in Science Teaching, 49*, 987–1011. doi:10.1002/tea.21031

Lavery, M. R., Nutta, J., & Youngblood, A. (2018). Analyzing student learning gains to evaluate differentiated teacher preparation for fostering English learners' achievement in linguistically diverse classrooms. *Journal of Teacher Education*. Advance online publication. doi:10.1177/0022487117751400

Lee, O., Adamson, K., Maerten-Rivera, J., Lewis, S., Thornton, C., & LeRoy, K. (2008). Teachers' perspectives on a professional development intervention to improve science instruction among English language learners. *Journal of Science Teacher Education, 19*(1), 41–67. doi:10.1007/s10972-007-9081-4

Lee, O., Llosa, L., Jiang, F., Haas, A., O'Connor, C., & Van Booven, C. D. (2016). Elementary teachers' science knowledge and instructional practices: Impact of an intervention focused on English language learners. *Journal of Research in Science Teaching, 53*, 579–597. doi:10.1002/tea.21314

Lee, O., & Maerten-Rivera, J. (2012). Teacher change in elementary science instruction with English language learners: Results of a multiyear professional development intervention across multiple grades. *Teachers College Record, 114*, 1–42.

Lee, O., Maerten-Rivera, J., Penfield, R. D., LeRoy, K., & Secada, W. G. (2008). Science achievement of English language learners in urban elementary schools: Results of a first-year professional development intervention. *Journal of Research in Science Teaching, 45*(1), 31–52. doi:10.1002/tea.20209

Lee, O., Penfield, R. D., & Buxton, C. A. (2011). Relationship between "form" and "content" in science writing among English language learners. *Teachers College Record, 113*, 1401–1434.

Lesaux, N. K., Kieffer, M. J., Kelley, J. G., & Harris, J. R. (2014). Effects of academic vocabulary instruction for linguistically diverse adolescents: Evidence from a randomized field trial. *American Educational Research Journal, 51*, 1159–1194. doi:10.3102/0002831214532165

Lewis, J. L., Ream, R. K., Bocian, K. M., Cardullo, R. A., Hammond, K. A. & Fast, L. A. (2012). Con cariño: Teacher caring, math self-efficacy, and math achievement among Hispanic English learners. *Teachers College Record, 114*, 1–42.

Li, N., & Peters, A. W. (2016). Preparing K-12 teachers for ELLs: Improving teachers' L2 knowledge and strategies through innovative professional development. *Urban Education*. Advance online publication. doi:10.1177/0042085916656902

Llosa, L., Lee, O., Jiang, F., Haas, A., O'Connor, C., Van Booven, C. D., & Kieffer, M. J. (2016). Impact of a large-scale science intervention focused on English language learners. *American Educational Research Journal, 53*, 395–424. doi:10.3102/0002831216637348

Loeb, S., Soland, J., & Fox, L. (2014). Is a good teacher a good teacher for all? Comparing value-added of teachers with their English learners and non-English learners. *Educational Evaluation and Policy Analysis, 36*, 457–475. doi:10.3102/0162373714527788

López, F., Scanlan, M., & Gundrum, B. (2013). Preparing teachers of English language learners: Empirical evidence and policy implications. *Education Policy Analysis Archives/Archivos Analíticos de Políticas Educativas, 21*(20), 1–35.

Love, B. J. (2004). *Brown* plus 50 counter-storytelling: A critical race theory analysis of the "majoritarian achievement gap" story. *Equity & Excellence in Education, 37*, 227–246. doi:10.1080/10665680490491597

Lucas, T., & Grinberg, J. (2008). Responding to the linguistic reality of mainstream classrooms: Preparing all teachers to teach English language learners. In M. Cochran-Smith, S. Feiman-Nemser, D. J. McIntyre, & K. E. Demers (Eds.), *Handbook of research on teacher education: Enduring questions in changing contexts* (pp. 606–636). New York, NY: Routledge/Taylor & Francis Group and The Association of Teacher Educators.

Lucas, T., & Villegas, A. M. (2011). A framework for preparing linguistically responsive teachers. In T. Lucas (Ed.), *Teacher preparation for linguistically diverse classrooms: A resource for teacher educators* (pp. 55–72). New York, NY: Routledge.

Lys, D., Ringler, M. C., & O'Neal, D. (2009). Changing teacher attitudes toward instruction of academic language through sustained school-university partnership. *International Journal of Educational Leadership Preparation, 4*(4). Retrieved from https://files.eric.ed.gov/fulltext/EJ1048067.pdf

Macleroy, V. (2013). Cultural, linguistic and cognitive issues in teaching the language of literature for emergent bilingual pupils. *Language, Culture, and Curriculum, 26,* 300–316. doi:10.1080/07908318.2013.852566

Manzo, R. D., Cruz, L., Faltis, C., & de la Torre, A. (2011). Professional development of secondary science teachers of English learners in immigrant communities. *Association of Mexican American Educators Journal, 5*(1), 41–48.

Martin, A., & Strom, K. (2015). Neoliberalism and the teaching of English learners: Decentering the teacher and student subject. *SoJo Journal, 1*(1), 23–43.

Martin-Beltrán, M., & Peercy, M. M. (2014). Collaboration to teach English language learners: Opportunities for shared teacher learning. *Teachers and Teaching, 20,* 721–737. doi:10.1080/13540602.2014.885704

Martínez, R. A. (2010). Spanglish as literacy tool: Toward an understanding of the potential role of Spanish-English code-switching in the development of academic literacy. *Research in the Teaching of English, 45,* 124–149.

Master, B., Loeb, S., Whitney, C., & Wyckoff, J. (2012). *Different skills: Identifying differentially effective teachers of English language learners.* Washington, DC: American Institutes for Research.

Matias, C. E. (2013). Tears worth telling: Urban teaching and the possibilities of racial justice. *Multicultural Perspectives, 15,* 187–193.

Matias, C. E. (2016). "Why do you make me hate myself?" Re-teaching whiteness, abuse and love in urban teacher education. *Teaching Education, 27,* 194–211. doi:10.1080/10476 210.2015.1068749

Matsuda, M., Lawrence, C., Delgado, R., & Crenshaw, K. W. (1993). *Words that wound: Critical race theory, assaultive speech and the first amendment.* Boulder, CO: Westview Press.

Matuchniak, T., Olson, C. B., & Scarcella, R. (2014). Examining the text-based, on-demand, analytical writing of mainstreamed Latino English learners in a randomized field trial of the Pathway Project intervention. *Reading and Writing, 27,* 973–994. doi:10.1007/s11145-013-9490-z

Maturana, H. R., & Varela, F. J. (1973). *Autopoiesis and cognition: The realization of the living.* Dordrecht, Netherlands: Springer.

Mellom, P. J., Straubhaar, R., Balderas, C., Ariail, M., & Portes, P. R. (2018). "They come with nothing": How professional development in a culturally responsive pedagogy shapes teacher attitudes towards Latino/a English language learners. *Teaching and Teacher Education, 71,* 98–107. doi:10.1016/j.tate.2017.12.013

Mitchell, K. (2012). English is not *All* that matters in the education of secondary multilingual learners and their teachers. *International Journal of Multicultural Education, 14*(1), 1–21. Retrieved https://files.eric.ed.gov/fulltext/EJ1105056.pdf

Mitchell, K., Homza, A., & Ngo, S. (2012). Reading aloud with bilingual learners: A fieldwork project and its impact on mainstream teacher candidates. *Action in Teacher Education, 34,* 276–294. doi:10.1080/01626620.2012.694020

Molle, D. (2013). The pitfalls of focusing on instructional strategies in professional development for teachers of English learners. *Teacher Education Quarterly, 40,* 101–124.

Moore, J., & Schleppegrell, M. (2014). Using a functional linguistics metalanguage to support academic language development in the English Language Arts. *Linguistics and Education, 26,* 92–105. doi:10.1016/j.linged.2014.01.002

Mosqueda, E., & Maldonado, S. I. (2013). The effects of English language proficiency and curricular pathways: Latina/os' mathematics achievement in secondary schools. *Equity & Excellence in Education, 46,* 202–219. doi:10.1080/10665684.2013.780647

Olson, C. B., Kim, J. S., Scarcella, R., Kramer, J., Pearson, M., van Dyk, D. A., . . . Land, R. E. (2012). Enhancing the interpretive reading and analytical writing of mainstreamed English learners in secondary school: Results from a randomized field trial using a cognitive strategies approach. *American Educational Research Journal, 49,* 323–355. doi:10.3102/0002831212439434

O'Neal, D. D., Ringler, M., & Rodriguez, D. (2008). Teachers' perceptions of their preparation for teaching linguistically and culturally diverse learners in rural eastern North Carolina. *The Rural Educator, 30*(1), 5–13.

Opfer, V., & Pedder, D. (2011). Conceptualizing teacher professional learning. *Review of Educational Research, 81,* 376–407.

Orellana, M. F., & García, O. (2014). Language brokering and translanguaging in school. *Language Arts, 91,* 386–392.

Ortega, I., Luft, J. A., & Wong, S. S. (2013). Learning to teach inquiry: A beginning science teacher of English language learners. *School Science and Mathematics, 113*(1), 29–40.

Paris, D. (2012). Culturally sustaining pedagogy: A needed change in stance, terminology, and practice. *Educational Researcher, 41*(3), 93–97. doi:10.3102/0013189X12441244

Pass, C., & Mantero, M. (2009). (UN)Covering the ideal: Investigating exemplary language arts teachers' beliefs and instruction of English language learners. *Critical Inquiry in Language Studies, 6,* 269–291. doi:10.1080/15427580903313520

Pawan, F. (2008). Content-area teachers and scaffolded instruction for English language learners. *Teaching and Teacher Education, 24,* 1450–1462. doi:10.1016/j.tate.2008.02.003

Pease-Alvarez, L., Samway, K. D., & Cifka-Herrera, C. (2010). Working within the system: Teachers of English learners negotiating a literacy instruction mandate. *Language Policy, 9,* 313–334. doi:10.1007/s10993-010-9180-5

Peercy, M. M., & Martin-Beltrán, M. (2012). Envisioning collaboration: Including ESOL students *and* teachers in the mainstream classroom. *International Journal of Inclusive Education, 16,* 657–673. doi:10.1080/13603116.2010.495791

Peercy, M. M., Martin-Beltrán, M., Silverman, R. D., & Nunn, S. J. (2015). "Can I ask a question?" ESOL and mainstream teachers engaging in distributed and distributive learning to support English language learners' text comprehension. *Teacher Education Quarterly, 42*(4), 33–58.

Pettit, S. (2011). Factors influencing middle school mathematics teachers' beliefs about ELLs in mainstream classroom. *Issues in the Undergraduate Mathematics Preparation of School Teachers: The Journal, 5.* Retrieved from https://files.eric.ed.gov/fulltext/EJ962628.pdf

Polat, N. (2010). A comparative analysis of pre-and in-service teacher beliefs about readiness and self-competency: Revisiting teacher education for ELLs. *System, 38,* 228–244. doi:10.1016/j.system.2010.03.004

Pu, C. (2012). Narrative inquiry: Preservice teachers' understanding of teaching English language learners. *AILACTE Journal, 9,* 1–18. Retrieved from https://eric.ed.gov/?id =EJ998629

Ross, K. E. L. (2014). Professional development for practicing mathematics teachers: A critical connection to English language learner students in mainstream USA classrooms. *Journal of Mathematics Teacher Education, 17*, 85–100. doi:10.1007/s10857 -013-9250-7

Russell, F. A. (2014). Collaborative literacy work in a high school: Enhancing teacher capacity for English learner instruction in the mainstream. *International Journal of Inclusive Education, 18*, 1189–1207. doi:10.1080/13603116.2014.884642

Russell, F. A. (2015). Learning to teach English learners: Instructional coaching and developing novice high school teacher capacity. *Teacher Education Quarterly, 42*(1), 27–47.

Sangster, P., Anderson, C., & O'Hara, P. (2013). Perceived and actual levels of knowledge about language amongst primary and secondary student teachers: Do they know what they think they know? *Language Awareness, 22*, 293–319. doi:10.1080/09658416.2012 .722643

Santau, A. O., Maerten-Rivera, J. L., & Huggins, A. C. (2011). Science achievement of English language learners in urban elementary schools: Fourth-grade student achievement results from a professional development intervention. *Science Education, 95*, 771–793. doi:10.1002/sce.20443

Schall-Leckrone, L., & McQuillan, P. J. (2012). Preparing history teachers to work with English learners through a focus on the academic language of historical analysis. *Journal of English for Academic Purposes, 11*, 246–266. doi:10.1016/j.jeap.2012.05.001

Schleppegrell, M. J., Greer, S., & Taylor, S. (2008). Literacy in history: Language and meaning. *Australian Journal of Language and Literacy, 31*, 174–187.

Shaw, J. M., Lyon, E. G., Stoddart, T., Mosqueda, E., & Menon, P. (2014). Improving science and literacy learning for English language learners: Evidence from a preservice teacher preparation intervention. *Journal of Science Teacher Education, 25*, 621–643. doi:10.1007/s10972-013-9376-6

Short, D. J., Echevarría, J., & Richards-Tutor, C. (2011). Research on academic literacy development in sheltered instruction classrooms. *Language Teaching Research, 15*, 363–380. doi:10.1177/1362168811401155

Sowa, P. A. (2009). Understanding our learners and developing reflective practice: Conducting action research with English language learners. *Teaching and Teacher Education, 25*, 1026–1032. doi:10.1016/j.tate.2009.04.008

Strom, K. (2015). Teaching as assemblage: Negotiating learning and practice in the first year of teaching. *Journal of Teacher Education, 66*, 321–333.

Strom, K., & Martin, A. (2017). *Becoming-teacher: A rhizomatic look at first-year teaching.* Rotterdam, Netherlands: Sense.

Strom, K., Martin, A., & Villegas, A. M. (2018). Clinging to the edge of chaos: The emergence of novice teacher practice. *Teachers College Record.* Retrieved from http://www. tcrecord.org/Content.asp?ContentId=22322

Swanson, L. H., Bianchini, J. A., & Lee, J. S. (2014). Engaging in argument and communicating information: A case study of English language learners and their science teacher in an urban high school. *Journal of Research in Science Teaching, 51*(1), 31–64. doi:10.1002/ tea.21124

Tandon, M., Viesca, K. M., Hueston, C., & Milbourn, T. (2017). Perceptions of linguistically responsive teaching in teacher candidates/novice teachers. *Bilingual Research Journal, 40*, 154–168. doi:10.1080/15235882.2017.1304464

Teemant, A., & Hausman, C. S. (2013). The relationship of teacher use of critical sociocultural practices with student achievement. *Critical Education, 4*(4), 1–20.

Turgut, R., Sahin, E. A., & Huerta, M. (2016). Changes in preservice teachers' perceptions of preparedness to teach English language learners (ELLs) in mainstream classrooms. *Journal of Ethnographic & Qualitative Research, 10*, 291–305.

Turner, E. E., Dominguez, H., Empson, S., & Maldonado, L. A. (2013). Latino/a bilinguals and their teachers developing a shared communicative space. *Educational Studies in Mathematics, 84*, 349–370. doi:10.1007/s10649-013-9486-2

Valencia, S., Martin, S., Place, N., & Grossman, P. (2009). Complex interactions in student teaching: Lost opportunities for learning. *Journal of Teacher Education, 60*, 304–322.

Van Laere, E., Agirdag, O., & van Braak, J. (2016). Supporting science learning in linguistically diverse classrooms: Factors related to the use of bilingual content in a computer-based learning environment. *Computers in Human Behavior, 57*, 428–441. doi:10.1016/j.chb.2015.12.056

Vaughn, S., Martinez, L. R., Linan-Thompson, S., Reutebuch, C. K., Carlson, C. D., & Francis, D. J. (2009). Enhancing social studies vocabulary and comprehension for seventh-grade English language learners: Findings from two experimental studies. *Journal of Research on Educational Effectiveness, 2*, 297–324. doi:10.1080/19345740903167018

Vázquez, V. P., López, J. A., Segador, A. G., & Mohedano, R. E. (2015). Strategic and organisational considerations in planning content and language integrated learning: A study on the coordination between content and language teachers. *International Journal of Bilingual Education and Bilingualism, 18*, 409–425. doi:10.1080/13670050.2014.909774

Vázquez-Montilla, E., Just, M., & Triscari, R. (2014). Teachers' dispositions and beliefs about cultural and linguistic diversity. *Universal Journal of Educational Research, 2*, 577–587. doi:10.13189/ujer.2014022806

Vygotsky, L. S. (1978). *Mind in society: The development of higher psychological processes.* Cambridge, MA: Harvard University Press.

Walker, D., Mahon, E., & Dray, B. (2017). Can we prepare culturally and linguistically responsive teachers online? A cross-case analysis of online and on-campus courses. *Urban Education.* Advance online publication. doi:10.1177/0042085917735970

Yoon, B. (2008). Uninvited guests: The influence of teachers' roles and pedagogies on the positioning of English language learners in the regular classroom. *American Educational Research Journal, 45*, 495–522. doi:10.3102/0002831208316200

Zhang, J., & Pelttari, C. (2014). Exploring the emotions and needs of English language learners: Facilitating preservice and in-service teachers' recognition of the tasks facing language learners. *Journal of Multilingual and Multicultural Development, 35*, 179–194. doi:10.1080/01434632.2013.822505

Chapter 12

How Does Changing "One-Size-Fits-All" to Differentiated Instruction Affect Teaching?

Rhonda S. Bondie
Christine Dahnke
Harvard University

Akane Zusho
Fordham University

This rigorous literature review analyzed how 28 U.S.-based research studies conducted between 2001 and 2015 have defined, described, and measured changes in teaching practices related to implementation of Differentiated Instruction (DI) in P–12 classrooms. Research questions examined frameworks that defined DI, classroom operationalization of DI, key barriers and facilitators, and how changes in teacher practices across studies did not lead to a common definition of DI. Extracted data were analyzed by study type, DI purpose, theoretical framework, research questions, methodology, analysis method, expected/reported change in teacher practice, expected/reported impact on student learning, key barriers, facilitators, contextual factors, and implications for teaching and research. Findings demonstrated how the many different frameworks used to define DI shaped a variety of changes to teacher practices and roles. The purpose of DI varied widely from a systematic response to policy to informal teacher perception of student differences. Barriers included the DI decision source (institution vs. teacher). Facilitators focused on teacher view of time, resources, control, and dispositions toward differences and ambiguity. The need for systematic replicable studies with greater methodological rigor is discussed and a more integrative definition of DI focused on teacher instructional reasoning and decision making is proposed for future research.

I n public school classrooms, student academic abilities can span across five different grade levels (Hertberg-Davis & Brighton, 2006). However, many teachers use a one-size-fits-all instructional approach (Latz, Speirs Neumeister, Adams, & Pierce, 2008) where teachers focus on the middle range of students' academic abilities

Review of Research in Education
March 2019, Vol. 43, pp. 336–362
DOI: 10.3102/0091732X18821130
Chapter reuse guidelines: sagepub.com/journals-permissions
© 2019 AERA. http://rre.aera.net

(Tomlinson, 1999), primarily using whole-class instruction (McIntosh, Vaughn, Schumm, Haager, & Lee, 1993). *No Child Left Behind* (NCLB, 2001-2015; Bush, 2001) required the disaggregation of test scores by student subgroup, increasing public attention to gaps in student achievement and illuminating the need to change teaching practices. One recommended change was Response to Intervention (RtI), an example of a multitiered support system used for instructional problem solving where students receive scientifically based interventions with frequent monitoring to measure student responses (McIntosh et al., 1993). Differentiated Instruction (DI) was a suggested practice for effectively implementing RtI to serve diverse learner needs in general classrooms (Gersten et al., 2008). However, given the pressures from policy to practice, did teachers change from a one-size-fits-all approach to DI?

DI was not new during the NCLB years. In fact, Washburne (1953) described DI as a school's constant dilemma, examining the question, "How can the teacher best meet—and most wisely use—the wide range of differences in [student] abilities, interests, and development . . .?" (p. 138). Although there are decades of articles examining DI, the changes in teaching practices remain unclear. There are no comprehensive evaluations of DI models (Hall, Strangman, & Meyer, 2003) and there are few large-scale experimental studies focused exclusively on its effects (cf. Brighton, Hertberg, Moon, Tomlinson, & Callahan, 2005; Reis, McCoach, Little, Muller, & Kaniskan, 2011). Thus, this rigorous literature review analyzed how U.S.-based research studies conducted between 2001 and 2015 have defined, described, and measured changes in teaching practices related to implementation of DI in P–12 classrooms. The following questions guided our analysis:

1. How did U.S. studies from 2001 to 2015 report changes in teacher practices related to implementing DI?
   (a) What frameworks or theories supported and defined DI?
   (b) How was DI operationalized in the classroom?
   (c) What were the key barriers and facilitators of intentional change to teacher practices aimed at DI?
2. Did changes in teacher practices across studies lead to a common definition of DI?

METHOD

This review followed rigorous, comprehensive procedures (Onwuegbuzie, Collins, Leech, Dellinger, & Jiao, 2010). Search terms were identified by consulting definitions of DI in reference encyclopedias and database thesauruses. Extant research literature was found through a computer-based search across ERIC, PsycInfo, and JSTOR, which was limited to peer-reviewed journal articles published from 2001 to 2015 inclusively. Table 1 displays the search results. In addition, a hand search of top-tiered journals—*American Educational Research Journal, Educational Researcher, Journal of Educational Psychology, Educational Psychologist, Contemporary Educational*

TABLE 1
Search Results

Source	Articles Found	Articles Included
ERIC	68	16
PsychINFO	10	1
JSTOR	79	11
Total	157	28

Psychology—was completed. Finally, a hand search of school and curriculum journals was completed. These journals included the following: *Social Education, Theory and Research in Social Education, Journal of Research in Mathematics Education, Research in the Teaching of English, Connected Science Learning, Journal of Special Education, Elementary School Journal, Middle School Journal*, and *High School Journal*.

Sample Search

((((((TI (differentiat* instruction OR individualiz* instruction)) OR (AB (differentiat* instruction OR individualiz* instruction))) OR (DE individualiz* instruction)) AND ((DE ("educational practice*" OR "teaching method*" OR "educational strateg*")) OR ((TI ("educational practice*" OR "teaching method*" OR "educational strateg*" OR "teach* practice*")) AND (AB ("educational practice*" OR "teaching method*" OR "educational strateg*" OR "teach* practice*"))))) AND (change*)) AND (study or research or quantitative or qualitative or mixed or case)

Inclusion and Exclusion Criteria

The authors independently evaluated all studies. Through ERIC, 68 articles were found, and 10 articles were found through PsychINFO. Seventy-nine articles were found in the JSTOR database using a full-text search with our key words. Of these 157 articles, 28 studies met the following inclusion criteria: (1) published between 2001 and 2015, (2) peer-reviewed journal articles reporting research, (3) the research investigated a change in teaching practice characterized by DI, and (4) took place in a general education P–12 setting in the United States.

As shown in Table 2, the majority of studies were classified as illustrative case studies, which described DI through classroom examples. Illustrative case studies had components identified by Yin (1994), including the following: the research question aimed to examine how or why teachers used DI, data collection was done within the context of the classroom, and the researcher did not control the classroom events. Very few of the reviewed studies were classified as experimental or quasi-experimental or even survey-based; indeed, only four identified studies had random assignment, which suggest varying quality of the research design across the studies reviewed. We nevertheless decided to include these articles in our review, given our goal of exploring how DI was defined and operationalized in the literature.

TABLE 2
Study Type and Definition by Year Published

Type	Definition	2002 and 2005	2006–2008	2009	2010–2012	2013–2015	Total
Illustrative case studies	Described DI through classroom examples	4	3	7	2	1	17
Experimental/ quasi-experimental design	Compared different treatments	1[a]			3	1	5
Action research	Examined practice of teacher researcher	1		1			2
Survey	Collects survey or interview responses			1	2	1	4
Total		6	3	9	7	3	28

Note. DI = Differentiated Instruction.
[a]No random assignment.

Organization of Studies

Two independent coders extracted information from each study and organized the data by study type, DI purpose, theoretical framework, research questions, methodology, analysis method, expected/reported change in teacher practice, expected/reported impact on student learning, key barriers, facilitators, contextual factors, and implications for teaching and research. Table 3 displays the studies organized by the framework supporting the studies' definition of DI, authors, date of publication, school level, and research study type. Eighteen studies or 64% of the studies reviewed used Tomlinson's framework to guide their definition and operationalization of DI in the classroom. (See the Findings section of this chapter for a discussion of the frameworks.) Nineteen of the 28 studies took place in elementary schools (68%), 7 in middle schools (25%), and 2 with participants serving students in a range of different grades, K–12 (7%).

Prior to analysis, data were sorted by the type, timeline, common elements, and source of data included in results. Visual organization of data aided in comparing/contrasting studies across various factors from which analytical themes emerged (Miles, Huberman, & Saldaña, 2014). Table 4 displays the included studies by the year conducted and grade level of participants. No research studies were found that were conducted between 2001 and 2015 using only high school participants. The participants in these studies ranged from the teacher and students in one classroom

TABLE 3

Frameworks Supporting DI Definitions for 28 Studies Reviewed

Framework	Author(s)	Year	School	Study Type
Bartlett	Beecher and Sweeny	2008	Elementary	Illustrative case studies
Black and Wiliam	Stewart and Houchens	2014	Middle	Illustrative case studies
Dunn and Dunn	Pitts	2009	K–12 range	Survey
Betts	Latz, Speirs Neumeister, Adams, and Pierce	2008	Elementary	Illustrative case studies
Renzulli	Grimes and Stevens	2009	Elementary	Illustrative case studies
Renzulli, Tomlinson	Reis, McCoach, Little, Muller, and Kaniskan	2011	Elementary	Experimental design
Renzulli, Tomlinson	Brimijoin	2005	Elementary	Illustrative case studies
RtI	Moats	2009	Elementary	Illustrative case studies
RtI	Geisler, Hessler, Gardner, and Lovelace	2009	Elementary	Illustrative case studies
RtI	Otaiba et al.	2011	Elementary	Experimental design
RtI	Connor et al.	2011	Elementary	Experimental design
RtI	Jenkins, Schiller, Blackorby, Thayer, and Tilly	2013	Elementary	Survey
Tomlinson	Werderich	2002	Middle	Illustrative case studies
Tomlinson	Brighton	2002	Middle	Illustrative case studies
Tomlinson	Brighton, Hertberg, Moon, Tomlinson, and Callahan	2005	Elementary	Experimental design
Tomlinson	Hurd and Licciardo-Musso	2006	Elementary	Action research
Tomlinson	Hertberg-Davis and Brighton	2006	Middle	Illustrative case studies
Tomlinson	Valli and Buese	2007	Middle	Illustrative case studies
Tomlinson	Patterson, Connolly, and Ritter	2009	Elementary	Action research
Tomlinson	Simpkins, Mastropieri, and Scruggs	2009	Elementary	Illustrative case studies
Tomlinson	Goodnough	2010	Elementary	Illustrative case studies

(continued)

TABLE 3 (CONTINUED)

Framework	Author(s)	Year	School	Study Type
Tomlinson	Connor, Lara, Crowe, and Meadows	2009	Middle	Illustrative case studies
Tomlinson	Goddard, Neumerski, Goddard, Salloum, and Berebitsky	2010	Elementary	Survey
Tomlinson	Tricarico and Yendol-Hoppey	2012	Elementary	Illustrative case studies
Tomlinson	Logan	2011	K–12 range	Illustrative case studies
Tomlinson	Dee	2010	Middle	Survey
Tomlinson	Poncy, Fontenelle, and Skinner	2013	Elementary	Experimental design
Tomlinson, Ladson-Billings	Santamaria	2009	Elementary	Illustrative case studies

Note. DI = Differentiated Instruction; RtI = Response to Intervention.

(7 studies, 25%), several classrooms within a school (4 studies, 14%), classrooms across schools (13 studies, 46%), and preservice teachers (4 studies, 14%).

In addition, data were extracted to identify the curriculum subject area where DI took place by year published and grade level. DI was implemented in nine different subject areas. Eight studies identified specific content areas, and two studies did not specify a subject focus within the elementary school day. Of the 28 studies included in this review, professional learning was the subject area for nine studies that included teacher preparation (four studies) and professional development (three focused on teacher learning and two on school administrators). Subject areas included eight studies examining DI in reading, four in math, two in general elementary school curriculum, and one study in each of five additional subject areas (humanities, writing, student thinking styles, science, and social studies). See Figure 1.

Additionally, we extracted the data sources used in the studies to understand the types of data collected that measured the implementation and impact of changing instructional practices to DI. Figure 2 illustrates the types of data by the number of studies using that type of data by the participants' school level. The data types were organized by perspective and proximity to DI, beginning at the student level with student work, interviews, and surveys and then the teacher with lesson plans, reflective journals, interviews, and surveys. Then researchers and others completed classroom observations. Next are curriculum-based and researcher-created measures to assess and monitor student learning. These assessments were not teacher made, requiring teachers to learn how to implement, interpret the results, and then use the data to plan DI. Finally, student scores on standardized tests were reported as a measure of DI's impact in 8 out of the 28 studies (29%).

TABLE 4
Studies by Year and Grade Level

Grade Level	Year															Total
	2001	2002	2003	2004	2005	2006	2007	2008	2009	2010	2011	2012	2013	2014	2015	
K–12 range														1		3
Middle		2			1	1			1		1					6
Elementary					3		1	1	7	2	3		2			19
Total	0	2	0	0	4	1	1	1	9	2	5	0	2	1	0	28

FIGURE 1
Number of Studies by Curriculum Subject Area

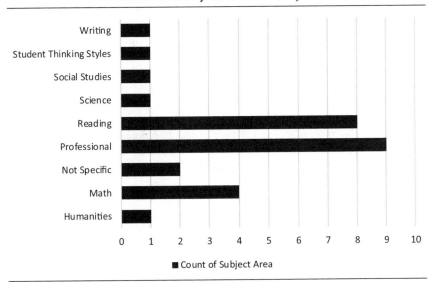

FIGURE 2
Data Types Listed by Source Type and the Number of Studies by Grade Level of Study Participants

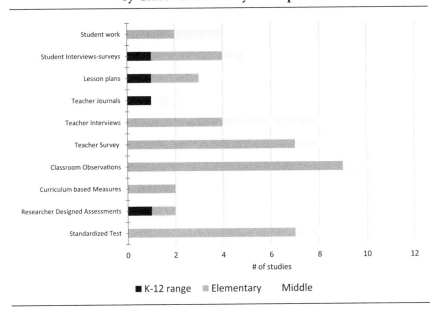

Examining the data sources used in studies illustrated how researchers measured changes in teacher practice when implementing DI and the impact on student learning. For example, although 19 studies took place in elementary schools, only 2 of the 19 studies (11%) examined student work and 4 out of 19 (21%) conducted teacher interviews as compared to 9 out of 19 (47%) that conducted classroom observations and 7 out of 19 (37%) that used standardized tests.

Data collection in the studies reviewed here took place during single moments in time and over the course of years. For example, one-time survey or interviews (5 studies) and semester-long (5 studies) comprise 36% of the studies in this review. In 11 studies (39%) data were collected throughout a school year. Finally, 7 studies (25%) took place over 3 to 8 years. The duration of data collection affected how changes in teacher practices were reported from a snapshot to examining increments of change over time and the sustainability of changes made to teacher practices.

Data Analysis

Two independent coders examined extracted data using Google forms and spreadsheets. From the extant data, a codebook was developed for each extracted field. The codebook included names, definitions, and examples (Saldaña, 2009). For example, the types of studies are listed in Table 2. Open-coding of the extracted data was followed by axial coding to relate initial codes to broader categories then selective codes were determined. The extracted data were then analyzed again using selective codes. Interrater reliability was established by each researcher completing axial coding independently and then comparing and discussing results until agreement was reached. Charts and tables were arranged with codes to uncover emergent themes. All studies were examined by both coders for patterns, replications, and common elements. Finally, unique elements were organized into themes and subthemes and recommendations were synthesized.

FINDINGS

We organized our findings by the two research questions. First, we examined changes in teacher practices by exploring frameworks and theories supporting and defining DI, operationalization of DI in the classroom, and reported barriers and facilitators of DI. Second, we examined patterns from the studies to define DI.

Changes in Teaching Practice

Our first research question examined how DI changed teacher practices in research conducted between 2001 and 2015. We used three steps to answer this question. First, we identified the framework or definition the researchers used to support their approach to DI. Then we used open and axial coding to identify how DI was operationalized in the classroom. Finally, we examined these descriptions for changes or shifts in teacher practice.

Frameworks Shape DI

We extracted data to determine the framework that researchers used to define their approach to DI. We identified key descriptions and patterns in the reported frameworks that affected changes in teacher practice to differentiate instruction.

Carol Tomlinson's (2001) definition of DI was used in 18 of the 28 studies (64%) to justify the approach to DI under investigation. Specifically, in 64% of the studies, DI was defined as adjustments to content (what is taught), process (how learning is structured), product (how learning is assessed), and the physical learning environment according to teachers' perception of student readiness, learning profile, and interests (Tomlinson, 2001). This definition was used to justify diverse approaches to meeting student needs from grouping students by independent reading level for instruction (Jenkins, Schiller, Blackorby, Thayer, & Tilly, 2013), to using an array of different classroom activities including extension tasks and choice of student-selected activities (Grimes & Stevens, 2009). For example, Brimijoin (2005) operationalized DI rooted in Tomlinson's framework as increased use of manipulatives, sheets with fewer problems, visuals, and tasks with greater challenge. This approach to DI embraced all teacher efforts to meet the perceived needs of students. Tomlinson's work was consistently referenced as the basis for the approach to DI in studies over 11 of the 15 years examined in this review, beginning in 2002 through 2013.

Three studies (Brimijoin, 2005; Grimes & Stevens, 2009; Reis et al., 2011) out of 28 (11%) referred to Renzulli as a foundation for their DI approach (two cited both Tomlinson and Renzulli; see Table 3). Renzulli's (1988) work defined a triad model for serving students with advanced abilities or those identified as gifted by (1) extending their skills, (2) fostering creative thinking, and (3) supporting their commitment to tasks. Both Renzulli and Tomlinson emphasize the importance of teacher response to perceptions of learner differences. Studies citing Renzulli and Tomlinson align with this framework by encouraging teachers to implement DI by changing their teaching from one task to a wide array of instructional activities.

By comparison, other studies were based on frameworks focused on helping teachers perceive student diversity. For example, Pitts (2009) referred to Dunn and Dunn's (1992) research on thinking styles. Dunn and Dunn's work focused on assessing and promoting critical thinking skills. Using this framework, DI consisted of assessing students as analytical or global thinkers and then asking teachers to provide feedback to students based on their thinking profile. This thinking styles survey was also cited in the Renzulli approach.

Additional frameworks supporting teacher perception included Black, Harrison, Lee, Marshall, and Wiliam's (2004) work on formative assessment. When basing DI in a formative assessment framework, teachers increased their perception of student differences by monitoring student learning needs, understanding, and progress through teacher-designed activities serving as informal assessments. Similarly emphasizing teacher perception, Ladson-Billings' (2009) culturally relevant pedagogy (CRP) was used along with Tomlinson's definition of DI by Santamaria (2009). In CRP, teachers made intentional efforts to connect curriculum and learning processes to students' cultural contexts. This approach relied on teacher perception of student learning styles, language, and culture and to help teachers plan curriculum. In addition, DI based in CRP emphasized clarifying concepts, emphasizing thinking, balancing choice among teacher and students, and using activities to increase student engagement. Studies rooted in thinking styles, formative assessment, and CRP frameworks all highlighted the importance of teacher perception of student variance and analysis of that variance. Then teachers were provided with a wide range of possible responses through instruction that reflected an awareness of the student differences that may affect effective learning.

Unlike the other frameworks focused on the teacher, Latz et al. (2008) cited the Betts' student mastery model to define DI. Latz et al. defined DI by combining Renzulli's triad model to guide teacher design of challenging learning activities with Betts' (2004) model of developing independent, self-regulated lifelong learners through mastery learning experiences. The Betts (2004) framework used a three-part continuum to shift the ownership for DI from the prescribed curriculum to teacher-adjusted curriculum (e.g., Renzulli), to finally a learner-driven curriculum (e.g., Renzulli plus self-regulated learning). Rooted in Betts' framework, DI was defined as not only providing learners with different activities but also activities were designed so that learners were not "passive consumers of information" (p. 2). DI according to this framework required learners to construct knowledge and work on tasks that they are passionate about, directed by themselves, and designed to fit their abilities. This framework demanded teachers change from seeing DI as individually teacher-assigned activities to teaching that dramatically increased learner responsibility to design their own learning within the constraints of standardized curriculum pacing and standardized testing.

Between 2009 and 2011, five studies (18%) rooted their approach to DI in Gersten et al. (2008) and/or the National Center on Response to Intervention (2010) recommendations that students receive DI in Tier I general classroom instruction (see Table 3). As part of RtI, DI was data driven, and used curriculum-based measurements (Deno & Mirkin, 1977) to systematically monitor student progress. Thus, systematic monitoring using researcher-developed assessments are emblematic of these studies.

In this framework, student differences were more narrowly defined primarily in terms of ability, and the need for teacher perception was reduced because teachers relied on researcher-designed ongoing assessments to detect student variance. In contrast, Tomlinson's framework encouraged teachers to notice a wide range of student differences including language, culture, and personal interests as factors that may influence teacher decisions in planning instruction to leverage student strengths or minimize challenges. However, the studies referencing Gersten et al. (2008) focused on DI as monitoring student ability and matching tasks to individual ability regardless of other factors of student variance, such as languages spoken, culture, and interests.

Given the expansive role of the researcher, the teacher's role shifted from perceiving student differences and creating curriculum that reflects a recognition of how those differences affect learning to implementing a mandated program. Teachers were charged with implementing assessments built by researchers unfamiliar with the teacher's specific classroom context and then assigning premade tasks that could be matched to a student's current skill level. This approach reduced the uncertainty of determining appropriate tasks for students to implement DI and increased teacher skills needed to interpret data, manage different activities, and implement a researched-based program with fidelity.

The type of teacher decision making required to implement DI was vastly different between Tomlinson's framework and the science-based RtI approach. Changes in teacher practices were different depending on the framework used to define DI. Bartlett's (2004) study illustrated how a constant mandate from a school district to implement DI changed the definition and the teacher's role from Tomlinson's approach to DI being a part of RtI. Although the primary purpose of Bartlett's research was to describe the impact of federal, state, and local policies on teacher roles, we included the article in this review because it provided data on how teachers thought about changes in their practice related to implementing DI over time as a mandate from the school district.

Bartlett's (2004) interviews of teachers and administrators illustrated how changes in teacher practice were dynamic because they reflected an evolving teacher understanding and application of DI over the 4 years. He determined that as NCLB was implemented, along with other policies such as Individuals with Disabilities Education Act (2004), DI increased, and teacher roles also increased, expanded, and intensified. Teachers reported increased tasks in five specific areas: instructional (assessing and assigning activities to students based on needs), institutional (curriculum pacing, curriculum alignment), collaborative (meeting/planning with other teachers), professional learning (interpreting data, research-based instruction), and relationship building (with students, families, and staff). Changes in teacher tasks also affected the definition and framework alignment of DI. For example, Bartlett described how curriculum control moved from teacher decisions to the district's pacing guide. Bartlett's study illustrated an important shift in control over decisions to respond to student differences from informal decisions in the classroom to highly institutionalized procedures. This study demonstrated how teacher change takes place within a complex dynamic context.

In summary, seven different frameworks explained the approach to DI used in these studies. The frameworks influenced the purpose of DI shaping the goals, materials teachers used or made, data type and interpretation skill required of teachers, level of teacher decision-making control, and necessary teacher professional knowledge to implement DI. The framework used to define DI affected teacher changes in practice.

DI Operationalized in the Classroom

In the studies reviewed, DI was operationalized in varying ways because of the alignment to different frameworks and implementation across contexts with unique goals. However, patterns in the ways that DI was implemented illuminate important shifts in the structure of instructional activities and teacher's decision making. Physical changes observed included teacher modification of instructional activities

(Beecher & Sweeny, 2008; Brighton, 2002; Reis et al., 2011). Teacher changes in instructional activities included shifts from whole group to small group, increased opportunities for student choice, and more learner-directed tasks. Changes in teacher decision making were found through many data sources including teacher journals (Logan, 2011; Valli & Buese, 2007), teacher interviews (Brighton, 2002), and survey statements (Dee, 2010; Geisler, Hessler, Gardner, & Lovelace, 2009; Jenkins et al., 2013). Changes in teacher decision making included changes in feelings of control of DI, use of an assessment cycle, and making decisions through collaboration with other educators.

All 28 of the studies reviewed described teacher grouping of students by a common characteristic as a change in teacher practices. Studies often described a physical change in seating arrangements from sitting in a whole group to small groups as evidence of DI. However, it was unclear as to whether the students worked collaboratively or individually while sitting in small groups or the extent that tasks were designed for collaborative learning. Only one study, Pitts (2009), operationalized DI in the whole class setting. Pitts surveyed student thinking styles and encouraged teachers to respond to students with feedback that matched their thinking style, either global or analytic. After calling on an individual student to provide an answer, teachers could provide this differentiated feedback based on the student's "thinking style." Although students were not required to move into small groups, this approach required teachers to consider students in terms of belonging to a group with a specific thinking preference. In every study, one change characterizing a shift from "one-size-fits-all" instruction to DI was grouping students for small group or individual tasks. However, the studies were not specific in how teacher instruction changed within the small groups. Furthermore, studies did not explore the possible impacts of grouping students on teacher expectations for achievement, bias, and fixed or growth mindsets in teachers.

Studies using the Tomlinson framework (see Table 3) generally reported increased student choice as a change in teacher practice. For example, Grimes and Stevens (2009) described teachers offering individualized enrichment projects to increase interest-driven challenging assignments. Other examples include Brighton et al.'s (2005) increased choice by offering students different prompts when writing in journals to increase student engagement through connecting to interests. Hurd and Licciardo-Musso (2006) allowed students to choose between different graphic organizers to facilitate work with a partner. In these studies, offering student choice was related to intentions to increase student engagement and appeal to student interests. No study measured pre–post student engagement with and without increased choice. In addition, teachers reported using choice opportunities to provide increased challenge to students with advanced skills. Similarly, no study measured how teachers changed the task to increase challenge for students such as a measure of task complexity with and without DI.

Teacher change to increase student choice (see above) and reports of increased student engagement (Brimijoin, 2005; Grimes & Stevens, 2009) suggest a shift in teacher practice from teacher-led activities to more learner-directed activities as a component of DI. For example, Goodnough (2010) described an approach to DI where students used a checklist to self-monitor vocabulary use in their writing. Patterson, Connolly, and Ritter (2009) describe the use of a self-directed assessment as the starting point for determining appropriate learning tasks for students. These studies reported activities and observations suggesting a change in teacher practice toward prompting student self-regulated learning as a component of DI. However, self-regulated learning prompts in teacher-designed lessons was not measured with or without DI.

All studies reported an increase in teacher decision making as a necessary step to the implementation of DI. Based on the framework used and the context, the type of decision making differed and teachers' feelings about making decisions to adjust instruction ranged from being empowered to overwhelmed. For example, studies rooted in Tomlinson's framework reported teacher difficulties in deciding to respond to student variance (Brighton et al., 2005; Hurd & Licciardo-Musso, 2006). Hertberg-Davis and Brighton (2006) examined teacher beliefs, specifically about equity as factors influencing the educators' implementation of DI. Conversely, some studies rooted in RtI reported teacher decisions regarding the interpretation of data to be challenging for participating teachers. In fact, Beecher and Sweeny (2008) reported that teachers felt like the curriculum pacing guide controlled their decisions. Yet using a sample of 616 teachers across 17 schools, Goddard, Neumerski, Goddard, Salloum, and Berebitsky (2010) reported that teachers suggested that when a principal expressed a clear definition of DI then it was easier to change their practice. As Goddard demonstrated, generally, teachers responded with stress when decisions to differentiate were moved to an institutional level; however, teachers did respond more favorably if the decision was clearly articulated and they felt supported to implement the change.

Hurd and Licciardo-Musso (2006) reported on a teacher team using lesson study to further their implementation of DI. Through careful watching of students in lessons led by other team members, teachers reported developing their own skills as assessors of student learning needs. Teacher collaboration to implement DI resulted in positive attitudes toward DI among the teacher team. In addition, Hertberg-Davis and Brighton (2006) pointed out that as more students with disabilities were included in general education classrooms, the collaboration with colleagues increased. This changed teacher practice to team instructional decisions rather than a classroom teacher making decisions alone. Teachers did not always report team collaboration as positive. Collaboration affected teacher decision making in different ways and also affected researcher ability to carry out studies. For example, Reis et al. (2011) and Brimijoin (2005) reported diffusion of the intervention between the control and treatment groups from teacher collaboration as a factor negatively affecting the validity of the results of their studies.

Changes in teacher practice were linked in complex ways to other social (collaboration), personal (beliefs), and professional (skills, knowledge, understanding of students) factors. Teacher change in practice often did not happen in these studies as researchers planned. Some researchers reported a gap between teachers' knowing how and why to use DI and actually implementing DI with students (Geisler et al., 2009).

Brimijoin (2005) illustrated how changes in teacher practice to implement DI was not always forward moving or sustained. In this case study, the teacher implemented DI one year and then a year later abandoned DI when pressured by standardized testing. Hurd and Licciardo-Musso (2006) and Valli and Buese (2007) reported that teacher decisions to change their practice varied based on perceived support from the principal. In addition, Valli and Buese (2007) and Brighton (2002) found that teacher decisions to change their practice reflected alignment with the fundamental purpose of DI for that specific school and teacher beliefs. Examining the changes in teacher practice when implementing DI during this time period provided a clear direction for variables that might measure how teacher practice has changed as a result of implementing DI in future studies. Particularly the relationships between the framework used to define DI and factors operationalized in observed teacher changes may assist researchers as well as practitioners in defining the purpose of DI and measuring changes in teacher practice.

Barriers and Facilitators of Teacher Change

We extracted reports of the barriers and facilitators of intentional teacher changes to differentiate instruction for each of the 28 studies. Figure 3 displays how the barriers identified in the studies were divided into categories and then organized into three conditions: institution decision on how to implement DI, teacher decision on how to implement DI, and barriers that appear in both conditions.

Taken together, the 28 studies identified several potential obstacles to the implementation of DI. The Brighton et al. (2005) study was especially useful in showing how contextual factors and teachers' personal beliefs about teaching and learning affect the quantity and quality of the DI implementation. Overall, their study highlighted the difficulties inherent in effectively differentiating instruction. As they state,

On their own, differentiation of instruction and assessment are complex endeavors requiring extended time and concentrated effort to master. Add to this complexity, current realities of school such as large class sizes, limited resource materials, lack of planning time, lack of structures in place to allow collaboration with colleagues, and ever-increasing number of teacher responsibilities, and the tasks become even more daunting. (p. 304)

This quote implied that teachers need adequate support (both material and psychological) to effectively differentiate instruction. For example, Brighton et al. (2005) found that teachers who worked in schools with encouraging and supportive administrators who helped provide resources (e.g., incentives for staff development opportunities, extra planning time) were more likely to differentiate their instruction. The study also suggested that teachers were more likely to implement DI when their beliefs about teaching and learning aligned with the school's definition of DI, and they felt more competent to implement DI effectively. Thus, DI would happen only if teachers were motivated to change their practices and were adequately supported to do so.

FIGURE 3
Barriers to Teacher Change by Condition for Differentiated Instruction (DI) Decisions (Institution vs. Teacher)

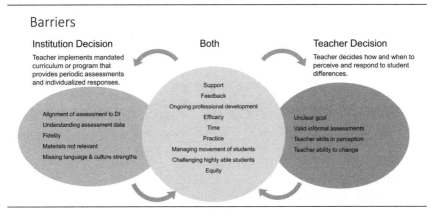

FIGURE 4
Facilitators Organized by Four Core Ideas

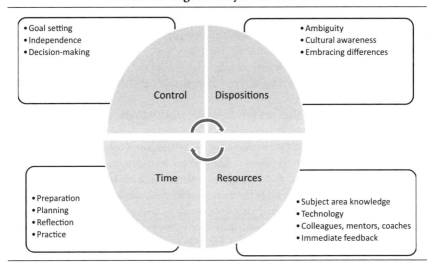

Each of the 28 studies also highlighted various facilitators of DI. Figure 4 displays how the identified facilitators were categorized into four core ideas: control, resources, time, and dispositions. Synthesized into bullet points are examples reported from the studies related to each core facilitator.

One supporting factor discussed in four studies was elements of control. This factor encompassed goal setting, independence, and the teacher as decision maker. Goddard et al. (2010) highlighted how a decentralized decision-making process within a school placed the teacher in the instructional driver's seat and facilitated the implementation of DI. The study highlighted how this approach empowered classroom instructors and created a scenario where "teachers are more likely to report that DI occurs in their schools" (p. 353).

Taking this a step further, in many of the studies, the role of effective leadership was central (Brighton, 2002; Grimes & Stevens, 2009; Hurd & Licciardo-Musso, 2006; Santamaria, 2009). Specifically, principal support, which was discussed in various forms—from setting the school-wide strategic plan and vision that centered on DI, to providing support for mentors and coaches, to aligning resources for professional development opportunities such as lesson study and for the creation and sustaining of professional learning communities within the school building—was a repeated theme throughout.

Other resources cited as facilitators were teacher subject area knowledge as well as immediate and consistent feedback from administrators and colleagues. Both Connor et al. (2011) and Otaiba et al. (2011) pointed to technology as a facilitating resource. In these studies, technology was used to implement ongoing monitoring of student learning. This use of technology influenced time positively with the amount spent calculating the results and negatively influenced time as a barrier requiring teachers to interpret data that resulted from these assessments.

The finite resource of time received its own category in this analysis because its impact is cited in terms of lesson preparation, planning, reflection, and practice. The use of existing materials (Patterson et al., 2009) and preparation for DI that did not significantly increase time required by the teacher (Goodnough, 2010) were highlighted as facilitators. Similarly, time provided for reflection, and in the Dee (2010) study for preservice teachers, it was noted as a supporting element to future and continued DI implementation.

The final category involves teacher dispositions and includes such concepts of dealing with ambiguity, willingness to reflect on and grow in cultural awareness, and, in general, the teachers' ability to embrace differences (Logan, 2011). Santamaria (2009) summarized how teacher disposition influenced teaching practices, stating, "The best teaching practices are those that consider all learners in a classroom setting and pay close attention to differences inherent to academic, cultural, linguistic, and socioeconomic diversity" (p. 241). Santamaria continued to discuss how culturally relevant pedagogy and DI are aligned and mutually supportive in meeting student needs.

To better understand how DI changed teacher practice, the barriers and facilitators were isolated, identified, and described. However, Figures 3 and 4 illustrate how these barriers and facilitators are interconnected. Factors such as time, feedback, practice, and decision making appeared both as facilitators and barriers to implementing DI. It may be useful to think of these factors along a continuum rather than in binary terms of being present or not. An awareness of common factors affecting the changes in teacher practice to implement DI may facilitate future researchers in designs that control for these factors as well as school personnel looking for levers to increase the use of DI.

DISCUSSION

Findings indicated that U.S. research studies that examined DI in general classroom settings from 2001 to 2015 primarily took place in elementary school settings. Although the subject areas varied, more than half of the studies focused on DI in reading and teacher professional learning. Data collected to measure changes in teacher practice included a range of sources spanning from examining student work, student and teacher surveys, teacher interviews, classroom observations, curriculum-based measurements, to standardized testing. Changes in teacher practice were related to the framework used to define DI. Analyzing how DI was operationalized in the classroom offered insight into how teaching practice changed. Considering barriers and facilitators identified in the studies reviewed provided levers for change that may be used to strengthen future studies. To explore the question, "Have we moved from a 'one-size-fits-all' to DI?" we considered three themes made visible by our findings: DI needs systematic replicable research, factors of DI left out of these studies, and the impetus for teacher change.

DI Needs Systematic Replicable Research

Analysis of these studies illustrated how, while "the reason for DI is commonly accepted, and the value is logical and empirically grounded, describing or defining DI has proved to be a challenge" (Reis et al., 2011, p. 4). For example, in Tomlinson's framework DI is based on learner readiness, interests, and learning profile and applied to ensure every task is a good fit for each student (Tomlinson, 2001). However, during NCLB years DI was defined as a tool to help teachers ensure all students made expected progress on standardized tests. In fact, "in schools at risk of inadequate yearly progress, bringing sufficient numbers of students in each designated category to proficiency became differentiation's primary goal" (Valli & Buese, 2007, p. 534). The desired result of DI ranged from a goal of achievement on standardized tests for students grouped by a common characteristic to increasing teacher learning about the student characteristics and connecting teacher understanding of students to learning tasks—such as linguistic diversity—and involving students in using their strengths to accomplish the task.

This lack of a consistent definition led researchers to identify very different classroom practices as DI. For example, DI was operationalized in terms of student choice prompts in learning journals (Brighton et al., 2005; Werderich, 2002), individualized worksheets (Connor et al., 2011; Connor, Lara, Crowe, & Meadows, 2009), sitting students with similar abilities in small groups to complete reading tasks, and teacher adjustment of feedback to match learner thinking preferences (Pitts, 2009). Differences in the definition of DI were present even when researchers grounded their studies in the same framework. For example, Patterson et al. (2009), citing Tomlinson's framework, examined teachers perceiving student differences, interpreting and analyzing those differences, and identifying and implementing an instruction response from a known repertoire that addresses the student learning needs. However, Hurd and

Licciardo-Musso (2006), also citing Tomlinson's framework, focused on teachers providing graphic organizers and sitting students in small groups but did not examine how instruction changed with the use of the material or structure for learning.

Studies focused on the use or nonuse of materials and activities rather than the instruction teachers used to illustrate DI in the classroom. For example, studies did not examine how teachers may have varied the use of the material, the teacher's decision of when to provide the material in lessons, or how instruction led to the material being faded over time as students developed skills. In addition, outcomes of DI varied across studies, reflecting the differing views of DI. Inconsistent definitions, outcomes, and changes to teacher practice taken together create a vague and confusing vision for how DI may ensure optimal challenge for all learners in a general education classroom. Clarifying the definition of DI and the operationalization of DI in the classroom is necessary to accurately measure how DI changed teacher practice.

Research based on an agreed upon purpose and approach to DI could investigate questions that were not asked in these studies, such as the following: How often, in what magnitude, and in what duration does DI occur? Is DI different at the beginning of a curriculum unit or the school year than it is at the end? How do teacher practices change when implementing DI among students and across grade level, subject area, and different school contexts? Greater clarity on the definition and desired results or outcomes of DI is necessary to facilitate replicable research.

Factors of DI Left Out in These Studies

The studies included in this review did not examine factors that might change teacher perception and expectations of students needed to implement DI effectively. Teacher beliefs were cited as obstacles for DI implementation. For example, Brighton et al. (2005) demonstrated how context and teachers' beliefs affect DI's quantity and quality. She summarized their findings stating that "If . . . educators practice elements and guidelines for DI by only acknowledging student differences without actually changing their practice (primarily because there are no guidelines on how to do so), teachers run the risk of practicing colorblind pedagogy" (p. 240). Taken together, studies highlighted the inherent difficulties of teacher beliefs and DI implementation. However, a more standardized approach to measuring beliefs that affect teacher decisions to use DI may be helpful. In addition, only Santamaria (2009) considered teacher perception of students' culture. Research tools could be developed to assist teachers in perceiving student cultural wealth as part of ongoing assessments to gain information used for DI. Furthermore, grouping students by perceived common characteristics may affect teacher expectations and student learning and should be investigated.

The population experiencing DI in the classroom that researchers studied was limited. Much of the research focused on students with advanced abilities and those struggling with reading skills in the elementary school. Absent from these studies were high school students and how DI may affect students who are progressing well in their learning.

Impetus for Teacher Change: Policy Mandate Versus Perception and Response

Finally, the collection of studies reflects the growth of a range of factors pushing teachers to use DI. In 2002, we found research studies where classroom teachers perceived student differences and responded through individualized instruction. This approach could be traced back in the literature to the 1953 article on adjusting instruction to student needs. However, as time progresses from 2002 to 2009 we saw some studies continue to reference Tomlinson while others shifted to a top down mandate where DI was implemented based on systematic monitoring of student variance on dimensions selected by researchers or curriculum designers.

During that time, the teacher expertise required to implement DI changed from an emphasis on formative assessment and being flexible or creative in assigning instructional activities and offering students feedback to administering standardized monitoring assessments using technology and interpreting the data. DI broadened from teacher-designed instructional responses to perceived student differences to include standardized procedures and materials. This approach was also fueled by the 2004 reauthorization of the Individuals with Disabilities Education Act that included RtI as a way for districts to identify students with learning disabilities and provided funding to start programs in states and districts (Mellard & Johnson, 2007). This approach shifted teacher responsibility and control from perceiving student differences and creating tailored instructional activities to implementing assessments mandated by the institution and providing instruction also mandated by the institution. Adding to the confusion, the National Center on Response to Intervention (2010) document listed in the recommendations for essential components of RtI, "differentiated learning activities (e.g., mixed instructional grouping, use of learning centers, peer tutoring) to address individual needs." This directive suggests a great variety of student variance could be addressed through a wide range of activities chosen by the teacher. Under the same framework of RtI, this approach to DI is very different than the specific individualized worksheets used in the reading studies (Otaiba et al., 2011; Reis et al., 2011). The teacher role and expertise required to implement DI changed depending on the definition of DI.

Although the definition of DI was varied, this review of the literature demonstrated changes in teacher practice moving from a "one-size-fits-all" approach with whole group instruction to DI with students working in small groups. Knowing these changes can be operationalized in the classroom and that academic diversity is only likely to increase leads to important next steps in future research.

FUTURE RESEARCH

Based on the limited number of research studies and the need for developing tools that can be tested across school contexts and disciplines, there seems to be more theorizing about the benefits of DI than tests of its claims. However, providing all students with optimal opportunities is among teachers' greatest challenges. Thus, future research must define DI with clarity so that we can extend our understanding of how and why teachers change their instructional practices to respond to the diverse needs of learners and the impact of these instructional changes on student learning.

Our review highlights a number of gaps in the literature on DI, including: (a) inconsistent theoretical framing and subsequent operationalization of DI, (b) uneven focus in terms of student populations, (c) and overall lack of methodological rigor in studies of DI that explore its effects on student outcomes. Thus, in this section, we propose a number of avenues for future research that are directly tied to these gaps.

Improving the Theoretical Framing of DI

As exemplified by the studies reviewed in this article, Tomlinson provides one of the most well-known definition of differentiation, which features modifying instructional content (what is taught), process (how students learn), and product (how students demonstrate learning) according to students' readiness, interests, and learning profiles (1999; Tomlinson et al., 2003). Although this definition is useful, our analysis also suggests that the unlimited combinations of possible teacher responses can overwhelm teachers, and can also possibly explain the lack of differentiation we see in schools. In this review, we also highlighted other equally important and useful theoretical frameworks of DI such as those that define differentiation on a continuum, or those that emphasize the use of formative assessments to tailor instruction and to develop lifelong, self-regulated learners (i.e., Betts, 2004; Black et al., 2004).

We propose an integrative framework of DI that can help teachers make more effective and efficient decisions about when, how, and what to differentiate, both in planning lessons and "on their feet" as they teach. In that spirit, we offer one such definition that has guided our own studies on DI (Bondie & Zusho, 2018). Specifically, we define differentiation as the outcome of a continuous decision-making process where teachers *look and listen* for academic diversity that will strengthen or impede effective and efficient learning, and then adjust instruction to increase *Clarity, Access, Rigor, and Relevance* (CARR) for *all* students within a learning community.

This definition reframes the research on DI from a focus on content-process-product to a focus on decision making. In line with the research on DI, which suggests that teachers often fail to adequately and accurately perceive student variability, this definition underscores the importance of providing teachers ample opportunities to listen and learn from their students. Indeed, it is reasonable to assume that if teachers are spending most of their time lecturing or running from table to table giving the same instruction to students, then teachers cannot possibly engage what the Nobel Laureate Daniel Kahneman (2013) calls System 2—the slower, analytic and rational side of the mind that is necessary for effective regulation of learning. Rather in those instances, they will be more inclined to make decisions based on System 1—the faster, intuitive side of the mind, which can result in instructional practices (i.e., interacting less with and providing less wait time and praise for struggling, marginalized students) that exacerbate gaps in achievement (Brophy, 1985).

Engaging routines that encourage looking and listening can have beneficial effects for any student, but it is especially critical when working with marginalized populations, as it can help teachers counteract their implicit biases. Biases are an inherent aspect of being human; thus, we do not mean to suggest here that teachers are any more biased than others. Nevertheless, research does suggest that teachers often hold stereotypical beliefs about marginalized students (Kumar & Hamer, 2013), and that these biases shape how teachers make decisions while teaching. For example, in a recent address given at the annual meeting of the American Educational Research Association, Deborah Ball counted 20 "micro-moments" where she needed to decide how to react in just a minute and a half of a lesson, and how some of these decisions were based on racial stereotypes (Barshay, 2018).

Thus, a focus on decision making may even lead to a greater awareness of how these instructional decisions affect not just academically gifted students, but *all* students in a community. Indeed, our review demonstrates that the empirical research on DI is limited when it comes to understanding how to promote the learning of (older) students at the lower extremes, who more often than not include emergent bilingual students and students with learning disabilities.

Another advantage of our definition of DI is that it is explicitly tied to learning outcomes. Unlike other models of DI, our definition provides a blueprint for how to improve the learning outcomes of students by increasing CARR for all members of a learning community. Research on CARR dates back to the 1970s and 1980s, when researchers became interested in documenting the effects of teacher behavior on student learning outcomes (Brophy, 1985; Brophy & Good, 1984). Collectively, these studies of teacher effects (also referred to as process-product studies) sought to examine how teacher variables such as the amount and quality of teaching affected student outcomes. Overall, these studies suggested that amount of academic learning time— time students spend actively engaged in academic tasks of appropriate difficulty levels—mattered, as did how (or how well) teachers performed common instructional tasks such as giving instructions, asking questions, and providing feedback (Brophy, 1985). Thus, the CARR framework is a useful tool (see Table 5) to remind us of these foundational teacher-related behaviors and to connect the research on DI to outcomes of student learning, thereby potentially increasing the significance of this research.

As mentioned earlier, implicit in our definition is the assumption that *all* students deserve instruction that is clear, accessible, rigorous, and relevant. Yet, we know that given prior experiences and differing background knowledge, not all students will have the same understanding of CARR—this is what makes teaching so challenging. What is clear for one student may not be for another; similarly, perceptions of relevance and rigor are likely to depend on the student. Thus, the challenge of DI is to find ways to meet this goal of CARR for all students. This is where the conceptualization of DI as being on a continuum becomes critical.

To that end, our model of DI (see Bondie & Zusho, 2018) distinguishes between three types of DI, which have different purposes (e.g., accessible engagement, closing gaps, and extending learning) and require different amounts of planning time. We assume that the majority of instructional time should be spent using *adjustable common instruction* where students are learning with the same goals, resources, and assessments so that

TABLE 5
CARR Check Questions for Teacher Reflection

C	Clarity	Is this task clear to ALL students? Are the words understandable by all students? Are students expected to understand vocabulary that may be vague, have multiple meanings, or are in unfamiliar contexts?
A	Access	Could ALL students complete the task independently and feel capable?
R	Rigor	How much effort is required of different students? What would students find complex?
R	Relevance	Would ALL students find this task important, interesting, valuable, and/or useful?

Note. CARR = clarity, access, rigor, and relevance.

teachers do not have to design anything new. With adjustable common instruction, the teaching approach relies mostly on routines that have been shown to have maximum impact on learning, such as those that promote self-regulated learning. The second type of DI is *specific resources* where the objectives and assessments are the same; however, some students (groups or individuals) are using different resources accompanied with a specific teaching approach to achieve the objective. Finally, the third type of DI is individualized, like a workout plan—not to be confused with specialized education that require Individualized Education Plans. *All* learners—not just those with Individualized Education Plans—at times, will need opportunities for individual workouts to review, practice, extend, or pursue an interest.

More Effective Studies of DI

Another major shortcoming of the research on DI is the overall lack of methodological rigor employed in studies. Our analysis suggests that few studies actually measure the frequency, magnitude, and duration of changes in teacher practice and the resulting impact of DI on student learning, which makes it difficult to ascertain its impact on student learning (see also Gersten et al., 2008). The Brighton et al. (2005) study is perhaps the most comprehensive experimental study; however, complications with sampling and study design, and the use of a limited set of teacher and student outcome measures, make it difficult to evaluate the effects of the intervention on student achievement outcomes. The operationalization of DI in this study also makes it difficult to determine the effects of specific instructional practices on outcomes, although overall the study does demonstrate that certain aspects of differentiation can positively affect teacher behaviors and beliefs. Other nonexperimental design studies (e.g., Beecher & Sweeney, 2008) also generally fall short in effectively addressing the frequency, duration, magnitude, and required flexibility of DI and how DI improves student outcomes. In short, these findings suggest that more targeted experimental studies on DI are warranted.

Also needed are frameworks of DI that include carefully considered routines that have been shown theoretically and empirically to have maximum impact on student learning outcomes. For example, considering that self-directed learning is an important goal of DI, it would be important for future research to consider the extensive work on self-regulated learning (SRL; Pintrich & Zusho, 2007; Zimmerman, 2008). Research on SRL routinely finds that self-regulated learners—students who are metacognitively aware of how they think, who set appropriate goals and plan for learning, monitor progress toward goals, adjust or regulate their thinking, motivation, and study habits—are more likely to achieve academic success than those who do not (Pintrich & Zusho, 2007; Zimmerman, 2008). Indeed, Hattie (2009) lists metacognition—a key aspect of SRL—as one of the top factors associated with achievement. Formative assessments are also considered to be a lever of SRL, which can further tie the research on DI to that of SRL.

Taken together, we propose that future studies of DI should be framed according to a more integrative definition of DI. A clear definition could prove useful in facilitating the kind of studies needed to fill the current gaps in the literature. By shifting our focus to the instructional reasoning and decisions teachers make, we can gain a more nuanced understanding of the underlying processes that result in more effective differentiation. Future studies should focus on differentiation for *all* students, intentionally, expanding the literature on how instruction can be adjusted to better serve the wide range of abilities diverse students bring to the classroom (see integrative examples in Kumar, Zusho, & Bondie, 2018). Finally, by explicitly tying the research on DI to actual student learning outcomes, we could gain critical information about the overall impact of this DI on achievement and broader learning outcomes.

ACKNOWLEDGMENTS

We acknowledge Carla Lillvik, Research Librarian, Monroe C. Gutman Library, Harvard Graduate School of Education, for her collaboration and support of our research.

REFERENCES

References marked with an asterisk were included in the review.

Barshay, J. (2018, May 7). 20 judgments a teacher makes in 1 minute and 28 seconds. *The Hechinger Report*. Retrieved from https://hechingerreport.org/20-judgments-a-teacher-makes-in-1-minute-and-28-seconds/

Bartlett, L. (2004). Expanding teacher work roles: A resource for retention or a recipe for overwork? *Journal of Education Policy, 19*, 565–582. doi:10.1080/0268093042000269144

*Beecher, M., & Sweeny, S. M. (2008). Closing the achievement gap with curriculum enrichment and differentiation: One school's story. *Journal of Advanced Academics, 19*, 502–530. doi:10.4219/jaa-2008-815

Betts, G. (2004). Fostering autonomous learners through levels of differentiation. *Roeper Review, 26*, 190–191. doi.org/10.1080/02783190409554269

Black, P., Harrison, C., Lee, C., Marshall, B., & Wiliam, D. (2004). Working inside the black box: Assessment for learning in the classroom. *Phi Delta Kappan, 86*(1), 8–21. doi:10.1177/003172170408600105

Bondie, R., & Zusho, A. (2018). *Differentiated instruction made practical: Engaging the extremes through classroom routines*. New York, NY: Routledge.

*Brighton, C. M. (2002). Straddling the fence: Implementing best practices in an age of accountability. *Gifted Child Today, 25*, 30–33. doi:10.4219/gct-2002-67

*Brighton, C. M., Hertberg, H. L., Moon, T. R., Tomlinson, C. A., & Callahan, C. M. (2005). *The feasibility of high-end learning in a diverse middle school*. Storrs: University of Connecticut, National Research Center on the Gifted and Talented.

*Brimijoin, K. (2005). Differentiation and high-stakes testing: An oxymoron? *Theory into Practice, 44*, 254–261. doi:10.1207/s15430421tip4403_10

Brophy, J. E. (1985). Teacher-student interaction. In J. B. Dusek (Ed.), *Teacher expectancies* (pp. 303–328). Hillsdale, NJ: Lawrence Erlbaum.

Brophy, J., & Good, T. L. (1984). *Teacher behavior and student achievement* (Occasional Paper No. 73). Retrieved from https://eric.ed.gov/?id=ED251422

Bush, G. W. (2001). *No Child Left Behind*. Retrieved from https://www2.ed.gov/nclb/landing .jhtml

*Connor, C. M., Lara, J. J., Crowe, E. C., & Meadows, J. G. (2009). Instruction, student engagement, and reading skill growth in reading first classrooms. *Elementary School Journal, 109*, 221–250. doi:10.1086/592305

*Connor, C. M., Morrison, F. J., Fishman, B., Giuliani, S., Luck, M., Underwood, P. S., & Schatschneider, C. (2011). Testing the impact of child characteristics × instruction interactions on third graders' reading comprehension by differentiating literacy instruction. *Reading Research Quarterly, 46*, 189–221. doi:10.1598/RRQ.46.3.1

*Dee, A. L. (2010). Preservice teacher application of differentiated instruction. *Teacher Educator, 46*(1), 53–70. doi:10.1080/08878730.2010.529987

Deno, S., & Mirkin, P. (1977). *Data-based program modification: A manual*. Retrieved from https://eric.ed.gov/?id=ED144270

Dunn, R. S., & Dunn, K. J. (1992). *Teaching elementary students through their individual learning styles*. Boston, MA: Allyn & Bacon.

*Geisler, J. L., Hessler, T., Gardner, R., & Lovelace, T. S. (2009). Differentiated writing interventions for high-achieving urban African American elementary students. *Journal of Advanced Academics, 20*, 214–247. doi:10.1177/1932202x0902000202

Gersten, R., Compton, D., Connor, C. M., Dimino, J., Santoro, L., Linan-Thompson, S., & Tilly, W. D. (2008). *Assisting students struggling with reading: Response to Intervention and multi-tier intervention for reading in the primary grades. A practice guide* (NCEE 20094045). Washington, DC: National Center for Education Evaluation and Regional Assistance, Institute of Education Sciences, U.S. Department of Education.

*Goddard, Y. L., Neumerski, C. M., Goddard, R. D., Salloum, S. J., & Berebitsky, D. (2010). A multilevel exploratory study of the relationship between teachers' perceptions of principals' instructional support and group norms for instruction in elementary schools. *Elementary School Journal, 111*, 336–357. doi:10.1086/656303

*Goodnough, K. (2010). Investigating pre-service science teachers' developing professional knowledge through the lens of differentiated instruction. *Research in Science Education, 40*, 239–265. doi:10.1007/s11165-009-9120-6

*Grimes, K. J., & Stevens, D. D. (2009). Glass, bug, mud. *Phi Delta Kappan, 90*, 677–680.

Hall, T., Strangman, N., & Meyer, A. (2003). *Differentiated instruction and implications for UDL implementation*. Wakefield, MA: National Center on Accessing the General Curriculum.

Hattie, J. (2009). *Visible learning: A synthesis of over 800 meta-analyses relating to achievement*. New York, NY: Routledge.

*Hertberg-Davis, H. L., & Brighton, C. M. (2006). Support and sabotage principals' influence on middle school teachers' responses to differentiation. *Journal of Secondary Gifted Education, 17*, 90–102. doi:10.4219/jsge-2006-685

*Hurd, J., & Licciardo-Musso, L. (2005). Lesson study: Teacher-led professional development in literacy instruction. *Language Arts, 82*, 388–395.

Individuals with Disabilities Education Act, 20 U.S.C. § 1400 (2004).

*Jenkins, J., Schiller, E., Blackorby, J., Thayer, S., & Tilly, W. (2013). Responsiveness to intervention in reading: Architecture and practices. *Learning Disability Quarterly, 36*(1), 36–46.

Kahneman, D. (2011). *Thinking fast and slow.* New York, NY: Farrar, Straus, & Giroux.

Kumar, R., & Hamer, L. (2013). Preservice teachers' attitudes and beliefs toward student diversity and proposed instructional practices: A sequential design study. *Journal of Teacher Education, 64,* 162–177. doi:10.1177/0022487112466899

Kumar, R., Zusho, A., & Bondie, R. (2018). Weaving cultural relevance and achievement motivation into inclusive classroom cultures. *Educational Psychologist, 53*(2), 78–96. doi:10.1080/00461520.2018.1432361

Ladson-Billings, G. (2009). *The dreamkeepers: Successful teachers of African American children.* Hoboken, NJ: John Wiley.

*Latz, A. O., Speirs Neumeister, K. L., Adams, C. M., & Pierce, R. L. (2008). Peer coaching to improve classroom differentiation: Perspectives from project CLUE. *Roeper Review, 31*(1), 27–39. doi:10.1080/02783190802527356

*Logan, B. (2011). Examining differentiated instruction: Teachers respond. *Research in Higher Education Journal, 13.* Retrieved from http://www.aabri.com/manuscripts/11888.pdf

McIntosh, R., Vaughn, S., Schumm, J. S., Haager, D., & Lee, O. (1993). Observations of students with learning disabilities in general education classrooms. *Exceptional Children, 60,* 249–261. doi:10.1177/001440299406000306

Mellard, D. F., & Johnson, E. S. (Eds.). (2007). *RTI: A practitioner's guide to implementing response to intervention.* Thousand Oaks, CA: Corwin Press.

Miles, M. B., Huberman, A. M., & Saldaña, J. (2014). *Methods of predicting qualitative data analysis: A methods sourcebook.* Thousand Oaks, CA: Sage.

*Moats, L. (2009). Knowledge foundations for teaching reading and spelling. *Reading and Writing, 22,* 379–399. doi:10.1007/s11145-009-9162-1

National Center on Response to Intervention. (2010). *Essential components of response to intervention.* Retrieved from https://rti4success.org/sites/default/files/rtiessentialcomponents_042710.pdf

Onwuegbuzie, A. J., Collins, K. M. T., Leech, N. L., Dellinger, A. B., & Jiao, Q. G. (2010). A meta-framework for conducting and writing rigorous comprehensive literature reviews for stress and coping research and beyond. In G. S. Gates, W. H. Gmelch, & M. Wolverton (Series Eds.), & K. M. T. Collins, A. J. Onwuegbuzie, & Q. G. Jiao (Vol. Eds.), *Toward a broader understanding of stress and coping: Mixed methods approaches. The Research on Stress and Coping in Education Series* (Vol. 5, pp. 169–211). Charlotte, NC: Information Age.

*Otaiba, S. A., Connor, C. M., Folsom, J. S., Greulich, L., Meadows, J., & Li, Z. (2011). Assessment data-informed guidance to individualize kindergarten reading instruction: Findings from a cluster-randomized control field trial. *Elementary School Journal, 111,* 535–560. doi:10.1086/659031

*Patterson, J. L., Connolly, M. C., & Ritter, S. A. (2009). Restructuring the inclusion classroom to facilitate differentiated instruction. *Middle School Journal, 41*(1), 46–52. doi:10.1080/00940771.2009.11461703

Pintrich, P. R., & Zusho, A. (2007). Motivation and self-regulated learning in the college classroom. In R. Perry & J. Smart (Eds.), *Handbook on teaching and learning in higher education* (pp. 55–128). Dordrecht, Netherlands: Springer.

*Pitts, J. (2009). Identifying and using a teacher-friendly learning-styles instrument. *Clearing House: A Journal of Educational Strategies, Issues and Ideas, 82,* 225–232. doi:10.3200/tchs.82.5.225-232

*Poncy, B., Fontenelle, S., & Skinner, C. (2013). Using detect, practice, and repair (DPR) to differentiate and individualize math fact instruction in a class-wide setting. *Journal of Behavioral Education, 22,* 211–228.

*Reis, S. M., McCoach, D. B., Little, C. A., Muller, L. M., & Kaniskan, R. B. (2011). The effects of differentiated instruction and enrichment pedagogy on reading achievement in five elementary schools. *American Educational Research Journal, 48,* 462–501. doi:10.3102/0002831210382891

Renzulli, J. S. (1988). The multiple menu model for developing differentiated curriculum for the gifted and talented. *Gifted Child Quarterly, 32,* 298–309. doi:10.1177/001698628803200302

Saldaña, J. (2009). An introduction to codes and coding. In *The coding manual for qualitative researchers* (pp. 1–42). Thousand Oaks, CA: Sage.

*Santamaria, L. J. (2009). Culturally responsive differentiated instruction: Narrowing gaps between best pedagogical practices benefiting all learners. *Teachers College Record, 111,* 214–247. Retrieved from https://www.tcrecord.org/Issue.asp?volyear=2009&number=1&volume=111

*Simpkins, P. M., Mastropieri, M. A., & Scruggs, T. E. (2009). Differentiated curriculum enhancements in inclusive fifth-grade science classes. *Remedial and Special Education, 30,* 300–308. doi:10.1177/0741932508321011

*Stewart, T. A., & Houchens, G. W. (2014). Deep impact: How a job-embedded formative assessment professional development model affected teacher practice. *Qualitative Research in Education, 3*(1), 51–82. doi:10.4471/qre.2014.36

Tomlinson, C. A. (1999). *The differentiated classroom: Responding to the needs of all learners.* Alexandria, VA: Association for Supervision and Curriculum Development.

Tomlinson, C. A. (2001). *How to differentiate instruction in mixed ability classrooms* (2nd ed.). Alexandria, VA: Association for Supervision and Curriculum Development.

Tomlinson, C. A., Brighton, C., Hertberg, H., Callahan, C. M., Moon, T. R., Brimijoin, K., . . . Reynolds, T. (2003). Differentiating instruction in response to student readiness, interest, and learning profile in academically diverse classrooms: A review of literature. *Journal for the Education of the Gifted, 27,* 119–145. doi:10.1177/016235320302700203

*Tricarico, K., & Yendol-Hoppey, D. (2012). Teacher learning through self-regulation: An exploratory study of alternatively prepared teachers' ability to plan differentiated instruction in an urban elementary school. *Teacher Education Quarterly, 39,* 139–158.

*Valli, L., & Buese, D. (2007). The changing roles of teachers in an era of high-stakes accountability. *American Educational Research Journal, 44,* 519–558. doi:10.3102/0002831207306859

Washburne, C. W. (1953). Adjusting the program to the child. *Educational Leadership, 11*(3), 138–147. Retrieved from http://www.ascd.org/ASCD/pdf/journals/ed_lead/el_195312_washburne.pdf

*Werderich, D. E. (2002). Individualized responses: Using journal letters as a vehicle for differentiated reading instruction. *Journal of Adolescent & Adult Literacy, 45,* 746–754.

Yin, R. K. (1994). *Case study research: Design and methods.* Thousand Oaks, CA: Sage.

Zimmerman, B. J. (2008). Investigating self-regulation and motivation: Historical background, methodological developments, and future prospects. *American Educational Research Journal, 45,* 166–183. doi:10.3102/0002831207312909

Chapter 13
Teaching Academically Underprepared Postsecondary Students

Dolores Perin (iD)
Teachers College, Columbia University

Jodi Patrick Holschuh
Texas State University

Only 25% to 38% of secondary education graduates in the United States are proficient readers or writers but many continue to postsecondary education, where they take developmental education courses designed to help them improve their basic academic skills. However, outcomes are poor for this population, and one problem may be that approaches to teaching need to change. This chapter discusses approaches to the teaching of academically underprepared postsecondary students and how teaching might be changed to improve student outcomes. A wide variety of approaches is reported in the literature, including teaching of discrete skills, providing strategy instruction, incorporating new and multiple literacies, employing disciplinary and contextualized approaches, using digital technology, and integrating reading and writing instruction. However, the field has yet to develop a clear theoretical framework or body of literature pointing to how teaching in this area might improve. Based on our reading of the literature, we recommend directions for future research that could inform changes in the teaching of underprepared students at the postsecondary level.

This chapter aims to identify ways in which the teaching of academically underprepared postsecondary students might be changed to enhance learning opportunities. The population of interest is students in postsecondary education with reading and writing skills below the level required for meaningful learning. Educational outcomes for this population are poor in terms of skill development, academic achievement, and persistence (Bailey, Jeong, & Cho, 2010; Perin, Bork, Peverly, & Mason, 2013; Perin, Lauterbach, Raufman, & Santikian Kalamkarian, 2017).

Review of Research in Education
March 2019, Vol. 43, pp. 363–393
DOI: 10.3102/0091732X18821114
Chapter reuse guidelines: sagepub.com/journals-permissions
© 2019 AERA. http://rre.aera.net

Strong literacy skills serve as a foundation of learning from early elementary grades through postsecondary education. However, in the United States, only 38% of students in the last year of secondary education are proficient readers and 25% are proficient writers, whereas 28% display low reading skills (National Assessment of Educational Progress [NAEP], 2015a; National Center for Education Statistics, 2012).

In the United States, underprepared postsecondary students may be referred for supportive courses and services designed to help them improve their literacy and mathematics skills and become familiar with academic expectations. These supports are referred to as "developmental education," which has been defined as "a comprehensive process that focuses on the intellectual, social, and emotional growth and development of all students. Developmental education includes, but is not limited to, tutoring, personal/career counseling, academic advisement, and coursework" (National Association for Developmental Education, n.d.). Developmental courses are often offered at several levels, with students placed based on assessments administered on college entry. In this chapter, we focus on postsecondary developmental education in postsecondary institutions coursework and interventions designed to improve reading and writing skills.

Course taking rates vary by type of institution, with an estimated 5.6% to 28.1% of students in public 2- and 4-year institutions taking at least one developmental reading or writing course (Chen, 2016; Skomsvold, 2014). Enrollments in these literacy courses are higher in community (2-year) colleges. For example, 28.1% of 2-year compared with 10.8% of 4-year college students enroll in developmental reading or writing courses (Chen, 2016). In fact, college policies vary considerably regarding whether students found to be academically underprepared on college entry are actually required to enroll in developmental education courses. For this reason, enrollments may be an underestimate of underpreparedness, as many students referred to developmental education elect not to attend but enroll in college-level courses instead (Perin & Charron, 2006).

Outcomes for entering postsecondary students identified as academically underprepared have been poor, especially for students of color, as measured by rates of course completion, persistence in college, grade point average, and degree attainment (Bailey et al., 2010). For example, a majority of Latinx students do not progress beyond developmental coursework (Acevedo-Gil, Santos, & Solórzano, 2014), and furthermore, the lower Latinx students are placed in the developmental English course sequence, the lower their likelihood of success in credit-bearing English classes (Acevedo-Gil, Santos, Alonso, & Solorzano, 2015). Although there are multiple causes for the poor outcomes (Cohen, Brawer, & Kisker, 2013), there have been calls for improvement of developmental instruction:

Little is known about what really goes on in developmental education classrooms, and even less is known about the attributes of effective teaching for this population. Principles of adult learning are often poorly understood by developmental education instructors, who are typically not offered professional development opportunities by their employers. Evidence-based instructional strategies used in high schools could be readily adapted for community colleges. Professional development for instructors and curricular reforms may be needed. (MDRC, 2013, p. 2)

Observations of developmental education classrooms have been reported, for example, by Norton Grubb and colleagues in California (Grubb, 2012; Grubb et al., 1999; Grubb & Gabriner, 2013), but they have been confined to single states, and more wide-ranging, systematic observational studies are needed. Lack of preparedness for postsecondary academic demands is a problem faced by many students. However, efforts to prepare secondary education graduates for the literacy demands of postsecondary education indicate the difficulty of dealing with this issue. For example, in a rare study reporting evidence bearing on this problem (Kallison, 2017), it was found that even after improving skills in an intensive high-school-to-college transition program that taught to state reading and writing standards, a group of underprepared secondary education graduates remained unready for college literacy demands.

PURPOSE AND QUESTIONS

There are many factors that underlie academic difficulty. The current chapter sets out to explicate one of these factors, approaches to teaching. Our purpose is to identify ways in which the teaching of academically underprepared students in postsecondary education might be changed to enhance students' learning opportunities. Based on the available literature, we identify the strengths and shortcomings of current approaches to teaching in postsecondary developmental settings to present directions for research and practice in instructional improvement. Three questions guide our discussion: (1) What approaches to the teaching of literacy skills to postsecondary students have been reported in the literature? (2) What ideas have emerged in the field concerning the improvement of teaching literacy skills to this population? (3) What implications can be drawn from the available literature for research and practice in improving the teaching of literacy skills to this population?

For context, we first present a conceptual framework for understanding reading and writing instruction and discuss the competencies needed in each area. We then summarize our identification of the literature and proceed to a discussion of the research. Finally, we present implications and future directions for research and practice bearing on the teaching of underprepared postsecondary students.

CONCEPTUAL FRAMEWORK

For the current purpose, *literacy* is conceptualized as the reading and writing of printed words to comprehend and express meaning. We acknowledge broader definitions, such as those that extend beyond the processing of print to the oral skills of speaking and listening (National Governors' Association and Council of Chief State School Officers, 2010), to the use of multimedia (Gee, 2012; Guzzetti & Foley, 2018; Mannion & Ivanic, 2007; Mulcahy-Ernt & Caverly, 2018), and, even more broadly, to social functioning, goal achievement, and the development of personal knowledge and potential (White, 2011). However, because literacy coursework for underprepared postsecondary students centers on the reading and writing of print, we assume the narrower definition here. Traditionally, reading and writing have been taught to underprepared postsecondary students in separate courses, but more recently, in a growing number of colleges, developmental education has been reformed to combine the two areas in single courses (Bickerstaff & Raufman, 2017). In this section, we present a conceptual framework for understanding reading and writing, and their integration.

Reading

Reading is multidimensional, goal directed, and developmental (Alexander, 2005, 2012) and involves multiple cognitive, metacognitive, affective, and sociocultural factors working in concert (Holschuh & Lampi, 2018; Pearson & Cervetti, 2015). Layered within each of these factors are other multidimensional constructs. For example, cognitive factors include decoding, predicting, and comprehending, and affective factors include motivation, self-efficacy, and self-regulation. All of these processes occur within social, cultural and contextual spaces, which favors those who understand academic discourse (Gee, 2012). Reading ability develops over time and involves both learning to read and reading to learn (Alexander, 2012; Rosenblatt, 1994). Learners develop flexibility, control, and experience to maneuver within the linguistic, cognitive, and sociocultural dimensions of literacy (Kucer, 2014).

Reading is developmental across the life span, and readers bring a variety of strategies, interests, and background knowledge to the text; making meaning requires the ability to critically analyze and interpret text (Alexander, 2012). In this sense, reading proficiency may not generalize to specific disciplinary areas that demand a good deal of content knowledge (Perin, 2018).

Key reading competencies include understanding literal and implied information in text, drawing appropriate inferences and conclusions; identifying and summarizing the main ideas; analyzing information as it unfolds over a text; interpreting the meanings of words and phrases; analyzing the text structure; understanding the purpose or point of view expressed in a text; making connections between the text and their own experience; comprehending information presented in diverse formats and media (i.e., engaging in multiple literacies, as mentioned above); assessing the arguments expressed in a text; comparing information across texts; analyzing an author's use of literary devices; and understanding complex texts (NAEP, 2015b; National Governors' Association and Council of Chief State School Officers, 2010).

Writing

Writing has been conceptualized as having two components, called "the task environment" and "the individual" (Hayes, 1996, p. 10). The task environment encompasses social aspects, such as the purpose of writing and characteristics of the readership of a written text, and physical aspects, including the medium, for example, pen and paper or digital means, and the text written so far, which provides context for writing for further composition. In the "individual" component are housed key cognitive and affective processes, including memory, schema for the act of writing, metacognition, understanding of core writing behaviors (planning, drafting, and revision), beliefs about writing, and motivation to write. An extension of Hayes's (1996) model includes executive functions in the self-regulation of the writing process, and the use of writing strategies (Berninger, Garcia, & Abbott, 2009).

Skills and processes that enable proficient writing are spelling, which requires phonemic awareness and the mapping of sounds and letters; knowledge of the conventions of a written language, including syntax, capitalization, and punctuation; and vocabulary knowledge (Berninger & Chanquoy, 2012; Rijlaarsdam et al., 2012). Also important is discourse knowledge, that is, awareness of the characteristics of and what is involved in producing well-written text (Olinghouse & Graham, 2009).

Key writing competencies include the ability to compose text in three major genres, that is, argumentative/persuasive, informational/explanatory, and narrative; use precise language and varied sentence structure; produce coherent text that demonstrates an awareness of the informational needs and basic assumptions of an assumed audience of readers; revise one's own text to improve clarity; use digital technology, such as the Internet, to communicate and collaborate with others; engage in multimodal, nonprint literacies in line with evolving practices in the 21st century; convey research findings; acknowledge the source of ideas—that is, avoid plagiarizing; and engage in both longer- and shorter-term writing tasks (Guzzetti & Foley, 2018; Mulcahy-Ernt & Caverly, 2018; NAEP, 2012; National Governors' Association and Council of Chief State School Officers, 2010; Paulson & Holschuh, 2018).

Integrated Reading and Writing

The integration of reading and writing instruction seems well supported from both theoretical and empirical perspectives. Reading and writing are not the reverse of each other (Stotsky, 1983) but share a number of important overlapping processes (Fitzgerald & Shanahan, 2000). Shanahan (2016) describes the relationship between reading and writing as "two buckets drawing water from a common well or two buildings built on a common foundation" (p. 195). Furthermore, two meta-analyses have shown mutually beneficial empirical relationships between reading and writing (Graham et al., 2018; Graham & Hebert, 2010).

IDENTIFICATION OF THE LITERATURE

The ProQuest, ERIC, EBSCO, and Google Scholar search engines; manual search of journals; and reference lists in the identified literature were used to generate an initial pool of studies for consideration. The search terms, used singly and in combination, were the following: *developmental education, remedial*, college, postsecondary, higher education, literacy instruction, reading instruction, writing instruction, reading* *skills, writing skills, integration,* and *integrated reading and writing.* Resources meeting the following criteria were selected for examination: (a) provided description, practitioner commentary, and/or data on the teaching of literacy skills to underprepared students in postsecondary education and (b) appeared in peer-reviewed journal articles, chapters in scholarly books, or technical reports produced by reputable organizations. A parameter of the years 2000 to 2018 was set, but a few earlier references were screened in because they offered important information not available in more recent work. The search yielded 199 studies, which were scrutinized for relevance to the current chapter; of these, 36 were relevant to our guiding questions. The literature identified included empirical studies, descriptive reports, and literature reviews. The work was organized by major theme, as shown in the next section. Where studies were thematically cross-cutting, they are presented below within a single theme for expediency. The large majority of studies identified were not designed as evaluations and thus did not report outcome data. Where evidence of effectiveness was reported, we include it in our discussion.

TEACHING LITERACY TO UNDERPREPARED POSTSECONDARY STUDENTS

Overview

The purpose of developmental reading and writing courses is to increase the proficiency of college students who are underprepared for college-level literacy (Paulson, 2014). Increasing the effectiveness of these courses is tied to pedagogical choices (Paulson & Holschuh, 2018). Although developmental educators use a variety of teaching approaches, two major approaches, discrete skills and meaning making, have been defined in the literature on teaching literacy to underprepared adults (Beder, Lipnevich, & Robinson-Geller, 2007; Perin, 2013). Though it has been claimed that many developmental education courses use a decontextualized, discrete skills approach (Grubb, 2012; Lesley, 2004; Weiner, 2002), and that when skills are taught in this way there is little use of authentic reading materials or literacy strategies (Rose, 2005), there have been few systematic analyses of instruction in developmental classrooms or comparisons of the outcomes of different teaching approaches.

One curriculum analysis found that developmental reading classes using discrete, decontextualized skills instruction may focus on finding the main idea, inferencing, and examining the paragraph structure while using workbook-style textbooks that feature mostly narrative text examples (Armstrong, Stahl, & Kantner, 2015). Textbooks used in these courses center on such skills, which are typically taught in isolation (Perin, 2013). This kind of "transmission" approach can lead students to use passive, surface-level strategies; they are unable to view reading as a conversation with the text and have difficulty adapting their reading strategies to the variety of task demands of college (Armstrong & Newman, 2011).

Courses using a meaning-making approach focus on problem solving and critical thinking using real-world examples and text (Perin, 2018), which may help students succeed by increasing their strategic cognitive, metacognitive, and affective approaches to learning (Holschuh & Lampi, 2018; Simpson, Stahl, & Francis, 2004). Being able to use cognitive strategies such as analyzing and synthesizing text can enable students to further develop metacognitive approaches such as self-questioning, self-regulation, and self-monitoring (Alexander & Jetton, 2000; Holschuh & Lampi, 2018; Zimmerman, 1995). We will now discuss the various teaching approaches reported in the literature.

We will organize our discussion according to the themes of teaching discrete literacy skills, strategy instruction, new and multiple literacies, disciplinary and contextualized approaches, digital technology, and integrated reading and writing.

Teaching of Discrete Literacy Skills

Instruction in discrete skills refers to the teaching aspects of literacy, such as vocabulary definitions, the morphological structure of words, or "getting the main idea," without relating them to one another or to meaningful acts of written communication. In this approach, teachers may assign repetitive drills using pre-prepared worksheets. It is difficult to determine the extent of discrete skills instruction in developmental education from the research literature, but given that it has been claimed to be widespread (Grubb & Gabriner, 2013), it is surprising that only three studies of this approach have been conducted (Ari, 2015; Atkinson, Zhang, Phillips, & Zeller, 2014; Curry, 2003).

Ari (2015) examined the effects of two reading fluency interventions, wide reading and repeated reading. The instructional materials consisted of binders with printed materials. The readings were 400 words long, which is not representative of the longer length of text typically assigned, and were not connected to the kinds of topics students encounter in postsecondary education. The students in the wide reading condition silently read four different grade-level passages, and the students in the repeated reading condition read one grade-level passage four times. The participants displayed gains in reading speed but not comprehension, which suggests that multiple readings without further strategic processing is insufficient for comprehension gains.

Atkinson et al. (2014) found that 5 weeks of word study instruction improved the orthographic knowledge of the developmental reading students. Explicit teaching was provided in spelling rules, suffixes, and past tense endings, using word sorts and word hunts, and was designed to meet the specific needs of the participants based on their pretest performance. The researchers found improvement in the students' orthographic knowledge despite the short duration of the intervention.

An ethnography of a basic writing classroom in which discrete writing skills were taught was conducted by Curry (2003). The students were English language learners, and the teacher taught skills such as sentence-level writing, grammar, punctuation, and simple one-paragraph writing. The students were asked to write an essay and a three- to five-page research paper on self-selected topics. All the writing assignments were brief, and none of the instruction modules observed by the researcher was related to the kinds of extended writing students would encounter in college coursework.

Two possible explanations for the lack of research on discrete skills instruction for academically underprepared postsecondary students are that (1) this approach is assumed to be effective and thus not worth studying or, from an opposite viewpoint, (2) discrete skills instruction is so damaging that it is not worth the effort to measure its (lack of) effectiveness. Ultimately, given the criticisms of discrete skills instruction (Grubb & Gabriner, 2013), in future research, this approach could serve as a control condition to be measured against more innovative approaches, analogous to the use of conventional grammar instruction in studies of writing interventions, in which the teaching of grammar has been used as a business-as-usual control and has been found in several studies to be ineffective (Graham & Perin, 2007).

Strategy Instruction

Strategy instruction involves explicit, structured teaching of specific steps for comprehending or composing text. Key components are teacher modeling and the use of graphic organizers and mnemonics to support metacognition and self-regulation. An underlying theme of strategy instruction is the gradual release of responsibility, with fading of scaffolding until the student reaches the designated literacy goals (Harris, Graham, Mason, & Friedlander, 2008; Pearson & Gallagher, 1983; Walker, 2012). Studies examining particular reading and writing strategies have reported largely encouraging results.

A strategy using the PLAN (*p*redict, *l*ocate, *p*lan, *n*ote) mnemonic reported by Caverly, Nicholson, and Radcliffe (2004) focused on the selection of information while reading and involved the gradual release of responsibility. Teaching began with instructor modeling and ended with the students transferring the strategy to a different context. Instruction included explicit teaching of the components of PLAN, that is, strategic reading strategies, metacognitive awareness, self-efficacy, recognizing text structure, and rehearsal strategies for recall. Teachers modeled the strategy using think-alouds with authentic text and supported student practice as a means to help students develop the skills to use the strategy independently in other college courses. The researchers reported increased scores on a standardized test of reading performance and comprehension and the likelihood of the use of the strategy in other contexts.

Armstrong and Lampi's (2017) PILLAR (*p*review, *i*dentify, *l*ist, *l*ook online, *a*ttempt, and *r*ead) mnemonic adds a disciplinary approach and is aimed at preparing students to read in situations where they have limited prior knowledge of a particular concept or topic. This strategy includes an online search component, which provides just-in-time information to the reader, encourages intertextual connections, and, as one student noted, "fits in with the current generation" (Armstrong & Lampi, 2017, p. 7). Instruction focuses on metacognition, specifically conditional and contextual knowledge, by teaching why, when, and where the strategy might be useful. It also centers on explicit instruction in metacognitive awareness and self-regulation as a way to build both disciplinary understandings and proficiency with reading strategies. Instructors guide students through systematic previewing of the text, purposeful terminology selection, engaging intertextuality, and reading for meaning. Although this was not an empirical study, the strategy has strong theoretical underpinnings from previous research.

This emphasis on metacognitive and self-empowering strategies is echoed in Gruenbaum's (2012) call to incorporate reciprocal teaching into developmental classrooms. Reciprocal teaching is a well-documented teaching method originally developed for adolescents to improve reading comprehension skills (Palincsar & Brown, 1984; Sporer, Brunstein, & Kieschke, 2009). Gruenbaum (2012) suggests that its combination of prediction, questioning, clarification, and summarization strategies can aid in comprehension and increase writing ability as students work together to bring meaning to text. Instruction in reciprocal teaching includes providing scaffolding, modeling, and using specific, concrete examples of reading and writing strategies. In a study examining the effects of instructions on university students' comprehension, Linderholm, Kwon, and Therriault (2014) found that sometimes less is more. When students were given instructions for reading, those who were given only a self-explaining definition during reading of multiple texts had greater comprehension scores than students who were provided with a definition and modeling of the strategy. This result suggests that the explanation was sufficient and even preferable to modeling as providing more support than students need may actually impede learning (Holschuh, 2014).

In a study examining the effects of traditional textbook-based instruction and strategic reading instruction on reading performance, Lavonier (2016) found that both approaches improved student scores on the Nelson-Denny Reading Test (Brown, Fishco, & Hanna, 1993). Textbook-based instruction involved using a traditional skill-focused textbook, with the instructor guiding the students through the skills contained in the text. Strategic reading instruction was conducted using Caverly et al.'s (2004) PLAN reading comprehension strategy. Although these results are encouraging, there are limitations as there was no report on participant skill levels prior to instruction. Furthermore, using the Nelson-Denny test as the measure of success is problematic for several reasons. It is not a particularly useful measure of real-world reading ability, some of the stimulus passages seem unreasonably difficult, the test's time limitations are unrealistic, and the norms are not nationally representative (Perkins, 1984; Smith, 1998). As with many other multiple-choice reading comprehension tests, some of the items can be answered from background knowledge without reading the passages (Coleman, Lindstrom, Nelson, Lindstrom, & Gregg, 2009; Ready, Chaudhry, Schatz, & Strazzullo, 2012). The issue of background knowledge is especially problematic for academically underprepared students and for students from diverse backgrounds (Lei, Rhinehart, Howard, & Cho, 2010) because it is hard to interpret a test score as reflecting background knowledge (or lack thereof) or reading comprehension ability alone.

Many studies of underprepared postsecondary students have used comprehension as the indicator of efficacy for a particular instructional strategy or approach. The results of such studies, however, need to be tempered not only by the criticisms just mentioned but also because comprehension is often depicted as merely extracting information, such as writing a summary or explaining the main idea. However, current literacy standards hold comprehension as a baseline (National Governors' Association and Council of Chief State School Officers, 2010). Students need to be able to analyze, critique, and argue as well. More compelling are the studies that showed gains on multiple outcome measures, such as strategy transfer, retention, and course grades, as well as those where instruction was contextualized.

Instructional practices mirroring real-world reading experiences are associated with learning gains. For example, Flink (2017) suggests that allowing students to self-select their reading choices improves motivation to read and promotes the idea of reading daily. Instruction involves allowing time in class for silent reading and a pedagogical change that views reading of self-chosen text as a valuable use of instructional time (Flink, 2017; Paulson, 2006). Flink (2017) argues that this requires training in ways to incorporate reading time into classrooms. Paulson's (2006) review of the literature cites barriers to implementing self-selected reading in the classroom, such as lack of access to books and lack of a curriculum for instruction, but states that there is evidence from K–12 studies that this approach yields gains in reading ability, which has potential for postsecondary settings. However, there is little empirical research on particular instructional approaches or on the effects of self-selected reading at the college level.

Paulson (2014) found that using analogical processes during reading—such as presenting the comparison of going to a movie and then describing that movie to someone unfamiliar with it as an analogy for reading a text and writing a summary—can help students make connections to their own knowledge and experiences while reading. Although this study focused on the efficacy of using analogies and not on classroom instruction, the results have pedagogical implications. Instructors can emphasize the importance of making connections between what students are reading and what they know. The results suggest that teaching of developmental reading designed to promote understanding embedded analogies and generating personal analogies may facilitate text comprehension. Strategic approaches have also been used in writing instruction. Simpson (1986) described a five-step writing strategy designed to prepare students for writing tests. Students were taught to use course texts to complete the steps described by the mnemonic PORPE: *P*redict potential essay questions, that is, generate questions that could be asked on an essay exam; *O*rganize key ideas; *R*ehearse key ideas; *P*ractice recall of key ideas in writing tasks; and *E*valuate the completeness, accuracy, and appropriateness of the written product using a rubric (p. 411). Each step was taught explicitly, with teacher modeling and class discussion. Although test preparation may seem a limited and unproductive approach to literacy instruction, passing tests is often uppermost in the minds of postsecondary students, especially developmental education students, who have a history of failing tests. Test preparation may be a productive direction for developmental literacy instruction if the teaching is consistent with evidence-based approaches.

A phenomenological study of the teaching of a writing strategy in developmental education classes was reported by Perun (2015). The purpose of the instruction was to improve students' ability to revise previously written papers. The students were given an assignment sheet, with detailed instructions on how to revise a paper, and a rubric. The students worked in small groups to annotate the assignment sheet to show understanding of the teacher's expectations. In the class discussion, teachers asked the students how they would approach the task and provided evaluative feedback. Teachers modeled the steps for revision on the board and had the students freewrite (write continuously without concern for grammar, spelling, or other writing conventions). Teachers also gave the students written feedback on their drafts. This descriptive study portrayed a comprehensive strategy made up of component procedures centering on the complex skill of revision of writing.

A quasi-experimental study comparing self-regulated writing strategy instruction with business-as-usual developmental writing instruction was conducted by MacArthur, Philippakos, and Ianetta (2015). Over one college semester, teachers used a researcher-developed curriculum to teach the steps of planning, drafting, evaluating, and revising essays in combination with the self-regulation strategies of goal setting, task management, progress monitoring, and reflection. The major academic writing genres of persuasive, descriptive, cause-effect, and narrative writing were included. Basic grammar and the use of English language conventions were taught along with editing and revision. This is a rare study in the literature for its rigor and the size of the research sample ($N = 252$, with 115 treatment and 137 comparison students). Pre-post measures included persuasive essays scored for quality, length, and grammar and a motivation questionnaire examining mastery goals, self-efficacy, beliefs, and affect. Two Woodcock Johnson–III (Woodcock, McGrew, & Mather, 2001) writing subtests were entered as covariates. The intervention showed positive effects on writing quality and length (effect sizes of 1.22 and 0.71, respectively), mastery goals (effect size 0.29), and self-efficacy for tasks and processes (effect size 0.27) but not for grammar, beliefs, or affect. (Confidence intervals for the effect sizes were not reported in this study.) A detailed description of the self-regulated writing strategy instruction tested by MacArthur et al. (2015) is found in Blake, MacArthur, Mrkich, Philippakos, and Sancak-Marusa (2016).

The pedagogy employed in the MacArthur et al. (2015) intervention borrows directly from a robust body of evidence on the effectiveness of writing strategy instruction in K–12 education (Graham, Harris, & Chambers, 2016). The field of developmental education would benefit considerably from testing literacy strategies documented as effective in K–12 and modifying them to build in principles of adult learning, such as tailoring instruction to students' immediate learning needs, capitalizing on students' motivation to learn, assumption of adults' self-confidence based on their family and community roles, and the need for self-determination (Barhoum, 2017; Knowles, 1984).

New and Multiple Literacies

In contrast to the discrete skill and strategy perspectives on literacy in postsecondary education is the new, or multiple, literacies framework, which views acts of reading and writing as socially constructed, communicative acts rather than a demonstration of skill (Relles & Duncheon, 2018). Studies of literacy conducted in this framework tend to examine how students express themselves and communicate with one other.

Hsu and Wang (2010) investigated the effects of the use of blogs on student motivation and reading comprehension in a developmental reading course. The instructors used the blogs as a way for students to respond to comprehension questions, write reflective essays, and perform other authentic learning tasks. Blogging activities were aligned with the course curriculum and emphasized critical thinking skills. Results were reported in comparison with nine sections of the same course that did not use blogs. Although no differences were found for reading performance or motivation, the students in the blogging group had higher retention rates. Instructor interviews indicated that they were not entirely comfortable integrating technology in their classrooms, which suggests a need for professional development.

In a description of how the multiple literacies approach can be used in writing instruction, Fernsten and Reda (2011) recommend a model of teaching using "reflective writing exercises [to help] students better understand the work of writing as they struggle to become more effective writers, negotiating multiple literacies" (p. 173). In one activity, students work together to compose a "group profile" (p. 176), the purpose of which is to help them see that they are not the only ones with writing problems and to view themselves as writers and critical thinkers. In another activity, students create "author's notes" (p. 177) to facilitate their reflection on their writing goals and creative processes. To guide the activity, the teacher provides 35 guiding questions, such as "What is the best thing (sentence, idea, section, etc.) in this draft? Why?" and "Where do you think readers might get stuck or need more information?" (pp. 177–178). This descriptive work provides interesting ideas on pedagogy that could be tested in future studies of effective writing interventions for academically underprepared postsecondary students.

Relles and Duncheon (2018) criticized teaching practices observed in developmental writing classrooms through the lens of new literacies. They observed the assignment of discrete, decontextualized activities, such as having students play a game involving the omission of unnecessary words from run-on sentences, designed to expose them to functional grammar. They suggest that students would increase their social identity as writers if instructional periods were lengthened, class sizes were reduced to allow more instructor feedback, and instructors created an environment for writing activity that promoted authentic discussion and interaction.

Disciplinary and Contextualized Approaches

On the hypothesis that connecting the teaching of literacy skills to material that is meaningful and useful to students will deepen learning, develop critical thinking skills, promote transfer of skill, and increase motivation to learn (Goldman et al., 2016; Perin, 2011; Shanahan & Shanahan, 2012), some postsecondary developmental instructors contextualize their instruction in academic disciplinary content, such as history and science. (We use the terms *contextualized* and *disciplinary* interchangeably here.) This approach gives students an opportunity to practice reading the type of materials and engage in the literacy tasks that they will encounter in the rest of their college courses (Armstrong & Newman, 2011). Disciplinary reading strategies may be taught to college students ranging widely in literacy proficiency (Hynd, Holschuh, & Hubbard, 2004), but here we will discuss this approach as used with underprepared students.

Armstrong and Newman (2011) suggest a model of intertextuality that includes explicit instruction to promote active reading, main idea identification, vocabulary development, and learning and studying of skills for application to a range of history texts, including primary and secondary sources, in a developmental reading course. They provide a description of the practical application of intertextuality in both community college and university settings, where students met in groups to discuss perspectives on topics drawn from the history texts they were using, used charts and graphs to represent the various authors' views, and wrote paragraphs and essays. The authors suggest that this model can help students in developmental education begin to view themselves as active participants in the reading process.

Leist, Woolwine, and Bays (2012) developed an assessment instrument that contained detailed instructions for applying reading and writing skills to content-area reading material. The instructions directed students to mark and annotate the content text and then write a summary that includes the main idea, supporting facts and data, the application to the subject area (history, biology, or psychology), and how the material is relevant to the student. The assessment was introduced, explained, and modeled and then used during a developmental reading course. Using a pre-experimental design with no control group, the researchers found a statistically significant increase in posttest scores on the COMPASS reading test (ACT, 2009), with greater gains achieved when more reading was assigned. This result is encouraging, but the COMPASS test is subject to the same criticisms leveled against the Nelson-Denny Test above.

Contextualized literacy instruction appears to benefit students in multiple contexts. In a rare study on Native American students, Toth (2013) described an approach to teaching developmental writing in a tribal community college. The course, according to the college catalog, aimed to advance "students' abilities to write well-crafted and grammatical essays, with appropriate and effective word choice" (p. 12) for the Diné (Navajo) students. In the contextualization of writing instruction, the teacher explained the cultural and historical aspects of language, with comparison of the lexical features of English and the home language. There was class discussion on history and language throughout the course. The author stated that the students' use of conventions improved by the end of the course. The Toth study suggests that contextualized approaches would be useful for this population.

Perin et al. (2013) examined the effects of providing contextualized practice in developmental reading and writing courses in several urban and suburban community colleges. The participants engaged in self-paced steps to practice reading comprehension, vocabulary development, written summarization, and other literacy skills before, during, and after reading science text from anatomy and physiology textbooks or generic reading passages from developmental textbooks. Statistically significant gains were found for a key outcome variable of written science summarization measured for both contextualized conditions compared with a business-as-usual comparison condition, with greater gains for participants whose practice was contextualized in science text.

Working within a new literacies framework, Tremmel (2011) proposed a move from a traditional approach where students are taught to write five-paragraph essays on isolated topics to project-based literacy instruction contextualized in meaningful topics, texts, and experiences both in and out of academic settings. The author gives as an example a project used in a college writing course that involved research, interviews, and writing in several genres on the topic of senior citizens. The products of this experience included collaborative multimedia presentations. Tremmel makes recommendations for reforming writing instruction that could be tested in future intervention research, such as having instructors develop their own curricula, reject deficit approaches to student writing, allow students to experience more control over their own learning process, stimulate student interest in writing rather than concentrating only on the development of skill, connect academic writing to nonacademic experiences, and reduce the focus on assessment.

Use of Digital Technology

There has been considerable interest in online teaching options in postsecondary education (Kebritchi, Lipschuetz, & Santiague, 2017). For example, with the aim of increasing motivation to read, critical thinking skills, and active learning among developmental reading students, Burgess (2009) implemented a hybrid course where the digital technology component consisted of a discussion board and online chat. The course design was based on principles of communication, feedback, and approach to learning (Testa, 2000). The discussion board was asynchronous; the students submitted posts at times of their own choosing and engaged in collaborative work. Online chat was synchronous; here, the teacher and students engaged in discussion. The students also communicated with the teacher via e-mail. The content of the reading course was not reported, but the researcher reported anecdotal evidence based on examination of the discussion posts, chat interactions, journal reflections, and student interviews that student motivation, critical thinking, and active learning improved over the period of the course.

Yang (2010) developed a Web-based reciprocal teaching interface for academically underprepared English language students enrolled in a developmental reading course in Taiwan. To teach the skills involved in reciprocal teaching, Yang used an online dialogue box, chat room, discussion forum, and annotation tool. Instructors initially led the students by facilitating discussion, but their input was gradually withdrawn as the students became better able to use both the technology and the critical thinking and reading processes of reciprocal teaching. A pre-experimental design showed gains on a reading test at the end of the course.

Social media platforms may be a useful venue for developing literacy skill. Ingalls (2017) examined the feasibility of using Facebook as a learning management system in a developmental writing course. The college had replaced leveled courses with a single course, and a tutor was present in the classroom. Using Facebook, the teacher aimed to create a community of learners, build students' confidence in writing, and promote sharing of writing. The teacher created a private Facebook page and established rules of interaction. Work on Facebook replaced face-to-face attendance at times. The students were required to post privately to the teacher and ask questions to clarify ideas and understanding of the assigned homework. Correct grammar was encouraged but not required. The students were required to use the platform to communicate with peers and teachers throughout the course. Ingalls concluded that this approach was feasible, and a review of the students' work showed improved writing, grammar, and spelling. Other instructors had reservations about using Facebook, expressing concerns about security and privacy, the purpose of social networking, and its educational value; these concerns have also been expressed in other venues (Kebritchi et al., 2017).

The use of digital material was investigated by Relles and Tierney (2013) as developmental writing students in a summer bridge program developed personal profiles. The course utilized an online social network platform that was similar to Facebook except that it permitted the creation of a closed community. The class lasted 80 hours over 4 weeks and took the form of an online community. In this descriptive, new literacies study, the authors analyzed the students' digital work, including text, image, and audio and video posts. There was no description of the teaching of writing in this study, but the authors discussed the importance of digital literacy proficiency for college literacy requirements.

Saidy (2018) conducted a case study of the use of podcasting in a developmental education summer bridge course whose purpose was to introduce underprepared students to the content and methods of study in the humanities through writing activity. Podcasting was used to provide opportunities for multimodal composing. A 1-week (18 hour) curriculum was organized around the topic of food. The podcasting was designed to encourage struggling writers to "jump into composing and take creative risks as they navigated the transition to college writing" (p. 262). The teacher first surveyed the students on their high school writing experiences and beliefs about writing. Then, the students listened to an existing podcast and worked individually and in pairs on a script for their own podcast. To develop podcast scripts, the students created an argument and identified genre elements such as opening, statistics, quotations, determination of credibility, statement of argument, analysis with evidence, and sound effects for the podcast. Based on peer review, the students revised their productions. Based on a qualitative examination of the students' work, the author concluded that podcasting encouraged critical thinking and self-reflection and promoted audience awareness and understanding of the nature of college writing.

Integrated Reading and Writing Instruction

The immediate, pressing problem for the teaching of literacy to academically underprepared postsecondary students is poor outcomes in terms of course completion, retention in college programs, and college graduation (Bailey et al., 2010). Reforms in developmental education have been reported, although rarely evaluated through rigorous comparative research. Based on the available literature, these reform efforts appear to center on structural rather than pedagogical efforts. A reform structure that has attracted a certain amount of attention is "acceleration," whereby students' moves through developmental education are hastened through reduction of course length or the number of courses that must be taken in a developmental education program (Brathwaite & Edgecombe, 2018; Cho, Kopko, Jenkins, & Jaggars, 2012; Edgecombe, Cormier, Bickerstaff, & Barragan, 2013; Edgecombe, Jaggars, Xu, & Barragan, 2014; Jaggars, Hodara, Cho, & Xu, 2015; Jenkins, Speroni, Belfield, Jaggars, & Edgecombe, 2010). Ideally, acceleration reduces the potential exit points for students and offers a quicker path to credit-bearing coursework (Bickerstaff & Raufman, 2017; Gerber, Miller, Ngo, Shaw, & Daugherty, 2017; Hodara & Jaggars, 2014; Jaggars et al., 2015). One method of acceleration that has direct pedagogical implications is the integration of reading and writing courses, replacing stand-alone courses in each of these areas (Hayward & Willett, 2014; Henson, Hern, & Snell, 2017; Hern, 2013; Kalamkarian, Raufman, & Edgecombe, 2015).

Pacello (2014) reported on a study in which reading and writing instruction was integrated by assigning writing tasks as responses to course readings. Various types of writing were assigned, including informal blogs and formal paragraphs and essays. The students kept "metacognitive reading blogs" (p. 127) for 3 weeks toward the end of the course, in which they practiced writing skills by reflecting on and summarizing their reading process. Prewriting, drafting, proofreading/revision, grammar, and punctuation skills were taught explicitly in the course, which appears to be conventional practice (Grubb & Gabriner, 2013), but the metacognitive focus on students' literacy process may help academically underprepared students make a transition from writing as an academic exercise to more authentic writing practices (Kucer, 2014).

In an approach to integrating reading and writing instruction studied by Falk-Ross (2001), the teacher assigned an inquiry writing task for the purpose of improving reading comprehension. The topics were self-selected and mostly related to the students' college major. As part of the instruction, the teacher explained the writing process. To gather information, the students held interviews, conducted Internet searches, and read journals and other texts. Reading strategies were taught, and 1 to 2 hours per week were spent in writing the inquiry paper. In small-group discussions, the students compared their papers. The teacher held writing conferences, and the students kept journals on their reading and writing process. The researcher's field notes, participant observation, and the students' reading scores suggested that the integrated inquiry activity was beneficial to the students. The students demonstrated increasing awareness of the connections between reading and writing and showed gains of approximately three grade levels on the TABE (Test of Adult Basic Education).

In another approach to reading-writing integration, Mongillo and Wilder (2012) assigned writing tasks in a developmental reading course. The integrated activity was conducted online through a discussion board. The students posted anonymously a written description of an object in a picture provided by the teacher. Peers in the class were asked to select one of six provided pictures to guess the picture being described, and to state in writing why they selected that picture. The writing assignment was to write a paragraph describing a situation currently being reported in the news without explicitly stating the topic. Peers in the class were asked to guess the topic based on the description and provide a written explanation for their guess. Correct peer guesses in both assignments were taken to indicate good descriptive writing skills on the part of the writer. A ceiling effect of 66% to 100% correct guesses was found, but it is possible that the integrated activity could be useful if it was more demanding.

Becket (2005) discussed a model where reading and writing were taught separately in two consecutive hours. The first hour was taught by a reading teacher and the second by a writing teacher, but the teachers collaborated on planning the instruction to create "interactive discussion classes" (p. 60) that drew in both literacy areas. The focus of the writing class was essay writing. The teacher encouraged the students to incorporate personal experience, but the topics came from text assigned in the reading class, such as on peer pressure in education, change that represented a "rite of passage" (p. 64), and experience of immigration. In one writing activity exemplifying the approach used in this class, the students practiced argumentative writing by applying personal experience to evaluate a television show from different perspectives. This model seems promising provided that instructors collaborate effectively to develop an integrated curriculum.

In the context of institutional pressure to accelerate students' completion of developmental education, there is often little guidance for integrating the current reading and writing curriculum, which leads some faculty to use an additive approach focusing on teaching discrete skills by adding new activities or assignments to previously used course materials, without a framework for integrating the curriculum (Bickerstaff & Raufman, 2017). In a case study on the use of adaptive technology including text-to-speech and graphic organizer software in integrated courses for students with learning disabilities, the instructors combined the content from separate reading and writing courses and taught reading strategies such as selecting the main idea, decoding, and understanding text coherence in conjunction with writing strategies such as summary writing, paragraph structure, and understanding the rhetorical structure (Engstrom, 2005). The use of adaptive technologies in the context of integrated reading and writing instruction aided a range of basic word-reading skills, as measured by several standardized measures.

Bickerstaff and Raufman (2017) investigated perceptions on integrating reading and writing courses using interviews, focus groups, and case studies. One writing instructor using an additive approach reported, "I thought, well, I'll just keep the comp quizzes. They used to be grammar and punctuation, and I can throw the reading in" (p. 9). This approach resulted in frustration because faculty were not able to cover all of the material they had taught when the courses were separate. Alternately, instruction that adopted a truly integrative approach to the courses was frequently structured around a theme on which all texts and tasks were centered. The themes were purposefully broad, such as "struggle" or "success." Often a single anchor text was used as the basis for reading and writing tasks and assignments that all connected back to the theme. Many of these tasks included text-based writing assignments, with strategy instruction embedded within scaffolding of students to complete the writing tasks (Bickerstaff & Raufman, 2017), and decisions on integrating assignments were purposefully made (Goen & Gillotte-Tropp, 2003). Instructors using the integrative approach reported more comfort and satisfaction in teaching and increased student understanding of the relationship between reading and writing (Bickerstaff & Raufman, 2017).

Implementing an acceleration model, a developmental program combined five separate courses into 1 year of integrated reading and writing that included both developmental coursework and the first credit-bearing composition course (Goen & Gillotte-Tropp, 2003). Instruction centered on making the connections between reading and writing explicit using a range of texts. Because instructors had a full year with the students they could introduce integrated strategies using increasingly complex material. Compared with a traditional instruction control group, the students receiving integrated instruction had higher course pass rates, reading and writing scores, and college retention rates.

Overall, research examining the efficacy of acceleration in integrated reading and writing courses has had mixed results. Although not describing classroom teaching, Paulson, Van Overschelde, and Wiggins (2018) examined the efficacy of accelerated integrated reading and writing courses in community college compared with nonaccelerated developmental reading and developmental writing courses. Using 10 years of data from 1.5 million community college students in Texas, they found that students who took two separate courses (developmental reading and developmental writing) were more likely to pass their first college-level intensive reading or intensive writing course than those who took the accelerated integrated reading and writing course. They caution that the results should not be used to imply that reading and writing processes should not be taught together but rather that the acceleration of these courses was not effective in the ways in which they were taught. An investigation of the actual teaching strategies used to integrate these two areas of literacy would help in the interpretation of the findings.

FUTURE DIRECTIONS FOR CHANGING INSTRUCTION

The purpose of the current volume is to explore the issues involved in changing teaching practice. Two key assumptions seem to underlie this goal, first, that teaching needs to change and, second, that teaching can change. In surveying the available literature on teaching of literacy to academically underprepared students in postsecondary education, we can hypothesize that teaching does need to change, because student outcomes for this population are historically poor. There is evidence that high-quality teaching is associated with strong student achievement (Darling-Hammond, 2000; Tyler, Taylor, Kane, & Wooten, 2010), although, admittedly, such evidence comes from the K–12 arena rather than postsecondary education. There has been much interest in reforming developmental education in recent years (Brathwaite & Edgecombe, 2018), but only one of eight current reforms described in a U.S. Department of Education report (Schak, Metzger, Bass, McCann, & Englis, 2017) clearly involves teaching, and furthermore, the report named one specific approach, contextualized instruction, rather than addressing the improvement of teaching as a whole.

Investigations of Current Teaching Practices

An important prerequisite for improving teaching is shared theoretical frameworks and operating principles, but these appear to be lacking in postsecondary developmental education. Eight years before this chapter was written, Paulson and Armstrong (2010) claimed that the field lacked a coherent theory, agreed-on terminology, and teacher preparation approaches. Unfortunately, this criticism is still warranted as there is no consistent research agenda or body of research that could guide pedagogical reform. Instead, studies of the teaching of developmental reading and writing are generally single, isolated efforts that do not build on prior instructional research. Although developmental instructors report a need to improve pedagogy to meet students' needs more effectively (Barragan & Cormier, 2013), the research literature at present does not offer clear directions for change.

The first step in understanding how teaching might change would be to know what teaching is actually like at the current time. The available literature presents a large number of approaches and strategies, mostly with minimal evidence, making it difficult to propose general recommendations on how the teaching of developmental literacy might change for the better. The approaches reported in the literature fall into two categories, teacher actions and student actions. Among the teacher actions reported are vocabulary and grammar drills; explicit teaching of strategies for reading, writing, or self-regulation; and integration of reading and writing instruction. Student actions include writing blogs and posting writing to social media platforms. At the present time, there is no sign that the field is coalescing around any one approach or that a critical mass of evidence is developing. However, there is general interest in connecting the literacy skills being taught to authentic college-level practices such as comprehension of academic text and writing of argumentative essays, which is consistent with a larger trend in literacy research (Purcell-Gates & Duke, 2016).

The majority of studies suggest that reading and writing instruction that is potentially effective involves much more than teaching discrete skills. Instead, teaching practices focusing more on cognitive, metacognitive, and motivational strategies provide encouraging results (Alexander, 2012; Pressley & Afflerbach, 1995). Additionally, the literature suggests that student gains may be achieved within a short instructional time frame, which is encouraging, although whether the gains hold would have to be investigated. There is also good evidence of a systematic approach to reading or writing instruction that includes a gradual release of responsibility from instructor to student, especially in the studies of strategy instruction (e.g., Armstrong & Lampi, 2017; MacArthur et al., 2015). Overall, current research suggests that contextualized and strategy-based approaches have more pedagogical promise than decontextualized or discrete skill approaches, but there may be other promising pedagogical practices that are not currently reported in the literature. However, appropriate literacy assessments for postsecondary students need to be developed that move beyond the skills-based assessments, such as the Nelson-Denny Test. There is long-standing criticism of these traditional reading tests, going back to the 1940s (Cronbach, 1946). The field seems ready for an overhaul of reading assessment of underprepared students, at least to bring measures closer to authentic reading practices.

Rigorous research designs, widely considered a prerequisite for improving teaching practice (Farley-Ripple, May, Karpyn, Tilley, & McDonough, 2018), are sorely lacking in studies on teaching literacy to underprepared postsecondary students. The most rigorous test of any teaching practice in the literature is the quasi-experimental study of writing instruction conducted by MacArthur et al. (2015), which provides evidence for the use of explicit teaching of both literacy and self-regulation procedures to help underprepared students improve their writing of academic essays.

Observations of purposive samples of developmental education classrooms have led to the conclusion that the field is marked by a preponderance of discrete skill instruction (Grubb et al., 1999; Grubb & Gabriner, 2013) and wide discrepancies between students' and teachers' definitions of good teaching (Cox, 2009). However, it is difficult to know what is being taught in developmental education classrooms when rigorous observation studies with representative samples of classrooms, teachers, and students are not reported in the literature. Thus, there is a need for more research on instructional approaches in developmental literacy courses. These could be either small-scale curriculum audits, similar to Armstrong et al.'s (2015), or larger-scale surveys, as called for by MDRC (2013). A useful preliminary step would be to conduct a national survey of developmental education teachers on their classroom practices, as has been done in K–12 education (e.g., Gilbert & Graham, 2010). Such investigations would aid greatly in understanding what is working and what modifications are needed in current practice.

There have been calls to change the instructional approaches in developmental education for decades. Rose (1983) argued that "a major skill in academic writing is the complex ability to write from other texts—to summarize, to disambiguate key notions and useful facts and incorporate them in one's own writing, to react critically to prose" (p. 119). This cannot be achieved using a part-to-whole approach (Grubb, 2012). Every one of Stahl, Simpson, and Hayes's (1992) recommendations for improving instruction in developmental education continues to be a needed change. Their calls for emphasizing transfer to new contexts, helping students broaden conceptual knowledge, explicit teaching of strategies, and promotion of self-regulation and metacognition align closely with the implications of the research discussed in this chapter.

An implicit goal of the literature on teaching literacy to academically underprepared postsecondary students seems to be to present teaching approaches that would help students learn more effectively than in (usually unnamed) conventional approaches. However, the authors rarely, if ever, place their teaching approaches in the larger context of reform of K–20 teaching in general. Instructional reform across educational domains has attracted and continues to attract much attention in the education literature (Hiebert & Stigler, 2017; Sykes & Wilson, 2016; Tschannen-Moran, Hoy, & Hoy, 1998); developmental education researchers would benefit from broadening their perspective to include theory and practice discussed in this larger body of literature.

Examining the Preparation of Literacy Instructors in Developmental Education

There is a need to examine the instructional approaches of successful developmental education classrooms and to provide meaningful professional development opportunities for instructors as well (Bickerstaff & Raufman, 2017; Paulson et al., 2018). One area in particular seems to need urgent attention—the preparation of instructors to teach both reading and writing in integrated courses as institutions increasingly adopt the integrated approach mentioned above. Traditionally, instructors have been trained to teach either reading or writing. Moreover, developmental reading and writing courses have typically been housed in different departments and guided by different theoretical understandings (Paulson & Armstrong, 2010). To prepare instructors to teach integrated reading and writing courses, some colleges have relied on cross-training between reading faculty and English faculty (Bickerstaff & Raufman, 2017). However, teaching integrated reading and writing may differ from teaching either reading or writing alone (Shanahan & Shanahan, 2012). For example, it would be important to teach text-based writing, using multiple sources as required in college education. Teaching text-based writing requires an equal focus on reading comprehension and writing skills, but it appears that few developmental instructors are prepared for this task.

There is little information on the preparation of developmental education instructors for integrated instruction or any other area of teaching academically underprepared postsecondary students. The few studies that have been conducted are based in single institutions and center on the perceptions of faculty and administrators with regard to professional development (e.g., Elliott & Oliver, 2016), rather than being rigorous tests of professional development approaches. In fact, the field of developmental education as an area of scholarly pursuit is relatively new, even though there have been studies on the constituent population for decades. One difficulty in this field is a disconnect between those who teach these postsecondary students and those doing research. For example, there is currently only one PhD program in developmental education in the United States (see http://www.education.txstate.edu/ci/dev-ed-doc/about/overview.html). Given the pressing need for better teaching of underprepared students, an important contribution of emerging scholars would be to identify effective approaches to professional development.

Such models may be adapted from the ample K–12 professional development literature. For example, investigations could focus on approaches in which teachers are included in a collaborative planning process (see, e.g., Miller, 2017), and the replacement of traditional short-term presentations by outside experts with the provision of ongoing classroom observation and coaching by individuals who have credibility among the instructors who are recipients of the professional development (see, e.g., Matuchniak, Olson, & Scarcella, 2014).

Examining Pedagogical Practices Based on Assumptions About the Developmental Education Population

Historically, much of the research on learners in developmental literacy has taken a deficit approach. It has been argued that this deficit thinking is "tantamount to 'blaming the victim'. It is a model founded on imputation, not documentation" (Valencia, 2012, p. X) and posits that the reason students do not do well in school is because they have some kind of internal deficiencies. In developmental education, these deficiencies are often described as low abilities, lack of motivation, lack of specific skills, and so on. Deficit thinking models are a form of pseudoscience, often lacking empirical grounding and rooted in classism and prejudice (Rose, 1983; Valencia, 2012). However, the more current developmental perspective, as indicated by the majority of the research discussed in this chapter, trends away from deficit thinking when a learner struggles with reading or writing by using theoretical approaches that center on helping students understand what they can do instead of focusing on what they lack.

Several researchers argue that infusing critical race pedagogy into developmental education coursework can create an environment that supports the success rates of historically underrepresented students (Acevedo-Gil et al., 2015; Williams, 2013). This includes implementing a curriculum that integrates culturally relevant themes and examples (Morris & Price, 2008; Williams, 2013) and "align[s] with a social justice lens that does not perpetuate deficit interpretations of cultural examples" (Acevedo-Gil et al., 2015, p. 119). However, there is a paucity of research examining the effectiveness of critical sociocultural instructional approaches in developmental courses.

Attempts to reform teaching may be affected by changes in state regulation and legislation (Paulson & Holschuh, 2018). Often, the suggested changes center on institutional changes, such as online delivery, nonmandated enrollment (Woods, Park, Hu, & Jones, 2017), or accelerated options, based on the assumption that developmental courses may not be beneficial. Research is needed to explore the effects of such institutional choices on how literacy is taught to underprepared students and how they, in turn, affect student outcomes.

CONCLUSIONS

Our discussion on how teaching might change to serve the literacy needs of academically underprepared students in postsecondary education points to a key problem that a wide range of instructional approaches is in use, with no central organizing theory or theme and a general lack of supportive evidence. However, change in teaching approaches seems to be needed based on the poor achievement outcomes that have been reported. It is encouraging that underlying the purposes of virtually all of the current literature is an interest in changing the way underprepared students are taught, with many of the studies aiming to illustrate specific changes. These studies can be viewed as a rich source of hypotheses on change in teaching practice. The next step to advance the field would be to test these practices in rigorous, controlled research that carefully documents and compares the new and conventional teaching approaches. Additionally, changing teaching requires the development and testing of professional development approaches, possibly adapted from the K–12 arena, with modifications for postsecondary education.

ORCID ID

Dolores Perin (ID) https://orcid.org/0000-0001-6833-4750

REFERENCES

Acevedo-Gil, N., Santos, R. E., Alonso, L., & Solorzano, D. G. (2015). Latinas/os in community college developmental education: Increasing moments of academic and interpersonal validation. *Journal of Hispanic Higher Education*, *14*, 101–127. doi:10.1177/1538192715572893

Acevedo-Gil, N., Santos, R. E., & Solórzano, D. G. (2014). Examining a rupture in the Latina/o college pipeline: Developmental education in the California Community College system. *Perspectivas: Issues in Higher Education Policy and Practice*, *3*(Spring), 1–19.

ACT. (2009). *COMPASS Reading Text*. Iowa City, IA: Author.

Alexander, P. A. (2005). The path to competence: A lifespan developmental perspective on reading. *Journal of Literacy Research*, *37*, 413–436. doi:10.1207/s15548430jlr3704_1

Alexander, P. A. (2012). Reading into the future: Competence for the 21st century. *Educational Psychologist*, *47*, 259–280. doi:10.1080/00461520.2012.722511

Alexander, P. A., & Jetton, T. L. (2000). Learning from text: A multidimensional and developmental perspective. In M. L. Kamil, P. B. Mosenthal, P. D. Pearson, & R. Barr (Eds.), *Handbook of reading research* (Vol. 3, pp. 285–310). Mahwah, NJ: Lawrence Erlbaum.

Ari, O. (2015). Fluency gains in struggling college readers from wide reading and repeated readings. *Reading Psychology, 36*, 270–297. doi:10.1080/02702711.2013.864361

Armstrong, S. L., & Lampi, J. P. (2017). PILLAR: A reading strategy for a new era of strategy instruction at the college level. *Journal of College Literacy and Learning, 43*(3), 3–17.

Armstrong, S. L., & Newman, M. (2011). Teaching textual conversations: Intertextuality in the college reading classroom. *Journal of College Reading and Learning, 41*(2), 6–21. doi:10.1080/10790195.2011.10850339

Armstrong, S. L., Stahl, N. A., & Kantner, M. J. (2015). Investigating academic literacy expectations: A curriculum audit model. *Journal of Developmental Education, 38*(2), 2–23.

Atkinson, T. S., Zhang, G., Phillips, S. F., & Zeller, N. (2014). Using word study instruction with developmental college students. *Journal of Research in Reading, 37*, 433–448. doi:10.1111/1467-9817.12015

Bailey, T. R., Jeong, D.-W., & Cho, S.-W. (2010). Referral, enrollment, and completion in developmental education sequences in community colleges. *Economics of Education Review, 29*, 255–270. doi:10.1016/j.econedurev.2009.09.002

Barhoum, S. (2017). Community college developmental writing programs most promising practices: What the research tells educators. *Community College Journal of Research and Practice, 41*, 791–808. doi:10.1080/10668926.2016.1231092

Barragan, M., & Cormier, M. S. (2013). Enhancing rigor in developmental education. *Inside Out, 1*(4), 1–5. Retrieved from http://tassr.org/uploads/3/4/2/3/3423105/enhancing-rigor-in-developmental-education.pdf

Becket, D. (2005). Uses of background experience in a preparatory reading and writing class: An analysis of native and non-native speakers of English. *Journal of Basic English, 424*(3), 53–71.

Beder, H., Lipnevich, A., & Robinson-Geller, P. (2007). A typology of adult literacy instructional approaches. *Adult Basic Education and Literacy Journal, 1*(2), 63–72.

Berninger, V. W., & Chanquoy, L. (2012). What writing is and how it changes across early and middle childhood development: A multidisciplinary perspective. In E. L. Grigorenko, E. Mambrino, & D. D. Preiss (Eds.), *Writing: A mosaic of new perspectives* (pp. 65–84). New York, NY: Psychology Press.

Berninger, V. W., Garcia, N. P., & Abbott, R. D. (2009). Multiple processes that matter in writing instruction and assessment. In G. A. Troia (Ed.), *Instruction and assessment for struggling writers: Evidence-based practices* (pp. 15–50). New York, NY: Guilford Press.

Bickerstaff, S., & Raufman, J. (2017). *From "additive" to "integrative": Experiences of faculty teaching developmental integrated reading and writing courses* (CCRC Working Paper No. 96). New York, NY: Columbia University, Teachers College, Community College Research Center. Retrieved from https://ccrc.tc.columbia.edu/publications/faculty-experiences-teaching-developmental-reading-writing.html

Blake, M. F., MacArthur, C. A., Mrkich, S., Philippakos, Z. A., & Sancak-Marusa, I. (2016). Self-regulated strategy instruction in developmental writing courses: How to help basic writers become independent writers. *Teaching English in the Two Year College, 44*, 158–175.

Brathwaite, J., & Edgecombe, N. (2018). Developmental education reform outcomes by subpopulation. *New Directions for Community Colleges, Summer*, 21–29. doi:10.1002/cc.20298

Brown, J. I., Fishco, V. V., & Hanna, G. S. (1993). *The Nelson-Denny Reading Test, Forms G and H.* Itasca, IL: Riverside/Houghton-Mifflin.

Burgess, M. L. (2009). Using WebCT as a supplemental tool to enhance critical thinking and engagement among developmental reading students. *Journal of College Reading and Learning, 39*(2), 9–33.

Caverly, D. C., Nicholson, S. A., & Radcliffe, R. (2004). The effectiveness of strategic reading instruction for college developmental readers. *Journal of College Reading and Learning, 35*(1), 25–49.

Chen, X. (2016). *Remedial coursetaking at U.S. public 2-year and 4-year institutions: Scope, experience, and outcomes* (NCES 2016-405). Washington, DC: U.S. Department of Education, National Center for Education Statistics. Retrieved from http://nces.ed.gov/pubs2016/2016405.pdf

Cho, S.-W., Kopko, E., Jenkins, D., & Jaggars, S. S. (2012). *New evidence of success for community college remedial English students: Tracking the outcomes of students in the Accelerated Learning Program (ALP)* (CCRC Working Paper No. 53). New York, NY: Columbia University, Teachers College, Community College Research Center. Retrieved from https://ccrc.tc.columbia.edu/publications/ccbc-alp-student-outcomes-follow-up.html

Cohen, A. M., Brawer, F. B., & Kisker, C. B. (2013). *The American community college* (6th ed.). Boston, MA: Wiley.

Coleman, C., Lindstrom, J., Nelson, J., Lindstrom, W., & Gregg, N. (2009). Passageless comprehension on the Nelson-Denny Reading Test: Well above chance for university students. *Journal of Learning Disabilities, 34*(2), 94–105. doi:10.1177/0022219409345017

Cox, R. D. (2009). *The college fear factor: How students and professors misunderstand each other.* Cambridge, MA: Harvard University Press.

Cronbach, L. J. (1946). Response sets and test validity. *Educational and Psychological Measurement, 6*, 475–494. doi:10.1177/001316444600600405

Curry, M. J. (2003). Skills, access, and "basic writing": A community college case study from the United States. *Studies in the Education of Adults, 35*(1), 5–18.

Darling-Hammond, L. (2000). Teacher quality and student achievement: A review of state policy evidence. *Education Policy Analysis Archives, 8*(1), 1–44. Retrieved from https://epaa.asu.edu/ojs/article/viewFile/392/515

Edgecombe, N., Cormier, M. S., Bickerstaff, S., & Barragan, M. (2013). *Strengthening developmental education reforms: Evidence on implementation efforts from the scaling innovation project* (CCRC Working Paper No. 61). New York, NY: Columbia University. Teachers College, Community College Research Center. Retrieved from http://ccrc.tc.columbia.edu/publications/strengthening-developmental-education-reforms.html

Edgecombe, N., Jaggars, S. S., Xu, D., & Barragan, M. (2014). *Accelerating the integrated instruction of developmental reading and writing at Chabot College* (CCRC Working Paper No. 71). New York, NY: Columbia University, Teachers College, Community College Research Center. Retrieved from https://ccrc.tc.columbia.edu/publications/accelerating-integrated-instruction-at-chabot.html

Elliott, R. W., & Oliver, D. E. (2016). Linking faculty development to community college student achievement: A mixed methods approach. *Community College Journal of Research and Practice, 40*(2), 85–99. doi:10.1080/10668926.2014.961590

Engstrom, E. U. (2005). Reading, writing, and assistive technology: An integrated developmental curriculum for college students. *Journal of Adolescent & Adult Literacy, 49*, 30–39. doi:10.1598/JAAL.49.1.4

Falk-Ross, F. C. (2001). Toward the new literacy: Changes in college student's reading comprehension strategies following reading/writing projects. *Journal of Adolescent & Adult Literacy, 45*, 278–288.

Farley-Ripple, E., May, H., Karpyn, A., Tilley, K., & McDonough, K. (2018). Rethinking connections between research and practice in education: A conceptual framework. *Educational Researcher, 47*, 235–245. doi:10.3102/0013189X18761042

Fernsten, L. A., & Reda, M. (2011). Helping students meet the challenges of academic writing. *Teaching in Higher Education, 16*, 171–182. doi:10.1080/13562517.2010.507306

Fitzgerald, J., & Shanahan, T. (2000). Reading and writing relations and their development. *Educational Psychologist, 35*, 39–50. doi:10.1207/S15326985EP3501_5

Flink, P. J. (2017). Adapting self-selected reading practices for college-level developmental reading courses. *Reading Improvement, 54*(3), 87–92.

Gee, J. P. (2012). *Social linguistics and literacies: Ideology in discourses* (4th ed.). New York, NY: Routledge.

Gerber, R., Miller, T., Ngo, F. J., Shaw, S. M., & Daugherty, L. (2017, April). *New approaches to developmental education pathways: Integrating reading and writing remediation.* Paper presented at the annual meeting of the American Educational Research Association, San Antonio, TX.

Gilbert, J., & Graham, S. (2010). Teaching writing to elementary students in Grades 4–6: A national survey. *Elementary School Journal, 110*, 494–518. doi:10.1086/651193

Goen, S., & Gillotte-Tropp, H. (2003). Integrating reading and writing: A response to the basic writing "crisis." *Journal of Basic Writing, 22*(2), 90–113.

Goldman, S. R., Britt, M. A., Brown, W., Cribb, G., George, M., & Greenleaf, C. L., . . . Project Read. (2016). Disciplinary literacies and learning to read for understanding: A conceptual framework for disciplinary literacy. *Educational Psychologist, 51*, 219–246. doi:10.1080/00461520.2016.1168741

Graham, S., Harris, K. R., & Chambers, A. B. (2016). Evidence-based practice and writing instruction: A review of reviews. In C. A. MacArthur, S. Graham, & J. Fitzgerald (Eds.), *Handbook of writing research* (2nd ed., pp. 211–226). New York, NY: Guilford Press.

Graham, S., & Hebert, M. (2010). *Writing to read: Evidence for how writing can improve reading: A report from Carnegie Corporation of New York*. Washington, DC: Alliance for Excellent Education. Retrieved from https://www.carnegie.org/publications/writing-to-read-evidence-for-how-writing-can-improve-reading/

Graham, S., Liu, X., Bartlett, B., Ng, C., Harris, K. R., Aitken, A., . . . Talukdar, J. (2018). Reading for writing: A meta-analysis of the impact of reading interventions on writing. *Review of Educational Research, 88*, 243–284. doi:10.3102/0034654317746927

Graham, S., & Perin, D. (2007). What we know, what we still need to know: Teaching adolescents to write. *Scientific Studies of Reading, 11*, 313–335. doi:10.1080/10888430701530664

Grubb, W. N. (2012). Rethinking remedial education and the academic-vocational divide: Complementary perspectives. *Mind, Culture, and Activity, 19*(1), 22–25. doi:10.1080/10749039.2011.632055

Grubb, W. N., & Gabriner, R. (2013). *Basic skills education in community colleges: Inside and outside of classrooms*. New York, NY: Routledge.

Grubb, W. N., Worthen, H., Byrd, B., Webb, E., Badway, N., Case, C., . . . Villeneuve, J. C. (1999). *Honored but invisible: An inside look at teaching in community colleges*. New York, NY: Routledge.

Gruenbaum, E. A. (2012). Common literacy struggles with college students: Using the Reciprocal Teaching technique. *Journal of College Reading and Learning, 42*, 110–116. doi:10.1080/10790195.2012.10850357

Guzzetti, B. J., & Foley, L. M. (2018). Social media. In R. F. Flippo & J. W. Bean (Eds.), *Handbook of college reading and study strategy research* (3rd ed., pp. 74–86). New York, NY: Routledge.

Harris, K. R., Graham, S., Mason, L. H., & Friedlander, B. (2008). *Powerful writing strategies for all students*. Baltimore, MD: Paul H. Brookes.

Hayes, J. R. (1996). A new framework for understanding cognition and affect in writing. In C. M. Levy, & S. Ransdell (Eds.), *The science of writing: Theories, methods, individual differences, and applications* (pp. 1–27). Mahwah, NJ: Lawrence Erlbaum.

Hayward, C., & Willett, T. (2014). *Curricular redesign and gatekeeper completion: A multi-college evaluation of the California Acceleration Project.* San Rafael, CA: RP Group. Retrieved from http://cap.3csn.org/files/2014/04/RP-Evaluation-CAP.pdf

Henson, L., Hern, K., & Snell, M. (2017). *Up to the challenge: Community colleges expand access to college-level courses.* Sacramento, CA: California Acceleration Project. Retrieved from http://accelerationproject.org/Portals/0/Documents/Cap_Up%20to%20the%20challenge_web_v4.pdf

Hern, K. (2013). *Instructional cycle for an integrated reading and writing class.* Retrieved from http://cap.3csn.org/files/2012/02/Instructional-Cycle-Integrated-Class-May-2013.pdf

Hiebert, J., & Stigler, J. W. (2017). Teaching versus teachers as a lever for change: Comparing a Japanese and a U.S. perspective on improving instruction. *Educational Researcher, 46,* 169–176. doi:10.3102/0013189X17711899

Hodara, M., & Jaggars, S. S. (2014). An examination of the impact of accelerating community college students' progression through developmental education. *The Journal of Higher Education, 85*(2), 246-276. doi:10.1080/00221546.2014.11777326

Holschuh, J. P. (2014). The Common Core goes to college: The potential for disciplinary literacy approaches in developmental literacy classes. *Journal of College Reading and Learning, 45*(1), 85–95. doi:10.1080/10790195.2014.950876

Holschuh, J. P., & Lampi, J. P. (2018). Comprehension. In R. F. Flippo & T. W. Bean (Eds.), *Handbook of college reading and study strategy research* (3rd ed., pp. 118–142). New York, NY: Routledge.

Hsu, H.-Y., & Wang, S. (2010). The impact of using blogs on college students' reading comprehension and learning motivation. *Literacy Research and Instruction, 50*(1), 68–88. doi:10.1080/19388070903509177

Hynd, C., Holschuh, J. P., & Hubbard, B. P. (2004). Thinking like a historian: College students' reading of multiple historical documents. *Journal of Literacy Research, 36,* 141–176.

Ingalls, A. L. (2017). Facebook as a learning-management system in developmental writing. *Journal of Developmental Education, 40*(2), 26–28.

Jaggars, S. S., Hodara, M., Cho, S.-W., & Xu, D. (2015). Three accelerated developmental education programs: Features, student outcomes, and implications. *Community College Review, 43*(1), 3–26. doi:10.1177/0091552114551752

Jenkins, D., Speroni, C., Belfield, C., Jaggars, S. S., & Edgecombe, N. (2010). *A model for accelerating academic success of community college remedial English students: Is the Accelerated Learning Program (ALP) effective and affordable?* (CCRC Working Paper No. 21). New York, NY: Columbia University, Teachers College, Community College Research Center. Retrieved from https://ccrc.tc.columbia.edu/publications/accelerating-academic-success-remedial-english.html

Kalamkarian, H. S., Raufman, J., & Edgecombe, N. (2015). *Statewide developmental education reform: Early implementation in Virginia and North Carolina.* New York, NY: Columbia University, Teachers College, Community College Research Center. Retrieved from https://ccrc.tc.columbia.edu/publications/statewide-developmental-education-reform-early-implementation.html

Kallison, J. M. (2017). The effects of an intensive postsecondary transition program on college readiness for adult learners. *Adult Education Quarterly, 67,* 302–321. doi:10.1177/0741713617725394

Kebritchi, M., Lipschuetz, A., & Santiague, L. (2017). Issues and challenges for teaching successful online courses in higher education: A literature review. *Journal of Educational Technology Systems, 46*(1), 4–29. doi:10.1177/0047239516661713

Knowles, M. S. (1984). *Andragogy in action.* San Francisco, CA: Jossey-Bass.

Kucer, S. (2014). *Dimensions of literacy: A conceptual base for teaching reading and writing in school settings* (4th ed.). New York, NY: Routledge.

Lavonier, N. (2016). Evaluation of the effectiveness of remedial reading courses at community colleges. *Community College Journal of Research and Practice, 40,* 523–533. doi:10.1080/10668926.2015.1080200

Lei, S., Rhinehart, P., Howard, H., & Cho, J. (2010). Strategies for improving reading comprehension among college students. *Reading Improvement, 47*(1), 30–42.

Leist, C. W., Woolwine, M. A., & Bays, C. L. (2012). The effects of using a critical thinking scoring rubric to assess undergraduate students' reading skills. *Journal of College Reading and Learning, 43*(1), 31–58.

Lesley, M. (2004). Refugees from reading: Students' perceptions of "remedial" literacy pedagogy. *Reading Research and Instruction, 44*(1), 62–85.

Linderholm, T., Kwon, H., & Therriault, D. J. (2014). Instructions that enhance multiple-text comprehension for college readers. *Journal of College Reading and Learning, 45*(1), 3–19. doi:10.1080/10790195.2014.906269

MacArthur, C. A., Philippakos, Z. A., & Ianetta, M. (2015). Self-regulated strategy instruction in college developmental writing. *Journal of Educational Psychology, 107,* 855–867. doi:10.1037/edu0000011

Mannion, G., & Ivanic, R. (2007). Mapping literacy practices: Theory, methodology, methods. *International Journal of Qualitative Studies in Education, 20*(1), 15–30.

Matuchniak, T., Olson, C. B., & Scarcella, R. (2014). Examining the text-based, on-demand, analytical writing of mainstreamed Latino English learners in a randomized field trial of the Pathway Project intervention. *Reading and Writing: An Interdisciplinary Journal, 27,* 973–994. doi:10.1007/s11145-013-9490-z

MDRC. (2013). *Developmental education: A barrier to a postsecondary credential for millions of Americans.* Retrieved from https://www.mdrc.org/publication/developmental-education-barrier-postsecondary-credential-millions-americans

Miller, A. (2017). Process for discovery. *Learning Professional, 38*(5), 35–39.

Mongillo, G., & Wilder, H. (2012). An examination of at-risk college freshmen's expository literacy skills using interactive online writing activities. *Journal of College Reading and Learning, 42*(2), 27–50.

Morris, D., & Price, D. (2008). Transformative teaching in a developmental reading program. *Journal of College Reading and Learning, 39*(1), 88–93. doi:10.1080/10790195.2008.10850314

Mulcahy-Ernt, P. I., & Caverly, D. C. (2018). Strategic study-reading. In R. F. Flippo & T. W. Bean (Eds.), *Handbook of college reading and study strategy research* (3rd ed., pp. 191–214). New York, NY: Routledge.

National Assessment of Educational Progress. (2012). *The NAEP writing achievement levels.* Retrieved from http://nces.ed.gov/nationsreportcard/writing/achieveall.asp

National Assessment of Educational Progress. (2015a). *2015: Mathematics and reading at Grade 12.* Retrieved from https://www.nationsreportcard.gov/reading_math_g12_2015/

National Assessment of Educational Progress. (2015b). *The NAEP reading achievement levels by grade.* Retrieved from https://nces.ed.gov/nationsreportcard/reading/achieve.aspx#2009_grade12

National Association for Developmental Education. (n.d.). *Mission, vision and goals.* Retrieved from https://thenade.org/Mission-Vision-and-Goals

National Center for Education Statistics. (2012). *The nation's report card: Writing 2011* (NCES 2012-470). Washington, DC: U.S. Department of Education, Institute of Education Sciences. Retrieved from https://nces.ed.gov/pubsearch/pubsinfo.asp?pubid=2012470

National Governors' Association and Council of Chief State School Officers. (2010). *Common Core state standards: English language arts and literacy in history/social studies, science, and technical subjects*. Washington, DC: Author. Retrieved from http://www.corestandards. org/ELA-Literacy/

Olinghouse, N. G., & Graham, S. (2009). The relationship between the discourse knowledge and the writing performance of elementary-grade students. *Journal of Educational Psychology, 101*(1), 37–50.

Pacello, J. (2014). Integrating metacognition into a developmental reading and writing course to promote skill transfer: An examination of student perceptions and experiences. *Journal of College Reading and Learning, 44*, 119–140. doi:10.1080/10790195.2014.906240

Palincsar, A. S., & Brown, A. L. (1984). Reciprocal teaching of comprehension-fostering and monitoring activities. *Cognition and Instruction, 1*, 117–175.

Paulson, E. J. (2006). Self-selected reading for enjoyment as a college developmental reading approach. *Journal of College Reading and Learning, 36*(2), 51–58. doi:10.1080/1079019 5.2006.10850187

Paulson, E. J. (2014). Analogical processes and college developmental reading. *Journal of Developmental Education, 37*(3), 2–13.

Paulson, E. J., & Armstrong, S. L. (2010). Postsecondary literacy: Coherence in theory, terminology, and teacher preparation. *Journal of Developmental Education, 33*(3), 2–13.

Paulson, E. J., & Holschuh, J. P. (2018). College reading. In R. F. Flippo & T. Bean (Eds.), *Handbook of college reading and study strategies* (3rd ed., pp. 61–73). New York, NY: Routledge.

Paulson, E. J., van Overschelde, J. P., & Wiggins, A. Y. (2018, April). *Do accelerated developmental integrated reading and writing courses in Texas prepare students for college-level coursework?* Paper presented at the annual meeting of the American Educational Research Association, New York, NY.

Pearson, P. D., & Cervetti, G. N. (2015). Fifty years of reading comprehension theory and practice. In P. D. Pearson & E. H. Hiebert (Eds.), *Research-based practices for Common Core literacy* (pp. 1–24). New York, NY: Teachers College Press.

Pearson, P. D., & Gallagher, M. C. (1983). The instruction of reading comprehension. *Contemporary Educational Psychology, 8*, 317–344. doi:10.1016/0361-476X(83)90019-X

Perin, D. (2011). *Facilitating student learning through contextualization* (CCRC Working Paper No. 29, Assessment of Evidence Series). New York, NY: Columbia University, Teachers College, Community College Research Center. Retrieved from https://ccrc.tc.columbia. edu/media/k2/attachments/facilitating-learning-contextualization-working-paper.pdf

Perin, D. (2013). Literacy skills among academically underprepared students in higher education. *Community College Review, 41*, 118–136. doi:10.1177/0091552113484057

Perin, D. (2018). Teaching academically underprepared students. In J. Levin & S. Kater (Eds.), *Understanding community colleges* (2nd ed., pp. 135–158). New York, NY: Routledge/Taylor Francis.

Perin, D., Bork, R. H., Peverly, S. T., & Mason, L. H. (2013). A contextualized curricular supplement for developmental reading and writing. *Journal of College Reading and Learning, 43*(2), 8–38. doi:10.1080/10790195.2013.10850365

Perin, D., & Charron, K. (2006). "Lights just click on every day": Academic preparedness and remediation in community colleges. In T. R. Bailey & V. S. Morest (Eds.), *Defending the community college equity agenda* (pp. 155–194). Baltimore, MD: Johns Hopkins Press.

Perin, D., Lauterbach, M., Raufman, J., & Santikian Kalamkarian, H. (2017). Text-based writing of low-skilled postsecondary students: Relation to comprehension, self-efficacy and teacher judgments. *Reading and Writing: An Interdisciplinary Journal, 30*, 887–915. doi:10.1007/s11145-016-9706-0

Perkins, D. (1984). Assessment of the use of the Nelson Denny Reading Test. *Forum for Reading, 15*(2), 64–69.

Perun, S. A. (2015). "What the hell is revise?" A qualitative study of student approaches to coursework in developmental English at one urban-serving community college. *Community College Review, 43*, 245–263. doi:10.1177/0091552115580593

Pressley, M., & Afflerbach, P. (1995). *Verbal protocols of reading: The nature of constructively responsive reading.* Hillsdale, NJ: Lawrence Erlbaum.

Purcell-Gates, V., & Duke, N. K. (2016). Teaching literacy: Reading. In D. H. Gitomer & C. A. Bell (Eds.), *Handbook of research on teaching* (5th ed., pp. 1217–1267). Washington, DC: American Educational Research Association.

Ready, R. E., Chaudhry, M. F., Schatz, K. C., & Strazzullo, S. (2012). "Passageless" administration of the Nelson-Denny Reading Comprehension Test: Associations with IQ and reading skills. *Journal of Learning Disabilities, 46*, 377–384. doi:10.1177/0022219412468160

Relles, S. R., & Duncheon, J. C. (2018). Inside the college writing gap: Exploring the mixed messages of remediation support. *Innovative Higher Education.* Advance online publication. doi:10.1007/s10755-018-9423-5

Relles, S. R., & Tierney, W. G. (2013). Understanding the writing habits of tomorrow's students: Technology and college readiness. *Journal of Higher Education, 84*, 477–505. doi:10.1353/jhe.2013.0025

Rijlaarsdam, G., van den Bergh, H., Couzijn, M., Janssen, T., Braaksma, M., Tillema, M., . . . Raedts, M. (2012). Writing. In K. R. Harris, S. Graham, T. Urdan, A. G. Bus, S. Major, & H. L. Swanson (Eds.), *APA educational psychology handbook: Vol. 3. Application to learning and teaching* (pp. 189–227). Washington, DC: American Psychological Association.

Rose, M. (1983). Remedial writing courses: A critique and a proposal. *College English, 45*, 109–128.

Rose, M. (2005). *Lives on the boundary: A moving account of the struggles and achievements of America's educationally underprepared.* New York, NY: Penguin Books.

Rosenblatt, L. M. (1994). The transactional theory of reading and writing. In R. B. Ruddell, M. R. Ruddell, & H. Singer (Eds.), *Theoretical models and processes of reading* (pp. 1055–1092). Newark, DE: International Reading Association.

Saidy, C. (2018). Beyond words on the page: Using multimodal composing to aid in the transition to first-year writing. *Teaching English in the Two Year College, 45*, 255–273.

Schak, O., Metzger, I., Bass, J., McCann, C., & Englis, J. (2017). *Developmental education challenges and strategies for reform.* Retrieved from https://www2.ed.gov/about/offices/list/opepd/education-strategies.pdf

Shanahan, T. (2016). Relationships between reading and writing development. In C. A. MacArthur, S. Graham, & J. Fitzgerald (Eds.), *Handbook of writing research* (2nd ed., pp. 194–207). New York, NY: Guilford Press.

Shanahan, T., & Shanahan, C. (2012). What is disciplinary literacy and why does it matter? *Topics in Language Disorders, 32*(1), 7–18. doi:10.1097/TLD.0b013e318244557a

Simpson, M. L. (1986). PORPE: A writing strategy for studying and learning in the content areas. *Journal of Reading, 29*, 407–414.

Simpson, M. L., Stahl, N. A., & Francis, M. A. (2004). Reading and learning strategies: Recommendations for the 21st century. *Journal of Developmental Education, 28*(2), 2–14.

Skomsvold, P. (2014). *Profile of undergraduate students: 2011–12* (NCES 2015-167). Washington, DC: U.S. Department of Education, Institute of Education Sciences, National Center for Education Statistics. Retrieved from http://nces.ed.gov/pubs2015/2015167.pdf

Smith, D. K. (1998). Review of the Nelson-Denny Reading Test, Forms G and H. In J. C. Impara & B. S. Plake (Eds.), *Thirteenth mental measurements yearbook* (Buros Institute of Mental Measurement). Retrieved from the Burros Institute's Mental Measurements Yearbook online database.

Sporer, N., Brunstein, J. C., & Kieschke, U. (2009). Improving students' reading comprehension skills: Effects of strategy instruction and reciprocal teaching. *Learning and Instruction, 19*, 272–286. doi:10.1016/j.learninstruc.2008.05.003

Stahl, N. A., Simpson, M. L., & Hayes, C. G. (1992). Ten recommendations from research for teaching high-risk college students. *Journal of Developmental Education, 16*(1), 2–4.

Stotsky, S. (1983). Research on reading/writing relationships: A synthesis and suggested directions. *Language Arts, 60*, 627–642.

Sykes, G., & Wilson, S. M. (2016). Can policy (re)form instruction? In D. H. Gitomer & C. A. Bell (Eds.), *Handbook of research on teaching* (5th ed., pp. 851–916). Washington, DC: American Educational Research Association.

Testa, A. (2000). Seven principles for good practice in teaching and technology. In R. A. Cole (Ed.), *Issues in web-based pedagogy* (pp. 238–243). Westport, CT: Greenwood Press.

Toth, C. (2013). Beyond assimilation: Tribal colleges, basic writing, and the exigencies of settler colonialism. *Journal of Basic Writing, 32*(1), 4–36.

Tremmel, M. (2011). What to make of the five-paragraph theme: History of the genre and implications. *Teaching English in the Two-Year College, 39*(1), 29–42.

Tschannen-Moran, M., Hoy, A. W., & Hoy, W. K. (1998). Teacher efficacy: Its meaning and measure. *Review of Educational Research, 68*, 202–248. doi:10.3102/00346543068002202

Tyler, J. H., Taylor, E. S., Kane, T. J., & Wooten, A. L. (2010). Using student performance data to identify effective classroom practices. *American Economic Review, Papers and Proceedings, 100*, 256–260. doi:10.1257/aer.100.2.256

Valencia, R. R.. (Ed.). (2012). *The evolution of deficit thinking: Educational thought and practice.* New York, NY: Routledge.

Walker, B. J. (2012). *Diagnostic teaching of reading: Techniques for instruction and assessment* (7th ed.). Boston, MA: Pearson.

Weiner, E. J. (2002). Beyond remediation: Ideological literacies of learning in developmental classrooms. *Journal of Adolescent and Adult Literacy, 46*, 150–168.

White, S. (2011). *Understanding adult functional literacy.* New York, NY: Routledge.

Williams, J. L. (2013). Representations of the racialized experiences of African Americans in developmental reading textbooks. *Journal of College Reading and Learning, 43*(2), 39–69. doi:10.1080/10790195.2013.10850366

Woodcock, R. W., McGrew, K. S., & Mather, N. (2001). *Woodcock-Johnson III Tests of Achievement and Tests of Cognitive Abilities.* Itasca, IL: Riverside.

Woods, C. S., Park, T., Hu, S., & Bertrand Jones, T. (2017). Reading, writing, and English course pathways when developmental education is optional: Course enrollment and success for underprepared first-time-in-college students. *Community College Journal of Research and Practice.* Advance online publication. doi:10.1080/10668926.2017.1391144

Yang, Y.-F. (2010). Developing a reciprocal teaching/learning system for college remedial reading instruction. *Computers & Education, 55*, 1193–1201. doi:10.1016/j.compedu.2010.05.016

Zimmerman, B. J. (1995). Self-regulation involves more than metacognition: A social cognitive perspective. *Educational Psychologist, 30*, 217–221. doi:10.1207/s15326985ep3004_8

Chapter 14

Components, Infrastructures, and Capacity: The Quest for the Impact of Actionable Data Use on P–20 Educator Practice

Philip J. Piety

University of Maryland at College Park

This chapter reviews actionable data use—both as an umbrella term and as a specific concept—developed in three different traditions that data/information can inform and guide P–20 educational practice toward better outcomes. The literatures reviewed are known as data-driven decision making (DDDM), education data mining (EDM), and learning analytics (LA). DDDM is grounded in K–12 settings, has a social orientation, and is shaped by policy. EDM and LA began in higher education using data provided by instructional tools. This review of more than 1,500 publications traced patterns in these communities revealing disciplinary disconnects between DDDM and EDM/ LA. Recognizing information's systemic nature, this review expanded the analysis from teacher practice to educator practice. While methodological progress has been made in all areas, studies of impact were concentrated in DDDM. EDM and LA focus on tools for current/future educational settings and leveraging data harvested for basic research while reconceiving learning practices. The DDDM impact studies did not support a directly beneficial model for data use. Rather, long timescale capacity factors, including cultural and organizational processes that impact data use were revealed. A complementary model of components, infrastructure, and capacity is advanced with recommendations for scholarship in education's sociotechnical future.

This review began by looking at *actionable data use* in prekindergarten through higher education (commonly called P–20) practice. Actionable data use is one umbrella term for several research traditions using data collected from educational practices to inform, alter, and guide those same practices. *Data-driven decision making* (DDDM) is largely focused on kindergarten through high school (K–12) settings. DDDM has developed with support from federal laws, policies,

Review of Research in Education
March 2019, Vol. 43, pp. 394–421
DOI: 10.3102/0091732X18821116
Chapter reuse guidelines: sagepub.com/journals-permissions
© 2019 AERA. http://rre.aera.net

and funding. Two other areas—*educational data mining* (EDM) and *learning analytics* (LA)—are more focused on higher education but are used in K–12 settings to a lesser degree. EDM and LA have developed by using information harvested from digital learning technologies. Although the communities studying these three areas are not tightly connected, they share important similarities. They all cast data as a principal resource for educational change and improvement and use emergent data analysis tools. Furthermore, they all have opportunities to address technological optimism and the expectation that information tools can help P–20 educator practices overcome long-standing challenges.

This review is important because of its topic and breadth. The introduction of data into any human endeavor often brings great expectations: education is no different. Significant funding and in some cases policy structures have encouraged greater data use across the educational enterprise. Leaders and policymakers have looked to data for solutions; this review has the potential to provide important answers about what can be expected. Natural and important questions arise about what the research shows about the difference these information tools make in the work of education, principally teaching. There are existing reviews of one or two of these data use areas, but never have all three been reviewed as they are here. Through more than 1,500 original sources, including more than 570 peer-reviewed journal articles, this review shows some of the broad similarities shared by these three areas and some of their differences, including that they are grounded in largely different communities with different venues, motivations, and research foci. In developing a common frame and integrative model, this review argues that despite substantive differences there are fundamental commonalities that make a complementary view productive.

This review began with a focus on impact: a warranted explanation of how actionable data use changes practice. Through this process, new ways of understanding the many complex ways information can be used emerged. It showed fields that are evolving, especially the newest and rapidly expanding LA. The review process culminated in synthesizing its findings into a general model that focuses on components, infrastructures, and capacity—issues that are discussed in more detail later in this chapter.

Prior reviews have commented on the variation in type and quality of the research. Any one of them can be akin to an academic yard sale: there is a wide range of items of varying scope and value. It is not always clear at first what a source's contribution is or sometimes at first even what kind of article it is. There are some methodologically rich studies providing meaningful insights. There are many that look from a distance to yield insights on practice but on examination are revealed to be something different. There are few standards for what counts as a typical empirical study in these three literatures and how to report findings in a comparable let alone replicable way, although there are emerging subgenres. Understanding this variation and mapping it is one contribution of this chapter. Another contribution is some recommendations for the reporting on data use in a transdisciplinary community. This chapter also adds to the understanding and problematizing of the concept of *impact on practice* that is the theme of this volume. This work expands the practice lens from teachers to educators, highlighting the work others do as administrators, coaches, and members of school groups such as professional learning communities to support instruction. A very specific definition of what constitutes impact on practice study in this review was used to reveal a set of 43 studies that were determined to show impact. This set comes predominately from the DDDM community; EDM and LA empirical work focused on other areas. This review confirms the challenges prior reviews found; rather than a consensus on the value of data use, the field maintains a range of positions on data use from positivist to cautionary. However, this review does yield insights into how the research into actional data use has evolved, further supporting an integrative and complementary view.

There are different approaches that could be taken to a review such as this. More credit could be given to inferences of changed practice or changes in practice that researchers hope would be enacted rather than actual impact empirically assessed. Perhaps other approaches would lead to different conclusions; possibly not. The criteria for impact in this review favored the DDDM community and what and how it studies. It is quite possible changes in practice through the use of data are actually occurring in ways that researchers are not studying or are being reported outside of peer-reviewed journals and therefore not included in academic reviews. In addition, two potentially important areas for data use—charter schools and comprehensive school reform models—were not studied.

The impact on educator practice that motivated this study is the tip of the iceberg in terms of educational data. In DDDM, much of the motivation for using data was based in policies directed at teachers and school teams, so studies of those settings do exist in DDDM literature. However, DDDM literature shows a significant and growing body of work studying *organizational capacity* for using data. Organizational capacity includes belief systems, cultural factors, and professional development. This part of the literature illuminates some of the factors that may make data use so difficult to see benefits from. There was little treatment of organizational capacity in higher education from either EDM or LA, revealing an important gap in the literature. As a technical parallel to the social construct of DDDM's organizational capacity, EDM and LA have developed legions of technical components that have the potential to be included in educational practices of the future. This study integrates these areas with a broad and systemic form of technology that operates over long timescales called *infrastructures*. The title of this chapter and the model presented near its end reflect this focus on components, infrastructure, and capacity that combine to create conditions for impact on practice.

This chapter starts with a brief historical background of these fields and summarizes what prior reviews have said. It will discuss this review process and decisions that were made. The report on findings includes a classification of the diverse literatures, which is another contribution of this work. It then summarizes the state of the knowledge base in terms of impact and some of the patterns and change that the literature shows. Rather than proposing a research agenda, this chapter will present a synthetic view with some thoughts about interdisciplinarity and leveraging insights from one subfield into others as well as important questions to consider. This discussion also suggests an evaluation model developed for this review that might help future researchers to report and design their studies to later report on the myriad of factors and impacts that are part of the educational data use practice.

BACKGROUND AND COMMUNITY SIMILARITIES

For decades, school systems and institutes of higher education have been required to collect information from summative end-of-year or end-of-semester tests, data about enrollment and outcomes, and other details about the populations they serve. These regulatory data were rarely used to inform or change the practices of the educators from whose work the data originated. Beginning with the introduction of the No Child Left Behind Act of 2001 (NCLB, 2002), the use of data from mandated tests became more consequential for students and educators in K–12 settings, which greatly increased DDDM activities that were related to evaluating school and teacher performances. While these efforts began by using test scores from a few areas of the curriculum as mandated by policy, the press to use data has been strong with a follow-on effort to use the same test data with so-called value-added models to evaluate teacher contributions to test score gains (Darling-Hammond, 2015).

Meanwhile, growing out of the proliferation of digital tools and mostly from higher education, EDM (and later LA) emerged not from a policy shadow but from opportunities presented to researchers by the abundant data that digital tools made available. These areas both complement and present a contrast to DDDM. They are broader than DDDM in terms of data types and more opportunistic in terms of using data to understand learning processes. However, their attention to how the data affect practice are less developed than DDDM where researchers draw on decades of experience studying what happens in classrooms, schools, and educational organizations.

In the years leading up to this review, there have been concrete steps taken to build and formalize these communities. In 2007, the annual International Educational Data Mining Conference began. In 2009, the *Journal of Educational Data Mining* was launched. In 2011, the Society of Learning Analytics and Research (SoLAR) held its first conference, and in 2014, the first issue of the *Journal of Learning Analytics* was published. DDDM has been active in the American Educational Research Association (AERA) since at least 2004, and in 2016, the first AERA special interest group dedicated to topics of data use was founded. While there is no journal currently for data use within AERA, several mainstream education journals have had special issues or well-cited articles, including *Educational Researcher, Teachers College Record*, and *American Journal of Education*.

Several high-quality literature reviews have contributed knowledge to each of these distinct areas, notably Marsh (2012), Datnow and Hubbard (2016), and Sun,

Przybylski, and Johnson (2016) on DDDM; Papamitsiou and Economides (2014) and Sin and Muthu (2015) on LA and EDM; and Peña-Ayala (2014) on EDM.

Few authors and no literature reviews have thus far looked across these areas with a unified lens. Siemens and Baker (2012) penned a well-cited essay describing the similarities and differences between EDM and LA. Piety, Behrens, and Pea (2013) and later Piety, Hickey, and Bishop (2014) described conceptually an education data sciences that encompasses these areas.[1] Moreover, Piety and Pea (2018) have proposed a similar unified framework under the title *Learning Analytics Across Contexts in Learning Analytics for Education*, which could be applied to almost any educational data program.

Despite this lack of a unifying label in these literatures, there have been various boundary-crossing authors whose publication orientation and topic broke the common patterns this review revealed. Streifer and Schumann's (2005) "Using Data Mining to Identify Actionable Information: Breaking New Ground in Data-Driven Decision Making" is an early example of EDM framing for K–12 contexts. More recently, Crossley, Allen, Snow, and McNamara (2016) wrote, in the *Journal of Educational Data Mining*, which is often focused on higher education, about automatic essay scoring models and writing quality for K–12 using data from public high school students. "What We Know About Data-Driven Decision Making in Higher Education: Informing Educational Policy and Practice" (Bouwma-Gearhart & Collins, 2015) appeared in a leading higher education conference, rather than in K–12, as the phrase Data-Driven Decision Making might suggest. Showing the limitations of these labels, *Learning Analytics Goes to School: A Collaborative Approach to Improving Education* (Krumm, Means, & Bienkowski, 2018) is largely targeted at K–12. Siemens (2012) in an early essay on LA identified its potential to serve multiple roles from supporting practice to providing insights for research.

Actionable Data

The term *actionable data* was not developed for this chapter. The term *actionable information* was used by Streifer and Schumann (2005) and later as actionable data by Wayman and Stringfield (2006) in the introduction to one of the earliest special issues on data use. Marsh (2012), in a comprehensive review of DDDM literature, altered the formulation to include *knowledge* rather than data or information, stating,

Unlike "evidence" or "information," the focus here is on raw data that must be organized, filtered, and analyzed to become information, and then combined with stakeholder understanding and expertise to become *actionable knowledge*. . . . The target "user" could include educators and other stakeholders at the school or district level. Thus, a teacher is expected to apply this knowledge to instructional practice or decisions, whereas administrators and other individuals may apply the knowledge to school or district-level administrative or managerial practice and decisions (e.g., school or district improvement efforts). (p. 3; emphasis added)

TABLE 1
Distribution of Sources in Initial Search

Publication Type	DDDM	LA	EDM
Book	25	2	5
Chapter	31	23	40
Journal	169	131	276
Paper	25	186	542
Report	29	17	11

Note. DDDM = data-driven decision making; LA = learning analytics; EDM = educational data mining. This table reveals the extent to which EDM and LA have large conference paper elements. DDDM may have a lower percentage of conference publications given that there has not been a conference dedicated to it.

Marsh also mentions the broader use of data to include district offices, school principals and leaders, professional learning communities, and others working to support classrooms, which aligns with the framing of educator, rather than teacher, practice used for this review.

REVIEW OF PUBLISHED LITERATURE

The literature review for this project involved three stages. The first stage was the development of raw lists of more than 1,500 initial sources from the three literatures as shown in Table 1.[2] The second stage focused on those pieces published in peer-reviewed journals. The third phase examined those that met the standard of impact on educator practice set for this review.

Figure 1 illustrates the growth in journal articles across all three areas. What appears to be declines in the past several years included is likely an artifact of the search process rather than a confirmed downward trend after 2016.

Differences in Venue

Research literatures are reflections of discourse communities. And the labels we use for them—DDDM, LA, and EDM—are to some extent arbitrary. As the boundary crossing literatures discussed above show there are not rigid criteria as to what kinds of topics can be included in any of these areas. However, if we look at the publications associated with these different labels, the outlines of these discourse communities become clear. Table 2 shows the journals that the three traditions utilized with three or more pieces. Only three journals are shared by more than one community and all three are shared between EDM and LA, illustrating the academic turf that these areas currently occupy.

FIGURE 1
Journal Articles by Category and Year in the Review

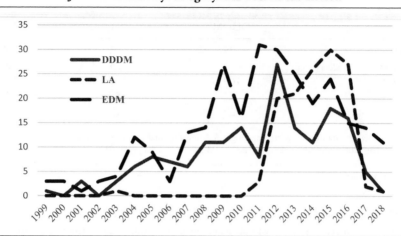

Note. DDDM = data-driven decision making; LA = learning analytics; EDM = educational data mining.

TABLE 2
Popularity of Journals for Journal Articles in This Study

DDDM	LA	EDM
• *Teachers College Record* (23)	• *Journal of Learning Analytics* (22)	• *Journal of Educational Data Mining* (53)
• *Teaching and Teacher Education* (14)	• **Computers in Human Behavior** (10)	• *Expert Systems with Applications Journal* (24)
• *American Journal of Education* (11)	• *Journal of Educational Technology & Society* (7)	• *Computing Education Journal* (17)
• *American Educational Research Journal* (10)	• *Educause Review* (6)	• **Computers & Education (15)**
• *Studies in Educational Evaluation* (8)	• **Computers & Education** (6)	• *User Modeling and User-Adapted Interaction* (9)
• *Journal of Education for Students Placed at Risk* (7)	• *British Journal of Educational Technology* (5)	• *Educational and Psychological Measurement* (8)
• *School Effectiveness and School Improvement* (6)	• *American Behavioral Scientist* (5)	• **The Internet and Higher Education** (4)
• *Educational Policy* (6)	• *Journal of Asynchronous Learning Networks* (4)	• **Computers in Human Behavior** (3)
• *Peabody Journal of Education* (5)	• **The Internet and Higher Education** (4)	• *Journal of Educational Technology & Society* (3)
• *Educational Administration Quarterly* (5)	• *International Journal of Technology Enhanced Learning* (3)	
• *Reading Research Quarterly* (4)	• *EDUCAUSE Learning Initiative* (3)	
• *Educational Researcher* (4)	• *Journal of the Learning Sciences* (3)	
• *Journal of Educational Administration* (3)		
• *Educational Management Administration & Leadership* (3)		
• *Educational Assessment* (3)		
• *Education Policy Analysis Archives* (3)		

Note. DDDM = data-driven decision making; LA = learning analytics; EDM = educational data mining. Bold text indicates journals shared by more than one community.

Determining Studies That Could Address the Question of Impact

At its most basic level, this review defined *impact on practice* as being a change in an existing practice that could be observed and was not fundamentally at some higher level of abstraction (e.g., the school system). *Impact* in this review did not only mean a change in an outcome variable with any quantitative confidence but rather *any positive or negative observable change in practice* resulting from the inclusion and use of some data in a regular educational activity rather than outside of a practice setting. A study that shows impact naturally differs from a study that suggests change might happen or presents a theory of change without empirical support; this review includes only the former of these.

Many important journal articles were not classified as having impact on practice. We classified some studies, largely from EDM and LA, as having *futuristic* titles: The title, and sometimes the abstract, indicated an impact on practice, but in reality the study addressed a technology that the researchers anticipated teachers would use, but there was no study of actual impact. For example, an EDM piece by Romero, Zafra, Luna, and Ventura (2013) is titled "Association Rule Mining Using Genetic Programming to Provide Feedback to Instructors From Multiple-Choice Quiz Data." The title suggests a potential change in practice, but the study does not research instructors in their classrooms (it was a technical pilot in a study context). Articles framed as promissory were excluded because they are difficult to compare and have uncertain utility in the daily work of educators.

Other articles that were important for understanding this movement are some important commissioned reports that inform the larger understanding of the field, including *Using Student Achievement Data to Support Instructional Decision Making* (Hamilton et al., 2009) and *Use of Education Data at the Local Level: From Accountability to Instructional Improvement* (Means, Padilla, & Gallagher, 2010). Both are federally funded projects and reflect not only important research and scholarship but also the commitment to this area that the federal government has had in recent years to the use of data. Similarly, Dede's (2015) *Data-Intensive Research in Education: Current Work and Next Steps*, which was the result of a National Science Foundation–funded conference looking at advanced data technologies and big data in education.

Excluded as specifically showing impact, but still informing the understanding of actionable data use, is a large randomized control study on a comprehensive data-driven school reform model by Slavin, Cheung, Holmes, Madden, and Chamberlain (2013). Clearly this kind of model uses actionable data and shows impact using rigorous methods. However, as a schoolwide program it fails to meet the criteria of a study of instruction or a school group. As a comprehensive school reform model, it represents a systemic approach that affects instruction, administration, and metrics at the same time. Whole school programs have their own literature that describes their benefits and challenges (Hopkins, Stringfield, Harris, Stoll, & Mackay, 2014, Rowan

& Miller, 2007). For this review, they present too large a change to be able to isolate the data use component.

Another source that was challenging to classify was Wayman, Shaw, and Cho (2017), who studied teacher use of a computer data system in relation to student achievement and found gains associated with system use. The teaching practice was not directly studied and indeed other explanations are possible for the change in student performance. It is an important piece for the field, however, because it suggests that greater engagement with data technologies will yield greater returns. In addition to being an example of a relevant study that did not meet the criteria for inclusion as a study of practice, but rather technology use, this study represents a possibly emerging example of techniques more typical of LA and EDM applied in the DDDM space.

Both Wayman et al. (2017) and Slavin et al. (2013) came from the DDDM tradition but share important features with EDM and LA pieces. They describe different approaches to educational delivery for which detecting change in traditional education practice is problematic. Slavin et al. (2013) examined data within a large social reform, whereas Wayman et al. (2017) looked through a technical lens. Both studies presented facets of a possible integrated educational practice where data are used as a systemic integrator rather than in isolated contexts.

Classifying the Peer-Reviewed Literature

Even though many journal articles did not meet the criteria for showing impact on practice, the process of finding which studies could show impact led to a search for a meaningful classification of all the sources. This process resulted in a taxonomy, shown in Figure 2, that illustrates the range of subgenres within these three communities.

This taxonomy may help illuminate some of the variation in research quality that some prior authors have noted (Coburn & Turner, 2011; Marsh, 2012; Piety, 2013). Some of the reported variation may be related to the inclusion of different kinds of pieces in complex literatures where many pieces are not actually empirical studies but addressing different characteristics of educational data use. Below, this taxonomy's categories are discussed with exemplars.

Essays

Essays were a large component of all literatures. Essays have no appreciable empirical component but instead present a report or argue for a position or perspective. The most basic of essays are *promotions* and *critiques*. A promotional essay extolls the virtues of a data use practice, while a critique raises questions about the entire endeavor or one aspect of it such as privacy. Some essays report on a particular technology or project. Others report on the state of the field. These *project reports, technology reports*, and *field reports* provide useful information about the nature of these

FIGURE 2
Taxonomy of Categorization for Source Items Included in the Search

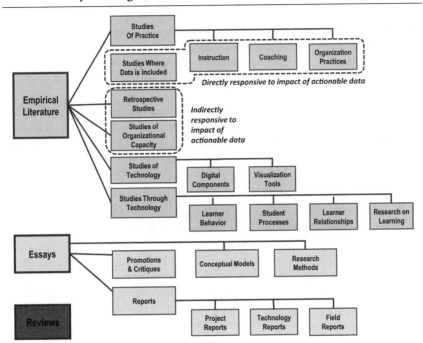

communities and the kinds of issues that are discussed but little information about the impact on practice.

The most numerous variation of essay in this study is the *conceptual model.* Conceptual models are varied in their focus. Many conceptual models focus on a particular aspect, for example, data literacy: Gummer and Mandinach's (2015) "Building a Conceptual Framework for Data Literacy" intended "to inform the discussions around data literacy so that continued refinement of operational definitions of the construct will emerge" (p. 1). Another conceptual model by Blikstein and Worsley (2016), titled "Multimodal Learning Analytics and Education Data Mining: Using Computational Technologies to Measure Complex Learning Tasks," looked at how different kinds of data support certain kinds of analyses. While most conceptual models will provide examples to illustrate their points, Scheffel, Drachsler, Stoyanov, and Specht's (2014) "Quality Indicators for Learning Analytics" is rare in that it is based on a literature review that informed the model's development. Some conceptual models describe series of transformations that information may go through or different kinds of stakeholders—a topic that emerges as potentially important for the field to consider, as discussed below.

Retrospective Studies

A retrospective study looks at how data had been used in practice but does not study data use as it is occurring. These pieces are usually based on analyses of surveys and interviews that ask practitioners how they had used data in their work and what kinds of issues using data raised. An example of a retrospective study is Park and Datnow (2008) that reviewed a prescriptive school reform model. Although these studies provided an important lens into the impact of practice, it was indirect, filtered by perceptions, and possibly affected by subject self-reports and researcher expectations. These studies can provide a wide and historical view that paints a portrait of how information has worked within an organization, especially when done as a systemic, multilayered study. While not counted as impact studies, findings from retrospective studies aligned well with those of the impact studies.

Studies of Organizational Capacity

Organizational capacity is a topic almost exclusively in the DDDM domain and relates to the various human factors likely to affect data use (Datnow & Hubbard, 2016). It includes studies where cultural attitudes or perceptions about data are considered rather than actually using data in practice (Anderson, Leithwood, & Strauss, 2010). Many organizational capacity studies are based on surveys, but in some cases observations of interactions are included. While these studies do not allow us to answer the primary question of impact on educator practice, they are important to understanding enabling/constraining conditions and show how researchers understand the challenges of data use within the complex social settings of educational institutions, including professional development and its relationships to educator data use. Some relevant studies were framed not as studies about the use of data but as relating to the use of *evidence* (Coburn & Talbert, 2006; Moss & Piety, 2007). Evidence can be inclusive of data collected from practice as discussed in this chapter but can also include inferences based on research that certain kinds of approaches are sound and "evidence based."

Studies of Practice: Instruction, Organizational Activities, and Coaching

This category is the one with the greatest ability to answer the overarching questions of impact on educator practice. All the literature in this group has a specific study of some aspect of educator work as it occurred. This group includes three subcategories: instructional, organizational, and coaching practices. *Instructional practice studies* are based in one or more classrooms or one or more online learning settings where data are used to guide or support teaching. An example of this category is Konstantopoulos, Miller, and van der Ploeg (2013), "The Impact of Indiana's System of Interim Assessments on Reading and Math Achievement." Not included in this group are some studies of online pedagogy that initially appeared to be instructional but instead involved data harvested from online courses used for other kinds of analysis rather than to guide instructional decisions. Many of those studies were classified as studies through technology, discussed below. *Organizational practice studies* included a range of organizational settings such as a principal's office, a professional learning community meeting (Stoll, Bolam, McMahon, Wallace, & Thomas, 2006), and a district office where decisions are taken that impact the practice of those organizational settings and with instructional implications. *Coaching studies* are those that occurred not in a classroom but feature a teacher and another teacher acting as a leader or an instructional coach. An example of this kind of study is Denton, Swanson, and Mathes (2007), "Assessment-Based Instructional Coaching Provided to Reading Intervention Teachers."

Studies of Practice Where Data Is Involved

This is one of the most interesting and analytically challenging categories that also occurs largely in the DDDM literature. Many of these pieces focus on elementary reading instruction. These studies include data use but do not foreground the data. Rather, the focus of these pieces are practices that may use data, for example, to reflect on student work (Burch & Spillane, 2003) or to support school-based inquiry teams (Gallimore, Ermeling, Saunders, & Goldenberg, 2009). These studies are challenging to analyze for a study such as this because they often weave data into the fabric of their account rather than making data a focus. While illustrating the extent to which data are now accepted as a regular part of some educational practices, a review such as this one framed around studies that are focused on data does not have neat categories for these kinds of studies. However, some of these studies may help understand the impact that data use can have on educator practice but others often require some additional analysis to be relevant to this review.

Studies of Technology Components: Visualizations and Embedded Algorithms

There is a significant portion of both the LA and EDM literatures that focus on a technology. Some of these have an empirical component that studies the technology in a laboratory or pilot context. There were two principal variations of these studies in the reviewed literature: *visualization tools* and *embedded algorithms*. Visualization tools are principally dashboards and other ways that information from practice could be viewed by practitioners. One example is Van Leeuwen, Janssen, Erkens, and Brekelmans (2014), "Supporting Teachers in Guiding Collaborating Students: Effects of Learning Analytics in CSCL," which looks at different ways student performance/progress can be presented to teachers. Embedded algorithms are discrete functions components that could be utilized within some practice activity to perform a specific task with data. One example is Cetintas et al.'s (2014) *A Joint Probabilistic Classification Model of Relevant and Irrelevant Sentences in Mathematical Word Problems*. Most are software components and/or models that, for example, make predictions, recommendations, or cluster/group students. For example, a common EDM artifact will cluster students using a formula. These tools do not constitute an educational delivery approach or technology. Rather, they are pieces to be embedded in an instructional or institutional setting. While hidden within systemic digital technologies—infrastructures—these tools could delegate consequential decisions such as selecting students for instructional groups and recommending various educational paths even without students and teachers being fully aware of their role.

Studies Through Technology: Student Processes, Learner Behavior, and Learning Relationships

There are three genres of studies found entirely in EDM and LA literatures where data collected in a digital environment were used to understand something about student educational progress. The first subcategory is *student process studies* that address students across courses. These studies tended to use data from multiple learning environments and administrative systems. Topics for these studies included academic persistence and retention. One example is Vialardi et al. (2011), "A Data Mining Approach to Guide Students Through the Enrollment Process Based on Academic Performance." A second subcategory is studies of *online learner behavior.* These were confined to the performance of students—learners—in a specific course or courses and examined the kinds of actions and decisions they took within those settings. One example is Muldner, Burleson, Van de Sande, and VanLehn (2011), "An Analysis of Students' Gaming Behaviors in an Intelligent Tutoring System: Predictors and Impacts." A third category is studies of *learning/learner relationships.* These are generally course specific and attempted to develop models that document relationships between certain kinds of behaviors and outcomes. Prediction and clustering were two common foci for these studies. These studies often share similarities with studies of technology components but the focus here is on the information rather than the tools. One example is Tempelaar, Rienties, and Giesbers (2015), "In Search for the Most Informative Data for Feedback Generation: Learning Analytics in a Data-Rich Context."

Research on Learning

Several studies were found in the EDM and LA literatures where the data collected from a digital tool were used to add to the knowledge base of how students learn in different kinds of situations. These studies show how data collected out of a digital infrastructure can be a resource for basic research. An example of this is Berland, Martin, Benton, Smith, and Davis (2013). These studies do not allow us to understand the impact of that data on practice directly, but their insights could help shape the design and delivery of educational offerings in the future.

Reviews

DDDM, EDM, and LA all had a similar percentage of their literature categorized as review pieces. Given that a review is a summary and analysis of other work rather than an original study, this category does not include pieces that have a review as part of a larger empirical objective, but rather substantially report on others' work. Most pieces classified as reviews were literature reviews but a few focused on technology components or other topics.[3]

Distribution of Types of Articles Across the Three Literatures

When utilizing this taxonomy of articles in the different communities of DDDM, EDM, and LA, some important similarities and differences are evident. As shown in Figure 3, in all three communities, reviews make up a similar percentage of their literature. Substantial and similar percentages are devoted to conceptual models, perhaps reflecting that all three communities are searching for adequate frameworks to guide their work. Their empirical work goes in different directions, however. The DDDM literature dominates the socially oriented research into practice while LA and EDM dominate the technology categories as well as leading in the use of infrastructures or educational tools to study learners and learning.

EVALUATING IMPACT, SEEING CHANGE

The quest for understanding how data impacts educator practice and for a clear model for how this impact is achieved was not successful in this review. No best practices were found and a generalizable theory that could productively guide practice was not developed. In these ways, this review aligns with prior research from the DDDM community that found success using data to be partial, at times counterindicated, and fundamentally complex. Marsh (2012), reviewing this space 6 years earlier, found that

among the limited number of studies examining the effect of interventions on student achievement there is mixed evidence of effects. Similarly, there is limited research on student achievement effects of data use more generally, and in fact, *little supporting evidence of positive effects* [emphasis added]. (p. 38)

These were strong statements when written and indeed still strong now. After over 15 years of research, this review confirms that, as a body of work, the studies looking specifically at impact have been unable to develop a clear picture of the value and risks of using data to support practitioners.

However, there is more to this issue. In addition to looking for the positive or negative effects of data in particular settings, broader patterns in the field were revealed that help understand more about the nature of these studies and the kinds of factors that may be present in them. The impact studies typically focused on specific areas such as classrooms, professional learning communities, or district meetings. Data use studies can look at one grade or several, one subject or many, and can focus on one part of an educational organization, such as a classroom or school group meeting, or across a wide organizational spectrum. In only a few cases did a study span contexts or subject areas, although these kinds of studies are more recent, indicating a field continuing to develop.

This development in the kind of research being undertaken can be illustrated with two quotations. Marsh (2012), looking back to the earliest DDDM research, found a

FIGURE 3
Distribution of Articles (by Percentage) Across the Three Literatures

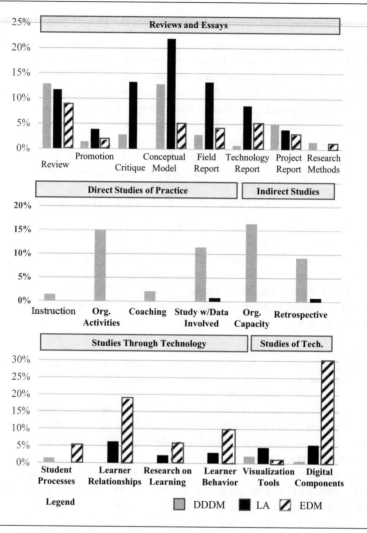

Note. DDDM = data-driven decision making; LA = learning analytics; EDM = educational data mining.

research base is limited in quantity and quality . . . [that] suggests the need for more methodologically rigorous research and greater attention to the organizational and student-level outcomes of interventions, comparative analyses, interventions helping educators move from knowledge to action, and specific ways in which the quality of data and leadership practices shape the effectiveness of interventions. (p. 38)

While this criticism of early research methods was echoed by others (Coburn & Turner, 2011; Marsh & Farrell, 2015; Piety, 2013), there are signs that this aspect of the DDDM movement may have evolved in recent years. Comprehensive and nuanced approaches are becoming more common in contemporary studies. Sun et al. (2016), in a review of teachers use of data, noted,

> From a research point of view, researchers are moving towards mixed methods from the typical approach to this topic more than 10 years ago when majority of the studies used a qualitative research design. This trend indicates a more matured approach to this problem, moving from describing what is going on in the early state of the inquiry towards examining relationships between teachers' use of data and its antecedents, shapers, and impacts. (p. 29)

An example of a broad systemic study is Farley-Ripple and Buttram (2014) that followed a state education department program that mandated professional learning communities in schools to monitor how the implementation in two different districts fostered collaborative data use. Similarly, Bowers (2009) compared data from two districts to explore the idea of using grades as a source for data use.

The nature of the data that are included in studies across these literatures has evolved along with the methods. DDDM began by largely focusing on assessments of student learning, either high-stakes tests or proxies for them. EDM and LA have largely utilized data drawn from technological environments. However, as Table 3 shows, conceptions of data have evolved in all three literatures, with increasingly varied kinds of information being considered in studies.

This aspect of the evolution of these three subfields is likely a result of at least two factors. One is that technology is constantly advancing: the technologies for educational data collection and dissemination are no exception. Second, as discussed above, research approaches are becoming more sophisticated over time and with new methods often come opportunities to consider new kinds of data and practices.

There are some potentially important topics that are not frequently covered in any of these literatures. The first is the systemic and organizational context in which it occurs. While systemic and organizational context, as well as policy, is discussed in conceptual essays and there is a significant literature category on organizational capacity, the studies specifically looking at practice sporadically describe policy and capacity issues. Rarely do they specifically describe what level the practitioners being studied might have reached in terms of building (or losing) capacity. A school system responding to a policy in the first year and in the fifth year of its existence can be different. More indexing of practitioner response within a longitudinal view of context or capacity of the issues is needed in the empirical base.

Similarly, within the studies of practice, the nature of the data was often lightly treated. Few pieces were clear about what the data were that were being studied—*as if all data can be considered through the same lens.* Similarly, in some organizational capacity pieces, there were generally low levels of exploration into the nature of the data being used. This is perhaps a more reasonable approach if the field were just

TABLE 3

Evolution of Data Types in Three Literature Areas

	Early Conceptions	More Recent Additions
DDDM	• High-stakes tests scores or high-stakes progress proxies, for example, formative/interim assessments • Fine-grained reading measures	• Demographics • Examples of student work • Goals • Data visualizations
EDM	• Trace data from cognitive tutors • Online course participation data • Web server logs	• Multimodal data (e.g., speech, gesture) • Game and simulation data • Administrative data sets
LA	• Log data from MOOCs and learning management systems • Social network data	• Personal experience telemetry • Complex visualizations • Game and simulation data

Note. DDDM = data-driven decision making; EDM = educational data mining; LA = learning analytics; MOOC = massive open online course.

beginning to encounter data in substantive roles, but we are in an era where the use of data, both generally and in education, has become commonplace. Some of the conceptual models discussed information transformations where raw data (test scores or event data from digital environments) are collected and subsequently go through a series of state changes to become more usable and connected to organizational decisions. This is reflected in Mandinach, Honey, Light, and Brunner (2008) and Marsh, Pane, and Hamilton (2006) and in several of the conceptual models on EDM where an analogous model of transformations was presented, albeit more technically and beginning with raw data that were cleaned, summarized, and put into an analytic format. However, few studies examining practice specifically link the concept of information transformation to practice or ask questions about what may be lost with each resemiotization (Iedema, 2003; Lemke, 2000).

COMPONENTS, INFRASTRUCTURES, CAPACITY LEADING TO DATA USE IN PRACTICE

The paucity of evidence that shows clear benefits (or costs) to using data in even one aspect of this broad terrain of research raises questions about how often actionable data use is a localized activity versus a systemic one. The significant research on organizational capacity supports a broad and systemic view, as does the evolution of research methods into data use that increasingly have a wide aperture on the landscape they study, the methods they use, and the kinds of data and information that are implicated in their research. The question of impact on practice(s) remains large but so do other important questions such as how to reconcile these literatures and how to leverage insights from different research agendas. Given these findings, a specific research agenda pointing to emerging questions and methods is premature. This review will suggest framing moves intended to support more integrated and rigorous practice.

By whatever label educational data use is called, it is a highly technologized activity. It is sociotechnical. It is therefore in constant transition. Using historical models of education and methods for research run the risk of missing important change, real and potential, that technology can bring. The structure of this review could lead to an incorrect inference that the work in EDM and LA is not relevant to impact on practice because it has paid little attention to studies of practice. This is problematic because parts of education's future may be represented in EDM and LA; at the same time, much of education's past is embedded within approaches used in DDDM because a practice must be stable to understand specifically how things change in it. Meanwhile, EDM and LA practice areas have the potential to become part of a more technologized educational landscape in the future, although that change is difficult to see in most studies.

Nevertheless, all three of these fields are dealing with technology and one of the constants of technology is change. Not only will the technologies change frequently, but in many cases, they alter practices. Email, having students search on the Internet, digital whiteboards, and one-to-one computing in schools are commonplace today, but were futuristic a few years ago. Platforms such as Google classroom are becoming ubiquitous despite researcher inattention. Similarly, one could incorrectly infer that issues of organizational capacity do not relate to higher education simply because the research has been done in K–12 settings. Rather, those areas have not been reported on in higher education data use literature.

A High-Level Cross-Community Model

To ground a discussion below on ways to holistically consider the different activities of data use, Figure 4 illustrates a tentative model that focuses on four kinds of factors or elements: technical components, infrastructures, capacity, and practices within a policy and systemic context.

The schematic in Figure 4 is not analogous to nor competes with the many conceptual models produced in different literatures. It is a high-level mapping of the kinds of elements that this review and other relevant studies have shown to be important for actionable data use. Although the schematic omits many important mechanisms and factors that conceptual models from across these literatures explicate, those conceptual models tend to focus on a subset of the factors that this review has shown are important. Elements in this model have been discussed earlier and in the literature but some details that could be added are briefly discussed below.

Environmental Contexts: Policy, System, Organization, and Institution

Data use does not happen in a vacuum. It occurs in response to pressures and initiatives. In the K–12 sector, many of these pressures have been carried through policy and funding programs, although the cultural expectations for data use are also present (Henig, 2013; Piety, 2013). Research that looked at the high-stakes environment of NCLB showed how schools under pressure from accountability policies used data

FIGURE 4
Conceptual Schematic of Data Use Research Landscape

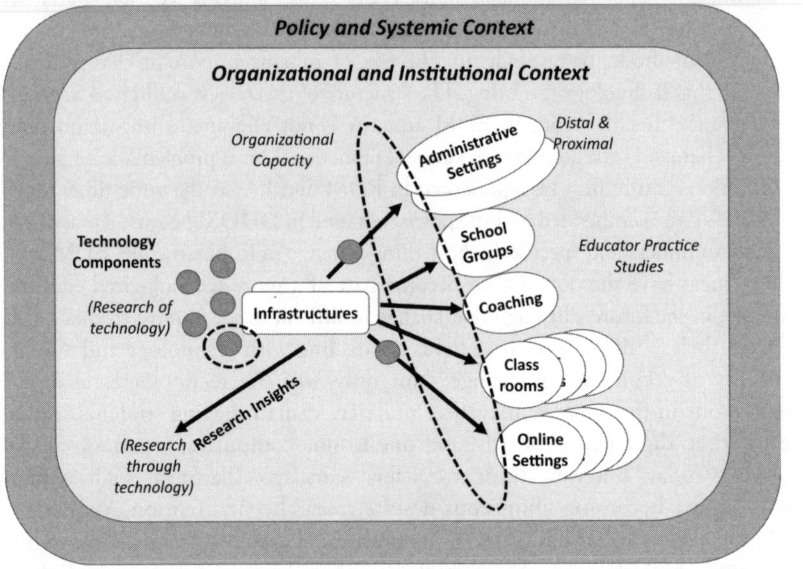

differently depending on how the schools stood in terms of potential sanctions (Diamond, 2007; Valli, Croninger, Chambliss, Graeber, & Buese, 2008). Because of the structure of federal education, these factors are more prominent in K-12 than in higher education. Still, there are contextual motivations for data use in higher education such as retention, remediation, and access. There may also be likely significant relationships between context and organizational capacity in ways that parallel K-12 schooling.

Related to the capacity and context is leadership and the role of data in the practice of instructional responsibility (Halverson, Grigg, Prichett, & Thomas, 2007; Knapp, Swinnerton, Copland, & Monpas-Huber, 2006). As with other topics that DDDM has some representation of, there was a gap in coverage of this perspective in EDM and LA, reflecting both the differences in K–12 settings and the predispositions of the different professional communities.

Technology Components and Infrastructure

Technology has a central role in this model and two kinds are highlighted: components and infrastructures. Technology components are discrete technologies that collect or modify information. They include the kinds of algorithms discussed earlier, such as clustering, prediction, and recommendation functions, which are often studied in isolation from their settings of use. Technology components cannot on their own impact anything but must be included in the systemic substrate and their outputs used for them to have even the potential for impact. Within this category of technology components could be assessments and learning tools that have the potential to create data streams for subsequent use. Even though many educational data streams begin with assessments, the field of measurement and assessment has been largely disconnected from the data use literature. This model creates a space for them.

Infrastructures are technologies that operate at the scales of systems: crossing classroom, school, and in some cases institutional boundaries. They also tend to be active for a long time, taking significant time to create and then replace. Digital infrastructures—data systems, learning management systems, digital textbooks, and assessment tools—provide linkages between different settings. Because infrastructures operate over long timescales taking time to build and become adopted (and in some cases, adapted) to different settings (Ribes & Finholt, 2009), they tend to be silent unless/until they break, when they often fade into background and then become harder to subject to critical investigation. The focus of infrastructures in this model is on the digital but are related to the institutional infrastructures described by Cohen, Spillane, and Peurach (2018), who highlight the importance of professional development, curriculum, and organizational routines that these scholars refer to as infrastructures but that in this study would align more with the concept of organizational capacity.

Using This Model

While a simple schematic, the model may help develop a stronger field studying the development and use of actionable data for the future. Below are five topics for building a stronger and more interdisciplinary and theoretically grounded field: transdisciplinary framing, timescales and expectations, leveraging the infrastructures for research, engaging and building theories, and reporting for comparability.

Transdisciplinary Framing

Currently, the majority of education data use researchers stay within their disciplinary lanes so that disconnects seen in the literature are self-reinforcing. To help the field leverage a larger knowledge base, when a study of technology components is undertaken, researchers may wish to look across this mapping of educational data use for relevant framing. For example, a recommendation algorithm might be framed using what researchers studying data use in the settings the recommender is to be used for to develop an understanding of the praxis environment the innovation is intended to support, for example a blended computer science course. Similarly, research into educational practice that looks at data might benefit from a more thorough examination of the technological components and infrastructures used by practitioners. Also, looking at issues of capacity and context that have been often treated lightly might be useful in describing the conditions that may affect the data use.

Timescales and Expectations

Teaching happens within social and organizational contexts. Data systems are technologies that operate within those same contexts and, as those systems are used, they may be affecting and altering the environment they are situated in. However, data use studies have often looked for a measurable impact at a relatively short period of time without an appreciation for the longer term, emergent characteristics of how infrastructures are adopted and, in some cases, adapted. Measuring impact is much easier quantitatively when many things are constant or assumed to be constant and so systemic relationships may make measurement complicated. As data are a systemic resource and agent, it is possible that their implementation may be altering those relationships over time.

With these systemic relationships in mind, we can ask to what extent impact on practice should hold a privileged place in the research on data use. Should broader questions be asked that illuminate more organizational factors and over longer time-scales than a semester or a year? Piety and Pea (2018) presented a programmatic view of LA that pointed to the fact that these data systems require a design and development effort as well as to be populated with data—all of which take time. Then, once there is an opportunity to collect and use some information, there may be new design and development efforts to refine existing data points and/or collect new *ones*. Unlike many fields, for example healthcare or finance, that can iterate through new data collection approaches in days, weeks, or months, the process in education is usually repeatable once or twice a year. Once a curricular topic has been covered, the next opportunity to improve the collection of information is with a new group of students the next time that topic is scheduled.

Using Contemporary Research Methods

What are the measures of impact that are representative of long-scale social outcomes? Test scores and self-reports of perceptions and attitudes have had a privileged position in education research for decades. However, the kinds of methods used in education research were established prior to the easy collection and management of data we are in today. While the research approaches into educational data are becoming more sophisticated, it is likely new technologies that leverage the strengths of current (and future) technologies and infrastructures will emerge. These new techniques will support different kinds of understandings about instructional and student processes across the praxis landscape. Much of education research and evaluation has been dominated by a "correctness" paradigm where student work is gauged against predefined correct scores (Behrens & DiCerbo, 2014). However, much of the learning lives of students does not fit into this framework, such as persistence, social networks, motivation, and goals. In the future, will we see these kinds of factors brought into considerations about data use? Will we see measures that are focused on process and more open with regard to different kinds of student contributions becoming part of the evidentiary landscape?

An important resource for learning broadly about impact are the very infrastructures that carry information from and to practitioners. While it is commonplace for technology concerns such as Amazon, Netflix, and Facebook to regularly mine their platform's interaction data, there are only a handful of examples of it being used in education—mostly in EDM and LA traditions.

Engaging and Building Theories

Mature fields are usually organized around theories and models that have followings and are challenged and critiqued and where those theories and models are elaborated/contradicted by research. What theories are guiding the questions that are answered by educational data? As this review showed, there are plenty of essays describing how data in education should work. However, there it is hard to find discussions of those same models; few seek to confirm or challenge the models. The kind of intellectual debate common in some areas of education research has not yet appeared in this one. One notable exception is the work of Bertrand and Marsh (2015), who sought to "complexify" the data use cycle models of Mandinach et al. (2008) and Marsh et al. (2006). These are rare examples, however. Perhaps one of the largest opportunities for the field is the development of testable theories that are refined through the empirical work similar to other sciences.

Reporting for Comparability

The broad framework presented above can be used to help structure the reporting of research for greater comparability. For publications reporting on impact on practice, the following elements may be useful:

1. *Context: Which practices are data being used with.* Context describes the conditions under which the data use is to occur and the activities in the educational enterprise that the data use is intended to address, including

    - *Educational level*, for example, fourth grade or undergraduate education
    - *Topical domain*, for example, math, science, or general studies
    - *The scale of the use* from individual students to classrooms to schools and districts
    - *The modality of instruction*, for example, face-to-face, online, or blended
    - *Instructional or organizational practice*, that is, the focus of the work from assessment to inquiry

The context details are all aspects of the educational practice that can be conducted with or without an inclusion of data or a study of those data systems.

2. *Artifact(s).* The artifacts that are part of any study are those elements that are being used to support decision making, data mining, or analytics. Artifacts can be test scores, activity trace data, surveys, or other information that may originate within the instructional settings or may be external to the activity(s) being studied. Artifacts usually have a life cycle and affordances for various kinds of uses. High-stakes tests, for example, are designed to make specific inferential claims, whereas other kinds of assessments developed by teachers or available on the Internet may have less inferential value (Behrens, Piety, DiCerbo, & Mislevy, 2018). As many conceptual models describe, artifacts frequently go through various transformation activities.

3. *Theories and methods of data use.* Data do not use themselves. They *can* be used in practices and according to theories or models about what their role and contributions of the data are. Some examples of the intended uses of these artifacts include identifying knowledge gaps, supporting conversations among teachers, and aligning instructional content across instructional settings. It is important to understand the ideas driving the data use, as those ideas may relate to the capacity for impact as much as the data themselves. It is important to know how the actual use of data and reports from researchers match with the theories and models that may guide their use. If one were taking an interventionist view of data and asking what the impacts of that data use are, then the artifacts combined with the theories and methods of data use together might constitute the treatment.

4. *Systemic and institutional context.* The systemic context entails other significant aspects of the kinds of pressures practitioners and decision-making educators are engaged in. As studies following NCLB, including Diamond and Spillane (2002), Valli et al. (2008), and others showed, when under pressure to meet accountability targets different schools may use data in different ways. There is a greater need for understanding the conditions that may affect data use. The systemic context represents important information about what else may be occurring that could influence the results that are reported.

5. *Evidence of impact(s).* The study design and kinds of evidence that can be evaluated are found here. This is the level often considered first. After reviewing the literature for this project, it became evident that there were other important aspects of studies that needed to be considered before the evidentiary perspectives. After the issues discussed above are taken into account can the research methods and any findings be best interpreted.

CONCLUDING THOUGHTS

This review had multiple aims. It was looking for evidence of the impact data can have on practice. It was also looking to build a common view of these three largely distinct activities but that are related in their temporal development, underlying logic models, and challenges in developing a consistent evidence base. While there was little evidence in the research literature of a widespread positive impact on practice, this review has shown some different ways to view these activities and their potential for synergy and to affect systems.

Much of what was hoped to be found in this study was not. This absence of evidence, while important, is not the same as evidence of absence. One of the things this review cannot say is that this dimension of the field—collecting, presenting, and making decisions with data—is unimportant. Indeed, the communities studying data use have grown in size and in the kinds of research they do. As the innovations, practice, and research into educational data use mature, the questions about methodological quality may need to be revisited as the norms of peer-reviewed communities take hold. One of the salient characteristics of technology, especially digital technology, is its pace of evolution. In many of the areas where EDM and LA operate, the same areas we have less evidence of impact on practice, the pedagogical approaches are still maturing.

This review leaves a lot of work undone. It took one focus on impact on practice and through it showed how the research landscape surrounding that focus is rich and relatable. In addition to presenting some information about the constitution of these communities, this review has presented synthetic lenses that can be used to make these areas of research stronger, thus supporting greater scientific debate and reflection on models and methods. As these areas of inquiry show no sign of diminished interest, this review will hopefully set the stage for a more coherent and respected field of exploring, understanding, and productively using actionable data.

ACKNOWLEDGMENTS

This chapter has benefitted from the contributions and comments of several people without whom this project would not have been possible. Principally Diane Ketelhut, Laura Hyde, and Scott Moses who provided invaluable thought leadership and in Laura and Scott's cases some initial literature collections to begin the review. Two anonymous reviewers, Fiona Jardine, and Terri Pigott provided useful feedback of various drafts, and Bob Mislevy, as he always does, provided keen insights into the field.

NOTES

[1] The results of the different lists were then brought together in a single source list that was coded for which original lists the pieces came from. When duplicates were found across these lists those items were assigned to multiple lists. Less than one half of 1% of the sources in this list showed an overlap between the lists with all of that coming between LA and EDM pieces and none shared by DDDM.

[2] In this version of the chapter, special issue introductions were classified as reviews leading to these numbers being slightly higher than if the category only included literature reviews.

REFERENCES

Anderson, S., Leithwood, K., & Strauss, T. (2010). Leading data use in schools: Organizational conditions and practices at the school and district levels. *Leadership and Policy in Schools*, *9*, 292–327.

Behrens, J. T., & DiCerbo, K. E. (2014). Technological implications for assessment ecosystems: Opportunities for digital technology to advance assessment. *Teachers College Record, 116*(11). Retrieved from https://eric.ed.gov/?id=EJ1040215

Behrens, J. T., Piety, P., DiCerbo, K. E., & Mislevy, R. J. (2018). Inferential foundations for learning analytics in the digital ocean. In D. Niemi, R. D. Pea, B. Saxberg, & R. E. Clark (Eds.), *Learning analytics in education* (pp. 1–48). Charlotte, NC: Information Age.

Berland, M., Martin, T., Benton, T., Smith, C. P., & Davis, D. (2013). Using learning analytics to understand the learning pathways of novice programmers. *Journal of the Learning Sciences, 22*, 564–599.

Bertrand, M., & Marsh, J. A. (2015). Teachers' sensemaking of data and implications for equity. *American Educational Research Journal, 52*, 861–893.

Blikstein, P., & Worsley, M. (2016). Multimodal learning analytics and education data mining: Using computational technologies to measure complex learning tasks. *Journal of Learning Analytics, 3*, 220–238.

Bouwma-Gearhart, J., & Collins, J. (2015). What we know about data-driven decision making in higher education: Informing educational policy and practice. In *Proceedings of International Academic Conferences* (No. 2805154). London, England: International Institute of Social and Economic Sciences.

Bowers, A. J. (2009). Reconsidering grades as data for decision making: More than just academic knowledge. *Journal of Educational Administration, 47*, 609–629.

Burch, P., & Spillane, J. P. (2003). Elementary school leadership strategies and subject matter: Reforming mathematics and literacy instruction. *Elementary School Journal, 103*, 519–535.

Cetintas, S., Si, L., Xin, Y. P., Zhang, D., Park, J. Y., & Tzur, R. A. (2014). *A joint probabilistic classification model of relevant and irrelevant sentences in mathematical word problems.* Retrieved from https://arxiv.org/abs/1411.5732

Coburn, C. E., & Talbert, J. E. (2006). Conceptions of evidence use in school districts: Mapping the terrain. *American Journal of Education, 112*, 469–495.

Coburn, C., & Turner, E. O. (2011). Research on data use: A framework and analysis. *Measurement: Interdisciplinary Research and Practice, 9*, 173–206. doi:10.1080/153663 67.2011.626729

Cohen, D. K., Spillane, J. P., & Peurach, D. J. (2018). The dilemmas of educational reform. *Educational Researcher, 47*, 204–212.

Crossley, S., Allen, L., Snow, E., & McNamara, D. (2016). Incorporating learning characteristics into automatic essay scoring models: What individual differences and linguistic features tell us about writing quality. *Journal of Educational Data Mining, 8*(2), 1–19.

Darling-Hammond, L. (2015). Can value added add value to teacher evaluation? *Educational Researcher, 44*, 132–137.

Datnow, A., & Hubbard, L. (2016). Teacher capacity for and beliefs about data-driven decision making: A literature review of international research. *Journal of Educational Change, 17*(1), 7–28.

Dede, C. (2015). *Data-intensive research in education: Current work and next steps.* Retrieved from https://cra.org/wp-content/uploads/2015/10/CRAEducationReport2015.pdf

Denton, C. A., Swanson, E. A., & Mathes, P. G. (2007). Assessment-based instructional coaching provided to reading intervention teachers. *Reading and Writing, 20*(6), 569–590.

Diamond, J. B. (2007). Where the rubber meets the road: Rethinking the connection between high-stakes testing policy and classroom instruction. *Sociology of Education, 80*, 285–313.

Diamond, J. B., & Spillane, J. P. (2002). *High stakes accountability in urban elementary Schools: Challenging or reproducing inequality?* (Working paper). Institute for Policy Research.

Diamond, J. B., & Spillane, J. P. (2016). School leadership and management from a distributed perspective: A 2016 retrospective and prospective. *Management Education, 30,* 147–154.

Farley-Ripple, E. N., & Buttram, J. L. (2014). Developing collaborative data use through professional learning communities: Early lessons from Delaware. *Studies in Educational Evaluation, 42,* 41–53.

Gallimore, R., Ermeling, B. A., Saunders, W. M., & Goldenberg, C. (2009). Moving the learning of teaching closer to practice: Teacher education implications of school-based inquiry teams. *Elementary School Journal, 109,* 537–553.

Gummer, E., & Mandinach, E. (2015). Building a conceptual framework for data literacy. *Teachers College Record, 117*(4), 1–22.

Halverson, R., Grigg, J., Prichett, R., & Thomas, C. (2007). The new instructional leadership: Creating data-driven instructional systems in school. *Journal of School Leadership, 17,* 159–194.

Hamilton, L., Halverson, R., Jackson, S. S., Mandinach, E., Supovitz, J. A., Wayman, J. C., ... Steele, J. L. (2009). *Using student achievement data to support instructional decision making.* Retrieved from https://ies.ed.gov/ncee/wwc/Docs/PracticeGuide/dddm_pg_092909.pdf

Henig, J. R. (2013). *The infrastructure of accountability: Data use and the transformation of American education.* Cambridge, MA: Harvard Education Press.

Hopkins, D., Stringfield, S., Harris, A., Stoll, L., & Mackay, T. (2014). School and system improvement: A narrative state-of-the-art review. *School Effectiveness and School Improvement, 25,* 257–281.

Iedema, R. (2003). Multimodality, resemiotization: Extending the analysis of discourse as multi-semiotic practice. *Visual Communication, 2*(1), 29–57.

Knapp, M. S., Swinnerton, J. A., Copland, M. A., & Monpas-Huber, J. (2006). *Data-informed leadership in education.* Seattle, WA: Center for the Study of Teaching and Policy.

Konstantopoulos, S., Miller, S. R., & van der Ploeg, A. (2013). The impact of Indiana's system of interim assessments on reading and math achievement. *Educational Evaluation and Policy Analysis, 35*(4), 481–484.

Krumm, A., Means, B., & Bienkowski, M. (2018). *Learning analytics goes to school: A collaborative approach to improving education.* New York, NY: Routledge.

Lemke, J. L. (2000). Across the scales of time: Artifacts, activities, and meanings in ecosocial systems. *Mind, Culture, and Activity, 7,* 273–290.

Mandinach, E. B., Honey, M., Light, D., & Brunner, C. (2008). A conceptual framework for data-driven decision making. In E. B. Mandinach & M. Honey (Eds.), *Data-driven school improvement: Linking data and learning* (pp. 13–31). New York, NY: Teachers College Press.

Marsh, J. A. (2012). Interventions promoting educators' use of data: Research insights and gaps. *Teachers College Record, 114*(11), 1–48.

Marsh, J. A., & Farrell, C. C. (2015). How leaders can support teachers with data-driven decision making: A framework for understanding capacity building. *Educational Management Administration & Leadership, 43,* 269–289.

Marsh, J. A., Pane, J. F., & Hamilton, L. S. (2006). *Making sense of data-driven decision making in education.* Santa Monica, CA: RAND.

Means, B., Padilla, C., & Gallagher, L. (2010). *Use of education data at the local level: From accountability to instructional improvement.* Washington, DC: U.S. Department of Education.

Moss, P. A., & Piety, P. J. (2007). Introduction: Evidence and decision making. In P. A. Moss (Ed.), *Yearbook of the National Society for the Study of Education: Vol. 106. Evidence and decision making* (pp. 1–14). Hoboken, NJ: Blackwell.

Muldner, K., Burleson, W., Van de Sande, B., & VanLehn, K. (2011). An analysis of students' gaming behaviors in an intelligent tutoring system: Predictors and impacts. *User Modeling and User-Adapted Interaction, 21,* 99–135.

No Child Left Behind Act of 2001. (2002). Public Law No. 107–110, 115 Statute 1425.

Papamitsiou, Z., & Economides, A. A. (2014). Learning analytics and educational data mining in practice: A systematic literature review of empirical evidence. *Journal of Educational Technology & Society, 17*(4), 49–64.

Park, V., & Datnow, A. (2008). Collaborative assistance in a highly prescribed school reform model: The case of success for all. *Peabody Journal of Education, 83*, 400–422.

Peña-Ayala, A. (2014). Educational data mining: A survey and a data mining-based analysis of recent works. *Expert Systems With Applications, 41*, 1432–1462.

Piety, P. J. (2013). *Assessing the educational data movement.* New York, NY: Teachers College Press.

Piety, P. J., Behrens, J., & Pea, R. (2013, April). *Educational data sciences and the need for interpretive skills.* Paper presented at American Educational Research Association Annual Meeting, San Francisco, CA.

Piety, P. J., Hickey, D. T., & Bishop, M. J. (2014). Educational data sciences: Framing emergent practices for analytics of learning, organizations, and systems. In *Proceedings of the fourth international conference on learning analytics and knowledge* (pp. 193–202). New York, NY: ACM.

Piety, P. J., & Pea, R. D. (2018). Understanding learning analytics across practices. In D. Niemi, R. D. Pea, B. Saxberg, & R. E. Clark (Eds.), *Learning analytics in education* (pp. 215–232). Charlotte, NC: Information Age.

Ribes, D., & Finholt, T. A. (2009). The long now of infrastructure: Articulating tensions in development. *Journal for the Association of Information Systems (JAIS): Special Issue on eInfrastructures, 10*, 375–398.

Romero, C., Zafra, A., Luna, J. M., & Ventura, S. (2013). Association rule mining using genetic programming to provide feedback to instructors from multiple-choice quiz data. *Expert Systems, 30*, 162–172.

Rowan, B., & Miller, R. J. (2007). Organizational strategies for promoting instructional change: Implementation dynamics in schools working with comprehensive school reform providers. *American Educational Research Journal, 44*, 252–297.

Scheffel, M., Drachsler, H., Stoyanov, S., & Specht, M. (2014). Quality indicators for learning analytics. *Educational Technology & Society, 17*, 117–132.

Siemens, G. (2012). Learning analytics: Envisioning a research discipline and a domain of practice. In *Proceedings of the 2nd international conference on learning analytics and knowledge* (pp. 4–8). New York, NY: ACM.

Siemens, G., & Baker, R. S. (2012). Learning analytics and educational data mining: Towards communication and collaboration. In *Proceedings of the 2nd international conference on learning analytics and knowledge* (pp. 252–254). New York, NY: ACM.

Sin, K., & Muthu, L. (2015). Applications of big data in education data mining and learning analytics: A literature review. *ICTACT Journal on Soft Computing, 5*(4). Retrieved from http://ictactjournals.in/paper/IJSC_V5_I4_paper6_1035_1049.pdf

Slavin, R. E., Cheung, A., Holmes, G., Madden, N. A., & Chamberlain, A. (2013). Effects of a data-driven district reform model on state assessment outcomes. *American Educational Research Journal, 50*, 371–396.

Stoll, L., Bolam, R., McMahon, A., Wallace, M., & Thomas, S. (2006). Professional learning communities: A review of the literature. *Journal of Educational Change, 7*, 221–258.

Streifer, P. A., & Schumann, J. A. (2005). Using data mining to identify actionable information: Breaking new ground in data-driven decision making. *Journal of Education for Students Placed at Risk, 10*, 281–293.

Sun, J., Przybylski, R., & Johnson, B. J. (2016). A review of research on teachers' use of student data: From the perspective of school leadership. *Educational Assessment, Evaluation and Accountability, 28*(1), 5–33.

Tempelaar, D. T., Rienties, B., & Giesbers, B. (2015). In search for the most informative data for feedback generation: Learning analytics in a data-rich context. *Computers in Human Behavior, 47,* 157–167.

Valli, L., Croninger, R. G., Chambliss, M. J., Graeber, A. O., & Buese, D. (2008). *Test driven: High-stakes accountability in elementary schools.* New York, NY: Teachers College Press.

Van Leeuwen, A., Janssen, J., Erkens, G., & Brekelmans, M. (2014). Supporting teachers in guiding collaborating students: Effects of learning analytics in CSCL. *Computers & Education, 79,* 28–39.

Vialardi, C., Chue, J., Peche, J. P., Alvarado, G., Vinatea, B., Estrella, J., & Ortigosa, Á. (2011). A data mining approach to guide students through the enrollment process based on academic performance. *User Modeling and User-Adapted Interaction, 21,* 217–248.

Wayman, J. C., Shaw, S., & Cho, V. (2017). Longitudinal effects of teacher use of a computer data system on student achievement. *AERA Open, 3*(1), 1–18. doi:10.1177/2332858416685534

Wayman, J. C., & Stringfield, S. (2006). Data use for school improvement: School practices and research perspectives. *American Journal of Education, 112,* 463–468.

Chapter 15

Trauma-Informed Practices in Schools Across Two Decades: An Interdisciplinary Review of Research

M. Shelley Thomas
Shantel Crosby
University of Louisville

Judi Vanderhaar
Kentucky Department of Education

Attention to childhood trauma and the need for trauma-informed care has contributed to the emerging discourse in schools related to teaching practices, school climate, and the delivery of trauma-related in-service and preservice teacher education. However, though trauma-informed systems of care include schools, empirical work informing trauma-informed teaching and teacher education that is reflected back to those audiences is less established. This interdisciplinary overview and synthesis of literature examined interventions used in schools to determine the dominant framework used for promoting and practicing trauma-informed care in schools and the effectiveness of school-based supports for trauma-affected youth to identify implications for changing teaching practice. While multiple disciplines conduct research using different methodologies examining trauma-informed practices in schools, educators are underexamined in this work. Additionally, education researchers began engaging in research on trauma-informed practices in schools more recently, and as such, research emanating from education researchers comprises a small portion of this review. Drawing across the work, we offer recommendations for a more robust, interdisciplinary research agenda with the intentional purpose to change teacher practice.

Literature around trauma-informed systems of care include schools, with the teachers and staff who work in them, as components of multitiered systems of supports (Chafouleas, Johnson, Overstreet, & Santos, 2016). However, the empirical work informing trauma-informed teaching and teacher education that is reflected back to education audiences is less established, "specifically studies that examine

Review of Research in Education
March 2019, Vol. 43, pp. 422–452
DOI: 10.3102/0091732X18821123
Chapter reuse guidelines: sagepub.com/journals-permissions
© 2019 AERA. http://rre.aera.net

particular moves educators make" (Alvarez, 2017, p. 55). This chapter includes an interdisciplinary overview and synthesis of literature examining interventions used in schools that attend to this need by explicitly analyzing and synthesizing existing work aimed at identifying implications for changing teaching practice.

Attention to childhood trauma and the need for trauma-informed care has contributed to the emerging discourse in schools related to teaching practices, school climate, and the delivery of trauma-related in-service and preservice teacher education (Cole et al., 2005; Crosby, 2015; Day et al., 2015; Oehlberg, 2008). Psychological trauma includes experiences or events that are perceived as harmful, create intense distress, and affect an individual's overall well-being (Substance Abuse and Mental Health Services Administration [SAMHSA], 2014). Complex trauma is the result of consistent or repeated traumatic exposure over a period of time, generally resulting in significant dysfunction or reduced well-being (Wolpow, Johnson, Hertel, & Kincaid, 2009). Research has shown that psychological trauma is commonly experienced by children and adolescents (Costello, Erkanli, Fairbank, & Angold, 2002). For example, almost two thirds of adults have reported experiencing adverse emotional events (i.e., trauma) during childhood (Anda et al., 2006). Research has also shown that such trauma in childhood is associated with impediments in school performance, as social, emotional, cognitive, and even brain development can be significantly impeded by traumatic stress (Perfect, Turley, Carlson, Yohanna, & Saint Gilles, 2016). Childhood trauma can negatively affect a students' capacity for self-regulation, organization, comprehension, and memorization (Wolpow et al., 2009), affecting students academically and socially throughout their school experiences.

In schools, trauma-informed education, also referred to as trauma-informed practices, requires administrative buy-in and support, trauma-sensitive classroom practices, positive and restorative responses to behavior, policy and procedure changes, teacher and staff professional development, and strong cross-system collaboration among school staff and mental health professionals (Oehlberg, 2008). Such an approach has been suggested as a means of improving student performance and retention as well as school climate (Oehlberg, 2008). Educators seeking information and resources for trauma-informed practices may locate advocacy and policy articles, as well as organizations that publish guides, toolkits, and best practices. These sources frequently build upon scientific literature to make the case for classroom or school-based recommendations, but few include empirical evidence to support the impact of those recommendations (Day et al., 2015). Indeed, the literature cited here (e.g., Oehlberg, 2008) demonstrates the siloed nature of the empirical work around trauma-informed practices and the subsequent need for interdisciplinary inquiry and dissemination to change teaching practice. Furthermore, implementation of successful trauma-informed approaches in and through schools requires attention to the complexities of school contexts (Chafouleas et al., 2016). The twofold purpose of this review is to examine: (a) lines and overarching methodologies of inquiry and related to trauma-informed school practice and (b) primary findings of the research. By looking across fields as well as where they intersect, we describe current empirical evidence, gaps, and recommendations for interdisciplinary research approaches. We intend this review to support communications of best practices as well as recommendations and advocacy to promote trauma-informed approaches to teaching.

FOUNDATION OF TRAUMA AND TRAUMA-INFORMED CARE

In a historical account of psychological trauma and societal responses, the SAMHSA's Center for Substance Abuse Treatment (2014) describes the origins of trauma conceptualization in the United States. They describe how ideas about trauma launched from literature on war veterans in the 1860s who returned home with physical and emotional stress from their experiences in combat. Early literature attributed such reactions to "moral weakness" (i.e., personal deficits on the part of the individual experiencing the distress) or "battle fatigue" (i.e., needing respite from the war environment). To address such conditions, talk therapy and physical rest were espoused as clinically appropriate treatments. Over a century later, in the 1980s, the American Psychiatric Association formally recognized posttraumatic stress disorder as a clinical diagnosis, marked by the experience of a specific tragic event and subsequently resulting in impaired functioning (American Psychiatric Association, 1980; Center for Substance Abuse Treatment, 2014).

While individual treatment and clinical methods were long seen as the most effective approach to addressing trauma and posttraumatic stress disorder, newer ideas began to emerge about the utility of empowerment and psychosocial models in the treatment of trauma-affected individuals (Center for Substance Abuse Treatment, 2014). For example, peer support became a strong supplemental treatment approach to aid individuals who had experienced catastrophic events. Eventually, as societal consciousness began to focus on the overwhelming plight of many marginalized and vulnerable populations in the United States, trauma's definition began to expand to include interpersonal forms of violence as well as perceived threat or harm. Aiding in the development of this new definition, research began to illuminate the prevalence of such adverse events, particularly among young people. This emergence of focus on youth is partially due to the work of Felitti et al. (1998), who found that more than 50% of adults in their study experienced at least one form of traumatic stress during childhood. They also found that these childhood experiences were positively correlated with significant health challenges later in life (Anda et al., 2006; Felitti et al., 1998). Today, childhood trauma is identified as "America's hidden health crisis" (ACEs Connection, 2016), as youth trauma has risen to the forefront of the trauma landscape. This work shed light on the importance of preventing childhood trauma and also recognizing and addressing the needs of youth exposed to adverse events prior to their journey into adulthood.

This research, in the fields of medicine and mental health services, along with the needs expressed by those receiving services, informed initial ideas about ways in which service agencies could better serve their clients through practices and policies that were sensitive to their traumatic histories (Center for Substance Abuse Treatment,

2014). These ideas, now termed "trauma-informed care," include a number of key features that are supported and promoted at the national level. For example, SAMHSA's trauma-informed approach includes acknowledging the prevalence of trauma, recognizing the impact of these experiences on all individuals, utilizing trauma-sensitive practices and policies, and avoiding practices that may retraumatize (Substance Abuse and Mental Health Services Administration, National Center for Trauma-Informed Care, 2015). In a review of trauma-informed care across various organizations, three core components of trauma-informed care emerged: (a) work-force/professional development, (b) organizational changes, and (c) practice changes (Hanson & Lang, 2016; Maynard, Farina, & Dell, 2017). Such trauma-informed approaches have become widely adopted in many public service sectors (e.g., mental health, child welfare) and have now come to the attention of schools and education authorities. In response to this emerging area of trauma-informed practice in schools, an abundance of resources and frameworks have been developed to address the needs of trauma-affected youth in schools, as described next.

TRAUMA-INFORMED PRACTICE IN SCHOOLS

In order to determine the most frequently promoted practices and approaches that are being recommended to districts to support the use of trauma-informed school practice, we conducted a practice analysis of the websites of national advocacy groups and state Department of Education (DOE) agencies for relevant resources, tools, and information. Some state DOE webpages range from including little information on trauma to virtually nothing mentioned across their website. Some state DOEs, in partnership with universities and nonprofit organizations, and state and federal grant initiatives are making concentrated efforts toward implementation and provide specific guidance on trauma-informed practice approaches. Furthermore, in many states, the content of trauma-informed practice is embedded in or connected to the domains of social and emotional learning, school safety, school discipline, and/or Positive Behavior Interventions and Supports (PBIS). Still, there is wide variation in the depth and breadth of resources and work reflected through each website.

There is also wide variation in the type of resources being provided on DOE webpages, including toolkits, research and/or practice briefs, guidebooks, PowerPoint slides, and online training and learning modules. Many key resources promoted are those developed in the medical, mental health, research/policy/advocacy, and social service fields. As such, they more so provide universal frameworks for implementing trauma-informed practice into any organization. For example, the American Institutes for Research provide a trauma-informed care curriculum to support organizations who seek to embed trauma-informed practices into all aspects of organizational programming (American Institute for Research, 2016). They provide guiding principles in five key domains (i.e., supporting staff development, creating a safe and supportive environment, assessing needs and planning services, involving consumers, and adapting practices). This allows for one to tailor practices, strategies, and training based on the context and population being served. In the plethora of resources being used, there is substantive overlap in the core content of the various frameworks, approaches, and principles. In many of the resources, such as the Wisconsin trauma-sensitive school initiative learning modules, the trauma work is promoted using the same tiered PBIS framework that so many administrators and educators are familiar with: Tier I (universal for 100% of students), Tier II (targeted students, 15%), and Tier III (intensive students, 5%; Wisconsin Department of Public Instruction, 2018). Resources from other state DOEs have either followed a similar PBIS framework or have directly cited Wisconsin's learning modules on their websites.

Much of the widely promoted content designed specifically for educators utilize the aforementioned trauma-informed approach developed by SAMHSA (Substance Abuse and Mental Health Services Administration, National Center for Trauma-Informed Care, 2015). These education-focused resources included various forms such as guidebooks, toolkits, and online learning modules. The most frequently cited and freely available trauma-related resources for educators were reviewed to identify common themes. In general, this content was related to one of the three following categories: (a) Building knowledge—understanding the nature and impact of trauma; (b) Shifting perspectives and building emotionally healthy school cultures; and (c) Self-care for educators. Several specific resources are provided in Table 1 for each of these three categories.

Building Knowledge: Understanding the Nature and Impact of Trauma

Providing educators interdisciplinary knowledge that they likely did not receive during their preservice training is a key feature in many of the state DOE resources. This includes findings from brain science, neurobiology, and mental health to help educators understand trauma's impact on students' social, physical, and psychological well-being, as well as how it may present in their school behaviors. One area of emphasis in the resources is on the "acting out cycle" and its relation to the fight, flight, and freeze response when a student perceives a threat to his or her safety. This information is provided through research briefs, presentations, online modules, videos, and so on, and is foundational for shifting the mindset of educators, administrators, and school staff.

Shifting Perspectives and Building Emotionally Healthy School Cultures

The resource literature places a strong emphasis on using new knowledge to employ empathetic responses to students who are trauma-exposed and avoiding approaching students from a deficit perspective when they exhibit behavior that is considered problematic or disruptive. One widely cited resource (e.g., Brunzell, Stokes, & Waters, 2016; Day et al., 2017; Dorado, Martinez, McArthur, & Leibovitz, 2016; Shamblin, Graham, & Bianco, 2016; West, Day, Somers, & Baroni, 2014), developed by Western Washington University and Washington Superintendent of Public Instruction, provides six principles for compassionate instruction and discipline in the classroom: (a)

TABLE 1
Trauma-Related Resources for Educators

Content Area	Resource	Resource Link
Building knowledge and understanding on the nature and impacts of trauma	Child trauma toolkit for educators from the National Child Traumatic Stress Network	http://www.nctsn.org/sites/ default/files/assets/pdfs/ Child_Trauma_Toolkit_ Final.pdf
	Trauma-informed care resources for educators from the Washington Education Association	https://www.washingtonea. org/pd/other-educator- resources/trauma-informed- resources/
	Trauma-informed schools learning network for girls of color from the National Black Women's Justice Institute and the Center on Poverty and Inequality, Georgetown Law	http://schools4girlsofcolor.org/
Shifting perspectives and building emotionally healthy school cultures	Compassionate schools: The heart of learning and teaching from the Washington Superintendent of Public Instruction	http://www.k12.wa.us/ CompassionateSchools/ HeartofLearning.aspx
	Helping Traumatized Children Learn 1 and 2 from the Massachusetts Advocates for Children and Harvard Law School	https://massadvocates.org/tlpi/
	Trauma-responsive educational practices project	http://www.trepeducator.org/
Self-care for educators	Self-care for educators from the National Child Traumatic Stress Network	https://www.nctsn.org/ resources/self-care-educators
	Secondary traumatic stress from the Treatment and Services Adaptation Center: Resiliency, Hope, and Wellness in Schools	https://traumaawareschools. org/secondarystress
	Secondary traumatic stress and self-care packet from the National Center on Safe Supportive Learning Environments	https://safesupportivelearning. ed.gov/sites/default/ files/Building_TSS_ Handout_3secondary_ trauma.pdf

always empower, never disempower; (b) provide unconditional positive regard; (c) maintain high expectations; (d) check assumptions, observe, and question; (e) be a relationship coach; and (f) provide guided opportunities for helpful participation

(Wolpow et al., 2009). The focus in this resource shifts educator perspectives from viewing students' undesirable behaviors (e.g., avoidance, aggression, disengagement) as inherently bad or oppositional toward viewing each student as having been affected in some way by their experiences.

Shifting Perspectives

Using a trauma lens when handling difficulties with students means shifting the question from "what is wrong with you?" to "what is happening with you?" While some specific Tier II and III school trauma interventions address trauma symptoms explicitly, the literature places greater importance on creating and maintaining a school environment where everyone is treated with compassion and understanding and is empowered and validated in who they are as students and educators. This includes intentionally building and sustaining meaningful relationships between staff and administrators, staff and students, and among the students themselves.

Self-Care for Educators

Educators working with students who are exposed to trauma can experience secondary traumatic stress. This stems from learning about students' trauma exposure, feeling empathetic yet having limited ability to change their situations. The resources emphasize the importance of maintaining self-awareness of secondary or vicarious trauma symptoms and engaging in self-care practices—a trauma-informed approach is a process and not a product—thereby not overemphasizing all the potential impacts/outcomes particularly as it relates to the universal strategies that support a trauma-informed environment in schools for all students and staff. In the large varied landscape of resources, a formally agreed upon approach and practices rooted in evidence should be promoted. Still, this approach should give specific attention to the health and well-being of teachers and other school staff, as they navigate the challenging roles they face with students.

REVIEW OF LITERATURE

The purpose of the review was to identify lines of inquiry related to trauma-informed school practice in empirical literature across disciplines and summarize those to identify implications for changing teaching practice. Teachers and other school personnel find working with students affected by trauma challenging (Souers, 2018), and though they are part of a larger child service system of care that includes the school (National Child Traumatic Stress Network, Schools Committee, 2017), they may not necessarily be fully integrated within those systems in terms of understanding their roles and responsibilities or in implementing or delivering practices (Perry & Daniels, 2016). In cases of natural disasters and other community-wide events, teachers and other school-based providers are also affected by the same challenges as students (Taylor, Weist, & DeLoach, 2012). Likewise, teachers may not feel prepared to take on those responsibilities or may resist doing so, particularly when considering contextual factors such as poverty (Blitz, Anderson, & Saastamoinen, 2016).

Given these challenges, this chapter examined the following research questions: What is the dominant framework used for promoting and practicing trauma-informed care in schools? How effective are school-based supports for trauma-affected youth at the school level (e.g., school climate and disciplinary incidents) and student level (e.g., attendance, academic achievement, sense of belonging)? To address these questions, we also considered the contexts where trauma-informed practices are promoted most heavily (e.g., high-poverty schools, alternative programs, large urban districts, and rural settings). Furthermore, the interdisciplinary nature of this review highlights the timeframes and suggests the mechanisms whereby knowledge and understanding about trauma in other fields migrated into the field of teaching and teacher education. Specifically, this review focused on peer-reviewed articles across disciplines, published between 1998 and 2018. The inclusion of two decades purposefully includes the timeframe prior to the emergence of the Cognitive Behavioral Intervention for Trauma in Schools around the year 2000 (see https://cbitsprogram .org/learn-more) and aligns with the timeframe of the work by Felitti et al. (1998) establishing a correlation between traumatic childhood experiences and challenges later in life.

As a team of researchers and practitioners in teaching and teacher education, social work education, and educational leadership at state and district levels, these lenses shaped decisions regarding how we bounded the review and conducted the descriptive analyses. We targeted studies describing *interventions* used in schools and classrooms and the *effects* of those interventions to determine how researchers outside of education as well as those from within designed research and described findings in order to change teaching practice in support of children affected by trauma. Importantly, selected studies had explicit, rather than implied, implications for classroom or schoolwide impact, involving school-based professionals, in order to change teaching practice.

Method

To examine the impacts, we employed the aforementioned research questions: What is the dominant framework used for promoting and practicing trauma-informed care in schools? How effective are school-based supports for trauma-affected youth at the school level and the student level? We conducted comprehensive searches using a university-based search engine inclusive of the targeted disciplines. Thus, each specific search used multiple databases available through EBSCO Web, Proquest, and ERIC; for example, Proquest searches 25 databases. Because each of the main databases used different terms and limiters, we predetermined these after trial searches. In general, we used "trauma-informed care" OR "trauma-informed practice" as well as variations on those phrases to finalize decisions. We intentionally balanced comprehensiveness and relevance through each trial and used results to inform the final search protocol. For our initial article retrieval, we used the following parameters as limits; again, the process for doing so varied by database: (a) peer-reviewed, empirical work inclusive of qualitative, quantitative, and mixed methods studies; (b) published between the aforementioned timeframe (1998-2018); (c) published in English; and (d) addressing school age (B–12) children. Searches with these parameters identified 4,056 articles for screening. To screen, we analyzed the titles, abstracts, and, in some instances, methods sections to arrive at 163 articles for eligibility.

Given the iterative nature of conducting a review (Moher, Liberati, Tetzlaff, Altman, & Prisma Group, 2009), we also made the following a priori decisions. First, we made decisions regarding, in essence, what we were looking for broadly, to both describe and inform "changing teaching practice in P–20 educational settings" in the spirit of the current *Review of Research in Education* volume. Next, we excluded work in medical journals, including those in psychiatry and nursing. To balance this exclusion, and because the pilot searches retrieved a low number of studies in school psychology, we modified school psychology to the broader field of psychology, which in a few circumstances include psychiatry. We also excluded dissertations but searched authors of dissertations through Google scholar to determine if they had published that specific research in a peer-reviewed outlet.

We added several recursive, intentional searches by identifying and screening articles cited within similar reviews of research, for example. We also targeted special editions in *Journal of Applied Schools Psychology, 28*(30), 2012, and *School Mental Health, 8*(1), 2016, and screening each article in those volumes not retrieved through previous searches as well as several education journals. We added approximately 52 articles through this method to bring the total to 215 articles screened for eligibility. To determine eligibility, we focused on the research, hypothesis, or purpose statements and methods sections and excluded ineligible articles if they (a) were not empirical, (b) were not school-based, (c) did not address trauma specifically, or (d) did not include an intervention. We interpreted "intervention" broadly but determined that studies needed to also (e) provide some type of results or impact of that intervention. Screening decisions eliminated potentially informative work describing processes and innovative directions, particularly in education (e.g., trauma studies; Dutro, 2008; Dutro & Bien, 2014; Wissman & Wiseman, 2011) because researchers did not frame their work as interventions or describe impact, a decision we recognize as a limitation. We also removed duplicates.

We ultimately included 33 articles in the analysis, which were published across 28 journals. To assign disciplines, we first accessed the journal website in June 2018. Next, we located journal information or aims and scope as described on each website. Finally, we categorized each journal into one of four disciplines: education, social work, psychology/psychotherapy, and inter-/multidisciplinary. We used descriptive coding for categorizing (Miles, Huberman, & Saldaña, 2014) and created a spreadsheet including the following: (a) year of publication; (b) outlet; (c) discipline; (d) methodology; (e) research design; (f) research questions/hypothesis/

purpose; (g) participant population; (h) participant demographics; (i) school context, geography, or other mitigating characteristics; (j) grade level or age of participants; (k) data sources; (l) intervention; (m) findings; and (n) implications for changing teaching practice. We also used holistic coding to consider the nuances of each inquiry and determined how they, individually and collectively, contribute to changing teaching practice across settings and push collaborations in the interest of increasing equity and access for children.

Findings

The 33 articles, identified through this review, published between 2001—three years after the earliest year (1998)—and 2018, represent several disciplines and methodologies. We considered each study broadly and individually in order to describe the landscape of empirical work around school-based, trauma-informed interventions and to make observations regarding how researchers intersect in terms of inquiries, contributions, or intended audience. Following general observations about the nature of the reviewed studies, we address the research questions regarding the dominant framework for promoting and practicing trauma-informed care in schools and the effectiveness of school-based supports. Next, we discuss implications for broad discussions on the research on trauma-informed practices in schools. Finally, we draw from across the body work to make recommendations for changing teaching practice and the research on those practices.

In light of the high percentage of school-aged children exposed to trauma (Jaycox et al., 2009) and the unique position of schools within the lives of students and their families as sites for identification and screening of children for services (Beehler, Birman, & Campbell, 2012; Fitzgerald & Cohen, 2012; Woodbridge et al., 2016), school-based interventions occupy a significant position in the continuum of care for these youth. That said, Saltzman, Pynoos, Layne, Steinberg, and Aisenberg (2001, 2003) described the results of a school-based program designed to address two specific challenges to providing services to trauma-exposed youth. First, youth are underidentified, even when school personnel are involved in the referral process, and second, those who are identified may not attend initial treatment. Furthermore, those who attend treatment initially may not remain for a sufficient time (Saltzman et al., 2003).

Even so, many of the studies included in this review highlight the success of school-based interventions in addressing challenges of identification, enrollment, and continuation of services. Indeed, several characteristics about schools create conditions conducive for provision of care, including routines and regularity (SAMHSA, 2014), and schools' geographical locations in or adjacent to disaster areas (Lee, Danna, & Walker, 2017; Mutch & Gawith, 2014) and war-torn regions (Baum et al., 2013). Schools serve communities that include families affected by terrorism (Berger, Pat-Horenczyk, & Gelkopf, 2007), the trauma of immigration (Beehler et al., 2012), and who are of refugee and asylum status (Ehntholt, Smith, & Yule, 2005). Students and their families experience regional conditions exacerbated by poverty in rural Appalachia (Shamblin et al., 2016) and urban areas (Dorado et al., 2016; Santiago et al., 2018); and they are shaped by their minoritized status by race, ethnicity, and language (Allison & Ferreira, 2017; Santiago et al., 2015). Some schools enroll students across all these conditions.

That said, service providers incur other challenges in schools. For example, evaluators identified barriers to school-based interventions and programs. Martin et al. (2017) listed a lack of support from administrators and teachers; competing teacher responsibilities; problems engaging parents, especially if the language about trauma-informed care felt threatening; and stigma regarding mental health concerns (Langley, Santiago, Rodríguez, & Zelaya, 2013). In addition, cultural and linguistic barriers may interfere with a staff's ability to recognize trauma-related symptoms, or to distinguish these symptoms from other challenges, such as cognitive or language delays or normal adjustment to a new language and culture (Langley et al., 2013).

To these, we add the conditions described by Mutch and Gawith (2014), who described schools struggling to cope with earthquake recovery as "too exhausted or more focused on returning to normalcy" (p. 59) to participate in research. Given the position and contexts of schools and the challenges inherent with school-based delivery of interventions, how might research across disciplines inform those involved in all systems to address these challenges while remaining effective and responsive as well as adaptable to local conditions and circumstances?

Some researchers considered contexts significant, as do we, particularly considering that circumstances as well as systemic and historical conditions shape the experiences of youth. Some studies were specifically focused on culturally relevant trauma interventions for oppressed, marginalized, and high-risk groups of students (e.g., racially minoritized immigrants, court-involved youth; Beehler et al., 2012; Day et al., 2017; Ijadi-Maghsoodi et al., 2017; Santiago et al., 2018). Other studies, nine in particular, occurred outside the United States, addressing various contexts, including war-related trauma, exposure to terrorism, natural disasters, violence, and disenfranchisement (Acevedo & Hernandez-Wolfe, 2014; Baum et al., 2013; Berger et al., 2007; Brody & Cohen, 2012; Ehntholt et al., 2005; Morgan, Pendergast, Brown, & Heck, 2015; Mutch & Gawith, 2014; Rønholt, Karsberg, & Elklit, 2013; Wolmer, Laor, Dedeoglu, Siev, & Yazgan, 2005). Additionally, 18 provided city or state locations inside the United States, while others named U.S. regions (e.g., Midwest, Northeast). On the other hand, six authors did not identify the exact locations for their studies though they took place in the United States. Table 2 lists the primary findings of each study, along with the discipline, location or context, method or research tradition, brief description of the participants including their grade or age, and the bounding of the study (e.g., the classroom, school, district, or state) as well as authors' implications for changing teaching practice.

TABLE 2

Overview of Included Studies

Authors and Date	Discipline	Location/ Context for the Study	Method or Research Tradition, Intervention	Participants, Grade or Age, Bounding for Study	Findings	Implications for Changing Teaching Practice
Acevedo and Hernandez-Wolfe (2014)	Interdisciplinary	Cali, Colombia	Qualitative, Consensual Qualitative Research methodology, working with students	21 teachers, elementary, middle school	Witnessing students cope constructively can result in subsequent teacher resilience	Attention to vicarious resilience may empower teachers
Allison and Ferreira (2017)	Social work	New Orleans	Quantitative, a pre-experimental pretest and posttest design, building resilience intervention	23 Latino youth, 14 females, 9 males, 4th, 5th, 6th grades, school	Participation in CBITS in Spanish contributed to significantly fewer symptoms	CBITS is a practical and effective intervention and resource for teachers
Alvarez (2017)	Teaching/teacher education	U.S./urban emergent city	Qualitative, instrumental case study, working with Holocaust curriculum	Black male director of school mentoring program, middle school	Documents effective practices of a successful educator	Need to broaden role of educators and prepare them for that role
Anderson, Blitz, and Saastamoinen (2015)	Interdisciplinary	Northeast United States	Mixed, researcher-developed workshop	16 school staff: 15 females; 15 White, elementary school	Concerns about school climate and the need to address students' trauma, barriers to staff implementation of skills[a]	Need for schoolwide plans, training, and implementation, university involvement can help
Bartlett et al. (2016)	Interdisciplinary	Massachusetts	Mixed, descriptive evaluation, Massachusetts Child Trauma Project	326 children 0-18, Systems—senior leaders, TILT ([trauma-informed leadership teams], e.g., mental health workers, school staff, pediatricians, and court personnel), children. $N = 5$ school personnel, state of Massachusetts	Participation in training linked to individual practices; After 6 months of treatment, children in treatment had fewer symptoms and behavior problems[a]	Those in TILT contributed to evidence-based treatment; collaborations linked to increase effectiveness

(continued)

TABLE 2 (CONTINUED)

Authors and Date	Discipline	Location/ Context for the Study	Method or Research Tradition, Intervention	Participants, Grade or Age, Bounding for Study	Findings	Implications for Changing Teaching Practice
Baum et al. (2013)	Interdisciplinary	Acre, Israel/ aftermath of Second Lebanon War	Quantitative, quasi-experimental, cluster randomized design employing intervention and wait-list control groups, Building Resilience Intervention	Teachers and 563 students, Grades 4–6, 4 elementary schools	Decrease in symptoms of students whose teachers participated in resilience building intervention	Teacher training in resilience building effective in reducing effects of traumatic exposure
Beehler et al. (2012)	Interdisciplinary	Clifton and Jersey City, New Jersey	Quantitative, correlations, random effects regression, Cultural Adjustment and Trauma Services (CATS)	149 immigrant students, high school, 2 school districts	Model was effective with different components affected different student outcomes	Providing an array of services and combining them from a comprehensive model is productive
Berger et al. (2007)	Interdisciplinary	Hadera, Israel	Quantitative, quasi-randomized controlled trial, overshadowing the threat of terrorism	142 students, 2nd to 6th grades, school	School-based training implemented within the curriculum effective	Intervention utilizing trained teachers and implemented within the regular school curriculum can be effective for children who may not otherwise be identified and consequently not have received treatment
Brody and Cohen (2012)	Teaching/teacher education	Israel	Qualitative, working with Holocaust curriculum	9 Elementary teacher preparation students, NA	TP students developed paradigms for dealing with the topic of the Holocaust over time	TP constructions of pedagogical content knowledge of traumatic content during their programs raise questions about teacher educators' possible interventions

(continued)

TABLE 2 (CONTINUED)

Authors and Date	Discipline	Location/ Context for the Study	Method or Research Tradition, Intervention	Participants, Grade or Age, Bounding for Study	Findings	Implications for Changing Teaching Practice
Crosby, Day, Baroni, and Somers (2015)	Social work	Large Midwestern city	Qualitative, focus groups, modified version of Heart of Learning and Teaching Compassion, Resiliency and Academic Success (HLT)	27 teachers, school	Prior to intervention, teachers identified challenges with student behaviors and needs including specific knowledge about trauma, how to manage, and how to balance their roles, after intervention they reported better understanding and connections between classroom behavior and trauma exposure	Need for improved communication and collaboration, and considerations of how to translate training into the classroom
Day et al. (2017)	Social work	Large Midwestern city	Qualitative, phenomenological, modified version of HLT, Monarch Room (MR)	45 females, 13–19 years old, school	Classroom dynamics, external trauma triggers, interpersonal factors, issues with peers, staff, and school personnel all promote and impede school engagement[a]	Importance of engaging youths' voices in how they are engaged or disengaged in schools
Dorado et al. (2016)	Interdisciplinary	San Francisco Unified School District	Quantitative, program evaluation, Healthy Environments and Response to Trauma in Schools (HEARTS)	46, 5–11-year-olds, 175 School staff	HEARTS as effective intervention, increasing staff knowledge and use of trauma-informed practices, decreased discipline referrals and suspensions, students' trauma related symptoms decreased[a]	Needs for more schools to implement, for district-wide approach, and for urban- and rural-specific models
Ehntholt et al. (2005)	Interdisciplinary/ psychology	London	Quantitative, control treatment, Children and War: Teaching Recovery Techniques	26 refugee or asylum-seeking children, 11–12 years, 2 schools	Improvements in treatment group compared with none in control group; however, follow-up with subset shows improvement was not maintained[a]	To sustain improvement, consider groups of students from same country/language, add booster sessions for children and parallel sessions for parents/caregivers

(continued)

TABLE 2 (CONTINUED)

Authors and Date	Discipline	Location/ Context for the Study	Method or Research Tradition, Intervention	Participants, Grade or Age, Bounding for Study	Findings	Implications for Changing Teaching Practice
Graham, Osofsky, Osofsky, and Hansel (2017)	Interdisciplinary	New Orleans	Quantitative, repeated-measures ANOVA, individual sessions with clinicians in social work or psychology	Children, 8–17 years, not specified	Students showed improvement after postdisaster treatment	Disaster-prone regions can benefit, need for flexibility and cultural sensitivity in implementation
Harber (2011)	Art therapy	Not specified	Qualitative, case study, art therapy	17-year-old male, writing, art, NA	Therapist-designed worksheets enabled participant to explore his feelings	Therapeutic process including art created a framework from which to understand past trauma and attachment
Holmes, Levy, Smith, Pinne, and Neese (2015)	Interdisciplinary	Not specified	Quantitative, evaluation, Head Start Trauma Smart (HSTS)	31 children, 31–76 months, nonspecific preschools	Preliminary support for the need for identification and the intervention[a]	HSTS, as an integrated intervention for young children, can be used as a curriculum along with other social emotional curricula with flexibility to address different settings and cultures
Hoover et al. (2018)	School psychology	Connecticut	Quantitative, implementation outcomes and pre–post test, CBITS	316 children, average age 12.2, state-wide	Students improved in PTSD symptoms, behavioral problems, some improvement in functioning, caregivers were very satisfied[a]	Successful scaling up of school-based model has implications for other states; implementation support included district and school support
Ijadi-Maghsoodi et al. (2017)	School psychology	Southwest United States/ urban	Mixed, evaluation, Resilience Classroom Curriculum adapted to the community	100 students, 9th grade, not clear	Students demonstrated improved resilience scores, both students and teachers received the curriculum well[a]	Use of students as participant/ researchers, teachers reported positive reactions, recommend future directions include teachers, even if passively

(continued)

436

TABLE 2 (CONTINUED)

Authors and Date	Discipline	Location/Context for the Study	Method or Research Tradition, Intervention	Participants, Grade or Age, Bounding for Study	Findings	Implications for Changing Teaching Practice
Jaycox et al. (2009)	Interdisciplinary	LASUD	Quantitative, pilot, Support for Students Exposed to Trauma (SSET)	78 students participated in the intervention, middle school	Teachers delivered SSET program with fidelity, intervention effective with high symptoms showed most reduction, students with low symptoms showed little reduction	SSET program delivered by teachers potentially effective and feasible in addressing PTSD and depression in low-income, urban students
Lawson and Alameda-Lawson (2012)	Education	Midsized city, western state	Qualitative, case study, CAN parent engagement program	32 parents, Spanish-speaking Latina, one elementary school community	Descriptions of barriers and traumatic experiences parents faced as well as their engagement	School leaders along with others can support engaging parents as communities of practice, reducing barriers to children's learning, while supporting parents' efforts, tapping into their insights
Lee et al. (2017)	Social work	New Orleans	Qualitative, Classroom–Community Consultation (C3)	5 adult females, not specified	Participants shared how and why they became involved with C3, the impact of the consultation, how C3 helped them grow as practitioners and connected them with additional resources, and their perspective on implications for linking community- and school-based mental health services	Linking school-based and community-based services can be beneficial for the professionals and students; investing in people important as is flexibility and responsiveness to community
Levendosky and Buttenheim (2001)	Interdisciplinary	Not provided	Qualitative, individual therapy and multimethod treatment	11-year-old female, individual	Use of relational, developmental, and trauma theories helpful in understanding and addressing child's symptoms and behaviors; school interventions effective	Development of relationships with teacher, who are among the primary adults in a patient's life, supported healthier internal growth

(continued)

437

TABLE 2 (CONTINUED)

Authors and Date	Discipline	Location/ Context for the Study	Method or Research Tradition, Intervention	Participants, Grade or Age, Bounding for Study	Findings	Implications for Changing Teaching Practice
Morgan et al. (2015)	Education	Queensland, Australia	Mixed, trauma-informed practice as shaping educator identity	20 teachers and staff, not specified	Identities are challenged and changed by exploring impact of trauma on students' development and learning; commitment to trauma-informed practice and relational pedagogy requires educator identities to be co-constructed and negotiated	Identity development in these educators can inform practice for educators in other settings
Mutch and Gawith (2014)	Teaching/teacher education	New Zealand	Qualitative, children engaged in research on their own experiences	Not specified, primary school, three schools	Children found projects helpful, supportive in contextualizing experiences	Schools can provide processing activities to help children's perspectives and recovery from disaster events
Perry and Daniels (2016)	Interdisciplinary	New Haven, Connecticut	Mixed, CBITS	32 school personnel, 17 students, pre-K to 8th, school level	Trio of Services Professional Development, Care Coordination, and Clinical Services described, foundation year important for sustaining	Understanding components and process essential in order to plan evaluations
Ronholt et al. (2013)	Multidisciplinary	Denmark	Quantitative, nonrandomized; noncontrolled, specifically designed intervention	108 children, Grades 1–9 (Denmark)	Children's PTSD symptoms reduced from pretreatment to posttreatment	Preliminary evidence of feasibility for screening instrument suitable for use by teachers and other school-based personnel; treatment may help to alleviate PTSD symptoms
Saltzman et al. (2001)	Psychology	Not specified	Quantitative, UCLA school-based trauma and grief-focused treatment	26 students, middle school	Participation in group treatment as an intervention may be related to improved academic and behavior measures[a]	Students exposed to community violence may not be identified or treated; this can impair school performance[a]

(continued)

TABLE 2 (CONTINUED)

Authors and Date	Discipline	Location/ Context for the Study	Method or Research Tradition, Intervention	Participants, Grade or Age, Bounding for Study	Findings	Implications for Changing Teaching Practice
Salzman et al. (2003)	Psychology	Not specified	Quantitative, UCLA school-based trauma and grief-focused treatment	26 students, 11–14 years, 68% Hispanic, 28% African American, 4% Caucasian	Significant barriers to receiving appropriate mental health services, at multiple levels, including at the school district level. Tentative finding that participation link to improvement in symptoms and increased academic performance. Lack of reduction in depressive symptoms[a]	A school-based model of identification and treatment may reduce symptoms and enable students to perform better in school
Santiago et al. (2015)	Interdisciplinary	Not provided/ urban	Quantitative/quasi-experimental, CBITS plus family	40 child-parent dyads, predominately Latino, low-income 5th to 8th grades	Parents who completed the family portion reported greater satisfaction and participation	Family involvement in CBITS may contribute to children's well-being
Santiago et al. (2018)	School psychology	Illinois/urban	Quantitative, Bounce Back program	52 first to fourth graders, predominately Latino, low income, 8 schools within one district	Bounce Back is an effective intervention; however, there were no significant effects for teacher-reported behavior[a]	Teachers are important in screening and they need training to do so; need to evaluate with different populations and include qualitative approaches to understand implementation process and challenges

(continued)

439

TABLE 2 (CONTINUED)

Authors and Date	Discipline	Location/ Context for the Study	Method or Research Tradition, Intervention	Participants, Grade or Age, Bounding for Study	Findings	Implications for Changing Teaching Practice
Shamblin et al. (2016)	Interdisciplinary	Appalachia/SE Ohio	Quantitative, pre–post, Early Childhood Mental Health Consultation (ECMHC), Project LAUNCH	217 preschoolers, 11 teachers, 11 classrooms in three schools	Improvement in teacher confidence and optimism toward affecting children, increased ratings of children's resilience, decreased ratings of negative attributes[a]	Teacher confidence and hopefulness affected students' behaviors. School–community partnerships created synergy; traumatic events and regional stressors related to poverty supported through ecological view
West et al. (2014)	Interdisciplinary	Large Midwestern city	Qualitative, phenomenology, modified version of HLT; MR intervention	39, 14- to 18-year-old females, alternative school	Students described behaviors, causes, and suggestions	Need for trauma-informed approaches in school settings and for alternatives to suspension/expulsion (Monarch room), importance of student voices
Wolmer et al. (2005)	Psychology	Turkey	Quantitative, controlled 3-year follow-up with multiple informants, school reactivation program (author designed?)	287 children, 9- to 17-year-old, three schools in disaster area	Severity of posttraumatic, grief, and dissociative symptoms of the two groups comparable; teachers blind to group assignment rated participating children significantly higher than the control group in terms of adaptive functioning, academic performance, and behavior[a]	Demonstrates necessity of early interventions postdisaster, teachers are capable to implement clinical interventions

Note. CBITS = Cognitive Behavioral Intervention for Trauma in Schools; PTSD = posttraumatic stress disorder.
[a]Explored effectiveness at school or student level.

Considerations of Frameworks

Overall, our review did not identify a particular framework as dominant among this research for either promoting or practicing trauma-informed care in schools or researching trauma-informed practices in schools. We based this determination on the types of interventions researched and the range of methods used by researchers to examine those interventions. Additionally, we identified methodological decisions regarding study participants and how studies were bounded within settings. Similarly, researchers selected a variety of disciplinary outlets for their work.

The 33 articles included the practices of 30 different interventions. We describe studies according to the most frequently used methods or research traditions as well as the most common disciplinary outlets for this work in order to identify gaps and future directions for research in education and other fields in order to change teacher practice.

Across these 33 articles, researchers used quantitative methodologies most frequently. Seventeen articles included quantitative inquiries, followed by 10 qualitative inquires. Researchers used mixed methods least often, as only six studies employed mixed methodologies. Authors explicitly identified eight studies, or just under 25% of the work reviewed, as evaluations; five of these used quantitative measures, two used mixed methods, and one was qualitative. The two quantitative evaluation studies used discipline and climate measures to determine program effectiveness (Dorado et al., 2016; Holmes et al., 2015), positioned their study toward "bringing a trauma lens to the 'school to prison pipeline' conversation" (Dorado et al., 2016, p. 164), and urged for "the creation of more safe and positive school climates" (Dorado et al., 2016, p. 173).

Based on our methodological criteria and descriptive coding, we categorized 19 articles published in inter-/multidisciplinary journals, the most of any category, followed by six in psychology/psychotherapy journals, five in education outlets, and three in social work publications. We raise questions, however, about which disciplines are included in inter- and multidisciplinary studies or published in outlets identified as such, as many research teams did not identify their disciplinary affiliations, nor explain how disciplinary frames informed their perspectives. Lawson and Alameda-Lawson (2012) serve as a notable counterexample of that trend.

Still, other studies approached trauma-informed practice from the lens of students. In particular, these studies (i.e., Acevedo & Hernandez-Wolfe, 2014; Anderson et al., 2015; Berger et al., 2007; Ijadi-Maghsoodi et al., 2017; West et al., 2014) utilized students' voices through focus groups or by incorporating students as participant-researchers.

Overall, studies across the aforementioned disciplines examined interventions that were derived from various, but similar, theoretical approaches and foundations. Seemingly, the emergence and rapid growth of trauma-informed care into the educational realm, as evidenced by these findings, has occurred with no standard, formally agreed upon terms or framework when it comes to implementing trauma-informed practices in districts and schools specifically. While there are some commonly identi-fied foundational resources and frameworks promoted through grants, legislation, and institutions, there in fact is currently no consensus on use or clear operationaliza-tion of the terms "trauma-informed approach," "trauma sensitive," "trauma- informed system" (Hanson & Lang, 2016; Maynard et al., 2017).

Through our review, we found that education research identified through the search parameters were published within the current decade, with the first two pub-lished in 2012, suggesting that date as when research on trauma-informed practices in schools migrated into education. However, Dutro's (2008) aforementioned trauma study along with similar work published in the field but excluded through our criteria were done within the timespan, raising questions about how trauma studies literature may inform interdisciplinary research.

As mentioned previously, because many research teams did not describe their dis-ciplinary perspectives, we cannot determine with certainty that researchers with edu-cation foci were not involved in other studies. That said, the five studies published in education journals described interventions that can be characterized as interventions of experience. That is, teachers/educators were shaped by their experiences working with trauma-affected youth (Alvarez, 2017; Morgan et al., 2015), preservice teachers were shaped by working through targeted curriculum over time (Brody & Cohen, 2012), and children engaged in their own participatory research processes (Mutch & Gawith, 2014). Similarly, Lawson and Alameda-Lawson's (2012) case study explored Latino parents' engagement through a communities of practice approach. Thus, we urge researchers across all disciplines to consider the potential for research using edu-cational lenses, described later.

Effectiveness of Trauma-Informed Practice

As mentioned, the 33 articles explored 30 different interventions. To highlight the different interventions included in this literature, we first list them here. A compre-hensive table provides details about each study (see Table 2).

- Bounce Back (Santiago et al., 2018)
- Cognitive Behavioral Intervention for Trauma in Schools (Allison & Ferreira, 2017; Hoover et al., 2018; Perry & Daniels, 2016; Santiago et al., 2015)
- Classroom Community Consultation (C3) (Lawson & Alameda-Lawson, 2012; Lee et al., 2017)
- Cultural Adjustment Trauma Services (CATS) (Beehler et al., 2012)
- Early Childhood Mental Health Consultation (ECMHC) along with project LAUNCH (Shamblin et al., 2016)
- Head Start Trauma Smart (Holmes et al., 2015)
- HEARTS (Dorado et al., 2016)
- Individual treatment (Graham et al., 2017)
- Monarch Room; Modified Heart of Learning and Teaching training (Crosby et al., 2015; Day et al., 2017; West et al., 2014)

- Resilience Classroom Curriculum (Ijadi-Maghsoodi et al., 2017)
- Support for Students Exposed to Trauma (SSET) (Jaycox et al., 2009)
- Trauma-Informed Leadership Teams (TILT) (Bartlett et al., 2016)

Thirteen of the 33 studies used school or student-level measures for effectiveness. Those researchers looked at reductions in symptoms of trauma and/or depression resulting from trauma-informed school-based practices (e.g., Allison & Ferreira, 2017; Baum et al., 2013; Graham et al., 2017), but more than half of the researchers did not use school-level measures of climate or disciplinary/behavior incidents, nor student-level measures of attendance, academic achievement, or students' sense of belonging to determine effectiveness. Still, researchers used other forms of evidence to support the effectiveness of each in the published work, with 32 of the 33 studies finding their respective interventions to be "effective" to some degree, duly noting important limitations. The one exception, Anderson et al.'s (2015) needs assessment, workshop implementation, and postworkshop survey and focus groups tapped the ongoing concerns of classroom staff around trauma-informed teaching and, significantly, school climate.

However, studies often underspecified contexts and demographics for their studies, giving too few details about participants, locations, and particularly the schools and/or classrooms where students received or participated in interventions. Along with researchers, we also recognize the nature of much of this work as pilots (Jaycox et al., 2009; Santiago et al., 2015) and preliminary studies (Holmes et al., 2015) rather than extensive randomized trials that provide more "rigorous" illustrations of effectiveness, with both "rigor" and "effectiveness" as terms interpreted differently across disciplines. That said, findings suggest that, within and across disciplines and interventions, more research is needed on the utility of trauma-informed practice, as well as the relationship between those and school disciplinary policies and practices.

DISCUSSION AND IMPLICATIONS

Given the findings that, at this point, there is no dominant or formally agreed upon framework for trauma-informed practices, as well as no consistent determination of effectiveness, it is important to examine what is informing understandings and implementation of trauma-informed practices occurring in states, districts, and schools. Additionally, we question how researchers and advocates attend to the complexities in school settings in general as well as in particular school contexts (Chafouleas et al., 2016). Furthermore, in many instances across the recommended practices promoted on DOE websites as well as in some of the research literature, authors and advocates were unclear or not explicit in providing evidence that the guidance offered was rooted in an empirical base. Furthermore, because disciplinary perspectives were underreported, disciplinary perspectives for "evidence" were not well grounded. This raises additional questions inherent in interdisciplinary work, such as, is the same term—"effective," for example, defined and understood the same in a mixed method evaluation as it is in a case study? Is "effectiveness" determined similarly within the field of education as it is in psychology or social work? With respect to language use, an established lexicon and protocol is needed to ensure clarity and consistency for the individuals involved and the researchers examining practices.

Directions for Research

We recognize and respect the necessary protections around human subjects in disseminating research. However, given the need for more research in this area as well as interdisciplinary research, we urge researchers to include demographic and contextual information and to do so ethically. Discussions of the ethics of deductive disclosure exist across many fields (e.g., Kaiser, 2009; Sanjari, Bahramnezhad, Fomani, Shoghi, & Cheraghi, 2014), providing the rationale for inclusion of demographic information and useful guidelines to avoid harm to particular populations (Schenk & Williamson, 2005).

We also recommend researchers to consider if and how they can provide significant contextual details so that subsequent researchers can appropriately continue along lines of research or identify gaps. For example, schools can be public, private, charter, alternative, and located in urban, suburban, or rural communities in different parts of the United States and other countries. Communities of minoritized youth and families experience both common and distinctive challenges and oppressions. While no experience of trauma is monolithic, as a community of researchers, we must grapple with questions at the system level as well as the granular level of the classroom; therefore, more contextual information is critical.

Implications Across the Research of Trauma-Informed Practices

We begin the discussion of implications across all disciplines of research by noting the dearth of empirical work within this review describing how teachers use their craft—teaching—as a component of the aforementioned systems of care (Alvarez, 2017), and leading up to that, considering how teachers' preservice experiences throughout their preparation programs can contribute to those practices. Rather, researchers positioned teachers as a source of referral or another service provider within the system of care (National Child Traumatic Stress Network, Schools Committee, 2017). Indeed, how might teaching practice, including instructional design, itself contribute to the system of care?

In advocating for trauma-informed positive education, Brunzell et al. (2016) urge providers to consider strengths approaches (e.g., how can educators/others build on students' positive attributes). Educators, including those in teaching and teacher education, frequently draw upon this perspective, and research in this review found that teachers also benefitted from their interactions and relationships with students (Alvarez, 2017; Morgan et al., 2015). We see this as an important framing for researchers outside education to consider. Additionally, several of the studies in this review (i.e., Acevedo & Hernandez-Wolfe, 2014; Anderson et al., 2015; Berger et al., 2014; Ijadi-Maghsoodi et al., 2017; West et al., 2014) speak to the significance of school climate from students' perspectives. Therefore, we also see value in exploring student perspectives in this research and practice, as student-guided attention to supportive and nurturing school climates is integral to trauma-informed school practices. It may also be worthwhile to consider ways in which district and school practices and policies, particularly around discipline and punishment, can cause retraumatization for students and replace exclusionary, deficit approaches with those that are informed by the science of trauma and recovery. In Table 2, we provide an exhaustive list of the practice implications derived from this review.

There is a noted trend-like nature among educational initiatives that are ever-changing and at times overwhelming to educators who may be tasked to implement multiple initiatives at once. Similar to trauma-informed school practice, there has been a noteworthy growth in interest and implementation of other approaches such as PBIS, social emotional learning, restorative practices, mindfulness, emphasis on school culture and climate, and so on. Many of these approaches provide healing, connection, support, and learning that are particularly helpful for trauma-exposed students. Trauma-informed practices in schools should not be perceived as just "another thing that will come and go"—rather due to the ever-increasing levels of adversity facing children and youth in our society, the need for providing environments where students feel cared for, safe, and empowered will continue to be tremendous.

Out of necessity, schools have pursued trauma-informed practices and interventions through partnerships with local mental health agencies and universities (e.g., Anderson et al., 2015). However, the core components of trauma-informed practices should also be considered at every level of the educational system. If schools are finding ways to ensure they are responsive to trauma, then districts, state, and federal education offices, and colleges of education should also consider how they are supporting widespread trauma-informed practices both internally and externally. This includes attention to all protocols and procedures, forms, accountability systems, partnerships, and trainings.

Recommendations for Changing Teacher Education Policy, Practice, and Research

Given the relatively recent entry of teaching and teacher education literature into discussions of trauma-informed practices in schools, identified as around 2012 through this review, we draw upon those contributions, the larger body of work identified, as well as the analyses of websites of national advocacy groups and state DOEs to recommend the following actions for research, policy, and practice in those fields.

Broaden Recognition and Understandings of Trauma and Its Impact

The system of care approach (National Child Traumatic Stress Network, Schools Committee, 2017) encompasses all individuals within programs and agencies that are in contact with young people. Furthermore, research demonstrates the need for consensus within schools implementing trauma-informed practices (Metz, Naoom, Halle, & Bartley, 2015). That said, school staff are called to participate in that system without explicit reference to their specific positions or types of interactions with young people. Schools are composed of caring adults in many roles, necessitating inclusion of a wider range of professionals in school-based care. All staff who interact with students, including but not limited to cafeteria workers, bus drivers, and custodial staff, are integral to school culture and may be the only people with whom students feel a connection. While we located individual districts in our professional experiences that are intentionally integrating these staff in trainings and school-wide practices, the experiences and perspectives of these individuals were virtually nonexistent in the literature as only two studies included school-based personnel who were not teachers or administrators: Anderson et al.'s (2015) study of professional development for classroom staff included teaching assistants, classroom aides, and paraprofessionals, and Alvarez's (2017) case study of an educator who serves as "program director of an in school mentoring program" (p. 58). Thus, the experiences and impacts of all school-based staff is underexplored. How can their experiences, skills, and contributions add to the research base?

Shifting From Deficit Notions of Trauma

As described previously, early literature on the impact of trauma positioned individual responses to trauma as "moral weakness." Though we are more than a century and a half from such framings, we need to recognize how contemporary conceptions re-inscribe deficit perceptions of individuals and essentialize their experiences. In his essay explaining the limitations of trauma-informed care, Shawn Ginwright (2018) described his experiences working with one youth in particular. After Ginwright explained to a group of youth how trauma can influence the brain and health, one young man stopped Ginwright, "I am more than what happened to me" (Para 5). Likewise, we urge educators along with others across systems of care to consider the implications of language and framings to include the voices of those effected (i.e., Acevedo & Hernandez-Wolfe, 2014; Anderson et al., 2015; Berger et al., 2014; Ijadi-Maghsoodi et al., 2017; West et al., 2014) and disrupt deficit notions of trauma-affected youth toward asset-based perspectives and actions. Ginwright refers to this approach as "healing centered" (The promise of healing centered engagement, Para 1). Indeed, Mr. Sellers, the educator in Alvarez's (2017) study, understood the nuanced, complex lives of students as he actively worked with them to understand and address structural inequities. Acevedo and Hernandez-Wolfe (2014) describe the "vicarious resilience" as a positive influence developed in teachers who worked with underserved learners in Colombia. Advocacy and policy pieces likewise call for asset or strengths-based approaches (Wolpow et al., 2009) and resiliency (Chafouleas et al., 2016) approaches. How might teacher education research methodologies using critical frameworks drive these calls forward?

Centering Culturally Responsive Instruction

Cultural responsiveness, or relatedly, culturally sustaining (Paris, 2012; Paris & Alim, 2017) practices assume the aforementioned calls to dismantle deficit notions. Additionally, several researchers (Beehler et al., 2012; Dorado et al., 2016; Lawson & Alameda-Lawson, 2012) include cultural responsiveness within program descriptions and recommendations from the research. We raise additional questions about how centering teaching that is culturally responsive/sustaining within trauma-informed classrooms might provide depth to the aforementioned research and opportunities to support students in positive directions.

Organizational Support to Promote Staff Well-Being

While self-care is noted in the resources as a critical element for educators who are exposed daily to students dealing with trauma and adversity, putting the full onus on individual staff members to support their well-being in light of the known effects of secondary trauma is not sufficient. SAMHSA (2014) recommends that leadership take action to promote organizational culture, policies, and practices to support staff. These include redesigning policies around training and scheduling, focus on prevention by being proactive in supporting stress management, building and reinforcing natural support systems for employees, and evaluating efforts. In education, the reality of secondary/vicarious trauma needs to be considered at every level of the system (federal, state, district, schools). In the high-poverty, high-stress schools, secondary trauma is underestimated. While self-care is promoted as component of trauma-informed practice, administrators at school and district levels should shoulder responsibility for embedding approaches and practices that encourage self-care and regulation for all adults in schools, including teachers and staff.

CONCLUSION

In summary, this chapter outlined the current, yet ever-evolving landscape of research informing trauma-informed practices in schools. To be sure, each study contributes to a collective understanding, but only by moving forward with a more robust, truly interdisciplinary research agenda can all stakeholders better understand and comprehensively address trauma through the schools. Given our finding that a key feature of state DOE resources centered on providing educators interdisciplinary knowledge that they likely did not receive during their preservice programs, we recognize the gaps in knowledge and practice among educators and call for an intentional, well-grounded, and methodologically sound research and practice agenda that drives changes in teaching practice. To that end, educators must also recognize their role and accept their responsibilities to ameliorate the consequences of trauma on youth.

Educational researchers along with school-based practitioners would be wise to incorporate pioneering research occurring in neuroscience, psychology, and social work to better inform their research and practice agendas. Likewise, we encourage researchers outside of education to position teachers and, specifically, teaching, as well as the other adults in schools (i.e., professional school counselors, teaching assistants, and bus drivers) and their activities more prominently in their research agendas.

Finally, we advocate for a truly systems-wide discussion in service of a research-informed practices approach that results in actionable recommendations and respect for all individuals and components of the system with explicit attention to schools. Because school-based practitioners confront the impacts of trauma in the lives of students on a daily basis, we urge that this work moves forward expediently with prevention and recovery at every level of the system in mind.

ACKNOWLEDGMENTS

This research was supported by the University of Louisville's Cooperative Consortium for Transdisciplinary Social Justice Research. The Consortium is directed by the Anne Braden Institute for Social Justice Research and the Muhammad Ali Institute for Peace and Justice, in collaboration with the Brandeis Laboratory for Citizenship, the Commonwealth Institute of Kentucky, and Health Sciences Center Office of Diversity and Inclusion.

ORCID ID

M. Shelley Thomas https://orcid.org/0000-0001-8796-1303

REFERENCES

References marked with an asterisk are included in the review.
ACEs Connection: A Community-of-Practice Social Network. (2016). *Childhood trauma: America's hidden health crisis.* Retrieved from https://www.acesconnection.com/g/los-angeles-aces-connection/clip/childhood-trauma-america-s-hidden-health-crisis
*Acevedo, V. E., & Hernandez-Wolfe, P. (2014). Vicarious resilience: An exploration of teachers and children's resilience in highly challenging social contexts. *Journal of Aggression, Maltreatment & Trauma, 23,* 473–493. doi:10.1080/10926771.2014.904468
*Allison, A. C., & Ferreira, R. J. (2017). Implementing cognitive behavioral intervention for trauma in schools (CBITS) with Latino youth. *Child & Adolescent Social Work Journal, 34,* 181–189.
*Alvarez, A. (2017). "Seeing their eyes in the rearview mirror": Identifying and responding to students' challenging experiences. *Equity & Excellence in Education, 50*(1), 53–67.
American Institute for Research. (2016). *Trauma informed care curriculum.* Retrieved from https://www.air.org/resource/trauma-informed-care-curriculum
American Psychiatric Association. (1980). *Diagnostic and statistical manual of mental disorders* (3rd ed.). Washington, DC: Author.
Anda, R. F., Felitti, V. J., Bremner, J. D., Walker, J. D., Whitfield, C., Perry, B. D., . . . Giles, W. H. (2006). The enduring effects of abuse and related adverse experiences in childhood: A convergence of evidence from neurobiology and epidemiology. *European Archives of Psychiatry and Clinical Neuroscience, 256,* 174–186. doi:10.1007/s00406-005-0624-4

*Anderson, E. M., Blitz, L. V., & Saastamoinen, M. (2015). Exploring a school-university model for professional development with classroom staff: Teaching trauma-informed approaches. *School Community Journal, 25,* 113–134.

*Bartlett, J. D., Barto, B., Griffin, J. L., Fraser, J. G., Hodgdon, H., & Bodian, R. (2016). Trauma-informed care in the Massachusetts child trauma project. *Child Maltreatment, 21,* 101–112. doi:10.1177/1077559515615700

*Baum, N. L., Cardozo, B. L., Pat-Horenczyk, R., Ziv, Y., Blanton, C., Reza, A., . . . Brom, D. (2013). Training teachers to build resilience in children in the aftermath of war: A cluster randomized trial. *Child & Youth Care Forum, 42,* 339–350.

*Beehler, S., Birman, D., & Campbell, R. (2012). The effectiveness of cultural adjustment and trauma services (CATS): Generating practice-based evidence on a comprehensive, school-based mental health intervention for immigrant youth. *American Journal of Community Psychology, 50,* 155–168.

*Berger, R., Pat-Horenczyk, R., & Gelkopf, M. (2007). School-based intervention for prevention and treatment of elementary-students' terror-related distress in Israel: A quasi-randomized controlled trial. *Journal of Traumatic Stress, 20,* 541–551.

Blitz, L. V., Anderson, E. M., & Saastamoinen, M. (2016). Assessing perceptions of culture and trauma in an elementary school: Informing a model for culturally responsive trauma-informed schools. *Urban Review, 48,* 520–542.

*Brody, D. L., & Cohen, H. (2012). "Touch it lightly": Israeli students' construction of pedagogical paradigms about an emotionally laden topic. *Journal of Early Childhood Teacher Education, 33,* 269–286.

Brunzell, T., Stokes, H., & Waters, L. (2016). Trauma-informed positive education: Using positive psychology to strengthen vulnerable students. *Contemporary School Psychology, 20*(1), 63–68.

Center for Substance Abuse Treatment. (2014). *Appendix C of treatment improvement protocol series, No. 57: Trauma-informed care in behavioral health services.* Rockville, MD: Substance Abuse and Mental Health Services Administration. Retrieved from https://www.ncbi.nlm.nih.gov/books/NBK207202/

Chafouleas, S. M., Johnson, A. H., Overstreet, S., & Santos, N. M. (2016). Toward a blueprint for trauma-informed service delivery in schools. *School Mental Health, 8,* 144–162.

Cole, S. F., O'Brien, J. G., Gadd, M. G., Ristuccia, J., Wallace, D. L., & Gregory, M. (2005). *Helping traumatized children learn.* Boston: Massachusetts Advocates for Children.

Costello, E. J., Erkanli, A., Fairbank, J. A., & Angold, A. (2002). The prevalence of potentially traumatic events in childhood and adolescence. *Journal of Traumatic Stress, 15,* 99–112. doi:10.1023/A:1014851823163

Crosby, S. D. (2015). An ecological perspective on emerging trauma-informed teaching practices. *Children & Schools, 37,* 223–230.

*Crosby, S. D., Day, A. G., Baroni, B. A., & Somers, C. L. (2015). School staff perspectives on the challenges and solutions to working with court-involved students. *Journal of School Health, 85,* 347–354.

*Day, A. G., Baroni, B., Somers, C., Shier, J., Zammit, M., Crosby, S., . . . Hong, J. S. (2017). Trauma and triggers: Students' perspectives on enhancing the classroom experiences at an alternative residential treatment-based school. *Children & Schools, 39,* 227–237.

Day, A., Somers, C., Baroni, B., West, S., Sanders, L., & Peterson, C. (2015). Evaluation of a trauma-informed school intervention with girls in a residential facility school: Student perceptions of school environment. *Journal of Aggression, Maltreatment & Trauma, 24,* 1086–1105.

*Dorado, J. S., Martinez, M., McArthur, L. E., & Leibovitz, T. (2016). Healthy Environments and Response to Trauma in Schools (HEARTS): A whole-school, multi-level, prevention and intervention program for creating trauma-informed, safe and supportive schools. *School Mental Health, 8,* 163–176. doi:10.1007/s12310-016-9177-0

Dutro, E. (2008). "That's why I was crying on this book": Trauma as testimony in responses to literature. *Changing English, 15,* 423–434.

Dutro, E., & Bien, A. C. (2014). Listening to the speaking wound: A trauma studies perspective on student positioning in schools. *American Educational Research Journal, 51,* 7–35.

*Ehntholt, K., Smith, P., & Yule, W. (2005). School-based cognitive-behavioural therapy group intervention for refugee children who have experienced war-related trauma. *Clinical Child Psychology & Psychiatry, 10,* 235–250.

Felitti, V. J., Anda, R. F., Nordenberg, D., Williamson, D. F., Spitz, A. M., Edwards, V., . . . Marks, J. S. (1998). Relationship of childhood abuse and household dysfunction to many of the leading causes of death in adults: The adverse childhood experiences (ACE) study. *American Journal of Preventative Medicine, 14,* 245–258.

Fitzgerald, M. M., & Cohen, J. C. (2012). Trauma-focused cognitive behavior therapy for school psychologists. *Journal of Applied School Psychology, 28,* 294–315. doi:10.1080/15 377903.2012.696037

Ginwright, S. (2018). *The future of healing: Shifting form trauma informed care to healing centered engagement.* Retrieved from https://medium.com/@ginwright/the-future-of-healing -shifting-from-trauma-informed-care-to-healing-centered-engagement-634f557ce69c

*Graham, R. A., Osofsky, J. D., Osofsky, H. J., & Hansel, T. C. (2017). School based post disaster mental health services: Decreased trauma symptoms in youth with multiple traumas. *Advances in School Mental Health Promotion, 10,* 161–175.

Hanson, R. F., & Lang, J. M. (2016). A critical look at trauma-informed care among agencies and systems serving maltreated youth and their families. *Child Maltreatment, 21,* 95–100.

*Harber, K. (2011). Creating a framework: Art therapy elicits the narrative. *Art Therapy: Journal of the American Art Therapy Association, 28*(1), 19–25.

*Holmes, C., Levy, M., Smith, A., Pinne, S., & Neese, P. (2015). A model for creating a supportive trauma-informed culture for children in preschool settings. *Journal of Child and Family Studies, 24,* 1650–1659.

*Hoover, S. A., Sapere, H., Lang, J. M., Nadeem, E., Dean, K. L., & Vona, P. (2018). Statewide implementation of an evidence-based trauma intervention in schools. *School Psychology Quarterly, 33*(1), 44–53.

*Ijadi-Maghsoodi, R., Marlotte, L., Garcia, E., Aralis, H., Lester, P., Escudero, P., & Kataoka, S. (2017). Adapting and implementing a school-based resilience-building curriculum among low-income racial and ethnic minority students. *Contemporary School Psychology, 21,* 223–239.

*Jaycox, L. H., Langley, A. K., Stein, B. D., Wong, M., Sharma, P., Scott, M., & Schonlau, M. (2009). Support for students exposed to trauma: A pilot study. *School Mental Health, 1*(2), 49–60.

Kaiser, K. (2009). Protecting respondent confidentiality in qualitative research. *Qualitative Health Research, 19,* 1632–1641. doi:10.1177/1049732309350879

Langley, A., Santiago, C., Rodríguez, A., & Zelaya, J. (2013). Improving implementation of mental health services for trauma in multicultural elementary schools: Stakeholder perspectives on parent and educator engagement. *Journal of Behavioral Health Services & Research, 40,* 247–262. doi:10.1007/s11414-013-9330-6

*Lawson, M. A., & Alameda-Lawson, T. (2012). A case study of school-linked, collective parent engagement. *American Educational Research Journal, 49,* 651–684.

*Lee, M. Y., Danna, L., & Walker, D. W. (2017). Classroom-Community Consultation (C3) 10 years after Hurricane Katrina: A retrospective look at a collaborative, school-based referral model. *Children & Schools, 39,* 119–127.

*Levendosky, A. A., & Buttenheim, M. (2001). A multi-method treatment for child survivors of sexual abuse: An intervention informed by relational and trauma theories. *Journal of Child Sexual Abuse, 9*(2), 1–19.

Martin, S. L., Ashley, O. S., White, L., Axelson, S., Clark, M., & Burrus, B. (2017). Incorporating trauma-informed care into school-based programs. *Journal of School Health, 87*, 958–967.

Maynard, B., Farina, N., & Dell, N. (2017). *Effects of trauma-informed approaches in schools.* Retrieved from https://campbellcollaboration.org/media/k2/attachments/ECG _Maynard_Trauma-informed_approaches.pdf

Metz, A., Naoom, S. F., Halle, T., & Bartley, L. (2015, May). *An integrated stage-based framework for implementation of early childhood programs and systems* (OPRE Research Brief; OPRE 2015-48). Washington, DC: Office of Planning, Research and Evaluation, Administration for Children and Families, U.S. Department of Health and Human Services.

Miles, M. B., Huberman, A. M., Saldaña, J. (2014). *Qualitative data analysis: A methods sourcebook* (3rd ed.). Thousand Oaks, CA: Sage.

Moher, D., Liberati, A., Tetzlaff, J., Altman, D. G., & Prisma Group. (2009). Preferred reporting items for systematic reviews and meta-analyses: The PRISMA statement. *PLoS Medicine, 6*(7), e1000097

Morgan, A., Pendergast, D., Brown, R., & Heck, D. (2015). Relational ways of being an educator: Trauma-informed practice supporting disenfranchised young people. *International Journal of Inclusive Education, 19*, 1037–1051.

*Mutch, C., & Gawith, E. (2014). The New Zealand earthquakes and the role of schools in engaging children in emotional processing of disaster experiences. *Pastoral Care in Education, 32*(1), 54–67.

National Child Traumatic Stress Network, Schools Committee. (2017). *Creating, supporting, and sustaining trauma-informed schools: A system framework.* Los Angeles, CA: National Center for Child Traumatic Stress.

Oehlberg, B. (2008). Why schools need to be trauma-informed. *Trauma and Loss: Research and Interventions, 8*(2), 1–4. Retrieved from http://www.traumainformedcareproject.org /resources/WhySchoolsNeedToBeTraumaInformed(2).pdf

Paris, D. (2012). Culturally sustaining pedagogy: A needed change in stance, terminology, and practice. *Educational Researcher, 41*(3), 93–97.

Paris, D., & Alim, H. S. (Eds.). (2017). *Culturally sustaining pedagogies: Teaching and learning for justice in a changing world.* New York, NY: Teachers College Press.

Perfect, M., Turley, M., Carlson, J., Yohanna, J., & Saint Gilles, M. (2016). School-related outcomes of traumatic event exposure and traumatic stress symptoms in students: A systematic review of research from 1990 to 2015. *School Mental Health, 8*(1), 7–43. doi:10.1007/s12310-016-9175-2

*Perry, D. L., & Daniels, M. L. (2016). Implementing trauma-informed practices in the school setting: A pilot study. *School Mental Health, 8*, 177–188.

*Rønholt, S., Karsberg, S., & Elklit, A. (2013). Preliminary evidence for a classroom based psychosocial intervention for disaster exposed children with posttraumatic stress symptomatology. *Child & Youth Care Forum, 42*, 617–631.

*Saltzman, W. R., Pynoos, R. S., Layne, C. M., Steinberg, A. M., & Aisenberg, E. (2001). Trauma- and grief-focused intervention for adolescents exposed to community violence: Results of a school-based screening and group treatment protocol. *Group Dynamics: Theory, Research, and Practice, 5*, 291–303.

*Saltzman, W. R., Pynoos, R. S., Layne, C. M., Steinberg, A. M., & Aisenberg, E. (2003). School-based trauma and grief intervention for adolescents. *Prevention Researcher, 10*(2), 8–11.

Sanjari, M., Bahramnezhad, F., Fomani, F. K., Shoghi, M., & Cheraghi, M. A. (2014). Ethical challenges of researchers in qualitative studies: The necessity to develop a specific guideline. *Journal of Medical Ethics and History of Medicine, 7*, 14.

*Santiago, C. D., Kataoka, S. H., Hu-Cordova, M., Alvarado-Goldberg, K., Maher, L. M., & Escudero, P. (2015). Preliminary evaluation of a family treatment component to augment a school-based intervention serving low-income families. *Journal of Emotional and Behavioral Disorders, 23*(1), 28–39.

*Santiago, C. D., Raviv, T., Ros, A. M., Brewer, S. K., Distel, L. M., Torres, S. A., . . . Langley, A. K. (2018). Implementing the bounce back trauma intervention in urban elementary schools: A real-world replication trial. *School Psychology Quarterly, 33*(1), 1–9.

Schenk, K., & Williamson, J. (2005). *Ethical approaches to gathering information from children and adolescents in international settings: Guidelines and resources.* Washington, DC: Population Council.

*Shamblin, S., Graham, D., & Bianco, J. A. (2016). Creating trauma-informed schools for rural Appalachia: The partnerships program for enhancing resiliency, confidence and workforce development in early childhood education. *School Mental Health, 8*, 189–200. doi:10.1007/s12310-016-9181-4

Souers, K. (2018). Responding with care to students facing trauma. *Educational Leadership, 75*(4), 32–36.

Substance Abuse and Mental Health Services Administration. (2014). *SAMHSA's concept of trauma and guidance for a trauma-informed approach.* Rockville, MD: Author.

Substance Abuse and Mental Health Services Administration, National Center for Trauma-Informed Care. (2015). *Trauma-informed approach.* Retrieved from http://www.samhsa.gov/nctic/trauma-interventions

Taylor, L. K., Weist, M. D., & DeLoach, K. (2012). Exploring the use of the interactive systems framework to guide school mental health services in post-disaster contexts: Building community capacity for trauma-focused interventions. *American Journal of Community Psychology, 50*, 530–540.

*West, S. D., Day, A. G., Somers, C. L., & Baroni, B. A. (2014). Student perspectives on how trauma experiences manifest in the classroom: Engaging court-involved youth in the development of a trauma-informed teaching curriculum. *Children and Youth Services Review, 38*, 58–65. doi:10.1016/j.childyouth.2014.01.013

Wisconsin Department of Public Instruction. (2018). *Trauma sensitive schools learning modules.* Retrieved from https://dpi.wi.gov/sspw/mental-health/trauma/modules

Wissman, K. K., & Wiseman, A. M. (2011). "That's my worst nightmare": Poetry and trauma in the middle school classroom. *Pedagogies: An International Journal, 6*, 234–249.

*Wolmer, L., Laor, N., Dedeoglu, C., Siev, J., & Yazgan, Y. (2005). Teacher-mediated intervention after disaster: A controlled three-year follow-up of children's functioning. *Journal of Child Psychology and Psychiatry, 46*, 1161–1168.

Wolpow, R., Johnson, M. M., Hertel, R., & Kincaid, S. O. (2009). *The heart of learning and teaching: Compassion, resiliency, and academic success.* Olympia: Washington State Office of Superintendent of Public Instruction Compassionate Schools.

Woodbridge, M. W., Sumi, W. C., Thornton, S. P., Fabrikant, N., Rouspil, K. M., Langley, A. K., & Kataoka, S. H. (2016). Screening for trauma in early adolescence: Findings from a diverse school district. *School Mental Health, 8*(1), 89–105. doi:10.1007/s12310-015-9169-5

Chapter 16

Teaching in Community Schools: Creating Conditions for Deeper Learning

JULIA DANIEL
University of Colorado, Boulder

KAREN HUNTER QUARTZ
University of California, Los Angeles

JEANNIE OAKES
University of California, Los Angeles; Learning Policy Institute

The community school strategy calls on teachers, families, and school staff to take on new and more challenging roles to collaboratively address existing educational inequities. For example, deepened family and community engagement in the schools can help incorporate the rich funds of community knowledge and experience, both in the classroom and in making plans and decisions about the school. As school and community stakeholders work together, they can develop learning opportunities and access to services that support student learning and development. Community schools are particularly well-positioned to take advantage of research-backed strategies like integrated supports that help students come to class more prepared to learn, hands-on and innovative teaching and learning opportunities to deepen and extend learning, and sustainable workplace conditions to promote teacher satisfaction and retention. Embracing the link between learning and community, teachers and community school staff ensure that students and communities have opportunities to access rich, challenging, and culturally relevant curriculum and pedagogy, while accessing resources and supports. This expanded conception of what it means to teach in a community school presents new ways for researchers to study and help advance the field as well as the larger community schools movement.

A s our society continues to educationalize the welfare state (Kantor & Lowe, 2016), we increasingly rely on schools to help ameliorate the ravages of concentrated poverty and racial discrimination, reducing pressure on the State to create

Review of Research in Education
March 2019, Vol. 43, pp. 453–480
DOI: 10.3102/0091732X18821126
Chapter reuse guidelines: sagepub.com/journals-permissions
© 2019 AERA. http://rre.aera.net

social policies that might more directly address inequalities. It is clear that for under-resourced schools to even begin to grapple with such a challenge requires deep investment to build sustainable schools that address the many needs of low-income students and communities. One clear example of this involves the growth of the community school strategy, which calls on teachers, families, and school staff to take on new and more challenging roles to collaboratively address existing educational inequities. For example, deepened family and community engagement in the schools can help incorporate the rich funds of community knowledge and experience, both in the classroom and in making plans and decisions about the school. As school and community stakeholders work together, they can develop learning opportunities and access to services that support student learning and development. Community schools are particularly well-positioned to take advantage of what we know from the learning sciences and education research to create integrated supports that help students come to class more prepared to learn, hands-on and innovative teaching and learning opportunities to deepen and extend learning, and sustainable workplace conditions to promote teacher satisfaction and retention.

Community schools can begin to address opportunity gaps by integrating community members into the classroom, creating learning spaces outside of the classroom, and aligning school and community resources (Biag & Castrechini, 2016; Fehrer & Leos-Urbel, 2016; Sanders, 2018). This can help enrich classroom experiences, making the curriculum relevant to students' lives and supporting students and communities in areas outside of the school. In addition, a collaborative professional learning environment can support teachers in improving their practice and sustaining them in the position (Podolsky, Kini, Bishop, & Darling-Hammond, 2016). For teachers to support students in historically underserved communities, they must understand the cultural background of the community, the political economy and bureaucratic structure of the schools, and the community and social service support networks available (Oakes, Franke, Quartz, & Rogers, 2002). While there is an increasing amount of research on community schools, there is not enough research yet on teaching and learning in community schools.

Drawing on research from the learning sciences and from community school literature, we explore in this chapter how community school teachers and other community school staff can collaboratively build new systems to deepen student learning for historically marginalized students and communities. We examine some of the ways that teachers in community schools can help create conditions in which low-income students have access to a wide array of learning opportunities similar to their more privileged counterparts. While the research reviewed is not exhaustive, we include studies that lift up best practices for teaching in community schools. Our goal is to advance a conversation about teaching and learning practices that can help create the conditions for meaningful learning among all students.

We also examine ways that community school teachers take on new roles, including being activists who work with the community to ensure equitable access to resources, and being partners who work with communities to strengthen curriculum and instruction. It can also mean that people who are not traditionally tracked into the teaching profession, such as parents from low income communities, are supported and developed into teachers, bringing rich knowledge and understanding of the community into the classroom. Finally, the community school strategy can transform the teaching profession into a sustainable and fulfilling career as it helps address many of the challenges teachers face by creating supportive school environments built on positive relationships and the belief that teacher voice and participation are foundational to school reform. With this in mind, this chapter examines existing research to begin to answer the following questions:

- In what ways can community schools address existing educational disparities by supporting students, teachers, families, and partners to collaboratively develop opportunities for learning grounded in challenging, culturally relevant, and sustaining curriculum and pedagogy?
- How is teaching practice conceptualized, evidenced, and analyzed in community school literature?
- What strategies for recruitment, preparation, development, and retention can community schools use to support teachers to effectively engage with families and community members for sustaining a community school strategy?

OPPORTUNITIES FOR DEEPER LEARNING IN COMMUNITY SCHOOLS

To enable and extend critical academic, social, and emotional learning, community schools aim to make sure that students have *sufficient learning resources and opportunities*. These resources include enough time to offer a rich, balanced curriculum that promotes deep learning and youth development, enabling young people to be community leaders, to critically analyze and address issues they might be facing, and to pursue various academic, civic, and career options. Community schools aim to ensure that students have the *academic and social supports* that they need for learning, either by providing additional support at school or by connecting them and their families with resources and services outside of school. Community schools also seek to create a *culture of trusting relationships* between adults and young people and their families by improving the school climate. In such cultures, every student is known well and feels cared for, conditions that foster engagement and learning.

Effective community schools are organized around four key features (pillars) that connect enriched academic learning with intentional support for children's social and emotional development. The community school pillars as identified by Maier, Daniel, Oakes, and Lam (2017) are (1) integrated student supports, (2) expanded and enriched learning time and opportunities, (3) family and community engagement, and (4) collaborative leadership and practice. These pillars together create learning and development opportunities similar to those to which wealthier students tend to have more access. This is how community schools create the structure that is needed to make good schools and teaching more equitably accessible and sustainable for all students.

The learning conditions made possible by the four community school pillars also parallel findings from the growing body of research in the learning sciences. Learning and development are ever-present, as people are constantly observing, thinking, and solving problems by connecting new experiences to their prior knowledge. Relationships are key to learning and development, and they involve many people and contexts that extend far beyond classrooms. As summarized recently by Darling-Hammond and Cook-Harvey (2018),

New knowledge about human development from neuroscience and the sciences of learning and development demonstrates that effective learning depends on secure attachments; affirming relationships; rich, hands-on learning experiences; and explicit integration of social, emotional, and academic skills. A positive school environment supports students' growth across all the developmental pathways—physical, psychological, cognitive, social, and emotional—while it reduces stress and anxiety that create biological impediments to learning. (p. v)

The four community-school pillars provide a framework that enables community school teachers and staff to create opportunities for deeper and engaged learning—building, in part, on deep connections with the community—that this body research suggests foster children's learning and development.

The Principles of Learning

Thinking about learning as active sensemaking grounded in experience is not new. The forefathers of today's learning sciences, Jean Piaget and Lev Vygotsky in the 1920s and 1930s, concluded that engagement within a social environment is a key to learning. Piaget observed that children's thinking *develops* as they make sense of experiences. Vygotsky pointed to the interconnectedness of social experiences and mental processes. He concluded that learning and problem solving occur in the interactions *between* a learner and others. Social participation is far more than external stimulation for thinking; rather, it is part of one's thought processes and can help develop, as well as express, ideas (Oakes, Lipton, Anderson, & Stillman, 2018).

By the mid-20th century, scholars from psychology, linguistics, and anthropology were conducting studies examining the mind and how it made meaning. Their work became the field of cognitive science. In later decades, other learning researchers, including Roland Tharp and Michael Cole, developed sociocultural theories based on their empirical work showing that social and cultural contexts determine learning and how knowledge emerges through activity during community participation (Cole, Engestrom, & Vasquez, 1997; Tharpe & Gallimore, 1988). They recognized that prior knowledge and preexisting mental schemes are not only "academic." They showed how people rely on cultural tools, symbols, and ways of knowing as they develop and make sense of the world and their experiences in it.

Contemporary learning theory also emphasizes the situated and social nature of meaning making, by which "mind, behavior, perception and action are wholly integrated." (Jonassen & Land, 2012, p. vi). That means that the social and emotional spheres are not independent of the cognitive. Humans learn more effectively when they are not anxious, fearful, or distracted by other pressing concerns; when the learning is connected to their prior knowledge and experience; when they are actively engaged; and when they have a reason to care about the content they are learning and can use it to deepen their understanding and to solve real questions or problems (Darling-Hammond & Cook-Harvey, 2018).

These views of deeper learning represent a dramatic departure from the views of learning that underlie traditional classroom instruction—views of learning as acquiring, retaining, and recalling new information—and they certainly contrast with behavioral perspectives of learning as conditioning. However, they are far more consistent with the ways that community schools seek to organize their learning environments and depend heavily on social relationships.

Community schools are well-situated to create learning environments that counter the negative stereotypes and deficit views of communities of color that too often influence teaching and learning, as evidenced by psychologists like Claude Steele (Steele & Aronson, 1995). Learning researchers Gloria Ladson-Billings (1995), Carol Lee (2008), and Geneva Gay (2010) have shown the power of protective factors such as affirmation, removal of stereotype threat, and cultural, racial, or ethnic socialization to counter these negative dynamics. When community schools build trusting relationships between school and communities, they set the stage for attending to and enacting these protective factors. Learning scientists are also pointing to the importance of developing curriculum and instruction that engage students in ways that are attentive to sociocultural factors and power dynamics (Lave, 1991; Nasir & Hand, 2006), and are also culturally relevant and sustaining (Gay, 2010; Paris, 2012). Here, too, the inclusive, community-based settings created by community schools are far more amenable to such practices than are traditional schools.

Together, this work offers a complex and nuanced picture of deeper learning. We know that learning occurs as people try to make meaning of the world and use what they have learned in new situations, and that usable knowledge requires an understanding of concepts that can be transferred to novel situations. Learning largely takes place in the context of the social interaction among people, problems, ideas, and tools in authentic settings, as people get feedback from their actions and about their ideas. It is also culturally embedded, developed through relationships and experiences— both neurologically and psychologically, and developmental. That is, each experience influences the possibilities and frameworks for future learning. The meaning that students bring to their experiences and the essential role their communities play in their lives provide context, value, and resources for the learning process. Young people are more likely to be engaged in learning—to invest attention and expend energy—when the content has personal meaning and builds on what they already know. Moreover, students are more likely to retain and transfer knowledge when given opportunities to apply what they are learning to real-world issues.

Community Schools Set the Stage for Deeper and Engaged Learning

Interpreting the four community school pillars from the perspective of research on learning provides a window into the core work of teaching in community schools. Each pillar supports the development of positive relationships with caring adults are so important for young people's learning and development.

By creating systems of *Integrated Student Supports*, community schools can help students and communities strengthen relationships and networks to better address the personal issues and social and emotional needs that are so interconnected with cognitive development. This can build a community of personalized support that ultimately aids in the learning process by increasing the number of adults and experiences that students are able to have in their lives. Integrating these supports into the culture of schools and classrooms can create the context for learning experiences that build on an ethic of caring and offer supports for social/emotional development, trusting relationships, and restorative practices. Community school coordinators can play important roles in coordinating such supports with school activities based on the needs and assets identified by families and the community. Because students are known well by school staff, learning experiences can build more easily on students' prior knowledge and experience, positioning them as active constructors of new knowledge and attending to both cognitive and socioemotional realms of knowing and learning. Additionally, the Integrated Student Supports pillar is a natural way to help offset adverse childhood experiences in a school setting where it can be easiest to access children, assess their needs, and provide support (as compared to community-based services).

By *Expanding Learning Time and Opportunities*, community schools can create extra time and opportunities for challenging and interesting learning that can happen in nontraditional ways, building critical thinking and problem-solving skills among students. As an intentional dimension of the curriculum, community-based learning helps students acquire, practice, and apply subject matter knowledge and skills. At the same time, students develop the knowledge, skills, and attributes of effective citizenship by identifying and acting on issues and concerns that affect their own communities. When implemented thoughtfully, these strategies create a pedagogy of engagement. Students invest time and attention and expend real effort because their learning has meaning and purpose. Community-based learning helps students build a sense of connection to their communities. At the same time, it challenges them to develop a range of intellectual and academic skills in order to understand and take action on the issues they encounter in everyday life. By intentionally linking academic standards to the real world of their communities, community schools are narrowing the gap between knowledge and action and between what students must learn and what they can contribute. Learning experiences promote critical thinking as students apply and transfer content knowledge to new and complex problems and connect abstract ideas to real-world problems through challenging, authentic activities that extend beyond classrooms.

Strong *Family and Community Engagement* can bring more expertise and local knowledge into the schools to support classroom practices and help shape the vision of the school to adequately reflect the needs of the community. As we describe in the next section, building partnerships with members and organizations from the community means that the schools can create new learning opportunities for students that are based in the community, such as project-based learning and apprenticeships. At the same time, these relationships enable learning experiences that are embedded in contexts that are meaningful for students, in connection with families and communities, and build on students' personal, cultural, and linguistic knowledge.

Collaborative leadership and practices support the inclusion of stakeholders in important decisions about learning as well as addressing nuts and bolts issues such as sharing classrooms and aligning classroom teaching with after-school programs. Teachers, school staff, and community members can collaboratively develop new ways of teaching and learning together, building each other's capacity to improve opportunities for students (Pais, Hurst, Lowe, Rosenblum, & Wadle, in press). Such collaboration provides opportunities to design high-quality, culturally responsive, and student-centered learning experiences that are based on the rich funds of knowledge of the local community and the students themselves. Such opportunities necessitate honest conversations around identity, power, and turf and can build pride and power among traditionally marginalized communities.

This view of the potential contribution of the community school pillars to deeper learning reflects the conclusions of highly esteemed researchers (including three panels commissioned by the National Research Council) who have reviewed the evidence from the learning sciences about how people learn and the effect of informal learning environments on student school-related and developmental outcomes (Bransford, Brown, & Cocking, 2000; Bransford & Donovan, 2005). The four pillars create a structure in community schools that enables the principles of deeper learning to flourish. Together, these pillars create more and better learning opportunities through which community members and teachers can incorporate local knowledge into the curriculum, provide opportunities for rich community-based learning, and develop a context for professional learning through collaboration.

TEACHING PRACTICES IN COMMUNITY SCHOOLS

We now explore a few examples of how teaching practices in community schools can create rich learning opportunities. We chose these examples out of numerous practices because we felt they represented a range of best practices aligned with the four community school pillars. Although these practices are not implemented in all community schools, they are effective ways for improving teaching and learning that community schools are particularly well-positioned to implement. Just as the four pillars mutually support each other, these practices also can reinforce the effectiveness of each other. For example, engaging families and communities in the schools can make curriculum and pedagogy more culturally relevant and offer new community-based learning opportunities.

The community school strategy can enable teaching and learning to happen in ways that follow what the learning sciences demonstrate as effective by creating learning opportunities that are collaborative, culturally sustaining, contextualized in students' previous experience and knowledge, and attentive to sociocultural conditions. We now turn to the growing body of pedagogical research to look at the instructional practices that bring these ideas to life. Understanding that relationships and prior knowledge are fundamental to learning, community schools bring community members into the schools, and bring students into the community for rich, engaging learning opportunities (Galindo, Sanders, & Abel, 2017). They offer an innovative approach to improving teaching and learning among diverse stakeholders, as community members and school staff work together to assess needs and develop solutions. Incorporating the prior knowledge and local norms of the students can improve the learning context for deeper learning (Oakes et al., 2018). Grounded in the theory that school and community success are inextricably linked, community schools work to integrate knowledge, teaching, resources, and opportunities in both schools and communities to strengthen them together (Fehrer & Leos-Urbel, 2016).

As community members are included in collaboratively planning and executing curriculum and pedagogy development, teaching can build on community knowledge and address community issues (Sanders, Galindo, & Allen, 2018). In this way, community schools can enhance an individual teachers' ability to teach well (Sanders et al., 2018), and turn learning into a social process in the schools and communities, involving many more adults in students' lives (Pais et al., in press; Quinn, 2005; Richardson, 2009; Sanders, 2016). The learning opportunities created that draw on students' preexisting understandings, interests, culture, and real-world experiences can make the curriculum more meaningful to them (National Research Council, 2003). When students are actively engaged in applying knowledge to real work problems, they tend to be more motivated (National Research Council, 2003).

Culturally Relevant Curriculum and Pedagogy

Expanded learning time and opportunities that are relevant to students' cultural backgrounds can be particularly engaging. Ladson-Billings and Tate's (1995) theory of culturally relevant teaching that develops students academically, nurtures and supports cultural competence, and develops critical sociopolitical consciousness has shown to be an essential way of meeting the learning needs of culturally diverse students (Gay, 2010; Howard, 2003). Paris (2012) has pushed the concept, calling for culturally sustaining pedagogy that supports and values the multiethnic and multilingual world we live in and seeks to perpetuate and foster "linguistic, literate, and cultural pluralism as part of the democratic project of schooling" (p. 93). While this is an emerging focus for many community schools, lacking a deep research base (Sanders et al., 2018), there is tremendous potential to build these pedagogies into the strategy of the schools because of the focus on community-engaged learning opportunities and family engagement in schools and classrooms (Khalifa, Gooden, & Davis, 2016). Grounding classroom teaching in previous knowledge and cultural backgrounds of students, while connecting this learning to real-world issues in the community can support culturally relevant pedagogy and curriculum in ways that teach cultural pride and builds the democratic leadership of students (Aronson & Laughter, 2016; Au, 1980; Sanders et al., 2018).

Community school teachers and other adults in the school ideally understand the sociocultural backgrounds of their students so that they can teach in ways that are culturally relevant and sustaining, engaging families and community members as local experts who can enrich the school and classroom using local funds of knowledge (Moll, Amanti, Neff, & Gonzalez, 1992; Sanders et al., 2018). Sanders et al.'s (2018) study of teaching in three community schools found that at one school that showed high academic gains and family and community engagement,

the teachers had come to understand and value the community schools approach and worked collaboratively with community partners to promote student success . . . [T]eachers at the case school were encouraged to engage in community partnerships that facilitated students' academic and social development. (p. 20)

Community partnerships can help shape learning opportunities and support teachers in improving discipline practices and classroom management by bringing new people into the school and classroom that can support teachers in developing culturally relevant practices (Sanders et al., 2018). While this work is not well-developed in many community schools, there is great potential for these schools to do an exemplary job creating such opportunities that support improved family and community engagement and out-of-school learning opportunities.

Engaging Families and Communities in Learning

One form of family and community engagement is including family members in teaching and learning opportunities. Creating culturally sustaining and community-based learning opportunities means that teachers are able to develop partnerships with families and community members that bring their expertise into the classroom as well as into decision-making bodies at the school level. Community schools can be well-designed to engage families and community members through various mechanisms in the schools such as through offering services, providing adult education, and creating opportunities for families to volunteer and take collaborative leadership in schools (Dryfoos, 2000) when they attend to power dynamics (Richardson, 2009). Extensive research demonstrates the importance of making spaces welcoming for families by creating space and competencies for trusting relationships, respect, and a sense of belonging in schools, which can in turn support improved student learning and engagement (Epstein, 2018; Henderson & Mapp, 2002; Kraft & Dougherty, 2013; Quezada, Alexandrowicz, & Molina, 2013; Sime & Sheridan, 2014). In community schools, family and community engagement has shown to lead to positive changes in academic achievement, improved social behavior and healthy youth development, reductions in substance abuse and student mobility, increases in families addressing housing food and financial issues, and lower violence and street crime in the communities (Biag & Castrechini, 2016; Castrechini & London, 2012; Dryfoos, 2000).

Family and community engagement is challenging to achieve, but because community schools have structures for collaborative leadership and multiple paths to involve families, they can demonstrate that they value their participation and role in teaching and learning (Pais et al., in press). This can create tremendous potential to incorporate local knowledge into the classroom through such engagement. To do so effectively, engagement efforts must challenge deficit-based ideas about families from low-income communities of color and involve them in schools through practices in which they have power to help shape the direction of the school (Alameda-Lawson & Lawson, 2016; Ishimaru et al., 2016; Mapp, 2002; Sanders, 2001; Stefanski, Valli, & Jacobson, 2017; Warren, Hong, Rubin, & Uy, 2009). Teachers' and families' emotional orientations toward each other also affect how relations develop, as a variety of political and normative forces (Welner, 2001) can support or erode trusting relationships between families, schools, and community members (Evans, 2011; Hargreaves, 2001). When schools have teams that engage teachers, families, and others to plan, implement, evaluate, and continually improve school-based programs, they can support family and community engagement in teaching efforts for improved student learning (Epstein et al., 2019). Similarly, when teachers do home visits to get to know families and community members, it can increase their empathy and reduce negative implicit biases, while helping parents to feel more confident about interacting with school staff (McKnight, Venkateswaran, Laird, Robles, & Shalev, 2017).

Out-of-School and Project-Based Learning Opportunities

Another form of expanded learning includes community-based learning opportunities such as academically based community service, civic education, environmental education, place-based learning, service learning, and work-based learning. These opportunities emphasize student-centered, hands-on, engaging learning experiences that include community partners (Murillo, Quartz, & Del Razo, 2017; Redd et al., 2012). Community school advocates point out how community-based learning opportunities help students develop important knowledge and skills of democratic participation through a pedagogy of engagement in their community:

Students invest time and attention and expend real effort because their learning has meaning and purpose. Community-based learning helps students build a sense of connection to their communities. At the same time, it challenges them to develop a range of intellectual and academic skills in order to understand and take action on the issues they encounter in everyday life. By intentionally linking academic standards to the real world of their communities, community schools are narrowing the gap between knowledge and action and between what students must learn and what they can contribute. (Melaville, Berg, & Blank, 2006, p. 3)

For example, service learning opportunities can support significant improvement in different areas like attitudes toward self, attitudes toward school and learning, civic engagement, social skills, and academic performance (Celio, Durlak, & Dymnicki, 2011). In the meta-analysis of 62 studies of service learning by Celio et al. (2011), the programs with the largest positive effects were those that incorporated academic and program curriculum or objectives, engaged students in planning, implementing, and evaluating activities (i.e., incorporated youth voice), involved community partners, and provided opportunities for reflection.

Engaging with real-world issues can also take the form of project-based learning. Project-based learning—defined as inquiry-based activities where the context of learning is provided through authentic questions and problems within real-world practices—engages students in creating an end product that represents their new understandings, knowledge, and attitudes regarding the question being investigated (Kokotsaki, Menzies, & Wiggins, 2016). Project-based learning can provide space for students to be reflective about their learning and ideas in relation to those of their peers. Barron et al. (1998) discuss how they scaffold their project-based learning in a way that helps students to "understand the relevance of particular concepts to activities in the world and to support inquiry skills, deep understanding, and the reflection on one's idea in relation to others" (p. 276). They point out that two key design principles for project-based learning curricula are that they provide multiple opportunities for students to engage in formative self-assessment and revision and that they promote participation and a sense of agency. Formative assessments are important to help teachers understand how to adapt their instruction to meet the needs of the students and using student self-assessment helps the students monitor their own understanding, making them active, reflective learners (Barron et al., 1998). When teachers give students resources and space to reflect on their learning, they can become agents in their own education, which is an important component of project-based learning (Barron et al., 1998). A 2016 review of research on project-based learning found that the design principles most commonly used in project-based learning are well matched to the goals of preparing students for deeper learning, higher level thinking skills, and intra-/interpersonal skills (Condliffe, Visher, Bangser, Drohojowska, & Saco, 2016). Out-of-school and project-based learning opportunities are best done in culturally sustaining ways, being grounded in local contexts and incorporating the knowledge of community members into the pedagogy and curriculum.

Community-Based Participatory Research

Another teaching and learning practice that community schools are well-positioned to offer as an opportunity for learning is that of community-based participatory research (CBPR), which includes youth participatory action research. This research, driven by students, families, and community members to address local issues, can be an effective way of both engaging young people in deeper learning and improving material conditions (Checkoway & Richards-Schuster, 2004; Fine & Torre, 2004; Israel, Schulz, Parker, & Becker, 1998). CBPR is what Fine (2008) calls an epistemological challenge that recognizes that expertise and knowledge are widely distributed. Through creating participatory spaces, methods, and opportunities for action, this practice disrupts normative beliefs and produces new knowledge and forms of participation by those often relegated to the margins and taught not to exercise their power (Fals-Borda, 1987). New knowledge based on social justice principles provide people "with a sense of hope and the drive to challenge inequities limiting their potential to help themselves as well as others to experience a full, unmitigated humanity" (Cammarota & Romero, 2009, p. 57).

Because people's knowledge is shaped by their experiences, CBPR uses those knowledges to shape questions, interpretations, and solutions as well as come to understand their experiences within institutions that attempt to make them racialized and gendered subjects (Cahill, 2007; Fine & Torre, 2004; Rios-Moore et al., 2004; Torre, 2009). Through analysis of power and discourse, new subjectivities are created by participants in the openings of existing power relations as they understand their personal experiences within political social relations (Cahill, 2007). In such a participatory form of transformative politics, people can struggle against oppressive material conditions and discourses.

For example, the Social Justice Education Project capitalizes on Latina/o students' "funds of knowledge" through youth participatory action research using photography and poetry to reclaim political spaces that have traditionally excluded their voices and influence decision makers (Cammarota & Romero, 2009). This practice can create both institutional and individual transformation in what Cammarota and Romero term a social justice epistemology in which students learn and create personal and social transformation. "The insights or knowledge foster an awareness of how to redefine one's self, community, and world in more positive and just terms" (p. 64). The process of redefinition facilitates participants to see themselves as agents of change.

Often connected to organizing work that seeks to disrupt unfair policies and practices, such research centers the knowledge and experiences of historically marginalized people in shaping the research questions, methodologies, and solutions (Cole & Simpson, 2016; Kirshner & Jefferson, 2015). By building power of marginalized communities and claiming the role of expert on issues that affect them, community-based research and organizing practices not only can improve policies and practices but also can reshape inequitable power relations so that communities have new mechanisms to demand change (Golob & Giles, 2013; Lopez, 2003; Warren et al., 2009). This helps students to see themselves as active citizens who can participate in shaping the local conditions in which they work and live, as they learn power through both research and organizing efforts (Ginwright & James, 2002; Oakes & Rogers, 2006; Warren, 2014).

Social Emotional Learning and Restorative Justice

Integrating student supports so that students are better prepared to learn can include implementing programs throughout the school to improve students' and teachers' emotional well-being and relationships. Community schools are set up to promote empathy and social cohesiveness, qualities that benefit both teachers and students, with the greatest benefits for economically disadvantaged students (Battistich, Solomon, Watson, & Schaps, 1997; Pais et al., in press). Schools that meet students' basic psychological needs for belonging, autonomy, and competence allow students to participate actively in a cohesive, caring group (Battistich et al., 1997). Comprehensive programs designed to create caring communities of learners in which students can participate in decision making are characterized by supportive relationships and collaboration among and between students, staff, and parents. They also tend to have a sense of common purpose and a clear commitment to salient norms and values of caring, justice, responsibility, and learning; responsiveness to students' developmental and sociocultural needs; and an accessible, meaningful, and engaging curriculum (Battistich, Schaps, Watson, Solomon, & Lewis, 2000).

As schools and teachers create safe, supportive learning environments within which all stakeholders are able to build self-awareness, social awareness, trusting relationships, and responsibility, it can improve instruction and achievement, and prevent teacher burnout (Durlak, Weissberg, Dymnicki, Taylor, & Schellinger, 2011; Jennings & Greenberg, 2009; Weissberg, Durlak, Domitrovich, & Gullota, 2016). Teachers' prosocial competencies can support teacher-student relationships (Pais et al., in press) and are associated with students' personal, social, and ethical attitudes, values, and motives (Battistich et al., 2000; Jennings & Greenberg, 2009; Solomon, Battistich, Kim, & Watson, 1996). Battistich et al. (1997) also found that when teachers are able to create a sense of community in their classrooms, students tend to have a more prosocial orientation and less disruptive behaviors. These important skills help students and teachers interact in better ways, support student development, and help teachers see and respond to student behavior in an empathetic way (Hughes, 2011; Jones, Bouffard, & Weissbourd, 2013; Noddings, 2005; Sibley et al., 2017). For example, Brophy and McCaslin (1992) found that teachers who were highly effective tended to work with students in order to develop long-term solutions to address the causes of behavioral issues.

Families and educators can work together to support children's academic, social, and emotional wellness (Albright, Weissberg, & Dusenbury, 2011). Similarly, restorative justice as an approach to discipline that focuses on repairing relationships, building accountability, and addressing harms has been shown to improve the learning environment by building trust and empathy within schools, and decreasing suspensions and arrests (Gonzalez, 2012). Restorative justice practices in community schools empower communities by building healthy relationships (Pais et al., in press).

[T]hese practices seek to empower students, parents, teachers, administrators, and community members. Unlike punitive models for regulating schools, restorative justice practice provides school communities with the flexibility to address, confront, and resolve conflicts. (Gonzalez, 2012, p. 335)

In addition to working with students to determine underlying issues that create challenges in schools, teachers can play a central role in supporting students' development and accessing resources, which in turn tends to improve student-teacher relationships, class environments, and relationships beyond the school (Sibley et al., 2017). Teachers' ability to access services for their students can help them build their skills to address students' nonacademic needs (Gutkin, Singer, & Brown, 1980). Teacher-student relationships improve when teachers are able to consult with counselors in the school and get support in addressing student concerns (Ray, 2007). A recent study of City Connects by Sibley et al. (2017) found that as teachers work with the comprehensive student support system, they learn more about the whole child, including the nonacademic spheres of their lives. Participating teachers reported being more patient because they understood how these nonacademic issues contributed to classroom struggles, and also reported feeling better equipped to dealing with challenging student behavior. Teachers viewed the coordinators of supports as helping to address issues so that teachers could focus on teaching and helping teachers follow through with nonacademic supports for the students (Sibley et al., 2017). Feeling supported by others in the school who can help students access outside services can reduce teacher stress, thereby helping retain teachers and improve teaching and learning practices. We turn now from effective teaching practices to look in more depth at the community school working conditions that can support teachers and their development.

SUSTAINING THE WORK OF COMMUNITY SCHOOL TEACHERS

The promise of community schooling lies in its distinct "whole child" approach to deeper learning, rooted in the power of a diverse group coming together to ensure the well-being and education of students and their families. Effective teachers in community schools embrace this approach to learning and serve as key members of diverse stakeholder groups to advance the practices reviewed above. However, the sustainability of these practices—many of which involve out-of-school time, coordination, leadership responsibilities, partnerships, and planning—is an important concern for the community schools movement, particularly for teachers working in large urban districts that serve neighborhoods of concentrated poverty, and increasingly in low-income rural communities that also deal with high levels of poverty.

Recent research confirms Ingersoll's (2001) characterization of high-poverty urban schools as churning "revolving door" organizations, with approximately two thirds of new teachers leaving their school within the first 5 years (Papay, Bacher-Hicks, Page, & Marinell, 2017). To explain the churn, research is shifting away from explanations that focus on the characteristics of students and/or teachers (e.g., Hanushek, Kain, & Rivkin, 2004) to the quality of schools as workplaces for adults (Simon & Johnson, 2015). Teachers are more likely to stay in schools when they experience administrative support, collaborative relationships, professional autonomy, and a positive school culture (Ingersoll & May, 2012; Simon & Johnson, 2015). However, large urban schools tend to have highly centralized bureaucracies, resulting in hierarchical settings in which educators have a limited amount of autonomy, constraining teacher participation and stakeholder collaboration (Weiner, 2000). The same schools also have a long history of being underresourced, including large class sizes, facilities disrepair, inadequate textbooks, and other factors that have been linked to teacher turnover (Loeb, Darling-Hammond, & Luczak, 2005).

For the community school strategy to succeed, the teaching profession must transform into a sustainable and fulfilling career, and the conditions that shape teachers' work each day must be improved to support this work. We briefly review how the community schools pillar of collaborative leadership and practice is foundational to stable and high-functioning workplace organizations. We also take up the other three pillars, suggesting that teachers' workload be considered in relation to the added student supports, extended learning time, and family and community engagement efforts that define community schooling.

Collaboration Is Foundational

Developing a comprehensive community school strategy requires distributed leadership and strong norms of collaboration among teachers as well as community members, school staff, service providers, parents, and others (Pais et al., in press). The fourth pillar identified by Oakes, Maier, and Daniel (2017), collaboration, is foundational to the success of community schools. When leadership is effectively shared, it offers different stakeholders the opportunity to bring their skills and knowledge into work that is oriented toward a common vision (Diamond & Spillane, 2016). This can improve practices such that school relationships and climates improve, while allowing stakeholders to engage in deeper ways in their work when other needs are being met by partners (Bryk, 2010; Maier et al., 2017). Robust ties between school actors like teachers and community school directors and families and community members tend to benefit schools and improve the learning environment (Bryk, Sebring, Allensworth, Easton, & Luppescu, 2010). When schools can support the development of new skills and knowledge in families and school staff, collaborative practices between stakeholders can improve the trust and the social base in the school community (Auerbach, 2009; Bryk et al., 2010; Mapp & Kuttner, 2014; Warren, 2005). Families and community members in community schools can share decision-making power with school staff and principals on topics including school budgets and curriculum (Henderson & Mapp, 2002; Pais et al., in press; Richardson, 2009; Sanders, 2001, 2016; Warren, 2005). Community participation in planning efforts and agenda setting for the school is important for their success (Richardson, 2009).

Collaboration between teachers and other school staff also plays an important role in school improvement efforts. Many challenges facing teachers today, including working in and creating positive school climates (S. M. Johnson, 2007); building trusting relationships with other teachers, with students, and with communities; and feeling supported at their job, can be ameliorated by a collaborative decision-making process at the school (Maier et al., 2017; Podolsky et al., 2016). Collaboration between teachers including their ability to be heard in decision making and to participate in professional learning environments is linked to greater consistency in instruction (Friedlander & Darling-Hammond, 2007), more sharing and experimenting with teaching practices (Snow-Gerono, 2005), improved job satisfaction (Stockard & Lehman, 2004; Hord, 1997), stronger desire to stay in the profession (Ware & Kitsantas, 2007), and improved teaching practices and student achievement (Kraft & Papay, 2014).

Teachers play important roles in shaping collaborative environments with other teachers as well as with family and community members. Lead teachers can help create professional learning communities through which teachers can learn from each other, improving trusting relationships, school climates, and instructional capacity. As engaged scholars, teachers can work with families and community members to incorporate the rich knowledge base of the community into the pedagogical and curricular practices (Galindo et al., 2017; Richardson, 2009). For example, collaborations can range from planning curriculum with community members and developing learning opportunities that build on students' cultural backgrounds, to making budgetary decisions for the school together (Sanders, 2018; Sanders & Lewis, 2005). As public intellectuals, teachers can work with community members to address local issues, advocating together for improved neighborhood and school conditions, access to resources, and other relevant issues (Oakes et al., 2002).

Caring school communities that promote empathy and social cohesiveness have benefits for both teachers and students (Battistich et al., 1997, Battistich et al., 2000). Strong relationships between teachers and communities facilitate all stakeholders' ability to participate and engage with each other as partners and understand each other's backgrounds (Pais et al., in press). To create caring and supportive school communities, these relationships must be intentionally nourished. Community schools engage families and communities through a variety of mechanisms (Sanders, 2001; Stefanski et al., 2017; Warren et al., 2009). For example, some schools with the support of teachers' unions train teachers to do home visits in order to build relationships and trust with families that can deepen engagement as well as help teachers better understand students' home and community context (Auerbach, 2009; E. J. Johnson, 2014).

Finally, teachers are more likely to remain in a school if they see themselves as part of a collaborative team and can have influence over their work environments (Allensworth & Easton, 2007; Podolsky et al., 2016; Seashore Louis, Leithwood, Wahlstrom, & Anderson, 2010). Policies designed to support teacher autonomy include initiatives such as charter and pilot school agreements that make it possible for groups of teachers, community members, and other organizations to start their own school, often as part of a broader district portfolio or school choice program. These autonomy initiatives have a complicated relationship with the broader community schools movement, which includes both new schools as well as long-standing neighborhood schools that are losing enrollment and resources as a result of market-based reform. The recent epidemic of urban school closures has ignited grassroots community organizing to support and sustain neighborhood community schools (Green, 2017; Urban Institute, 2017). Teacher unions are playing a large role in this fight, taking up community schools as a collective bargaining issue. Strong union-management partnerships have the potential to translate into increased school-level collaboration and infrastructure for the collective problem solving that undergirds community schooling (Rubinstein & McCarthy, 2016).

Reasonable Workloads, Adequate Compensation, and Collective Bargaining

Community schools are designed to give teachers more control over their work, but they also require supports and structures to ensure the work is sustainable and productive. In a qualitative study of teachers' working conditions in two types of autonomy models, pilot and charter schools, S. M. Johnson and Landman (2000) describe how stress, exhaustion, arbitrary treatment, and other factors underscored the need for "sensible guidelines and reasonable parameters that would free them to work as professionals" (p. 112). This is especially important in community schools given teachers' expanded roles and responsibilities. Kraft et al. (2015) examined how teachers and administrators in high-poverty urban schools orient the work of their school as an open system that is shaped by students' environment and experience outside of school. This orientation expanded the work of teaching to include serving on student support teams, engaging with parents, and interacting with the many uncertainties related to the complex social, health, and economic factors facing students living in poverty. The authors found that teachers' ability to manage work in this environment depended on systematic organizational responses for supporting instruction, promoting discipline, engaging parents, and supporting students' socioemotional well-being.

One of the most often cited organizational supports for teacher professionalism, leadership, and retention is time during the school day to plan and collaborate (Darling-Hammond, 1999). Recommendations from more than 2,000 National Board–certified teachers who were brought together to examine research on recruiting and retaining teachers in high-needs schools included the following: "schedule protected, uninterrupted, common planning time (e.g., through regular planning periods, early dismissal or late arrival times, substitute coverage, etc.) so colleagues can share ideas, plan/observe lessons, and assess student work" (Berry, 2008, p. 17). In community schools, the need for time may be heightened given the expanded responsibilities teachers may have for coordinating with social service professionals, extended learning providers, and families. Teachers must also receive adequate compensation for their time, especially if their work hours increase as a result of expanded responsibilities. This is especially pressing because teachers' salaries have been declining since the 1990s and represent only about 70% of the salaries of other workers with a college degree (Sutcher, Darling-Hammond, & Carver-Thomas, 2016). Research is needed to understand the time spent by community school teachers on these and other collaborative activities considered part of their job.

Efforts to ensure reasonable working conditions for community school teachers include both locally developed work rules as well as collective bargaining agreements between teachers' unions and school boards. Working conditions in pilot schools, for example, are formalized in local teacher-developed elect-to-work agreements that allow teachers to remain in their unions while also creating work rules and provisions suited to their schools. For example, a community pilot school in Los Angeles moved up the start date of the school year to better serve its community (Fauci & Quartz, 2018). The freedom to make these sorts of decisions locally depends on the flexibility of collective bargaining agreements, which varies widely, with large and urban districts having more restrictive contracts overall (Strunk, 2012; Strunk et al., 2018). As part of their national campaign, the American Federation of Teachers (2017) advocates using "collective bargaining agreements, memoranda of understanding and/or consultation agreements to introduce language supporting community schools to ensure that both the community school coordinator position and the local site-level decision-making team are in place at each school" (p. 2). These two provisions are seen as key to the sustainability of teachers' work in community schools.

PREPARING THE NEXT GENERATION OF COMMUNITY SCHOOL TEACHERS

Looking to the future, the community school movement will depend on a workforce of teachers and other community school professionals that embraces the four pillars and the opportunities for deeper learning that they afford. We conclude with a brief look at research on the policies and practices that can establish a pipeline of high-quality teachers likely to stay and be successful in community schools serving high-needs populations. Increasingly, preservice teacher education programs offer specialized preparation for urban, high-poverty school contexts that are applicable to many community schools. These programs are driven by a commitment to social justice and equity and provide a framework for novice teachers to learn their craft (Cochran-Smith, 2010; Darling-Hammond & Oakes, in press; Oakes et al., 2018).

For example, Murrell's (2001) Community Teachers framework defines a community teacher as "an accomplished urban teacher who develops the contextualized knowledge of culture, community, and identity of children and their families as the core of their teaching practice" (p. 340). The Community Teachers framework uses situated identity theory to help teachers focus on the social and cultural contexts that shape student learning and identity. Teacher education practices aligned with this sociocultural and asset-based framework include field-based placements in community organizations (Varelas et al., 2018), guided immersive programming (R. E. Lee, 2018), working in solidarity with parents and families (Zeichner, Bowman, Guillen, & Napolitan, 2016), and residency programs that immerse novices in the life of a school and community to develop strong relationships and local knowledge (Guha, Hyler, & Darling-Hammond, 2016). These and other preparation experiences teach candidates to challenge deficit conceptions of low-income culturally diverse students and learn firsthand how to engage the community cultural wealth of students and families to advance learning. Teachers who have these specialized preparation experiences may also be retained at higher rates in high-poverty schools (Lyons, 2007; Quartz & the TEP Research Group, 2003).

Recruitment is a critical component of social justice teacher education, as many programs seek to enroll teaching candidates with a firsthand knowledge and experience of the challenges facing students in high-poverty communities. Research on "Grow Your Own" teacher education programs describe the process of recruiting and preparing nontraditional teaching candidates from local communities, including paraprofessionals, after-school staff, and community members. These programs are particularly well-suited to community schools because they affirm the value of prior experience in learning to teach, particularly the experiences related to extended learning and integrated services. For example, community school teachers with experience managing after-school programs will be better prepared to connect students' learning across contexts and work alongside other community school professionals. In addition to bringing this valuable work experience to the role of community school teacher, Grow Your Own programs also aim to develop teachers of color who share the background and experiences of their students (Carver-Thomas, 2018; Gist, White, & Bianco, 2018). Teachers' race and ethnicity have important consequences for students of color that underscore the need to diversify the teaching workforce. In addition to serving as role models for students, teachers of color improve the academic outcomes and school experiences of students of color (Villegas & Irvine, 2010). In addition to the promise of Grow Your Own programs to diversify the workforce, other policies such as loan forgiveness, mentorship, scholarships, and residencies can help create high-retention pathways for teachers of color into community schools (Carver-Thomas, 2018).

NEW DIRECTIONS FOR RESEARCH

We have found that community schools create conditions in which teachers, students, families, and communities can collaboratively participate in engaging teaching and learning opportunities. These conditions offer the potential to address opportunity gaps between low-income students of color and their privileged counterparts.

While we have examined research that in many cases represents best practices for community schools, we recognize that successful implementation can be challenging and requires a high degree of support and engagement at all levels of the school system. Effectively supporting teachers, students, families, and communities to create and take advantage of educational opportunities is a wise choice for districts who want to create equitable access to such learning opportunities, and it requires normative and political shifts in how we develop and sustain teachers and schools. While this research is promising, we outline research questions below that will help us further understand how community schools can support conditions for deeper teaching and learning opportunities.

Learning

- How do teachers in community schools take advantage of the structures and relationships to embed learning in contexts that extend far beyond classrooms?
- How do community-school learning activities position students' out-of-school knowledge and the essential role their communities play in their lives as context, value, and resources for the learning process?
- How do relationships among teachers, families, and community leaders facilitate the use of cultural symbols and tools in learning activities?
- How do the community partners enable teachers to make authentic connections between academic principles and real-world learning?
- How do the community school pillars serve to strengthen relationships among school stakeholders, thereby supporting healthy development and learning?

Teaching Practices

- What supports can help teachers develop cultural competencies in order to create culturally sustaining curriculum and pedagogies?
- How can we support teachers to develop trusting relationships with families and community members in order to support authentic partnerships for collaboration and development of rich learning opportunities for students?
- What deficit-based normative ideas need to be challenged among school staff in order to build trusting relationships between schools and communities?
- What training and supports can help teachers build skills for restorative practices to supplant punitive measures for discipline? Recognizing that their time is limited, and that punitive measures are normative in many schools, how can teachers receive coaching and continuous support to make these shifts?

Retention-Oriented Workplaces

- What roles, responsibilities, and collaborative efforts are required of community school teachers to embrace the four pillars? How can we use this information to help the field understand whether and how the community schools strategy is sustainable over time?

- What is the relationship between teachers and other community school professionals, including the community school coordinators who are considered central to the movement?
- As community schools mature and develop, it will be important to study whether and how teachers experience professional rewards associated with having an impact beyond the classroom. How do community school teachers participate in the broader democratic struggle for educational equity and justice?

Community School Teacher Preparation

- What and how do novices learn in residence when they are full members of a community school? What implications does this learning have for teacher preparation programs?
- How do community schools create grow your own pathways into teaching as well as other community school roles?

A CLOSING QUESTION: WHAT DOES IT MEAN TO BE A COMMUNITY SCHOOL TEACHER?

Enacting the principles of deeper learning as a community school teacher involves extending what it means to be a teacher, beyond traditional classroom-based conceptions of work and identity. Oakes et al. (2002) demonstrate that effective teachers who work with low-income students in urban contexts are skilled classroom practitioners as well as public intellectuals who understand the local culture, political economy, and community and social service networks so that they can work with other stakeholders for educational equity. To be effective, they argued, teachers must also demonstrate a deep caring and commitment to democratic participation so that they can work with others and negotiate common understandings that support collective action. Embracing the link between learning and community, teachers in community schools similarly must demonstrate a commitment to collaboratively working with diverse stakeholders to improve conditions both inside and outside of the school so that students and communities have opportunities to access rich, challenging, and culturally relevant curriculum and pedagogy, while accessing resources and supports that might be helpful. This expanded conception of what it means to teach in a community school presents new ways for researchers to study and help advance the field as well as the larger community schools movement.

REFERENCES

Alameda-Lawson, T., & Lawson, M. A. (2016). Ecologies of collective parent engagement in urban education. *Urban Education, May*, 3–12. doi:10.1177/0042085916636654

Albright, M., Weissberg, R., & Dusenbury, L. (2011). *School-family partnership strategies to enhance children's social, emotional, and academic growth*. Newtown, MA: National Center for Mental Health Promotion and Youth Violence Prevention, Education Development Center.

Allensworth, E., & Easton, J. (2007, July). *What matters for staying on-track and graduating in Chicago public high schools* (Research report). Chicago, IL: Consortium on Chicago School Research. Retrieved from https://consortium.uchicago.edu/sites/default/files/pub lications/07%20What%20Matters%20Final.pdf

American Federation of Teachers. (2017). *Successful and sustainable community schools: The union as an essential ingredient.* Retrieved from https://www.aft.org/sites/default/files /wysiwyg/sustainablecommunityschools.pdf

Aronson, B., & Laughter, J. (2016). The theory and practice of culturally relevant education: A synthesis of research across content areas. *Review of Educational Research, 86*, 163–206.

Au, K. H. P. (1980). Participation structures in a reading lesson with Hawaiian children: Analysis of a culturally appropriate instructional event. *Anthropology & Education Quarterly, 11*, 91–115.

Auerbach, S. (2009). Walking the walk: Portraits in leadership for family engagement in urban schools. *School Community Journal, 19*, 9–31. doi:10.1177/0042085907300433

Barron, B. J., Schwartz, D. L., Vye, N. J., Moore, A., Petrosino, A., Zech, L., & Bransford, J. D. (1998). Doing with understanding: Lessons from research on problem- and project-based learning. *Journal of the Learning Sciences, 7*, 271–311.

Battistich, V., Schaps, E., Watson, M., Solomon, D., & Lewis, C. (2000). Effects of the Child Development Project on students' drug use and other problem behaviors. *Journal of Primary Prevention, 21*, 75–99.

Battistich, V., Solomon, D., Watson, M., & Schaps, E. (1997). Caring school communities. *Educational Psychologist, 32*, 137–151.

Berry, B. (with Rasberry, M., & Williams, A.). (2008). *Recruiting and retaining quality teachers for high-needs schools: Insights from NBCT summits and other policy initiatives.* Chapel Hill, NC: Center for Teaching Quality.

Biag, M., & Castrechini, S. (2016). Coordinated strategies to help the whole child: Examining the contributions of full-service community schools. *Journal of Education for Students Placed at Risk, 21*, 157–173. doi:10.1080/10824669.2016.1172231

Bransford, J. D., Brown, A., & Cocking, R. (2000). *How people learn: Mind, brain, experience, and school.* Washington, DC: National Research Council.

Bransford, J. D., & Donovan, M. S. (2005). Scientific inquiry and how people learn. In M. S. Donovan & J. D. Bransford (Eds.), *How students learn: History, mathematics, and science in the classroom* (pp. 397–420). Washington, DC: National Academies Press.

Brophy, J., & McCaslin, M. (1992). Teachers' reports of how they perceive and cope with problem students. *Elementary School Journal, 93*(1), 3e68. doi:10.1086/461712

Bryk, A. (2010). Organizing schools for improvement. *Phi Delta Kappan, 91*(7), 23–30. doi:10.1177/003172171009100705

Bryk, A. S., Sebring, P. B., Allensworth, E., Easton, J. Q., & Luppescu, S. (2010). *Organizing schools for improvement: Lessons from Chicago.* Chicago, IL: University of Chicago Press.

Cahill, C. (2007). The personal is political: Developing new subjectivities through participatory action research. *Gender, Place and Culture, 14*, 267–292. doi:10.1080/09663690701324904

Cammarota, J., & Romero, A. F. (2009). A social justice epistemology and pedagogy for Latina/o students: Transforming public education with participatory action research. *New Directions for Youth Development, 23*, 53–65. doi:10.1002/yd

Carver-Thomas, D. (2018). *Diversifying the teaching profession: How to recruit and retain teachers of color.* Palo Alto, CA: Learning Policy Institute.

Castrechini, S., & London, R. A. (2012, February). *Positive student outcomes in community schools.* Retrieved from https://files.eric.ed.gov/fulltext/ED535614.pdf

Celio, C. I., Durlak, J., & Dymnicki, A. (2011). A meta-analysis of the impact of service-learning on students. *Journal of Experiential Education, 34*, 164–181.

Checkoway, B., & Richards-Schuster, K. (2004). Youth participation in evaluation and research as a way of lifting new voices. *Children, Youth & Environments, 14*(2), 84–98. doi:10.7721/chilyoutenvi.14.2.0084

Cochran-Smith, M. (2010). Toward a theory of teacher education for social justice. In A. Hargreaves, A. Lieberman, M. Fullan, & D. Hopkins (Eds.), *Second international handbook of educational change* (pp. 445–467). Dordrecht, Netherlands: Springer.

Cole, M., Engestrom, Y., & Vasquez, O. (Eds.). (1997). *Mind, culture, and activity: Seminal papers from the Laboratory of Comparative Human Cognition.* Cambridge, England: Cambridge University Press.

Cole, M., & Simpson, K. (2016). A symposium on community-based research on learning and development. *Mind, Culture, and Activity, 23*, 2–4. doi:10.1080/10749039.2015.1107743

Condliffe, B., Visher, M. G., Bangser, M. R., Drohojowska, S., & Saco, L. (2016). *Project-based learning: A literature review.* New York, NY: MDRC.

Darling-Hammond, L. (1999). Target time toward teachers. *Journal of Staff Development, 20*(2), 31–36.

Darling-Hammond, L., & Cook-Harvey, C. M. (2018). *Educating the whole child: Improving school climate to support student success.* Palo Alto, CA: Learning Policy Institute.

Darling-Hammond, L., & Oakes, J. (in press). *Preparing teachers for deeper learning.* Cambridge, MA: Harvard Education Press.

Diamond, J. B., & Spillane, J. P. (2016). School leadership and management from a distributed perspective: A 2016 retrospective and prospective. *Management in Education, 30*, 147–154. doi:10.1177/0892020616665938

Dryfoos, J. (2000). *Evaluation of community schools: Findings to date.* Washington, DC: Coalition for Community Schools. Retrieved from http://www.communityschools.org/assets/1/AssetManager/Evaluation%20of%20Community%20Schools_joy_dryfoos.pdf

Durlak, J. A., Weissberg, R. P., Dymnicki, A. B., Taylor, R. D., & Schellinger, K. B. (2011). The impact of enhancing students' social and emotional learning: A meta-analysis of school-based universal interventions. *Child Development, 82*, 405–432.

Epstein, J. L. (2018). *School, family, and community partnerships: Preparing educators and improving schools.* New York, NY: Routledge.

Epstein, J. L., Sanders, M. G., Simon, B. S., Salinas, K. C., Jansorn, N. R., Van Voorhis, F. L., . . . Greenfield, M. D. (2019). *School, family, and community partnerships: Your handbook for action* (4th ed.). Thousand Oaks, CA: Corwin Press.

Evans, M. P. (2011). Revisiting emotional geographies: Implications for family engagement and education policy in the United States. *Journal of Educational Change, 12*, 241–255. doi:10.1007/s10833-011-9155-0

Fals-Borda, O. (1987). The application of participatory action-research in Latin America. *International Sociology, 2*, 329–347. doi:10.1177/026858098700200401

Fauci, J., & Quartz, K. H. (2018). *A decade of innovation: How the LAUSD Pilot School movement is advancing equitable and personalized education.* Los Angeles: UCLA Center for Community Schooling. Retrieved from https://ucla.app.box.com/s/tma1u9jd17nb9mc3z9f2cbr3t2bnbo67

Fehrer, K., & Leos-Urbel, J. (2016). "We're one team": Examining community school implementation strategies in Oakland. *Education Sciences, 6*(3), 26. doi:10.3390/educsci6030026

Fine, M. (2008). An epilogue, of sorts. In J. Cammaroto & M. Fine (Eds.), *Revolutionizing education: Youth participatory action research in motion* (pp. 213–234). New York, NY: Routledge.

Fine, M., & Torre, M. E. (2004). Re-membering exclusions: Participatory action research in public institutions. *Qualitative Research in Psychology, 1*, 15–37. doi:10.1191/1478088704qp003oa

Friedlander, D., & Darling-Hammond, L. (2007). *High schools for equity: Policy supports for student learning in communities of color.* Palo Alto, CA: School Redesign Network at Stanford University.

Galindo, C., Sanders, M., & Abel, Y. (2017). Transforming educational experiences in low-income communities: A qualitative case study of social capital in a full-service community school. *American Educational Research Journal, 54*(1 Suppl.), 140S–163S. doi:10.3102/0002831216676571

Gay, G. (2010). *Culturally responsive pedagogy* (2nd ed.). New York, NY: Teachers College Press.

Ginwright, S., & James, T. (2002). From assets to agents of change: social justice, organizing, and youth development. *New Directions for Youth Development, 96*, 27–46. doi:10.1002/yd.25

Gist, C., White, T., & Bianco, M. (2018). Pushed to teach: Pedagogies and policies for a Black women educator pipeline. *Education and Urban Society, 50*, 56–86.

Golob, M. I., & Giles, A. R. (2013). Challenging and transforming power relations within community-based participatory research: The promise of a Foucauldian analysis. *Qualitative Research in Sport, Exercise and Health, 5*, 356–372. doi:10.1080/21596 76X.2013.846273

Gonzalez, T. (2012). Keeping kids in schools: Restorative justice, punitive discipline, and the school to prison pipeline. *Journal of Law & Education, 41*, 281–335.

Green, T. (2017). "We felt they took the heart out of the community": Examining a community-based response to urban school closure. *Education Policy Analysis Archives, 25*(21). Retrieved from https://epaa.asu.edu/ojs/article/view/2549/1882

Guha, R., Hyler, M. E., & Darling-Hammond, L. (2016). *The teacher residency: An innovative model for preparing teachers.* Palo Alto, CA: Learning Policy Institute.

Gutkin, T. B., Singer, J., & Brown, R. (1980). Teacher reactions to school-based consultation services: A multivariate analysis. *Journal of School Psychology, 28*, 127–134.

Hanushek, E. A., Kain, J. F., & Rivkin, S. G. (2004). Why public schools lose teachers. *Journal of Human Resources, 39*, 326–354.

Hargreaves, A. (2001). Emotional geographies of teaching. *Teachers College Record, 103*, 1056–1080.

Henderson, A. T., & Mapp, K. L. (2002). *A new wave of evidence: The impact of school, family, and community connections on student achievement.* Retrieved from https://www.sedl.org /connections/resources/evidence.pdf

Hord, S. (1997). *Professional learning communities: Communities of continuous inquiry and improvement.* Austin, TX: Southwest Educational Development Laboratory.

Howard, T. C. (2003). Consciousness and self-reflection in preservice teacher education. *Theory Into Practice, 42*, 181–187. doi:10.1207/s15430421tip4203

Hughes, J. N. (2011). Longitudinal effects of teacher and student perceptions of teacher-student relationship qualities on academic adjustment. *Elementary School Journal, 112*, 38–60.

Ingersoll, R. M. (2001). Teacher turnover and teacher shortages: An organizational analysis. *American Educational Research Journal, 38*, 499–534.

Ingersoll, R. M., & May, H. (2012). The magnitude, destinations, and determinants of mathematics and science teacher turnover. *Educational Evaluation and Policy Analysis, 34*, 435–464.

Ishimaru, A. M., Torres, K. E., Salvador, J. E., Lott, J., Williams, D. M. C., & Tran, C. (2016). Reinforcing deficit, journeying toward equity: Cultural brokering in family engagement initiatives. *American Educational Research Journal, 53*, 850–882. doi:10.3102/0002831216657178

Israel, B. A, Schulz, A J., Parker, E. A, & Becker, A B. (1998). Review of community-based research: Assessing partnership approaches to improve public health. *Annual Review of Public Health, 19*, 173–202. doi:10.1146/annurev.publhealth.19.1.173

Jennings, P. A., & Greenberg, M. T. (2009). The prosocial classroom: Teacher social and emotional competence in relation to student and classroom outcomes. *Review of Educational Research, 79,* 491–525. doi:10.3102/0034654308325693

Johnson, E. J. (2014). From the classroom to the living room: Eroding academic inequities through home visits. *Journal of School Leadership, 24,* 357–385.

Johnson, S. M. (2007). *Finders and keepers: Helping new teachers survive and thrive in our schools.* Indianapolis, IN: Jossey-Bass.

Johnson, S. M., & Landman, J. (2000). "Sometimes bureaucracy has its charms": The working conditions of teachers in deregulated schools. *Teachers College Record, 102,* 85–124.

Jonassen, D., & Land, S. (Eds.). (2012). *Theoretical foundations of learning environments.* New York, NY: Routledge.

Jones, S. M., Bouffard, S. M., & Weissbourd, R. (2013). Educators' social and emotional skills vital to learning. *Phi Delta Kappan, 94*(8), 62–65. doi:10.1177/003172171309400815

Kantor, H., & Lowe, R. (2016). Educationalizing the welfare state and privatizing education: The evolution of social policy since the New Deal. In W. J. Mathis & T. M. Trujillo (Eds.), *Learning from the federal market–based reforms: Lessons for ESSA* (pp. 37–59). Charlotte, NC: Information Age.

Khalifa, M. A., Gooden, M. A., & Davis, J. E. (2016). Culturally responsive school leadership: A synthesis of the literature. *Review of Educational Research, 86,* 1272–1311. doi:10.3102/0034654316630383

Kirshner, B. E. N., & Jefferson, A. (2015). Participatory democracy and struggling schools: Making space for youth in school turnarounds. *Teachers College Record, 117*(6), 1–26.

Kokotsaki, D., Menzies, V., & Wiggins, A. (2016). Project-based learning: A review of the literature. *Improving Schools, 19,* 267–277.

Kraft, M. A., & Dougherty, S. M. (2013). The effect of teacher–family communication on student engagement: Evidence from a randomized field experiment. *Journal of Research on Educational Effectiveness, 6,* 199–222.

Kraft, M. A., & Papay, J. P. (2014). Can professional environments in schools promote teacher development? Explaining heterogeneity in returns to teaching experience. *Educational Evaluation and Policy Analysis, 36,* 476–500.

Kraft, M. A., Papay, J. P., Johnson, S. M., Charner-Laird, M., Ng, M., & Reinhorn, S. (2015). Educating amid uncertainty: The organizational supports teachers need to serve students in high-poverty, urban schools. *Educational Administration Quarterly, 51,* 753–790.

Ladson-Billings, G., & Tate, W. (1995). Toward a critical race theory of education. *Teachers College Record, 97*(1), 47–68.

Lave, J. (1991). Situating learning in communities of practice. In L. B. Resnick, J. M. Levine, & S. D. Teasley (Eds.), *Perspectives on socially shared cognition* (pp. 63–82). Washington, DC: American Psychological Association.

Lee, C. D. (2008). Wallace Foundation Distinguished Lecture—The centrality of culture to the scientific study of learning and development: How an ecological framework in education research facilitates civic responsibility. *Educational Researcher, 37,* 267–279.

Lee, R. E. (2018). Breaking down barriers and building bridges: Transformative practices in community- and school-based urban teacher preparation. *Journal of Teacher Education, 69,* 118–126.

Loeb, S., Darling-Hammond, L., & Luczak, J. (2005). Teacher turnover: The role of working conditions and salaries in recruiting and retaining teachers. *Peabody Journal of Education, 80*(3), 44–70.

Lopez, M. E. (2003, December). *Transforming schools through community organizing: A research review.* Retrieved from http://youthjusticenc.org/download/education-justice/prevention-intervention-alternatives/Transforming%20Schools%20Through%20Community%20Organizing:%20A%20Research%20Review.pdf

Lyons, K. B. (2007). *Preparing to stay: An examination of the effects of specialized preparation on urban teacher retention* (Unpublished dissertation). University of California, Los Angeles.

Maier, A., Daniel, J., Oakes, J., & Lam, L. (2017, December). *Community schools as an effective school improvement strategy: A review of the evidence.* Palo Alto, CA: Learning Policy Institute. Retrieved from https://learningpolicyinstitute.org/sites/default/files/product-files/Community_Schools_Effective_REPORT.pdf

Mapp, K. L. (2002, April). *Having their say: Parents describe how and why they are involved in their children's education.* Paper presented at the annual meeting of the American Educational Research Association, New Orleans, LA.

Mapp, K. L., & Kuttner, P. J. (2014). *Partners in education: A dual capacity-building framework for family–school partnerships.* Retrieved from http://www.sedl.org/pubs/framework/

McKnight, K., Venkateswaran, N., Laird, J., Robles, J., & Shalev, T. (2017). *Mindset shifts and parent teacher home visits.* Berkeley, CA: RTI International.

Melaville, A., Berg, A. C., & Blank, M. J. (2006). *Community-based learning: Engaging students for success and citizenship.* Washington, DC: Institute for Educational Leadership.

Moll, L., Amanti, C., Neff, D., & Gonzalez, N. (1992). Funds of knowledge for teaching. *Theory Into Practice, 31,* 132–141.

Murillo, M. A., Quartz, K. H., & Del Razo, J. (2017). High school internships: Utilizing a community cultural wealth framework to support career preparation and college-going among low-income students of color. *Journal of Education for Students Placed at Risk, 22,* 237–252. doi:10.1080/10824669.2017.1350182

Murrell, P. (2001). *The community teacher: A new framework for effective urban teaching.* New York, NY: Teachers College Press.

Nasir, N. S., & Hand, V. M. (2006). Exploring sociocultural perspectives on race, culture, and learning. *Review of Educational Research, 76,* 449–475. doi:10.3102/00346543076004449

National Research Council. (2003). *Engaging schools: Fostering high school students' motivation to learn.* Washington, DC: National Academies Press.

Noddings, N. (2005). What does it mean to educate the whole child? *Educational Leadership, 63*(1). 8–13.

Oakes, J., Franke, M. L., Quartz, K. H., & Rogers, J. (2002). Research for high-quality urban teaching: Defining it, developing it, assessing it. *Journal of Teacher Education, 53,* 228–234.

Oakes, J., Lipton, M., Anderson, L., & Stillman, J. (2018). *Teaching to change the world.* New York, NY: Routledge.

Oakes, J., Maier, A., & Daniel, J. (2017). *Community schools: An evidence-based strategy for equitable school improvement.* Boulder, CO: National Education Policy Center.

Oakes, J., & Rogers, J. (2006). *Learning power: Organizing for education and justice.* New York, NY: Teachers College Press.

Pais, E., Hurst, S., Lowe, D., Rosenbaum, J., & Wadle, J. (in press). Community school teacher leaders enhance learning. In J. Ferrara & R. Jacobson (Eds.), *The community school book series: A strategy for connecting hearts and minds.*

Papay, J. P., Bacher-Hicks, A., Page, L. C., & Marinell, W. H. (2017). The challenge of teacher retention in urban schools: Evidence of variation from a cross-site analysis. *Educational Researcher, 46,* 434–448.

Paris, D. (2012). Culturally sustaining pedagogy: A needed change in stance, terminology, and practice. *Educational Researcher, 41,* 93–97.

Podolsky, A., Kini, T., Bishop, J., & Darling-Hammond, L. (2016, September). *Solving the teacher shortage: How to attract and retain excellent educators.* Palo Alto, CA: Learning Policy Institute. Retrieved from https://learningpolicyinstitute.org/product/solving-teacher-shortage

Quartz, K. H., & the TEP Research Group. (2003). Too angry to leave: Supporting new teachers' commitment to transform urban schools. *Journal of Teacher Education, 54*, 99–111.

Quezada, R. L., Alexandrowicz, V., & Molina, S. (2013). Family, school, community engagement, and partnerships: An imperative for k-12, and colleges of education in the development of twenty-first-century educators. *Teaching Education, 24*, 119–122. doi:10.1080/10476210.2013.786888

Quinn, J. (2005). The Children's Aid Society community schools: A full-service partnership model. *New Directions for Youth Development, 107*, 15–26, table of contents.

Ray, D. C. (2007). Two counseling interventions to reduce teacher-child relationship stress. *Professional School Counseling, 10*, 428–440. Retrieved from https://www.researchgate.net/publication/232418798_Two_Counseling_Interventions_to_Reduce_Teacher-Child_Relationship_Stress

Redd, Z., Boccanfuso, C., Walker, K., Princiotta, D., Knewstub, D., & Moore, K. (2012). *Expanding time for learning both inside and outside the classroom: A review of the evidence base.* Washington, DC: Child Trends. Retrieved from https://www.childtrends.org/wp-content/uploads/2013/10/2012-48ExpandedTimeLearningFullReport.pdf

Richardson, J. W. (2009). *The full-service community school movement: Lessons from the James Adams Community School.* New York, NY: Palgrave Macmillan.

Rios-Moore, I., Allen, S., Contreras, J., Jiang, N., Threatts, T., & Cahill, C. (2004). *Makes me mad: Stereotypes of young urban women of color.* New York, NY: Center for Human Environments, City University of New York. http://web.gc.cuny.edu/che/che.htm

Rubinstein, S. A., & McCarthy, J. E. (2016). Union–management partnerships, teacher collaboration, and student performance. *ILR Review, 69*, 1114–1132.

Sanders, M. (2016). Leadership, partnerships, and organizational development: Exploring components of effectiveness in three full-service community schools. *School Effectiveness and School Improvement, 27*, 157–177. doi:10.1080/09243453.2015.1030432

Sanders, M. G. (2001). The role of "community" in comprehensive school, family, and community partnership programs. *Elementary School Journal, 102*(1), 19–34. doi:10.1086/499691

Sanders, M. G. (2018). Crossing boundaries: A qualitative exploration of relational leadership in three full-service community schools. *Teachers College Record, 120*(4).

Sanders, M., Galindo, C., & Allen, K. M. (2018). Professional capital and responses to student diversity: A qualitative exploration of the role of teachers in full-service community schools. *Urban Education.* Advance online publication. doi:10.1177/00420859 18770719

Sanders, M. G., & Lewis, K. C. (2005). Building bridges toward excellence: Community involvement in high schools. *High School Journal, 88*(3), 1–9. doi:10.1353/hsj.2005 .0005

Seashore Louis, K., Leithwood, K. A., Wahlstrom, K. L., & Anderson, S. E. (2010). *Learning from leadership: Investigating the links to improved student learning.* Retrieved from https://www.wallacefoundation.org/knowledge-center/Documents/Investigating-the-Links-to-Improved-Student-Learning.pdf

Sibley, E., Theodorakakis, M., Walsh, M. E., Foley, C., Petrie, J., & Raczek, A. (2017). The impact of comprehensive student support on teachers: Knowledge of the whole child, classroom practice, and teacher support. *Teaching and Teacher Education, 65*, 145–156. doi:10.1016/j.tate.2017.02.012

Sime, D., & Sheridan, M. (2014). "You want the best for your kids": Improving educational outcomes for children living in poverty through parental engagement. *Educational Research, 56*, 327–342. doi:10.1080/00131881.2014.934556

Simon, N. S., & Johnson, S. M. (2015). Teacher turnover in high-poverty schools: What we know and can do. *Teachers College Record, 117*(3), 1–36.

Snow-Gerono, J. L. (2005). Professional development in a culture of inquiry: PDS teachers identify the benefits of professional learning communities. *Teaching and Teacher Education, 21,* 241–256.

Solomon, D., Battistich, V., Kim, D., & Watson, M. S. (1996). Teacher practices associated with students' sense of the classroom as a community. *Social Psychology of Education, 1,* 235–267.

Steele, C. M., & Aronson, J. (1995). Stereotype threat and the intellectual test performance of African Americans. *Journal of Personality and Social Psychology, 69,* 797–811.

Stefanski, A., Valli, L., & Jacobson, R. (2017). Beyond involvement and engagement: The role of the family in school–community partnerships. *School Community Journal, 26,* 135–160.

Stockard, J., & Lehman, M. B. (2004). Influences on the satisfaction and retention of 1st-year teachers: The importance of effective school management. *Educational Administration Quarterly, 40,* 742–771.

Strunk, K. O. (2012). Policy poison or promise: Exploring the dual nature of California school district collective bargaining agreements. *Educational Administration Quarterly, 48,* 506–547.

Strunk, K. O., Cowen, J. M., Goldhaber, D., Marianno, B. D., Kilbride, T., & Theobald, R. (2018). It is in the contract: How the policies set in teachers' unions' collective bargaining agreements vary across states and districts. *Educational Policy, 32,* 280–312.

Sutcher, L., Darling-Hammond, L., & Carver-Thomas, D. (2016). *A coming crisis in teaching? Teacher supply, demand, and shortages in the U.S.* Palo Alto, CA: Learning Policy Institute.

Tharpe, R. G., & Gallimore, R. (1988). *Rousing minds to life: Teaching and learning in social contexts.* Cambridge, England: Cambridge University Press.

Torre, M. E. (2009). Participatory action research and critical race theory: Fueling spaces for nos-otras to research. *The Urban Review, 41,* 106–120. doi:10.1007/s11256-008-0097-7

Urban Institute. (2017). *Subtracting schools from communities.* Retrieved from https://www.urban.org/features/subtracting-schools-communities

Varelas, M., Morales-Doyle, D., Raza, S., Segura, D., Canales, K., & Mitchener, C. (2018). Community organizations' programming and the development of community science teachers. *Science Education, 102,* 60–84.

Villegas, A. M., & Irvine, J. J. (2010). Diversifying the teaching force: An examination of major arguments. *The Urban Review, 42,* 175–192.

Ware, H., & Kitsantas, A. (2007). Teacher and collective efficacy beliefs as predictors of professional commitment. *Journal of Educational Research, 100,* 303–310.

Warren, M. (2005). Communities and schools: A new view of urban education reform. *Harvard Educational Review, 75,* 133–174.

Warren, M. R. (2014). Transforming public education: The need for an educational justice movement. *New England Journal of Public Policy, 26*(1), Article 11. Retrieved from http://search.ebscohost.com/login.aspx?direct=true&db=buh&AN=99746977&site=ehost-live

Warren, M. R., Hong, S., Rubin, C. H., & Uy, P. S. (2009). Beyond the bake sale: A community-based relational approach to parent engagement in schools. *Teachers College Record, 111,* 2209–2254.

Weiner, L. (2000). Research in the 90s: Implications for urban teacher preparation. *Review of Educational Research, 70,* 369–406.

Weissberg, R., Durlak, J. A., Domitrovich, C. E., & Gullota, T. P. (2016). *Why social and emotional learning is essential for students.* Retrieved from https://www.edutopia.org/blog/why-sel-essential-for-students-weissberg-durlak-domitrovich-gullotta

Welner, K. G. (2001). *Legal rights, local wrongs: When community control collides with educational equity.* Albany: SUNY Press.

Zeichner, K., Bowman, M., Guillen, L., & Napolitan, K. (2016). Engaging and working in solidarity with local communities in preparing the teachers of their children. *Journal of Teacher Education, 67,* 277–290.

About the Editors

Terri D. Pigott is associate provost for research and professor of research methodology at Loyola University Chicago. She was formerly dean of the School of Education at Loyola University Chicago. She received her PhD in Education from the University of Chicago, specializing in measurement, evaluation, and statistical analysis. Her research focuses on the methods for meta-analysis, including handling of missing data, power analysis in meta-analysis, and individual participant data meta-analysis.

Ann Marie Ryan is an associate professor of education in the School of Education at Loyola University Chicago. She received her PhD in curriculum and instruction from the University of Illinois at Chicago. Her teaching and research concentrate on the preparation and professional development of educators. She also researches the history of Catholic schooling in the United States from the early to mid-20th century with a focus on the intersections between Catholic schools and public education reforms.

Charles Tocci is an assistant professor of education at Loyola University Chicago. He earned his doctorate at Teachers College, Columbia University, where he also worked as senior research associate at the National Center for Restructuring Education, Schools, and Teaching. His research explores the ways teaching practice has changed and remained consistent over time. His work has been published in *Review of Research in Education, Educational Philosophy and Theory*, and *The Washington Post*.

Review of Research in Education
March 2019, Vol. 43, p. 481
DOI: 10.3102/0091732X19839404
© 2019 AERA. http://rre.aera.net

About the Contributors

Arnetha F. Ball, PhD, is the Charles E. Ducommun Professor in the Graduate School of Education at Stanford University. Her research advances sociocultural theories through studies that integrate sociolinguistic and ethnographic approaches to investigate ways in which semiotic systems serve as a means for mediating teaching and learning in linguistically complex settings and the processes of teacher change and development.

Lívia Barros Cruz, a doctoral research fellow, is currently pursuing a doctoral degree in early childhood education in the Department of Curriculum and Teaching at Teachers College, Columbia University. Her current interests include languages, critical literacies, multimodalities, and poetry.

Rhonda S. Bondie is a lecturer at the Harvard Graduate School of Education and faculty chair for the professional education program Differentiated Instruction Made Practical. She taught general and special education in public schools for over 20 years. Her research examines equitable instructional practices and teacher decision making in inclusive classrooms.

Nancy Bradt is a doctoral student in the Department of Curriculum and Teaching at Teachers College, Columbia University. She is interested in curriculum studies, social studies education, and postcolonial theories and disability studies, especially as they pertain to understanding and working with transnational students.

Nancy Cardwell, PhD, is a psychologist and educator with expertise in human development, unpacking implicit bias, neuroscience, and intergroup relations. Her research examines the interplay between culturally based, experiential knowledge and learning the professional knowledge of teaching. She is an assistant professor at The City College of New York.

Martyna Citkowicz is a senior researcher at American Institutes for Research. Her work focuses on study design, methodology, meta-analysis, and program evaluation.

Review of Research in Education
March 2019, Vol. 43, pp. 482–488
DOI: 10.3102/0091732X19840655
© 2019 AERA. http://rre.aera.net

David K. Cohen is the John Dewey Collegiate Professor of Education and Professor of Public Policy at the University of Michigan and a visiting professor at the Harvard Graduate School of Education. His research concerns the relations between policy and instruction, teaching, school improvement, and systems of schooling.

Shantel Crosby, PhD, LCSW, is an assistant professor in the Kent School of Social Work at the University of Louisville. She previously practiced as a community mental health clinician with children and families. Currently, she conducts interdisciplinary research focused on adverse childhood experiences among high-risk youth and trauma-informed practice in youth-serving systems.

Christine Dahnke is a doctoral candidate in education leadership at the Harvard Graduate School of Education. From her experiences as a classroom teacher, coach, and district administrator in urban school districts, she brings specialized expertise in leading change on behalf of English learners.

Julia Daniel is a doctoral candidate in the School of Education at the University of Colorado, Boulder. Her research and organizing center on community participation in equity-oriented educational reform as essential for deep, sustained, and just social change.

Beverly Falk is a professor and director of the Graduate Programs in Early Childhood Education at The City College of New York. She is also the director of the High Quality Early Learning Project (https://highqualityearlylearning.org), an online platform of multimedia resources for developmentally appropriate, culturally and linguistically responsive pedagogy for early childhood education.

Miranda Suzanne Fitzgerald is a postdoctoral research fellow at the University of Michigan. Her research focuses on ambitious and equitable literacy instruction. Her specific interests include the design and study of learning environments for diverse learners that integrate science and language literacy instruction and meaningful uses of digital tools.

Naomi Flynn, PhD, associate professor of primary English education at the University of Reading, UK, researches teachers' pedagogy and subject knowledge for teaching multilingual learners, and the relationship between policy and classroom practice. She is co-director of Bilingualism Matters@Reading (https://www.reading.ac.uk/celm/bilingualism-matters/).

Rachel Garrett is a senior researcher at American Institutes for Research. Her work focuses on impact evaluations of programs to support instructional effectiveness, English learner students, and mathematics learning.

Louis M. Gomez is a social scientist dedicated to educational improvement. His research and design efforts are aimed at helping support community formation in schools, and other organizations, so that they can collaboratively create new approaches to teaching, learning, and assessment. He currently serves as professor of education and information studies at University of California, Los Angeles, and as a senior fellow at the Carnegie Foundation for the Advancement of Teaching.

Steve Graham is the Warner Professor in Teachers College at Arizona State University. He studies how writing develops, how to teach it effectively, and how writing can be used to support reading and learning. He is the current editor of the *Journal of Educational Psychology*.

Svenja Hammer, PhD, research associate at the Department of Educational Science at Leuphana University Lüneburg, Germany, researches professional competencies of (preservice) teachers of multilingual learners. By modeling, measuring, and internationally comparing competencies, she is trying to better understand opportunities to learn in teacher education.

Jodi Patrick Holschuh, PhD, is a professor of developmental education and chair of the Department of Curriculum and Instruction at Texas State University. Her research interests include students' beliefs about learning, the transition from high school to college learning, developmental education, strategies for academic success, learning in the sciences, and disciplinary literacy.

Lauri D. Johnson is an associate professor and chair of the Department of Educational Leadership and Higher Education at Boston College. Her research interests include culturally responsive and race-conscious school leadership in national and international contexts, historical studies of school-community activism and multiculturalism in urban school reform, and successful school leadership in high-poverty schools.

Mary M. Kennedy is professor emeritus in the Department of Teacher Education at Michigan State University. She has received numerous awards for her scholarship, including awards from the American Educational Research Association (AERA), the American Association of Colleges of Teacher Education, and the Association of Teacher Educators. She served as vice-president for AERA's Division on Teaching and Teacher Education from 1993 to 1996, and in 2011 she became a fellow in that association.

Cindy Hammer Linzell, MA, graduate teaching and research assistant in teaching, learning, and teacher education at the University of Nebraska-Lincoln, researches teacher preparation for multilingual learners in mainstream classrooms.

Dina López is an assistant professor at The City College of New York. She has written extensively about bilingual education, immigration, and adolescent literacy both in Latin America and the United States. Her research examines the situated nature of educational policies and practices.

Maritza Lozano is an assistant professor in educational leadership at California State University, Fullerton. In her teaching and research, she investigates the micro- and macro-level processes that support learning and the design of equitable learning experiences in schools that serve historically minoritized students.

Katrina Liu is an assistant professor at the University of Nevada, Las Vegas. Her research focuses on theory, practice, and innovation in preparing quality teachers to teach in diverse classrooms. Her current research includes critical reflection for transformative learning in teacher education, preparing and supporting teachers and teacher educators of color, and preparing globally minded teachers. Her interdisciplinary work appears in journals such as *Educational Review, Journal of Teacher Education and Technology,* and *Reflective Practice.*

Meghan McGlinn Manfra, PhD, is an associate professor in the Department of Teacher Education and Learning Sciences at North Carolina State University. She is the editor of the *Handbook of Social Studies Research* and author of the forthcoming book *Action Research for Classrooms, Schools, and Communities.*

Jessica Masterson, PhD, is a postdoctoral research associate with the International Consortium for Multilingual Excellence in Education at the University of Nebraska-Lincoln. Her research concerns articulations of literacy and justice in public schools.

Nicole McGowan is a doctoral candidate at Teachers College, Columbia University. A former kindergarten teacher in Detroit, Michigan, she is passionate about exploring positive learning experiences of students of color, particularly Black boys. Currently her research focuses on relationships between Black boys and Black male teachers in early childhood education.

Jessica Mitchell-McCollough, MA, doctoral candidate and a graduate teaching and research assistant in teaching, learning, and teacher education at the University of Nebraska-Lincoln, researches the interaction of top-down and bottom-up language policies and language ideologies surrounding heritage languages, and the relationship between policy, ideology, and classroom practice.

Rebecca Colina Neri is a PhD candidate in the Graduate School of Education and Information Sciences at University of California, Los Angeles. She utilizes an equity-centered, data-driven, and practice-oriented research approach for both investigating the systems that produce complex problems in education and working within and across these systems to improve the educational and life trajectories of nondominant students.

Jeannie Oakes is Presidential Professor in Educational Equity Emeritus at the University of California, Los Angeles, and senior fellow in residence at the Learning Policy Institute. She is a past president of the American Educational Research Association and a member of the National Academy of Education.

Yoon K. Pak is an associate professor and acting head in the Department of Education Policy, Organization and Leadership at the University of Illinois at Urbana-Champaign. Her research and teaching interests are in the history of education, citizenship, and immigration issues in K–12 contexts.

Annemarie Sullivan Palincsar is the Jean and Charles Walgreen Jr. Chair of Reading and Literacy and Arthur F. Thurnau Professor in the School of Education at the University of Michigan. She is a teacher educator and instructional researcher who studies instructional contexts that support sensemaking and knowledge building.

Aura Perez is a doctoral student, an instructor in the early childhood education preservice program, and a teacher of infants at the lab school at Teachers College, Columbia University. Her research explores the role of race in the relationships between student teachers and mentor teachers within the context of fieldwork experiences.

Dolores Perin, PhD, is a professor of psychology and education, chair of the Health and Behavior Studies Department, director of the Reading Specialist Program, and a senior research associate at the Community College Research Center, Teachers College, Columbia University. Her research centers on the literacy skills of adults with reading and writing difficulties.

Donald J. Peurach is an associate professor of educational policy, leadership, and innovation at the University of Michigan and a senior fellow at the Carnegie Foundation for the Advancement of Teaching. His research examines the production and use of knowledge to improve practice and outcomes in educational networks and systems.

Philip J. Piety, PhD, teaches in the University of Maryland's College of Information Studies (iSchool) where he directs the Maryland Educational Digital Infrastructures and Analytics Lab. He has written about education data science and learning analytics and authored *Assessing the Educational Data Movement*, published by Teachers College Press in 2013.

Karen Hunter Quartz directs the Center for Community Schooling at the University of California, Los Angeles, and is a faculty member in the UCLA Graduate School of Education and Information Studies. Her research, teaching, and service support community school development, teacher autonomy and retention, and educational reform.

Ayesha Rabadi-Raol, a doctoral research fellow, is an instructor in the preservice early childhood teacher education program at Teachers College, Columbia University. Her research focuses on issues of equity and justice in early childhood education and teacher education, attending to how immigrant and transnational students and teachers are positioned by educational institutions.

Elizabeth Rollins is a doctoral student in the Department of Curriculum and Teaching at Teachers College, Columbia University. She is an instructor in the pre-service early childhood education and early childhood special education programs. From a critical perspective, her research prioritizes equity and inclusion in early childhood teaching and teacher education.

Mariana Souto-Manning, PhD, is a professor in the Department of Curriculum and Teaching, and founding co-director of the Center for Innovation in Teacher Education and Development (CITED) at Teachers College, Columbia University. Her research critically examines inequities and injustices in early childhood teaching and teacher education, (re)centering methodologies and pedagogies on the lives, experiences, and values of intersectionally minoritized individuals and communities.

James P. Spillane is the Spencer T. and Ann W. Olin Professor in Learning and Organizational Change at the School of Education and Social Policy at Northwestern University. His work explores the policy implementation process and organizational leadership in school systems. He is a member of the National Academy of Education.

Kathryn Strom, PhD, assistant professor of educational leadership at California State University, East Bay, employs critical posthuman theories to study teacher learning and the translation of that learning into classroom practice. She currently serves as a senior researcher with the International Consortium of Multilingual Excellence in Education.

M. Shelley Thomas, EdD, is an associate professor in middle and secondary education at the University of Louisville. She conducts research on transdisciplinary social justice approaches to educational challenges including culturally responsive, trauma-informed teaching. She is currently the principal investigator of a transdisciplinary grant, infusing trauma-informed teaching into teacher preparation.

Judi Vanderhaar, PhD, works in the Kentucky Department of Education, Division of Student Success. She conducts training on trauma-informed care for educators in partnership with the University of Kentucky Center on Trauma and Children

Educator Learning Collaborative. Her previous research centers on racial disparities in school exclusion.

Kara Mitchell Viesca, PhD, associate professor of teaching, learning, and teacher education at the University of Nebraska-Lincoln, researches advancing equity in the policy and practice of educator development, particularly for teachers of multilingual learners. She currently leads the International Consortium for Multilingual Excellence in Education (https://cehs.unl.edu/icmee/).

Ryan Williams is a principal researcher at American Institutes for Research. His work focuses on impact evaluations and research syntheses of teaching and learning programs. He also conducts methodological research on methods for meta-analysis and quasi-experimental design.

Maxwell M. Yurkofsky is a doctoral candidate at the Harvard Graduate School of Education. His research draws on organizational and new institutional theory to understand how school systems, and the educators who inhabit them, make sense of and respond to reforms related to deeper learning and continuous improvement.

Akane Zusho is a professor in the Graduate School of Education at Fordham University. She has written extensively on the intersection of culture, achievement motivation, and self-regulated learning, and she has conducted numerous studies exploring the relation of cultural, cognitive, and motivational processes to learning.